SELECTING THE RIGHT ANALYSES FOR YOUR DATA

Also Available

When to Use What Research Design
W. Paul Vogt, Dianne C. Gardner,
and Lynne M. Haeffele

Selecting the Right Analyses for Your Data

Quantitative, Qualitative, and Mixed Methods

W. Paul Vogt
Elaine R. Vogt
Dianne C. Gardner
Lynne M. Haeffele

THE GUILFORD PRESS
New York London

A Division of Guilford Publications, Inc.
72 Spring Street, New York, NY 10012
www.guilford.com

Printed in the United States of America

This book is printed on acid-free paper.

Last digit is print number: 9 8 7 6 5 4 3 2 1

Library of Congress Cataloging-in-Publication Data

Vogt, W. Paul.
Selecting the right analyses for your data : quantitative, qualitative, and mixed methods / W. Paul Vogt, Elaine R. Vogt, Dianne C. Gardner, Lynne M. Haeffele.
pages cm
Includes bibliographical references and index.
ISBN 978-1-4625-1576-9 (paperback) — ISBN 978-1-4625-1602-5 (hardcover)
1. Social sciences—Research—Methodology. 2. Quantitative research. 3. Qualitative research. I. Title.
H62.V6228 2014
001.4′2—dc23

2014011278

Preface and Acknowledgments

Using the right analysis methods leads to more justifiable conclusions and more persuasive interpretations of your data. Several plausible coding and analysis options exist for any set of data—qualitative, quantitative, or graphic/visual. Helping readers select among those options is our goal in this book. Because the range of choices is broad, so too is the range of topics we have addressed. In addition to the standard division between quantitative and qualitative coding methods and analyses, discussed in specific chapters and sections, we have dealt with graphic data and analyses throughout the book. We have also addressed in virtually every chapter the issues involved in combining qualitative, quantitative, and graphic data and techniques in mixed methods approaches. We intentionally cover a very large number of topics and consider this a strength of the book; it enables readers to consider a broad range of options in one place.

Analysis choices are usually tied to prior design and sampling decisions. This means that *Selecting the Right Analyses for Your Data* is naturally tied to topics addressed in our companion volume, *When to Use What Research Design,* published in 2012. In that book we introduced guidelines for starting along the intricate paths of choices researchers face as they wend their way through a research project. Completing the steps of a research project—from the initial idea through formulating a research question, choosing methods of data collection, and identifying populations and sampling methods to deciding how to code, analyze, and interpret the data thus collected—is an arduous process, but few jobs are as rewarding.

We think of the topic—from the research question to the interpretation of evidence—as a unified whole. We have dealt with it in two books, rather than in one huge volume, mostly for logistical reasons. The two books are free standing. As in a good marriage, they are distinct but happier as a pair. It has been exciting to bring to fruition the two-volume project, and we hope that you too will find it useful and occasionally provocative as you select effective methods to collect, code, analyze, and interpret your data.

To assist you with the selection process, the book uses several organizing techniques to help orient readers, which are often called *pedagogical features:*

- Opening chapter previews provide readers with a quick way to find the useful (and often unexpected) topic nuggets in each chapter.
- End-of-chapter Summary Tables recap the dos and don'ts and the advantages and disadvantages of the various analytic techniques.
- End-of-chapter Suggestions for Further Reading are provided that include detailed summaries of what readers can find in each one and why they might want to read them for greater depth or more technical information.
- Chapter 14 concludes the book with aphorisms containing advice on different themes.

It is a great pleasure to acknowledge the help we have received along the way. This book would not have been written without the constant support and advice—from the early planning to the final copyediting—of C. Deborah Laughton, Publisher, Methodology and Statistics, at The Guilford Press. She also recruited a wonderful group of external reviewers for the manuscript. Their suggestions for improving the book were exceptionally helpful. These external reviewers were initially anonymous, of course, but now we can thank at least some of them by name: Theresa E. DiDonato, Department of Psychology, Loyola University, Baltimore, Maryland; Marji Erickson Warfield, The Heller School for Social Policy and Management, Brandeis University, Waltham, Massachusetts; Janet Salmons, Department of Business, School of Business and Technology, Capella University, Minneapolis, Minnesota; Ryan Spohn, School of Criminology and Criminal Justice, University of Nebraska at Omaha, Omaha, Nebraska; Jerrell C. Cassady, Department of Educational Psychology, Ball State University, Muncie, Indiana; and Tracey LaPierre, Department of Sociology, University of Kansas, Lawrence, Kansas.

The editorial and production staff at The Guilford Press, especially Anna Nelson, have been wonderful to work with. They have been efficient, professional, and friendly as they turned our rough typescript into a polished work.

This book and its companion volume, *When to Use What Research Design,* were written with colleagues and students in mind. These groups helped in ways too numerous to recount, both directly and indirectly. Many of the chapters were field tested in classes on research design and in several courses on data analysis for graduate students at Illinois State University. We are especially grateful to students with whom we worked on dissertation committees as well as in classes. They inspired us to write in ways that are directly useful for the practice of research.

We have also had opportunities to learn about research practice from working on several sponsored research projects funded by the U.S. Department of Education, the National Science Foundation, and the Lumina Foundation. Also important has been the extensive program evaluation work we have done under the auspices of the Illinois Board of Higher Education (mostly funded by the U.S. Department of Education).

Although we had help from these sources, it remains true, of course, that we alone are responsible for the book's shortcomings.

Abbreviations Used in This Book

The following is a list of abbreviations used in this book. If a term and its abbreviation are used only once, they are defined where they are used.

ACS	American Community Survey
AIK	Akaike information criterion
ANCOVA	analysis of covariance
ANOVA	analysis of variance
AUC	area under the curve
BMI	body mass index
CAQDAS	computer-assisted qualitative data analysis software
CART	classification and regression trees
CDC	Centers for Disease Control and Prevention
CFA	confirmatory (or common) factor analysis
CI	confidence interval
COMPASSS	comparative methods for systematic cross-case analysis
CPS	Current Population Survey
CRA	correlation and regression analysis
CSND	cumulative standard normal distribution
DA	discriminant analysis
d-i-d	difference-in-difference
DIF	differential item functioning
DOI	digital object identifier

DV	dependent variable
E	estimate or error or error terms
EDA	exploratory data analysis
EFA	exploratory factor analysis
ELL	English language learner
ES	effect size
ESCI	effect-size confidence interval
FA	factor analysis
GDP	gross domestic product
GIS	geographic information systems
GLM	general (and generalized) linear model
GPA	grade point average
GRE	Graduate Record Examination
GSS	general social survey
GT	grounded theory
HLM	hierarchical linear modeling
HSD	honestly significant difference
ICC	intraclass correlation
ICPSR	Inter-University Consortium for Political and Social Research
IPEDS	integrated postsecondary education data system
IQ	intelligence quotient
IQR	interquartile range
IRB	institutional review board
IRT	item response theory
I-T	information-theoretic analysis
IV	independent variable
IVE	instrumental variable estimation
JOB	Job Outreach Bureau
LGCM	latent growth curve modeling
LOVE	left-out variable error
LR	logit (or logistic) regression
LS	least squares

M	mean
MANOVA	multivariate analysis of variance
MARS	meta-analytic reporting standards
MC	Monte Carlo
MCAR	missing completely at random
MCMC	Markov chain Monte Carlo
MI	multiple imputation
ML or MLE	maximum likelihood (estimation)
MLM	multilevel modeling
MNAR	missing not at random
MOE	margin of error
MRA	multiple regression analysis
MWW	Mann–Whitney–Wilcoxon test
N	number (of cases, participants, subjects)
NAEP	National Assessment of Educational Progress, or the Nation's Report Card
NES	National Election Study
NH	null hypothesis
NHST	null-hypothesis significance testing
NIH	National Institutes of Health
OECD	Organization for Economic Cooperation and Development
OLS	ordinary least squares
OR	odds ratio
OSN	online social network
PA	path analysis
PAF	principal axis factoring
PCA	principal components analysis
PIRLS	Progress in Reading Literacy Study
PISA	Program for International Student Assessment
PMA	prospective meta-analysis
PRE	proportional reduction of error
PRISMA	preferred reporting items for systematic reviews and meta-analysis
PSM	propensity score matching

QCA	qualitative comparative analysis
csQCA	crisp set qualitative comparative analysis
fsQCA	fuzzy set qualitative comparative analysis
QNA	qualitative narrative analysis
RAVE	redundant added variable error
RCT	randomized controlled (or clinical) trial
RD(D)	regression discontinuity (design)
RFT	randomized field trial
RQDA	R qualitative data analysis
RR(R)	relative risk (ratio)
SALG	student assessment of learning gains
SD	standard deviation
SE	standard error
SEM	structural equation modeling; simultaneous equations modeling; standard error of the mean (italicized)
SMD	standardized mean difference
SNA	social network analysis
SNS	social network sites
STEM	science, technology, engineering, and math
TIMSS	Trends in International Math and Science Study
URL	uniform resource locator
WS	Web services
WVS	World Values Survey

Brief Contents

Extended Contents

General Introduction

In this General Introduction we:

- Describe our main goal in the book: helping you select the most effective methods to analyze your data.
- Explain the book's two main organizing questions.
- Discuss what we mean by the remarkably complex term *data*.
- Review the many uses of ordered data, that is, data that have been coded as ranks.
- Discuss the key role of visual/graphic data coding and analyses.
- Consider when the coding process is most likely to occur in your research project.
- Discuss the relation between codes and the world we try to describe using them: between "symbols" and "stuff."
- Present a graphic depiction of the relation of coding to analysis.
- Give examples of the relation of coding to analysis and where to find further discussion of these in the book.
- Look ahead at the overall structure of the book and how you can use it to facilitate your analysis choices.

In this book we give advice about how to select good methods for analyzing your data. Because you are consulting this book you probably already have data to analyze, are planning to collect some soon, or can imagine what you might collect eventually. This means that you also have a pretty good idea of your research question and what design(s) you will use for collecting your data. You have also most likely already identified a sample from which to gather data to answer the research question—and we hope that you have done so ethically.[1] So, this book is somewhat "advanced" in its subject matter, which means that it addresses topics that are fairly far along in the course of a research project. But "advanced" does not necessarily mean highly technical. The methods of

[1]Designs, sampling, and research ethics are discussed in our companion volume, *When to Use What Research Design* (Vogt, Gardner, & Haeffele, 2012).

analysis we describe are often cutting-edge approaches to analysis, but understanding our discussions of those methods does not require advanced math or other highly specialized knowledge. We can discuss specialized topics in fairly nontechnical ways, first, because we have made an effort to do so, and, second, because we emphasize *choosing* various analysis methods; but we do not extensively discuss how to implement the methods of analysis you have chosen.

If you already know what data analysis method you want to use, it is fairly easy to find instructions or software with directions for how to use it. But our topic in this book—deciding when to use which methods of analysis—can be more complicated. There are always options among the analysis methods you might apply to your data. Each option has advantages and disadvantages that make it more or less effective for a particular problem. This book reviews the options for qualitative, quantitative, visual, and combined data analyses, as these can be applied to a wide range of research problems. The decision is important because it influences the quality of your study's results; it can be difficult because it raises several conceptual problems. Because students and colleagues can find the choices of analysis methods to be challenging, we try to help by offering the advice in this book.

If you have already collected your data, you probably also have a tentative plan for analyzing them. Sketching a plan for the analysis before you collect your data is always a good idea. It enables you to focus on the question of what you will do with your data once you have them. It helps ensure that you can use your analyses to address your research questions. But the initial plan for analyzing your data almost always needs revision once you get your hands on the data, because at that point you have a better idea of what your data collection process has given you. The fact that you will probably need to adjust your plan as you go along does not mean that you should skip the early planning phase. An unfortunate example, described in the opening pages of Chapter 1, illustrates how the lack of an initial plan to analyze data can seriously weaken a research project.

WHAT ARE DATA?

What do we mean by **data**? Like many other terms in research methodology, the term *data* is contested. Some researchers reject it as positivist and quantitative. Most researchers appear to use the term without really defining it, probably because a workable definition fully describing the many ways the term *data* is used is highly elusive. To many researchers it seems to mean something like the basic stuff we study.[2] It refers to perceptions or thoughts that we've symbolized in some way—as words, numbers, or images—*and* that we plan to do more with, to analyze further. Reasonable synonyms for *data* and *analysis* are *evidence* and *study*. Whether one says "study the evidence" or "analyze the data" seems mostly a matter of taste. Whatever they are, the data do not speak for themselves. We have to speak for them. The point of this book is to suggest ways of doing so.

[2]Literally, *data* means "things that are given." In research, however, they are not given; they are elicited, collected, found, created, or otherwise generated.

TWO BASIC ORGANIZING QUESTIONS

To organize our suggestions about what methods to use, we address two basic questions:

1. *When you have a particular kind of data interpretation problem, what method(s) of analysis do you use?* For example, after you have recorded and transcribed what your 32 interviewees have told you, how do you turn that textual evidence into answers to your research questions? Or, now that the experiment is over and you have collected your participants' scores on the outcome variables, what are the most effective ways to draw justifiable conclusions?
2. A second, related question is: *When you use a specific method of analysis, what kinds of data interpretation problems can you address?* For example, if you are using multilevel modeling (MLM), what techniques can you use to determine whether there is sufficient variance to analyze in the higher levels? Or, if you are using grounded theory (GT) to analyze in-depth interviews, what kinds of conclusions are warranted by the axial codes that have been derived from the data?

These two questions are related. One is the other stood on its head: What method do you use to analyze a specific kind of data? What kind of data can you analyze when using a specific method? Although the questions are parallel, they differ enough that at various points in the book we stress one over the other. We sometimes address them together, because these two different formats of the question of the relation of evidence and ways of studying it appear often to be engaged in a kind of dialectic. They interact in the minds of researchers thinking about how to address their problems of data interpretation.

Your options for analyzing your data are partly determined by how you have coded your data. Have you coded your data qualitatively, quantitatively, or graphically? In other words, have you used words, numbers, or pictures? Or have you combined these? If you have already coded your data, the ways you did so were undoubtedly influenced by your earlier design choices, which in turn were influenced by your research questions. Your design influences, but it does not *determine*, your coding and analysis options. All major design types—surveys, interviews, experiments, observations, secondary/archival, and combined—have been used to collect and then to code and analyze all major types of data: names, ranks, numbers, and pictures.

RANKS OR ORDERED CODING (WHEN TO USE ORDINAL DATA)

We add **ranks** to the kinds of symbols used in coding because ranks are very common in social research, although they are not discussed by methodologists as much as are other codes, especially quantitative and qualitative codes. Ranking pervades human descriptions, actions, and decision making. For example, a research paper might be judged to be excellent, very good, adequate, and so on. These ranks might then be converted into A, B, C, and so forth, and they, in turn, might be converted into numbers 4, 3, 2, and so forth. If you sprain your ankle, the sprain might be described by a physician as severe, moderate, mild, or with combinations such as "moderately severe." Similar ranks are often used by psychologists describing symptoms. Severity rankings of psychological symptoms or conditions are often based on numerically coded inventories. Ankle sprains are usually judged with visual data; the eye is used to examine an X-ray, a magnetic resonance image (MRI), or even the ankle itself. The arts are no exception to the ubiquity of ranked descriptions; quality rankings by critics of plays, novels, paintings, and so on are routine. In music, composers indicate the tempo at which musicians should play a piece using such ranked tempos as "slowly" (*lento*), "fast—but not too much" (*allegro, ma non troppo*), or "as fast as possible" (*prestissimo*).

Sometimes ranks are given numbers. At other times, numerical continua are divided into categories using cut scores in order to create verbal ranks. Ranks are about halfway between categories and continua. Ranked codes and data can be thought of as a bridge between qualitative categorical codes and quantitative continuous ones. And it is a two-way bridge, with much traffic in both directions. For example, you might describe an interviewee's response to your question by saying that she seemed somewhat hesitant to answer the question—not *very* hesitant or *extremely* hesitant, but *somewhat.* Other interviewees could be described as being willing to answer, whereas still others were eager to do so. If you code your interview responses in this way, you have an implicit or explicit set of ordered categories—or a continuum—in mind. You give those categories (or points on the continuum) labels; they might range from "very eager" to "extremely reluctant" to participate in the interview or to answer particular questions.

Social scientists routinely use concepts and theories based on ranks: psychological conditions, density of social networks, trends in the economy (from mild recession to severe depression), and so on. Ranks are indispensable to social research. Theories,[3] even theories describing relations among quantitatively coded variables, are most often stated in words. Very often the words are descriptions of ranks. Coding using ranks is usually expressed in words or numbers, and it can also be symbolized graphically. Ranked codes are not purely qualitative, quantitative, or visual. Like most codes, they can be arrived at by researchers intuitively and impressionistically or by using fairly strict rules of categorization. Although you have several options when matching concepts to symbols, it is important to be meticulous in recording what you have done in a codebook. It is also important to be certain that you are using analysis techniques appropriate for your codes—for example, different correlations are used for ranked and interval-level data (see Chapter 8).

VISUAL/GRAPHIC DATA, CODING, AND ANALYSES

Visual/graphic data and analyses pervade everything that we write. This is in part because there are so many types and uses of visual/graphic data and analyses. Visual/graphic images can be fairly raw data, such as photographs or video recordings of

[3]We discuss the much-contested term *theory* at several points in the book, most systematically in Chapter 10. Here we can say that a theory is a general description of the relations among variables. An example from social psychology is "expectation states theory": Hierarchies grow up in small groups because of members' expectations of other members' likely contributions to the group's goals.

interviews or interactions. They can be a way to recode other types of data, as when logic models describe a theory of change and a program of action or when bar graphs describe a statistical distribution. And they can be an effective tool of analysis, as when concept maps are used to interpret ideas or when path diagrams are employed to investigate relations among variables. Thus visual/graphic images can be a form of basic data, a way to code data collected in other forms, a way to describe data, and a tool for analyzing them. Although visual/graphic data, codes, and analyses to some extent form a distinct category, they are also discussed in every chapter of this book, because they are indispensable tools for handling and describing one's data as well as for interpreting and presenting one's findings.

A note on terms: We use the terms *visual* and *graphic* more or less interchangeably because that is how they are used in practice by prominent writers in the field. For example, the classic work by Edward Tufte is called *The Visual Display of Quantitative Information*, and his early chapters discuss graphical excellence and integrity. Howard Wainer covers similar topics in *Graphic Discovery*, which recounts several "visual adventures." Nathan Yau's *Visualize This* reviews numerous techniques in statistical graphics, and Manuel Lima's gorgeous *Visual Complexity* mostly uses the term *visual* but calls many of the images he produces *graphs*. Lima pursues the goal of visualizing information—quantitative, qualitative, and visual—which he identifies as the process of "visually translating large volumes of data into digestible insights, creating an explicit bridge between data and knowledge."[4]

AT WHAT POINT DOES CODING OCCUR IN THE COURSE OF YOUR RESEARCH PROJECT?

Although there is no universal sequence, choices about approaches to a research project often occur in a typical order. First, you craft a research question and pick the design you will use to collect the data. The design, in turn, will imply an approach to coding your data. Then your coding choices direct you to some analytical procedures over others. But this order can vary.[5] For example, you may know that your research question requires a particular form of analysis. That form of analysis, in turn, can require that you collect your data and code it in specific ways. For example, if your research question concerns the influence of contexts on individuals' behaviors, you will need to collect data on contexts (such as neighborhoods) and on individuals' behaviors (such as socializing with neighbors, shopping locally, or commuting to work).

Coding data is crucial because an investigation of a research question cannot move ahead without it. When you code your data, you make decisions about how to manage the interface between the reality you are interested in and the symbols you use to think about that reality and to record evidence about it. Two phases are typical in coding.

---

[4]See, respectively, Tufte (1983), Wainer (2005), Yau (2011), and Lima (2011, quotation on p. 18). A note on footnotes: Based on research with users (graduate students in research methods courses) of books such as this one, we use footnotes rather than in-text citations. For a brief account of that research, see the blog entry "Citation Systems: Which Do You Prefer?" at *http://vogtsresearchmethods.blogspot.com*.

[5]For further discussion, see the Introduction to Part I.

First you define your concepts[6] specifically enough to identify relevant phenomena and collect relevant data. Second, you assign values, such as names or numbers, to your variables in order to prepare them for analysis.[7] The first step in coding is to decide how you will identify your variables (a.k.a. attributes) in order to collect data: Is this a neighborhood? What are its boundaries? The second step is deciding on the coding symbols you will use to produce values you can use in your analyses: Is this neighborhood densely populated? Are particular instances of socializing in the neighborhood organized or spontaneous? The coding symbols can be pictures,[8] words, numbers, ranks, or some combination of these.

CODES AND THE PHENOMENA WE STUDY

Whatever coding scheme you use, a fundamental question is the relation between the symbols and the phenomena they represent. Linguistic philosophers have called the relation between reality and the symbols we use to express it "words and the world."[9] We think of the relationship more broadly to include numbers and pictures as well as words; in our shorthand we call it "symbols and stuff," or, more formally, representations and realities. The key point is that without symbols, you can't study "stuff." The symbols you choose surely influence your understanding of stuff, but not in ways that can be easily specified in advance. The quality of the symbols, their validity, importantly determines the quality of any conclusions you draw from your data.[10]

Most research projects can, and frequently should, involve coding, and therefore analysis, with all three major types of symbols: quantitative, qualitative, and graphic or visual (such as color coding). Often, in any particular project, one of these will be the dominant mode of coding and analysis, but the others generally have a valuable, and perhaps unavoidable, role. Our own beliefs about using multiple forms of coding and analysis are not quite uniform. Our opinions range from the hard position that "it is impossible to think about anything important without using all three" to the softer "there are often many advantages to combining the three in various ways." Although we don't want to digress into epistemology or cognitive psychology, we think that hard and fast distinctions between verbal, numerical, and graphical symbols are difficult to maintain and not particularly useful.[11] In most studies we have conducted, we have

---

[6]These definitions are often called operational definitions by researchers collecting quantitative data. Fuller discussion of these terms can be found in relevant sections of this volume.

[7]These processes have been described several ways, and different methodologists prefer different terms. For example, some qualitative researchers resist the term *variables* for the things they study; others think that the term *coding* is inappropriate. Helpful descriptions of the processes of coding concepts from different perspectives are given by Jaccard and Jacoby (2010) on the more quantitative side and by Ragin (2008) on the more qualitative.

[8]Network diagrams might be especially useful for this example. For an overview, see Lima (2011) and Christakis and Fowler (2009). Genograms could be even more useful; see Butler (2008).

[9]The classic texts are Austin (1962) and Searle (1969).

[10]For a discussion of valid data coding, see the Introduction to Part I of this book and the Conclusion to Vogt et al. (2012).

[11]See Sandelowski, Voils, and Knafl (2009) on "quantitizing."

combined them. Sometimes we have used formal techniques of mixed method analysis to devise common codes for verbally and numerically coded data. More often we have used graphic, verbal, and numerical data coding sequentially to build an overall interpretation.

Because we think that combined or mixed data are so often helpful for effective analysis and interpretation, we discuss multimethod research throughout this volume rather than segregating it in a separate part of the book.[12] The examples of coding and analysis recounted in the upcoming section drive home the point by illustrating how natural it is to move from one form of coding and analysis to another as you traverse a research project and to unite them in an overall interpretation.

A GRAPHIC DEPICTION OF THE RELATION OF CODING TO ANALYSIS

The typical sequence in a research project leads from coding to analyses. This is illustrated in Figure 1, which also describes how we organized our thinking as we wrote this book. We look at coding and choices among verbal, numerical, graphic, and combined codes (see the left side of the figure; discussed in Part I) and then we review choices among qualitative, quantitative, graphic, and combined modes of analysis (see the right side, as discussed in Parts II and III). Please note that this figure should *not* be read to imply a necessary thematic unity of coding types and analysis methods. It may be more common for attributes coded with words to be analyzed qualitatively or for variables coded with numbers to be analyzed quantitatively, but this is a tendency, not a logical entailment. Researchers have more choices than would be the case were these relations between codes and analyses logical necessities. Because they are not necessary relations, the burden of choice—or, more positively, the freedom to choose—is great.

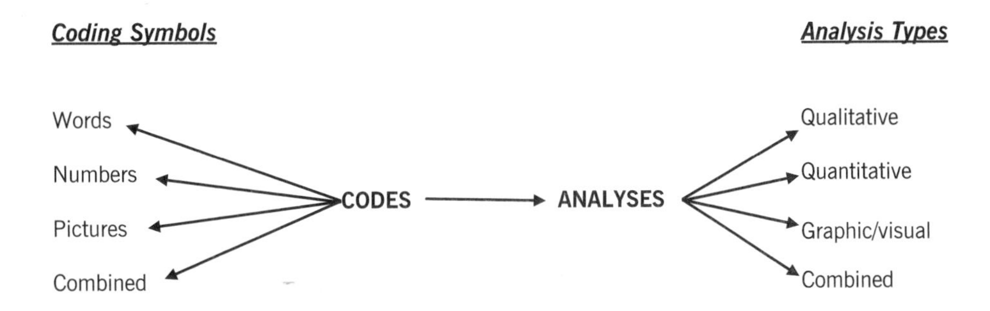

FIGURE 1. The relation of coding to analysis. (*Note.* For an explanation of why the arrows in the figure point in the directions they do, see the discussions of factor analysis [FA] and principal components analysis [PCA] in Chapter 9. The figure is modeled after FA, not PCA.)

---

[12]The one exception is Chapter 13, in which we address some of the more technical considerations in combing data that have been coded in different ways.

EXAMPLES OF CODING AND ANALYSIS

Rather than continuing to discuss coding and analysis abstractly, we present some brief examples of approaches that one could take to data coding and analysis. There is one set of examples for each of the chapters on coding, and these are tied to relevant chapters on analysis. Each brief example illustrates the interaction between selecting coding and analysis methods and how effective choices can lead to compelling interpretations of your data.

Example 1: Coding and Analyzing Survey Data (Chapters 1 and 8)

Although surveying is usually considered a method of collecting and analyzing quantitative evidence, this is a simplification. Say that you are conducting survey research to investigate attitudes. You collect data about each of the attitudes. But what are attitudes? They are theoretical constructs expressed in *words*. To study them, you could ask respondents to react to statements about attitudes by picking options on a Likert *ranking* scale, which typically uses the following *words*: *strongly agree, agree, neutral, disagree*, and *strongly disagree*. At this point you might assign *numbers* to those words: 5, 4, 3, 2, and 1 are typical. Once numbers are assigned to the words on the scale, you can use quantitative techniques, such as factor analysis, to see whether the items in your presumed scale actually hang together. Using that *quantitative* method, which usually employs *graphic* techniques (such as scree plots), you may find that the items actually form two quite distinct numerical scales. You label those quantitative scales using *words* to identify your new theoretical constructs.[13] This example illustrates how it can be nearly impossible to avoid applying qualitative, quantitative, ranked, and graphic coding and analysis to the same research problem. It also illustrates the pervasiveness of mixed or combined methods of coding and analysis and why we discuss them in *every* chapter of the book.

Example 2: Coding and Analyzing Interview Data (Chapters 2 and 11)

Say you are interviewing people to ask them about their reactions to a social problem. Your main method of data collection is verbal interaction, which you audio- and videotape. You make a transcript of the words, which you analyze using textual techniques. Using your audio or video recording, you analyze gestures, tones of voice, pauses, and facial expressions. You might count and time these (as numbers) or assign ranked verbal codes, such as *strong, moderate*, and *weak* reactions, which you then enter into your notes. You might use grounded theory for the analysis of transcripts, or one of the more quantitative forms of content analysis, or one of the qualitative computer packages (such as Ethnograph) to help you organize and analyze your data.[14] And you might combine these with one of the more quantitative approaches to textual analysis. This example

[13]For an example of this kind of coding and analysis, see Vogt and McKenna (1998).

[14]Some grounded theory researchers embrace computer packages; others reject them; see Chapter 11. The old standbys remain a good place to start when coding interview data (Miles & Huberman, 1994; Spradley, 1979).

illustrates the wide range of choices open to researchers, as well as, again, the pervasiveness of opportunities to apply combined or mixed methods of analysis.

Example 3: Coding and Analyzing Experimental Data (Chapters 3 and 7)

Experiments have a prominent place in most lists of quantitative methods. But the interventions or treatments in experimental social research are not usually quantitative, although they are often coded with a 1 for the experimental group and a 0 for the control group. Here are three quick examples of experimental research and the wide range of coding and analysis methods that can be applied to experimental data. In a survey experiment,[15] respondents were shown two versions of a video depicting scenes of neighbors interacting; the scenes were identical except that the actors in the two videos differed by race. Respondents answered survey questions in which they rated the desirability of the neighborhoods; their ratings were coded with a rank-order variable and analyzed quantitatively. Race importantly influenced individuals' ratings of neighborhood desirability.[16] Another example is a study of the so-called Mozart effect (that listening to Mozart supposedly makes you smarter). The treatment was listening to different types of music (or other auditory phenomena). The dependent measure was obtained with a nonverbal (progressive matrices) IQ test, which resulted in a numerical score. Listening to Mozart had no effect.[17] As a final example, Kahneman discussed studies in which participants briefly looked at photos of political candidates to judge their "trustworthiness." Trustworthiness was coded *verbally* and was associated with other *visually* observed traits (e.g., type of smile). Those qualitative, verbal judgments of visual phenomena were good predictors of election results; that is, they were used in *quantitative* analyses of voting outcomes.[18]

Example 4: Coding and Analyzing Observational Data (Chapters 4, 11, and 12)

In observational studies of organizations, fieldnotes and documents can be used to collect and code data on quality, duration, and number of interactions of members of the organization. Sociograms or other graphic depictions of interactions among people in the organization's networks might be constructed.

For example, in her study of novice teachers, Baker-Doyle investigated each of her participants' social and professional support networks, and she coded these as network diagrams.[19] With these network diagrams, she was then able to characterize the social capital of individual teachers and to come to some useful conclusions about helping new teachers to be successful. The network diagram is becoming a common way to

---

[15] See Chapter 3 for a discussion of this method.

[16] Krysan, Couper, Farley, and Forman (2009).

[17] Newman et al. (1995).

[18] Kahneman (2011); see especially pages 90–91.

[19] Baker-Doyle (2011).

code interactions of all kinds as a means of understanding human social capital and the powerful role it plays.[20]

Example 5: Coding and Analyzing Archival Data—or, Secondary Analysis[21] (Chapters 5 and 6–8)

Archival data are collected and paid for by someone other than the researcher.[22] One of the most common types of archival research is the literature review. A meta-analysis is a literature review that results in a *quantitative* summary of research findings; this means that numbers predominate in coding and analysis. But the first step in a meta-analysis is a *qualitative* determination of the eligibility of studies for inclusion. And *graphic* techniques, such as funnel plots, are usually considered essential for discovering important patterns in the data and for depicting a summary of the findings of research articles. The qualitative assessments of eligibility are combined with graphic depictions of patterns and numerical statistical summaries of results to produce an overall summary. Another important field of research using archival data is the study of social media. Millions of messages can be gathered, coded, and analyzed quantitatively, qualitatively, and visually. Visualizing information is often indispensable for discovering comprehensible patterns in the huge amounts of data available from social media, as well as from other archival sources.

Example 6: Coding and Analyzing Data from Combined Designs (Chapter 13 and throughout)

Our general point in the first five sets of examples is that combined methods of coding and analysis are common in all designs, even those ostensibly tied to quantitative, qualitative, or graphic methods of analysis. A fortiori, if it is true of unitary designs, it will be even truer of explicitly combined/mixed designs. In combined designs, it is especially important to ensure that your coding methods are compatible. It is crucial that you do not assign incompatible coding schemes to data that you intend to merge for analysis. If you intend to unify your analysis only at the more theoretical and *interpretation* stages, then the coding for quantitative and qualitative *data* may remain distinct.

Here are two examples: Say you are investigating the quality and quantity of food available in low-income urban neighborhoods. Both quality and quantity are important attributes of food availability, but your coding must reflect the interaction of both attributes. Is a lot of poor-quality food better than a little high-quality food? Is quantity better measured by weight, volume, or calories? What attributes of food indicate "quality"? If your coding decisions skew your analysis, you might even conclude that a small amount of bad food is a good thing. Or to take a second example: Say you are trying to determine the adequacy of school facilities for the next 20 years. You use school-age population projections from census data. You determine population trends by county and then create qualitative categories, such as *rapidly increasing, increasing, stable, declining*, and *rapidly declining*. You might then create a color-coded map by county to

---

[20] Cross and Parker (2004); Castells (1996).

[21] For secondary analysis of "big data" from the Census Bureau, see Capps and Wright (2013).

[22] This definition comes from the classic discussion in Webb, Campbell, Schwartz, and Sechrest (1966).

determine regions of the state in which schools may not be able to house their students or in which school buildings may be empty in coming years. Where you place the "cut scores" to determine the category boundaries matters greatly; it could mean the difference between accurately or inaccurately determining school capacity and could greatly influence policy decisions affecting many people.[23]

LOOKING AHEAD

The preceding six sets of examples correspond to chapters in Part I on coding choices and are related to how those choices link to selecting analysis methods in the remaining chapters of the book. Each chapter on coding choices includes suggestions about which chapters to consult for analysis options (in Parts II and III). Those analysis chapters also discuss interpreting and reporting your analytic results by addressing the questions: How do you make sense of your analytic results, and how do you convey your interpretations to others? Although the coding and analysis sections of the book are closely related, there are important differences among them.

The chapters in Part I on coding are organized by design; each is relatively free-standing and can be read independently of the others. The chapters in Parts II and III, on methods of analysis, are more closely tied together. This is especially true of Part II, on quantitative analysis. The later chapters in Part II often assume knowledge of the earlier. Also, the analytic techniques in Part II are routinely used together in practice; researchers frequently use all of the types of quantitative methods—descriptive, inferential, and associational—in a single project. The inductive and deductive methods discussed in Part III, on the analysis of qualitative data, are less often employed together in a formal way. But they are often used together informally, perhaps even autonomically. Induction and deduction are, like inhaling and exhaling, ultimately inseparable, as are, we believe, qualitative and quantitative concepts.

Probably the most exciting moment in a research project occurs when the results from the data analysis start to become clear and you can actually begin to interpret the findings.

That is what it was all about. You've struggled devising a good research question, selected an appropriate design for gathering the data, identified a justifiable sample, and had it all approved by the institutional review board. And now, at last, you are going to see how it turned out. Will the painstaking and detailed work pay off? Your work is more likely to yield something interesting and important if you have given serious consideration to alternate methods of analysis. If you have done that, your choices were made knowing the options. It is hard to make a good decision otherwise. Our goal in this volume is helping with that penultimate, and crucial, step in a research project—choosing the most effective methods of data analysis.

---

[23]For an example of this type of population prediction being used in a policy context, see Simon (2012). For a discussion of how population predictions based on prior trends and assumptions may be misleading and therefore require adjustments in analysis methods, see Smith (1987).

PART I

Coding Data—by Design

In this Introduction to Part I we:

- Define coding.
- Describe two main phases of data coding: for data collection and for data analysis.
- Provide an example: coding attitudes and beliefs.
- Review recurring issues in coding: validity, judgment, reliability, symbols, persistence, and justification.

INTRODUCTION TO PART I

Coding is a kind of "translation" of your data into symbols. The symbols can be words, numbers, letters, or graphic markers (such as + for more or ↓ for decreasing). You use these symbols to conduct an analysis. Coding differs by design. For example, in a participant observation, you might observe social interactions, describe them in your fieldnotes, and then label the descriptions of interactions in your notes with codes on a continuum ranging from "casual" to "intense." By contrast, in survey research, coding might involve assigning words to create predetermined response options and then assigning numbers to those words, such as *strongly agree* = 5, *agree* = 4, and so on. These examples illustrate one of the ways coding differs by design. In observational research, coding occurs mostly after data gathering, whereas in survey research much of it occurs before the data are collected. However, in both designs, additional recoding of the initial codes is common.

In most research projects, coding falls naturally into two phases. First, you need to make coding decisions to determine how you will collect your evidence. In this first phase, coding involves answering such questions as: How will you recognize a phenomenon when you see it? How will you record what you observe? In the second phase, after the data collection, you refine your initial coding to get your data ready for analysis.[1]

[1] Researchers who collect quantitative data often call this phase *measurement*. A common definition of measurement is assigning numerical codes to data. That definition means that measurement is a subcategory of coding, which is how we treat it in this book.

For example, in interviews and in surveys, in the first phase you write the questions, and you expect the questions to elicit certain types of answers; the questions imply codes. In the second phase, you make adjustments in the coding to prepare your data for analysis. In observational research you first decide how you will record your observations (when and how will you write your fieldnotes?), and, second, you determine how to turn those notes into analyzable data. In experiments you decide first how you will collect data on an outcome measure (perhaps verbal responses to questions) and then how you will code those responses for analysis.

In the first phase—coding for data collection—the focus is on validity or appropriateness of the codes that you use to label your study's attributes or variables. Validity refers you back to your research question. The goal is to be sure you are coding data in ways that allow you to address your question; you need appropriate links between your concepts and indicators. In the second phase—coding for analysis—you put more emphasis on reliability[2] or consistency; the links between your indicators and your data need to be dependable. Without consistency in coding, the logic of analysis disintegrates. Reliability of coding makes possible (it does not guarantee) effective data analysis and, ultimately, interpretation.[3]

Our emphasis in this book is more on the second phase of coding: for data *analysis*. We have already discussed coding for data *collection* in our companion volume;[4] there we stressed that coding decisions should be determined by the nature of your research questions and by the ontological character of the phenomena you are planning to study. Here, in this volume, in which we focus on coding for analysis, our emphasis is slightly more technical. But coding for analysis is never as straightforward and algorithmic as it is sometimes portrayed. The distinction between coding for data collection and coding for data analysis is a real one, but it simplifies an ongoing process, sometimes with feedback loops. Still, the earliest collection decisions might affect your final analysis options. For example, if you decide that the most valid way to code a variable is categorically—yes or no—because that is most appropriate for your research question, your decision will strongly influence the analysis options open to you. But these early decisions are not always fixed for the life of the research project. Preliminary exploratory analyses can lead you to decide to recode your data to improve your chances for effective final analyses and interpretations.

An Example: Coding Attitudes and Beliefs in Survey and Interview Research

An example can help make the discussion of the typical complications in the coding process more concrete. Say your general research question is, Do political attitudes influence scientific beliefs, and, if so, how? The research literature offers several theories and interpretations of data on the question. You decide to investigate further by studying

[2]Many researchers who collect and analyze qualitative data use the terms *trustworthiness* and *dependability* for validity and reliability. We use the latter as our generic terms because they tend to be familiar to more readers.

[3]It is increasingly common to use multiple coders, especially for complicated qualitative data. See Chapter 2.

[4]*When to Use What Research Design* (Vogt et al., 2012).

whether and how political conservatism and liberalism influence or predict beliefs about biological evolution and global warming. Beliefs about evolution and global warming will probably be comparatively easy to code. Most people either believe that evolution is a good description of the origin of species or that it isn't, although some people may be undecided or indifferent. And most people seem to have similarly firm beliefs about global warming. Coding these outcome variables could be fairly uncomplicated. On the other hand, conservatism and liberalism are notoriously slippery concepts. Are they clear categories, or do they range on a continuum from very liberal on the left to very conservative on the right? Are there views more left wing than very liberal or more right wing than very conservative? How much difference is there between slightly liberal and slightly conservative, or do such views constitute another category, say, moderate?

How would you gather the data to code? Would you ask people to tell you about their political views in an interview or in a survey, or in some combination of the two? We assume in this book that you have already made that basic design decision: survey, interview, or both. Now you are ready to move to coding decisions to implement your choice. One key difference between interviewing and surveying is that coding decisions come earlier in survey research. Typical forced-choice survey questions determine the answers and how they can be coded and analyzed much more than do typical semistructured interview questions. For instance, if you surveyed, you might ask respondents to identify their political positions by having them select a point on a conservative–liberal continuum. If you interviewed, you might ask a series of broad questions about politics, hoping to encourage extensive comments and narratives from interviewees. One of your coding activities with the interview data might eventually be to place the interviewees on a conservative–liberal continuum, rather than having survey respondents pick the point on a continuum themselves.

To continue with the example, say that as you review the responses and your initial coding of them, it begins to look like the scientific beliefs you are studying are not distinct or separate. Perhaps what you are really investigating are not individual scientific *beliefs* but general *attitudes* toward science; and these attitudes, in turn, are related to political tendencies. In your surveys, you find that answers to the question about global warming predict answers to the question about evolution, and vice versa. In your interviews you discover that many people think of the two topics as related and, furthermore, that quite a few interviewees bring up other beliefs that they understand as being part of the "same thing," most prominently their beliefs about the effects of and need for vaccinations. You begin to ask yourself, Do most people who reject evolution also reject global warming and the need for vaccinations? And do most people who agree that vaccinations are a good idea also believe in global warming and evolution? You were not looking for these clusters when you framed your original research questions. You had thought of evolution and global warming as separate examples of scientific beliefs from different scientific fields.

On the face of it the two beliefs are unrelated: whether humans and chimps have a common ancestor and whether atmospheric pollution is changing climates. And neither appears to have much to do with the effectiveness of vaccination. But this does not seem to be how your interviewees and survey respondents see things, and you need to change your codes to reflect *their* views if you want to code *their* responses validly. That recoding will also probably lead you to refine your initial research question and review the theories on which it was based. Perhaps you are dealing with a syndrome or a cultural pattern, not distinct beliefs. Coding and analyzing syndromes and general attitudes require different techniques than coding and analyzing separate beliefs.

In short, coding straddles data collection and data analysis. That is why we ended our companion volume on research design with a chapter on coding and why we begin this one on data analysis with chapters on coding for different designs. To collect data, you have to make initial coding decisions. To analyze them, you may need to make further decisions, which, together with the initial decisions, influence the analysis options open to you. Coding begins with your research questions so that you can code the data you collect appropriately. It continues as you build your analysis strategies so that you can code your data in ways that enable you to use the most effective methods of analysis and interpretation.

In brief, coding varies considerably depending on the research design you have used to collect the data. Coding responses to interview questions will raise a conceptually different set of problems than will, for example, coding research articles for a meta-analysis. Because coding issues emerge out of and are shaped by your design, we review them that way in the coming chapters as we discuss coding for surveys, interviews, experiments, observational studies, archival studies, and combined designs. However, we conclude this introduction by discussing ways in which all forms of coding are analogous. All of them share similar problems and raise related questions.

Recurring Issues in Coding

Validity[5]

How do you capture the essence of a variable or attribute with a code? It is in the nature of coding for the code to be simpler than the phenomenon it attempts to represent. Deciding what simplifications do the least damage and which are the most appropriate for the research questions is challenging. As has been said of statistical models, so too of codes: All are wrong, some are useful. Codes that lead to data that are most analyzable are not necessarily those that are most appropriate or relevant to your research question or truest to the phenomena being studied. Conscious trade-offs are sometimes required. To return to the example of coding conservatism and liberalism: You could present respondents to surveys or interviews with a scale having 10 options, ranging from very liberal on the left to very conservative on the right, and have them identify the point on the scale that best describes their beliefs. Most respondents could do it, and probably would. Their answers would generate data that would be easy to handle and would have nice statistical properties that would facilitate analysis. But does this approach capture the underlying reality? And would one person's score of, say, 8 on the 10-point scale mean the same thing as another person's score of 8?

Judgment

How much judgment is required when you do your coding? All coding involves some judgment; there are no easily applied algorithms. One can think of the process of coding

[5]Validity is an exceptionally complicated and contested topic. One review, by Adcock and Collier (2001), found more than 30 types of measurement validity used for qualitative and quantitative data.

as ranging from low- to high-inference judgments. In an experiment to teach writing, an example of questions that would generate answers that could be coded with minimal inference would be, Can participants distinguish grammatically correct sentences (yes–no)? How many? An example of a question that would require high-inference coding would be, Can participants write a *persuasive* essay? The answer might be a simple yes or no, but the process of determining the code for persuasiveness of essays would involve much more judgment than the code for grammatically correct sentences. Or, in an observational study of interaction, a low-inference coding question would be, Did *X* hit *Y*—yes or no? A high-inference question would be, If yes, was *X*'s action assault, intimidation, self-defense, horsing around, a pat on the back, an unintentional contact, or something else?

Reliability

How do you attain consistency without rigidity? Without some form of consistency from one bit of data collection to the next, and from one act of preparation of data for analysis to the next, your results become literally meaningless. But consistency in coding can come at the cost of less validity. To make your coding plan work, you may have to use categories that are too broad. Or, to implement the coding plan, you might have to whittle down too many square pegs to fit them into the round holes of your coding scheme.

The three broad types of reliability are (1) *interrater* reliability, which refers to the consistency of more than one coder; (2) *test–retest* reliability, which refers to the consistency of the same test over time; and (3) *internal consistency* reliability, which refers to the consistency of multiple questions probing aspects of the same concept. This third one is the most complicated of the three; it can be illustrated with our political attitudes example. Say you think that liberalism is not one belief but is rather a cluster of related beliefs, so you ask respondents or interviewees about each belief in the presumed cluster. If you are correct about the cluster, respondents or interviewees will tend to answer the questions consistently (reliably). If you are wrong, they won't.

Symbols

How do you decide whether to use names, ranks, numbers, pictures, or combinations? This is a key choice both when determining the codes you will use to collect data and as you prepare them for analysis. It can importantly determine the data analysis options open to you. That is why these choices involve (or should involve) much more complicated decision making than is sometimes realized. The choices should not be treated casually. When they are made deliberately, we think it is best to decide on the basis of the nature of the phenomena being studied rather than in an effort to follow an overarching ideology or epistemological stance—constructivism, neopositivism, or some other, broader worldview belief. Constructivism might lead one to prefer categorical or qualitative codes, whereas neopositivism might lead one to prefer continuous or quantitative codes, but such personal preferences for words or numbers are poor criteria for making this important choice.

Persistence

How do you manage the phases of coding that occur throughout the research project? Coding will be crucial in preparation for data collection, in the actual act of collection, and then as a step in the preparation of data for analysis. Sometimes the codes might not change from stage to stage. In that case your initial decisions carry through to the final analysis stages. At other times, operational definitions that enable you to recognize a phenomenon will not be the best codes to use to record an observation, nor will they necessarily be the most felicitous codes for data analysis. When your coding procedures change from the collecting through the analyzing phases, it is important to maintain detailed fieldnotes or a codebook (usually it's more of a list than a "book"), or, in grounded theory terms, memos that enable you to maintain an "audit trail" (see Chapter 11). Reconstructing codes after the fact can be embarrassingly difficult if you haven't recorded your coding steps and why you took them.

Justification

How do you explain the rationale for or defend the appropriateness of your coding decisions? We have found that novice researchers and even some experienced investigators breeze over this aspect of the research process. If you have decided, for example, to code conservatism using categories rather than a continuum, it behooves you to explain why. At minimum, you need to record what you did so that you'll remember (you might think you'll have no problem remembering, but in our experience, you'll be wrong). Making this information, and the reasoning behind it, available enables your readers to interpret and possibly replicate your study. Although you'll want to be meticulous in your record keeping and will often want to share those records, many outlets for research reports have insufficient space for you to provide details. One solution is to write two papers, one about coding issues and solutions and a second paper addressing the substantive findings of your research. A more practical solution, perhaps, is to keep good records, give readers a quick overview in the research report, but put the coding details on an open-access Web page.

In the chapters that follow, we look at how these perennial questions arise and can be addressed in each design. We also discuss more specific issues and examples of specialized problems in coding and how to solve them. But the specific issues and specialized problems will always raise versions of or be subcategories of the six recurring questions we have just reviewed. Each of the chapters in Part I, "Coding Data by Design," concludes with guidelines for appropriate analysis options and references to the chapters in which they can be found.

When coding survey data (discussed in Chapter 1), the emphasis is usually on writing valid and reliable questions with predetermined answers and then on summarizing those answers into codes that can be conceptually linked to your research questions (open-ended questions are an exception, of course). Coding in interview research (Chapter 2) is often closely tied to the technology used to record what the interviewees have said: notes, audio recordings, video recordings, and so on. Whatever the collection method, the data usually become textual. Those texts then need to be transformed through coding into units of data and concepts that can be analyzed. In experimental research (Chapter 3) the main issues in coding tend to center on justifiable causal inference and therefore on valid and reliable coding of outcome variables;[6] also of concern is coding for analytic techniques that can increase statistical power, which is an especially worrisome issue when the number of experimental participants is small. Observational research (Chapter 4) comes in many forms—overt–covert and participant–naturalistic are two continua—and observational researchers collect many types of data. Often the major coding issues tend to center on how to integrate varieties of data and their multifarious codings. Because archival research (Chapter 5) uses data that were not generated by the researcher, coding issues are often constrained by the nature of the primary records from which the researcher obtains the data. Coding involves, first, the criteria to be used when extracting the data from records (which have not usually been compiled with the needs of researchers in mind) and, second, translating those data into codes appropriate for the chosen method of analysis. Combined designs (Chapter 13 and throughout) by definition touch on at least two, and often more, of the issues discussed in Chapters 1–5. Combined designs also raise the special problem of coordinating and integrating these codings for analysis and interpretation (Chapter 13).

Coding is using symbols (words, numbers, or graphics) to define, label, and prepare your data for analysis. In some research designs, such as surveys and experiments, you do much of the coding work up front; the codes are written before the data are collected. In other research designs, such as interviews and participant observations, you do the coding of transcripts and notes after the data are collected. In combined/mixed data you often do both types of coding—planned and post hoc. In any case, the quality of your analyses and conclusions can be no better than the quality of your data and how you have coded them. That is why coding has a prominent place in this book.

[6]Coding for fidelity of implementation and the strength of the independent variables is also important; see Century, Rudnick, and Freeman (2010).

SUGGESTIONS FOR FURTHER READING

Any thought that data coding and editing is a cut-and-dried, noncontroversial issue will be quickly dispelled by the eye-opening article "Diversity in Everyday Research Practice" by Leahey, Entwisle, and Einaudi (2003). Practicing researchers in psychology, anthropology, and sociology who responded to a hypothetical problem about coding and editing messy data differed sharply about proper data coding and appropriate procedures for data handling.

Social Science Concepts: A User's Guide by Gary Goertz (2006) is a terrific review of the main questions that face social scientists engaged in the processes of concept formation and coding. The book transcends squabbles between the "quants" and "quals" and focuses on the common problems involved in tying theorizing about concepts to empirical data coding and analysis.

A classic, which is still very much worth reading and not really superseded by newer work, is *Unobtrusive Measures: Nonreactive Research in the Social Sciences* by Webb, Campbell, Schwartz, and Sechrest (1966). The authors call for triangulation, multiple operations of concepts, and "multimethod research." It is especially important, they argue, to combine unobtrusive research with more intrusive methods—such as interviews, surveys, and experiments—in order to control for the biases that arise when people are aware that they are being studied.

A useful article that speaks to interrater reliability in a general way and describes a coefficient that can be determined with an SPSS/SAS macro is Hayes and Krippendorff's "Answering the Call for a Standard Reliability Measure for Coding Data" (2007). It is especially interesting because it could be used across design types that employ content analysis: text, visual, and audio.

Guidelines for quantitative data coding are somewhat more widely available than those for qualitative coding. A very handy book that partly fills the gap for qualitative coding is Saldaña's (2012) *The Coding Manual for Qualitative Researchers*. Although it is general in scope and reviews a broad range of coding approaches, it is, like much of qualitative coding, importantly influenced by grounded theory.

Graphic representation and coding of data have recently become more important in social research. It has long been central in the natural sciences, in which, since the 18th century, many disciplines have been defined by large, elaborately produced atlases—in fields such as anatomy, astronomy, archeology, botany, chemistry, and crystallography (and that's just the ABCs). As the epistemological basis of disciplines changed, so, too, did the way each depicted its subject matter. Changes in graphic coding give us a window on the "epistemologies of the eye," which are brilliantly described by Daston and Galison's (2007) *Objectivity*. Concepts of objectivity in the natural sciences were not static. They evolved. And they always evolved in concert with concepts of subjectivity. The social sciences went through similar phases, although these were less *visible* in most social science disciplines in part because these disciplines less commonly employed graphic representation.

CHAPTER 1

Coding Survey Data

In this chapter we:

- Present an example of pitfalls to avoid when constructing surveys.
- Discuss what methods to use to write an effective questionnaire, including:
  - Considerations when linking survey questions to research questions.
  - When to use questions from previous surveys.
  - When to use various question formats.
    - When should you use open-ended or forced-choice questions?
    - When should you use reverse coding?
    - How many points do you need in a scale?
    - When should respondents be given neutral response options?
  - When mode of administration (face-to-face, telephone, or self-administered) influences measurement.
  - Steps you can take to improve the quality of questions.
    - Checklists, focus groups, expert review, linking survey questions to research questions, cognitive interviews, pilot tests, and survey experiments.
- Review coding and measuring respondents' answers to questions.
  - When can you sum the answers to questions (or take an average) to make a composite scale?
  - When are the questions in your scales measuring the same thing?
  - When is the measurement on a summated scale interval and when is it ordinal?
- Indicate where in this book to find further analysis guidelines for surveys.

If you have decided that your research question can be best addressed through survey research, you have chosen to use the iconic method for quantitative social research. When people think of gathering quantitative social science data, survey research often comes to mind, and it is true that more quantitative social science data have been collected through survey research than in any other way. Survey research has been a social science success story in fields as diverse as network analysis and election prediction. That success and widespread use has led to much accumulated wisdom about how to code survey questions and answers. So you will have many standard resources on which to rely.

Coding for surveys usually focuses on quantitative data, and we do so in this chapter, even though survey researchers often collect qualitative data when they ask open-ended questions. For such qualitative survey data, see Chapters 2, 4, and 11. Methods for coding quantitative survey data are often parallel to methods used to code quantitative experimental data. Although the two can differ in important ways, it can be helpful to compare them, and we do so at several points throughout this chapter. For an overview, compare the Summary Table in this chapter and the one in Chapter 3 on coding experimental data.

As in many other research designs, coding and measurement in surveys falls naturally into two phases: first, before the data collection, as you write the questionnaire;[1] and second, after the data collection, as you sort and categorize the responses to prepare them for analysis. In the first phase you construct the questions and, with forced-choice questions, you precode the answers (coding occurs later with open-ended questions, of course). In the second phase you continue coding the answers to prepare them for analysis. Surveys differ from most other designs in that the work in the first phase is more extensive. The contrast with coding semistructured interview questions is particularly sharp: In interviews, almost all the coding is done after the data are collected; in surveys, nearly all of it is done before.

The first phase of coding in survey research focuses on what questions to ask respondents, how to format the questions, and how to code the answers so that they can be analyzed and interpreted. Addressing the content and format of the items in a survey you write includes taking steps to increase the chances that the response options are actually measuring what you want to measure. In other terms, the focus in the first phase of coding in survey research is the **content validity** of the questions. The questions have content validity to the extent that they address your research questions and the theoretical substratum on which they are built.

In some disciplines, especially psychology and related fields, it is probably more common to use a preexisting survey than to construct one. For example, some 3,000 commercially available instruments are indexed in *Tests in Print* and reviewed in its companion volume, the *Mental Measurements Yearbook*. And many more, such as *General Social Survey*, are essentially in the public domain or are available from individual scholars at no cost. We begin by discussing constructing a survey rather than reusing one.

AN EXAMPLE: PITFALLS WHEN CONSTRUCTING A SURVEY

It is crucial to do all that you can to write a good questionnaire. No one would disagree, but sometimes researchers appear to forget that the answers to survey items can only be as good as the questions. You can't get good answers unless you ask good questions.

[1]We use the term *questionnaire* in the generic sense of any standardized list of questions, not only in the strict sense of a list that respondents read and answer in writing.

Writing survey questions requires a great deal of thought, skill, and attention to detail. It is something that almost no one working alone and writing only one draft can do well. As consultants helping people with their research, we have seen a remarkable number of nearly useless surveys. A consultant is usually brought in to help in the analysis phase, that is, after the survey is written, administered, and the responses collected. This is too late. What you should do before it is too late—before the analysis phase—is the focus of this chapter. The following example of a survey we were asked to help with (details are disguised to ensure anonymity) illustrates some pitfalls of putting off crucial work until it is too late.

The survey was self-administered. Instructions were ambiguous for some questions.[2] Because these questions could be, and actually were, interpreted in more than one way, the same was true of the answers. There was nothing to be done but to discard those questions. For some other questions, the response categories were not appropriate. One question, for example, did not have a "does not apply" option, although the question clearly did not apply to a large number of the respondents. On some other questions, the responses either were not mutually exclusive or were not exhaustive. **Mutually exclusive** answers contain no possible overlap; more than one answer cannot logically be chosen. For example, "How old are you: (a) 20–30, (b) 30–40, (c) 40–50, (d) 50–60?" does not provide mutually exclusive answers; someone who is 30 could answer either (a) or (b). **Exhaustive** answers cover all possible options. "Are you Protestant or Catholic?" is not exhaustive; it leaves out, among others, Jews, Moslems, Hindus, and the nonreligious. Mutually exclusive and exhaustive are perhaps the two best-known criteria for question options, as well as for any system of categorization, but it is remarkably easy to slip up and write a poor question with answers that are not exhaustive and/or mutually exclusive.

Of the 65 questions on the survey we were helping with, 40 seemed to have no major problems. After pointing this out to the client, he said, "Okay, could you help me analyze those 40?" Our reply was: "Sure, what do you want to know?" He stared at us blankly. He could not easily articulate the research questions that he hoped to answer with the responses to his survey questions. He thought that his research questions were implicit in his survey questions. We explained as gently as possible that with 40 questions, he had 760 bivariate relationships that he could examine and many more multivariate relationships. For example, Question 3 asked about respondents' education levels. Question 11 asked about political party identification, and Question 21 asked about attitudes toward a new law. Did he want to know about education's relationship to attitudes, or party identification's relationship to attitudes, or the effect of education on attitudes controlling for party identification—or what? Eventually, we were able to work with him to construct some research questions—questions that had been in the back of his mind when he wrote the survey. We could then relate these research questions to some of the survey questions, but the process was frustratingly inefficient for the client.

Because the survey author did not attend to the first phase of coding and measurement, he had largely wasted his time. Even worse, he had wasted the time of the hundreds of survey respondents who answered his survey questions. And, had the survey been better constructed, our time would also have been spent more effectively; but,

[2]See the later discussion of steps to improve the quality of questions.

unlike the survey respondents, at least we got paid for our efforts. The survey author was very intelligent, but he was ignorant of or did not pay sufficient attention to some basic procedures for writing survey questions. In survey research, the "up-front" work is exceptionally important, more so than most people realize. It determines everything else.

Numerous excellent books are available to guide researchers in writing questionnaires. It would be foolish not to spend at least a few days consulting such works on question design before drafting your survey.[3] In the following pages, we outline some of the steps to take in order to avoid disasters such as those in the preceding example. However, the treatment here is necessarily brief, so once you have settled on your general approaches, you will want to consult more specialized and detailed works; those we have cited are meant to suggest places to start. A book such as ours is like a regional map for someone traveling to a city. It is good for orienting yourself and getting there, but to find your way around the city once you have arrived, more detailed maps are needed.

WHAT METHODS TO USE TO CONSTRUCT AN EFFECTIVE QUESTIONNAIRE

Considerations When Linking Survey Questions to Research Questions

First, if you have decided to use a survey design, you should have already judged that potential respondents are likely to have knowledge sufficient to answer your questions or that they have beliefs that are clear enough to respond meaningfully. For example, if you asked us whether we favored proposed tariff regulations concerning the import of mineral ores, we wouldn't have enough knowledge to have a belief. We might be able to offer an opinion based on vague attitudes about tariffs, but is this what you would want to know?

Second, if you have chosen to conduct survey research, you have thereby already decided to use mostly structured questions designed to yield structured answers. Questions that might be just the ticket for an interview—such as, "What's it like living around here?"—would not work well on a survey. A survey question on the same topic might take the form, "In comparison with other neighborhoods where you have lived, would you say this one is safer, less safe, or about the same?" Survey questions are written to produce easily codable responses, and you should have already decided when you settled on a survey design that your research questions could be answered, for the most part, by short, structured responses. If the questions cannot be so answered, then survey research is probably the wrong design for your purposes.

There are two broad categories of surveys and survey questions: those that ask for facts and those that ask for attitudes, beliefs, or opinions. The kind of questionnaire you write will depend on your research question(s). These two types of survey questions

[3]Two classics are Sudman and Bradburn (1982) and Fowler (1995). A more recent and comprehensive treatment is Presser et al. (2004). See also Fowler (2008).

collect what can be called either **objective data** or **subjective data.**[4] The terms *objective* and *subjective* can be hard to define and are often quite controversial, but in the context of survey research, there is a clear distinction. If you can only reasonably get data from the *subjects* of the research (respondents to the survey), then the data are subjective. Opinions are a good example. If it is possible to get data other than from the respondents, such as their place of residence or age, then the data are objective. To answer your research questions, do you need objective or subjective data? Most often, perhaps, you will need both, and your survey questionnaire will seek to gather both kinds of data. Even when the focus is on subjective data, such as beliefs and attitudes, factual, objective information is usually collected as well, such as respondents' ages, genders, education levels, incomes, and so on.

Coding issues can differ for objective and subjective survey data. For objective data, knowledge and memory can be big issues. For subjective data, they hardly ever are. Coding usually is not much of a problem with objective data, assuming respondents know or remember what you ask them: How many times did you visit the dentist last year? When did you first become employed full time? The answers are easily coded, but it would also be easy for respondents to forget the exact details. To help respondents, it is often useful to ask them about a range of values rather than exact values—for example, *not at all, once or twice, . . . more than 5 times.*

By comparison, memory and knowledge are not as often a problem when survey researchers ask respondents for subjective data. It is usually safer to assume that people know how they feel, and surveys rarely ask them to remember how they felt in the past. On the other hand, coding and interpreting answers to questions seeking subjective data can be very complicated. In brief, for objective data, knowledge and memory can be problems, but coding is usually easy. For subjective data, coding is usually hard, but the knowledge and memories of respondents usually are not at issue.

How do you link your survey questions to your research questions? It would hardly ever be appropriate simply to turn your research question into a survey question. Say that your research question is, What is the relationship in this population between age, education level, and income? It would probably not be productive to ask respondents an open-ended question about this. Rather, you would ask short factual questions of respondents and make inferences yourself. Even when seeking answers to questions about subjective matters, such as respondents' feelings, it is rare to have respondents speculate on this. The research question might be, What is the relation between job satisfaction on the one hand and feelings of anxiety on the other? A good research question is almost never a good survey question for respondents. To answer the research question about job satisfaction and anxiety, you might ask as many as a dozen questions, half of them to measure job satisfaction and half to measure anxiety. The dozen questions would constitute your operationalizations of the variables *satisfaction* and *anxiety*.

To move from your research questions to your *first draft* of the survey questions, the first step is to determine what your variables are. These should either be explicit or

---

[4]Some researchers object to the use of these terms, mostly because the distinction between them can be drawn more sharply than is warranted. But we find the concepts useful and can think of no equally good labels. The concepts and labels are much debated; for enlightening discussions, see Hammersley (2011); Letherby, Scott, and Williams (2013); and Daston and Galison (2007).

implicit in your research questions. Make a complete list of these variables. Put them into one column of a two-column table. In the second column, write a draft of the question or questions you will use to gather data on each variable, or find questions from previous surveys to use to answer your research questions.

When to Use Questions from Previous Surveys

It is rare to plan to do survey research on variables that have never been studied before. Because writing your own questions is hard work, and work with many pitfalls, it is crucial to review the literature in your field before deciding to compose your own questions. Think hard about how your variables have been coded and measured by others. Literature reviews yield precious information not only about substantive findings but also about methodological procedures, such as ideas about how to construct your measurement instrument.

Variables such as anxiety and job satisfaction have been studied and measured by many researchers. Give serious consideration to asking your respondents questions used in previous studies. There is a strong presumption in favor of using instruments (in whole or in part) developed by other researchers. If they have done good measurement work on their questions, this can save you an enormous amount of time. You will still have to do some of this work with your data, such as examining the reliability of any scales as they were answered by your respondents. Here is a *very important* point: You should not use others' questions as an excuse to skip testing for reliability. Rather, you use others' questions because they serve as a sort of pilot test for your survey and because it is very helpful to be able to compare your results with previous work.

Another advantage to using existing measurements is that doing so facilitates the study of change. Perhaps you want to investigate whether the relation between job satisfaction and anxiety changes with economic conditions. If you have an effect size for the relationship based on data collected during a previous recession, you can compare that with the effect size of the relationship in more prosperous times or in a current recession. You complicate your work greatly if you use a different measure. As the old saying goes, "If you want to measure change, don't change the measure."

However, just because there is a preexisting measure of a variable, it does not necessarily follow that it is appropriate for your purposes and that you should use it. One of your important hypotheses might be, "The reason researchers studying my topic have gone astray is that they have used poor measurements." Although there are many benefits to reusing items, don't be afraid to revise another researcher's questions. However, there is much to be gained from using the same questions. In brief, one rarely has to and rarely should start from scratch when writing survey questions. Much can be learned through replication and through modification and reanalysis of responses to existing survey questions.[5] Of course, if you use others' questions, you will need to obtain permission (from the author and/or the publisher) to do so, perhaps paying a fee, and to cite their work as appropriate.

---

[5]Replication can be tricky; accuracy depends on exercising extreme care. See Altman and McDonald (2003).

When to Use Various Question Formats

The range of possible formats for questions is wide. The first division is open-ended versus forced-choice questions. Do you want your respondents to answer questions freely in their own words, or do you want them to select among a set of predetermined options? Say that you are asking questions of clients of the Job Outreach Bureau (JOB) in order to evaluate that office. An open-ended question might be as follows:

1. Please tell me, in your own words, what you think of the Job Outreach Bureau (JOB). Write on the back of the page if you need more space.

Questions such as this one have much to recommend them, but you will want to make limited use of such open-ended questions on a survey, for two main reasons. One has to do with measurement; the other concerns resources. First, respondents tend to skip such questions, and that raises problems of response bias and missing data. Second, open-ended questions take many more resources than forced-choice questions to code and analyze. Just as survey respondents tend to think it is too much work to answer open-ended questions, you may think it is too much work to code and analyze the answers to them. You may have decided to do a survey because your research question requires responses from a large, representative sample. If so, you probably have already determined that in order to code and analyze answers from hundreds of respondents to dozens of questions, you have to use forced-choice questions almost exclusively. You are willing to pay a price for that. You lose the depth and nuance possible with open-ended questions. But you gain the breadth and generalizability possible with a large sample survey.

If you decide you need to use a forced-choice question to obtain a general evaluation of the JOB, you could give respondents a rating scale such as the following:

2. On a scale of 1 to 10, with 10 being high or positive, how would you rate JOB?

   1 2 3 4 5 6 7 8 9 10

   (Please circle the number that best expresses your opinion.)

In an ideal world in which both you and your respondents had a great deal of time, you might want to ask both Question 1 and Question 2. Comparing the answers to the two questions could be very informative. If you can draw the same conclusions from the two types of questions, this provides cross-validation. You can be more confident about what you have learned than if you had used only one of the questions. Or, what you learn in the open-ended paragraph could help you explain the answers to the forced-choice rating scale. It is also possible that respondents will give conflicting answers to the two questions, perhaps giving a good "grade" on the rating scale but complaining about the inadequacies of the bureau in the open-ended answer. If your resources allow you to gather your evidence in more than one way, you are better off having both types of questions on your survey. You could also make your choice about type of question not on substantive grounds about what you'd like to know but because you believe that respondents would be more likely to answer some kinds of questions than others. Combining broad statistical approaches with in-depth methods that yield qualitative data is a good idea whenever you have the resources. Teams of researchers working on projects may have resources sufficient to do extensive multimeasurement work. Solo investigators can rarely afford to do a great deal of it. But they can do more than was once the case because of the wide availability of computer software packages for textual analyses and the increased possibilities for combining the analysis of qualitative and quantitative data.[6]

Surely the most common question format in survey research today is the **Likert scale**, named after Rensis Likert, the investigator who pioneered it. Respondents are given a series of statements with which they agree or disagree. The familiar set of choices is a 5- or 7-point scale that ranges from *strongly agree* through *neutral* to *strongly disagree*. Returning to our example, the clients of the JOB could be asked to agree or disagree with the statements in items 3 through 6, as follows:

3. JOB found opportunities for me that I wouldn't have been able to find on my own.

   Strongly agree Agree Neutral Disagree Strongly disagree

4. JOB increased my self-confidence in employment interviews.

   Strongly agree Agree Neutral Disagree Strongly disagree

5. JOB was less helpful than I expected it to be.

   Strongly agree Agree Neutral Disagree Strongly disagree

6. It would be better to replace JOB referrals with an actual training program.

   Strongly agree Agree Neutral Disagree Strongly disagree

This format is widely used because it has many positive features. Scores on the questions can be summed to get an overall assessment of the JOB office, but each question's score provides specific information about an aspect of the office.[7] This is more informative than an overall rating scale alone. One can test sets of questions for reliability, and one can learn from the scale's component questions why respondents tend to rate it as they did. Perhaps those who gave the JOB high rankings were especially fond of the way it helped them with their self-confidence and those who gave it low ratings did so because they thought it should focus on training, not on referrals. It is also helpful that the statements can be positive (such as Questions 3 and 4) or negative (Questions 5 and 6). This enables you to avoid the kind of bias that might occur if respondents liked to agree or to disagree with whatever is said to them. Some researchers think yea-saying or nay-saying is a big problem. It should be headed off by wording some questions positively and others negatively. (Of course, when you do so, you will code the negative question responses on a reverse scale, as we discuss subsequently.)

The Likert-type format is also preferable to the one that asks respondents to check all of the options that apply. Evidence from survey experiments very powerfully

---

[6]For an example of the very fruitful integration of survey and interview data, see Pearce (2002). For an account of the possibilities of software approaches to uniting text and numerical data, see Bazeley (2006).

[7]Likert scales have a long history of use in the social sciences; see Spector (1992). Typically the means of scales are analyzed, but more advanced options using other characteristics of the responses (such as their skewness and kurtosis) can also be very revealing; see Camparo and Camparo (2013).

demonstrates the superiority of the forced-choice format, in which respondents have to answer a question about each part of the topic. By contrast, the check-all-that-apply format is less likely to encourage respondents to take the questions as seriously or to think about their responses carefully.[8]

When Should You Use Reverse Coding?

This is one of several measurement issues with a set of questions, such as the four on the JOB office, that involve the wording of questions and the assigning of numbers to the answers (coding). It is often advisable to use both negatively and positively worded items, as there are some grounds for worry that some respondents like to check "agree" just to be agreeable—or to disagree to be disagreeable.[9] If you do use positively and negatively worded items, you will need to use reverse coding before summing the scores on items to make a scale. For example, for Question 3 you might give a 5 to *strongly agree*, a 4 to *agree*, and so on. In this case, for Question 6 you would give a 1 to *strongly agree*, a 2 to *agree*, and so on. This reverse coding is required because someone who says "strongly agree" to Question 3 likes the JOB office, but someone who says "strongly agree" to Question 6 dislikes it. One of the most common sources of puzzling results, such as an item that is highly inconsistent with others in the scale, is the investigator's having forgotten to reverse code an item. This is a rookie mistake, but one that is also made surprisingly often by veterans.

How Many Points Do You Need in a Scale?

The short answer to the question of how many points or options you should provide is that you should provide as many as are meaningful. If you err, it is better to include too many than too few. Neither is ideal, but you can always combine answers if you have too many options. Of course, after the survey, it is impossible to expand the number of options if you have too few. For some simple questions, *agree–disagree–unsure* may be enough. For others, on which you think respondents might have many levels of feeling or opinions, a scale with as many as nine *agree–disagree* intervals might be appropriate. Some researchers use a "feeling thermometer," on which respondents can pick a point on a thermometer ranging from 0 to 100. Commonly on Likert scales, one uses a range either of 5 or 7 points. An odd number of points on the scale makes it possible to have a neutral response choice in the middle.

When Should Respondents Be Given Neutral Response Choices?

Should the questions include neutral responses such as "don't know" or "unsure"? Measurement specialists disagree about this. Many researchers recommend eliminating all neutral, wishy-washy options. They argue that by forcing respondents to take a stand, you get better answers, that is, scores with bigger variances. Although it is true that you get bigger variances this way, that alone does not justify eliminating the neutral option

[8] Smyth, Dillman, Christian, and Stern (2006).

[9] One classic study found that such yea-saying and nay-saying differed by respondents' race (Bachman & O'Malley, 1984).

in all questions. For some questions, "don't know" or "don't care" are real opinions worthy of investigation. If you use a forced-choice format, the choices you force respondents to make should be good ones. In addition to being exhaustive and mutually exclusive, the choices have to be *valid*, which means that the question options should capture what the respondents actually believe. Forcing respondents to act as though they know or they care, even when they do not, reduces validity. Researchers may find it inconvenient if respondents frequently pick the neutral response; it tends to reduce variances and make it more difficult for researchers to get statistically significant results. But that is the researchers' problem, not the respondents' problem.

When Does Mode of Administration (Face-to-Face, Telephone, and Self-Administered) Influence Measurement?

Advantages and disadvantages of various modes of surveying are reviewed in our companion volume on choosing a research design.[10] Here we briefly mention some of the more frequent coding and measurement problems that are associated with particular modes of survey administration.

Face-to-face surveying raises the issue of the gender or color or age of the faces. There is no doubt that at least some respondents react to the characteristics of the survey interviewer, as well as to the questions. To compensate for this, you could randomly assign survey interviewers to respondents, which could randomly distribute such biases. You can also investigate whether responses vary with the characteristics of interviewer and respondent. It is often possible to check to see whether responses vary according to the age, gender, and ethnicities of respondents and survey interviewers. If they do, you can statistically control for these variations. Of course, every control variable you add means that you will need to increase your sample size. And there are other interviewer characteristics that could be considered, such as accent and mode of dress.

Telephone surveys—we might call them "ear-to-ear"—are very common for obvious reasons: They greatly reduce the time and cost of surveying large numbers of respondents spread over a wide geographical area. Some respondents will find the telephone intrusive, but others will prefer it or will only be willing to be contacted by telephone.[11] And, like the face-to-face survey, the telephone researcher is available to clarify survey questions that the respondent does not understand. Respondents may still react to gender, ethnicity, and tone of voice differences in telephone surveys, so it remains important to statistically control for any such biases in responses.

One of the important advantages of **self-administered** surveys is the elimination of this kind of bias. You should try to design self-administered questionnaires so that it will be *extremely* difficult to misinterpret the instructions. But some respondents will almost certainly misinterpret them. Never underestimate the inattention of respondents. They will almost never find your survey as interesting as you do. Probably the most frequent form of misinterpretation of survey instructions occurs when there are **skip patterns**: "If you answered yes to Question 14, go on to the next question; if you answered no, skip ahead to Question 18." A remarkable number of people can be inconsistent when faced with this kind of question. They will answer "no" to Question 14, forget to skip

[10] Vogt et al. (2012, Ch. 1, pp. 19–23).

[11] Stephens (2007).

ahead, and answer Questions 15, 16, and 17 as if they had answered "yes" to Question 14. For example, Question 14 might be, "Did you work while in college?" Questions 15, 16, and 17 might be about how much you worked and the nature of the work. If you answered: "No, I didn't work," then questions about the number of hours worked and the nature of the work are inapplicable, but sometimes people will answer them anyway. Such logically inconsistent responses are generally not usable, and you have to discard the data—never a pleasant experience.

If you must use skip patterns, consider face-to-face or telephone survey administration in which the interviewer does the skipping. Another alternative is self-administered electronic Web surveys; these can be designed so that the program does the skipping. That way the respondents never get a chance to answer questions they should have skipped.

The key point to remember is that survey experiments have shown that very small differences in question format can produce big differences in results, sometimes bigger even than those produced by differences in the content of the questions. Reviewing the results of such research on survey research is always time well spent.[12] A classic example of the influence of wording is: "Should the government not allow *X*?" versus "Should the government forbid *X*?" Although not allowing and forbidding seem logically equivalent, many more people will agree that the government should not allow something than that it should forbid it. The two apparently have different connotations for many people.

What Steps Can You Take to Improve the Quality of Questions?

After you have written your initial draft of questions based on your literature review and on your research questions, there are several steps you can take to improve the quality of your questionnaire. By *quality*, we refer here to the meaning of the questions, not to their technical aspects, such as when you need to use reverse coding. Constructing a good survey—one in which the questions are valid and truly ask about what you want to know—is a difficult process that requires many steps.[13] Most solo researchers will not be able to do all of them that we list, but doing them all should be kept in mind as an ideal. After each step you make the necessary revisions and proceed to the next step. In order, the steps are:

1. Review your draft using a checklist designed for the purpose.
2. Conduct focus groups with people who would qualify as potential respondents to help you make sure you have not omitted important items.
3. Have a small panel of experts review your questions; ideally, they would have expertise in question design, as well as in the topics being studied.
4. Review your revised questions in terms of your research question and your analysis plan, specifically, how you will be able to tie the responses to your research questions.

[12]A good example is Christian, Dillman, and Smyth (2007).

[13]See Sanders et al. (2010) for a discussion of the numerous ways survey respondents interpreted the phrase "had sex" and the implications of multiple meanings for misclassification bias.

5. Interview people who would qualify as potential respondents to ask them about the content and quality of the questions.
6. Pilot-test the survey with a sample of real respondents.
7. For questions that remain unclear, conduct survey experiments.

1. **Review your draft survey using a checklist.** This is the minimum first step. Writing surveys is a complicated business, and it is easy to omit something important or to make an easily corrected mistake. An excellent checklist is the one by Gordon Willis.[14] We have worked on several surveys over the years and still find it useful, as have many of our students. There are too many elements to the process of constructing survey questions—both their format and content—to trust things to memory. Even pilots who have flown planes for decades do not skip their checklists—or they are foolishly (and maybe criminally) negligent if they do.

2. **Conduct focus groups with potential respondents.** Focus groups sometimes come up with insights that the same people answering questions individually do not. The idea is to get a group of similar people (their similarity will be that they are the sorts of folks you will sample for your survey) to focus on something, in this case the scope of your questionnaire. Focus groups are a good place to ask and learn about problems with the overall presentation of the survey—clarity of instructions, length, question order, and so on.

3. **Have a small panel of experts review your questions.** Anybody is better than nobody. But it is nice to have someone who knows about the subject and somebody (it could be the same person, of course) who knows about survey design. Doctoral students have a ready-made panel—the members of their dissertation committees. Three or four experts are usually enough, but if you can importune half a dozen or more, that would usually be an advantage. Even when you get contradictory advice, you can use it to stimulate your thinking about your survey. And you will almost certainly get contradictory advice—about reverse coding, neutral options, question wording, question order, and so on.

4. **Review your revised questions in terms of your research questions and analysis plan.** Make sure that you have a sufficient number of questions for each of the variables and concepts contained in your research questions and that the questions will be such that you can use the answers to address your questions in the analysis phase. For example, if your dependent variable is measured with one yes–no question, you will not be able to use ordinary regression analysis to interpret it. In general, scales are better than individual questions. The more important the variable and the more difficult it is to measure, the more important it is to use multiple measurements of the variable, that is, multiple questions. Generally best practice for turning the multiple measures into a scale is to use structural equation modeling, because it allows you to construct a continuous latent variable out of categorical indicators (see Chapter 9).

---

[14]The checklist is available in Willis (2005); for an online discussion see: *http://appliedresearch.cancer.gov/areas/cognitive/interview.pdf*. For further discussion in the context of cognitive interviewing (Step 5), see Beatty and Willis (2007).

5. **Interview potential respondents to ask them about the content and quality of the questions.** This is often referred to as **cognitive interviewing**, which is usually more targeted than interviews with focus groups, which tend to be done at an earlier, more exploratory, stage of the question writing. Cognitive interviewing focuses on whether survey questions are eliciting from respondents the kind of information that the researcher means to elicit. In a word, cognitive interviewing is about the validity of questions. Evidence about validity is obtained by asking a small sample of respondents to tell survey interviewers what they meant and what they were thinking as they answered questions. The researcher uses what is learned from their responses to revise questions.

6. **Pilot-test the survey with a sample of real respondents.** We have never successfully anticipated every problem with a survey, but we have come closest after having conducted serious pilot testing. If you are developing your own scales, you *need* quite substantial pilot testing. Indeed, scale development is itself a discipline. Not infrequently, a researcher trying to learn about a topic has to develop an instrument to study it, and the instrument can be an important contribution to knowledge in its own right. Sometimes a good instrument has made a more lasting contribution to research than the findings of the research project on which it was first used.

7. **For questions that remain unclear, conduct survey experiments.**[15] It is often the case that issues and uncertainties remain even after the previous steps have been taken. Here is where **survey experiments** become very helpful. For example, to study the effects of different question wordings or question orders in your survey experiment, you would randomly assign members of the sample to different question wordings or question orders and test the effects of these differences. If there is no difference in response patterns between the different wordings or orders, combine them and analyze them together. If there is a difference, you have learned something psychometrically interesting. One of your findings will be how different wordings made a difference. Report any differences. Finally, the survey experiment has one special strength: It is one of the few research designs that commonly attains the ideal of combining random sampling with random assignment. The special strength of experiments is internal validity achieved through random assignment. The special strength of surveys is external validity achieved through random sampling. A survey experiment can unite the two in one study.

CODING AND MEASURING RESPONDENTS' ANSWERS TO THE QUESTIONS

After you have produced the best survey you can using guidelines such as those just discussed, and after you have received the responses, then what do you do? As Phase 1 tied the survey back to the research questions and was mostly related to validity, Phase 2 looks forward to the analysis and is mostly related to reliability.[16]

[15] Gaines, Kuklinski, and Quirk (2007) are superb on survey experiments.

[16] For a general discussion of validity and reliability in data coding, see Vogt et al. (2012, pp. 317–333).

Your first step is to enter the responses into a spreadsheet or a statistical package. Each row is a respondent; each column is a variable or question. This is a very straightforward process. Open-ended questions are somewhat more complicated, and you have more choices. The answers to the questions could simply be entered into word processing software to prepare them for analysis. Software packages for text data are also useful for the purposes of integrating qualitative and quantitative data analysis.[17] On the other hand, if the answers to the open-ended questions are fairly short, they can be entered directly into a spreadsheet or statistical package. Of course, if you have coded open-ended questions into briefer codes, probably as categorical or rank-order variables, you will usually want to enter those codes into a statistical package so that you can link the numerically coded to the categorically coded answers.

When Can You Sum the Answers to Questions (or Take an Average of Them) to Make a Composite Scale?

Summing the answers to questions with Likert scale responses (*strongly agree, agree . . .*) is the usual practice. Returning to our questions about the Job Outreach Bureau (JOB), if you added together the numerical codes of the answers, you could construct a "summated scale." The highest possible score would be 20 (5 times 4 questions = 20), and the lowest possible score would be 4 (1 times 4 questions). The advantages of using a scale, rather than studying individual items one at a time, are considerable. The meaning and interpretation of any one question are uncertain. Scales are generally more reliable and valid. It is easy to see why. Think of a multiple-choice examination on your knowledge of a subject. One question, no matter how good, would almost certainly be a poor measure of your knowledge. To measure what you really know about the subject, a fairly large number of questions would be needed, and, within reasonable limits, the more questions, the better. The same is true of respondents' beliefs and attitudes on complex matters. One question will hardly ever do the job well. When you use a scale, you should test for reliability using a technique such as Cronbach's alpha (see the next subsection) or factor analysis.

On the other hand, when you sum a group of items into a scale, you may lose important information about differences in individuals' scores. For example, on the four questions in the preceding illustration, someone who answered neutral on all four questions would get a total score of 12 ($4 \times 3 = 12$), whereas another respondent who answered "strongly agree" on two of the four and "strongly disagree" on the other two would also get a score of 12 ($5 + 5 + 1 + 1 = 12$). But the two response patterns are *dramatically* different—as different as they could possibly be. The first respondent has given uniformly neutral answers, whereas the second has given sharply discordant responses. This is the reason that, when summing items in a scale, you should also explore patterns in the responses with exploratory data analysis (see Chapter 6).

Also, although there is general consensus that scales are better than single items, the common practice of summing Likert scale items is more than a little controversial. Can Likert scale items correctly be treated as interval-level data, in which case they can correctly be summed, or should they be treated as ordinal, in which case they cannot?

[17]One popular program is NVivo; see Bazeley (2007).

Although the practice of scaling ordinal variables is widespread, it has been challenged. It is hard to justify the assumption that the distance between, for example, *strongly disagree* and *disagree* is the same as the distance between *disagree* and *neutral*. If the distances between the points on a Likert scale are not equal, then summing items is at best dubious, though widely practiced by applied researchers.[18]

When Are the Questions in Your Scales Measuring the Same Thing?

Because of the increased reliability and validity that can result from multiple measures of a variable, it is generally advisable to write several questions, the answers to which you expect to combine into a more general measure. But how do you know whether you have been successful in writing questions that consistently measure aspects of the same variable? This is a question of **reliability**. The most common measure of reliability for survey scales is **Cronbach's alpha**. Cronbach's alpha is a correlational measure of the consistency of the answers to items in a scale. For example, it would tell you the extent to which people who answered some questions favorably or unfavorably about the JOB tended to do so on all of the items. If they did not, then it is probably the case that the items are not really measuring aspects of the same thing, and the items should not be summed up to make an overall rating scale. If your items seem not to be measuring aspects of the same thing, don't discard them. They may be measuring two or more distinct things. And you can always analyze the answers to the individual questions, even when adding their scores together would be inappropriate. Your intention to write questions that can be summed into a scale is no guarantee that the questions will work as you intended. You cannot know in advance whether your efforts to write questions that are related have succeeded. They may be related in your mind, but are they related in your respondents' minds? To find out you have to probe their minds by collecting and analyzing their answers to the questions.[19]

Cronbach's alpha ranges from 0 to 1.0—from answers that are completely unrelated to those that predict one another perfectly. A common threshold for scale reliability in survey research is .70. An alpha that high or higher is evidence that the questions on the scale are measuring the same underlying concept.[20] Quite often, as you read survey research reports, you will see much lower reliabilities. Any conclusions drawn from scales with reliabilities lower than .70 should be treated with extreme skepticism. A reliability score of .70 is the *minimum* acceptable. For example, imagine that in the real world, one variable *completely* determines a second variable. But, if your measures of the two variables have reliabilities of .70 and .60, the highest possible correlation between the two would be .65. The r^2, or coefficient of determination—the extent to which you can predict one variable using the other—would be .42—and this for variables that should be, if accurately measured, perfectly correlated: $r = 1.0$. In short,

[18]One classic discussion is Duncan and Stenbeck (1987). If you want to use multiple Likert scale items, many scholars would advise that it is better to use the items as multiple indicators of a latent variable in a structural equation model (see Chapter 9).

[19]For a summary of reliability measures, including Cronbach's alpha, as they are used for experimental data, see Chapter 3, Table 3.1, page 82 in this volume.

[20]For a good and highly cited overview, see Cortina (1993); for a more advanced discussion, consult Sijtsma (2009).

the more important the variables and their accurate measurement are to your research questions, the higher the reliability you should try to attain.

How do you tell whether your set of questions, which you intended to be one scale, is actually two or more scales? Factor analysis can be used for this purpose (see Chapter 9). Factor analysis is most appropriate for longer scales with numerous questions, and it requires a substantial sample size. Although it is more complicated than Cronbach's alpha, the principle behind the two measures (and other measures of reliability) is the same. And the reason for their importance is the same: Measures of reliability are crucial for validity, because a completely unreliable scale measures nothing and therefore cannot be a valid measure. Both exploratory and confirmatory factor analysis can have an important place in assessing and improving the coding and analysis of your survey.[21]

When Is the Measurement on a Summated Scale Interval and When Is It Rank Order?

The distinction between a rank order scale (very high, high, medium, low, and very low) and an interval scale (5, 4, 3, 2, and 1) can be murky. When you add together the rank order answers from several questions, does that transform them into interval answers? Not really, but the answers are treated by many researchers as if they were an interval scale. Strictly speaking, you should treat the scale of 4–20 from the above-discussed JOB survey as a rank order scale and use the appropriate rank order statistics.[22] On the other hand, the 20-point scale seems like more than a mere rank order scale. Many measures of many variables in the social sciences are treated as continuous, interval-level scales but might more correctly be thought of as "approximately interval." A rating scale composed of several Likert-like questions that has a high Cronbach's alpha can reasonably be treated in your analyses as a true interval-level measure even though it does not quite measure up, so to speak. In such cases we advise computing statistics using both the ordinal-level and the interval-level statistics (it only takes a few extra mouse clicks). Report and interpret *both* the ordinal and interval results—not just the one that conforms better to your biases.[23]

CONCLUSION: WHERE TO FIND ANALYSIS GUIDELINES FOR SURVEYS IN THIS BOOK

Writing good survey questions and effectively coding the responses is more difficult than many beginning researchers believe. Surveys are so pervasive in modern society that it is hard for people not to think that they know more than they do about what makes a good survey. On the other hand, some of the basic steps for increasing the quality of your survey are fairly clear, and we have reviewed those in the previous pages. They are also reviewed in the Summary Table on page 39. The more advanced steps for writing valid survey questions in such a way that you can code, analyze, and interpret

[21]Brown (2006).

[22]For example, Spearman's rho rather than Pearson's *r*; see Chapter 8.

[23]Spector (1992) is a good introduction.

the answers meaningfully are quite demanding. See the last paragraph in the Suggestions for Further Reading at the end of this chapter for some key sources.

Now that we have discussed how to code your survey data, it is time to make some suggestions about how to analyze the data thus coded. Virtually *all* analysis techniques can be used, and have been used, to analyze and interpret survey data. If you ask open-ended questions—and for your most important variables, we think this is a good idea whenever practicable—then you can use one or more of the techniques for coding and analyzing textual data. Both qualitative and quantitative approaches to the study of texts are available and are discussed herein, along with several software options (see Chapters 2, 4, 11, and 12). For analyzing answers to the more typical forced-choice survey questions, the most widely used techniques are associational methods based on correlation and especially regression (see Chapters 8 and 9 in this volume). Multiple regression is particularly suited to survey research, which usually gathers data about multiple variables and which often collects these data from samples large enough that multivariate analyses are possible.

Descriptive and exploratory methods of data analysis (Chapter 6) always have an important role to play when investigating any data, including survey data. And inferential, or hypothesis testing, techniques (Chapter 7) are routinely applied to most calculations of correlation and regression-based statistics. If your time is limited and you want to go to the most applicable (*not* the *only* applicable) analysis options, Chapters 8 and 9 are likely to be most useful for many readers planning to analyze survey data. In those chapters you will find details for specific types of correlations and regression analyses to use when investigating data coded in specific ways. If you are really short of time, you can get a quick overview of your data analysis options by consulting the Summary Tables in Chapters 8 and 9. Although the tables are integrated within and discussed in the texts of the chapters, we have done our best to make them freestanding.

The up-front work in survey research is very demanding, and, as compared with other forms of research, you often have to wait a long time until you begin to see some results or have any idea about how it will all turn out. Except for some hints you get during pilot surveys and other activities linked to writing the questions, the survey responses and preliminary data usually come in a rush. And the results of the first analyses can also come all at once. Thus surveys can require huge amounts of work with little payoff until the end, but the rewards at the end can be momentous. Of course, the quality of the answers you get from your survey questions is directly determined by the quality of the work you have done in preparatory stages described in this chapter.

Survey development occurs in two phases: constructing an effective questionnaire and coding respondents' answers to the survey questions. The Summary Table illustrates key considerations in each phase.

SUGGESTIONS FOR FURTHER READING

If you search the Internet for guidelines to coding your survey data, you will most likely find the Web pages of several companies offering to do this work for you—for a fee, of course. There are many reasons we do *not* generally recommend using such products. If you are a student, doing so may constitute academic dishonesty. Check the rules of your institution before spending the money. But the main reason we advise against using one of these services is that doing so severs the mental link between writing a survey and interpreting the results. It would be like planning a long hike, say on the Adirondack Trail, with the aim of writing a book reflecting on your experiences. But, rather than going on the hike, you hire someone to follow your planned route, keep a diary, and make extensive video recordings. Writing a book in this way would certainly be easier. However, most potential readers might not be interested if they knew that you did not actually experience the hiking described.

Many guidelines to writing, coding, analyzing, and interpreting survey data exist. In addition to those mentioned in the footnotes, the following works are also helpful with specific aspects of survey coding.

Quantitative coding for survey analysis is a highly developed field with many books at many levels. One of the best, though quite advanced, is the third edition (2011) of DeVellis's *Scale Development: Theory and Applications.*

Coding open-ended survey questions is most easily approached as a form of textual or content analysis. A good general text is Krippendorff's (2004) *Content Analysis: An Introduction to Its Methodology.*

A good short book that discusses several of the topics in this chapter is Blair, Czaja, and Blair's (2013) *Designing Surveys.* Chapter 9 on "reducing sources of error in data collection" is particularly helpful.

We conclude our recommendations with three fairly technical, but quite indispensable, articles on aspects of survey coding and measurement. They all focus on the most important question: How does one write *valid* questions—questions the answers to which accurately tap into respondents' beliefs? On the issue of social desirability bias—whether respondents fake answers and how to detect and correct for this if they do—see Ziegler and Buehner, "Modeling Socially Desirable Responding and Its Effects" (2009). On consulting with members of the target population, specifically by using focus group interviews, to improve the content validity of survey questions, see Vogt, King, and King, "Focus Groups in Psychological Assessment: Enhancing Content Validity by Consulting Members of the Target Population" (2004). Finally, King and Wand, in "Comparing Incomparable Survey Responses: Evaluating and Selecting Anchoring Vignettes" (2007), very persuasively make the case for a method—vignettes—currently being used by the World Health Organization to improve the validity and cross-cultural comparability of survey responses. This issue is particularly important when respondents interpret identical questions in different ways. King and colleagues explain methods for discovering and correcting for this complication, principally through interpreting responses to vignette-based questions. We know of no single article on survey research validity more likely to repay readers' efforts.*

*See also King, Murray, Salomon, and Tandon (2004).

CHAPTER 1 SUMMARY TABLE

CONSTRUCTING AN EFFECTIVE QUESTIONNAIRE	
When linking survey questions to research questions (pp. 24–26)	• Examine your research questions to determine whether you will collect objective or subjective data—or both. • Determine your research variables and make sure you have sufficient survey questions to answer them. • Use your survey questions to operationalize your variables.
When to use questions from previous surveys (p. 26)	• When you are examining variables studied previously by other researchers. • When you want to study whether change has occurred since a previous survey study was conducted.
When choosing question formats (pp. 27–29)	• Choose between open-ended and forced-choice formats, considering research questions, variables, and resources. • For forced-choice, choose among response types (e.g., multiple choice, Likert scales). • Consider when neutral and does-not-apply options are appropriate and/or necessary.
When redrafting questions to improve quality (pp. 31–33)	• Use a checklist. • Conduct focus group research. • Have a panel of experts review your draft. • Revisit your research questions and analysis plan. • Interview potential respondents about survey quality. • Pilot-test the survey with a sample of real respondents. • Conduct survey experiments.

CODING RESPONDENTS' ANSWERS TO QUESTIONS	
When to make a composite scale across related questions (p. 34)	• When you want to increase reliability and validity.
When you want to know whether items measure the same aspects of a variable (pp. 35–36)	• For most surveys, use Cronbach's alpha as a correlational measure of consistency. • For surveys with numerous questions per variable, use factor analysis.
When to report measures as interval or rank order (p. 36)	• Compute both ways, reporting both ordinal and interval results.

CHAPTER 2

Coding Interview Data

In this chapter we discuss:

- Interviews in the context of other types of research.
- Goals: What do you seek when asking questions?
- Your role: What should your part be in the dialogue?
- Samples: How many interviews and with whom?
- Questions: When do you ask what kinds of questions?
- Modes: How do you communicate with interviewees?
- Observations: What is important that isn't said?
- Records: What methods do you use to preserve the dialogue?
- Tools: When should you use computers to help code your data?
- Getting help: When to use member checks and multiple coders.

Interviewing is the original form of social science research. The first book-length social science monograph is Herodotus's *The Histories*, written some 2,500 years ago. Based almost entirely on interviews, it described the war between the Greeks and Persians that changed power relations in the area for centuries. So, if you have decided that your research question is best answered with interview data, you will be following a time-honored tradition. You have determined that you need to ask people questions and carefully record, code, and analyze what they say. Although there have been many refinements in the coding and analysis of interview data since the 5th century B.C.E., the core of the method has not changed greatly.

Herodotus mostly gathered testimony; he wanted to learn what his interviewees knew or believed. Modern interviewers have in addition investigated the interviewees themselves, viewing them not only as sources of information about external events but as people whose experiences are worthy of investigation in their own right. Another focus in modern interviewing is the structure of the interviewees' knowledge, beliefs, and cultures. Thus, today, there are three broad classes of questions:

1. What do interviewees know or believe?
2. Who are they?
3. How does their culture structure their knowledge, beliefs, experiences, and so forth?

The three areas of interest are distinct. But they are also related. Although many studies touch on all three, the researcher typically emphasizes one of them. That emphasis is determined by your research question, which in turn shapes the questions you ask interviewees.

In other words, the discourse you obtain to code in your interview research will depend on the questions you ask; your questions will shape, more or less directly, the responses you receive to record and code. The same is true of survey research, of course, and it is natural to compare and contrast these two to get a better understanding of each. One source of overlap or confusion is the so-called **survey interview**. This is a survey in which the researcher asks survey questions face-to-face, which is the typical context for interviews. The survey interview usually requires the respondent to answer forced-choice questions that will be coded quantitatively, as is typical in surveys. By **interview** we mean interactions between researchers and participants in which the questions and answers are open-ended and in which the answers are usually coded qualitatively. The differences between interviews (usually open-ended questions) and surveys (usually forced-choice questions) tend mostly to be a matter of degree. In both cases you ask people questions; your data are their answers. The differences are in the number of people you ask, the number of questions you ask, and the degree of freedom respondents have in answering. In surveys you tend to ask a lot of people a lot of questions and give them little choice in how they answer, most typically structuring the questions to require forced-choice answers. By contrast, in interviews you tend to ask fewer people fewer questions but give them greater latitude in how they answer. Despite these differences, many of the issues with asking questions and interpreting answers in the two designs are similar. They both involve uncovering and clarifying the meanings in what people tell the researcher.

Two phases are typical in the coding work of researchers using interview designs. First, you decide on the questions you will ask; the questions imply coding strategies. Then, you record and code the answers. Although these two phases parallel the stages of survey research, there are important practical differences in emphasis between the two. One of them concerns the degree of effort required in the two phases. In surveys, composing the questions is more challenging, but gathering the data and analyzing it can be fairly routine activities. Analysis might only take a few days. In interviews, writing the questions is often comparatively easy. In many interviews, the initial questions are few in number and general in scope; they are frequently designed mainly to open up the dialogue between the interviewer and interviewee. Collecting the data, a process usually completed in a few weeks in surveys, routinely takes many months in interview research. And analyzing it often takes even longer.

Despite these differences in the stage at which the most demanding work occurs in interviews and surveys, the similarities remain important. Both survey and interview researchers formulate research questions that require answers from people; they choose people to ask; they struggle to make the questions asked relevant to the research questions; and they try to make sense of what respondents and interviewees have told them. Not surprisingly, therefore, many of the issues we encountered in the chapter on coding survey data recur in this chapter on coding interview data. Also, many of the topics discussed here are relevant for observational research (Chapter 4). Coding interview transcripts often has much in common with coding observational fieldnotes, and interview researchers often supplement their data with observational fieldnotes. We divide the discussion of coding and analysis in interviews at the same point as we do for observations: Your work up to the establishment of the final interview transcripts (or fieldnotes) is coding for preparing and ordering the transcripts. Some think of this as **precoding** or coding that occurs during the data collection phase. Once the interview transcripts have been transcribed and checked for accuracy, one then engages in coding for analysis (see Chapter 11).

The parallels between interviews and other designs are particularly consequential because interviews are often combined with other methods of data collection. Of all major design types, interviews are more likely to be used in conjunction with others—surveys, observations, experiments, and archival investigations. They are very likely to be one of the elements of a multimethod design; or, if the combination crosses the word–number barrier, interviews become part of mixed methods designs. In short, in addition to being a natural primary way to investigate research questions, and one with a long history, interviews are a natural complement to other types of research (see Chapter 13).

Much coding in interview research is precoding; it occurs during data collection, and such coding is a large part of what the researcher needs to analyze interview transcripts. Still, collecting, coding, and analyzing are distinct—and they interact. Before you begin collecting data, there are several coding-relevant questions, given in the following list, that you should try to answer at least tentatively. And you should continue to pay attention to them, and collect fieldnotes in answer to them, in the course of your interviewing. Your answers will strongly imply or shape the early steps in your coding.

- What are your *goals* in conducting the research?
- What *roles* should you play in the interview?
- *How many* interviews do you need to conduct—and *with whom*?
- How many *questions* of which kinds will enable you to achieve your goals?
- What technologies or *modes of communication* work best for the kinds of questions you are asking of your interviewees?
- In what *contexts* will the interviews be conducted, and what are the interviewees' reactions to you and the contexts?
- What methods will you use to *record* your dialogues on these kinds of questions with these respondents in these contexts?
- What *help* might be available from computer tools, interviewees, and other researchers?

Answers to these questions provide the structure for the remainder of this chapter. They are the bridge between your design and coding choices. Textbooks too often describe the process of coding interview data as something that *starts* after you have had someone type up your audio recordings to turn them into interview transcripts.

Most of what we discuss in this chapter can be thought of as processes of precoding, that is, the kinds of coding that mostly occur *before* the final transcript is prepared. The goal is to obtain better data and to be prepared to code it more effectively once the transcript is ready.

In the vast majority of cases, the codes for interview data will be words. As with any coding, when you use words for codes it is important to focus on consistency. The only practical way we know to do that is to construct a codebook/glossary.[1] The term **codebook** is more commonly used by researchers handling quantitative data, but the process is equally important, and probably more so, for researchers coding qualitative data.[2] For example, if you describe your interview questions as *structured, semistructured*, or *unstructured*, what do you mean by those terms? If you say you used *purposive* sampling to find and recruit interviewees, what were your purposes and how did you implement them? Too often researchers will say little more than "semistructured questions were asked of a purposive sample of 31 participants." That doesn't tell your reader much, nor is it specific enough to help you sort out your interview data. The reason is that the term *semistructured* covers a wide range of structures, and the term *purposive* covers a wide range of purposes. Or, to take another example, if you describe interviewees as "a little," "moderately," and "somewhat" reluctant to answer particular questions, what do you mean exactly? Are these synonyms, or is moderately more than a little? It is essential to keep good fieldnotes or a journal to make sure you know what you have coded in what ways and to help you use terms consistently when doing so.[3] This kind of rigor is probably even more important in observational research (see Chapter 4).

GOALS: WHAT DO YOU SEEK WHEN ASKING QUESTIONS?

Your research question leads you to focus on certain types of responses from your interview participants. Sometimes you seek **information** that they can provide. Then, you look for respondents such as witnesses to an event you are studying or who are members of an organization you are investigating. You might also want to know *why* the event occurred or why the organization functions as it does; in that case, you pursue reasons or **explanations**. These can be obtained directly from interviewees, or they can be inferred by you from what the interviewees say; most likely, you will do some of each—record interviewees' explanations and make explanatory inferences from interview data.

One common way that people provide explanations, the way they convey the why of something, is to tell a story. In that case you might seek **narratives**. And even if you do not seek them, you are likely to obtain them anyway, because telling stories seems the favored way for most people to give reasons, to make sense, to offer an explanation.[4] If

[1] When you use the interviewees' own words as codes, this is called *in vivo* coding.

[2] A codebook can be part of, but does not replace, a field journal, in which you include observations and reflections of many kinds. See Chapter 4.

[3] When your codes are rank orders, it is sometimes easiest to use numbers as a shorthand notation, such as 0–4 for *not at all, a little, somewhat, a lot, always*. Be sure to define these in your codebook.

[4] See the brilliant discussion in Tilly (2006). Bruner (2002) is a strong advocate of the pervasiveness of narratives in human communication.

your interview questions yield many narrative responses, you will probably want to use some of the techniques of **narrative analysis**.

Closely related to narrative analysis is **discourse analysis,**[5] in which individuals' use of language is employed to understand their culture or lives. The narratives or discourses are often **autobiographical**, even when they are offered in response to a question seeking information about, for example, how an organization functions. Question: "How does this organization handle employee problems?" Answer: "Well, when I first had a problem with . . . ." The interviewee tells you a story. Instead of giving you a personal story, the interviewee *could* tell you about the organization's rules for resolving disputes or provide a description of the organization's decision hierarchy and power structure. And some interviewees will. But you will be more likely to obtain such information embedded in a story. Of course, a story can be used to illustrate a general explanation or causal account—not just to take the place of one. Indeed, ultimately, one form of storytelling is a causal theory—at least causal theories are very often expressed in ways that closely approximate a narrative form: when *X* brought about an increase in *Y* that caused *Z* to decline.

As an aside, it is worth noting that one common way to conclude a story is often very annoying to an information- or reason-seeking interviewer: a story the moral of which is "everything happens for a reason." When an interviewee tells you that everything happens for a reason, it is actually a way of saying that there is a reason, but it is a mystery. The phrase may actually be a social signal that the interviewee wants to end the discussion. In that case, it is not an attempt to communicate something of substance about the question asked. Or, it could also be, and probably is, a way for interviewees to communicate their feelings about the meaning of life and hopes for certainty in a complex and confusing world.

When collecting narratives as data, your goals direct your focus. Is your goal to learn about external phenomena the narrator is describing, to learn about the narrator, or to learn about the nature of narratives? As always when we ask this kind of question, the answer is "some of each," but you should have a focus shaped by your research question. If, for example, you are writing a biography, many details about the interviewee's life will be important, but such details would be only marginally relevant to an account of an event or a description of the power structure in an organization. For whatever reason, individual narrations of life experiences are extremely popular. Memoirs (sort of self-interviews) are one of the most common types of books published in the 21st century. Ironically or puzzlingly, the surge in the urge to tell all about oneself in blogs or other social media seems to have grown in parallel with the crisis of concerns about privacy.

Narratives are not only a way for interviewees to answer questions; they also are a possible format for constructing your research report. Even when the data are not narratives, the researcher may arrange them to tell a story. Historians and biographers often do this. In many research reports shaped as narratives, a common approach is using events in a personal life to explain something broader. Perhaps the best known example is biographies of famous people in which childhood and adolescent events (often narrated in meticulous, sometimes excruciating, detail) are used to explain the psychological roots of adults' accomplishments. Other biographies focus more on the accomplishments and

[5]See Clandinin (2007) on narrative analysis and Gee (2005) on discourse analysis.

less on their psychological roots.[6] In either case, a principal method to gain the information used to write biographies of living and recently deceased individuals is interviewing.[7] Comparing the details in the stories provided in many interviews allows the author to arrive at a more "definitive" narrative account.

Knowing that you will collect narrative accounts of respondents' lives still does not very specifically answer the question of your goal in doing the research. For example, do you want to study homelessness or homeless people? You could approach the people's stories as examples of the phenomenon of homelessness. Or you could make the people the focus of the study and investigate how they are influenced by the condition of being homeless. Your research questions might be: How is homelessness structured in this city? Or, how does becoming homeless change people's lives? Or, how do people become homeless? Or, what are the employment experiences of homeless people? How do those employment experiences differ between men and women? You might pursue several of these as subquestions. If you do, they will constitute **preliminary codes** for categorizing the responses of your interviewees. Your research questions entail your goals; they direct you to ask some kinds of questions and to omit others; and they help you sort and code the answers you receive.

YOUR ROLE: WHAT SHOULD YOUR PART BE IN THE DIALOGUE?

In addition to your goals, you need to decide how you envision your role in the interview process. You also need to be sure to code any variation in your role from one interview to the next. And there will almost certainly be variation; one of the delights and challenges of interview research is that the interaction between the participants in the interview (you and the interviewees) rarely occurs as you had planned. Even if you do not have conscious plans, you probably have implicit ones. One marker of implicit plans or expectations occurs when you are surprised by the kinds of replies your questions elicit.

Improvisation in the face of the unexpected is one of the strengths of a good interviewer. Although you should have a general approach in mind, you should also expect the unexpected and expect to be called upon to improvise. Do you intend to be fairly passive, gently eliciting replies, or do you mean to be an active participant in a dialogue with the interviewee? Do you share things about yourself in the hopes of encouraging the interviewee to respond in kind, or do you maintain a more business-like, or therapist-like, formal attitude, with you playing the role of questioner or elicitor and the interviewee playing the role of answerer or reflector?[8] Roles that work nicely in some interviews will flop in others. A good interviewer can recognize that the initial role/approach is not working and make adjustments.

---

[6]Skidelsky's (2000) biography of John Maynard Keynes uses the details of Keynes's personal life to set the context for the examination of his work; the work drives the rest of the biography. The same is true of Herbert Simon's (1991) autobiography.

[7]Max (2012) studies the life of David Foster Wallace the better to understand his literature; the personal details are interesting because they are seen as shaping the work.

[8]Regarding "self-disclosure" during interviews, opinions are strong, but the evidence is weak. Our best advice is to reflect on the experiences and suggestions of experienced interviewers to help you decide on your role. See Reinharz and Chase (2002).

Sometimes your role in an interview will be similar to that of a physician "taking a history." When you have adopted the history-taking role,[9] your part in the dialogue might read as follows: "When did you first become homeless? How did it happen? Where did you live before that? Whose apartment was it? Were you employed at the time? Were you able to hold onto your job?" Pause. "I hope you don't think I'm being too nosy here. I ask all these questions because I want to learn about you and about homelessness and want to make sure I'm getting it right." When taking this rapid-fire information-seeking approach, the questions need not be scripted, and they will surely change depending on the replies, sometimes because a participant provides the answer before you get around to asking the question. One of the signs of an inexperienced, inflexible, or nervous interviewer is doggedly persisting in asking a question because it is next on the list, even though the interviewee has already answered it.

When you are focusing on keeping replies directed toward a particular topic, it is important that you do not appear to be a police interrogator. Much has been written and quite a bit is known about interrogating suspects and eliciting confessions. Indeed, one of the most popular textbooks about interview techniques, originally written in 1962 by Inbau and others and now in its fifth edition,[10] provides guidelines on how to take an adversarial role and wrest information from a reluctant suspect. The famous nine interrogation steps are meant to be used only when the officer is "sure" the suspect is guilty, which obviously begs the question, because the interview is ostensibly used to investigate whether the suspect is guilty, not to trick him or her into admitting something that the interviewer already "knows." Psychological manipulation and deceit are a key part of the nine-step method. It is pretty gruesome stuff, and ethical social researchers would be reluctant to use it, even if they were allowed to do so by the institutional review board (IRB). Many scholars think that the nine-step Inbau method has been very effective at eliciting confessions, but, unfortunately, that includes false confessions pried from innocent suspects.

Interview guidelines for interrogating suspects are a good example, a cautionary tale, illustrating that the role you play as a researcher can greatly influence participants' responses to interviews. A more benign example is **motivational interviewing**, which is a therapeutic technique designed to help people deal with problems and change behaviors.[11] These examples make it very clear that researchers need to specify the nature of their goals and roles. Because roles affect the researcher–interviewee interaction, they are a very important part of data generation—and one that *must be coded*. Research on interviewer effects is most extensive in survey interviews. Even in that environment, more controlled than in the typical qualitative interview, "the only reasonable answer" to the question of how interviewers affect replies "seems to be that absolutely anything can happen."[12] As with **interaction effects** in numerical data, so too with interaction effects in qualitative data; when the data interact (or the participants interact), it is *impossible* to analyze their separate effects. In short, in interviews, you have to code and

[9]A similar approach used with survey data is event history analysis. See Chapter 11.

[10]Inbau, Reid, and Buckley (2011).

[11]Miller and Rollnick (2013) is a well-known text.

[12]Schaeffer and Maynard (2001, p. 579).

analyze both halves of the dialogue and also attempt to interpret how each influences the other.

How objective should you try to be? **Objectivity** is a hotly contested topic, especially, perhaps, because it is difficult to define. "Objectivity" is definitely not synonymous with quantitative data. Attempts to attain objectivity have a long history in qualitative research; phenomenology's "analytic bracketing" is a case in point.[13] However, most researchers would agree that there is no method of gathering data in which objectivity is more difficult than interviewing. By design, interviewing is characterized by a lack of standardization, unpredictable interactions between participants, and the highly subjective nature of the topics typically pursued. For most kinds of interview, there is no external referent against which to gauge accuracy. The researcher usually seeks to learn what the interviewee actually thinks, believes, or feels at the time of the interview. The "objective" truth in that case might be what the interviewee really does *subjectively* feel. You might even help some interviewees to uncover their feelings and beliefs.

Writers on methodology in interview research sometimes flatly deny any possibility of objectivity and lightly toss around statements to the effect that interviewers "hear *only* what their own intellectual and ethical development has prepared them to hear [italics added]."[14] Although statements like that are common, if they were literally true it would mean that interviewers could never be surprised by what they hear, that they could never alter their initial beliefs, and, ultimately, that they could never learn anything. Although it might be true that some researchers are so biased that they are incapable of systematic analysis of evidence, it does not follow that everyone is or must be. On the other hand, what could objectivity mean in recording, coding, and analyzing interview data? One criterion would be fidelity to the meanings of the interviewee. You want to write your version of what was said so that, if asked, the interviewee might say, "Why yes, that captures it well; that is a good account of what I believe." Of course, through "member checking" (discussed later), the interviewees' reactions do not have to be imagined; they can be directly investigated.

The criterion of whether or not the interviewee would agree with what you have written would be more difficult (and often less appropriate) to apply at analysis and interpretation stages. But making clear how what you say is supported by your evidence is hardly an impractical or "epistemologically" impossible demand. We think it is possible for researchers to be aware enough of their biases and attentive enough to their evidence to exercise some self-control and not let their biases and preferences completely corrupt the research process. Other ways of moving toward the goal of objectivity include being very explicit about your goals and roles and coding these—which means including your half of the interview dialogue. Self-questioning and self-evaluating are crucial. When you have made audio recordings, listen critically to yourself, not only to the interviewees. One indicator of objectivity is "intersubjectivity," which means agreement among researchers working on the project. The opportunity to assess intersubjectivity is one of the benefits of having multiple coders (discussed later in this chapter and in Chapters 11 and 12).

---

[13]The concept of bracketing as enabling unprejudiced description originated in Husserl's (1913/1962) work.

[14]Johnson (2001, p. 106).

SAMPLES: HOW MANY INTERVIEWS AND WITH WHOM?

Judgment sampling, also known as **purposive sampling**, is something of an embarrassment in survey research. But, as long as you specify the criteria used to make the judgments in judgment sampling or explain your purposes in purposive sampling, these approaches are ideal in interview research. Many sampling issues are settled at the design stage. However, in interviews it is common to use leads from one interviewee to learn of other people to contact for later interviews.[15] Of course, haphazard, casual, and catch-as-catch-can sampling are just as inadvisable in interviews as in surveys. A researcher will surely learn something, even from participants chosen thoughtlessly, but it will be hard to discern and convincingly portray what has been learned. The main point about sampling when coding interview data is to *code for any differences in how interviewees were selected.* Did you begin by interviewing a few people you knew, perhaps friends, who were appropriate for the study? Were some interviewees recruited by advertisements asking for volunteers? Were later participants found by referrals from earlier ones? Were any or all of them paid for their efforts? You should code all sources and types of participants. It may be that interviewees who were friends, volunteers, referrals, or paid recruits all replied to your questions in similar ways. But perhaps they did not; it is important to know. So check for and code any differences.

Are your interviews repeated with some or all participants, or are they one-time events? Particularly interesting coding issues occur with multiple interviews. Say you have conducted three interviews with each participant—one introductory interview to set the context with each interviewee and two follow-ups. Initially, your categorization and reading and coding of the transcripts will probably be *by interviewee.* But it can also be instructive to categorize *by stage* in the interview cycle; read together and code the set of second and the set of third interview transcripts. Reading and coding by stage is definitely worth exploring. And it is greatly facilitated by having your data indexed in grid-like formats, with each interviewee occupying a line and each attribute of the interviewees and of the interview format, context, and so on occupying the columns. (See Chapter 4 for illustrations of grids and matrices.)

QUESTIONS: WHEN DO YOU ASK WHAT KINDS OF QUESTIONS?

The content of your questions, at least your initial questions, tends to be determined fairly early in the design stages. In this section we focus more on the format and the number of questions. A successful approach to deciding what and how many questions to ask and in what format is to begin with your research questions and your goals (informational, exploratory, theory-testing, etc.), as discussed previously. Ask yourself what you need to learn from the study's interviewees to help you answer your research questions. Usually a research question includes several concepts; interview questions should include queries to address each of these concepts.

---

[15]Formal versions of this approach to finding participants include respondent-driven sampling and snowball sampling. See Vogt et al. (2012, Ch. 8) for overviews. See also Wejnert and Heckathorn (2008).

When Do You Use an Interview Schedule/Protocol?[16]

Do you arrive at the interview with a detailed series of questions, including follow-up questions scripted to match likely or expected replies? How strictly should you plan to stick to the script? Do you use the schedule mostly before the interview, reviewing it to remind yourself of the topics on which you want to touch, or do you use your list of questions more formally and visibly? No matter how detailed an interview schedule is, some room to improvise is always needed. That is one reason it is useful to pilot-test your questions with at least a few interviewees. Sometimes you'll discover that your questions are unclear, that they elicit answers you don't expect, or that they hardly elicit any answers at all. Pilot testing of questions can reduce but never eliminate surprises in interviewing. We have conducted many interviews, some with quite strict schedules, but every one of those interviews has required some improvisation because of unexpected replies to questions on the schedule. Occasionally, we have found that answers to the follow-up questions—made up on the spot in response to unexpected replies—proved to be most interesting and informative in the final analysis. How detailed your list of questions is and how closely you adhere to it is in part a matter of personal style; it also depends on your memory and ability to stick to the point without written guidelines. We certainly differ among ourselves in this regard. One of us has trouble simultaneously focusing on what the interviewee is saying, remembering the guiding concepts in the schedule, thinking about follow-up questions, and restraining from participating in the discussion a bit too much. For him, the schedule is a necessary crutch.

In terms of coding, the most important thing is to *be explicit about what you have done.* This is important both for your own analytical purposes and for your readers' understanding and evaluation of your results. One typical description of lists of questions for interviewees is to say that they are unstructured, semistructured, or structured. This is far too uninformative either for your own purposes or for those of your readers. Indeed it is hard to imagine using anything but semistructured questions in a qualitative interview: Fully structured questions would constitute more of a survey than an interview, and unstructured questions would be more of a chat than a research dialogue. We discussed the degree of structure of the questions in the beginning of this chapter as one example of the need for explicitness and consistency when coding types of questions. Of course, the degree of structure is but one of several ways to categorize questions. Previous scholars have described types of questions and have given them labels. It can be very useful to review one or more of their lists to help you devise your own typology.[17]

Even when the *questions* are not highly structured, we often engage in preliminary coding and indexing by structuring the *responses* in a matrix. For example, in one study the researcher interviewed a total of 22 participants and asked a total of 18 questions.[18] In that study, it was very helpful, even before making a transcript, to create a grid as part of the fieldnotes. In such a grid, the rows can be the interviewees (1–22 in this case)

[16]Strictly speaking, an interview *schedule* is the list of questions with places for the researcher to write down the answers. An interview *protocol* is a list of questions and guidelines for how to ask them. We use *schedule* to cover both concepts. Another term used by many researchers is *interview guide.*

[17]Spradley's (1979) text contains one of the better known and widely used categorizations of questions.

[18]This example is based on the work of one of P. Vogt's doctoral dissertation advisees when she was interviewing graduate students in different departments.

and the columns the questions (1–18 in this example). The cells in the grid can include checkmarks to indicate who answered which question, and/or they can include brief characterizations of their replies.[19] In this example, although 11 of the questions were asked of and answered by every participant, others were less frequently asked and/or answered. (A question can be asked, but not answered; *be sure to code for that.*) One of the early questions was dropped because, upon reflection, the researcher judged that it was confusing and misleading and was not yielding useful answers. One of the later questions on the list was answered by only a few interviewees because it emerged out of the interview process and was added fairly late in the research; it was raised by perceptive interviewees toward the end of the first round of interviews.[20] The valuable replies to this question subsequently led the researcher to ask it in some reinterviews with the original group of participants and in some new interviews with additional interviewees in a follow-up project.

If you do any even moderately elaborate and systematic coding, you will surely generate several transcripts. They might contain the same data from one master set of transcripts that have been organized in different ways. The two most common organizational principles are: (1) all the answers from each interviewee and (2) all the answers to each question. In addition to organizing by interviewee and by question, types of answers to each question—such as informational, attitudinal, emotional, contextual, and narrative—are also very important to code. And you would probably want to code by background differences among the interviewees, such as gender and age. This way you could read, for example, all the answers by female interviewees to Question 14 and compare them with the male interviewees' replies to the same question. Cross-classifying all of these data categories all but requires computer help, and your work will almost never fit onto 8½″ × 11″ pages. It is much easier to scroll through them on a computer screen. (See the later section on computer assistance in coding.)

MODES: HOW DO YOU COMMUNICATE WITH INTERVIEWEES?

The ideal type of a model of an interview is a face-to-face conversation in a quiet and private place. This was also long considered the best setting for a survey. Survey researchers have probably been less reluctant than interview researchers to move away from the face-to-face model, which is still considered by many to be the best way to communicate. It is undoubtedly easier to adapt forced-choice survey questions to other modes of communication, such as individual telephone interviewing, teleconferencing, and e-mail interviewing. Even those who see the face-to-face interview as the principal method of data collection—and they are probably in the great majority among interviewers—are likely to supplement this approach with others. For instance, it is common to communicate by e-mail or telephone to set up an initial appointment or a follow-up interview.[21]

[19] See Chapter 4 for an example of such a data matrix.

[20] This is the reason it is important to do preliminary coding before having finished the interviews. Schwalbe and Wolkomir (2001) propose a 20% rule: Do preliminary coding after the first 20% and after each subsequent 20%. Iterative coding and recoding are also very important in grounded theory. See Chapter 11.

[21] For example, Vogt and Nur-Awaleh (1999), in a postal mail survey, asked respondents to respond by e-mail if they were willing to be interviewed by telephone.

Such communications often turn out to be more than a way to make appointments; conversations relevant to the research frequently occur as part of these exchanges. If so, there is no point in discarding the information obtained in this way, but you do need to label the e-mail responses and the telephone conversations *using different codes* in order to distinguish them from responses to interview questions.[22]

Other forms of **text-to-text** communication and interviewing can also be important. Still, some researchers believe that the disadvantages of not having face-to-face interactions are too great to surmount. But others find the advantages of electronic, text-to-text communication compelling, and they are many: being unconstrained by geography; eliminating the need to schedule meetings and to find a place to hold them; having the opportunity to think before you ask the next question; and giving interviewees a chance to think before they answer. Finally, and perhaps most important, the interviewees' replies arrive on your desktop already transcribed, thus saving hundreds of hours of work.[23]

If your interviewees are busy, they may not be willing to be interviewed in any way other than by telephone or via the Internet, and some prefer to avoid face-to-face meetings for other reasons, such as privacy. You often have to accommodate your interviewees' wishes.[24] Here the point is that it is crucial for you to *code for those accommodations*, even fairly minor ones. For example, one of us found codable differences in length and detail between the transcripts of interviews conducted in a quiet office versus those that occurred in a busy coffee shop. The interviewer found the interviews in the office more tiring and even a little stressful, but the transcripts were more complete and richer in detail than the transcripts of the interviews conducted in the coffee shop.

There may be no substantive differences in what you learn in different types and settings of interviews. If there are not, then you can pool and analyze responses together, but it is unwise to simply assume there will be no differences. You can learn whether there are differences by using codes to specify the variety in types and settings and investigating whether they coincide with substantive differences in interviewees' replies. As with other such coding problems, we like to arrange the coded categories in a grid or matrix. For example, each line on the grid would be an interviewee, and each column would be one of the variables we have been talking about: face-to-face, telephone, in the office, in the coffee shop, and so on. The grids can easily become too large to handle on paper. The easiest way we know of to manipulate such data occurring in many categories is to use a spreadsheet program (see the later section on tools).

One mode of communication with interviewees is a special case and raises specific issues of coding: the focused group interview, or **focus group**, for short. The basic idea of a focus group interview is for the researcher to moderate a discussion focused on a particular topic. The participants usually share some characteristic that makes them suitable for answering the research question. They may be potential customers for a new product, graduate students working on dissertations, undecided voters in

---

[22]This may raise ethical issues involved as well, because most consent forms we have seen do not cover such incidental sources of information. They should. See Warren et al. (2003).

[23]Markham (2007).

[24]On e-mail interviewing, see Hessler et al. (2003) and Menchik and Tian (2008); for telephone interviewing, see Stephens (2007).

the next election, and so on. Most of the issues in coding and analyzing focus group data closely parallel those for analyzing individual interview data.[25] But there are also important differences. The most salient of these is your unit of analysis. Is your focus on the groups or on the individuals in the groups? This is determined by your research question. Does your question involve, for example, how groups deal with problems, or does it address how individual beliefs are influenced by the group discussions? Or are you using focus group data as a kind of survey data, to generalize to a broader population?[26]

Some researchers think of focus groups as a cost-effective way to interview many individuals. Indeed, 10 focus groups could easily yield data from 100 individuals. But if you are really interested in individuals as individuals, you would almost certainly be better off conducting 20 full interviews with individuals. What people will say in a dyad composed of interviewer and interviewee is likely to differ importantly from what people will say in a discussion with several other people. On the other hand, focus groups are particularly appropriate for studying group phenomena. You could be interested in groups, or in interindividual dynamics in groups, or in group learning,[27] or in the formation of collective identities.[28] Finally, using evidence from focus groups to improve survey questions or to help interpret them is another frequent practice, and one that has been very fruitful of insights.[29]

The practical issues with coding focus group data mostly revolve around the fact that it can be hard to keep straight who said what. As in any discussion, people in focus groups talk at the same time, talk to their neighbors but not the group as a whole, lose interest and check their cell phones, and so on. A good moderator can keep these problems to a minimum, but they can probably never be eliminated without exerting so much control over the group discussion that it loses most of its spontaneity value. Most focus group researchers recommend having an assistant moderator so that the two of you can divide up the tasks of guiding the discussion and making a record of it. Teleconferenced focus groups are possible, and the technology may eventually improve to the point that these become more common. In the current state of technology, we have found that textual focus groups—for example, using online bulletin boards—are more effective than teleconferences. But this is a personal observation; we know of no research on the topic.

Finally, it can be quite difficult, more than with individual interviews, to keep the group sessions distinct in one's mind, especially if the group interviews are all conducted in the same room at the same time of day. That means that it is very helpful to immediately take fieldnotes that include memory aids, such as distinguishing characteristics (and perhaps a nickname) for each group. Video recordings are also often a useful supplement to an audiotape for helping you recall which group was which and for sorting out who said what.

---

[25] A good source for coding focus group data is Krueger (1998), especially Chapter 8. See also Macnaghten and Myers (2007).

[26] Eby, Kitchen, and Williams (2012) provide an example.

[27] Wibeck, Dahlgren, and Oberg (2007).

[28] Munday (2006).

[29] For very good examples, see Goerres and Prinzen (2012) and Lindsay and Hubley (2006).

OBSERVATIONS: WHAT IS IMPORTANT THAT ISN'T SAID?

Your interview transcripts should always be combined with your observations in formal fieldnotes (see Chapter 4). One of the most important kinds of observations is of interviewees during the interviews. In the example discussed earlier, in which interviews were conducted with 22 doctoral students, the following summary of observations was made. Of the 22 interviewees, 13 were eager to communicate and were the kinds of participants the researcher had expected. Three were perhaps too eager to communicate: They were delighted to have someone listen to them; they often free-associated about all manner of topics, many of which were only tangentially related to the specific questions they were asked. Another three were nervous or shy or embarrassed or otherwise reluctant; it was hard to specify why exactly, but they were somewhat uncommunicative. Two others were "super-participants," who were as interested in the research as the researcher; they volunteered to fact-check notes and recruit other participants and said they were looking forward to reading the study; one even said that maybe she'd do something similar for her dissertation someday. These two super-participants were the kinds of people anthropologists refer to as "key informants."[30]

Finally, and at the other end of the spectrum, two interviewees seemed hostile during the interviews, perhaps seeing the questions as an invasion of privacy; one of them quit the interview after about 10 minutes. Maybe not coincidentally, these two interviewees were male. The specifics of this example do not matter greatly, and we have no way of knowing whether these proportions of types of responses to an interview are typical. What they do exemplify, however, is that you are missing something if you just transcribe all that was said and treat all transcribed text as identical. The researcher needs to *code observations about the interviewees*, including basic background information (age, gender, occupation, etc.). It is surely meaningful to describe their types of responses, demeanors, and attitudes and to cross-classify these with background categories. These attributes and characteristics of the interviewees and their responses to the interview setting provide important interpretive clues that you can use in your subsequent coding and analysis.

RECORDS: WHAT METHODS DO YOU USE TO PRESERVE THE DIALOGUE?

Interviews are live. Coding is done using records of live interviews. Researchers mostly treat interviews as verbal and aural, but face-to-face interviews are also visual experiences for both participants—researcher and interviewee. It is very hard to use only one sense at a time. The room is hot, the lights are bright, the interviewee speaks very softly, and so on. Expressions of surprise, sighs, and laughter can all be important but are comparatively hard to record, or, if recorded electronically, hard to convert into text. Something is always lost between the events and the records of them; therefore, coding and analysis are inevitably based on imperfect records.

[30]One researcher (Irwin, 2006) dated, married, and eventually divorced her key informant. That is an extreme example, but relations with participants may change, and when they do *the changes need to be coded.*

The first record is the interviewer's memory. But memory is fickle. The greater the distance from the remembered event, the less reliable is the memory. Hence fieldnotes and the implicit codes they contain need to be written as soon as possible after the conclusion of the interview. It is also usually a good idea to clean up the notes taken during the interview (fill in gaps, correct illegible sections, etc.) while your memory is fresh. We have found that it is very helpful to type your notes and preliminary codes into a computer. As the days pass, you will have fewer reliable memories beyond those you have committed to writing. When we have compared our notes and our memories, we have found our memories sometimes to be unreliable after a surprisingly few days, particularly when during those days we have conducted more than one interview. In short, you will soon have little left to work with but your notes—plus, of course, any mechanical recordings you have made, such as photos and audio and/or video recordings.

Language is primary in interview research mainly because it can be used to *translate* other symbols and representations—such as gestures and body language or nonverbal sounds such as laughter or a sigh. The primacy of language is the reason that the typical records used to code and analyze interview data are texts: fieldnotes and transcriptions. The interviewer usually takes notes before and after the interview to describe contexts: settings, dates, times, and so on. These become fieldnotes.[31] Similar notes can be taken during the interview, at which time the focus is usually on recording what the interviewee is saying.

Notes during the interview are especially important, of course, if audio and visual recordings cannot be made. For reasons of confidentiality, interviewees may not wish to leave a direct record. They may be willing to be part of the study and to talk to you but not to be recorded, nor to allow you to take notes during the interview or even to sign a written consent form. After all, a signed consent form could be construed as a threat to privacy. In these kinds of cases, you have to make as complete a "memory transcript" as you can immediately after the interview. The data you have available as a researcher to code and analyze is importantly shaped by recording technologies you have used. When you only have notes and/or a memory transcript, your data are quite different than when you have electronic recordings from which you have made notes. Be sure to let your readers know of any such differences in your notes—for example, memory transcripts versus transcripts of audio recordings.

To a considerable extent, the history of interviewing as a research method has been shaped by the history of recording technologies—from stenographers sitting behind a screen to videotaping of a focus group through a two-way mirror.[32] Usually, the fieldnotes and transcribed texts are the final form of the data. Sometimes researchers go back to the original record, such as audio- and videotapes, to review important points, but when they do so they convert their observations and codes into texts so that they can be analyzed. We think you should audio and/or video record your interviews whenever you can. For interviews that are worth in-depth analysis, electronic recording is almost always a good idea. Often you will want to go back to these original records, so don't destroy the audio- or videotapes or files unless the IRB absolutely insists. Just as you will want to read your notes and transcripts more than once, you are also likely to want to listen to audio or visual recordings more than once. A further, and distinct, advantage

[31]See Chapter 4 and the sources cited therein for a fuller discussion of fieldnotes.

[32]See Lee (2004) for a fascinating review.

of the recorder is that it enables you to go "off the record." Turning off the recorder provides a clear signal. Interviewees generally understand this signal to mean that you will not use what is said with the machine off.[33] And, of course, you should not do so. So if you can't use what they say "off the record," how is this information useful? Maybe it can inform analysis or future interviews?

But from the many advantages of an electronic record, it does not necessarily follow that it is always necessary to make a full verbatim transcript of the interview. Sometimes the tapes are not made with the goal of constructing a transcript but only as an aid to memory. For example, if your research question mostly leads you to ask informational questions about matters of fact and interviewees' interpretations, notes may suffice. But even here we like to have the tapes if we can. And we have found them especially helpful for observing ourselves to make sure of the questions we have asked, not only of the answers. It provides a way of self-monitoring to check for such problems as "observer drift," which is the tendency for the researcher's attention to stray.

Who Should Prepare Transcripts?

If transcripts are being prepared, who should prepare them? As we argue elsewhere about quantitative data, so too with qualitative: Do not trust your data to someone who has little understanding of or interest in your work. Generally, if it's worth preparing a transcript, it's worth preparing it yourself. In addition to confidentiality issues raised by allowing a nonresearcher access to recordings, preparing the transcript yourself is a great opportunity to get familiar with your data and to jot notes (we use footnotes) about how you think you might want to code what you are listening to and typing. It is also an opportunity to integrate your observations and fieldnotes into the transcript (we use text boxes). It is possible that voice-to-text software will eventually become good enough that no one will ever *have to* type audiotapes again.[34] But even if that were to come to pass, we think it could still be helpful to do it yourself. You will probably want to listen to your tapes all the way through at least once after you have finished conducting the interviews. And you will certainly have to read the transcripts several times. Thus, if you can type moderately well, it is often well worth the effort to create your own transcription.

Looking at it negatively, if it's not worth doing yourself, maybe it's not worth doing. Is it *really* worth the effort to prepare a full, verbatim transcript? A modest number of interviews, say 20, will yield hundreds of pages of text. With space for notations and symbols for pauses, grunts, and so forth, it is not uncommon for 1 hour of interviewing to yield 30 pages of typewritten text. There is a lot to be said for using summaries or abbreviated transcripts instead. One option is to selectively transcribe recordings, transcribing only the dialogue specifically related to the research questions. In short, there are several alternatives to full transcripts. For example, in information-gathering interviews in which we asked state officials to discuss their perceptions of policies, we seldom needed to analyze transcripts in great depth. We mostly used our notes. We took **process notes** about the date and time of day, the setting for the interview, and

[33] See Warren et al. (2003).

[34] Because voice-to-text software transcripts usually require extensive editing, this may provide the best of both worlds: preparing the transcript, but not having to do most of the typing.

so on. We also, of course, took **content notes** on the questions we asked and the interviewees' responses to them. Finally, we included **context notes** about the interviewees' demeanor, cooperativeness, interest in making time for us, and so on. Those notes were usually sufficient for our purposes. We reverted to the recordings only occasionally to clarify a point or to make sure that our quotations were accurate.[35] And you should always try to retain your original records so that you and others can verify your summaries.

Of course, in other research settings with other interviewees, and focusing on different kinds of research questions, the verbatim transcript might be indispensable. But what does "verbatim" mean? Does a verbatim transcript correct grammar? Probably not. What does the transcriber do about pauses, inflections, grunts, and nonverbal vocalizations? If a video recording is being used, how are gestures and facial expressions handled? You certainly would not want to exclude them, and you surely would not want them to be interpreted by someone who is not on the research team. Because coding guidelines for such nonverbal communication are not well established, researchers resort to quite a bit of improvisation. Sometimes they simply give up. If nonverbal communication has been important in your interviews, make some attempt to describe this in fieldnotes, even if what you describe may be difficult to code.

Finally, the researcher does not generate all the records. Sometimes interviewees will bring along artifacts—perhaps photos to show you or documents to give you. If they do, you need a strategy for using this kind of evidence as well.

TOOLS: WHEN SHOULD YOU USE COMPUTERS TO CODE YOUR DATA?

One must begin by saying that computer software *cannot* code the typical interview transcript or other texts—not yet, and not well enough, although information scientists and others keep trying to devise appropriate software.[36] *You have to do the coding*, to think up good labels for attributes of the data. Once that is done, you have to figure out how to sort your data using those codes. You might hand-code using paper and colored pencils or highlighters. Many people begin this way or alternate between computer-generated work that is printed, then worked over by hand, and then reentered into the computer.

Spreadsheets, such as Excel or Gnumeric,[37] allow you to easily include all the questions, differences in rapport with the interviewees, different modes of interviewing, and so on. Spreadsheets are probably underutilized for qualitative information, perhaps because they were originally designed for quantitative data. Most of our students collecting interview data do not realize that spreadsheets are easily adapted to the needs of qualitative data analysis. Spreadsheets are simpler to learn to use than many other forms of software, and they are wonderfully handy all-purpose grids into which you can insert words as easily as numbers. The purpose of recording and coding the many features of

[35] See Hammersley (2010) for an extensive discussion of theoretical issues involved in interpreting interview transcripts.

[36] See Laver, Benoit, and Garry (2003); Simon and Xenos (2004); and Franzosi (2010).

[37] See the Suggestions for Further Reading at the end of the Introduction to Part II.

your interview data in spreadsheets is not to engage in statistical analysis, although we would not necessarily rule that out. Rather, the basic idea is to keep track of your notes and organize your coding decisions.

The amounts of data that researchers engaging in all but the simplest of projects need to collect and classify rarely fit easily on 8½″ × 11″ sheets of paper. When we have tried to do complex coding of interview data on ordinary sheets of paper, we have found it very hard to keep track of everything. As with contingency tables in quantitative data, if you try to cross-classify more than a few attributes, each with a few categories, the table quickly becomes unmanageably large and complex. But if you place your classifications and their codes in a spreadsheet, they become dramatically more searchable, manipulable, and viewable. And they can be revised quickly. In general, the kinds of problems modern researchers tackle are increasingly difficult to squeeze onto the confines of the printed page.

It is much easier to be systematic using some kind of computerized help. One way or another you are going to have to reduce hundreds of pages of transcripts and fieldnotes into something more manageable. If you are not systematic, there is a good chance you will be biased—or whimsical. If you do not start sorting, indexing, and coding right away, you run the risk of having to reread transcripts far too many times to stimulate clear thinking. Underlining with different colored pencils or cutting a copy of the master text of fieldnotes and transcripts into pieces that could be sorted and rearranged were once common tools. But for some time now all of this work can be much more easily handled by using computer software; for example, most spreadsheets allow you to color-code columns, rows, and/or cells. Word processing software is also of great help in searching, splicing, highlighting, and making multiple copies. Spreadsheets raise your ability to construct grids and tables to a much higher level; for qualitative data they take only a few hours to learn how to use.

The next question, of course, is whether interview data can be best handled with software specifically dedicated to qualitative analysis—usually called **CAQDAS** (computer-assisted qualitative data analysis software). Again, no software can do your analysis for you. Essentially, what software enables you to do is index, sort, and cross-reference your notes with great efficiency. But you have to provide the labels and codes that are used for indexing, sorting, and cross-referencing. As we have repeated in several contexts, we think you should at minimum consider using a spreadsheet for managing data, for setting up an indexing system, and for the early stages of coding. CAQDAS packages are more versatile than spreadsheets, but they require more time to learn to use well. They have the same conceptual advantages as spreadsheets or other matrix-based approaches. To use them requires researchers to systematically classify their data and thus add rigor to their qualitative data analysis. We discuss CAQDAS in somewhat more depth in Chapter 4. Here we simply say that whether to use one particular package and, if so, which one, has quite a bit to do with personal preferences.[38] We usually recommend—all else equal—that, if you are interested in exploring the possibilities of CAQDAS, you start with one of the freeware packages. As usual, the R collection of programs is one of the best places to begin, specifically the R qualitative data analysis (RQDA) package.

[38]See Kelle (2007a) for an excellent review stressing the theoretical benefits of using CAQDAS.

Finally, the need to be systematic and the benefits of being so are also greater when more than one person participates in the coding. The two main ways this occurs are through member checks and using multiple coders.

GETTING HELP: WHEN TO USE MEMBER CHECKS AND MULTIPLE CODERS

Will you use **member checks**, and, if so, how do you incorporate them into the data you code and analyze? The practice of member checking (also called *respondent validation* or *informant feedback*) was pioneered by ethnographers.[39] The basic idea is straightforward. The researcher asks the interviewee to review a summary or an abbreviated transcript of the interview and uses what the respondent says to improve the text and its interpretation. What could be more helpful, who could know better than the interviewees themselves what they said or meant? The benefits of member checking can be considerable, but in practice it can be more difficult to implement successfully than it might at first seem. One question is whether the interviewees are likely to be willing and/or able to review documentary summaries of their interviews. Another question is what to do when an interviewee disagrees with your account of the interview, especially if you are not persuaded that your version is incorrect. Some researchers have been incautious and, on ethical grounds, have given research participants veto rights over their research. This is a fairly widespread practice, but we think it is highly inadvisable. In any case, planning for member checks needs to be done early in the research, even though the actual checking occurs late—after summaries of the research have been written. Basic research ethics requires that if you decide to conduct member checks, you must be willing to live with the consequences and not discard responses that you find inconvenient. Also, because it is rare for all members to agree to review your work, you need a *code to identify those transcripts or summaries that have been checked and those that have not.*

Using **multiple coders** is another way to obtain help with the arduous process of coding interview data. Additional coders usually become involved in coding after the transcript stage has been reached, so we discuss them again in Chapter 12 on analysis. Here we point out what we see as one of the biggest advantages of using multiple coders. Coding is the least visible part of the process of analyzing and interpreting interview data. When teams do the coding, the work necessarily becomes more visible and explicit. The team's members have to explain their reasoning processes to one another. Some teams have shared their discussions by publishing them.[40]

Team coding makes the process of coding explicit and thereby more rigorous, and we recommend it. We think it should begin not after the transcripts have been constructed but before. For maximum benefit, multiple coders should participate during the processes of arranging the data in preliminary grids, as well as indexing the procedural and contextual notes and fieldnote data. The main problem with team coding is that

[39] Although the term is used broadly, it comes from anthropology, in which the people studied are often *members* of tribes, societies, groups, and so forth.

[40] Weston et al. (2001) provide rich detail, as do Millery et al. (2011). Note that NVivo will provide a quantitative measure of interrater reliability.

it can be very labor intensive. But that intensity also reveals the need for it when practicable. Different researchers often produce very different codes and coding schemes, and reconciling these can be laborious, even when it is a labor of love. But if the team is dedicated to the research, it is hard to think of a more valuable approach. Some teams have had considerable success discussing the initially different codes and producing an agreed-upon set of categories and codes. Multiple coding may not be objective, but it is at least intersubjective. We think the best approach to coding in social research is to employ multiple coding by skilled researchers who strive for intersubjective agreement by using explicit and public criteria of judgment.[41] Here as elsewhere, we believe that social research can benefit from becoming more social and being less based on ad hoc individual methods.

CONCLUSION

Nothing seems more natural to many beginning researchers than to plan to interview people to learn what they think, believe, feel, or have done. And beginning researchers are right. Interviewing is certainly one of the most straightforward approaches to research. But the difficulties of using interviews to obtain good answers to research questions are formidable. Some of these are reviewed in this conclusion.

Coding interview data most often involves coding written materials. The texts to code can be your notes or, if you have recorded the interviews, transcriptions of those recordings. It is important to be as thorough as possible because, as most experienced reviewers will attest, memory is not very reliable. We have several times been surprised to learn, by checking notes, that very clear memories were simply not true. For example, one of us remembered that Smith in Phoenix insisted on a particular point when in fact, according to our notes, it was Jones in Tucson who was insistent. The memory was right about the trip, but wrong about which individual in which city was insistent.

What is true of the researchers' memories is also true of interviewees' recollections. So, when we suggested earlier that one criterion of objectivity was fidelity to what the interviewee said, this does not provide terribly solid ground on which to base a claim of objectivity. You might be accurate in recording what interviewees say, but have they told the truth about what they believe? Are their memories accurate about what they did, or are they telling you what they think you want to hear? It is always impossible to know. In the midst of all this uncertainty, it is important to do your best to accurately record what you and the interviewee actually said. Being reasonably certain that you have accurately captured the spoken words and transcribed them correctly, do you know what the interviewee *meant* by them? If you have interviewed people who differ from you, perhaps precisely because you wanted to learn about the differences, how will you know that you have correctly *interpreted* what they said?[42] Plain speaking on your part is almost always helpful. If you have spent too much time in graduate school, you

[41] Of course, this approach is usually impossible when you are conducting an individual research project for individual academic credit. It can be difficult to align good professional practice, which often involves teamwork, with good approaches to grading *individual* student work.

[42] Tavory and Swidler (2009) discuss creative methods for addressing the semiotics of meaning.

might have come to think of yourself, for example, as a research *instrument* that studies *participants* in *venues*, but such jargon could lead to trouble when interviewing. Try instead to think of yourself as a *person* who studies *people* in *places*.

However you code interview data, our experience and the descriptions in the literature suggest that it is a lengthy, demanding process. Researchers coding qualitative data have comparatively fewer agreed-upon guidelines to consult and fewer established routines to follow than do their quantitative cousins. This is what makes coding qualitative data more exciting—and more difficult. One indication of the difficulty involved is the fact that when teams tell the story of their coding efforts, they almost always describe much initial disagreement among coders, followed by arduous efforts to construct common coding schemes.[43] These experiences, together with our own, we take as strong evidence that coding by individual researchers flying solo is fraught with possibilities for error and uncertainty.

Finally, as a researcher you have to be guided by your research question, but not so constrained by it that you are unprepared to investigate something new. This dichotomy generates a tension, perhaps a creative tension, between seeking specific kinds of data on the one hand and, on the other, exploring paths of discovery with interviewees. The old term for this tension, going back to Socrates, is the **paradox of inquiry**: If you already know what you are looking for, why are you bothering to look? This question is an implied critique of **deductivist** approaches (see Chapter 12). On the other hand, if you don't know what you are looking for, how will you recognize it if you see it? This question is an implied critique of **inductivist** approaches (see Chapter 11).[44] Researchers gathering and coding interview data have to be especially flexible as they engage in dialogues with interviewees. They also have to be alert to the challenges of another kind of dialogue—the kind that occurs between research perspectives. The paradox of inquiry can lead to fruitful interactions between being guided by initial ideas and being ready to learn something new.

In this chapter we have focused on what we think of as precoding, the kind of coding decisions that are typically made before an interview transcript is prepared. This kind of precoding involves asking yourself numerous questions. The answers to those questions constitute the initial set of codes, which you then use to index your data. These questions are discussed in detail in the corresponding sections of this chapter and in the Summary Table.

---

[43]Hruschka et al. (2004) are especially systematic. See also Weston et al. (2001); Kurasaki (2000); Wasserman, Clair, and Wilson (2009); and Creese, Bhatt, Bhojani, and Martin (2008). See also the works cited in Chapter 5 on meta-synthesis.

[44]Socrates was not impressed by the paradox, which he considered a rhetorician's device, not a serious problem.

SUGGESTIONS FOR FURTHER READING

As always, one of the best ways to learn about any research method is to see it in action in an outstanding book or article. It is harder to do so for coding interviews, because coding is usually the least visible part of interview research publications. One of the main points in this chapter is that coding is too important to be the invisible foundation of interview research. Michèle Lamont's books are methodologically interesting in many respects; among them is that she reveals more about her coding methods than is the norm. See her *Money, Morals, and Manners* (1992) and *How Professors Think* (2009). Another good example of coding complex data is Erikson's *Everything in Its Path* (1976).

Coffey and Atkinson's (1996) *Making Sense of Qualitative Data: Complementary Research Strategies* is a very nice volume that exemplifies the variety of ways the same set of data (24 interviews with graduate students and 25 with their faculty advisors) can be coded and analyzed. Although the various approaches to coding and analysis differ and can be seen as conflicting, the authors stress how the various approaches can be thought of as complementary, as completing one another, rather than as warring paradigms. A recent and more thorough approach to conflict and complementarity in the analysis of qualitative data is *Five Ways of Doing Qualitative Analysis* by Wertz et al. (2011).

It is often very instructive to read widely in the interview literature drawing from diverse fields that employ interviewing for a variety of goals. Just as traveling to other countries can be broadening, so can reading beyond the borders of your field. Research interviewers can learn a great deal, although much of it may not be *directly* applicable, by reading about interview methods in clinical psychology or even police interrogation. We have mentioned in this chapter books in those fields (by Miller and Rollnick and by Inbau et al.). Journalists' methods also provide food for thought. Woodward's works, *The War Within* (2008) and *Obama's Wars* (2010), are particularly interesting because they cover some of the same ground as did Herodotus. Interview methods are diverse enough and flexible enough that research interviewers can learn by reading expansively about the methods used by investigative journalists, therapists, interrogators, and others.

Another broadening resource is the *Workshop on Interdisciplinary Standards for Systematic Qualitative Research* compiled by Lamont and White (2009). This workshop was sponsored by the National Science Foundation and contains discussions by leading qualitative researchers in sociology, anthropology, and political science. The appendices include papers prepared by participants that are especially helpful. Although not confined to interview research, as is usual in discussions of qualitative research, interviewing holds a central place in the volume.

CHAPTER 2 SUMMARY TABLE

CODING ISSUES IN INTERVIEW DATA: QUESTIONS TO ASK YOURSELF	
1. GOALS: What do you seek when asking questions? (pp. 43–45)	• Do you seek information or explanations? • Do you hope to construct a theory or test a theory or neither or both? • Do you seek narratives? What do you do when you get narratives when you are not seeking them? • Is your goal biographical? Do you focus on the persons interviewed or their situations, organizations, or cultures?
2. ROLES: What should your part be in the dialogue? (pp. 45–47)	• Should you plan to be passive or engaged? Formal or informal? • How will you adjust when your role/approach seems ineffective? • Should you seek objectivity, and what do you mean by that? • How are your roles likely to influence replies to your questions?
3. SAMPLES: How many interviews, and with whom? (p. 48)	• In judgment sampling, what specifically are your criteria of judgment? Or in purposive sampling, what are your purposes? These should be included as part of your coding. • Will you conduct single or multiple interviews with each participant? Why, and how will you code any differences between early and later interviews?
4. QUESTIONS: When do you ask which kinds of questions? (pp. 48–50)	• Will you use an interview schedule/protocol? If so, how detailed is it, and how strictly do you adhere to it? • How will you sort and code questions asked but not answered, or questions not asked of all interviewees, or replies from different types of interviewees?
5. MODES: How do you communicate with interviewees? (pp. 50–53)	• How will you code so that you can distinguish differences in answers using different modes of communication, such as face-to-face, telephone, and Internet, including e-mail? • If you use focus groups, is your unit of analysis the groups or the individuals in the groups? If groups, how will you code for individual differences? If individuals, how will you code for group influences on the individuals?
6. OBSERVATIONS: What is important in the interview that isn't said? (p. 53)	• How will you code for potentially important differences among interviewees, such as their demeanors in the interview or their backgrounds? • How will you code so that you can determine whether there are differences among different categories of interviewees?

7. RECORDS: What methods do you use to preserve the dialogue? (pp. 53–56)	• How will you balance the use of your various recording methods: memory, notes, audio recordings, and video recordings? • Can the coding be done directly from electronic records, or will you transcribe the data first? • Will complete transcripts be necessary in your research, or might you write summary notes using recordings to check your memory as needed? • How verbatim will your transcripts be? What will you do about grammatical mistakes, nonverbal expressions, gestures, and so on?
8. TOOLS: When should you use computer tools to help you code your data? (pp. 56–58)	• How will you manipulate the codes *you* generate so that they can be used for analysis? • Will you hand-code using paper and colored pencils or highlighters? • Will you mainly use word processing software? Will you use spreadsheets as an indexing tool? Will you use software specifically designed for qualitative data, i.e., CAQDAS?
9. HELP: When will you use member checks and multiple coders? (pp. 58–59)	• Will you use member checks? How will you use them? How will you code for the differences in transcripts that have and have not been checked? • Will you use multiple coders? How will you use them and how will you reconcile differences in their initial codings?

CHAPTER 3

Coding Experimental Data

In this chapter we:

- Discuss the similarities and differences in coding among experiments and other designs.
- Consider coding and measurement techniques that apply to all experimental designs, including when to:
  - Categorize continuous data.
  - Screen for and code data errors, missing data, and outliers.
  - Code different types of independent variables.
  - Include and code covariates/control variables.
  - Use propensity score matching and instrumental variable estimation.
    Assess the validity of variable coding and measurement.
  - Assess variables' reliability.
  - Use multiple measures of the same concept.
  - Assess statistical power.
  - Use difference/change/gain scores for your dependent variable.
- Address coding and measurement issues that vary by type of experimental design:
  - Survey experiments.
  - Randomized controlled trials.
  - Multisite experiments.
  - Field experiments as compared with laboratory experiments.
  - Longitudinal experiments.
  - Natural experiments.
  - Quasi-experiments.

Surveys, interviews, and experiments (Chapters 1, 2, and 3) are the three most employed research designs in social research, and effective coding of their data has been examined by many methodologists (as we show, this is less true for observational and archival designs). Among the trio of widely recognized designs, experiments are most often held up as exemplars worthy of imitation by researchers using other methods, particularly when researchers are interested in investigating causal relationships. In part because of pressure from federal funding sources, this honored place in the suite of research methods has been reinforced by governmental muscle, which, in turn, has led to recent impressive increases in the number of randomized controlled trials (RCTs) and randomized field trials (RFTs) in several disciplines, including psychology, criminology, social policy, and education. Education has a considerable lead over the others.[1]

The advantages of experiments in causal research are that—uniquely among the major designs—experimenters create, manipulate, and control the variables/interventions that they study. And they determine who receives them. These features of experimentation raise some unique coding and measurement issues. In other ways, however, this chapter on experimental data coding parallels the other chapters on data coding. The parallels are perhaps closest between experimental and survey coding, because experiments and surveys often focus on quantitative data. Although surveys and experimental designs are also used to collect qualitative data (such as open-ended questions on surveys and debriefing interviews in experiments),[2] we discuss coding such qualitative data in Chapters 2, 4, and 12. We focus in this chapter on coding experimental data that are quantitative.

To review, coding means getting your evidence ready to analyze. You need to find appropriate symbols to label your data and to do so in a way that helps you to keep track of your data and ultimately to make sense of them. Coding tends to vary by design. Your research question leads you to a design for collecting data pertinent to answering the question. When you choose an experimental design, this tends to generate particular types of data and raise specific coding and measurement issues. Some issues of data coding in experiments are generic to all types of experiments. Other coding and measurement issues tend to be specific to one of the many varieties of experimental designs.[3] Consequently, this chapter has two main sections on coding and measurement, covering issues that are pertinent (1) in all experimental designs and (2) in particular types of experimental designs.

CODING AND MEASUREMENT ISSUES FOR ALL EXPERIMENTAL DESIGNS

Although there are many coding measurement questions that are especially important for specific types of experimental designs, others are important for all varieties of experimental data and, indeed, for many types of quantitative data, whether obtained

[1]The statement that the field of education research leads in the adoption of experimental methods may come as a surprise. Just the opposite has been widely reported. The reports were wrong, but the reporting error has, rumor-like, been repeated often. See the account in Skidmore and Thompson (2012). We know about these four disciplines in particular because they are the ones covered in the Cochrane Collaboration. See Chapter 5.

[2]For a good example of a double-blind experiment in which the dependent variable was qualitative (preferences of experienced violinists for new vs. classic old violins), see Fritz, Curtin, Poitevineau, Morrel-Samuels, and Tao (2012).

[3]In what follows we discuss experimental designs only to the extent necessary to address coding issues; for more design details, see our companion volume, *When to Use What Research Design* (Vogt et al., 2012, Ch. 3). Other good sources include Murnane and Willett (2011) and Gonzalez (2009).

through experiments or with other designs. Some of what we say about experimental coding overlaps with the guidelines in Chapter 1 about good procedures for analyzing quantitative survey data. We point out several parallels as we go along. It may also be worth your while to consult the Summary Tables for Chapter 1 to review more links.

When to Categorize Continuous Data

Almost never. Categorizing continuous data is *data mutilation*. When you categorize a continuous variable, you *throw away information*. The unfortunate practice of turning a continuous variable into crude categories (e.g., high, medium, and low) seems especially prevalent among researchers conducting experiments. That may be because the independent variable (IV) in an experiment is naturally categorical: treatment or no treatment. Even when the researcher is using a more complicated IV, it is almost inevitably categorical—for example, training A versus training B versus no training.[4] The fact that the IV in an experiment is most often naturally categorical should not distract you from the key point concerning control variables and dependent variables: Categorizing continuous control and dependent variables reduces statistical power and makes any estimates of the size of experimental effects less precise. Categorization reduces effect sizes and makes it more likely that an important experimental effect will be missed. Sometimes continuously measured data are naturally clustered; in that case, it can be appropriate to categorize them. The graphic methods of exploratory data analysis (see Chapter 7) are especially helpful for discovering breaks in continuous data that define more or less categorical groups.

Two or three generations ago, before computers, categorizing continuous data reduced the burdens of calculating test statistics by hand. That excuse has long since lost its justification. But the tradition of categorizing continuous data is remarkably persistent. Such categorizing may be useful when *reporting* findings to a general audience. But don't confuse what might be helpful in reporting results for popular consumption with good methods for analysis and interpretation. If you want to introduce cut scores to describe your findings in Goldilocks' categories (too little, just right, too much), do so *after* the analysis.[5] In general, we are not persuaded by an argument claiming that it is better to use weak data to produce a bad analysis on the grounds that more people might be able to understand the bad analysis. Surely it would be better to use the best data to draw solid conclusions, and then make the effort to describe these in lay terms.

Finally, if you are going to use cut scores, one version or another of **Angoff procedure** is often recommended. There are several types, and controversy exists among experts about which is best, but the basic method is clear and sensible: Use a panel of experts to establish the cut score at which a person could be judged competent, or at risk, or depressed, or proficient, and so forth.[6] Expert judgment hardly settles all issues, of course. Well-known examples include the striking inconsistencies in wine tasters'

---

[4]Ranks are also common, such as 2 weeks versus 4 weeks versus no training.

[5]The classic source for this point is Cohen (1983). Butts and Ng's (2009) more recent discussion is broader and even less compromising in its opposition to "data chopping." Taylor, West, and Aiken (2006) demonstrate that the mistake of coarsely categorizing a continuous dependent variable cannot be repaired by using logit and/or probit regression, as many researchers apparently believe.

[6]Cizek (2001) reviews the Angoff procedure and other standard-setting methods.

ratings and, a favorite example among statisticians, bias in the judging of Olympic events.[7]

When to Screen for and Code Data Errors, Missing Data, and Outliers

Errors

Before beginning your analysis, it is important to screen your data for possible errors. All your work reviewing the literature, setting up the experiment, finding participants, and collecting the data can be spoiled by skipping this easy (but easily ignored) step of correcting errors in your dataset. And errors are inevitable. Minimizing them is crucial. The analysis can only be as good as the data, and error-ridden data will lead to weak and possibly misleading conclusions. All the major statistical packages contain routines to help you screen, clean, and correct your data. It is essential to use them.[8] The most obvious types of errors are values that are impossible, such as a score on the verbal reasoning part of the Graduate Record Exam (GRE) of 50 or 5000 or 150. But wait! A score of 150 would be a possible, and a fairly typical, score if the exam had been taken in 2012, but it would be impossible if it had been taken in 2010. That's because, in mid-2011, the GRE folks changed the scoring metric from one odd, but familiar, range (200–800) to an even odder, and unfamiliar, range (130–170). Changes in the way data are coded and reported are fairly common, and you need to remain alert to them.

Errors can be multivariate. With the simplest experimental designs, the focus is on finding individual errors. With more complex designs that include control variables, looking for multivariate errors is important. Scores that are perfectly possible when taken individually can be impossible or highly unlikely in combination. Say that among your variables are the ages, heights, and weights of school students in the 1st through 12th grades. Your data screening indicates that one student is 6 years old, weighs 60 pounds, and is 6 feet tall. Looks like a data entry error! You'd want to go back to the original data for that student. You might suspect that the data row should be 6 years, 60 pounds, and 4 feet; or 16 years, 160 pounds, and 6 feet. If you can't figure out the source of the error and correct it, the data cannot be used. They become missing data.

Missing Data

Missing data constitute a special kind of error. In this section, we address only coding issues. We review how missing data can provide clues for analysis in the section titled "When to assess statistical power, and what does this have to do with coding?" on pp. 84–85; and we consider special analytical imputation techniques in Chapter 8. But it is useful to illustrate with one of the simple ways to tell whether the missing data matter for your analysis. Say, for example, that quite a few of the participants in your experiment did not respond to the item on the background questionnaire asking for age. Divide the sample into two groups: those who gave their ages and those who did not. Conduct a *t*-test. The IV is "Answered the question," yes or no. The dependent variable

[7]See Emerson and Arnold (2011) for a probing examination of the scores of figure skating judges.

[8]A good source is Chapter 4 in Tabachnick and Fidell (2001) on data cleaning and screening, which both describes techniques and compares software routines for implementing them.

(DV) is the score on the outcome measure. Use the *t*-test to see whether there is a statistically significant difference between the two groups on your outcome, or dependent, variable. If there is, that tells you that the data are not missing at random.

Reviews and corrections of your data are greatly facilitated when you plan to code your missing data before the analysis phase. It is exceptionally important to track and report on your missing data.[9] Doing so says much about the seriousness with which you take your work and thus about how seriously your readers should take it. Our impression, which is backed up by some empirical studies,[10] is that the majority of published articles are far too casual about reporting and addressing missing data problems. But neither you nor your readers can accurately judge the quality of your work without knowledge of the character and degree of missing data. You will want to address and code for such basic questions as: Are the missing data more frequent in the control or the experimental group(s)? Are missing data equally distributed among demographic or other pretest variables? The more control variables you include in the design, the more likely it is that you will be able to code, analyze, and understand missing data rather than merely taking last-minute corrective actions to improve estimates.[11] The importance of planning for missing data is greater in more complicated designs, such as Latin squares. It is also very salient in repeated measures studies that span a considerable amount of time (see the section titled "Coding Data from Natural Experiments" on pp. 96–98).[12]

What codes do you enter on your datasheets and in your datafile when data are missing? It depends on *why* the data are missing. Say that one of your outcome variables is a score on a 5-item test. What if a participant refused to take the test; what if she took it but you lost her answer sheet; what if she took it but skipped a question; or what if she moved to a different town and withdrew from the experiment? You might code these kinds of missing data 66, 77, 88, and 99 for *refused, lost, skipped*, and *withdrew*, respectively. Using 0 for the missing data is *not* a good idea, because 0 is a possible score on the test. There are big differences between a participant's refusing to take a test, her getting a score of 0 on the test, and your losing her data. It is also not a good idea to code missing data by simply leaving the cell blank. When you go back over your dataset and encounter a blank, you won't know whether you forgot to enter something there, whether the participant refused, whether she withdrew, and so forth. Using numbers such as 66, 77, 88, and 99—which are far outside the possible range of 0–5 on the 5-point test—helps you to retain maximum information that could later be useful in your analysis and helps you in preventing later mistakes.

Outliers

It is also important to screen for outliers. These are scores on variables that are so extreme that leaving them in the dataset would make summary statistics misleading. Sometimes outliers are merely data entry errors and can be handled as such. At other

[9]Newton and Rudestam (1999, pp. 156–173) provide a thorough, nontechnical review of methods for detecting and reporting missing data.

[10]Rousseau, Simon, Bertrand, and Hachey (2012).

[11]See Huber (2012) for a thorough review.

[12]Ryan (2007).

times they are real scores, but require special consideration. A cluster of outliers for a small number of participants is often an indicator of a subgroup that should be considered in the analysis (see the section titled "When to Include and Code Covariates/Control Variables" on pp. 71–73). Also, outliers may mean that statistical assumptions necessary to analyze the data are violated. We review, in the chapters on analysis, cases in which specific analytical techniques require that certain assumptions about your data be met. Here it is worth noting that experts disagree about whether and when outliers should be removed or data transformations used to make the data more amenable to analysis and more in conformity with statistical assumptions.[13]

Everyone agrees, however, that deleting outliers to make your results come out the way you want is fraud. This kind of fraud may be quite common. It is so easy to do, and the results are so pleasing! It is also fairly easy to detect—if the detective has access to the original data.[14] This is the reason that scholarly journals are increasingly requiring that authors make their data available to other researchers—a trend we strongly support. Eliminating extreme scores does not always improve results. Deleting extreme scores can reduce linear correlations and therefore the likelihood of a correlation being statistically significant.[15] But, when comparing means, which is the most common approach in experiments, discarding extreme scores reduces within-group variation. That, in turn, makes it easier to increase t- and F-ratios and thereby to attain a significant p-value. What to do? First, it is helpful to have an extreme-score strategy *before* looking at the data; this makes it harder to handle your data in ways that (perhaps unconsciously) merely confirm your biases. Second, tell your readers what you have done and why. Third, run your data both with and without deleting outliers and present the results *both* ways.

The most useful techniques for reviewing and rebuilding your dataset are exploratory data analysis and other descriptive techniques described in Chapter 6. All of these methods rely heavily on graphic reviews of your data, such as stem-and-leaf displays and scatterplot matrices. Graphic displays are often the easiest and sometimes the only way to spot errors, such as our earlier example of the 6-foot-tall 6-year-old.[16] Detecting outliers involves graphic methods and statistical routines. Figuring out where they came from and what to do about them often demands more work and judgment. The key point about coding and correcting errors is to take the process seriously. No matter how pristine your experimental design and how advanced your analytical techniques, messy data can ruin the analysis. It is irresponsible not to review and repair your dataset before beginning an analysis and even more irresponsible to tidy it up in ways that help you confirm your prejudices—and sometimes only a fine line separates the two. Full disclosure about how you have coded and analyzed your data is always the best policy.

[13]See Osborne (2008, Chs. 13 and 14). For a thorough discussion of removing outliers in questionnaire data, which has many applications to experimental data, see Zijlstra, Van der Ark, and Sijtsma (2011).

[14]See the revealing discussion in Yong (2012). Note that transforming your data so that they meet statistical assumptions, such as normality, is very distinct from discarding inconvenient data.

[15]The correlational technique Cronbach's alpha is also affected in this way: Outliers inflate alpha estimates; see Liu, Wu, and Zumbo (2010).

[16]Multivariate outliers can be detected using a statistical technique called the *Mahalanobis distance*. The concepts involved are somewhat complicated, but given modern software, the Mahalanobis distance is fairly easy to use.

Finally, it is often useful to maintain two or more datasets: the original messy one with the data as they were collected and one or more others in which the errors have been corrected, the outliers removed, and the data transformed for purposes of analysis. Some analysts recommend keeping all versions of the data in one master file (variables in the original form, with errors corrected, with outliers removed, etc.). It is a matter of personal preference; we use separate files because we make fewer errors that way.

What to Consider When Coding the Independent Variable

Normally one doesn't think of coding decisions as concerning the independent variable (IV), which is why most of the discussion in this chapter is directed to dependent variables (DVs) and control variables. The usual coding for an IV is: experimental group, 1; control group, 0. However, the methods of implementing the IV can vary from experiment to experiment. Seemingly small differences in the procedures (protocol) can have large effects; the "same" IV can have different effects on the DV depending on how it is implemented.[17] So if you conduct a series of experiments, which is fairly common practice, and you vary the instructions for implementing the IV, these variations should be recorded and coded. This means also that in your review of the literature, don't just note *that* the "same" IV was used, but also code for *how* it was implemented. Finally, if incentives were used to recruit participants and/or to encourage them to follow the protocol, this should be noted and coded, especially if there were any differences in the incentives offered to different groups or at different stages of the research.

One important variation in design effects that should be described and coded is the degree of "blinding," that is, the extent to which the participants do not know whether they received the experimental or the comparison treatment (single-blind). When the researchers also do not know, this is called double-blind. Blinding is not possible in many quasi-experiments or experiments conducted in natural settings rather than in laboratories. Surprisingly, blinding status is often left unclear in research articles. When researchers do report that their study was blinded, they often do no more than state this in the narrative. This would be fine except that several different definitions of "blinding" exist. If you have done blinding, you need to explain exactly who was blinded (participants, researchers, and/or data analysts) and how. This is especially important in a series of experiments or in multisite experiments in which the blinding procedures may vary. Identifying these differences should be part of the coding process so that the differences can be incorporated into the analysis.[18]

Evaluation researchers often discuss the concept of **fidelity of implementation,** and this concept has implications beyond the field of program evaluation. Rather than describing *differences in* protocols, a lack of fidelity has more to do with *departures from* an agreed protocol. A related concept is **intensity of implementation**, which is often an issue with multisite studies and quasi-experiments. Are the experimenters just going through the motions, or are they gung ho? Do they have the enthusiastic support of other people in the organization, or are they lonely pioneers? Attending to fidelity and intensity of implementation is easier said than done. There are no well-developed

[17]Kalkhoff and Thye (2006) have demonstrated this in a review of 26 separate experiments studying the same variables, but with variations in the treatment protocol.

[18]Haahr and Hrobjartsson (2006) provide a sobering review.

scales or scaling procedures, as there are, for example, for assessing reliability of scales or applying techniques such as propensity scoring. That lack of standardization means that researchers often have to invent something for the specific purpose and often to use more or less subjective assessments. One practice (it should be more common) is the **manipulation check**, in which the researcher investigates whether the IV was delivered as per instructions or agreement.[19] This is usually coded as a categorical "yes–no." More useful on many occasions would be fuzzy sets or rank order categories that reported the degree to which the IV was effectively implemented.

Much of what is usually *described* in the narrative description of the experiment can also be *coded* and included in the dataset for subsequent analysis. Experimenters work with volunteers. Note any differences between the target population and the subgroup composed of members of the population who volunteered. How many were recruited? How were they determined to be eligible? Were there any differences in types of eligibility? Were different techniques used to assign them to treatment/experimental versus comparison/control groups? How well did the participants comply with the researchers' instructions? Did the participants stay in their assigned groups? If the treatment was considered a benefit, were those assigned to the comparison group more likely to withdraw? Sometimes, especially in field experiments, participants can find ways to alter their assignment; for example, parents might move so their children are in the experimental district. "No-shows," people assigned to treatment but who do not participate, are also a potential complication. The existence of no-shows usually indicates that the assignment methods did not produce an unbiased group. Ways to rescue a biased sample, to make it more random, have long engaged the attention of methodologists.[20] When the assignment mechanism does not work perfectly, you can sometimes adjust for this by using techniques such as instrumental variable estimation (IVE; see the section titled "When to Use Propensity Score Matching and Instrumental Variable Estimation" on pp. 73–77).

When to Include and Code Covariates/Control Variables

A **control variable** or **covariate** is a variable that the researcher wants to control for, because doing so can sometimes increase statistical power and improve the accuracy of effect-size estimates. It is a variable that influences the outcome but is not relevant to the research question. A covariate correlates with the DV; controlling for a covariate means statistically subtracting the effects of the control variable from the effects of the IV. Remaining effects of the treatment on the DV will be "purified" of misleading outcomes due to the covariate.[21] For example, in a study of an experimental method of teaching computer programming, we added the students' cumulative GPAs as a covariate to control for variance not taken care of by assignment to control and experimental groups; this was done to control for students' prior academic ability and achievement.

[19] See Mowbray, Holter, Teague, and Bybee (2003) for an excellent review.

[20] Bloom (1984).

[21] Including covariates is even more important when the treatment is a policy intervention in the real world (not the laboratory world), where random assignment is difficult or impossible. See Manski (2001). A blanket recommendation to use covariates conceals much variation in correct application to specific problems; for a thorough discussion see Steiner, Cook, and Shadish (2011).

Adding such control variables is especially important when membership in the control and experimental groups is not determined by random assignment, but it is useful even when random assignment is used, because random assignment can result, purely by chance, in skewed groups of experimental participants.

Why would you need covariates in a randomized experiment? Isn't the whole idea of random assignment to eliminate the need for statistical controls? Haven't you controlled irrelevant variance through randomization? Yes, but even with random assignment, including important covariates will improve the precision of your estimates of experimental effects. And you will increase your statistical power, too. (It is for these reasons that experimenters often use designs such as matched pairs.) So, if you have good data on covariates available, include them. But, to repeat our earlier warning, do not code them by dichotomizing or otherwise mutilating your data. When you include covariates, you usually use multiple regression (see Chapter 8) to analyze your data rather than terminating the analysis with one of the simple significance tests such as analysis of variance (ANOVA) or the *t*-test (see Chapter 7).

In addition to controlling for subgroup variables such as gender, ethnicity, and age, it is also very important to study how the treatment might vary across groups or individuals. The default focus in experiments is on mean differences between the control and experimental groups, but a corollary to *controlling for* group differences is to *test for* group differences. It could be the case that an experimental treatment has outcomes that vary by group in strength and sometimes even in direction. A treatment that had a positive effect on one group could have a negative effect on another. For example, a study of a high school curriculum designed to promote tolerance for diversity found that it worked fairly well on average but that it had negative effects for some students, particularly males with low self-esteem.[22] What subgroups should you code so that you can test for the effects of subgroup membership? That depends on your theory and substantive knowledge. For example, in the aforementioned study, the authors knew that a long line of research indicated that low self-esteem correlated with intolerance, so a measure of self-esteem was included in the experimental design.

Another example is the experiment on the so-called Mozart effect mentioned in the General Introduction to this book. Simply put, the presumed effect is that listening to Mozart makes you smarter. This had been reported in previous research, was much ballyhooed in the media, and led many parents to purchase classical CDs and music lessons for their children. More specifically, the claim was that listening to Mozart increases spatial reasoning ability. A group of investigators that included one of us attempted to replicate the previous research finding. The treatment was listening to Mozart or to other auditory phenomena. The dependent measure was obtained with a nonverbal (progressive matrices) intelligence test, which resulted in a numerical score. To improve the specificity of the experimental results, the authors added covariates that arguably could have influenced any effect of listening to the music, specifically the participants' prior experience with classical music, whether and how long they had studied a musical instrument, and the type of music they most enjoyed. In this experiment, listening to Mozart had no effect either for the participants as a whole or for any subgroups among them.[23]

[22] Avery, Bird, Johnstone, Sullivan, and Thalhammer (1992).

[23] Newman et al. (1995).

Note that some subgroups are hard to code. For example, most ethnic categories are neither mutually exclusive nor exhaustive, which means that they violate the principles of accurate categorization. The same individuals can reasonably be coded, or can label themselves, in different ways. To take a famous (presidential) example, if your mother is from Kansas and your father from Kenya, you might call yourself black, white, mixed, African American, American African, or one of several other labels. Data on income are clearer, but often hard to obtain, and when you can get information about incomes it often comes in crude categories. Other codes, such as those for gender or age, usually are more straightforward. The basic point is that the average effects of an experimental intervention might not be the most important outcomes. Average effects might not even be visible because they have been canceled out by subgroup variety. With random assignment and a large sample, some of these problems are not likely, but they are still possible. When pure random assignment is not used—and it is much rarer in social research than textbooks might lead one to expect—it is crucial to check for subgroup differences. The typical experimental design in social research is a quasi-experiment, often with group randomization, and for these experiments subgroup differences between treatment and comparison groups need to be coded and analyzed.[24]

When to Use Propensity Score Matching and Instrumental Variable Estimation

These two advanced methods are discussed here together because they both address the same problem: how to undertake causal analysis when the assignment to control and experimental groups has not been done at random, as in a randomized controlled trial (RCT). The methods also can be used when assigning treatments to intact groups (group rather than individual randomization), as in most quasi-experiments. Both allow experiment-like analyses when selection effects and other design implementations result in nonrandomness—at least in some special circumstances.

Propensity Score Matching

Propensity score matching (PSM) is an elaboration on the basic matched-pairs experimental design in RCTs. In RCTs, matching is a supplement used to improve on simple random assignment by increasing the similarity of control and experimental groups beyond what it would be with simple random assignment. Such matching designs are especially important when sample size is small and simple random assignment is therefore less likely to produce equivalent control and experimental groups. In the most familiar approach, the matched-pairs design, potential experimental participants are first ranked on a variable that correlates with the outcome variable. Then the top-ranked two are assigned at random to control and experimental groups; then the third- and fourth-ranked participants are assigned; and so on. The ranking is done *before* the assignment. For example, in a statistics learning experiment, participants might be ranked on math aptitude and then assigned (by matching) to control and experimental groups.

[24]See Poulson, Gadbury, and Allison (2012) for a revealing account of how to handle treatment effects that differ in strength, and even in direction, for different groups and individuals.

With PSM the matching is done *after* the experiment has been conducted or after nonexperimental data have been gathered. PSM amounts to *virtual* assignment to control and experimental groups. For example, say you want to study the effects of a new method of instruction on learning as measured by an achievement test. If you can assign students at random to use the new method (experimental group) or not use it (control group), you can proceed with an RCT. But assigning students to instructional groups is difficult except for short-term laboratory experiments. If you are studying classroom learning rather than laboratory learning, over a semester rather than for an hour or two, random assignment is usually impossible. Rather, some instructors volunteer to try out the new method (experimental group), and others might agree to teach as usual and let their students be measured on the outcome variable, such as an achievement test (control group). Say there are 10 instructors in each group and each of their classes enrolls 30 students. You have 300 students in each group. But the real comparison is 10 classes in the control versus 10 classes in the experimental group.

Any conclusions drawn from this study will be limited, especially if your goal is to study the effects of the new method on individual students. You would, or should, have limited confidence in any inferences you make, because the students are not randomly sampled or assigned, nor are the instructors. You can increase your confidence in conclusions by controlling for important variables, such as the students' prior academic achievement. PSM involves using control variables but takes the use of control variables to a higher level. PSM uses a *set of* control variables to form a composite variable, which is used to compute a **propensity score** (propensity to learn the subject matter, in this case). Students with similar propensity scores are matched across treatment groups. Presuming that the variables used to compute the propensity score are important predictors of the outcome variable, and presuming that the study has a sufficient number of participants (300 in each group would be sufficient in most cases), PSM is a very powerful technique and one of the few good methods to use to draw solid conclusions from the data in such a study.[25]

Instrumental Variable Estimation

Instrumental variables are tricky to define and hard to use. And when you can define them and know how to use them, you still have to be able to *find* them, which is usually quite difficult. But when you can find an appropriate "instrument," instrumental variable estimation (IVE) is one of the most important ways to compensate for the lack of random assignment in the forming of control and experimental groups. Like PSM, it is a method of *virtual* assignment of individuals to control and experimental groups. And even when random assignment has actually been used, an instrumental variable can be employed to rectify imperfections in the way the random assignment was implemented.[26] Because IVE is so helpful in the study of natural experiments and other archival data, we discuss it briefly again in the section titled "Coding Data from Quasi-Experiments" (pp. 96–98). Here we sketch in the basic idea in order to clarify when you might want to use the method to address a problem of noncomparability of

[25] See Stuart and Rubin (2008) and Rudner and Peyton (2006) for good brief overviews. To code and analyze the data in this example, you would also want to use multilevel modeling. See Chapter 9.

[26] See Shin and Raudenbush (2011) for a persuasive example.

control and experimental groups resulting from the lack of, or imperfections in, random assignment. IVE is an intricate and subtle technique. However, if you can find a candidate instrumental variable, and if you can make a case that it truly functions as it must if it is to fulfill its function, then it is a very powerful method of analysis.

An **instrumental variable** is a kind of control variable that can substitute for a randomly assigned IV. To be an instrument, a variable *must* be related to the predictor variable, or IV, but *not* related to the outcome variable, or DV.[27] If you can find one of these (and, to repeat, this is the hard part), then you code it as an instrument and go ahead with the analysis. If at this point the explanation of when you might want to use IVE seems unclear, we would not be surprised. An example might help.[28]

Political scientists have often hypothesized that education fosters civic engagement, such as voting. The data in this example come from a nationally representative sample of individuals in their late 20s. As in most such studies, there was a strong positive correlation between education level of these young adults and their probability of civic engagement as measured by registering to vote. Does this correlation indicate a causal relationship between the two? A valid and consistent correlation between two variables, *X* and *Y*, is an indicator that

1. *X* causes *Y*, or
2. *Y* causes *X*, or
3. *X* and *Y* are both caused by one or more other variables, say *A* and *B*.

In this example, *X* is going to college and *Y* is young adults' probability of registering to vote. (Registering to vote isn't likely to cause going to college, so option number 2 can be eliminated.) Say that we added two control variables: Variable *A* is parental education, and variable *B* is parental income. It could be that the higher the young adults' parents' educations (*A*) were and the higher their parents' incomes (*B*) were, the more likely young adults were to register to vote (*Y*). This relation could hold whether the participants went to college (*X*) or not. Or it could be that parents' educations and incomes influence the likelihood of going to college *and* that going to college increases the tendency to register. To sort out the possibilities, the typical solution is to study the basic relation *X* (college) → *Y* (registering) with regression analysis while controlling for the effects of *A* and *B* (parents' educations and incomes). Of course, *A* and *B* might not be the only other variables that could have an effect on young adults' tendency to register to vote. If we have reason to believe that there are other influences, and if data are available, we can "just" add the extra variables to the regression equation. "Controlling for everything" is a long tradition in regression analysis. But it is a crude approach with several problems (see Chapter 8 for some discussion). The advantages of IVE over this crude approach can perhaps best be appreciated by comparing causal diagrams of the relationships in our example, first using the traditional regression approach and second using IVE.

---

[27] Remember that a good *control* variable is correlated with the outcome variable but not highly correlated with the predictor variable, which is just the opposite of a good instrumental variable.

[28] Our discussion summarizes (and simplifies) the account in Murnane and Willett (2011) of the research by Dee (2004) on which the example is based.

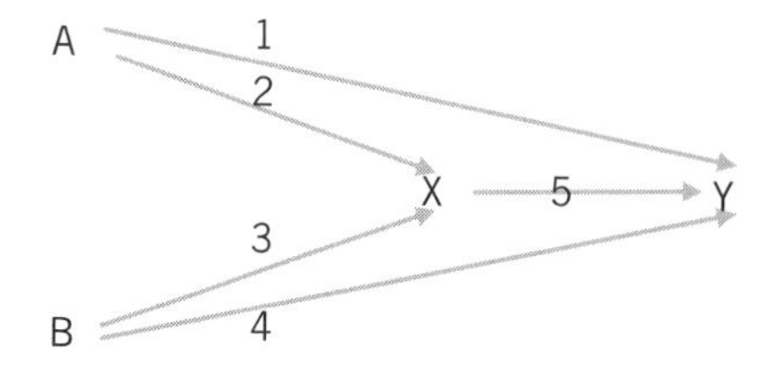

FIGURE 3.1. Causal diagram of the relation of parents' income and education on young adults' probability of attending college and registering to vote.

Figure 3.1 shows the basic set of relations discussed thus far. Arrow 5 is the one that we're interested in: the effect of college on registering to vote. Arrows 1 and 4 are the direct effects of parents' educations and incomes on registering, and arrows 2 and 3 are the possible indirect effects (through college) of parents' educations and incomes. For example, parents' education levels are related to going to college (line 2), and college in turn is related to registering (line 5). The complications mount when we realize that the two control variables discussed so far are hardly the only ones that previous research has shown to be associated with both going to college and registering to vote. Examples include the verbal aptitudes and the self-efficacy levels of young adults. Both of these have been shown to increase the tendency to go to college *and* to engage in civic behavior such as voting. If we include those variables in the analysis, calling them variables *C* (verbal ability) and *D* (self-efficacy), the diagram would begin to get very intricate. Finally, consider that all of these control variables—young adults' verbal ability (*C*), their self-efficacy (*D*), their parents' educations (*A*), and their parents' incomes (*B*)—are themselves probably intercorrelated. That means that lines connecting them to one another could be added. The whole thing could start to look pretty murky—a mess that the human eye and brain could have trouble grasping. How can IVE improve on this situation? Figure 3.2 makes it clear. When using IVE, you add one instrumental variable (*Z*). It replaces *all* four connecting intersecting arrows in Figure 3.1 with one arrow, arrow 1 in Figure 3.2.

As in Figure 3.1, here, too, the main relation we are interested in is $X \rightarrow Y$, now arrow 2, which addresses the research question, Does education lead to civic engagement? But the rest of the complications in Figure 3.1 (which arose from adding variables *A* and *B*) are nowhere to be seen in Figure 3.2. They are replaced by the one simple arrow from *Z*. What is *Z*, and how can it replace the earlier mess? *Z* is the "instrument." It functions like the application of simple random assignment to control and experimental groups. How does it do this? That is the key question.[29]

Note first that there is no arrow from *Z* to *Y*. Although *Z* is correlated with the predictor *X* (college), it is not correlated with the outcome *Y* (registering). In this example,

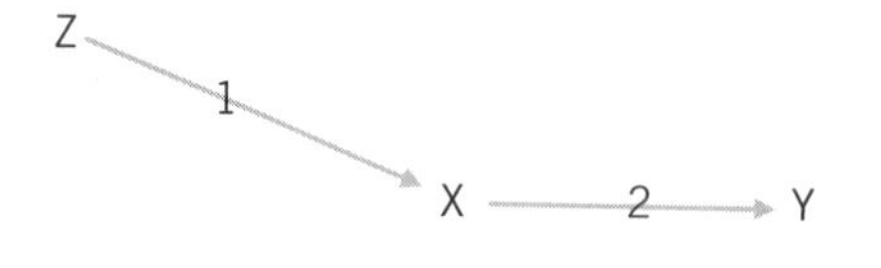

FIGURE 3.2. The influence of going to college on young adults' probability of registering to vote controlled by instrumental variable *Z*.

[29]The clearest explanation we know is in Murnane and Willett (2011), whose Venn diagrams are the first really lucid nontechnical explanation we've seen. Angrist and Pischke's (2009) discussion is lighthearted but quite a bit more technically advanced.

the instrument Z is the distance of the young adults' homes from a college when they were in high school. Distance from a college (Z) is associated with going to college upon high school graduation for the simple reason that living close to a college makes it somewhat easier to attend one. But, and this is important, there is no reason to expect that distance from a college is correlated with the likelihood of registering to vote. How does this help? To answer, we summarize Murnane and Willett's argument.[30] When it is possible (and it occasionally is) to locate a variable that you can show is uncorrelated with the residuals or error terms in the regression analysis of the relation of X and Y (in our example, college and registering to vote, respectively), then you can use that variable (the instrument) to calculate an unbiased estimate of the causal relation of X (college) and Y (registering). Finding a variable that truly meets the requirements of an instrumental variable is difficult. But when one can be found, it can greatly reduce the bias in an estimate of causal effects that arises from nonrandom assignment to control and experimental groups.

In sum, PSM and IVE are two of the best solutions to a common problem. The common problem is lack of random assignment to control and experimental groups and the consequent lack of certainty about causal effects. Both PSM and IVE can be used to analyze data from quasi-experiments and even archival survey data, which, through recoding, can become evidence in a natural experiment. Both PSM and IVE are relatively new methods, and neither method is easy to apply, but when they are feasible, it would usually be unwise to ignore them.

When to Assess the Validity of Variable Coding and Measurement

Validity is a central issue at all stages of a research project. At the design stage, the chief concern is whether the study is set up so that you can reach justifiable conclusions about your topic. This is usually referred to as **internal validity**. It addresses the question, Do my conclusions apply to my sample? By contrast, **external validity** asks the question, Do my conclusions apply to anyone else? In other words, can you generalize your conclusions beyond the participants in the experiment? The answer depends on the quality and the appropriateness of your sample.

After design and sampling comes coding and measurement. Valid codes and measures accurately capture the essence of the phenomena you are interested in so that you can record those phenomena and assess them in ways that allow you to address your research questions.[31] Some variables are fairly easy for researchers to measure directly, such as height, weight, and gender. For them, validity of coding and measurement is often not much of an issue. Gauging the validity of a measure is more problematic when a variable cannot be measured directly. And most variables in social research cannot be measured directly by researchers: for example, ability, aggression, ambition, anxiety, autonomy, and so forth—and that's just the A's.

---

[30] Murnane and Willett (2011, pp. 217–218).

[31] An elementary overview is in Vogt (2007). A more advanced review of measurement validity, with particular attention to statistical techniques for assessing types of validity, is Bryant (2000). Adcock and Collier (2001) synthesize the dozens of types of measurement validity of both quantitative and qualitative variables. For all aspects of validity in experimental designs, the *locus classicus* is Shadish, Cook, and Campbell (2002).

Like other types of validity, measurement validity is a matter of degree. No coding scheme or measurement is perfectly valid, but different approaches can be more or less valid. It is easier to identify problems with (or threats to) validity than it is to assert that a measure is clearly valid. One of the easiest threats to measurement validity to avoid is data mutilation. An excellent way to *reduce* measurement validity is to categorize a continuous variable (see the section titled "When to Categorize Continuous Data" earlier in this chapter). Doing so makes your measurement crude and thereby less valid.

Validity is difficult to measure, in large part because it is hard to define. And measuring a measure's validity may be doubly so. One indicator of how hard validity is to define is that many different and contested definitions and measures of validity have been proposed, and each of these comes with distinct coding schemes for types and subtypes of validity. Labeling disputes and alternative taxonomies aside, measurement validity addresses the questions, Do your measures and the way you have coded them yield information about what you intend to study? Does a particular code or measure capture what you want it to? Statistical methods for answering these questions are limited because using them implies an independent criterion against which to compare the measure. For example, a common practice for validating a new measure of something is to compare it with a previous measure of the same thing. But this procedure is a valid way to measure validity *only* if the previous measure is itself known to be valid. How could you know that? By comparing it with a pre-previous measure? This is why validity is much more a matter of reasoning and judgment than statistical routines. Because the concept of validity is a conceptual jungle and it is hard to define and measure, many studies do not in fact report on what they have done to guard against problems with validity or whether they have done anything at all to assess measurement validity.[32]

The main type of validity relevant to coding and measurement is **construct validity**. Some methodologists argue, and we are inclined to agree, that all other types of validity are subtypes or clarifications of construct validity. Construct validity addresses the question, Are the concepts being coded and measured in ways that enable us to study what we aim to study? One of the most important subtypes of the construct validity of a measurement is **content validity**. Content validity addresses the issue of whether the measure is thorough or representative of the thing being measured. If content validity is lacking—because, for example, a test covers only a small portion of what it should—then the construct validity of the test would also be lacking.

For example, if your research question leads you to study learning as an outcome variable, what are the most valid ways to measure the kinds of learning you are interested in? If you are studying a program meant to promote the learning of job skills, is the best measure whether participants get jobs, whether they could demonstrate the skills on a practical test, the quality of their resumes, or whether they can pass an objective exam on knowledge relevant to particular lines of work? Or is it some combination of all of these? It seems that researchers often decide questions such as this nonsystematically, perhaps even by picking the easiest way to code and measure the variable. A step up from "convenience coding" is to put on your thinking cap and reason it through as best you can. Even better is to consult a panel of experts. This is frequently done, but there is not much research literature on how such experts are or should be chosen. For students working on a dissertation, the dissertation committee is a good place to start.

---

[32]Hogan and Agnello (2004).

For practitioners in most fields, consulting with colleagues makes sense. Although there is a lot of quantitative research on the *reliability* (consistency) of experts' judgments, deciding whether someone is actually an expert is a qualitative decision. One way to judge consensus among research colleagues is to use a measure of a variable that has been frequently used before. A measure that has been used before by experts can be thought of as encapsulating their judgments.

Assessment of validity is often coupled with gauging reliability. It is incontestably true that the two are tied. A completely unreliable, or inconsistent, scale cannot be a valid measure of anything—"reliability precedes validity" is the old saw. Another way to put it is that the degree of validity is limited by the degree of reliability. Because reliability can often be assessed with relatively straightforward measurements, it is much more routinely gauged and reported than validity. We now turn to this precondition of validity: reliability.

When to Assess Variables' Reliability

Reliability is consistency or agreement among measures. As compared with validity, it is much easier to define and, consequently, much easier to gauge. Reliability assessments are measures of measures. There are many ways that coding and measurement can be consistent, and each of them is associated with a type of reliability. Unlike a lot of methodological terms, the majority of the labels used to describe types of reliability are clear indications of what they measure. Interrater reliability is the consistency of two or more raters, test–retest reliability is the consistency of results on repeated tests, and so on.

As with scales in survey research, you need to check the reliability of the measurement of all variables. Typically, the IV in experimental research is a matter of treatment versus control, and it isn't as much of an issue in terms of reliability as are DVs and control variables. However, whether the assignment to treatment and control groups has been consistent, whether the participants have withdrawn or have managed to move from one group to another, and so forth, is a matter of reliability and must be monitored carefully. For example, if the treatment is valued, participants might try to find ways to get into the treatment group; or if the treatment is onerous, they might drop out of the experiment. (See the earlier section titled "What to Consider When Coding the Independent Variable.")

Outcome and control variables are often continuous and studied with compound measures, so they frequently raise more coding and measurement complications than do IVs. For example, in a quasi-experiment at several universities, we investigated the effectiveness of a new method of teaching computer programming to undergraduates. The outcome variable was student learning, which was measured two ways, by student self-assessment and by an objective examination.[33] To improve the assessment of the impact of the new method on learning, we used a range of control variables; one of these was student self-efficacy. Self-efficacy is a psychological construct that gauges how much a person believes that effort is likely to lead to success. Not surprisingly, people who think that their efforts won't be rewarded tend neither to try nor to succeed.

---

[33]We use this study as a recurring example because, although the basic idea of the study was simple, implementing it illustrates many of the methodological choices discussed in this book. For details see Lim, Hosack, and Vogt (2012).

Many studies have shown that self-efficacy is an important predictor of achievement. To investigate its impact on learning computer programming, we developed a 11-question self-efficacy scale tailored to the tasks and content of the courses in which the new method of instruction was being tried. To ensure validity, we patterned this scale closely after several other frequently used and well-regarded self-efficacy scales.[34] We did this as a way of incorporating into our scale the experience and expert opinions contained in those scales. Was the self-efficacy scale in our study reliable, and therefore potentially valid? We used Cronbach's alpha to assess its reliability (see the discussion in Chapter 1). The scale worked well; it had an alpha above .90.

When using an existing scale, even one that has repeatedly been tested for reliability, you must still conduct your own tests of the reliability of the scale in *your* study with *your* participants. Reliability is not an invariant property of scales but always varies from one group of participants to the next and/or from one investigation to the next. As we discussed in Chapter 1, reliability is important because it is harder to detect effects with less reliable measures, and a completely unreliable scale can measure nothing. In our quasi-experiments on computer programming instruction, one of the measures of learning was a well-known student self-assessment scale.[35] It has several subscales, and we also checked these with Cronbach's alpha.

Of more interest to our discussion at this point are our efforts with a second measure of student learning, which was created by the investigators and had not been used before. The measure was composed of a 20-item objective test written by the investigators. Using this exam involved trade-offs. Specifically, we gave up some degree of validity to achieve an acceptable level of reliability. Our validity experts, instructors in computer programming courses, generally believed that the most valid measures of student learning involved having the students write actual computer programs to solve problems. We agreed. But grading such exercises raised considerable difficulties of intercoder reliability, especially because dozens of different instructors, teaching at a score of universities, would have to grade such problem-based exams using comparable measures of achievement. Our alternative was to use a common objective exam that all student participants took. This exam was graded centrally by the project. It was highly reliable in the sense that, regardless of who graded it, individual students would always get the same scores. We tried to make the exam valid by addressing the main concepts or domains of introductory programming, by modeling the questions closely on those used in certification examinations in programming, and by having the exam reviewed by experts in the field (professors who taught introductory computer programming). We undertook this work because, without a common, objectively gradable exam, the lack of reliability in this measure of our DV would have been so great that we would have had no valid measure at all.

How good was this common exam at assessing students' knowledge? Test theory, whether classic or modern, is built on the assumption that all the items on a test are measuring the same "domain" or construct. To check on this assumption, we used factor analysis (see Chapter 9) and, as expected, determined that ours was a cluster of subtests, each of which we then analyzed separately using test theory. The state-of-the-art

[34]Bandura (2006).

[35]It is the Student Assessment of Learning Gains (SALG). For a description see Seymour, Wiese, Hunter, and Daffinrud (2000).

approach in test theory is a suite of methods called **item response theory** or, most often, **IRT.**[36] Rightly considered an important advance on "classical test theory," modern IRT provides much better information but at the cost of being considerably harder for non-experts to understand or to conduct on their own. Adding to this complexity is the fact that modern test theory is divided into two camps: IRT and Rasch modeling.[37] But the general outlines of test theory are clear regardless of camp. The main difference between classical test theory and IRT is that, rather than working with raw scores of the number of questions correct, as in the classical approach, IRT investigators work with the *probabilities* that students who have attained particular scores on the exam will answer specific questions correctly.

Test theory involves two basic components: item difficulty and the likelihood that, by virtue of their difficulty, test items will reliably differentiate among students in terms of how well they know the subject matter. In short, students who really know more will reliably (with discernible consistency) score higher on a good test. To differentiate among students, there has to be variety in their responses. If all students get a question right, or if they all get it wrong, the question tells you nothing you can use to differentiate among students, nor is it useful for assessing how much a group of students has learned. In either IRT or classical analyses, one indicator of a bad question would be a question that the high-scoring students tended to get wrong.[38] When IRT can be used to test the reliability of a set of test questions and to determine how well the test distinguishes among knowledge, skill, and ability levels of test takers, it is far superior to other approaches. But, like many of the more advanced approaches we recommend, it is more difficult to apply, and it requires larger sample sizes. If IRT is impossible for your data, the simpler methods of classical test theory are far better than nothing for judging the reliability of examinations.

We conclude the discussion of reliability with Table 3.1, in which the most common approaches to assessing reliability are listed, along with guidance about when to use them. The research literature on measuring reliability is vast. This summary, although a good place to start and perhaps all that most beginning investigators will need, only scratches the surface of the options available.[39]

What is an acceptable level of reliability? Reliability coefficients generally range from 1.0 for a perfectly reliable[40] measure to 0 for one that is completely inconsistent from one rater or test or observation to the next. Reliability coefficients can be interpreted as the part of the variance in a series of measures that is accurate, that is not

[36] For brief overviews that require limited technical knowledge, see Finch (2010) and Chapter 16 in Vogt (2007). For a comprehensive text see Embretson and Reise (2000).

[37] The best general introduction to the Rasch approach is Bond and Fox (2001). One important journal in the field, *Rasch Measurement Transactions*, is freely downloadable.

[38] A special feature of IRT is differential item functioning (DIF), which enables you to determine whether test items are answered differently by subgroups in your sample. For example, we are using DIF to investigate whether the new method is equally effective for men and women in the sample.

[39] In addition to the works already cited, see the more advanced and influential article by Bland and Altman (1999); it introduces several effective graphic techniques for judging reliability. Strube (2000) explores advances in reliability assessment, particularly generalizability theory.

[40] No measure is ever perfectly reliable. An excellent example is inconsistency in repeated measures of the same object—the International Prototype Kilogram; the exact weight is *literally unknowable.* See Freedman, Pisani, and Purves (1998).

TABLE 3.1. Common Measures of Reliability and When to Use Them

Measure	When to use
Cronbach's alpha (α)	When you want to know whether the items in your scale or index are measuring aspects of the same thing. • The "scale if item deleted" feature helps identify items that could be removed or analyzed individually (see IRT). • .70 is usually considered the minimum acceptable level; higher levels are needed when results are used for high-stakes decisions.
Cohen's kappa (κ)	When you are comparing ratings of two raters on one categorical variable or, less frequently, ratings of two variables by the same rater. It is a measure of agreement that corrects for chance (random) agreement. • + 1.0 = perfect agreement; – 1.0 = perfect disagreement; and 0 = the amount of agreement you would expect by chance alone.
Pearson's *r*	When you want to compare scores on two or more continuously scored scales by the same sample of individuals, as in test–retest reliability. • The reliability measure is the correlation or the squared correlation. • See Chapter 8.
Factor analysis (FA)	When you want to determine whether your measure might be measuring more than one thing. • FA can find more than one cluster of items that could be subscales; Cronbach's alpha identifies only one cluster/factor. • See Chapter 9.
Item response theory (IRT)	When you want to improve a test by identifying weak items for deletion. • Can be used to differentiate between subgroups by using differential item functioning (DIF).

erroneous. In other words, unreliable measures have more error—and they lead to error in the estimates of the outcomes we are interested in. Unreliable measures result in lower effect sizes in bivariate analyses.[41] Ultimately, the practical question about measurement error confronting a researcher is, How much error can you tolerate? The answer depends on the purposes of the measure. Some error is inevitable in any measurement, but if it is used for high-stakes judgments (e.g., eligible or not, graduate or not), the reliability should be considerably higher than what researchers often say is acceptable for scales on attitude surveys: a Cronbach's alpha of .70. The acceptable level of reliability is a matter of judgment and context, not statistics.

Remember also that what you are measuring when you investigate the reliability of a particular measure is the pattern of responses of the participants *in your research.* That is why you need to compute the reliability coefficients for your study, even when you are using a measure that has been widely used and studied. Past reliability scores are important for indicating how well a scale has functioned in past research. Whether

[41]Lower effect sizes are the kind of error most often discussed, but in multiple regression, controlling a variable that is not reliably measured can result in effect sizes that are too high.

it works well in your research and whether the results can be generalized from your sample of participants to a broader population are separate questions.

Finally, using more than one observer/rater is preferable whenever possible and when your resources allow. If you use more than one rater, you should conduct one version or another of interrater reliability: typically, Cohen's kappa for categorical ratings or Pearson's *r* for continuous ones. If you are a lone observer/rater, there are ways of testing your own reliability, that is, the stability of your judgments, called **intrarater reliability**. An example from radiology can illustrate. Give a radiologist a stack of 100 X-rays to read; 20 of the X-rays are duplicates. The question with this kind of reliability measure is, How often does a rater agree with him- or herself on the 20 duplicates? We have had modest success using versions of this approach with essay- and problem-grading experiments. Note, however, that, like all measures of reliability, this method of studying intraobserver reliability does not speak to the *correctness* of a rating, only to its *consistency*. Observers/raters can get perfect reliability scores by consistently making the same errors. Correctness is a matter of validity, not reliability.

An advance on common methods of assessing reliability, especially Cronbach's alpha, is **generalizability theory**. It breaks down measurement error, or lack of reliability, into components rather than treating it as one thing that can be described with one statistic. Although even Cronbach argued that Cronbach's alpha was inferior to generalizability theory,[42] it seems not to have caught on among applied researchers, who continue to make heavy use of Cronbach's alpha despite Cronbach's advice that it is much better to identify the sources of error in measurement rather than merely estimating total error. Generalizability theory is both computationally and conceptually more complex than alpha and most other measures discussed in Table 3.1.

When to Use Multiple Measures of the Same Concept

Given that any measure of anything is imperfect—whether in experiments, surveys, or other designs—it is better to have more than one measure whenever practicable. Of course, to be valuable, the measures must be valid and reliable (see the previous two sections). When your multiple measures agree, this helps you be more confident in your conclusions. This is what is meant by **cross-validation**, which is an important concept in multimethod research. When your measures do not agree, the disparity often provides useful clues for interpretation. When you have multiple measures, they can be especially effective if some are quantitative and others qualitative. Combine them using mixed method techniques. If both are quantitative, and if you have a large sample of participants, the state of the art methods for combining assessments are confirmatory factor analysis (CFA) and its sibling, structural equation modeling (SEM); these are discussed in Chapter 9.

Note also that it often adds comparatively little to the overall cost of an experiment to collect data on several outcome variables or multiple measures of the same outcome variable. Typically, most of your time, effort, and money in experiments are used recruiting participants and administering the experiment. Adding additional relevant measures once you have the participants signed up and in place can be comparatively easy. It seems a shame not to do so. And doing so can greatly increase understanding of

[42]Cronbach and Shavelson (2004). For a good overview, see Strube (2000).

any effects of the IV on your outcome measures. However, if you use multiple outcome variables and test multiple hypotheses, you *absolutely must* make statistical adjustments in reporting the results of your hypothesis tests. Failure to do so leads to misleading results—claims that outcomes are statistically significant at a particular alpha level when they are not. Not adjusting for **multiple comparisons** is one of the most inexcusable errors a researcher can make. The adjustments are easy, well known, and a routine part of all statistical analysis packages. See Chapter 7 for details.

In our study of computer programming instruction discussed earlier, we used two measures of learning, a student self-assessment and an exam designed by the investigators. Each was imperfect in some ways. But confidence in the conclusions could be enhanced if the two imperfect measures agreed. Disagreement among the measures could mean several things. For example, many students believed that as a result of their work in the class, they made substantial gains in the understanding of a particular concept; but some of them did not correctly answer the exam questions on the concept. This disparity in the two measures of concept understanding could be due to a problem with the exam questions or a problem with the self-assessment measure or to students' inaccurate assessment of their own learning. Because the two measures of learning are both quantitative (they are scored numerically), there are well-known, though not uncomplicated, methods that can be used to combine them into a more reliable measure of learning. If we postulated a latent variable, the learning of programming—or learning of a particular concept in programming—measured in different ways, we could combine sets of self-assessment questions into scales and groups of questions on the exam into additional sets of scales. Because the two sets of scales were measured in different ways, a method of common coding would have to be devised. This would make it possible to use SEM to determine the effects (if any) of the new method of teaching on learning. The last few sentences are written using conditional verbs because we have not as yet gathered data on enough cases for a valid analysis, and SEM is very case-hungry.[43]

When to Assess Statistical Power, and What Does This Have to Do with Coding?

Statistical power is, in essence, the ability to detect an effect. More formally, it is the probability of detecting an effect in the sample when it exists in the population. Powerful experimental designs and procedures are roughly equivalent to powerful microscopes. The more powerful the microscope, the smaller the things it can detect.[44] The analogy isn't perfect, but it is close: The more powerful the statistical test, the smaller the effects it can detect. Power calculations make sense and are appropriate for random samples drawn from known populations. Power is also calculated for other kinds of samples, but it is harder to interpret the results of those calculations.

Most people we know use the freeware G*Power to compute statistical power estimates for common statistical tests, including the *t*-test, *F*-test, and chi-squared families

[43]Hosack, Lim, and Vogt (2013).

[44]Strictly speaking, statistical power is the probability of rejecting the null hypothesis when it is false and should be rejected; see Chapter 7. Motulsky (2010) provides an excellent brief account.

of tests (see Chapter 8).[45] You can use power calculations to *plan for* the sample size you will need in your study in order to be able to detect the effects you are interested in. It is also possible to calculate **observed power** (also known as **post hoc power**), which describes the power of the test you used in your study. This is fairly widely advocated, and some journals require you to do so if you have obtained results that are not statistically significant. On the other hand, most statisticians argue against using observed power calculations because they have no meaningful interpretation. But they are a routine part of the output of several statistical packages.[46] Power is important in planning to use a sample size big enough to detect effects, but observed power calculations after the study is conducted are controversial.

As argued earlier, mutilated data (such as continuous data that have been categorized) lead to lower power. Power is also strongly affected by sample size. To improve power, increase sample size and/or include covariates (control variables). Remember, however, that there is a trade-off; adding variables reduces power unless you increase the sample size to compensate. These steps are mostly taken at the design stage, but proper coding and measurement is also a factor (once more: avoid converting naturally continuous variables into categories). Power is also influenced by the quality (reliability) of measurements. A scale with a Cronbach's alpha of .90 will be able to detect smaller effects than will a scale with an alpha of .70. In sum, in addition to using reliable measures, there are two main ways to improve statistical power and heighten the precision of your estimates of effect sizes: increase the number of participants[47] and add relevant covariates. The second often requires many fewer resources. The power of the tests you use should be reported, as well as their effect sizes and their levels of significance.

When to Use Difference/Gain/Change Scores for Your DV

The most basic experimental design compares the outcomes on the DV of the control and experimental groups after the treatment, and this suffices for many purposes. But it is often a good idea to include pretest data as a covariate; as with all covariates (see the earlier section titled "When to Include and Code Covariates/Control Variables"), pretests can increase the power and precision of your estimates. For example, if the experiment is meant to increase knowledge or to change attitudes, then a pretreatment measure of the participants' knowledge or attitudes provides very pertinent information. If the pretests are scales, they need to be assessed for reliability (see the earlier section titled "When to Assess Variables' Reliability"). How do you code the pretest and its relation to the posttest? The most obvious solution is to plan for a simple difference

[45]Another good freeware package, covering design issues including power, is Optimal Design; see Raudenbush (2011).

[46]See Faul, Erdfelder, Lang, and Buchner (2007) for a good review of the G*Power program and its uses; it also includes discussions of several technical matters that are beyond the scope of this book. Schochet (2008) provides a thorough discussion using examples from program evaluation. Most statisticians recommend against using observed power calculations; a succinct and persuasive account is Hoenig and Heisey (2001).

[47]Slavin and Smith (2009) report the counterintuitive finding that small-*N* published experimental studies tend to have *larger* effect sizes than large-*N* studies. One possible reason is a kind of publication bias; effect sizes in small studies are more variable (contain more random error), and only those with large effect sizes get published.

or gain score or a change score arrived at by subtracting pretest from posttest scores. You would expect the gain to be nil for the control group, but if the treatment had an effect, you would predict a substantial change for the experimental or treatment group.

The simple subtraction method for coding and analyzing differences is controversial. The titles of two research papers can illustrate this. The first asks, "Are Simple Gain Scores Obsolete?" Not as much as commonly believed, say the authors.[48] In the second, "Ten Difference Score Myths," all of the myths, says the author, are mistaken beliefs that it is necessary or OK to use simple difference scores.[49] We believe that change measured as a simple difference between pretest and posttest scores can be a reasonable approach in some limited circumstances, such as in a preliminary exploration of the data; but the general consensus among research methodologists is that it is better to treat the pretest scores as covariates in a regression analysis. When experts disagree, the best choice is to code, analyze, and report both ways—both as a simple arithmetic difference and as a postscore in which prescores have been controlled.

Two more advanced techniques useful for measuring change while controlling for prescores are regression discontinuity and difference-in-differences regression. As their names indicate, they are both regression-based methods. Both are more complicated than simply adding control variables to a regression analysis, but they can produce more reliable estimates of the effects of IVs. **Regression discontinuity** (**RD**) methods are used when you have a series of measures of an outcome variable. A break or a sharp bend in the regression line indicates the presence of a causal effect. Although RD methods can be applied to the analysis of archival data, they are typically used only when you have planned for them at the design stage; the reason is that they are based on a method of assignment of participants to experimental conditions.[50] **Difference-in-differences** (**d-i-d**) regression does not require planning for special approaches to data collection at the design stage. Indeed, d-i-d regression is often used in natural experiments in which the researcher has not generated the data; it is illustrated in more detail in the section titled "Coding Data from Natural Experiments" (pp. 96–98). But d-i-d methods can be used in any circumstance when you have control variables for the study of at least two groups measured at two points in time. The difference between the two groups in the before–after measures is the difference in the difference, and that difference is calculated while taking control variables into account.[51]

CODING AND MEASUREMENT ISSUES THAT VARY BY TYPE OF EXPERIMENTAL DESIGN

Although many coding and measurement methods are generic and can be used in most types of experiments, some methods are more closely associated with particular approaches to experimentation. The association is not perfect, so even those methods

---

[48] Williams and Zimmerman (1996).

[49] Edwards (2001).

[50] Shadish, Cook, and Campbell (2002) and Murnane and Willett (2011) each contain excellent discussions that emphasize different aspects of the method.

[51] Card and Krueger (2000) provide a good discussion and an excellent example. Of course these points about coding longitudinal data apply to nonexperimental longitudinal data as well.

we discuss as mostly associated with specific designs—RCTs, natural experiments, quasi-experiments, and so on—are also used more generally. Thus this section on coding data obtained from specific designs will sometimes contain elaborations of points made in the first section on generic approaches to coding experimental data. Indeed, for many types of experimental designs, the first part of the chapter contains much of what needed to be said. Still, the amount of design-specific coding work is great enough to demand a separate section. Some of this coding work involves specifying how the experiment has been conducted so that appropriate analytical methods can be used.

As we discuss coding data from different experimental designs, some of our discussion refers back to issues of experimental design and some of it looks forward to coming chapters on analytical methods. Such overlap is inevitable in discussing the acts that are located on the continuum running from design and sampling through coding and analysis.

Coding Data from Survey Experiments

Survey experiments are experiments conducted within surveys (see Chapter 1). Respondents are randomly assigned to control and experimental groups; the groups are then asked different versions of questions or the same questions in different orders or in different formats, and so on.[52] This kind of experiment is often conducted for measurement purposes to better understand the properties of the survey questions and modes of administering surveys. Most of what we know about question order and wording effects comes from survey experiments. Taking advantage of a random sample of survey respondents, survey experiments can also provide key insights into substantive issues (not only measurement questions), such as the relative importance of race and class in respondents' neighborhood preferences.[53]

In some ways survey experiments are the purest form of the randomized experiment. By consenting to the survey, respondents have also consented to be experimental participants. And survey researchers usually have an easier time controlling the randomization process than do experimenters using other designs. This control makes coding the IV very straightforward (see the earlier section, "What to Consider When Coding the Independent Variable," pp. 70–71). It is mostly a matter of meticulous reporting of what was done. Also important in survey experiments, as in all experiments, is to report carefully on what the intended or **target population** and the **effective sample** actually were. The reason why this is important can be illustrated with the example of Web-based survey experiments. Web-based companies such as Amazon, Microsoft, and Netflix conduct very large numbers of survey experiments and tend to put the results to use very quickly.[54]

A typical example of a Web-based survey experiment might be asking customers who have just used a company's product or service to rate their experience and satisfaction. The experiment might be to ask for the information in two different formats so as to compare the response rates and levels of approval using the two formats. The sample

[52]See the discussion in Gaines et al. (2007).

[53]For a compelling example using respondents' reactions to different video depictions of neighborhoods, see Krysan, Couper, Farley, and Forman (2009).

[54]For a fascinating review, see Kohavi, Longbotham, Sommerfield, and Henne (2009).

might be formed by picking a start date and asking the next 10,000 customers who use the service to rate it, randomly assigning half to one format and half to the other. The target population would be all customers. The recruitment pool would be the next 10,000 customers. The effective sample would be those who accepted the invitation to rate the service, perhaps 6,000 of the 10,000. Half of the 6,000 would be assigned at random to use each format. How broadly could you generalize the results? The key point is that you could only generalize about responders or volunteers, not about all customers. Perhaps the 4,000 who didn't accept the invitation to rate the service were satisfied and didn't want to waste their time, or perhaps they were disgusted with the inferior service and gave up on the company.[55]

Although the assignment was random, the sample really was not. While survey experiments are one of the few designs in which both conditions for valid statistical inferences are often met—both a random sample from a population *and* random assignment of members of that sample to control and experimental groups—whether those conditions are met in any particular experiment is an empirical matter. Conscientious researchers report on the extent to which their samples and assignment mechanisms were random. Although the felicitous combination of random sample and random assignment is probably more common in survey experiments, it is not guaranteed even there.

Coding Data from RCTs

Some differences in coding in RCTs depend on the role of the variables or where the variables come in the sequence of a randomized experiment: before, during, and after. Some variables are most important before the experimental intervention or treatment; others are the main focus during it; and still others come into play mostly after the treatment and lead most directly to analysis. All must be coded, of course. We consider each in turn.

Before Treatment

Before the treatment or experimental intervention, three variables come into play. In order of importance, they are selection variables, matching variables, and participant equivalency variables. **Selection variables** are used to identify and select participants who are eligible for the study. Depending on the research question, they could include such variables as age, gender, area of residence, or work experience. These variables are almost always coded categorically for selection purposes, even when they are continuous variables such as age, so that a potential participant is coded as eligible or ineligible for the study. For example, a hypothetical study might select only females 21 years old or older who are employed full time and have one or more children in day care. **Matching variables**, discussed earlier in the section "When to Use Propensity Score Matching and Instrumental Variable Estimation" (pp. 73–77) are usually continuous and are used to improve the results of random assignment. In the hypothetical study,

[55]Of course, if those who declined to reply to the survey after they looked at it differed by the format to which they were assigned, this could be important information, though somewhat difficult to interpret. On questions of nonresponse and consequent missing data, see Chapter 7.

one might match eligible participants (over 21 years old) by age before assigning them to control and experimental groups. Finally, after assignment, a final check of **participant equivalency**, using variables not used for selection or matching, may be conducted to determine, for example, whether the women in the control and experimental groups in the hypothetical study had similar numbers of children.

All of these variables are used to improve upon or to correct for any imperfections in random assignment. They are used to identify the population to which generalizations about the sample can apply and to improve on the external validity of RCTs. If you are doing serious experimental research, you will want to do all that you can to address the main criticism of RCTs—that their findings are hard to generalize beyond the samples studied; in other words, that they have limited external validity. Even in medical research it is easy to find concern about the external validity of findings, illustrated in such titles as "Randomized Controlled Trials: Do They Have External Validity . . . ?"[56] or, in a report on clinical trials, in a section head such as "A Strategy's Effect on a Risk Factor May Not Predict Its Effect on Patient Outcomes."[57] An article on the cost effectiveness of using data from randomized trials or clinical practice concluded that studying actual practice was superior.[58] These references are given to caution researchers that care is needed in generalizing results of an RCT; carefully coding selection, matching, and participant equivalency variables improves the quality of potential generalizations.

During Treatment

When you are conducting the experiment, the focus will shift to the independent, or treatment, variables and the dependent, or outcome, measures. We have addressed most of the coding issues pertaining to them in the first section of this chapter. Here we add two further considerations: (1) implementation of the assignment to control and experimental groups and therefore the definition and coding of the IV and (2) whether a fixed effects or a random effects model was used.

It is very important to describe and code the various elements in your sample and, therefore, how you have identified the control and experimental groups. A state of the art approach is to use the **intention-to-treat** methods.[59] This approach is easiest to describe with an example. Say you have designed a program to improve the persistence in college of first-year students. Your outcome variable will be persistence to the sophomore year. The predictor variable will be participation in the program. Say you recruit 2,000 students who are willing to participate in your experiment. Half (1,000) are assigned to the control group and the other 1,000 are members of the experimental group. Upon conclusion of the program you find that only 800 in the experimental group actually participated; the other 200 did not show up. Whom do you compare? Not the 800 participants to the 200 no-shows, and not the 800 participants to the 1,000 in the control group, even though these codings for group membership are not unknown. Rather, it is much preferable to compare the 1,000 in the control group with *all* 1,000 students

[56]Fortin et al (2006).

[57]Krumholz and Lee (2008).

[58]Van Staa (2009).

[59]Hollis and Campbell (1999) argue that although intention-to-treat analyses are often referenced in research articles, in fact they are often inadequately applied.

in the experimental group, *including* the 200 who did not participate. Those 200 are coded as missing data. That approach is what is meant by intent-to-treat. You intended to treat the 200 no-shows and dropouts. They are not likely to be a random sample of those randomly assigned to the experimental group; excluding them would make the assignment process biased. You will have all 2,000 recruits in your database.

Another coding and measurement issue that pertains mostly to the IV is whether you have used a random effects or a fixed effects model. This is usually settled by design or the researchers' intentions, but it has important coding and analysis implications. In the random effects model, the "levels"[60] of the IV are selected at random from the population of all levels. In the fixed effects approach, the levels have been selected in some other way, usually because they are of particular interest to the researcher or are especially relevant to the research question.

This choice is mostly a design issue, and it is a decision that's made quite early, but it is one that has to be carefully noted (coded) so that the right analysis techniques can be used. The choice of whether to use fixed or random effects models can be controversial. It also tends to be quite important in cluster randomized designs (discussed in "Coding Data in Multisite Experiments").

For Analysis after Treatment

After the study is concluded, you will want to determine whether the IV had an effect on the DV and, if so, whether it was large enough (effect size) to be important, whether it is measured with enough precision (margins of error or confidence intervals) to be useful, and whether it is statistically significant. Codes for covariates for statistical control and propensity score matching are used posttreatment so that these variables can be applied in the analysis to improve the accuracy of the effect-size measurement, to narrow the margins of error around the estimate of the effect size, and to increase statistical power, that is, to increase the probability that a false null hypothesis will be rejected (see earlier discussion in this chapter, and see Chapter 8 for further discussion).

Coding Data in Multisite Experiments

Multisite experiments are fairly common, and the coding and analytical issues they raise can be complicated. They involve issues of coding for differences among sites before implementation and then, during the study, coding differences among the sites in their fidelity of implementation (see the earlier section, "What to Consider When Coding the Independent Variable," pp. 70–71). Typically these differences are coded with dummy variables for categories such as public–private (see Chapter 8) or with rank order codes for variables such as small–medium–large. It is our impression that researchers do a better job at controlling for differences among sites before implementation. These are more often noted and coded than are departures from the research protocol; such departures are harder to track and code but are very important. Deviations in how the experiment was implemented are inevitable. Extreme deviations mean that data from the site are

[60]The term *level* is used to mean a value of an independent variable in an experiment, such as number of counseling sessions; level is also used even when the value is categorical, such as Treatment A versus Treatment B.

no longer eligible to be included in the analysis (except under intent-to-treat methods; see the preceding section). Lesser departures should be noted and coded whenever you know them; typically you would add dummy variables or rank order codes for departures from the protocol.

Multisite experiments usually employ **group-randomized designs** (also called cluster-randomized). This means that rather than assigning individual participants to control and experimental groups, sites or groups are randomly assigned to receive the experimental treatment or to be in the control/comparison group: Students are not randomly assigned, schools are; clients are not, clinics are; employees are not, businesses are; and so on. Most often, this means that group-randomized experiments are also quasi-experiments (see the section "Coding Data from Quasi-Experiments," pp. 98–99). However, if the units of analysis are the groups (e.g., the school, the clinic, or the business), then group randomization is compatible with an RCT. On the other hand, if the units of analysis are individuals (e.g., the students, clients, or employees), then group-randomized experiments should probably be thought of as quasi-experiments. The label matters less, of course, than does taking into account the special coding and analysis issues that group randomizing raises. Group randomizing is very common in education and medicine; much of the best research on how to make that design most effective has been done in those fields. Group randomization greatly reduces statistical power; it also reduces effect sizes and makes them less precise (increases their margins of error or confidence intervals).[61] In brief, the single *most inexcusable error* is to code and analyze data from group-randomized experiments as if the individuals had been randomized.

Perhaps the key issue is assessing statistical power in group-randomized designs.[62] To do this, the basic question is whether the sites in your research are studied with fixed or random effects models. This is determined at the design and sampling stages and is based on how sites were selected for inclusion in the study. If the sites/groups were randomly selected from a broader population of sites, and the sites were randomly assigned to control and experimental groups, then the random effects model is appropriate. Our sense of the research literature is that it is rarely the case that the sites in a study can be considered a random sample from a population of sites. Usually the difficulties of the recruitment process, combined with the search for volunteers, greatly reduce the likelihood of being able to randomly sample and assign sites. You might *wish* you could make statistical inferences about a larger population of sites, but this wish is hard to fulfill. A consolation prize of sorts (the good news) is that when using a fixed effects model, your study will have greater statistical power to detect effects—but *only* (this is the bad news) as those effects can be generalized to the sites actually studied. You can't legitimately generalize to a broader population. This is not as much of a limitation as it might seem. For many studies, the goal is to establish that an IV can have an effect somewhere, not whether it can be generalized or scaled up to a broader population. For establishing that an intervention can be effective somewhere, even judgment samples and enthusiastic volunteers can be appropriate. What is not appropriate is using a sample that is fine for

[61] Hedges (2011) provides an excellent review and a list of five different effect-size measures that can be employed.

[62] For power, see Spybrook and Raudenbush (2009) and Konstantopoulos (2009).

establishing the internal validity of an effect to make conclusions about the generalizability or external validity of the effect.

When your data come from experiments that have randomized groups rather than individuals, the best analysis choice is to use multilevel modeling (MLM), which is also called hierarchical linear modeling (HLM; see Chapter 9 for a brief discussion). MLM allows you to separate the effects of the group or site (e.g., the school, the clinic, or the business), which is called Level 2 in the analysis, from the effects of the Level-1 individuals (e.g., the students, clients, or employees). In other words, if you are interested in individuals but they come clustered in groups and you have to do your randomization at the group level, then you need to use MLM. This means that you have to have group-level variables, as well as individual-level variables, which are the actual focus of your efforts. Being sure to code variables so that the levels are distinct is facilitated by the use of different Latin and Greek letters in the formulas for the different levels, but it is easy for a first-time user of MLM to make a mistake.

The random assignment of participants to control and experimental groups *within* each site, rather than across sites, is typically easier to achieve and more commonly implemented. And it is good to do so, but it does not eliminate the fact that the study has not used true randomization of the participants in the study. The distinction between the proper multilevel analysis of sites (Level 2) and participants (Level 1) is an important one. The how-tos of it are beyond the scope of this book, but for an overview see Chapter 9 and the references cited therein. The take-home message is, in short, if you have clustered data, you must use one of the advanced methods discussed in Chapter 9 such as MLM, and using these methods adds another level of complexity to your work as a data coder.

Coding Data from Field Experiments as Compared with Laboratory Experiments

The complexity of implementing an experiment and coding the data collected is increased when the experiment is conducted in natural settings rather than in more controlled laboratory settings. A chief reason to conduct field experiments is the opportunity they provide for enhancing the external validity or generalizability of findings. The chief barrier to successful field experiments is a potential lack of internal validity, or the ability to draw justifiable causal conclusions about the effects of the treatment. Therefore, the main challenge for the field experimenter is to make sure that the advantages in external validity of field experiments are not drastically offset by their possible lack of internal validity. This means that part of the early coding process has to do with describing the field settings or sites and coding for any differences among them.

Field experiments with random assignment—randomized field trials, or RFTs—are often very difficult to arrange. In most of the well-documented and persuasive RFTs, the experimenters have been governmental agencies.[63] It is unlikely that a graduate student working on a dissertation, or even a small group of professors, will be able to conduct the kind of RFT that is usually held up as an exemplar. Examples include the Tennessee class-size experiment in which students across the state were more or less randomly

[63] See the superb review of RFTs of social welfare programs in the United States in Moffitt (2004). Sabates and Feinstein (2008) describe an interesting program and its evaluation in the United Kingdom.

assigned to attend classes of varying sizes. We say "more or less" randomly because, even in this much-praised example, randomization fell far short of the ideal.[64] When the randomization is imperfect, the imperfections have to be noted and coded.

More typical of the modest scope of, and many of the problems with, field experiments are illustrated in our already mentioned study of the effects of using a Web services (WS) approach to teach computer programming; it was conducted by a small group of professors assisted by a few graduate students. For this research, a laboratory-based RCT would have been of little interest. The WS approach had already been shown to be effective in some circumstances. What was of interest was whether it would work in regularly scheduled classes in a wide range of universities taught by volunteer professors who were interested in trying a new teaching method in their classes. This sample had a lot of external validity because it was composed of the target population: volunteers teaching regularly scheduled classes across types of higher education institutions.[65] However, this variegated design led to many small differences in how the design was implemented, each of which had to be coded before analysis.

Even when random assignment is used in field experiments, the participants are not under the control of the experimenters to the degree they typically are in laboratory experiments of short duration. The whole idea of a field experiment is to study real settings in real time. Field experiments, in this sense, have much in common with naturalistic observations (see Chapter 4). Participants in uncontrolled contexts might engage in any number of behaviors that could undermine the ability to gauge the effects of a treatment. Volunteers who agree to try a new weight-loss drug might begin an exercise program or otherwise change their behavior in ways likely to affect the outcome variable. These confounding effects are often discussed using such terms as *history effects* or *threats to validity*, and they tend to be a greater problem the longer the duration of the field experiment. If there are differences in duration of the treatment at different sites, this is one of the variables researchers should be certain to code. Despite all the potential problems, successful field experiments have been conducted. We give two examples, one simple classic study and one more recent complicated investigation, both of which were modest enough in size that they did not require government intervention to implement.

Stanley Milgram, best known for his controversial laboratory experiments, was also a pioneer in field experiments in social psychology. A well-known little study nicely illustrates how researchers with modest resources could experimentally study behavior in the field rather than the lab.[66] The investigators and a group of their students in a graduate research seminar went to a particular spot on a busy sidewalk in New York City to study the effect that crowd behavior had on pedestrians walking past. The research question was whether the actions of passersby would be influenced by the behavior of crowds of different sizes. The treatment was to have the crowd stand on the pavement and look up for 60 seconds at the sixth-floor window of a building where nothing was happening. The IV was the size of the crowd, which was 1, 2, 3, 5, 10, or 15 gawkers. The DV was the percentage of the passersby who looked up or who stopped and joined

[64]The experiment is described in Finn and Achilles (1999). Problems with randomization are discussed in Murnane and Willett (2011).

[65]What would be the alternative population—perhaps professors from only one type of institution compelled to teach irregular classes?

[66]Milgram, Bickman, and Berkowitz (1969).

the crowd gazing at nothing. The behaviors were video recorded and coded for analysis. The size of the crowd of gazers had sizable effects on each of the behaviors: looking up and stopping. Most people looked up as soon as the crowd was 2 or 3 persons, and the percentage didn't increase much once the crowd increased to 5. It was harder to get the pedestrians to stop than to merely look up, but the number of pedestrians who did stop was directly related to the size of the crowd. When the crowd reached 15 gazers, nearly 40% of the pedestrians stopped, but the rest hurried on regardless. The study remains a model, is still cited with some frequency decades after it was written, and serves as a useful little primer on coding data from experiments conducted in the field rather than the lab. Perhaps the main distinction between coding data in field versus lab experiments is the lack of the researchers' control in the field over the research site and the people who are studied in it. Much improvisation is typically required.

Our second example is a field experiment to study the market behaviors of buyers and sellers. Experimental studies of market behavior have usually been done in laboratory settings in colleges and universities using artificial markets and artificial customers (students). The experimenters in this example took the theories they wanted to test to a real market, specifically, to a coin show in which coins were bought and sold by dealers and customers.[67] Real coins were used (U.S. silver dollars) that had been graded for quality according to a widely used scale (quality grading was an IV). The experiment is too complex to summarize here, but the key points and advantages of the procedure are clear. Field experiments, the authors conclude, can provide "a useful bridge between the lab and the field." Experiments with student participants are highly controlled and have all the benefits to researchers of that control. By contrast, real markets and the data they generate are completely uncontrolled by researchers. The field experiment has a natural place in the gap between the small, comprehensible laboratory world of simulations with college students and real markets in which an unknown number of confounding variables are at work. The challenge to coding data from field experiments is designing a study in a realistic setting with codable variables. In this example, the researchers used, as the DV, the price that real customers were willing to pay for coins of different grades.

Coding Longitudinal Experimental Data

Many longitudinal studies are not experimental; they involve neither the investigator's manipulating of variables nor assigning of participants. We focus here on longitudinal studies that are experimental. But the "right" label is not always perfectly clear. If you did a computer search of the literature on the key words *experimental* and *longitudinal*, you might be surprised at the variety of methods in some of your search results. For example, a study of the effects of receiving a college scholarship on students' time allocations was longitudinal in that students were measured at three points: before college, in their 1st year, and in their 3rd year. The authors call their study a quasi-experimental investigation.[68] We would say that because the authors neither assigned the students to control and experimental groups nor manipulated the IV, their study would be better called a natural experiment (see the next section) or simply a secondary analysis of

[67]Harrison, List, and Towe (2007).

[68]DesJardins, McCall, Ott, and Kim (2010).

archival data (see Chapter 5). But researchers' uses of labels vary, and on the whole, it is good that attempts to set up a vocabulary police have not been very effective.

For an experiment to qualify as longitudinal, the outcome variable would have to be measured at least two times. An experiment with a before–after pretest and posttest would be the minimum. This is also often called a **repeated measures** design. Usually, in most researchers' minds, for an experiment to merit the label *longitudinal*, the number of repeated measures would need to be larger than two and separated by a considerable period of time. One early type of longitudinal design, although not much in current use, nicely illustrates the concept: the interrupted time series design. In this design measures of the outcome variable are taken several times before and after the treatment. The trend line is examined to see whether a significant bend in the trend line occurred at the time of the treatment. This is usually determined by examining the trend line visually. It can also be analyzed statistically by calculating whether there was a significant curve in the regression line coinciding with treatment (see Chapter 8 on curvilinear regression).

Variants of this approach can be used in **single-case experiments**, which are most often employed in therapeutic settings. Single-case experiments are usually aimed at finding an effective therapy for a particular individual. With only one participant, there can be no random assignment to control and experimental groups. Rather, a schedule of treatments is assigned to a particular individual. The focus is on what works for an individual, not on what works on average for groups. You might take three baseline measures before the treatment, three during, another three after the treatment has stopped, and a final three when the treatment is resumed. An effective treatment would be one in which the participant showed improvement during the treatment, a decline in the gains that had been made when the treatment is suspended, and continued improvement when it is resumed. The results are usually analyzed and presented graphically, although some statistical measures can also be used.[69]

Introducing time as a variable raises numerous complicated coding and analysis issues. Even storing your data in a spreadsheet or statistical software program requires special techniques when you use longitudinal data. In the typical layout for quantitative data, each person or case is placed in a single row that contains all the data for that case; the variables are placed in columns. More effective, when the outcome variable is measured several times, is to give each person several rows, one for each time the variable is measured. This greatly facilitates analysis.[70]

Once the data are properly entered, then a wide range of analysis options are open to the researcher; the choice depends in part on the research question and the nature of the DV. The two main options are MLM and SEM. Both of these are discussed in Chapter 9. The number of additional analysis options is large, but most are too specialized for more than brief mention in Chapter 9.

[69] A thorough and very readable overview is Kennedy (2005).

[70] For a discussion of the advantages of this form of coding the data, see Singer and Willett (2003); this is probably the best single volume on analyzing longitudinal data. The two data layouts are sometimes referred to as the wide format—one row for each case/person—and the long format—giving each case/person several rows, one for each time point. Some programs, e.g., STATA, will convert the data between the two.

At this point we want to stress the most important consideration in longitudinal experiments when gathering and coding data prior to analysis and interpretation—the problem of missing data. In the face of too much missing data, all methods rapidly lose their effectiveness. Not surprisingly, missing data issues are particularly pressing in longitudinal studies in which people have more time to drift away and researchers have more opportunities to make recording mistakes. The longer the term of the longitudinal study, the more likely the problem of missing data is to be severe. We discuss some "statistical fixes" for missing data in Chapter 7. But no matter how advanced some of these methods may be, they all rest on assumptions about the missing data that are hard to verify because, well, the data are missing, unknown, unobserved. The best one can do at the coding stage is to ensure that you have a good system for identifying, recording, and classifying missing data.[71]

Coding Data from Natural Experiments

The opportunity for a natural experiment arises when a "natural" event seems to have randomly assigned some people, places, or organizations to control and experimental groups. Examples include disasters, such as hurricanes or tornados, which damage some towns but have no effect on very similar neighboring towns (the between-groups approach). A variant is to compare towns just before and just after an event (the within-groups approach). The two kinds of comparisons (within- and between-groups) can be combined by using d-i-d methods, discussed briefly in what follows.

We put "natural" in quotation marks because many, perhaps most, of the natural events in published natural experiments are actually deliberately created by governments. What makes them natural from our perspective as researchers is that we did not create the control and experimental groups. Rather, the method of creation was similar to what researchers using randomization methods *might have* done. The event only becomes a natural experiment when researchers recognize that what has happened approximates an experimental situation with experimental and control groups determined by something approximating a random assignment. The strongest kind of example arises when a lottery is used to assign access or obligations, as with the draft lottery for the Vietnam War in the early 1970s.

The distinction between a natural experiment and an archival study is usually a matter of degree. The data already exist, and they were not created by the researcher; that makes them archival. How strongly can a researcher argue that archival data generated by naturally occurring events are what has been called "arguably exogenous,"[72] by which is meant that the participants had no say about whether they were in the virtual control or virtual experimental group? Thus one of the key components of a natural experiment is that the researcher has to *make an argument* that the events are similar to what an experimenting researcher might have devised. Having to make an argument has been the foundation of natural experiments since the first one was "conducted" in the mid-19th century. In the 1850s John Snow was able to demonstrate that

[71]See the earlier section "When to Screen for and Code Data Errors, Missing Data, and Outliers" (pp. 67–70) and Ibrahim and Molenberghs (2009) for a very thorough review.

[72]Murnane and Willett (2011).

the cause of cholera was drinking contaminated water. The people of London got their water from two sources, one highly contaminated, the other less so. His demonstration was a milestone in the history of epidemiology, as well as of research methods. Indeed, Snow simultaneously invented both epidemiology and the natural experiment by convincingly arguing that "no experiment could have been devised"[73] that would have better made the case that the cause of cholera was drinking water polluted by fecal matter. In a natural experiment, the initial "coding" of the IVs and DVs is done by making a case, by putting forth an argument, not by manipulation—as in an unnatural experiment.

In natural experiments, as with any other experiments, you still can strengthen the analysis—increase statistical power and the precision of effect-size estimates (see the earlier section "When to Include and Code Covariates/Control Variables," pp. 71–73)—by adding and properly coding control variables (covariates). Indeed, it is more typical to do so with natural experiments than with laboratory experiments. And it is even more common still in archival research, in which control variables are really all that you have as IVs (see Chapter 5). So studies can be ranged on a continuum of how much you need to rely on, code, and analyze control variables. In laboratory experiments, they are a helpful supplement to the IV but often not considered necessary; in natural experiments, they are frequently needed to make the case stronger; and in archival studies, there is really no difference between independent and control variables except the intent of the researcher.

Natural experiments are often geographical. An example could be a study of the effects of daylight savings time by investigating similar communities located near one another but on opposite sides of a boundary between time zones. Natural experiments are also often longitudinal—the measures of the outcome variable are made just before and after a policy change, for example—and thus require longitudinal methods of analysis. One important design/coding question is how long the interval is between "just before" and "just after"—weeks, months, years?[74] The wider the time gap, the harder it is to claim that differences between before and after are likely to be due to the naturally occurring IV. But natural experiments need not be either geographical or longitudinal.

We conclude the discussion of natural experiments with two recent examples of assessments of the effects of policy interventions. Both of them used one of the most common and effective coding and analysis strategies for natural experiments: difference-in-differences or d-i-d methods. The question to be answered using these methods is: What is the difference between individuals in the experimental group and those in the control group before and after the treatment? The d-i-d approach thus combines between-group and within-group coding and analysis.

The first study investigated the effects of a guaranteed tuition policy instituted in 2004 by the State of Illinois for all public 4-year colleges and universities. Although universities set their own tuitions and fees, once a student entered a particular university, tuition was fixed by law at the entry-year rate for 4 academic years. It was hoped

[73]The example has been discussed many times by epidemiologists, and statisticians have often reanalyzed the data, but Snow's (1855) work remains the most interesting source. The story is much more complicated and interesting than we have conveyed here; see Johnson (2006).

[74]Of course, this applies to all longitudinal studies, not only experiments.

that this change, widely supported by elected officials, would reduce tuition costs for students and families, or at least slow tuition growth, and that it would do this without the state having to spend any more money in support of public higher education. To examine the effects of the policy, the authors used data from the 1999–2000 through the 2010–2011 academic years to study trends in the cost of tuition and fees in Illinois as compared with national trends and as compared with a group of states in the region (Indiana, Ohio, Michigan, and Wisconsin) that did not have guaranteed tuition policies. The policy did not have the hoped-for effects. Indeed, comparing the differences before and after and the differences among states, the evidence indicates that guaranteed tuition *probably* had unintended negative effects. Tuition and fees were higher after guaranteed tuition than before it, and they went up faster in Illinois than in other states without guaranteed tuition.[75]

The second example of a natural experiment using d-i-d methods shows that it is possible to add a third layer of differences, resulting in a difference-in-differences-in-differences approach. The study examined the impact of prescription drug insurance, specifically Medicare Part D, on hospitalization rates. The hypothesis was that prescription drug insurance would lead to more regular use of medications and, in so doing, improve patients' health. As an indicator of improvements in patients' health, the researchers used hospitalization rates. If health improved as a result of Medicare Part D's prescription drug insurance, hospitalization rates should decline. The three differences were: (1) before and after the introduction of Part D in 2006; (2) for people 65 or older, who were eligible, versus those ages 60–64, who were not; and (3) states with high versus low rates of other types of prescription drug insurance in 2005. The authors' conclusion was that Part D reduced hospitalization rates; the greater availability of prescription drugs had positive effects by reducing the incidence of hospitalization and reduced overall health care costs because prescriptions are less expensive than hospitalizations.[76]

The range and quality of natural experiments, many of them using d-i-d methods, has expanded greatly in recent years. Examples can be found that examine many topics in diverse disciplines, and each raises particular coding challenges. In political science, the effects of a Supreme Court decision on the third-party candidates' chances of getting on the ballot were investigated. Using a major earthquake as a naturally occurring IV, a demographer studied the effects of maternal stress on birth outcomes. The influence of an increase in minimum wages on rates of employment was examined by economists. And the introduction of a school choice lottery was used to measure the effects of school choice on students.[77]

Coding Data from Quasi-Experiments

We discuss **quasi-experiments** briefly, not because they are less important—quite the opposite. Our impression is that the vast majority of experiments in social research are in fact quasi-experiments, whether or not they are labeled that by the investigators.

[75] Dean and Vogt (2012).

[76] Afendulis, He, Zaslavsky, and Chernew (2011).

[77] Respectively, Drometer and Rincke (2009); Torche (2011); Card and Krueger (2000); and Cullen, Jacob, and Levitt (2006).

Various dictionary definitions of *quasi* are “almost but not quite,” “to some degree,” or “resembling.” What quasi-experiments *resemble to some degree* is the pure ideal of the experiment in which the researcher controls the administration of the IV, assigns participants to control and experimental groups at random, and ensures that the expectations of participants, experimenters, and data analysts cannot influence the measurement of the DV because they are all blinded to which participants have received what treatments (experimental, control, placebo, etc.). If that description is used as the standard, then most of our experiment-based knowledge in the social sciences has been gained through quasi-experiments, not “true” or “full” experiments. A quasi-experiment is a study that meets at least one of the characteristics of a pure or true experiment, but not all. One common type occurs when the experimenter is able to manipulate the IV and determine how it is implemented but is not able to assign individual participants to control and experimental groups. For example, investigators might want to test the effectiveness of a new after-school program; they receive a grant to provide and manage the program, so they have control over the implementation. But the schools, the students, and their parents would all be volunteers.

Most discussions of quasi-experiments focus on their shortcomings as compared with true experiments. Discussed at greatest length are the threats to the internal validity of causal conclusions that ensue from using a quasi-experiment, with its lack of random assignment, rather than a true experiment.[78] Quasi-experiments are a good point at which to conclude this chapter, because they employ all the methods of coding and measurement discussed herein.

To summarize, as with all forms of experimental research, so too with quasi-experiments, researchers should rarely categorize continuous variables, and they should always screen data for errors and outliers, including missing data. It is especially important to consider the fidelity of the implementation of the research protocol in a multisite quasi-experiment and to code any departures from it. Using various forms of participant matching, including PSM, is helpful in any type of experiment but is particularly beneficial in quasi-experiments. All quantitative research projects, including quasi-experiments, should assess the study variables’ reliability and validity, and it is especially important in quasi-experiments to carefully describe the study’s external and ecological validity, as well as its internal validity. Adding control variables helps improve the investigation’s precision and statistical power. Results of statistical power calculations should be used to estimate needed sample size before the experiment and to interpret results after. Concerning the participants in a quasi-experiment, the researcher needs to specify which portions of the experiment used random methods—sampling, assignment to groups, or both. Finally, the researcher should carefully monitor the experiment to determine whether any unintended selection effects, including losing track of participants,[79] has partially invalidated the randomization (individual or group) since the experiment began. When applicable, IVE can be used as an alternative means of data analysis in these circumstances.

[78]This tradition began with Campbell and Stanley (1963), became a staple of the American research culture with Cook and Campbell (1979), and was brought to its highest development with the superb volume by Shadish et al. (2002).

[79]This is an easy problem to underestimate, and the usual statistical fixes used to compensate for such missing data are of limited value. See Ware (2012) for some suggested improvements.

CONCLUSION: WHERE IN THIS BOOK TO FIND GUIDELINES FOR ANALYZING EXPERIMENTAL DATA

Now that we have addressed when to use what methods of coding for your experimental data, you are ready to turn to the question of how to analyze the data thus coded.

Because experimenters collect data in many forms, most analysis techniques can be and have been used to analyze and interpret experimental data. Sometimes experiments generate qualitative data, for example, by asking participants to discuss their reactions to the experimental treatment or, in field experiments, intervening and observing what people do in more or less natural settings. Even when the outcome data for an experiment are wholly quantitative, the data from debriefings are often qualitative and can be analyzed with the methods for studying verbal and other qualitative data discussed in Chapters 11 and 12.

The typical randomized experiment is analyzed using inferential methods discussed in Chapter 7. Descriptive methods are nearly as essential, because the statistics that are tested for statistical significance or upon which one builds effect-size estimates are typically descriptive statistics, such as means and standard deviations. See Chapter 6 for an account of these. When controlling for background variables or matching participants on them, regression techniques are often used (see Chapter 8), and regression is essential in quasi-experiments and natural experiments. When the measures of an experiment's outcome variables are complex—for example, when several questions or scales are used to construct an outcome variable—then SEM (see Chapter 9) is commonly used. When the experiment uses group randomization—for example, randomizing classes to study individual students—then the most common approach is MLM, also discussed in Chapter 9. As always, using the Summary Tables at the end of each chapter can help you find analysis options quickly.

SUGGESTIONS FOR FURTHER READING

Coding data from experimental designs is a good topic under which to quickly review the issue of whether one can draw justifiable causal inferences from data that were not generated by experimentalists who controlled the delivery of the IV and who assigned participants to control and experimental groups at random. This kind of experiment remains an ideal. However, much of the work in quantitative research methods addresses the question of what can be done when the ideal cannot be met. And it *very* often cannot be met. Whether for practical or for ethical reasons, experimenters in the social sciences seldom have complete control over treatments of interest or over assigning people or institutions to these treatments.

It is possible to arrange the recommended readings for this chapter on a spectrum from works whose authors are exceptionally cautious about drawing causal conclusions from data not generated by RCTs, to those who are happy to (carefully) try alternative methods such as IVE, to those who are rather enthusiastic about the opportunities for causal inference in not fully controlled and not fully randomized experimental data. Statisticians tend to be our guardians of rectitude in these matters—perhaps because although they advise experimenters, they do not usually have to be involved in the troublesome details of rounding up people to study and herding them into randomly determined groups. People resist being treated in this way. Economists tend to be libertines—perhaps because their main subjects of study are rarely amenable to experimental approach, so they don't use experiments very much (the exception is so-called experimental economics, which is the psychology of decision making). Most of the rest of us fall somewhere in between.

Angrist and Pischke's (2009) *Mostly Harmless Econometrics* is refreshing because, like many economists, they do not approach causal inference from nonexperimental data with fear and trembling. Their book is very witty, but still quite advanced, particularly when it comes to instrumental variables. They are properly cautious, but they don't think causal inference from nonexperimental data is taboo; this is something of an occupational trait of economists, especially macroeconomists, who seldom can gather experimental data relevant to their most pressing research questions. More typical of the very cautious approach, which seems an occupational trait of statisticians, is Freedman's (2009) *Statistical Models: Theory and Practice.*

In the "just right" category, not too cautious and not too enthusiastic, we recommend Murnane and Willett's (2011) *Methods Matter.* Their book is cited frequently in this chapter because their conclusions and practical suggestions are remarkably well supported. And they work in the difficult area of program evaluation, which, because it is mostly done outside of the laboratory, has to address most of the tricky problems that can trip up the would-be experimenter. A final noteworthy and welcome feature of these three books is that they rely heavily on graphics as analytical and as explanatory tools.

Finally, Song and Herman's (2010) checklist and discussion of "critical issues and pitfalls" is a basic, but very thorough, set of guidelines for experimental studies, particularly RCTs. They fall more on the cautious than on the daring end of the spectrum of willingness to draw causal conclusions from non-RCT data.

CHAPTER 3 SUMMARY TABLE

CODING AND MEASUREMENT ISSUES FOR ALL EXPERIMENTAL DESIGNS	
When to categorize continuous variables (pp. 66–67)	• Almost never. Unless there is empirical support for validly categorizing continuous data, this is a form of "data mutilation." • If categorizing for purposes of reporting results, do this *after* the analysis.
When to code missing data and outliers (pp. 67–70)	• Always. It is crucial to screen for and code errors, missing data, and outliers. • Code missing data to specify their origins. • Be sure to check for multivariate errors and outliers.
When coding the independent variable, consider (pp. 70–71)	• Fidelity of implementation of the IV vs. departures from the protocol. • Whether and how "blinding" was done. • Differences between the target population, volunteers who were eligible, and volunteers who participated.
When to use and code covariates (pp. 71–73)	• To improve the similarity of experimental and control groups and thus increase precision of estimates. • PSM and IVE are special cases (see next entry). • To identify subgroup differences in the effects of the IV on the DV.
When to use PSM and IVE (pp. 73–77)	• Use PSM to create *virtual* assignment to control and experimental groups using a set of control variables to combine into a propensity score. • Use IVE when you can find a control variable related to the IV but not the DV to achieve *virtual* assignment to control and experimental groups.
When to assess variables' measurement validity (pp. 77–79)	• Whenever possible to assess whether your measures provide accurate information about your construct. • Note that reliability is a necessary precondition of validity.
When to assess variables' reliability (pp. 79–83)	• Always assess all variables' reliability. • Assess all relevant types of reliability (intercoder, test–retest, etc.). • Assess reliability for your study even when using variables and measures tested in other studies.
When to use multiple measures of the same concept (pp. 83–84)	• Any single measure is imperfect, so use multiple measures whenever practical; combining multiple measures often requires recoding.

When to assess statistical power (pp. 84–85)	• Because power is the ability to detect an effect, you should assess your study's power and report the results.
When to use gain or difference or change scores for the DV (pp. 85–86)	• When pre–post changes in a DV are the outcome measure, they can be reported as simple change scores, or the prescore can be used as a control variable, with the postscore as the dependent variable.

CODING AND MEASUREMENT ISSUES THAT TEND TO VARY BY DESIGN

When coding data from survey experiments (pp. 87–88)	• Specify both the target population and the effective sample. • Describe the survey sample's randomization and the assignment of respondents to control and experimental groups.
When coding data from RCTs (pp. 88–90)	• Code selection variables, matching variables, and participant equivalency variables. • Code dropouts, no-shows, etc., so as to use intention-to-treat analysis.
When coding data from multisite experiments, including randomized groups/clusters designs (pp. 90–92)	• Be sure your coding distinguishes between group randomization and individual case randomization. • Be sure to distinguish between group variables and individual variables.
When coding data from field experiments (pp. 92–94)	• Code differences in the field sites. • Code site-to-site differences in implementation of the protocol and measurement of outcomes.
When coding data from longitudinal experimental designs (pp. 94–96)	• Remember that missing data and history effects are especially likely in longitudinal designs.
When coding data from natural experiments (pp. 96–98)	• Attempt to find and code instrumental variables to use in the analysis (see "When to Use PSM and IVE"). • Use PSM when sufficient covariates can be coded and combined into a propensity score (see "When to Use PSM and IVE"). • Code data for d-i-d regression analysis when the design is longitudinal.
When coding data from quasi-experiments (pp. 98–99)	• It is especially important to use codes that describe and enable you to analyze ways in which the data are quasi- rather than purely experimental.

CHAPTER 4

Coding Data from Naturalistic and Participant Observations

In this chapter we:

- Introduce observational research by comparing it to other forms of data gathering.
  - o Discuss naturalistic and participant observation.
- Discuss the three main phases of coding observational data.
  - o Phase 1: Observing
    - ▪ Your research question.
    - ▪ Your roles as a researcher.
      - —Active/passive.
      - —Overt/covert.
  - o Phase 2: Recording
    - ▪ The main ways to record observational data.
    - ▪ First steps in note taking.
    - ▪ Early descriptive notes and preliminary coding.
    - ▪ Organizing and culling your early notes.
    - ▪ Technologies of recording observational data.
    - ▪ When to make the transition from recording to coding.
    - ▪ When to use an observation protocol.
      - —Appendix 4.1: Example of a Site Visit Protocol.
  - o Phase 3: Coding
    - ▪ When should you use computer software for coding?
    - ▪ Example of a data organizing and coding grid.
    - ▪ Recommendations.
    - ▪ Teamwork in coding.
    - ▪ Future research topics.
- Conclude with tips for completing an observational study.
  - o From observation to fieldnotes.
  - o Coding the initial fieldnotes.

INTRODUCTION TO OBSERVATIONAL RESEARCH

If you have decided that your research question is one that can be best answered by onsite observation of events and people in natural settings, then you have collected or will soon be collecting data using the methods of observational research. More than in any other research design, in observational research, most of the work of coding and analysis is "entangled" with data gathering, and it is also "back loaded." What we mean by entangled and back loaded is best highlighted by a comparison with survey research (see Chapter 1). In surveys the questions have to be written before any data can be collected; the questions strongly imply codes, and the codes suggest analysis plans. By contrast, in observational studies, data collection and recording precede coding; collection and recording begin to suggest codes as you prepare fieldnotes after each observation session. This is an **inductive** approach to coding, which we discuss further in this chapter and in Chapter 11. In brief, in surveys, much of the work of coding comes before data gathering; in observational research, most of it comes during and after.

The term **observational research** is used in more than one way by methodology writers.[1] We use it to mean studying phenomena as they occur without the researcher intervening. The oldest of the observational sciences is astronomy, which has generated data usable by modern researchers dating back thousands of years to ancient China and Mesopotamia. Astronomy pioneered in another sense: It was the first observational method to systematically employ photography to record data. Of course, all research involves observation of one sort or another, but astronomical observations, like the observations studied in this chapter, are not based on manipulations of, or interventions in, the phenomena observed. Experimenters observe participants' reactions to their treatments, and survey researchers and interviewers observe respondents' answers to their questions. The researchers discussed in this chapter are distinguished from experimenters, interviewers, and surveyors because they observe without shaping the phenomena studied. In other words, observational researchers seek to study human phenomena as they occur naturally, as if the researchers were not present. The meteor that crashed into Jupiter on September 10, 2012, would have done so had amateur astronomers not observed and documented it.[2]

Other terms besides *observational research* are also used to identify investigations aimed at studying social phenomena as they occur more or less naturally, without the kinds of interventions typical of surveys, interviews, and experiments. **Field methods** and **ethnographic research** also denote the same class of approaches to research as those discussed in this chapter. We prefer *observational* only because other terms can be somewhat less descriptive. For example, *field methods* may be too narrow and connote a particular anthropological approach, and the term *ethnographic* may have become, through widespread use, too broad.[3] In its original sense of long-term onsite observation

[1] Often "observational" is used as a crude residual category to label any research that is not experimental—a designation that is less than helpful.

[2] Only one actually observed it; another had made a video recording that captured the event and was able to confirm the observation.

[3] See Culyba, Heimer, and Petty (2004) for a study of the use of the term and Gans (1999) for a critique of newer trends in ethnography, such as autoethnography. A case for autoethnography is made in Hughes, Pennington, and Makris (2012).

of human cultures, ethnographic research was most highly developed by anthropologists, and we have relied heavily on their work.[4]

Some **naturalistic observers** of social life try to be as unobtrusive as possible, if not by interfering as little as an astronomer bent over a telescope, then at least by being as inconspicuous as the proverbial fly on the wall. The investigator's goal of neutral, observer-free research is seldom if ever totally met, because, to one degree or another in social research, the observers' presence usually affects the phenomena being observed (even a fly on the wall can be a distraction). But effect-free observation remains an ideal for many researchers. In **participant observation**, in which the researchers join the social activities that they are studying, their purpose is not to alter the phenomena,[5] although they inevitably do so. Rather, the goal is to gain a closer, insider perspective on the phenomena. In practice, participant and naturalistic observation are often less distinct than their names suggest. Differences are a matter of degree. The extent to which the researcher participates in the phenomena being studied ranges on a continuum from minimal (naturalistic) to extensive (participant). Finally, one type of participant observation is important in most types of research: The observations made by researchers as they are conducting their surveys, interviews, and experiments frequently provide important insights that complement the main method of data gathering.

By saying that pure observation is a goal, we do not mean to suggest that there can be an immaculate perception, an observation free of any prior researcher knowledge or filtering concepts or motivations. While admitting that all observation is, to use the popular term, "theory-laden," we think it is possible and desirable to keep observations from becoming *theory-obliterated*, to be nothing other than poorly disguised extensions of ideological commitments. We would not want to work in social research if we believed that there was no reality that could be observed credibly, that no observation was more accurate than any other, or that one could not improve the quality of one's observations through study and practice. If there was really nothing in the world apart from various epistemological posturings, what would be the point? Practically, we think it is possible to learn to use the phenomenological approach called *bracketing*, which means suspending judgment by recognizing and temporarily setting aside one's assumptions in order to better conduct a study.[6]

One key characteristic of observational researchers is that they tend to use several kinds of observation in the same study. Because observational researchers often have to improvise, as they conduct their investigations with minimal researcher control, they almost always resort to more than one way of gathering data—listening at a meeting, watching people interact in a social setting, or making a comment in a discussion and noting how it is received. Therefore, multiple sources and types of observation are typically used in data collection, and researchers frequently employ **triangulation**[7] to confirm and analyze their data. Improvisation and multiple types of observation are important advantages of observational research, but they make it somewhat more difficult for

[4] See Bernard (2000), Van Maanen (2011), and Chapter 11 in this book.

[5] Action research is an exception.

[6] Fischer (2009) is a recent discussion.

[7] The term comes from trigonometry, in which distances and angles between two points are used to calculate a third. In research methodology, it is used loosely to refer to the combined use of two or more methods or types of data.

text and reference book writers to systematize their advice, especially since the multiple types of observation are used to investigate many types of phenomena.[8]

Probably the most frequently studied kinds of phenomena investigated in observational research involve verbal interactions: conversations, discussions, debates, meetings, shouting matches, and so on. These verbal interactions, like interviews, are often recorded and transcribed. The difference is that, unlike in interviews, the researcher rarely directs the course of the verbal interactions by asking questions. Rather, researchers watch and listen as the verbal exchanges develop. Of course, observational researchers also often conduct interviews, both as formal interviews and as informal conversations. But interviews (see Chapter 2) and observations are distinct enough that we have found it helpful to discuss them in separate chapters. Perhaps the greatest of the distinctions between the two is that in interviews the emphasis is more on what interviewees *say*; the researcher *interprets the interpretations* of the interviewees and analyzes what the interviewees' words reveal about what they think or feel. In observational research, the emphasis is more on the *actions* of "observees," on what they *do*. Of course, one of the things they do is talk, sometimes to the researcher. So this distinction, like many others, is a matter of degree rather than kind.

Because observational researchers intervene least and have the least control over the phenomena they study, it is difficult to systematize descriptions and recommendations about effective research methods. Also, observational researchers are least likely to have already gathered their data before they begin the work of coding and analyzing them. The codes tend to emerge in the data collection and the review of records. Of course, this can happen in surveys, interviews, experiments, and archival research, too. All researchers make adjustments as they go along, but in observational research more emphasis is usually placed on learning by doing. We have assumed in writing this book that many readers will have already collected their data and are now thinking about how to code and analyze them. This assumption is probably less applicable to observational researchers. Because the processes of gathering and recording data are more fundamentally involved in coding them, we go back to stages of a research project earlier than those we looked at for surveys, interviews, and experiments.

In this chapter we examine three phases of gathering and preparing data for analysis in observational research: (1) methods of *observing*, (2) methods of *recording* the observations, and (3) approaches to *coding* the recorded observations. The phases overlap and can be cyclical. For instance, early observations may suggest ideas to use in coding; or the work of coding recorded observations often leads researchers to want to engage in further observation and to pay attention to different or additional things when they do.[9] Such overlaps, returns, and repeats occur in all types of research, quantitative or qualitative, but they tend to be more extensive in observational research. After discussing the three phases of preparing data for analysis in observational research—observing, recording, and coding—the chapter concludes with recommendations about where in the book to seek advice about effective analysis techniques for data from observational research, recommendations for research on observational practice, and suggestions for how to avoid common barriers to success.

[8]Zussman (2004) provides many examples of this variety.

[9]Yin's (2011) felicitous term for this process is the "analytic cycle"; Creswell (2007) uses and illustrates the "data analysis spiral."

PHASE 1: OBSERVING

There are many ways to observe and many occasions, settings, and persons that can be observed. Where and when will you observe whom doing what? Everything cannot be observed, even with the aid of excellent recording equipment. Selection is always involved. In addition to practical considerations, there are two important ways in which the selection of what, where, when, and who to observe is shaped in a research project: (1) by your research question and (2) by your role as a researcher.

Your Research Question

What you observe is inevitably and appropriately influenced by your research question and its relation to the theory or sensitizing ideas undergirding it. Different varieties of theories and types of research questions can lead to different foci in your observations. If your research question is exploratory, you may be concerned with *building* a theory; in your observations you might seek perceptions of phenomena that will give you ideas. Looking for ideas is a mysterious process, to be sure, but it is one many researchers have pursued. As your initial research question you might ask, Why does this occur? That question is based on a simple initial theory: It occurs; therefore it can be explained. The question also implies your initial codes. For example, the question might be, Why are some clinics more successful than others? This presumes that there are differences in success and that the reason(s) for the difference can be discerned through observation. You have to have some kind of working definition of, or code for, success so that you can recognize it when you see it.

If the question involves *assessing* a theory, you may be looking for confirming or disconfirming instances and for insights into what features of the phenomena being observed lead them to be confirming or disconfirming instances. For example, if the theory is that crime rates are lower in some neighborhoods because of the presence of certain kinds of social capital, you would observe neighborhoods for social patterns that confirmed or disconfirmed the salience of social capital in those neighborhoods. What kinds of neighborhood institutions and interactions would constitute the type of social capital specified in your research question? How will you observe them? If you observe them in different ways (e.g., attending a block meeting, having lunch in a popular restaurant), these have to be noted, and they become some of your first codes.

Whatever the type of research question and its underlying theory (e.g., exploratory or confirmatory), the *sites* of the research and the observations made at those sites must both be relevant to the research question and the theory upon which it is built.[10] A site might not be relevant because it is not representative of the category of phenomena being studied. For example, the success rate at some of the clinics might be high only because of unusual methods of recording outcomes. Or the crime rates in some of the neighborhoods might not take into account an important category of crime.

And the *observations* at the sites also need to be representative and relevant. If you visit a site at an unusual time or observe atypical people and places, you will not

[10]These issues are also important at the design and sampling stages of the research; see Vogt, Gardner, and Haeffele (2011), especially Chapters 4 and 10, for further discussion.

be observing "business as usual." For example, if you wish to investigate the organizational climate of a particular company, you need to observe it over an extended period and at different times of the day and week. Otherwise, you may be observing only the short-term weather, not the long-term climate. Your efforts to make your observations representative and relevant also need to be recorded and included in your final research report. They are forms of sampling that have to be included as part of your early coding.

Your Role as a Researcher

The kinds of observations, recording, and coding that are possible depend on the status of the observer in the social situation being studied. Observers can be active participants in the situation or passive observers. Also, observers can conduct their observations overtly or covertly. Two continua can be used to describe the roles and positions of researchers conducting observational studies: active–passive and overt–covert. One continuum reaches from full participation in the social situation being studied at one end to the role of a completely passive observer at the other. The other continuum extends from the researcher being clearly identified as such to the researcher who is "under cover" (see Figure 4.1). If you imagine 5 points on each continuum, there are 25 possible combinations. Of course, many more subtle shadings and nuances are possible. What you will be able to observe, record, and therefore code will differ depending on your positions on these two continua and how they are combined. Reading the observational research literature, it is possible to find examples of all possible combinations of active–passive and overt–covert researcher roles.

Opinions differ about which approaches are best in what circumstances. Beliefs are strong, debates are spirited, but the evidence is weak.[11] Your choice is, of course, constrained by what is possible in a particular setting. Among the possible options, you choose those that are most effective for answering your research question. The range of roles that are feasible may not always include the options you believe would be most effective. Observational research begins with the art of the possible. In brief, there are three questions: (1) Should you participate or be passive, (2) should you do this overtly or covertly, and (3) how do you best combine the two choices in specific settings? We provide some examples of the different ways researchers have made these choices that fall at various points of the active–passive and overt–covert continua illustrated in Figure 4.1. Briefly, the extremes of an overt but passive researcher (1–5 in the figure) would be studying law enforcement through police "ride alongs."[12] An active but covert

1. Active/Passive	Active Participant	<----1----2----3----4----5--->	Passive Observer
2. Overt/Covert	Openly Researching	<----1----2----3----4----5--->	Covertly Researching

FIGURE 4.1. Continua describing observational researchers' roles.

[11] One study that presents some systematic evidence is Tope, Chamberlain, Crowley, and Hodson (2005).

[12] Spano (2006); Van Maanen (1982).

researcher (5–1 in the figure) would be taking a job in order to study what it was like to do that job but not informing your coworkers that you are a researcher as well as an employee.[13]

The researcher's roles may not be stable. For example, researchers have described, sometimes rather poignantly, how challenging it is to maintain an outsider role when observing, especially when it seems that it is hard to gain people's trust if you don't participate.[14] At other times you might want to participate, but everyone knows you are an outsider, "just" there to do your research, so your involvement is viewed with suspicion.[15] In general, it can be very difficult to maintain a purely passive external observational role; it can be equally difficult to be a full participant; and the fluidity of roles in ongoing social interaction means that you might not always be sure exactly what your role is or how it is evolving. It is not entirely up to you. An excellent example is Duneier's study of the culture of street vendors in New York City. Over the several years of his research, he played several more or less active roles—even, at the close of the project, partnering with one of the members/participants to teach his course on research methods.[16]

One of the ways that your role is not entirely up to you is the requirement to clear your research with institutional review boards (IRBs), which are the official guardians of research ethics, as well as propagators of bureaucratic rules. One of the biggest changes in social research as a result of IRB activities is that covert observation is *probably* much less common than it once was. We emphasize "probably" because we know of no systematic evidence one way or the other. But it seems highly likely that ethical considerations and the bureaucratic slowness attendant upon IRB paperwork often limit the possibility of studying important events and processes covertly, especially rapidly unfolding events. It is sometimes amusing to imagine what would be required were one to want to study, for example, the reactions of the police and soldiers to various political movements and demonstrators—Tea Party, Occupy Wall Street, or pro-choice and right-to-life groups, for example. Imagine asking a truncheon-wielding, pepper-spray-squirting member of the riot police, "Excuse me officer, would you sign this consent form so that I can use my observations of your actions in my dissertation?" Not surprisingly, the field of research "where the action is" has mostly been ceded to journalists, who are constrained by many fewer rules.[17] But some courageous social scientists have persisted in this important type of research, in which the risks are born by the researchers, not by the "human subjects."[18]

Another once common observational role occurs when the researcher takes a job in order to study the life and work and social situations of a particular type of worker and

[13]Ehrenreich (2011).

[14]Spano (2006); Bosk (2008); Vogt (2012).

[15]Venkatesh (2008).

[16]Duneier (1999). The roles of participant observers have long been a topic in the methodology literature; see Becker (1958) and Gans (1968) for classic discussions.

[17]For example, replicating the shocking Milgram experiments on conformity, which no psychologist could get past an IRB, was done on NBC's *Dateline* in the name of "infotainment" (Shermer, 2012).

[18]The need sometimes to take a side and the difficulties of gaining consent in intensely controversial settings is nicely discussed in Drury and Stott (2001). See also Jacobs (2006).

workplace setting.[19] Sometimes this research is done covertly; this was once common and resulted in pioneering books in social research.[20] This kind of research, in which researchers pose as something they are not, or in which they have dual roles (worker and researcher), one of which is hidden, has an impact on the recording and coding of observations. Establishing a record of events, usually in the form of fieldnotes, will typically be done at the end of the day and will depend heavily on the author's memory. Because of IRB regulations, and perhaps for other reasons, this type of covert participant observation seems to have become quite rare. Whether the loss of insights stemming from the decline in covert participant observation has been balanced by the gains to the rights of research subjects is a topic of some debate among active researchers.

Nonparticipant covert observation (coded 5–5, passive–covert, in the continua in Figure 4.1) also seems to have become rare. As an example of this type, one of us (W.P.V.) conducted nonparticipant naturalistic covert observation in a large, popular, and busy student–faculty cafeteria at a university. It was easy to be an unobtrusive researcher in that setting because many other cafeteria patrons were, like the researcher, hanging out, drinking coffee, and writing in their notebooks. There seemed to be no expectation of privacy; indeed, loud talking, easily heard beyond the tables, was frequent. The topic of the research was social and ethnic interactions and diversity as influenced by physical surroundings. About half of the seats in the cafeteria appeared to have been tacitly "assigned" to different ethnic, professional (student or faculty), and gender groups. The rest of the seats in the cafeteria were usually open, which made it easy for the researcher to move around and observe.

Day after day, week after week, a core group of five to eight students or faculty members would assemble at a particular table—or, if it were occupied, one close by. This core would often be joined by a roughly equal number of secondary or rotating members of the table group. The social interactions were remarkably restrained by the size of the tables: five seats on each side, one on each end, with the possibility of squeezing in two or three more; a group was never bigger than 15 for more than a minute or two before extra members wandered off or formed a satellite group. Different ethnic groups sat at particular tables with remarkable regularity. In casual conversation with the cafeteria's patrons, the researcher found that one of the things people liked about that cafeteria was its "diversity." But it was diversity between, not usually within, tables. One rarely saw students interacting with faculty or students from different ethnic groups at the same tables. At another cafeteria, less than 200 yards away, the tables were smaller; each had four chairs. Sometimes students would push tables together to form larger tables, but this was fairly rare. Couples and threesomes, almost always transitory in the first cafeteria, were all very common in the second (with four-person tables). Interestingly, there was more within-table ethnic diversity in the cafeteria with smaller tables.[21]

Another type of heavily observational research is conversation analysis. Based on **ethnomethodology**, the idea behind conversation analysis is to understand the

---

[19] A well-known example is Ehrenreich (2011). Examples of delayed note taking in different settings include Calvey (2008) and Stewart (2006).

[20] Goffman's (1961) *Asylums* is probably the best known.

[21] See Vogt (1997) for a brief discussion. Duneier's (1994) study of the patrons of a neighborhood cafeteria is a classic in the field.

methodologies ordinary people (the ethnos) use to interact with and understand one another.[22] The researcher's role is usually passive but overt—frequently to engage in video recording. For example, one scholar obtained consent to videotape a small dinner party. She got the consent forms signed, set up the video camera, turned it on and left; she collected the recording the next day. This is an example of overtly researching through completely passive observation of a natural (not manipulated or staged) occurrence—which would be coded 1–5 using the schema of Figure 4.1. It was a natural setting in that the people would have had their dinner party whether the researcher had set up her camera or not. The data coding and analysis consisted of extremely detailed empirical examination focused on one particular type of conversational interaction (self-deprecation). The text included a somewhat standardized set of markings or "transcription symbols" to indicate pauses, grunts, and so on. This text was analyzed and presented to an audience of researchers with the videotaped interaction playing in the margins of the text.

A less natural setting, also using video recording to collect the data, is exemplified by a study of the interactions of mothers with their daughters in which one of us (E. V.) was a data coder. The coder of the audiovisual tape sees a female member of the research team escort a mother and her 5- or 6-year-old daughter into a room and seat them on two chairs in front of a computer. The researcher leans over the child and gives her a few brief verbal directions and points to the keyboard and screen to show the child how to make objects on the screen move by manipulating the keys. The researcher leaves the room and the pair of participants, mother and daughter, are left alone together. Later, the coder watches and listens to the interactions of mother and child as the child involves herself in the computer activity while the mother watches. Coding the interactions of the several mother–daughter pairs first involved transcribing the dialogue between them. But the words alone were inadequate to describe the event. Coding also required noting the tone and volume of each voice. The body movements of the mother and child provided essential information, such as impatience of the mother or a silent pleading on the part of the child for help as she looked at her mother—or the mother giving unasked-for direction to her child. When coding such video data in words (or other symbols), consistency is, of course, crucial.

Another example comes from Wally Lamb, a noted novelist, who used his role as an educator teaching a writing class in a women's prison to become a participant observer/facilitator. In his capacity as teacher, he encouraged and assisted female prisoners to develop their writing skills as they composed the stories of their lives. The students in the workshop wrote autoethnographies with Lamb as facilitator. Lamb's role was important, but he had virtually no coding to do. The participants in his class generated the data, so Lamb did little recording and coding; he was mostly an assistant and compiler. When he arranged for the women's stories to be published, after considerable resistance from the prison authorities (who actually sued some of the authors), the royalties went to the authors of the autoethnographies.[23]

In some ways Lamb's work is an extension of **diary methods** that sociologists and others have long used to study individuals' experiences and their reflections on them.

---

[22]The *locus classicus* for ethnomethodology is Garfinkel (1967); a recent overview is Sidnell (2010); the specific example is from Hayano (2012).

[23]Lamb (2004, 2007).

Today, researchers using diary methods usually ask participants to complete a once-a-day diary entry on the Internet. Another approach, similar to diary methods, reminds us that observational researchers, conducting investigations of daily life in natural (not laboratory) settings, by no means confine themselves to collecting qualitative data. One of the most highly developed of these methods is called **experience sampling**. Research participants wear or carry a device similar to a pager. At random intervals throughout the day, they are asked to report on what they are doing, with whom, in what settings, and how they feel about it. In some ways this is a form of survey research. It is survey research on the go, in which the experiences, as well as the respondents, are sampled. And the coding of responses is much more akin to coding survey questions than coding observations. But it is unlike typical surveys in that the people being studied with experience sampling go about their normal activities. Because technologies for conducting this kind of research have improved greatly and become much cheaper and more familiar to more people, experience sampling has expanded greatly in recent years. It is one of several inventive methods researchers have devised to conduct naturalistic observations in the real world.[24]

Reading over the previous several paragraphs on researchers' roles, the reader may have been struck by how much the roles were intertwined with their methods for recording observations. From writing in notebooks during events through fieldnotes written up after the events to various electronic means of collecting and recording data, what researchers have done and been able to do has been tied to how they turned their perceptions into records that could be analyzed.

PHASE 2: RECORDING

Etymologically, the word *recording* stems from Latin and French words for recalling or remembering. This word origin was especially apt a couple of generations ago, when most records of observations were fieldnotes constructed as recollections *of* perceptions (and reflections *on* recalled perceptions) that had occurred some time before—as when participant observers compiled their fieldnotes at the end of each day. This practice is still widely used by researchers whose roles are types of participant observation. It is especially common when conducting covert participant observations, which makes it difficult at best to take notes while observing. But observational data may be recorded in many different ways, and it typically is. For example, a video recording of an event is inevitably made simultaneously with the phenomena being observed, not after it. Each method of recording has strengths and weaknesses, and each raises questions of coding for collection and of coding for analysis.[25]

This second phase of the observational research process (recording) is usually closely tied to the first (observing), but recording is conceptually and often practically distinct from observing. The main ways of recording observational data are:

[24]The handbook by Mehl and Conner (2012) provides an excellent overview and much useful detail on methods of coding and analysis.

[25]For a superb account of how recording technologies have influenced interview research (the insights can easily be extended to observational methods), see Lee (2004).

- Transcribing memories into fieldnotes after the observation.
- Taking notes during an observation.
- Correcting and revising notes taken during the observations.
- Audio recording of your notes.
- Audio recording of participants' words or other sounds (singing, etc.).
- Drawing.
- Photographing.
- Video recording.

We can provide no succinct if–then advice on when to use these various recording technologies. The choices depend importantly on what is practical to use in particular settings, what is allowable given ethical considerations, and what your abilities and preferences are. Another reason that we do not prescribe clear-cut recommendations is that many researchers use a combination of several methods of recording. And it is often best to do so. Indeed, one recommendation we can make at this point is that you try methods you are not familiar with in order to become adept enough to know whether you want to add them to your tool kit.

The first point to make about approaches to recording is that before you can *analyze* any of these forms of recording, you usually have to convert them into text. A partial exception is video recordings. You can *code* data from video recordings without first turning them into text, but the codes you create are almost inevitably composed of language or other written symbols. If you have photos, they cannot be coded and analyzed by simply pasting them into your texts. To analyze the data in the photos, you'll have to say something about them, to code them as text. Without text they are data, but not readily useful information. Another partial exception is that some researchers prefer to use audio recorders to dictate their observations and reflections, but eventually these, too, will have to be transcribed. Software for turning spoken notes or other audio recordings into text is gradually improving, almost to the point of usefulness for making transcriptions, but this software does not allow you to escape from the written word. Writing remains an "essential technology of the intellect."[26] As one field guide to fieldnotes put it, "lived experience must eventually be turned into observations and reduced to textual form."[27] Some researchers prefer to get to the textual stage as quickly as they can. Others wait, wanting to leave the data in a raw state as long as possible. In either case, as an observational researcher, your job is not only to observe; you must also write—the sooner the better, we think.

A key characteristic of written records is that they are fixed and permanent, at least as compared with ideas and memory. To rephrase the old Chinese saying, the writing of the palest toner cartridge is more trustworthy than the strongest memory. Another formidable advantage of textual data is the speed with which it can be scanned and rearranged. If you've ever reviewed dozens of hours of audiotape trying to find a particularly salient comment or incident, you may have come to appreciate, as we have, that the eye can scan much faster than the ear. To put it another way, you can read (and skim)

---

[26]Goody (1986).

[27]Emerson, Fretz, and Shaw (1995, p. 38).

much faster that someone can talk or you can listen. If your notes are in computer word processing software, you can search for key words in seconds. One final qualification—because the eye is quicker than the ear, scanning videotapes for particular images is usually much faster than scanning audiotapes for particular sounds. However, many audio recorders allow you to increase the speed of the playback; if you don't mind the high-pitched voices, you can review the material somewhat more quickly.[28]

In short, when it comes to coding and analysis, texts are the nub of the matter. We always tell students contemplating dissertations using naturalistic or participant observational methods: "If you don't like to write and to rewrite and to think about what you've rewritten so that you can organize it in various ways and rewrite it again, you are going to find observational data analysis very unpleasant." It is a writer's game. The actual work of the observations themselves can seem so "real world" and so very unlike hunching over a desk in a quiet place and writing. And it is true that at the data collection stage, observational research could hardly be more different from library document research and the work of the traditional scholar/scribe. But at the recording, coding, analysis, and interpretation stages, the two kinds of research are very similar.

One common operational definition, put variously by different commenters over the years, is that an observational researcher is someone who writes fieldnotes at the end of the day. Because the shelf life of memory is short, observing is only half the work. Memories need to be recorded at the end of every day at minimum. If you are doing more than one observation session per day, it is important to leave time between them for fieldnotes; otherwise, sessions can get confused in your mind. If you don't set aside substantial time at the end of each observation session to record, the observations won't yield much data for you to code and analyze. One rule of thumb is that for every hour in the field observing, you need *at least* one hour writing. Practically, this requirement can lead to a surprising conclusion: In order to do your writing, you might have to cut back on your observations. The situation is very different when interviewing (see Chapter 2), in which the goal is frequently to make a verbatim transcript. When you have used audio and/or video recording, the transcripts can be created well after the event—but not your *observations* of the interview setting and participants, which, like other observations, need to be firmed up immediately. Still, in interview research, recording is comparatively less complicated, and you can move more quickly and unproblematically to coding.

First Steps in Note Taking

How do you, as an observational researcher, get from your first perceptions/observations to notes that will help as an aid to your memory and eventually become the data you will analyze? This can be a hard question to answer, but there is plenty of practical shared wisdom—rules of thumb and pitfalls to avoid—about which many researchers agree. We summarize some of these in the next few paragraphs. Our first recommendation is that it is very useful to talk with as many knowledgeable people as possible about tips for how to proceed—to compare notes on notes, as it were, with other students, with faculty, and/or with colleagues.

One tricky question is whether to take notes *while* you are observing—under what circumstances can you, should you? In some cases the choice is easy. If you are a covert

[28] We were reminded of this last point by an anonymous reviewer.

naturalistic observer, as in the cafeteria study mentioned earlier, of course you will. Even if you are an overt naturalistic observer, say at a meeting of an organization, you probably will, and it could seem odd to the members[29] if you did not do so; not taking notes might seem to imply that you were not taking their doings seriously. On the other hand, you will not be able to write down everything. If you spend all your time writing (or photographing), you risk not seeing and hearing. The strain can be considerable when you try to write down an account of what you just saw and heard in the immediate past while you attempt to continue to see and hear what is going on in the present and to prepare for what you are likely to observe next.

What about circumstances in which it would not be natural to take notes? If you are a covert participant observer, you are likely to "blow your cover" if you take notes. Even if you are an overt participant observer, taking notes can get in the way not only of seeing but also of participating. The only general rule is that, if it is obtrusive to take notes and if doing so changes what you are observing, you'll have to rely mostly on your memory and take notes later. On the other hand, even in busy participant-observation research, you might be able to take brief notes to help you remember important things (names, times, facts) or phenomena that you want to remember to write about more extensively after you leave the site. These brief notes or "jottings"[30] might be taken on a napkin, in the margins of a newspaper, or, given the ubiquity of cell phones, you could send a quick text message to yourself or use the cell phone as an audio recorder for quick notes to aid memory. If notes cannot be taken onsite, they might be written in a stairwell or a bathroom.

Early Descriptive Notes and Preliminary Coding

The jottings help you keep perceptions and observations in short-term memory until you can put them into a more permanent form. Eventually your notes have to be clear and permanent enough that you can use them weeks or months later. Still, making even minimal jottings might not be wise in some settings where members might view you as a "spy" or as otherwise invading their privacy. We've had members say to us, "Hey, why are you writing this down?" But, in other circumstances and just as insistently, "How come you're not writing this down?" If the situation is one in which you have trouble taking notes, you will also have trouble using other forms of recording, such as audio- or videotape—at least if you are ethical, not sneaky about it. In any case, whether you can make "jottings" or not, while observing try to think about what you will write when you are alone. Also, keep in mind, when you are participating, that you are a researcher, not only a participant.

If, as is often the case, your note taking onsite has been minimal, then you need to create a written record of your observations at the first opportunity. At least try to quickly jot down what you'll need later to help you remember—perhaps in the parking lot before driving home. At the end of the day, every day, turn your memories—and jottings if you have them—into proper notes. At this first stage of constructing fieldnotes,

[29] *Members* is the term anthropologists usually prefer; psychologists more often use *participants*, as in members of the group being studied or participants in the study.

[30] The term is from Emerson et al. (1996), who have the most extensive discussion of this crucial part of note taking that we know of.

you'll want to keep your descriptions separate from your commentary and interpretation. To separate them, you might use facing pages of a spiral notebook or, if you are typing, you could use footnotes, brackets, different fonts, whatever helps you keep descriptions and commentary distinct. But they fade into one another, rather like osmosis. For example, in the cafeteria study mentioned earlier (Vogt, 1997), the researcher noted:

1. "When observing a group of a dozen young men today, I had trouble distinguishing between friendly, boisterous banter and a more mocking hostile exchange."
2. "Maybe the members of the group themselves didn't know; they seemed uncertain, and their tone varied over the course of 5 or 10 minutes. Sometimes their broad smiles looked genuine enough, at other times forced."
3. "Such ambiguity in banter, bluff, and bluster seems common in groups of young men."

Those three numbered passages range from descriptive (a dozen young men) to interpretive (smiles looked genuine enough) through theoretical and/or stereotypical (common in groups of young men). The sentences move from description to analysis and interpretation. Such sentences all have a place in your notes, but you need to keep them distinct and keep the distinctions clear in your mind. Still, they all have the same origins—your perceptions and your reflections on your perceptions: "these contrasting terms—description and analysis—refer more to recognized kinds of writing than to separate cognitive activities."[31]

As you transform your jottings into more complete and readable fieldnotes and then revise those into codable and better organized fieldnotes, be sure to keep your original versions and drafts. In working with qualitative data, as with quantitative, we have found it crucial from time to time to be able to go back to earlier versions and drafts. To be sure, most of the early stuff becomes useless, but not all of it does, and you won't know for a long time what was truly useless and what turned out to be useful after all. So follow "the first rule of data handling": make a copy. Also, follow the second rule: "do it again."[32] Photocopy your handwritten notes or scan them into a computer file. E-mail the file to yourself or save it on a thumb drive (a.k.a. flash drive, memory stick, dongle). Keep copies of everything, and be sure you can distinguish or track successive revisions.

Organizing and Culling Your Early Notes

You won't use everything you observed. First, some of your perceptions won't make it into your jottings or memory, and all your jottings and memories during the day will not make it into your notes at the end of the day. Even your initial drafts of fieldnotes might be cut to improve later write-ups. How do you decide what to include and what to discard? At the beginning of each fieldnotes writing session, you might ask yourself a common set of questions, such as: Did I observe phenomena relevant to my research

[31] Emerson et al. (1996, p. 195).

[32] Davidson (1996).

question today? What did I observe that seems important to me, but I'm unsure why? What did I observe that surprised me? What is missing? Having a set of questions (perhaps even a checklist) like this to ask yourself at each writing session can help with the construction of a few categories of fieldnotes. Some researchers would say that such questions shape the notes too much in advance. One dispute among researchers has to do with how theory-free you can be as you come into the world of observation. But all agree that ultimately you must be selective.

One approach we have often found useful is to start out organizing fieldnotes in two ways. First, make a brief chronological outline of times and events. This is often very helpful for remembering what happened over the day. It can also be very useful for remembering, months later, which day was which. Second, into your hour-by-hour list of the day's happenings, you can insert longer descriptions of the three to five main events or interactions or other phenomena that are especially pertinent to the themes of your research or that raise interesting questions. Even if you could record everything, you do *not* want to. Think of the analogy of taking notes on a book; you write down the most important ideas and information and perhaps some significant quotations. But, even if you have time, you don't copy, verbatim, the whole book. That is not taking notes; it is useless drudgery. To be useful your notes must be selective. The same is true of attempting to write down everything that occurred during an observation session. Similarly, when you collect documents as part of your observational investigation, you need to be selective, not only about what documents to collect but also about what to do with them. If you simply photocopy them and stick them into a file folder, you risk collecting a heap of paper too large to be useful. As soon as possible, read, highlight, and take notes to convert the raw data in the document into more useful information.

Another useful analogy, parallel to the contrast between early jottings and mature fieldnotes, is the difference between late-breaking news on television versus an account of the same events in a weekly magazine. The former is immediate and vibrant, but also often confused, contradictory, and repetitive. Viewers might be fascinated, but they struggle to grasp what is going on. By the time the event has been described in the weekly magazine, the outlines of what actually happened are clearer. In 15 minutes of reading you can get a firmer grasp of what took place than you first obtained in 2 hours of watching breathless reporters and jiggling video images. Your fieldnotes eventually, as you observe and understand more, become something like a thoughtful magazine article, but they begin as confused, contradictory, and repetitive memories and jottings.

One way to help determine what to include in your notes is to keep in mind for whom the notes are being written. At first, you write them for yourself to help you remember what you have observed and to organize your thinking about it. Most people find that they don't really *know* something until they have written about it. Writing makes the gaps in memory, narrative, and logic stand out so that you can fill in where you are able and admit what you don't know. Although your notes are initially for you, ultimately your writing is for others. The difference between, say, a tourist keeping a diary and researchers observing social phenomena is that the researchers are writing for others—others in their discipline or in a broader community of scholars. If you are a student, you are writing for your professors; if you are a doctoral student, then your writing is for your dissertation committee and also for other researchers who might read your dissertation. For example, we took extensive fieldnotes as part of a multiyear, multiproject program evaluation. The notes were first for each of us individually. Then we wrote them up for other members of the team. The fieldnotes were then consolidated into team fieldnotes, which were then used to write for a broader audience of evaluation researchers, as well as for the state agency funding the program of which the projects were a part.[33]

Technologies for Recording Observational Data

When the research setting is conducive to their use, various electronic recording technologies can be enormously helpful tools. We have already discussed audio recording in Chapter 2 on interviews, in which it typically plays a fundamental part. Here we focus more on visual recording, which can also be important in interviews but tends to be even more helpful in observational settings. Rather than discussing generally the issues of the relationship of recording technologies to coding for analysis, we briefly describe an example of a relatively new subdiscipline, visual sociology.

The term **visual sociology** denotes both a means of recording research observations and a topic of investigation. Researchers using the techniques of visual sociology[34] use three broad and fairly distinct approaches. Visual representations are used as (1) documents that refer to the phenomena of study that they depict, (2) examples of how a topic is understood or stereotyped in society, and (3) indicators of how social contexts affect our representations of reality. For example, photographs taken by the researcher could be used as documents to record data about people and situations, such as events in the lives of migrant workers or the conditions in which they work. Similar photographs, especially as taken by others, could be employed as data when the researcher's focus is less on the reality of the lives of the workers and more on how they are depicted by those who have taken the photographs. Finally, photographs with the same or similar subject matter could be used to investigate how changes in social and political contexts influence which photographs are selected for display in the popular media (e.g., magazines and advertisements). Visual sociology also sometimes concerns itself with how visual technologies are used in art and society, such as in the emergence of photography as a middle-class art.[35]

Visual social research seems underutilized. Rigor in the coding and analysis of visual data does not appear to us to have progressed much beyond nor often attained the levels demonstrated in the classic by Gregory Bateson and Margaret Mead, *Balinese Character: A Photographic Analysis*, published more than 70 years ago. Mead and Bateson did not simply illustrate, they integrated photographic data into their analyses.[36]

With the easy availability of photographic technology, for example on cell phones, one might expect visual sociology and anthropology to have become more widespread. Perhaps visual recordings have remained underutilized because of regulations regarding

---

[33]For a brief description of the project, see Vogt, Gardner, Haeffele, and Baker (2011). For a strong case that keeping the audience in mind is one of the keys to good research writing, see Booth, Colomb, and Williams (1995).

[34]The term *visual psychology* usually refers to studies of perception.

[35]Bourdieu (1965) is a foundational work. The journal *Visual Studies*, established in 1985, is the official journal of the International Visual Sociology Association. Harper's (1988) oft-cited article is a good overview.

[36]Bateson and Mead (1942).

research ethics, particularly maintaining the anonymity of research participants. It is certainly much more difficult to ensure members' anonymity when researchers use video rather than audio recordings. One consequence, probably unintended, is that the culture of research is becoming increasingly distant from popular culture and journalism, in which visual—still photo and video—representations abound. Consequently, if researchers study popular visual culture, they usually do so *not* through images they themselves have made but rather by commenting on images made by others. Despite some barriers to the use of images in social research, they can be exceptionally helpful. For example, one modest and simple, but important, use of photo images is as a form of visual "jotting," a way to preserve memories. Quick snaps or videos taken with a cell phone or other device can be very helpful in recollecting and distinguishing in your mind's eye persons and places when you write up fieldnotes. They can often make it possible to reconstruct memories weeks or months later.[37]

When to Make the Transition from Recording to Coding

It is widely recognized that recording observations and coding them are naturally linked. It can be hard to say where one activity ends and the other begins. When you record, as in writing up your notes, you also and inevitably start coding. Merely to write (or to think), you have to use basic categories/codes such as *similar* and *different, few* and *many, close* and *distant.* Consider the following excerpt from the notes for the cafeteria study, mentioned earlier: "They looked quite similar, and they sat physically very close to one another; didn't notice them at first—perhaps because there were only a few of them." The elementary codes (*similar, close, few*) are embedded in the description.

Another way you begin coding early is in the simple process of storing your records (notes, tapes, photographs, etc.) in an orderly way so you can retrieve them later. At minimum, records will be labeled by date, time, and place. These labels are often important because human life naturally has different rhythms that vary by times of the day and/or seasons of the year.[38] At first you might see yourself as merely following simple routines of good record keeping, but your filing system markers often become the basis of some of your most important initial codes. In the same way, part of your record keeping should include observations of yourself while observing. Where and with whom were you sitting or standing? If you asked questions, what questions did you ask? How did you decide? When you arrived at the site, what, if anything, were you planning or expecting? The answers to these questions entail some initial coding by keeping track of what you did when gathering information. Finally, your coding will be influenced by how much your preparations have led you to precode. If you have specific things you are looking for at the observational site, such as instances of particular kinds of behavior, you will want to identify these in your written notes; if you use electronic recording, insert the appropriate indicators, such as track numbers on a video recording.

[37]We know more than one researcher who has used stealth recording (without the knowledge or permission of the members). Recording technologies, such as cell phones, make this ever easier; but even when used only by the researcher as an aid to memory, the ethical violation is grave. And it is especially so if the members have cultural or religious objections to being photographed or videotaped.

[38]The classic study is by Mauss (1950/2004) on the seasonal variations of Eskimo social life.

When to Use an Observation Protocol

Our final question in this section on recording observational data is, When should you use an **observation protocol** or a site visit protocol, and what are the implications for coding of doing so? The advantages and disadvantages of an observation protocol are similar to the pros and cons of an interview schedule. There are differences between the two. The interview schedule will often contain the actual questions you will ask interviewees, as well as ideas about follow-up questions (see Chapter 2). The observation protocol will more often contain questions you ask yourself that you want to try to answer. Sometimes you will ask members or participants a question that is on the protocol, but mostly the protocol's list of topics and questions are meant to direct your attention; they are reminders of your purposes and research questions.

Observation protocols are most necessary when a project is big and complex. For example, in the multiyear evaluation research project mentioned before, three observers visited numerous sites and observed different phenomena (meetings, classrooms, physical settings) over several years. The observation protocol was indispensable. The researchers needed a structure for what was to be observed and for how to observe it. The protocol is presented in Appendix 4.1 at the end of this chapter.[39] It is as much an observation guide as a coding guide. As you can see, the heart of the protocol is a list of questions we wanted to answer, rather than a list of questions that we directly asked the members. Reading the protocol vertically, the questions in the columns formed a checklist of what we wanted to learn. Reading horizontally, the rows indicated how and when we were going to try to learn it. The protocol was not devised at the very beginning. First, we had to do some observation and become more familiar with the people and settings. But the protocol was written well before most of the actual data collection. Like many protocols, this one looked forward to the data collection, implied an analysis strategy, and was helpful at the end for analysis and organizing the write-up.

A key part of any observation protocol is to identify and code participant feedback, member checks, or whatever you call reactions to your observations. How much feedback did you use, how did you decide who you would ask to provide it, how was it gathered, and how did you use it? If you have a research or observation protocol, this information should be included in it. Such coding helps the reader judge the value of the member checks[40] and of your methods for obtaining them. Finally, the protocol also helps identify, at least indirectly, where the researcher has had to improvise.

Of course, on a shorter solo-researcher project you would be very unlikely to use anything like the 3-page list employed in our multisite, multiyear evaluation program, but we think it is useful (at least if your memory is as bad as ours) to have some guiding questions and a checklist of things you eventually want to try to observe and learn. Of course, in the early stages, when you are just trying to figure out what to do, you can "wing it" until you are familiar enough with the phenomena to ask intelligent questions. Regardless of whether it is minimal or elaborate, if you have used an observation protocol, it should have a prominent place in your records and thus in your coding. If you are writing a dissertation, your faculty committee members would appreciate it if you

---

[39] See also the examples in Yin (2011, pp. 105–106).

[40] See Chapter 2 for a discussion of member checks in interview research.

would provide something like this; the more explicit you can be, the more constructive feedback the committee members can offer.[41]

In concluding this section on recording, we should point out that none of the preceding suggestions is very relevant to the *quality* of the fieldnotes you construct as your main record or dataset. We have provided many suggestions about when various methods are likely to be helpful in ensuring accuracy. But all that leaves open a different kind of question: What makes some notes vivid and interesting and others dreary chronicles? In other terms, what does it take to be a good writer? If you are engaged in observational research, it could easily be worth your time to take a writing workshop or a journalism course.[42] Talent is part of good writing to be sure, but even the greatest writers have asserted that they had to work hard at it. "Easy reading is damned hard writing," is how Nathaniel Hawthorne put it; he attributed that aphorism to Alexander Pope, who also said that the opposite was true: "Easy writing makes for hard reading." And our favorite: "Excuse me for writing such a long letter; I did not have time to write a short one" (Pascal). Clear, concise writing takes a lot of time, effort, and practice.

PHASE 3: CODING

Some people bristle at the idea that observational data, or any qualitative data, should be coded—and even that the outcome of observational research is in any sense data. We would agree if by coding one meant assigning numbers to observations. But our definition of data coding is broader; it refers to converting your observations into symbols so that you can analyze them. For example, if you take notes on what you have observed, you have had to do some minimal coding by assigning words to phenomena; if you make marginal notes on those notes, you have recoded them. One can call these activities reconceptualizing or rethinking or any of several other terms. We use "code" as a handy shorthand term and mean nothing positivistic or otherwise sinister about it. Usually in observational research coding means nothing other than writing up your observations, generating text. Of course, observational research often also involves collecting texts, such as meeting minutes or other documents, but before documents can be used in analysis, they have to be repurposed or recoded.

The steps from recording to coding can be fairly short and direct, and the distinction between data records and coded data can be less than perfectly clear. For instance, while transcribing into text the audio recording of a conversation, you can insert (in brackets or in the margins) your initial codes. Coding is usually more complicated when you code a videotape of the same conversation. The data are richer, because facial expressions, gestures, and so on are recorded and can be coded.

Coding almost always involves recoding—adjusting your codes as you gain more insight into and familiarity with your data. Furthermore, the observation, recording, and coding are often quite fluid, especially in the early stages. You will have to have some idea of what you are looking for, as guided by your research questions, and those

[41] We owe this observation to one of our anonymous reviewers.

[42] For an excellent account by a veteran journalist of how to structure masses of notes into a coherent narrative, including comparisons of scissors-and-paste (with real scissors and paper) methods versus software, see McPhee (2013).

initial ideas function as precodes, but you will probably change your precodes as you learn more through your explorations. Once you collect your data—fieldnotes, interview transcripts, document collections, photos, videos, and so on—then you'll need to figure out how to code them for analysis. You usually begin with descriptive codes and then start to conceptually code these descriptive codes. Such categorizing of codes, or higher-level coding, is the first truly analytical step and is discussed in Chapter 11.

Another part of coding that is easy to ignore or underestimate stems from the fact that most of the data and the analysis categories are words. Many words have multiple meanings, can mean different things in different contexts,[43] and can have different meanings in ordinary language versus "researcher-speak." You will often have to stipulate what you mean by key terms. Many of the words in your notes will be quotations from your research participants, but their terms might not be the ones you eventually use for coding.[44] One technique for deciding on the definitions of terms to use is to employ the ones most common in your home discipline. But remember, even within a discipline, would-be vocabulary police have often been unsuccessful. For example, *attitude* is defined quite differently by different camps in social psychology. And terms such as *recursive, nested*, and *tolerance* have remarkably different meanings in qualitative and quantitative data analysis.

When you are using particular words as codes and you are sorting your evidence so that it is organized compatibly enough that you can link and think about evidence drawn from many sources, it is crucial that you don't use ambiguous codes. There is a lot of ambiguity in the world, which gives life and language much of their charm, but ambiguity in coding causes big headaches. In our own research and in working with students on dissertations, we have found that analysis problems very often originate in inconsistency in the definitions of the words used for coding and the terms used to describe concepts. If there are words or codes that you use frequently, it is generally a good idea to build a glossary of these. Building the glossary or codebook helps catch inconsistencies of usage and helps your readers when they are uncertain of your meanings. The list of terms in your glossary may not be part of your final research report, but you will probably need it for your analysis.

As with any system of categorization, separate categories or codes should usually be mutually exclusive. An exception occurs when you are coding phenomena using a continuum, such as codes ranging from *extremely* to *not at all*. In that case, however, it is important to know whether you mean the same thing or different things by terms such as *extremely, a great deal*, and *very much*. Variety in word use can make for a pleasing literary style but can lead to confusing research codes. Categorical codes should also be exhaustive, that is, they should cover all phenomena of a certain type. Often you will not observe the full range of types or will not know how to categorize certain observed phenomena. In these circumstances, codes such as *unknown* or *not observed* are indispensable for rounding out the coding scheme and for helping you keep track of what you did not see or do not know. For example, in the observations of the university cafeteria discussed earlier, the social backgrounds of the people interacting at the tables usually could not be determined by the observer. Thus generalizing about any relationships

[43]The classic example is "time flies like an arrow, but fruit flies like bananas."

[44]When you do use their terms, it is sometimes called "in vivo" coding.

between social backgrounds and social interactions were tempered by this missing data, by the fact that some of the codes and categories were empty.

When Should You Use Computer Software for Coding?

Ultimately this is a personal choice. One generalization is that the larger and more complex your study, the more likely computer tools are to be helpful. We avoid making specific software recommendations because these can quickly go out of date.[45] The right software depends on your needs, interests, and budget, so we confine ourselves to a few guidelines that are likely to be generally useful. One generalization is that it is hard to imagine coding data from any moderately complex qualitative research project without using word processing software. Ultimately all data become text. Text files recorded on computer internal and/or external drives are a must. We know people (even people who can type well) who put this step off and work as long as possible with handwritten notes and codes, and there is no harm in that. We usually prefer to get notes into the computer sooner rather than later because even the slowest typist among us can type faster than he can write legibly. Typewritten text is superior because it is easier to read and, more important, because it is easier to rearrange. In most projects on which we have worked, our notes are converted into files in a word processing software program in the early stages of recording data—often well before the systematic coding begins.

We also frequently use tables and grids to organize our data, codes, and ideas about codes. Often we do this using the table options of word processing software, but spreadsheets (such as Excel) and database programs (such as Access) are very helpful when the number of rows and columns is large. We have found spreadsheets very useful when working with data complex enough that the research requires more than a dozen rows and columns and indispensable when the rows and columns cannot possibly be squeezed onto a physical page.[46] When using one of these grid programs, you might designate each row (often called a "record") as an instance of something observed (a day, a place, a person, an event, etc.). Each column would then contain information about that record; for example, if each row is a place, the columns might be the time it was observed, its location, size, shape, purpose, furnishings, and so on. Usually, the rows and columns can be switched depending on what is most convenient for your records on a particular project.

The categories and labels in the rows and columns in grids or matrices for organizing data can take many forms. What you put in rows versus columns depends on your research questions and observation strategies. As an example, here is a brief, simplified extract from a grid used to organize observations at numerous sites over a period of several weeks (see Table 4.1).

The questions the researcher wanted to answer were designated by the row titles. The column titles indicated each observation, as well as where and when it took place. Site 1 was observed three times (on the 18th, the 20th in the morning, and the 20th in the afternoon). Observation 4 was conducted at Site 2. The *X*'s in the cells of the

---

[45] A very useful website that compares several alternatives is the CAQDAS Networking Project at the University of Surrey: *www.surrey.ac.uk/sociology/research/researchcentres/caqdas/support/choosing/*. See also Friese (2006).

[46] Miles and Huberman (1994) provide many suggestions about how to use a matrix for displaying data.

TABLE 4.1. Example of a Data Organizing and Coding Grid

	1 Obs 1, Site 1, 10/18, 1–4 P.M.	2 Obs 2, Site 1, 10/20, 8–11 A.M.	3 Obs 3, Site 1, 10/20, 3–6 P.M.	4 Obs 4, Site 2, 0/23, 1–4 P.M.
Question 1	X	X		X
Question 2	X	X	X	X
Question 3	X	X	X	X
Question 4		X	X	X
Question 5	X	X	X	
Question 6	X (notes)			X
Question 7		X (notes)	X (notes)	X

grid represent answers to the researcher's questions. The blanks indicate that nothing relevant to a question was observed—for example, data relevant to Question 4 was not observed during Observation 1. The researcher began with five questions gleaned from a literature review on the research question. Questions 6 and 7 first occurred to the researcher during Observation 4. She then went back to her notes and was able to find in them information relevant to Question 6 from Observation 1 and relevant to Question 7 from Observations 2 and 3.

Of course, in the actual data grid, unlike in this skeletal extract, the questions were written out, and the cells describing the observations relevant to the questions contained two or three sentences describing each answer. One of the reasons that spreadsheets are preferable to tables drawn by hand or with word processing software is that they are much more flexible in what they can hold and display. The final version of this table, which contained more than 40 columns and 15 rows, would have been unmanageable except maybe on a scroll of butcher paper, but all was neatly displayed and easily searchable on the computer screen. Columns and rows can easily be extracted for separate review and analysis.

The general shape of this grid was determined before the data collection, because the researcher began with five questions based on what was learned in a literature review. More questions were eventually added. The first five questions and categories were decided in advance. The others emerged while engaging in the process of observation. Deciding to use a grid-like data display does not commit you to preparing any questions or categories in advance. You could write the questions or determine themes or categories only after reviewing all the fieldnotes of the observation sessions. You could also decide to put nearly all of your fieldnotes into a data grid, or you could wait until you have done some initial coding and categorizing (which is conceptual coding of descriptive codes) before resorting to the grid.

Another advantage of this kind of coding and display of data is that it makes **missing data** stand out. You might want to go back and make more observations to fill in some important blanks in the grid, or you might want to temper your conclusions because they are based on a limited number of observations relevant to a question or category.

It is important to identify and code missing data not only for your own purposes but also for accurate reporting to your readers about the limitations of your conclusions. If the data are missing because a site became unavailable or withdrew from the study, this is important information, especially if there is a pattern to the missing data that could influence the conclusions of your study.

Ultimately, the most important advantage of this kind of approach is its flexibility. For example, if you decide you want to insert comments and reflections next to the observations, it is an easy matter to insert additional columns for the purpose. Also the spreadsheet grid can be used for organizing and coding data relevant to many kinds of research projects. For example, it is a very effective way to organize information from literature reviews.[47]

The grid in Table 4.1 is a brief extract from a large file that was compiled using spreadsheet software. But when somebody asks the question, "Should I use software for coding my qualitative data?" he or she usually means, "Should I use one of the CAQDAS [computer-assisted qualitative data analysis software] packages?" Several versions of CAQDAS have become available and have been around long enough (since the 1990s) to have been revised and improved numerous times. Some types of combined or mixed method approaches may require using one of the CAQDAS programs when the mixed methods involve devising codes compatible across qualitative and quantitative data.[48]

We know many people who like one of the CAQDAS programs and use them extensively, but we also know quite a few other researchers, not just older colleagues, who do not. The choice often seems to be mainly a matter of personal inclination. For example, one of us still uses handwritten note cards to gather some initial data, especially when extracting data from long documents. His reaction to one type of CAQDAS software was that it was a nifty way of automating the complex process of sorting the note cards but that it took so long to type in all the notes first, to say nothing of the time needed to learn the quirks of the particular brand of software, that it remained quicker to do the initial sorting by hand.

As with quantitative software, so too with qualitative: There is no substitute for in-depth knowledge of your subject matter, using a valid design to collect relevant data, and thinking about it. Software cannot design a good project, determine data relevance, or replace thinking.[49] Indeed, software cannot even write your codes for you. But it can be of great help in organizing your thoughts, and it makes data retrieval and recoding much easier. For example, if you want to mark every place where you have used the code *attitude* in your fieldnotes and see how often those codes coincide with your codes for *intention*, CAQDAS can be very handy, though you might be able to get along well enough using search routines in your word processing software.

Qualitative software allows you to give a chunk of text multiple codes, whereas with nonelectronic methods you would have to rewrite the text multiple times in order to put it in separate piles.

One final suggestion about how to decide about software: If you are planning to follow a career path that involves frequently working on large qualitative data analysis

[47] For a discussion of how this can be done, see Vogt (2007, Ch. 17) and Chapter 5 in this volume.

[48] See Bazeley (2006, 2007). See also Pellegrini (2103, Ch. 12).

[49] Concept mapping is usually most useful comparatively late in the analysis process; software called Cmap-Tools is freely available at *http://cmap.ihme.us*.

projects, it is probably worth the effort to become familiar with one of the major CAQ-DAS packages. But, if you don't expect to be doing much research after you have finished the project you are currently working on, such as a dissertation, it may not be worth the time and money. And we always recommend starting with freeware; in this case the R Qualitative Data Analysis (RQDA) package is a good place to begin. On the other hand, if your university has a site license for a particular software package, which means that you have access to it for free, and if many of your friends and colleagues also use that software, it could be the better choice.

RECOMMENDATIONS

We have two main recommendations. The first is for implementation by researchers conducting studies now. The second is to be pursued by the community of scholars conducting observational research in the future. The two are linked: (1) use multiple coders whenever feasible; (2) study the effects of using different coders and/or different methods of recording data.

Teamwork in Coding

Observational research is probably (we know of no studies of this) the least likely of the main design types to be undertaken as teamwork using multiple coders. Survey, interview, experimental, archival, and multimethod research are all more likely to be conducted by teams of researchers. By contrast, observational fieldwork, coding, and analysis seem more likely to attract solo researchers. We are not sure of the reasons. Perhaps it is tradition, or perhaps it has to do with the difficulty of dividing the research into clear components that can later be assembled. Whatever the reason for the prevalence of the lone researcher in observational research, we think that both immediate and long-term gains are possible by making observational research more social. Just as we recommended more teamwork in the coding of interview research data, we also advocate team coding of observational research data. Such teamwork may be more common in interview research, because working on the same verbatim texts of interview transcripts is quite straightforward.[50]

The reason to use multiple coders is to improve the quality of coding, and that in turn requires consistency or reliability among coders. Most work on consistency among coders has focused on various quantitative indices of agreement.[51] Qualitative approaches to the reliability of coding seem to focus more on working together to reach a consensus rather than measuring the presence or absence of consensus after the fact. But the broad purposes of the two approaches are largely the same. Although solo researchers have been the norm in observational methods, we have found some examples of research teams working together to code and analyze the same data. The emphasis in these teams has mostly been on textual analysis, specifically fieldnotes. One example is ongoing research over a 30-year period begun in the 1970s concerning

[50] A good example is Kurasaki (2000).

[51] A very useful Web source is Lombard, Snyder-Duch, and Bracken (2010).

life on plantations in Brazil.[52] The team members each undertook their own individual projects on the same topic, but they sometimes worked as a team. The most important part of their teamwork was not mainly the ability to have more observations in more places but the opportunity to have more analytical resources for coding and interpreting the fieldnotes.

A second example of the advantages of teamwork, which again were especially salient in constructing and interpreting fieldnotes, occurred in the process of agreeing on the text of the notes and their interpretations. The work of constructing, coding, and interpreting the fieldnotes was performed by several researchers. It was fully as arduous as constructing the original notes had been in the first place.[53] But the benefits in terms of understanding the topic (special schools in a British city) seemed worth the effort.

If the improvements in quality of the coding and analysis that resulted in these two studies are typical of what can be achieved, and we suspect that they are, this gives support to the recommendation for more teamwork. By extension, it leads to concerns about the value of research that relies only on one person's interpretations. Interpretation is difficult. It can be facilitated when a research team treats the problem of coding and interpreting data as a common goal. This approach can increase the extent to which research on social topics is addressed by social groups of researchers. Differences in interpretation among researchers on the team can become a resource that can lead to better quality research.

Eventually, your notes become "objective" in the sense that they could be analyzed by someone other than yourself; they do not depend only on your personal or "subjective" experience. Even your personal reflections will often come to be examined by you with some objective distance. Can you analyze someone else's notes? Can a colleague code and analyze yours? We think such collegial work is possible and desirable.

On the other hand, when using multiple coders, the "Rashomon problem" can arise, in which different observers see, describe, and code the same event in contradictory ways.[54] And we have encountered examples in which different coders were unable to reach consensus. However, when multiple coders work together to devise a common coding scheme, the Rashomon problem might become the Rashomon opportunity to create something better. We conclude with some research we would like to see to illustrate how a problem can be a solution. Our message, in brief, is: *Observers, observe yourselves.*

Future Research Topics

How much do the differences in observations and codings vary with different observers and recording methods? One type of research we would like to see is systematic observation by observers of themselves and of other observers. For example, one team of researchers[55] compared three approaches to the study of work: participant observation, nonparticipant observation, and offsite interviews. They made their comparisons by

---

[52] Sigaud (2008).

[53] Creese et al. (2008).

[54] The name comes from the classic Japanese film *Rashomon*, by Akira Kurosawa.

[55] Tope et al. (2005).

reviewing the research literature on the subject. Although they saw advantages to each approach, they concluded that participant observation had the highest "information yield."

Studies based on systematic observations of differences in methods of data collection and recording could even be experimental. Experiments need not be quantitative; they could, rather, use a type of focus group discussion of different observations and how they varied by technology and types of observers. One such approach to conducting research on observational research is suggested by the study, mentioned earlier, that used audio and video recordings of mothers interacting with their daughters while the daughters worked at computers. The researcher observed her own observing and determined that she could see some interactions better with the sound turned off; she also sometimes could hear certain verbal interchanges (tones of voice) better when only listening to the audio portion and not looking at the video. This was one set of observations by one observer. We would like to see more systematic research on the possibilities opened by separately observing each component of an audiovisual tape, as well as observing them together. How is coding influenced by looking only at the video or by listening only to the audio, and how do they differ from using the full audio–video recording? Are there differences by type of coder? There will surely be individual differences; for example, gender of coders might matter for some topics, such as the one that triggered this proposal—mothers interacting with their daughters. Investigations of methodological questions such as these could easily become an important subfield in observational research.

CONCLUSIONS AND TIPS FOR COMPLETING AN OBSERVATIONAL STUDY

As in the other chapters in Part I, we conclude with suggestions about where in this book to seek advice about effective analysis techniques. Methods for analyzing data from observational research are discussed in Chapter 11 for mainly inductive approaches and in Chapter 12 for more deductive approaches. The descriptive and exploratory methods for qualitative/categorical data analysis methods, discussed in Chapter 6, are likely to be helpful on many observational projects. We wind up this chapter with a discussion of some barriers to completing a study based on observational research. This provides a review of some of what we have said in this chapter (recapitulated in the summary table at the end of the chapter) and helps provide a transition to the chapters on analysis.

In our experience, people often have trouble finishing a big observational research project, such as a dissertation. Getting into the field and making observations is not usually the source of problems with completion, although it is easy to underestimate how much time and effort fieldwork can take. The more serious stumbling blocks have to do with knowing what to do with your observations once they have been made. What steps do you take in order to turn observations into a research article or dissertation? Because there are comparatively few agreed-upon routine steps for coding and analyzing data from field observations, researchers often encounter barriers along the way that are hard to surmount. They get stuck; they have to devise their own coding and analysis steps; they confront obstacles that are in part psychological and that in part stem from a shortage of agreed-upon "recipes." The three main points at which impediments to completion are likely to be encountered are (1) turning your recollections, jottings, photos, and so on into full fieldnotes; (2) deciding how to code these notes at the end of fieldwork; (3) analyzing the coded fieldnotes so that you can interpret your observational experiences and write up a research report. In our own work and in working with students and other colleagues, we have found that all three of these barriers stem from a tendency to underestimate how hard it is to turn observations into data that can be analyzed—and then to analyze them. The third of these roadblocks is discussed in Chapter 11. Here we focus on the first two.

From Observation to Fieldnotes

Observations and records of observations, such as notes and recordings (audio and video), are almost always incomplete and not fully compatible. You have jotted down a few lines but don't quite remember what they meant, parts of the audio recordings are inaudible, the lighting was poor during some parts of the video recording, and a few key events occurred off camera. If you are to have any hope of tying together these disparate records, you must do it very soon after the observations so that you can fill in the blanks with memories. Memories fade quickly. Those that don't fade become unreliable.

After you have made the first draft of fieldnotes as complete as you can make them, they are still largely undigested. You are still writing mainly for description rather than to prepare the notes for interpretation. After an exhausting day or week of field observations, it is hard to realize that the really difficult work still lies ahead. That really difficult work is, in a word, writing. When questioned about the keys to their success, well-known writers agree on one main point: In order to get any writing done, you have to schedule time to do it. "Well, duh," you might say. But writing time can be very difficult to schedule, especially for busy, socially active people, the kinds of people drawn to observational research. Scheduling writing time can be very different from scheduling other kinds of activities. It requires that you abstract yourself from the world so that you can deal with the abstractions that are words, concepts, and codes.

People (friends, partners, spouses, colleagues at work) who don't do much writing may not understand why you need to block out time, and to block them out, so that you can do this work. Most students and colleagues we know who have had trouble getting their writing done are busy people who are determined that, as soon as they get some free time, they will devote it to their writing—but they never quite get some free time, or, when they do, like everyone else, they have to devote some of it to rest and recreation, not writing. To schedule or to plan is to *make* time. Writers need to decide, for example, that on Tuesday, Thursday, and Saturday mornings they will not check their e-mail, answer the phone, agree to attend any meetings, or have coffee with friends. That kind of regularity is often impossible, but some approach to determining fixed time in advance is required. Put writing and coding your fieldnotes on your calendar or in your planner so that it does not look to you or to others as though you have nothing scheduled.

Coding the Initial Fieldnotes

The first phase of coding is managing your records or evidence; the second phase is getting the records ready for analysis. Initially, your fieldnotes will be organized by types of evidence, such as jottings in situ, audio recordings, photos, photocopied documents, notes on documents you've reviewed, and so on. They will also initially be organized by the times and places that the notes and other records were made. To analyze all this, you need to make the transition from organizing by types of evidence (jots on the spot, audiotapes, etc.) and by time and space (Wednesday morning in the break room) to topics, categories, and themes. This is very intellectually demanding work because it involves sorting through a lot of different kinds of materials and because the categories have to emerge out of or be imposed upon recalcitrant data. The topics often "sort of" fit but not quite; sometimes it's hard to tell categories from subcategories, and you have to reorganize and re-reorganize your notes and categories without losing data. It is demanding and often frustrating work that is particularly hard to do without support. Schoolwork can rarely be teamwork—mostly because the grading and credentialing system is focused on ranking the work of individuals working unaided—but sharing ideas (and complaints and tears) with colleagues and fellow students is one good way around these barriers.

One approach to taming seemingly uncontrollable problems with coding is to realize that coding texts such as fieldnotes and interview transcripts is little more than **indexing**. The basic techniques of indexing are almost as old as the written word. Ancient Babylonian, Greek, and Roman libraries all had reliable indexing systems. And modern nonfiction books have indices that serve as guides to readers wanting to search the book for particular topics. Most of what you need to do with your notes can be greatly facilitated using nothing more complicated than the "find" or "search" or "find and replace" commands in your word processing software. As you read your notes, insert descriptive words (or short phrases) near passages you want to be able to find. Make these preliminary codes distinct in some way: for example, caps, italics, or underlining.

Your initial codes will come from your research questions; the concepts in the research questions constitute the first broad codes. As you add more detailed codes, try to organize these in some sort of logical way. This can be done by thinking in terms of a taxonomy, a concept map, or an index: Smaller topics are subsumed under bigger ones. As we suggested for coding survey data, make a two-column list or table. In the first column put your research questions' concepts and codes; in the second insert the observations you have made that are relevant to these concepts and codes. If you have observations without codes, add the codes. If you have codes without observations, delete the codes or make more observations.

The goal in coding and indexing is to make searching your own notes no more complicated than the electronic searches you conducted for your literature review. In the literature review the codes were the key words. With interview transcripts, most of the text in which you search will have come from the interviewees; your words will be added as index terms or codes, and it is helpful if these codes are distinct in some way, perhaps by employing terms that are not often used in ordinary discourse. With fieldnotes, most of the words will be yours; to these you add index terms (codes or key words). The idea behind the coding/indexing process tends to be clear in concept, but it requires painstaking attention. We have found that the more systematic our efforts—the more we use grids, lists, schedules, and so on—the easier it is for us to turn an ordeal requiring huge intellectual and psychological resources into some modest tasks that can be managed one at a time.

Appendix 4.1. Example of a Site Visit Protocol

Project Name: ______________________

	Establish initial understandings ↔		Fill out and elaborate understandings ↔		
	Background		**Fieldwork**		
Collaborative Elements ↓	*Proposal*	*Telephone Interview*	*Observation(s)*	*Documents/Artifacts*	*Interviews*
Structure—General • ***Entities:*** Who are the collaborating institution(s), district(s), and school(s)? What are the internal and external connections among them? What connecting structures exist? • ***People:*** Who are the people involved from each entity? Who is connected to whom? • ***Hierarchy:*** What are the levels of decision making and authority? • ***Sociogram:*** Map the structures and interactions among entities and people.	Use the proposal to create the initial identification of entities, people, and relationships. Create initial sociogram.	Clarify and verify the sociogram information. Indicate any new information not included in the proposal.	Document observations of project structures (sociogram elements).	• Project organizational charts • Participant lists • Project brochures, handouts, and Web pages	Document collaborators' views of project structures.
Structure—Roles and Relationships • Who plays key roles within the collaborative? (e.g., trainers, participants, designers, consultants, decision makers) • Who are "boundary spanners"? • Who is getting paid to do what? • Who is not paid but critical to the project work?	Use the proposal to create initial list of key players, boundary spanners, paid and unpaid players.	Clarify lists of players and roles.	Observe various players and document their respective roles.	• Project budget (who gets paid for what?) • Job descriptions • Project brochures, handouts, and Web pages	Document key players' views of roles and relationships.
Structure—Rules and Expectations • What are the formal rules governing the collaborative and its activities? • How did the formal rules evolve? Were they developed among the partners or unilaterally?	Use the proposal to create an initial list of formal project rules.	Clarify formal rules and inquire about informal rules and behavioral norms.	Observe partner activities and document the presence, use, and	• Policy manual • Meeting handouts • Financial agreements • Memoranda of Understanding	Document key players' views of the formal and informal

• What are the informal rules and behavioral norms? How are these developed and adopted?			effects of formal and informal rules.	• Subcontracts • Individual contracts • Space arrangements/ agreements • Accountability requirements • Reports/audits	rules and norms.
Structure—Resources • ***Financial***: How does the money flow (e.g., top down, shared among partners)? How financially dependent is this collaborative upon the Title II funds? Are other financial resources being put to use? • ***In-kind***: What other types of resources are being donated to the collaborative by the partners? How are they being used? • ***Knowledge:*** Which type of model is operating: dependent (one-way knowledge flow), independent (self-directed), or interdependent (reciprocal—one cannot occur without the other)?	Use the proposal to create initial lists of financial, in-kind, and knowledge resources and how they are being applied.	Clarify and verify initial resource lists.	Observe the actual use of financial, in-kind, and knowledge resources during project activities. Document how the knowledge model is operating.	• Project budget • Subcontracts • Activity descriptions • Project brochures and handouts • Time and effort charts	Document key players' views of the project's resource networks. Document key players' views of the knowledge model, its features, and its effects.
Processes—Prehistory • What kinds of relationships existed among the collaborators prior to this project? • Sociogram: What did the preproject sociogram look like? What differs from the current sociogram? • What happened to create the current sociogram?	Use the proposal to glean any available information about the prehistory of the project.	Gather additional information about prehistory from the project director.	Document any observable remnants (operating or vestigial) from the project's prehistory.	• Historical descriptions • Prior grant proposals (some may be in Eisenhower archives) • Historical partnership agreements	Document key players' knowledge and views about the project's prehistory.

(continued)

Collaborative Elements ↓	*Proposal*	*Telephone Interview*	*Observation(s)*	*Documents/ Artifacts*	*Interviews*
Processes—Current • ***Planning:*** What current processes operate in the project related to planning? • ***Decision making***: How are decisions made within the project? • ***Implementation:*** How are project processes (e.g., activities, interactions, communication, data collection, modifications) occurring? • ***Institutionalization:*** What processes are occurring that lead to (or have the potential to lead to) sustained action?	Use the proposal to determine the intended planning, decision making, implementation, and institutionalization processes. ***Use rubric for this section***. →	Gather additional information about intended and actual planning, decision making, implementation, and institutionalization processes.	Document observable planning, decision making, implementation, and institutionalization processes	• Meeting agendas • Decision documents • Activity records • Communication records • Collected data • Project revisions	Document key players' views of how current processes are occurring.
Processes—Future What plans does the project have for continuing and improving current processes?	Use the proposal to determine projected future project processes.	Gather information regarding future project processes.	Document observable examples of future process continuation and improvement.	• Planning docs • Vision statements • Additional grant proposals • Other contributions	Document key players' views of future project processes.
Goals, Outcomes, and Measures • ***Goals:*** What are the project goals? • ***Outcomes***: What are the intended outcomes for each goal? • ***Measures:*** How are project goals and outcomes being measured? Are the measures adequate to determine project effects? • ***Evaluation:*** To what extent does the evaluation plan include both formative evaluation related to processes and summative evaluation related to outcomes? Is the plan adequate to provide feedback to the project participants and accountability information for the Illinois Board of Higher Education?	Use the proposal to determine intended goals, outcomes, and measures. **Coordinate with program evaluator and individual project evaluators. →	Gather additional information and clarification regarding goals, outcomes, and measures.	Document observable occasions at which goals, outcomes, and measures are discussed and utilized.	• Databases • Reports • Project records	Document key players' views of goals, outcomes, and measures.

SUGGESTIONS FOR FURTHER READING

A good way to learn about research methods, regardless of the design, is to read and study classics in the field. This seems to us especially sound advice when it comes to observational research, including the often underdescribed and underanalyzed processes of coding observational data. Some of our favorites are Erving Goffman's *Asylums*, Kyle Erikson's *Everything in its Path*, Michèle Lamont's *Money, Morals, and Manners*, and Mitchel Duneier's two works, *Slim's Table* and *Sidewalk*.

Among texts and reference books, some of the best are Miles and Huberman's and Anthony Pellegrini's. If you had to confine yourself to using only one "how-to" book to guide you through the intricacies of qualitative coding and analysis, what would it be? Our choice would be Miles and Huberman's *Qualitative Data Analysis: An Expanded Sourcebook*. Few books that old (2nd ed., 1994) have had as much staying power.

Pellegrini's *Observing Children in Their Natural Worlds* (3rd ed., 2013) is quite thorough for a fairly short "methodological primer." Although focused on observational studies of children, it has much broader implications. Especially relevant for coding observational research are his chapters on "Choosing a Perspective" and on "Coming Up with Categories."

Finally, *The Craft of Research* by Booth, Colomb, and Williams (1995) contains just about every hint, tip, or suggestion about good research writing we have ever made to our students and quite a few that had not occurred to us. The recommendations are organized in a marvelously clear way—uncommonly clear and accessible to teachers of research writing and to their students.

CHAPTER 4 SUMMARY TABLE

CODING AT THE OBSERVATIONAL STAGE	
Research questions (pp. 108–109)	• Your first codes are the concepts in your research question(s). • Does your question lead to building a theory or assessing one? The answer will lead to different sites, times, and types of observation.
Your role as a researcher (pp. 109–113)	• Will you be a passive observer or a participant observer? Will your research role be open or covert? How do these roles interact and evolve? The answers will determine what you can observe and code.

CODING WHILE RECORDING	
First steps in note taking (pp. 115–116)	• Jot a few notes while observing, if this can be done without interfering with the phenomena you are observing.
Descriptive notes and early codes (pp. 116–117)	• Focus on notes and codes that help you remember the broader set of events; record these as soon as possible.
Organizing and culling notes (pp. 117–119)	• Chronologies are good aids to memory. • Remember that the notes are ultimately being made and prepared for a broader community of researchers.
Technologies of recording (pp. 119–120)	• Visual records are easier to make than ever before, but are still comparatively underused.
Transition from recording to coding (p. 120)	• Start by keeping good records. Codes begin to emerge out of date, time, and place records. • Be sure to observe yourself as an observer, and record those observations.
When to use an observation protocol (pp. 121–122)	• The greater the size and complexity of the research project, the greater the need for a list of topics and questions that you want to address.

CODING FIELDNOTES	
Basics (pp. 122–124)	• Classifying and labeling phenomena effectively requires consistency in the use of codes. • Often codes/categories need to be mutually exclusive and exhaustive.

Using software (pp. 124–127)	• It is almost impossible to proceed without word processing software. Spreadsheets can be equally important. • CAQDAS is optional, and opinions about its importance vary. Investigate by starting with freeware.
RECOMMENDATIONS	
Teamwork in coding (pp. 127–128)	• Multiple coders can improve the quality of coding. • Teamwork in coding allows observers to observe their thought processes.
Future research on observation (pp. 128–129)	• Investigations of methodological questions based on observers observing themselves and others as they observe should become an important subfield in observational research.
CONCLUSIONS AND TIPS FOR SUCCESS	
From observation to notes (p. 130)	• Make time for writing and coding.
Coding the initial notes (pp. 130–131)	• Compare codes and observations. • Make sure there are codes for each important observation and observations for each important code.

CHAPTER 5

Coding Archival Data

Literature Reviews, Big Data, and New Media

In this chapter we discuss what constitutes archival research and outline its main types: reviews of the research literature, big data, and new media. Each is discussed in a separate section. Highlights are provided at the start of each.

Archival data, in the classic definition, has neither been paid for nor created by the researcher.[1] Therefore, coding archival data is almost always recoding or reclassifying; often, it is coding secondary data, which have been previously coded in another way. When you generate your own data, you do so in ways designed to answer your research question, and you code them accordingly. But the data in an archive were not assembled with your research question in mind, for the obvious reason that those data were assembled before that question entered your mind. Data assembled by others, for purposes other than yours, will have to be rearranged and recoded so that it can be used to accomplish your goals. And if your research question requires measurement as an important part of your task, you will usually have to construct the measurement criteria and methods to fit the type of data with which you are working. Of course, the details of your recoding and measurement will vary with the type of archive, depending on whether it is, for example, an oral history archive, a newspaper archive, a set of institutional records, a collection of research articles to review, a statistical database, or a network of social media messages.

This is a long chapter for one reason: The topic is huge. The quantity of archival data is extraordinarily large. Archival data easily outweigh the total data generated by researchers conducting surveys, interviews, experiments, and naturalistic/participant observations. What is the scope of archival data? To borrow from taxonomy, the family of archival research, which consists of data not generated by the researcher using it, is composed of three genera that we examine here—literature reviews, big data, and new media. Each genus contains several species, and we address, at least briefly, several of the main species of each genus. Because the chapter is long and because the topic is large, we were tempted to break it into three separate chapters but decided instead that

[1] Other terms for archival research include *ex post facto research* and *observational research*.

it was better to keep the family together—much as we discussed the separate species of experiments (randomized controlled trials [RCTs], natural, quasi-, longitudinal, single-case, etc.) in one chapter. Discussing different types of archival data in one chapter allows us to focus on common issues and themes in coding them.

The coding of archival research is shaped both by the specific genus or type of archive and by the researchers' purposes as encapsulated in their research questions. Each genus is reviewed in a section of the chapter: (1) reviewing the research literature; (2) using big data, including textual data[2] and database archives; and (3) mining the new media, especially Web sources such as blogs and social networking sites. Each type of archive contains different kinds of data and therefore each raises somewhat unique coding problems. But they overlap in many ways.

Unless the archival data are a mere heap, they will already be arranged in some order (chronological, alphabetical, etc.), and that will help you find the particular data of interest to you. Disorganized heaps exist, and sometimes they are very important,[3] but they are comparatively rare. Most often you can use the organizational scheme of those who created the data to help you with your sorting and coding. Your first coding step will usually involve a qualitative sorting of the data by relevance, often into two or three categories—*yes, no, maybe*. Such initial coding is parallel to sampling. It is all but universal, but it varies considerably with the types of archival data with which you are working. We now turn to a consideration of those types.

REVIEWS OF THE RESEARCH LITERATURE

In this section we discuss:

- Types of literature reviews
  - Introductory and investigatory reviews
  - Traditional and/or narrative reviews
  - Theoretical reviews
  - Systematic reviews or research synthesis
  - Meta-analysis
  - Meta-synthesis
- Features of good coding for all types of literature review
- Coding in meta-analysis
  - Additional/Advanced topics in coding meta-analyses
    - Changes in scales or coding and measurement practices
    - Using multiple coders
    - Fixed-effect or random effects models
    - Summing results from multivariate studies
    - Biases in primary sources
- A note on software for literature reviews

[2]Not all textual data would qualify as big data, but we focus on big textual data here, in large part because we have discussed methods for coding textual data on a smaller scale elsewhere—in Chapters 2, 4, and 11.

[3]Guzmán (2011).

In our companion volume, *When to Use What Research Design*,[4] we discussed approaches to sampling in reviews of the research literature, including meta-analyses, and the kinds of samples different approaches were likely to yield. In this chapter, we assume you have a good plan for collecting the literature you plan to analyze or perhaps have even collected most of it. Now you want to know how to code it to prepare for the analysis. You will be coding the work of others, often recoding for your purposes what they had coded for theirs.

What you code and how you code it depends importantly on your purposes for conducting the review. One common distinction is whether the purpose of your review is to analyze evidence to guide practice or to guide future research. To guide practice, for so-called **evidence-based practice**, you want to focus on research findings that are fairly certain, that is, on what is *known*. To guide future basic research, you might be mainly interested in what is *unknown*, such as gaps in knowledge, unexamined variables, neglected populations, and so on. Generally, the sources you focus on and how you code the data in them are determined about equally by your goals in writing the review and by the nature of your sources. The two—goals and sources—interact with and shape one another in your research project.

Types of Literature Reviews

Descriptions of methods for coding reviews of the research literature are dominated by discussions of techniques appropriate for meta-analysis. The reason is that meta-analysis is the most developed (even algorithmic) set of methods for literature reviews. What is true of meta-analysis can sometimes be a guide for other types of review, but often meta-analytic techniques are not directly applicable. What types of literature reviews are there? Lists of types differ, and so do their labels. We discuss four types: (1) introductory and investigatory, (2) traditional and/or narrative, (3) theoretical, and (4) systematic review or research synthesis. The fourth type is divided into two major subtypes, quantitative and qualitative approaches, specifically, meta-analyses and meta-syntheses. It is important to realize that following a particular approach is a choice. One's choices are not limitless, but neither are they wholly determined by the sources. For example, it is possible to review the same set of sources using the approach of a traditional narrative review, a theoretical review, or a research synthesis. Your choice will be shaped by your purposes and your research question. And that choice will, in turn, importantly influence the type of coding that is appropriate.

Introductory and Investigatory Reviews

This type of review is usually appropriate only for researchers who are working on a topic for the first time. The review often includes introductory works, such as encyclopedia entries and textbooks, as well as a few well-known or classic research articles. For an introductory review we suggest that you use the three following criteria for selecting and coding sources. They can be important for any review, but they are especially helpful in an introductory review. The more closely these three criteria can be followed in an introductory review, the better:

[4] Vogt et al. (2012).

- *Recency.* Your review should be based on up-to-date, not antiquated, sources. When finding sources through electronic searches, you might sort citations by date and work backward, starting with the most current. Recent sources can be a good guide to the older sources that they cite.

- *Importance.* Your review should be built on important, not obscure or marginal, sources. Importance, or at least influence, could be determined by the number of citations the source has received or the journal's "impact" rating. Both of these can be investigated with Google resources. *Google Scholar Metrics* can be used to gauge a journal's popularity as measured by how frequently articles in the journal are cited. An article's popularity can be ascertained by entering the article's name into Google Scholar, which will then provide the number of works that have cited the article, as well as their citations (and, not infrequently, a link to a pdf copy). Some researchers think that Thomson Reuters's resources are better. Having used both, we think the verdict is unclear.[5]

- *Breadth.* When your time for reviewing is limited, include existing sources that discuss your topic broadly, not narrowly. One of the best sources for this kind of breadth is other literature reviews. You can and should use previous reviews of the literature on your topic when you write your own review. Then you would be reviewing reviews, which is not as unusual as it might sound.

There usually is little coding involved in an introductory review, such as a class project in which you review 10 sources on a topic, because there is seldom enough data to code. We do not discuss this type of review further except to say that the more it can approximate one of the other types discussed here, the better it is likely to be.

Traditional and/or Narrative Reviews

This term is mostly a residual category that includes everything that is not one of the other types. Like most residual categories, it is defined negatively and is not very helpful. For many writers, what makes a review "traditional" is the absence of an organized, prespecified searching and sampling plan. What makes it "narrative" is the absence of quantitative techniques for summarizing the data. *Traditional* also usually suggests "out of date," but the traditional review remains very common and important. It probably still is the type of review most often conducted by degree seekers writing dissertations and theses in the social sciences. Another place to see traditional reviews is in the introductory paragraphs of a typical research article, in which a brief narrative about previous research on a subject might be used to set the context for the research reported in the article.[6]

What coding methods are good for this type of review? The steps are fairly obvious, but that does not mean they are easy:

---

[5]The Thomson Reuters/ISI resources are proprietary and not cheap, although the costs may often be borne by your university; Google Scholar's resources are, of course, free. See van Aalst (2010) on Google Scholar; on the validity of citation counts compared across disciplines, see Najman and Hewitt (2003).

[6]Some journals (e.g., *Lancet*) require that to introduce your original research you must cite a research synthesis or conduct one of your own.

1. Read broadly and deeply on a topic, think while doing it, and take good notes.
2. Then proceed as with fieldnotes (see Chapter 4): Review your notes and thoughtfully take more notes on the notes until you feel able to draw some conclusions.

Traditional narrative reviewers could presumably use techniques of coding developed for textual analysis methods and perhaps those developed in grounded theory, but this is not often done. As always, our recommendations for choosing methods are based on extant methods, and the existing choices specifically tailored for traditional/narrative literature reviews are meager. The best guidelines are probably those developed for other kinds of textual data, such as interview transcripts and fieldnotes (see Chapters 2 and 4).[7] Another recommendation for traditional reviewing is to find a few good reviews, ones that you think are particularly effective, and emulate their methods. We give some sources subsequently.

Although criticized as biased and antiquated, the traditional/narrative review persists and remains influential. One reason is that obtaining broad knowledge of a field through traditional reading and thinking is usually a necessary preamble to conducting a meta-analysis or systematic review.[8] Despite the fact that it is widespread, we do not discuss the traditional/narrative review extensively here because the methodological literature is mostly silent on this type of review—except to criticize it and recommend against it. That is a shortcoming of the methodological literature. Researchers conducting extensive traditional reviews often engage in a great deal of coding by classifying the findings they review, but there is little guidance in the research or textbook literature about how to do so. Very often writers begin from scratch using their own methods derived from thinking about examples of reviews they have read and considered persuasive.

Theoretical Reviews

Theoretical reviews are not usually featured in lists of types of literature reviews, but they constitute a very important subtype. Most commonly the theoretical review is a version of a traditional or narrative review, but with the specific purpose either of *synthesizing* previous theories or of *generating* new ones. Thus there are two types of theoretical reviews. The first focuses on understanding, synthesizing, and critiquing other theories, as when a social or political theorist reviews the works of other theorists. The second type involves reviewing empirical studies on a topic with the goal of identifying and devising a new explanation (theory) of empirical phenomena. Of course, these two types can be combined, but usually in practice one or the other approach is emphasized. Theories do not drop from the sky into the minds of theorists, nor do they emerge fully developed from your head like Athena from the head of Zeus. Theories are based on research, and that research is usually one form or another of literature review. Examples of these kinds of literature reviews, which use coding in the technical sense of the term,

---

[7] On content analysis more broadly, see Krippendorff (2004).

[8] This link between the traditional and the systematic is discussed in detail by Jesson, Matheson, and Lacey (2011).

are mostly conducted by scholars working in the field of comparative social and political analysis.[9]

Both theoretical and traditional reviews are much more common than one might believe were one to base one's judgment on textbook guidelines. Indeed, several highly prestigious journals and annuals specialize in publishing them. Reviews in these journals and annuals provide many examples of good practice that one would do well to consult in planning to conduct a traditional or a theoretical review. For example, *Annual Reviews* is a nonprofit company that publishes volumes of reviews in a wide variety of fields, including several in the social and behavioral sciences, specifically in anthropology, economics, political science, psychology, and sociology. Review articles in these annuals are invited, and the authors are well-respected authorities in their fields. When new developments in a subject occur, the subject is often re-reviewed. Although these reviews tend to be very systematic, they are not "systematic reviews" in the strict sense of the term (see the next section). Rather, they are narrative and/or theoretical reviews, which are often important and influential contributions to a field and thus are widely read by its practitioners. The publications offered by *Annual Reviews* are probably the best known, but there are other outlets for narrative and theoretical reviews, such as the *Review of Educational Research* and the *Journal of Economic Literature*. Such journals often deal with broader topics than do other journals.[10] For example, one widely discussed review of 21 books on the causes of the financial crisis of 2008 was published in the *Journal of Economic Literature*. The topic is obviously an important one, but the sources reviewed were not the kind most amenable to synthesizing in a meta-analysis—typically, an experiment with one dependent variable that can be summarized with a mean difference effect size.[11]

Systematic Reviews or Research Syntheses

These two terms are almost synonyms, but there is a difference in emphasis in how they are used. **Systematic review** is used frequently to refer to evidence-based practical applications, whereas **research synthesis** more often refers to basic research that is not necessarily tied to practical applications. They are similar in that the chief feature of both is that the researcher states in advance the procedures for finding, selecting, coding, and analyzing the data. Meta-analyses are a subtype: Meta-analyses are reviews/syntheses that use quantitative methods to summarize and analyze quantitative data. Meta-syntheses take the same approach to research sources reporting qualitative data.

META-ANALYSIS

More is written about coding and analysis for purposes of meta-analysis than any of the other types of literature review. In a meta-analysis the results of primary research studies on a specific topic are coded so that the findings can be pooled in a secondary

---

[9]See Ragin (2008); Rihoux and Ragin (2009); George and Bennett (2005).

[10]Two other journals specializing in this type of review are the *Psychological Review* and the *Journal of Family Theory and Review*.

[11]Lo (2012).

analysis and interpretation of the topic. Specific *quantitative* methods have been developed to code and meta-analyze quantitative research studies. The basic idea is to use a standardized **effect size** (ES) with which you can compare results across studies and/or average results of several studies to come up with an overall effect size. ES statistics come in several forms, and the ones that are most appropriate for the sources you are studying depend a great deal on how the primary studies report their results and whether, if needed, you can recode these reports. We discuss these topics in a separate section because the available discussions of coding for meta-analysis are extensive.

META-SYNTHESIS

Meta-synthesis is probably the most common term used to describe attempts by researchers to conduct systematic reviews of *qualitative* data. We use the term here generically to cover other labels, including meta-ethnography, qualitative meta-analysis, and qualitative research synthesis. Progress in developing methods for coding and analyzing qualitative data from literature reviews has been quite modest, at least if we define progress as agreement among researchers. And there is much controversy among researchers in the field of meta-synthesis on basic methodological principles and techniques. There is controversy in the field of meta-analysis, too, but it usually is built on a foundation of broad agreement about basic principles; disputes tend to be about recently developed specialized and advanced techniques. In other words, quantitative meta-analyzers are working within a common paradigm. But qualitative meta-synthesizers have not come to the same level of consensus.

Although one can disagree about whether following a paradigm is progress, it is clear that researchers reviewing qualitative studies have not reached consensus on a set of coding and analysis methods for meta-synthesis. Guidelines and taxonomies have been suggested by various scholars, but none seem persuasive enough to convince many other researchers to use them. In one study surveying 16 years of published reports in peer-reviewed journals in health and health care, the authors were able to retrieve only 42 qualitative syntheses; they found little consensus about important issues. And they could not even agree among themselves about what issues were in fact important or even what counted as "qualitative."[12] In light of this lack of a disciplinary consensus and the consequent difficulty novice researchers have in finding coding and analytical guidance for meta-syntheses, we offer two suggestions.

We suggest that researchers conducting meta-syntheses consider adapting one of two well-developed methods of coding and analyzing qualitative data. These are grounded theory (GT) and qualitative comparative analysis (QCA). Doing so has many potential advantages: Each comes with a methodological tool kit, and each is supported by a virtual community of scholars discussing and debating appropriate methods and techniques. The two methods are quite distinct. GT is very inductive in that it approaches and emphasizes coding data and building theories from the ground up. One advantage of GT for this purpose is that its methods and terminology are already familiar to many researchers; indeed, many researchers have borrowed the terminology of GT without following the methods very closely. QCA is more deductive in that it works best when

[12]Dixon-Woods et al. (2006) and Dixon-Woods, Booth, and Sutton (2007) demonstrate this in the course of thorough reviews of qualitative syntheses in health care research.

you have a preliminary theory to test. One attraction of QCA for literature reviewers is that it is built on Boolean logic, which has long been widely employed for searching citation databases and which is very well suited to categorical/qualitative data. For details, see Chapters 11 (for GT) and 12 (for QCA). For the earlier phases of qualitative data coding, before applying the analysis methods of GT and QCA, see Chapters 2 and 4 for coding interview transcripts and fieldnotes, respectively. We make these suggestions as a way of providing guidelines because, as researchers in the field have noted, "no firm meta-synthesis guidelines exist."[13]

Features of Good Coding for All Types of Literature Reviews

Despite the great differences among types of literature reviews, the processes for effective coding in literature reviews are based on some common principles. We discuss these under five headings: relevance, redundancy, role, quality, and diversity.

Relevance

The first issue is sorting the research literature for *relevance* to your research question. What literature should you include? This initial coding, in which you decide whether a particular research report should be included in your review, is at the outset a question of identifying a population and selecting or sampling from it. Although much of the sorting will already have been done at the sampling stage, the processes of selection, rejection, and classification of sources are hardly ever one-time tasks. For example, you might find publications on your topic that are not actually research articles reporting original results. They might be opinion pieces or policy briefs that report the research of others in support of a position. These should be treated differently from reports of primary research. Or you might find that a research article that you initially decided (based on the key words and the abstract) was relevant to your subject is not really on your topic. This can happen in several ways, one of which occurs when the research literature contains sharply different concepts or definitions of a variable or a term. For example, studies of tolerance sometimes focus on putting up with crime and deviance; thus, in the National Youth Survey, a respondent with a high tolerance score thinks it's OK to steal, destroy others' property, and so on. Other studies of the "same" concept, tolerance, investigate social conditions that encourage respect for the rights of others, such as their freedom of expression. If you did a search using the key term *tolerance*, you would find examples of both: *contempt* for and *respect* for the rights of others.[14]

In addition to different phenomena being given the same name in the research literature, the same phenomenon can be given different names. This makes it difficult,

[13]The quotation is from Finfgeld (2003). Several frameworks for qualitative research syntheses have been offered, but we found insufficient agreement among them to allow us to extract a general set of guidelines. For those who wish to read further, we recommend Zhao (1991), which is a frequently cited and somewhat pioneering taxonomy, and the more recent overview of 177 studies by Major and Savin-Baden (2011), which recommends a constructionist approach. And for one more good effort to tackle the problem of generating common qualitative standards for literature reviews, see McCormick, Rodney, and Varcoe (2007).

[14]For examples, see, respectively, Raudenbush and Chan (1992) and Avery, Bird, Johnstone, Sullivan, and Thalhammer (1992); these two studies of adolescents' beliefs use very different definitions of the same key term. Tolerance is defined in other ways as well; see Vogt and Johnson (2011, p. 401).

if not impossible, to conduct an effective literature search on the phenomenon. When you are planning to work on a project, probably the most important kind of research literature would indicate that the research you are planning to do has already been done by others. This happens more often than one might think. In one interesting example, two researchers who had used the theory of games to devise a system of stock market portfolio management found that their "discovery" had been discovered over a dozen times since the 1950s, and "every researcher who made [the] discovery had given it a different name and description."[15]

Most discussions of naming confusions that have led to multiple "discoveries" focus on the natural sciences, but such confusion is probably more frequent in the social sciences, in which there is little agreement on how to label phenomena. As a coder of literature review data, you have to devise ways to label phenomena that may have been inconsistently labeled in the primary sources. When looking for candidate articles, it is essential to use search engines such as SocioFile, PsychINFO, and Google Scholar. These resources search only in titles and abstracts for matches to the terms you specify. Once you have downloaded articles, then you can conduct full-text searches for those terms, as well as others you think might have been used to label phenomena of interest.[16]

Redundancy

As you become more familiar with your data (primary research reports), you will likely find yourself revisiting your earlier decisions about specific sources. One reason is *redundant* data, which is a frequent problem when conducting literature reviews. You are very likely to find relevant articles that repeat data already provided in an earlier article. You have to be careful in an empirical summary not to include the same data more than once. In a more impressionistic summary, in which the findings cannot easily be combined quantitatively, you will still want to be sure that your impressions have not been overly influenced by, say, three versions of the same research reported in different formats—a conference paper, an article in a research journal, and a chapter in a collection. There is nothing wrong with an author presenting data in a preliminary form in a conference paper, in more complete form in a research article, and as a popularization or part of a summary in a chapter in a book. But you need to be sure not to code these as three separate chunks of evidence. Again, although redundancy is in some ways more of a sampling problem than a coding issue, you are not likely to know your sources in enough detail to recognize duplication (or triplication) until you are examining your evidence more closely than can usually be done in the initial sampling.

Roles

Different research reports that are both relevant and nonredundant may play quite distinct *roles* in your literature review. Is a particular article centrally relevant, important mostly for background, or only needed for a subsidiary point? Many articles not directly addressing your topic can be important for context or background or for insight about possible mediating variables. Very often, in our reviews, we find sources that seem

---

[15] Kolata (2006).

[16] On the value of full-text searching, see Kostoff (2010).

too important to put aside, but we don't quite know what to do with them yet. The roles particular sources play in your review will often differ depending on whether you are mainly interested in summarizing what is known—to guide practice, for example—or are mainly interested in building on the review to guide your own primary research investigations.

Quality

Should you code for *quality*, giving extra weight to the better quality data and studies? You will definitely want to keep track of the features of studies that contribute to their quality. Among these are sample sizes and study designs. In two otherwise similar studies, you should give more weight (qualitative or statistical) to the one with the bigger sample. That adjustment is a routine part of meta-analytic procedures. Design is as important as, perhaps more important than, sample size, but it is harder to code. Still, putting more emphasis on well-designed studies is imperative. A study based on short one-time interviews with interviewees selected haphazardly will naturally carry less weight in your summary and explanations than a study based on in-depth interviews, repeated as necessary, with interviewees purposely chosen to provide relevant evidence. Or, when reviewing two otherwise similar studies on the effects of a treatment or a program, you would want to give more explanatory weight to the one with a control group.

But there is no way to automatically rank the quality of studies. How do you rank, weight, or code a mediocre little laboratory experiment as compared with an excellent reanalysis of archival data on a topic? All other things being equal, experiments with control groups are preferable, but what if things are not equal, as indeed they seldom are? Judgment and justification are always involved. It is not a good idea to simply exclude excellent studies because they were conducted with diverse designs. For example, we concluded in our companion volume[17] that a much-cited Tennessee experiment about the effects of class size on learning was less persuasive than a study comparing international data from database archives: The experimental data were from a smaller sample, and the data were older and less representative. We did not think that the advantages of its experimental design compensated enough to make up for its use of comparatively small amounts of old and unrepresentative data. But other researchers would surely disagree. In short, judging quality is, well, *qualitative*—even when judging research reports based exclusively on quantitative data.

If you are sure that a few studies among those you are reviewing in your sample are much better than the rest, and if your thinking is formed by them and you keep returning to them again and again, don't ignore your impression. Rather, reflect deeply on the features of these superior studies. This reflection can lead to a form of coding—and interpretation. Maybe, upon reflection, you will see that the studies you think are superior all confirm your prior opinions; having discovered your possible bias, you can try to take it into account as you interpret your results. But maybe you will find explanations other than your biases—perhaps a particularly insightful design or a revealing comparison group or a team of very smart researchers who have a knack for persuasively interpreting their data. Some articles are better than others, or at least more influential.

[17]Vogt et al. (2012, pp. 52, 237). See Finn and Achilles (1999) for the experiment and Pong and Pallas (2001) for the archival study.

Some define a field. Others are adequate contributions at best. Meta-analysis guidelines usually argue against coding for article quality by assigning numerical ranks to the quality of articles and treating these numbers as data.[18] This is good advice because the numbers that could be assigned would usually be artificial or impressionistic. On the other hand, there is no point in pretending that powerful pieces of research are the same as mediocre ones.

Diversity

Diversity among research studies occurs in several ways, the two most important being different designs and conflicting conclusions. What do you do when, as is typical, research on your topic uses different designs and/or comes to different conclusions? Often—too often in our view—literature reviewers confine themselves to reviewing research done using one design. We think it is better to conduct a combined-methods review, recognizing that this will complicate your work. A good example of what we mean by a combined-methods review is one that summarized the research on programs (called induction programs) intended to prepare new teachers for their professional positions. The studies varied too much in data and methods to be summarized using typical meta-analytic techniques. As the authors explain:

> Some were evaluations of specific district or state mentoring programs. Some involved close-up examination of small samples of classrooms. Others used secondary analysis of large-scale databases to statistically investigate the association of induction with outcomes. The nature of the data reported across the studies reviewed did not permit a meta-analysis without eliminating a significant number of studies, along with the useful information they provide.[19]

It is important to engage in systematic thinking about, and to weigh evidence from, different designs. This is not mainly a matter of recoding some studies so they can be combined with others, although that is often a fruitful thing to do. Rather, it is a matter of theoretical reasoning about the conclusions and the evidence that supports them and then weaving the whole into a set of more systematic conclusions. Confining oneself to finding all the research results that can be averaged into an overall effect size and ignoring the rest does not strike us as the best strategy.

Finally, of course, you don't want to "simply ignore conflicts among findings"; it is better "to try to provide explanations to reconcile contradictory findings and also suggest future research needed to test such hypotheses."[20] The most intellectually fruitful and challenging parts of literature reviewing often come as a result of trying to reconcile, or at least to explain, differences in the evidence and conclusions researchers have drawn from it. Conducting a thorough review of the literature—in which you code for differences in the quality of the research and note the features (qualities) of the articles that could explain those differences—gives you a chance to make an important contribution to your field.

---

[18] See Ahn and Becker (2011) for a thorough examination of the issue.

[19] Ingersoll and Strong (2011, pp. 210–211).

[20] Ingersoll and Strong (2011, p. 226).

To prepare to make such a contribution, it is usually helpful to begin with a list of attributes, features, or qualities of research reports—perhaps organized in a spreadsheet to keep track. Your list of qualities of the research literature to code for will almost certainly grow as you read and reread the literature.[21] Guidelines for reporting results can also serve as checklists to use when planning your coding strategies. Two good ones are PRISMA (Preferred Reporting Items for Systematic Reviews and Meta-Analyses) and MARS (Meta-Analytic Reporting Standards).[22] Reviewing the literature is a labor-intensive and brainware-intensive job; it is too complicated to tackle without using checklists or other such guidelines.

Coding in Meta-Analysis

Many of the same issues we just discussed concerning the general coding of research literature also occur in meta-analysis, but in a form distinct enough that they require some elaboration. Coding in meta-analysis is itself the subject of a large and technically complex literature. Here we review the main points and provide references for works describing more advanced methods.

Coding in meta-analysis comprises all the steps up to and including computing each study's ES.[23] *Analysis* is combining and interpreting the ES's you have computed. The ES is, unlike many statistical terms, aptly named. It is a measure of the size of an effect. More specifically, it is a *standardized* measure (see Chapter 6). Standardized measures are often stated in standard deviation units. This means that they can be used to compare and combine results across studies. Comparing and combining across studies is the whole point of meta-analysis.

When you code in meta-analysis, you do so planning for the outcome measure you will use to summarize the data. Numerous outcome measures, or ES's, are available. The choice is not wholly yours to make because you are limited by the data available in the original studies. By far the three most common are correlation, standardized mean difference, and odds ratio. The **correlation** is used when the two variables, predictor and outcome, are continuous. The **standardized mean difference** (SMD) is used when the predictor is categorical and the outcome is continuous. And the **odds ratio** (OR) is used when both variables are categorical. These usage choices are summarized in Table 5.1. You will have noted that all these ES measures are designed for use with two variables.[24] Not many investigations in the social sciences are two-variable studies. But as always, we start with the basic techniques to establish general principles and then apply these principles to more complicated topics.

Whatever the design of the studies you meta-analyze, you will always need to record the sample size for each study. If your research question has mostly been studied by researchers doing laboratory experiments, your choice of ES measures and the coding you need to do to collect data to calculate them *might* be very simple. In addition to the sample

[21] Various lists of features to code for in literature reviews are available. For a checklist of questions to ask yourself when critiquing research reports, see Vogt (2007, p. 300); it is partly based on several other such lists.

[22] See, respectively, Moher, Liberati, Tetzlaff, and Altman (2009) and Cooper (2010).

[23] For a thorough overview, see Card (2012).

[24] Dozens of ES measures exist; for a thorough review see Grissom and Kim (2005).

TABLE 5.1. Different Effect Sizes Used for Data Coded Differently

	Independent variable	Dependent variable
Correlation[a]	Continuous	Continuous
Standard mean difference	Categorical	Continuous
Odds ratio	Dichotomous	Dichotomous

[a]Forms of correlation are available for categorical variables, which is one reason some researchers suggest using them as the ES statistic in all cases.

size, you will need information on the independent variable (IV) and the dependent variable (DV). If there is one categorical IV—such as treatment versus control group(s)—you need to know the number of groups and the size of each group. If the DV is continuous, such as score on an achievement test, it is most common to use one version or another of an SMD. Perhaps the most common is Cohen's *d*; another is Hedges's *g*.[25] Different authors recommend different SMDs. Our recommendations are to choose based on (1) the data available in your sources, (2) the best method for clear reporting in the specific circumstance, (3) the measure that most authors in your field use, and (4) what we call *the principle of inclusion*: report several, discuss any major differences among them, and let the readers choose. Any controversy among proponents of various ES measures for meta-analysis is muted by the fact that it is usually quite easy to convert one into another.

If both the IV and the DV are two-value categorical, such as treatment versus control (IV) and surviving versus not surviving (DV), then the typical ES measure is the odds ratio. But there are others; a common one for categorical data is **area under the curve** (AUC). The AUC seems most widely used when studying the effectiveness of various medical treatments for preventing death. And meta-analysis has its historical roots in medical research on the effectiveness of these treatments. Meta-analysis got its conceptual and practical beginnings with Pearson's (of Pearson *r* correlation fame) efforts to determine the effects of inoculations on preventing death. Predicting death continues to be a central concern of meta-analysts over a century later.

The AUC metric—specifically, the area under receiver operating characteristic curve—is an excellent outcome measure for such studies. The beauty of the AUC for summarizing the data is that in addition to providing an easily understood statistic, the results are depicted graphically in ways that enhance the readers' understanding. A perfect predictor model would get an AUC score of 1.0; a model no better than chance would get 0.5. An AUC of 0.80 is usually thought of as good, and 0.90 is considered excellent. Many different models have been developed to predict mortality. The results of one thorough review using the AUC are not encouraging about their quality.[26] Even with an outcome variable that can be measured with very low ambiguity (survival) and dealing with a very important issue (literally a matter of life or death), the accuracy of these predictive models was only somewhat better than flipping a coin.

[25]For discussions see Card (2011), Lipsey and Wilson (2001), and Rosenthal, Rosnow, and Rubin (2000); the latter recommends using correlations, including for experimental data, for which the SMD is much more common.

[26]Siontis, Tzoulaki, and Ioannidis (2011).

Additional/Advanced Topics in Coding in Meta-Analysis

Although coding issues in systematic reviews are somewhat distinct and some specific statistics have been developed for coding in meta-analysis, nearly all analytical methods are familiar to researchers and were originally developed for more general purposes.[27] Therefore, those methods are discussed more fully in the chapters in Part II. For ES measures, as well as descriptive and inferential statistics to use in literature reviews, see Chapters 6 and 7. For ES statistics, based on correlation and regression, see Chapter 8. For forms of meta-analysis based on more elaborate techniques, such as structural equation modeling (SEM) and multilevel modeling (MLM), see Chapter 9.[28] We conclude this section by touching on some quantitative coding and measurement issues that apply mainly to fairly advanced problems in meta-analysis.

CHANGES IN SCALES OR CODING AND MEASUREMENT PRACTICES

A meta-analysis is inherently retrospective,[29] often summarizing results from sources dating back 20 years or more. A kind of history effect can occur in the way the data are reported in the original sources; this kind of threat to validity could result in identical scores or ratings referring to different underlying conditions. This happens when a coding or measurement technique is changed. It also happens when practices in applying the technique have evolved. Some examples are in social psychology (such as measurements of prejudice and racism[30]), in clinical diagnoses (such as criteria for defining autism in the *Diagnostic and Statistical Manual of Mental Disorders* [DSM]), or in radiology, in which practitioners' applications of the same scales or definitions might drift.[31] Meta-analysts are not likely to learn about such changes until they are well immersed in the sources. Correcting for such changes, or at least trying to code for them, is crucial, but it is often not possible. This problem is similar to the naming problem discussed earlier in which the same term was used to label different things or different terms were used to label the same thing. But in this case it is more a matter of inconsistency in coding and measuring rather than in naming in the primary sources. These kinds of measurement and coding problems can occur within one study, of course, but they are especially likely to occur, and to be missed, in attempts to synthesize multiple studies. Measurement reliability across studies is a key issue in meta-analysis and in any other form of systematic review.[32]

---

[27]This is a point made in the pioneering article by Glass (1977).

[28]For qualitative analysis methods that can be used for meta-syntheses, see Chapters 11 (on inductive approaches) and 12 (on deductive approaches).

[29]It is possible to plan to conduct a prospective meta-analysis, but this is quite uncommon; see Schaefer (2008).

[30]McConahay (1983); Dovidio et al. (2004).

[31]For example, the ways pathologists rated tumors using the Gleason score seems to have experienced grade inflation; see Ghani, Grigor, Tulloch, Bollina, and McNeil (2005) and Tsivian et al. (2009). We owe this observation to Michael Abern.

[32]For a well-known approach to measurement reliability in meta-analysis, see Vacha-Haase (1998), and for an update, Howell and Shields (2008).

USING MULTIPLE CODERS

It is increasingly common in meta-analyses to use multiple coders. The practice is driven by the growing number of original research reports to be synthesized and by the increasing emphasis on leaving no stone unturned during the search for possible sources to be examined. Sometimes the majority of the work is screening—reviewing and coding studies as eligible or ineligible for inclusion in the synthesis. It is not uncommon for candidate studies to number in the hundreds, but it is rare for more than a few dozen of those to be included in the meta-analysis. The advantage of multiple coders is the chance to delegate some of the work or at least to divide the labor among colleagues. The disadvantage is that doing so requires reliability checks. Paradoxically, this can also be an advantage. Here as elsewhere we recommend against multiple coders unless they are coauthors and thus have a stake in the quality and accuracy of the work. Generally, using poorly paid employees to help you with research work is a false economy. If you do use such helpers, such as student assistants, use more than one, have them double code at least some of the sources, and conduct intercoder reliability checks on their work.[33] Even when multiple coders are experienced researchers, reliability checks are beneficial. If, for example, all primary sources are coded by three colleagues, this gives the researchers the opportunity to find, discuss, and adjust for any discrepancies and, more generally, to improve the quality of the analyses. The gains from multiple perspectives can be substantial.

Many textbooks seem to assume that using multiple coders is standard operating procedure; this has led some of our students to forget that in a modest meta-analysis it is simple enough to do the coding and analysis themselves. For example, if the final count of research reports included in your study is 30, this would add up to perhaps a total of 1,000 pages. Reading these is the equivalent of reading three or four medium-sized books. Given all the advantages of gaining deep familiarity with your data and the extra certainty that coding standards are being applied consistently, why wouldn't you simply do this work yourself? One reason is that you might not be as trustworthy as you think. We have found that our own *intra*coder reliability is well short of perfect. To check on your intracoder reliability, code some of your sources a second time, without first checking how you originally coded them. Review your coding for consistency.

In any case, if multiple coders or codings are used, the research report should include explanations of how the multiple coding was done and how any discrepancies were found and rectified. A common approach is to discuss discrepancies to find a consensus. Specific measures of intercoder reliability are also very important, but studies of practice in fields such as communications and education indicate that the number of research reports that actually calculate and report the results of intercoder reliability tests is less than half.[34] Perhaps the most common standard of good practice is to have two coders, who are coauthors of the research, independently code all studies and resolve disagreements by bringing in a third author and/or by consensus.

---

[33] Different types of intercoder reliability are used for different types of data (categorical or continuous); see Lombard, Snyder-Duch, and Bracken (2010). Very useful online Web service software for calculating the most common measures is available at *dfreelon.org*; for a discussion see Freelon (2010).

[34] For communications, see Lombard, Snyder-Duch, and Bracken (2002) and for education, Raffle (2006).

FIXED-EFFECT OR RANDOM EFFECTS MODELS[35]

A key analytical decision that has important consequences for coding in meta-analysis is whether to use a fixed-effect or a random-effects model. Like most coding and measurement issues, this one is important in areas of research beyond meta-analysis (it is discussed again in Chapters 9 and 10). Here we explain what the choice of models means for meta-analysis. The basic question to answer in deciding whether to use a fixed-effect or a random-effects approach is, Is it reasonable to assume that the effects of the IVs on the DVs in your source studies are the same, or do the effects vary from study to study? If the effects of the IV on the DV are assumed to be identical in the primary studies, then the fixed-effect (or common-effect) model should be used. If the effects are assumed to vary among studies, then the random-effects (or variable-effects) model should be used.

In the absence of a strong reason to presume the opposite, it is safer to assume that the effects vary from study to study and, therefore, that the random-effects model is preferable. Common causes of variation in the effect of the IV on the DV are differences in the way the IV was implemented and/or differences in the studies' participants (e.g., their ages, education levels, and so on). Because these differences are very frequent, the random-effects model is generally the better choice. Another reason to prefer the random-effects model is that it is more versatile; it is an appropriate tool when the effects of the studies are in fact fixed, but the reverse is *not* true.[36]

One might be tempted to use the fixed-effect model because it is easier to obtain a statistically significant result by so doing, but except when the studies being summarized can be considered virtually identical in their methods and samples, it is inappropriate to do so. Another reason the fixed-effect model is sometimes used is that the number of studies might be too small to use the random-effects model. But, when the number of primary studies is small, there are better alternatives than using an inappropriate model. The main alternative is to report the studies' separate effects and not summarize them in an overall ES. This means, in other words, that you have determined that the studies are not amenable to meta-analysis; they have to be synthesized using more traditional conceptual rather than statistical methods. Another alternative is to compute a summary fixed-effect ES but carefully explain to the reader that it cannot be generalized beyond the studies in the sample. Because of the possibility of reader misinterpretation, we do not advise this.[37]

SUMMING RESULTS FROM MULTIVARIATE STUDIES

Most quantitative studies in social research are multivariate. They have multiple IVs and/or multiple DVs. The basic methods for computing ES summaries that we have discussed, and that are most widely used, are designed for simple, bivariate studies, such

---

[35]For excellent detailed discussions that do not require a great deal of technical background, see Card (2012, Ch. 10) and Borenstein, Hedges, Higgins, and Rothstein (2010).

[36]There are interesting parallels here with two-tailed versus one-tailed *t*-tests and with oblique versus orthogonal factor rotation; like random-effects models, two-tailed tests and oblique rotations are more versatile.

[37]See Borenstein et al. (2010, p. 107) for other alternatives.

as an experiment with one IV. Summing multivariate results can be easily accomplished *only* if the set of multiple variables is *identical* in each study and if each variable is defined, coded, and measured in the same way. For example, if one wanted to meta-analyze a group of primary studies using multiple regression and they all included the same IVs measured the same way, one could compare and average standardized regression coefficients. But finding such a group of primary studies—all including the same variables coded and measured in precisely the same way—is highly unlikely. This, in turn, means that the majority of quantitative studies, which are multivariate, are not susceptible to the basic ES approaches to meta-analysis.

In short, when different studies use different models, it is hard and perhaps impossible to sum them quantitatively. But, of course, it is possible to compare them more qualitatively. Perhaps the most active area of research in methods for meta-analysis concerns devising ways to compare and summarize multivariable studies quantitatively. This ongoing area of research focuses on applying advanced techniques based on matrix algebra, SEM, and multiple correlation and regression.[38] Various promising lines of research for approaching this problem are being undertaken, but there is as yet little consensus among researchers. It is not an area of research that a novice meta-analyst will undertake lightly. Learning the techniques and deciding which among the evolving methods to use demands serious and fairly advanced study.

BIASES IN THE PRIMARY SOURCES

The most intriguing and fundamental issues in meta-analysis concern biases in the primary studies, how to detect them, and how to correct for them—or at least to code them. Usually, the first step in a research summary is to be sure that you have found all the research. And you must report the sources used for searching and the query strings with which you searched them. But a second crucial, and more difficult, step is to undertake a critical review of the studies and their designs and sampling plans to see if these evince bias. This kind of work will necessarily be more theoretical than analytical; there are no algorithms. No matter how adept researchers are at summarizing the existing literature correctly and without bias, if that literature itself is biased, then paradoxically a perfectly unbiased summary will simply replicate that bias. If, for example, in the studies being reviewed, women or people from particular age groups are underrepresented,[39] then *an accurate and unbiased summary will replicate the bias in the primary studies.*

A frequently discussed type of bias in the primary sources is publication bias, which is the tendency for some types of studies to be more likely to get published. The two most common forms of this bias are favoring studies with positive rather than negative outcomes and/or favoring studies with statistically significant findings. There are statistical tests to check for such biases,[40] but even the inventors of these tests caution

[38] For an overview, see Card (2012, Ch. 12); for the SEM approach, see Cheung and Chan (2008, 2009). For correlation approaches, see Rosenthal and Rubin (2003), Gilpin (2008), and Aloe and Becker (2011). For overviews of regression approaches using MLM, see Van Den Noortgate and Onghena (2003) and Denson and Seltzer (2011).

[39] Age-group differences in the study participants may be part of what is behind the continuing controversy over hormone replacement therapy and its effect on cardiac health. See Swern (2010) for a superb review.

[40] Ioannidis and Trikalinos (2007).

that they are imperfect indicators and that they cannot be applied to the majority of meta-analyses. A further form of publication bias occurs in the authorship of studies. For example, women remain underrepresented as lead authors of research articles in many fields.[41]

Of particular concern in meta-analyses and quantitative research syntheses are implications for practice; this focus on practice has greatly outdistanced the use of meta-analysis to guide further basic research. The focus on practice is an especially predominant feature of meta-analysis in applied fields such as medicine and education and in program evaluation more generally.[42] This focus can itself be considered a kind of bias, as can any focus. Implications for practice tend, understandably, to zero in on positive results. Practitioners are often more interested in what to do than in what not to do. And unclear results—such as "there are no clear advantages of *X* over *Y*"—are easy for practitioners to ignore, especially when they challenge standard practices. Such studies are common, and they are often contradictory enough that practitioners can "cherry-pick" results favorable to their biases.

Further possible biases in meta-analysis concern appropriate sample sizes and power in the individual studies.[43] Sample sizes are especially important variables, not only because they figure into all formulas for calculating summary ES statistics but also because they have counterintuitive consequences for the ES statistics of individual studies. Power increases as a function of increased sample size, but an inverse relation between sample size and ES has been found in both education and medicine—that is, the larger the sample, the smaller the ES. And it is a substantial inverse relationship. It is not perfectly clear why this paradoxical inverse relation exists, and what the nature of the implied bias is, but there is a strong and clear tendency for small and large studies to produce these surprising outcomes: an inverse relation between the amount of evidence and the effect size, that is, the more evidence, the smaller the effect. A closely related problem is that large effects found in early small-*N* studies often fade in later, larger studies.[44]

Sometimes the earlier, positive studies with the improbably large effects will be the ones that continue to get cited long after they have been superseded. This problem occurs not just in primary studies. Meta-analyses are afflicted by some of the same biases. And they certainly can produce contradictory results. Here is a striking example of wildly contradictory findings of meta-analyses on the same topic (the use of steroids in patients with bacterial meningitis) over several years:

1994: No question about benefits, but beware of harm.
1997: Definite benefit only for some bacteria, limit to 2 days to avoid harm.
2003: Definite benefit only for children, no increase in harm.
2003: Correction: Actually benefit is seen also in adults.
2007: Benefit in high-income countries, but not in low-income countries.

---

[41] For data on medical research authors, see Jagsi et al. (2006).

[42] See Anderson et al. (2011), Pawson (2002), and Slavin (2008).

[43] A good overview of current practice in psychology and recommendations is Cafri, Kromrey, and Brannick (2010).

[44] See Slavin and Smith (2009); Ioannidis (2008); and Pereira, Horwitz, and Ioannidis (2012) for a discussion of the origins of the problem and possible corrective actions.

2009: Clear benefit, give it to all, this is it.
2010: No benefit at all.[45]

When undertaking literature reviews and advising students to do so, we have sometimes felt that the general approach seems very straightforward. Although it might be arduous, arriving at some reasonably firm conclusions ought to be possible. The plan is simple: We will review the good studies, extract the valuable findings, and summarize the results for practitioners or for future researchers. In reality, the biases in the primary sources and the technical problems in synthesizing them make our naïve optimism seem dangerous. The world is enormously complex. Studies, by comparison, are always drastic simplifications of some small part of the world. Studies that summarize those simplified efforts help reintroduce complexity to some degree, but they cannot eliminate the intractable complexity of the social world.

A Note on Software for Literature Reviews

Should you use, or do you need, special meta-analysis software? As with any software, qualitative or quantitative, so too with software for meta-analysis and other forms of literature review: Software will usually operate on whatever you give it. It does not know any better; it trusts you. And, as with any software, if you give it poorly coded junk, the analysis cannot be valuable. To avoid the garbage-in-garbage-out (GIGO) syndrome, most of our teachers in graduate school advocated first learning to do coding and computations by hand, so that we would understand what we were doing; only then were we allowed to use computerized versions. Many textbook writers still advocate this approach. For a student who plans to specialize in research methods and data analysis, this remains good advice. But for someone who is not aiming to be a methodologist but is instead mostly interested in using data analysis methods to investigate social research problems, following that advice is likely to seem too costly in time and effort.

You will almost surely need to use software of some type if you conduct extensive literature reviews, and especially if you conduct a meta-analysis with more than a small number of sources (say, 10 or so). Even when engaging in purely qualitative meta-syntheses of numerous sources, we have found it extremely helpful to keep track of our sources and their qualities using a spreadsheet program. Ultimately, of course, at the interpretation and presentation stages of your research, you will have to rely most heavily on "brainware." Software recommendations tend to go out of date quickly, so our first recommendation is to look for recent reviews of software for meta-analysis[46] and computer-assisted qualitative data analysis (CAQDAS).[47]

As of this writing, commercial software packages for literature reviews and meta-analysis do not seem to us obviously superior to general purpose analysis packages, nor do they appear better than freeware packages for meta-analysis; but some specific software resources have their advocates. Here follow a few sources for freeware. The R Project for Statistical Computing contains several literature review statistical packages,

---

[45] Ioannidis (2010).

[46] For example, see Bax, Yu, Ikeda, and Moons (2007). A newly available and advanced program is OpenMetaAnalyst; it can be downloaded at *www.cebm.brown.edu/open_meta*.

[47] A good general text is Lewins and Silver (2007). See also the suggestions in Chapter 4.

both for meta-analysis and CAQDAS; they are available in the R open-source software archive at *www.r-project.org*. David Wilson, a coauthor of a meta-analysis text cited in this chapter, has a website that contains macros for use with SPSS, STATA, and SAS. The same site also has spreadsheet programs for computing ES statistics in Excel; it is available at *http://mason.gmu.edu/~dwilsonb/ma.html*. Finally, Charles Ragin's website for QCA offers free software that could be adapted to synthesizing qualitative literature, although, to the best of our knowledge, no one has done this yet. It is available at *www.u.arizona.edu/~cragin/fsQCA/software.shtml*.

Conclusion on Literature Reviews

Upon completing their first extensive literature review, whether a meta-analysis or one of the other formats discussed previously, many researchers find that they have gained an appreciation for excellence in reporting research results in primary studies. Doing a careful review of the literature tends to make one acutely aware of how helpful it is when researchers thoroughly explain how they conducted their research and give complete accounts of the data analyses that led them to draw their conclusions. Standards for literature reviews have increased in recent decades. One of the most important consequences of more rigorous literature reviews is heightened sensibility to accurate reporting of research in primary studies. As an individual literature reviewer, reviewing the problems you have had in summarizing the results of others' studies can provide you with a good beginning list of practices to follow in your own research.

Looking at it from a different perspective, remember that your study is destined to become part of a virtual data archive. Users of data archives are dependent on those who established the archives to provide as much information as possible so that researchers can make effective use of the contents of the archive. Sometimes there will not be sufficient space in a published article to present what you should, such as correlation matrices for quantitative studies or full accounts of how multiple coders were used to code interview transcripts. A simple solution is to place such material on a Web page or a blog so that researchers can access it easily. This open approach to research reporting is often discussed as part of "meta-analytic thinking." We also view it more broadly as an ethical obligation or an implied social contract that we all have made with the community of scholars. As we have benefited from the work of past researchers, so too we all have an ethical obligation to do everything possible to help future researchers benefit from ours. Generally, the obligation can be fulfilled by taking great care to be thorough and conscientious when writing research reports.[48]

From Literature Reviews to Big Data and Web-Based Research

The links between coding and analyzing the research literature and the coming sections of this chapter on coding and analyzing big data and Web-based data are nicely illustrated by a discussion in *Nature* on the study of social networks.[49] One of the most frequently cited contributions to the research literature in sociology is Granovetter's study

---

[48] For a superb discussion of this point of view, particularly as it pertains to quantitative research and meta-analyses, see Zientek and Thompson (2009).

[49] Giles (2012).

of the central importance of weak ties in social networks.[50] Over the past few years, one of the kinds of networks most often analyzed is citation networks of the authors writing the research articles summarized in a literature review. These citation networks are very important for understanding scholarly disciplines and the influence of ideas. Until the emergence of big data and computational social science, it had been largely impossible to test Granovetter's ideas on large social networks. But many such studies have recently been done. Granovetter's reaction to learning that very often his insights from four decades ago were being confirmed using heavily computational Web-based big data is instructive. He said: "Even the very best of these computational articles are largely focused on existing theories." By contrast, he reports that his weak-ties paper "didn't result from data analyses, it resulted from thinking about other studies. That is a separate activity and we need to have people doing that."[51] Granovetter here refers to what we called previously a theoretical review and highlights the importance of such reviews.

The activity of "thinking about other studies" is, of course, the heart of the research literature review. Finally, new media and the Web are important resources for encouraging and facilitating more high-quality thinking about research studies. For example, it is easy to imagine Facebook-like networking sites in various disciplines and subfields devoted to publishing early drafts of research articles. Members could get e-mails announcing new postings, and a discussion thread would be linked to each new posting.[52] Feedback could be very quick and extensive. Attribution and credit for new ideas would be clear because contributions would be dated. Sites for instantaneous electronic publication, notably *arXiv*, already exist. It is hard to imagine that such social networking resources for researchers will not continue to grow.

BIG DATA

In this section we:

- Discuss various definitions of big data.
- Examine coding of textual big data.
- Review the use of survey archives.
- Compare various national and international test data.
- Consider the use of data from the U.S. Census, including
  - Current Population Survey (CPS).
  - American Community Survey (ACS).
- Look at examples of government and international agency reports.
- Consider publicly available private (nongovernmental) data.
- Discuss the opportunities provided by geographic information systems (GIS).

[50] Granovetter (1973).

[51] Quoted in Giles (2012, p. 450).

[52] For a more elaborate discussion of how a social researcher site could work, see Rohe (2012).

Archival data sources are among the most commonly used in social research, and they are surely the biggest source by far of what is loosely called "big data," which has emerged as the main label used to describe coding of the kind of data discussed in this section. Although Big Data is often written with capital letters, as though it were a proper noun, there is no established definition of the term.[53] It is clear that what was once regarded as big, and still is big for some practical purposes, can look paltry by today's standards. A decade ago a megabyte was a lot of data. Now thousands of them, or gigabytes, can be stored on inexpensive memory sticks (a.k.a. thumb drives, flash drives, etc.). So far, terabytes (thousands of gigas) and petabytes (thousands of teras) mostly describe institutional storage (e.g., Facebook or Google). Next on the list of prefixes (established by the International Bureau of Weights and Measures) to describe inflated amounts of data are exabytes and zettabytes. As we write this book in 2013, those terms are rarely used, but by the time the book is published and you read it, they will probably have become more familiar.

Our working definition of big data is "an amount of information impossible for one individual to code and analyze in less than a year without computer help." This is a very inclusive or minimalist definition; it includes amounts of data to which some would deny the label "big." But from the standpoint of a working social researcher, it is a good practical standard. Applying this standard, we can see that it is still the case that much data used in contemporary research is not, in fact, big; the data can be handled in a reasonable amount of time, with only minimal computer use, by a solo researcher. For example, typical experiments in social psychology involve perhaps 100 or 200 participants who are subjected to a handful of conditions and measured on a few outcomes. A full analysis of the data generated by such experiments (significance tests, effect sizes, confidence intervals, etc.) could be done by hand in several days. We would not recommend this because hand analyses are much more likely to contain errors, but the work is still on such a scale that it *could be* one individual's hand-coding and calculation job. Similarly, the analysis of interview data gathered during 20 or 30 interviews can be an individual-sized project completable in a year; coding and analyzing transcripts could be done by hand (mind, actually) without computer assistance—if you don't count as computer assistance word processing and digital recording. As one last example, a simple meta-analysis of a score of articles could be conducted without computer assistance in a reasonably short time; however, a thorough search for research reports probably could not be.

An alternate working definition of big data implicit in many discussions is "data whose amount and complexity is sufficiently great that one of the researcher's main problems is how to manage the sheer mass of it." Sometimes, even with computer assistance, it appears that we have *too much* data. Very often the reason is that the data have come from Web-based sources that include millions of cases; indeed, some commentators see big data as predominantly Web-based.[54] There is so much big data of so many kinds that we can do little more than list major categories and briefly discuss some general principles and paradigm examples. Most big data is quantitative and uses statistical

[53] A loosely associated term is metadata, which is used in several ways—either as data about data, such as where and how it is stored, or methodological documentation, such as design and sampling information.

[54] Capps and Wright (2013).

techniques to analyze textual and graphical data. Statistics as a discipline is striving to catch up to big data.

Textbook guidance on coding and analyzing quantitative data sometimes still bears the marks of its origins in the late 19th and early 20th centuries.[55] The discipline of statistics for analyzing data was long dominated by the concerns of experimentalists, and the experiments were, for the most part, conducted on small samples, examined very few variables, and used hand calculations to analyze the data. The emphasis of most statistical methods was on guarding against overgeneralizing from small samples. In recent decades large samples have become prevalent, and in recent years their growth has accelerated rapidly. Coding and analysis methods have been adjusted to accommodate the kinds and amounts of data modern social scientists are more likely to use; increasingly, those data are big data, variously defined. And virtually all big data have not been collected by the researcher; they are archival. We begin with a species of big data that some might consider surprising—textual archives.

Textual Big Data

Big data, in our definition, have been around much longer than the term. Much of it is text. Soon after the invention of printing, and surely by the 18th century, vast amounts of published materials were available for analysis. So the first kind of big data we examine, because of its temporal priority, is textual. Of course, we have already examined textual data in our discussion of literature reviews. In recent decades, the amount of published literature and even the number of meta-analyses have themselves become "big," too extensive to be coded and analyzed by one researcher in a year. Not only are there more research publications, but they are also increasingly more accessible, which means, in practical terms, that there are more of them that researchers can be expected to investigate. A generation ago, it was often quite difficult for a researcher who did not have access to a major research library to do a thorough review of the literature on a topic. That is one reason literature reviews were often modest in scope.

Today, the number and availability of research publications has increased dramatically; they, too, have become big. Data and publications that were once available only at major research institutions can now be consulted via the Internet at almost any small-town library—or in a coffee shop with a wi-fi connection. (We occasionally access Google Scholar and even read pdfs of articles on our cell phones.) Similarly, the quantity and quality of freely accessible online journals is rapidly increasing. Examples of those we have used while writing this book include the *International Journal of Qualitative Methods; Forum: Qualitative Social Research; arXiv;* the *PLoS* (Public Library of Science) series; and *Methodological Innovations Online*. Their availability is also part of a general trend toward open-access publishing.

A strong and clear general trend exists in Europe and North America toward increasing public access to all government-sponsored research publications and data. For example, the National Institutes of Health (NIH) require public access to research publications that were funded by the NIH. The basic argument is that because the research was publicly funded, it belongs to the public. Within 12 months of being

---

[55]Big data such as the use of government statistics was not rare at the time; for example, see Durkheim's (1897/2010) sociological study.

published elsewhere, NIH-funded research has to be republished in PubMed, which is freely searchable and downloadable by anyone with an Internet connection.[56] Ironically, perhaps, open-access publishing has sometimes led to more private funding, because individuals increasingly have to bear the costs of publishing. Funding sources for publications seem to be shifting from a subscription model to an author-funded model; the authors pay, the readers do not.

In brief, texts continue to be an important category of big data. Some texts are ancient, dating even to the era before printing. For example, the sources for Needham's multivolume *Science and Civilization in China* were often manuscripts rather than printed texts. Using his considerable knowledge of science and of the Chinese language, he collected rare and endangered texts that were the basis of his multivolume history, which by most accounts is the single most important history of science in the English language.[57] Although textual data can be ancient, they grew enormously with the printing press and more dramatically still via the new media (see later in the chapter).

All texts—ancient manuscript, modern printed, and new media—are astonishingly more accessible and analyzable with use of computers. Even traditional documents, such as published books or journal articles, are available as computer files or can be scanned into computer files so that they can be searched electronically. For example, millions of books can be searched at Google Books. This is a remarkable source, especially useful for trends in the history of language and ideas. The Google Labs "Ngram" viewer provides longitudinal data in very clear graphics, describing the number and percentage of books that mention a particular word or phrase; access to the raw data is available, and the data can be explored in many ways. How do you sample when using such a vast resource as Google Books? As we think about such sources, we again realize that the problem is often not too little data but too much. An early goal in coding has to be making effective decisions about sampling and data reduction. Traditional methods of statistical significance testing—mostly designed to make sure that one does not overgeneralize from too little data—are of limited relevance for this work.

Sampling strategies are initially determined by your research question. A political scientist or historian might be interested in the evolution of political discourse in the 20th century—did it become more contentious over the decades? Like all archival research questions, this one is dependent on what has been saved. The Congressional Record might be used as the source for speeches in the Senate and House. But for political discourse in the general population, that source would not be highly useful. The general population's speech has been much less systematically recorded. If you were interested in 21st-century political discourse, blogs might be a good source. For earlier periods, letters to the editor might be the best choice. If you used letters to the editor, which newspapers would you investigate? How do these papers determine which letters get published? And how would you determine which of the published letters were political discourse? That would be the first coding question. If you were interested in political discourse among specific groups—for example, women or African Americans—you would have different set issues concerning finding, sorting, and coding data. For

[56]For example, one of the sources we cited earlier reviewing software for meta-analysis (Bax, Yu, Ikeda, & Moons, 2007) was obtained through PubMed.

[57]Needham (1954–1998).

example, how will you identify the gender and ethnicities of the authors? Members of Congress have done a better job at preserving their speech than other citizens, so by default, their discourse is much more often studied. Coding their texts is easy compared with coding that of most other groups.

Once you have established the dimensions of your textual dataset, what do you search for in that dataset? What are you looking for in your documents? This again is a sampling question that is invariably linked to coding issues. Are you interested in the *content* and what your documents tell you about phenomena in the real world? Or are you interested in the *authors* and what the documents say about those who wrote them? Or are the texts' *readers* your main emphasis? For example, can you make inferences about newspaper readers by the content of articles under the presumption that newspapers adjust their content to conform to their readers' interests so as to maintain sales? Finally, you might be interested in the *genre*—how have newspapers evolved over a period of time, perhaps as they have had to compete with other forms of news and entertainment? Often researchers will attempt to discuss several of these (content, authors, readers, genres), but in order to manage the project, an emphasis on one is usually required. The others become background or context. Thus one form of coding is distinguishing the foreground from the various types of background or context.

More technical issues are also influenced by your research questions. For example, when focusing on content in textual analysis using computer programs, some searchers delete all the prepositions, articles, and pronouns, as well as common verbs (such as forms of *to be* and *to have*). This can reduce the number of words by half or more and makes it easier to focus on the substantive *content*.[58] Other researchers focus on precisely what this first group has eliminated—pronouns, articles, and other "function words"—because of what they can reveal about their authors.[59] Others try higher-order searching and sorting using concepts such as "lexical cohesion" and "ontology-based information extraction."[60] Some are looking for specific phenomena, while others take a more GT approach and immerse themselves in the text to generate ideas that can then be followed up in later rounds of increasingly more directed searching.

Still other researchers do more brute force searching,[61] but this is actually not very common. To search, you need some concepts or categories to go on before you start. For example, one computer analysis of political manifestos, designed to see whether political parties changed their positions, had to begin with "qualitative decisions by the researchers" in which they identified the baseline or reference texts against which change was assessed via the use of a computer program.[62] Even text mining, often considered a brainless form of data dredging, frequently requires a great deal of knowledge about the texts being mined and is often greatly improved by preliminary hand (brain) work to find concepts to guide the computer program. And testing the quality of the text mining is often done by hand (brain) work to see whether the results are credible. Short

---

[58] Goldschmidt and Szmrecsanyi (2007).

[59] See Pennebaker (2011) for a discussion of this approach.

[60] Respectively: Klebanov, Diermeier, and Beigman (2008) and Wimalasuriya and Dou (2010).

[61] This is a computer science term for trial-and-error searching.

[62] Laver, Benoit, and Garry (2003). See Lampropoulou and Myers (2013) for an example of text mining of interview transcript data in the Qualidata Archive.

pre- and posttests using traditional read-and-think methods are a key part of nearly all machine-based work.[63]

This highlights a key point. Computers have not taken over. Although they are increasingly indispensable assistants, they remain assistants. They are limited in what they can do (so are humans, of course).[64] There is still enough uncertainty in computer analyses that the kinds of studies just mentioned routinely compare their categorizations, done with heavy data crunching methods such as factor analysis, with those of traditional human coding. Traditional human coding is still the most common standard against which new computer approaches are judged. It is the main way to assess the validity of what the computer program has produced. Of course, human coding is possible only by using a small number of comparatively short texts. If you are doing computer analyses, we strongly recommend that you take a random sample of the texts and use it to compare the computer program's coding with traditional human coding. For comparison purposes, the coders should be skilled and experienced[65] in coding but blind to the "answers" the computer program has provided. In sum, you will start with human coding to discover the themes, concepts, terms, and so forth that will guide the computer search. And you will often finish with human coding as a validity check on the computer's work.

One set of early coding decisions, and another type in which human coding is crucial, will probably have to be revised, using human coding, as you gain familiarity with your textual data: that is, classifying sources into primary, secondary, tertiary, and so on. An example of a **primary source** could be the testimony of a participant in an event. A **secondary source** would be the account of an observer able to see the event but not to participate in it. A **tertiary source** might be the work of a scholar or reporter who combined the primary testimonies and secondary observations into a general account of the event. That tertiary account could be the "best" one in some senses of the term, in part because it is based on more information, but there is a presumption in the research literature that primary sources are the firmest type of evidence.

The distinctions between primary, secondary, and other sources are not absolutes. What would be primary for one research question could be secondary for another. A collection of newspaper articles or blogs would be primary for studies of articles or blogs. The same sources would be secondary for a study of their authors' intentions or psychological states and tertiary for a study of the sociopolitical context in which they were written. Whether any source can be accepted as "true" and whether any researcher can be objective in establishing what the source really says or implies are issues long discussed in documentary scholarship.[66]

Generally, the more primary the source, the more solid the source is considered for making inferences, which is why your readers need to know how you have sorted

---

[63] Cohen and Hunter (2008).

[64] It was mathematically/logically proven (by Turing in 1937, and the proof stands) that computers are not capable of performing certain tasks; this has parallels to Gödel's proof (in 1931) that basic axioms in mathematics are unprovable.

[65] Deciding who is sufficiently skilled and experienced is mostly a matter of human judgment—made by people who are skilled and experienced as determined by those recognized as having skill and experience, and so on.

[66] See Butterfield (1931) and Becker (1931) for classic and still widely read discussions.

and coded your sources. The hardest inferences to make about the state of the world usually are those based on secondary or tertiary documents. Or, to put it another way, the closer (or more proximal) the source is to the phenomenon, the safer the inferences. For example, it is safer to draw conclusions about an author's intentions than about the readers' intentions. But quite a lot of research is done using secondary and tertiary sources, especially if they are scholarly sources. For example, political scientists conducting comparative analyses and interested in the truth about what they are studying often use secondary accounts, such as well-known scholarly articles and books relevant to their topics. This kind of research can be effective because the information sought is fairly uncontroversial: Was the inflation rate increasing at the time of the revolution? Was emigration increasing? Did the country have compulsory military service? The secondary sources are used to determine relatively clear facts about societies or nations or other entities in order to build a theory.[67]

One example of a study using big textual data examined some 70,000 blog posts just before and just after the attacks of September 11, 2001, to study the changes in writing styles and the emotional reactions of the bloggers. These are very good primary sources for how people reacted to the events of 9/11, but they would be nearly useless as sources for describing the events themselves or what occurred in their aftermath. This study is also, of course, an example of using new media; much traditional text material is available through new media. Methods inspired by new media studies can also be used on more traditional historical and literary documents, such as the correspondence between Freud and Jung or between Elizabeth Barrett and Robert Browning.[68] Another ambitious use of more traditional data is quantitative narrative analysis (QNA), in which, one author explains, he quantifies "simply because I have too much information to deal with qualitatively."[69] What this author studied was the rise of Fascism in Italy in the period 1919–1922. The sources were newspaper articles on the topic.

These last two examples (correspondence between famous people and newspaper articles on an important event) were all conducted with *dedicated* software for particular types of analysis. These kinds of software are more theory loaded and coded. All coding systems are, in the last analysis, theoretical systems, but the software used in the last two examples (by Pennebaker and Franzosi) contrast with more general versions of CAQDAS programs discussed in Chapters 2 and 4. Those more general types of software are more flexible but require more precoding on the part of the researcher. The book by Franzosi, cited in footnote 69, is particularly instructive on the choice of types of programs because the author systematically compares several alternatives for coding textual data.

A final, very ambitious example of textual media study will serve to conclude this section. The author studied some 50,000 newspaper articles and television transcripts written between 2001 and 2008 to examine the evolution of media discourse about Islam following the 9/11 attacks.[70] The newspapers and television stations were selected

---

[67]See Chapter 12 in this volume.

[68]See Pennebaker (2011, pp. 116–121) both for the study of the bloggers and the Brownings.

[69]Franzosi (2010, p. 5). This book is a superb overview of the various computer programs applied to textual data and how those approaches can be linked to another computer analysis approach, QCA; see Chapter 12 in this volume.

[70]Bail (2012).

to represent a range of conservative-to-liberal news outlets. The author was particularly interested in the influence of "civil society organizations," which are a type of nonprofit, nongovernmental institution in which people unite to foster common interests. One of the main goals of such organizations is to influence public opinion through press releases and media campaigns. The author found 120 such organizations, which, in the period under study, produced 1,084 press releases about Muslims. To gauge the influence of these press releases on the newspaper articles and television program transcripts, the author made innovative use of plagiarism detection software (the author also did considerable human coding). Most of the civil society organizations had no influence on the press as measured with these techniques. Those that did have an influence were disproportionately anti-Muslim fringe groups. The coding for the political message (pro–anti, fringe–mainstream) was mostly determined by human researchers; the coding for influence-cum-plagiarism was mostly done by machine. A key element of the analysis was conducted with network visualization software. This study would not have been possible without using both human coding and computer coding, and its effectiveness was due to innovative combinations of quantitative, qualitative, and graphic methods.

Survey Archives

Of all types of archival data, social researchers are probably most familiar with survey archives. These quantitative database archives have been widely used by social researchers. They are an example of **older big data.** Our working definition of "older" is "before the broad availability of the World Wide Web, that is, prior to about 1995." Examples of well-established surveys, used by political and social researchers for decades, include the General Social Survey (GSS),[71] which is mainly an attitude survey, and the National Election Study (NES), which comprises pre- and postelection surveys, available from the Inter-University Consortium for Political and Social Research (ICPSR). The NES asks respondents about their intentions and behaviors (Who do you intend to vote for in the next election? Who did you vote for in the last election?), as well as about their beliefs and attitudes. The data in survey archives are either publicly available or can usually be purchased or licensed for a reasonable fee. As with big textual data, the field of big survey data is so vast that we can do no more than indicate some general categories and the typical coding problems associated with a few paradigm examples.[72]

Coding using survey archives begins with learning the coding systems used by the survey organizations. Coding might end there, because recoding possibilities are sometimes limited. One option for recoding is to combine individual questions so that they can be analyzed as scales (see Chapter 1). The coding tasks involved with using survey archives can actually be quite a lot of work, more than beginning researchers often realize. Coding archival survey data so as to answer your research question requires much perusal of the technical documentation to learn how the coding and sampling were done. Recoding is especially likely to be necessary when combining data from different survey archives. One well-known example involves combining the results of political

[71]For an example of using the GSS to study 30,000 cases over 36 years (1974–2010), see Gauchat (2012); and for another example on the 9/11 theme, see Schuman and Rodgers (2004).

[72]Several survey archives are discussed in Chapters 5 and 11 of Vogt et al. (2012). Herrera and Kapur (2007) review survey archives and governmental databases, putting particular emphasis on data quality.

polls to produce predictions that are more accurate than any individual poll. Merging the polls and weighting them according to quality—and taking into account the different **sampling weights** when they were used[73]—often requires using quite complex algorithms, but it enables greatly enhanced quality of prediction.[74] Sampling weights are used to adjust for the fact that most survey samples are not created using simple random sampling. The basic idea behind this advanced procedure is to give more weight to some categories of response and less to others in order to make the overall sample more representative. The complexities become especially great, and often insurmountable, when you try to merge different sources using different methods of weighting.

Recoding data so as to merge information from more than one database archive is quite common. For example, a study of the religiosity of males and females and its relation to other behaviors combined data from the GSS and the World Values Survey (WVS). The surveys asked similar but not identical questions addressing what were arguably the same concepts. The response options to the questions were often similar but not identical scales (e.g., 0–8 vs. 0–6).[75] Another study of religiosity used an author-developed national survey in which the data were collected through random-digit dialing. Because the response rate to such telephone surveys is often quite low (in this case, it was about 36%), the authors compared the results of their survey with responses to well-established surveys—the ubiquitous GSS and an equally important survey, the Current Population Survey (CPS).[76] More technical coding problems can arise when the data available to the researcher come in different software formats, such as Excel, SQL, Access, SAS, SPSS, and so forth. The usual solution is to download and recode or reformat the data so that you can study the data with your favorite software. Often your software can save the data in a different format, which means that you need not do recoding in this case.[77]

Another common area of research in which investigators routinely use data from different survey and other database archives is the relation between health outcomes and socioeconomic differences such as gender, education, ethnicity, and income. The CPS is often used to obtain income and education data; it is available at the state level annually. The U.S. Census provides these data at the county level, which is a more finely grained measure, but it does so only once every 10 years, which is a cruder measure. Health outcomes are measured in numerous ways, and deciding how to code health outcomes (e.g., subjective feelings of well-being or death rates or life expectancies) will lead researchers to different databases, such as the Health and Retirement Survey,[78] the National Vital Statistics System, and the most comprehensive of these, the Integrated Health Interview Series (IHIS). This is a consistently coded version of nationally representative data. It is freely available on the Web and contains thousands of health-related variables for the period 1963 to date.

---

[73] See Pfeffermann (1993) and Winship and Radbill (1994).

[74] Silver's (2012) work is probably the best known example.

[75] Roth and Kroll (2007).

[76] Edgell, Gerteis, and Hartmann (2006).

[77] We were reminded to include these important points by one of the manuscript's anonymous reviewers.

[78] To review or download the IHIS, go to *www.ihis.us*.

Another problem when combining data from several survey archives (as well as from other databases) is missing data. The education levels will be missing for some cases in one source, the mean incomes will not be available for some cases in another, and the causes of death will be incomplete from yet another.[79] Coding for missing data is crucial in these instances. Analytical options include discarding all cases with data missing from any source, but this can rapidly deplete even very large datasets. When feasible, a better option can be one form or another of imputing missing data. Missing data imputation can be seen as a type of coding because it involves preparing your data for analysis. (The most effective methods are inferential and are discussed in Chapter 7.)

Surveys of Knowledge (Tests)

One special kind of survey, often available in data archives, is a survey of knowledge, that is, a test. A test is typically a *sample* survey in two senses: first, because the knowledge is sampled (not everything in the field is covered on the test) and, second, because many tests that provide archival data are administered to samples, not an entire population.[80] The most extensive of these testing programs in the United States is the National Assessment of Educational Progress (NAEP), also known as the "Nation's Report Card." Dating back to the 1970s, it is the best available source for longitudinal data on U.S. students' educational achievement, and the data archive is quite extensive. Because a great deal of information about students and their schools is available to researchers, many different approaches are possible, and these lead to different coding strategies.

Important among researchers' options is merging NAEP data with other databases, particularly international studies that parallel the U.S. data collection in topic and methodology. For example, the Trends in International Mathematics and Science Study (TIMSS) collects international data from some 60 nations, including the United States. Also relevant is the Progress in Reading Literacy Study (PIRLS). The Program for International Student Assessment (PISA) gauges the achievement of 15-year-old students in the member countries of the Organization for Economic Cooperation and Development (OECD), including the United States. The advantage of all these sources being available is that they allow cross-validation of concepts and conclusions by studying similar concepts assessed in somewhat different ways.[81] Because different age groups in different years and in different nations take tests on different subjects, the researcher has a great deal of data coordination and coding to do in order to merge data from these and other related sources.

One interesting use of such archival data is to devise standards for what count as "large" and "small" effects in school outcomes research. By providing an empirical source for the range of variation in actual outcomes over the past several decades, studying data from the NAEP and similar sources can help determine reasonable ranges for

---

[79] Examples include Ezzati, Friedman, Kulkarni, and Murray (2008); Jemal, Ward, Anderson, Murray, and Thun (2008); Krieger et al. (2008); and Link, Phelan, Miech, and Westin (2008).

[80] State-level proficiency tests in the United States are often administered to the entire population of a state's students.

[81] For a study using international data to study the effects of class size on mathematics achievement see Pong and Pallas (2001).

what might be achievable and thus provide a context for interpreting effects of interventions.[82] Researchers often want to define in advance what would count as success in improvements for students, programs, or schools. Criteria for success may be set for political reasons and are often well outside the range of the probable, if by probable one means what has been achieved by the most effective interventions in the past. Looking at it the other way around, after the fact, an improvement in outcomes that might seem insubstantial could be interpreted differently when put in the context of changes that have in fact actually occurred somewhere in the real world. Outcomes judged to be too small to be of interest are sometimes at the top end of the range of variation that has occurred in actual practice.

The Census

We discuss the U.S. Census together with surveys because the main difference between the two is a matter of sampling, not coding. A census attempts to collect data from an entire population, whereas a survey collects data from a sample. Coding issues with the two forms of data are largely the same. Indeed, the U.S. Census Bureau also conducts two important supplementary surveys, and many researchers find these survey data more valuable than the census data. The two surveys are the Current Population Survey (CPS) and the American Community Survey (ACS). Like the Census, both of these surveys focus mainly on matters of fact rather than on beliefs, opinions, and attitudes.

Current Population Survey (CPS)

The CPS focuses on the employment status of the population. It began in 1940, and it currently surveys the residents, ages 15 and over, of approximately 60,000 households about their employment status and related matters, such as age, gender, race, ethnicity, income, and education. Its most familiar use is to compute the official monthly unemployment rate. Because of the size and quality of the sample and the frequency of the survey, it is an exceptionally valuable resource for the variables it covers. Because the CPS has been around for many decades, it can be used to address longitudinal questions, but, as with most such data, the coding schemes change over the years, and considerable effort is required to recode consistently if one is trying to follow trends. But for many topics, it is the best source. The CPS contains multiple observations within the same household. Thus the observations are not independent. One way to handle this is with MLM (see Chapter 9). More advanced is dyadic coding and analysis, which can be used to handle reciprocal effects of replies to survey questions by members of the same family.[83]

In one case of using longitudinal CPS data, one of us (P. V.) worked on a project to construct an index of the cost of gaining access to higher education as a percentage of family income. We wanted to compare trends in tuition over time (three decades) among the 50 states. The index was computed using average public tuition, average public student support, and annual family income in each state. The state income figures were

[82]Konstantopoulos and Hedges (2008) is a good guide to effective practices in using archival data for standard setting.

[83]Kenny, Kashy, and Cook (2006).

obtained by recoding data from the CPS. The CPS was much better than the Census for this purpose, because we were studying trends over time and state by state. The Census figures, collected only every 10 years, were too crude a measure for comparing with our annual tuition trend data. But using the CPS data, we were able to compute an index to compare the costs for students and their families of access to public higher education in the 50 states. The changes over time and the differences between the states were quite dramatic.[84]

American Community Survey (ACS)

Many researchers think that the nation would better use its resources by replacing the decennial Census with the ACS. The Census is quite expensive and has too many data collection problems. Although the Census will probably persist because it is constitutionally mandated, the ACS has essentially replaced the long-form portion of the Census. Beginning in the 1990s on an experimental basis, the ACS was fully operational in its current form by 2005. Because the ACS is still comparatively new, it has mostly been used as a source of governmental decision-making data, such as deciding how federal funds are to be allocated to communities. It has not yet been used by researchers as extensively as the CPS and the Census. But given the large size of the sample (250,000 addresses per month, or 3 million per year) and its sophisticated sampling methods, and given that the response rate is very high (like the Census, it is mandatory), the ACS will probably become one of the most widely used of the big data archival sources.[85] Many coding issues when using the ACS will be familiar to users of Census data, especially long-form data, and several free training workshops are available for researchers interested in learning how to use this vast data resource.

We have found that it is often useful to combine information from the three sources: the Census, CPS, and ACS. Although there is overlap, they collect data in different ways and ask different questions. As always, when combining across sources, much meticulous attention to detail is needed. It can be hard to figure this out on your own, but there are many resources that can be tapped. Free seminars are available to the public. One of our favorites was "The Census, the Origins of Data Processing, and the Challenge of Big Data." And, like the Census, the ACS provides much online guidance for beginning data users[86] and opportunities for more advanced researchers to attend summer seminars.

Government and International Agency Reports

Some governmental agency reports are sample surveys, and others, while using a survey format, require participation of all. Following are a few examples to illustrate the range of what is available. For example, all U.S. institutions of higher education that participate in federal student financial aid programs (which is virtually all) are required by statute to provide data for the U.S. Department of Education's Integrated Postsecondary

---

[84]Vogt and Hines (2007).

[85]One good example of the use of the ACS on the link between income and health is Minkler, Fuller-Thomson, and Guralnik (2006).

[86]An excellent place to start would be the booklet What General Data Users Need to Know, available at *www.census.gov/acs*. For seminars see *www.census.gov/research/seminars*.

Education Data System (IPEDS). This program has been collecting data on a wide range of variables using a uniform (though not unchanging) format since 1993. Public users can access a wide range of data, including tuition, graduation rates, institutional resources, and faculty salaries, for individual institutions comparatively and over time. Qualified researchers can obtain permission to probe more deeply.[87]

Coding issues with IPEDS include changes in codes over time and in how some variables were measured. More fundamental have been controversial questions of whether individual student-level data should be collected and, if so, to whom they should be available and whether social security numbers or other unique identifiers can be used for individual-level data. Thus far, institutions have been required to report student data as aggregate-level data (rates and percentages). This has meant, for example in our own work, that many questions could be pursued only at the single-institution level and then only when it was possible to obtain individual-level data from university officials. Privacy concerns with individual data can be addressed by deidentifying the data and using specially generated case numbers relevant only for one project.

Centers for Disease Control and Prevention

The Centers for Disease Control and Prevention (CDC) collect huge amounts of data, most of it from mandatory reports of vital statistics (on birth and death). These have important uses for addressing questions in political and social research. In one recent report, for example, the CDC examined the effects of motorcycle helmet laws on survival in traffic accidents. The specific data were from the National Highway Traffic Safety Administration's Fatality Analysis Reporting System, which is a census (not a sample) of fatal traffic crashes in the United States.[88] Because there has been considerable change in helmet laws, with states passing, repealing, weakening, or strengthening helmet laws over the last four decades, the data for assessing the effects of this legislation are particularly strong. They can be used to conduct a natural experiment that meets what we think of as **Snow's test** for an effective natural experiment: *No experiment could be devised that would more thoroughly test the effect.*[89] The results from this natural experiment are clear: Helmet laws increase helmet use, and helmet use sharply reduces the death rate, serious injuries, and hospital costs arising from motorcycle accidents. As is common when using archival data to conduct a natural experiment, considerable historical research about the specific timing of the independent variables (e.g., when laws went into effect, when and where they were revised or repealed) has to be combined from several sources. By comparison, it is relatively easy to obtain CDC data, because they are publicly available, usually on the Web. But it can be tricky to code them. As is often the case with data from public archives, data collection can be easier than coding.

Such coding work can be especially heavy for international comparisons.[90] Sometimes international data are collected in more or less the same ways by international

---

[87]The best place to get started is *www.nces.ed.gov/ipeds*.

[88]Centers for Disease Control and Prevention (2012).

[89]Snow (1855).

[90]See Herrera and Kapur (2007) for an excellent review of potential data coding problems.

agencies such as the United Nations and the European Union's Statistical Agency. A good source of data in which some of the coding comparability work has already been done for you is the OECD. This is an international economic organization that today is composed of 34 economically developed nations, including the United States. The basic goals of the OECD are to provide ways to compare policy experiences, to seek answers to common problems, to identify good practices, and to coordinate domestic and international policies of its members.[91] For studying its member nations, the OECD is an excellent source and has some data going back to the 1960s. Because its focus is comparative, many of the typical comparability problems of coding international data are lessened.

Publicly Available Private (Nongovernmental) Data

Although government sources are very important, they by no means exhaust the options for the archival researcher. One of the busiest areas of analysis of private data is sports. Economists and statisticians often work on sports data (one suspects that part of the reason is the opportunity to combine entertainment with work).[92] Sports data are usually in more raw form than data from survey archives or government databases; this means that opportunities for and the burden of coding can be greater. Sports data are especially interesting because they are generated by what can be thought of as little field experiments in group behavior. Like social psychology laboratories, they are artificially simple: The number of players is fixed, the rules are known by all in advance, only specifically designated individuals can participate, and there are clear outcome variables—such as wins. In addition to wins, sports analysts also study numerous **surrogate end points**,[93] such as defensive activity, points scored, and so forth. Because the data are raw records and have not been collected with the needs of researchers in mind, much more coding work is required before analysis can begin. Such data have entertainment value, but they also have economic value. They are especially pertinent for team owners and coaches: When we play against a team with such-and-such a statistical profile, which strategies should we adopt, which players should we use more heavily?

Statistical analysis of sports variables is now a big business; many teams have consultants or buy data and analyses from data analysis firms. The data are used to decide whom to try to recruit, how much to pay them if they are recruited, and whom to play in which circumstances. The richest pool of data is probably on professional baseball. The teams are large, so data exist about many players (many more than, say, in professional basketball), and the game has had essentially the same rules for over a century.

---

[91] OECD data are available at *www.oecd-ilibrary.org/statistics*. For use of United Nations data, see the examples in Chapter 9.

[92] For baseball, the best known example is Lewis (2003); see also Silver (2012). Berri, Schmidt, and Brook (2007) is a good source of serious academic analyses, by economists, of several other sports.

[93] A surrogate end point (a term used mostly in medical research) is data about an intervening variable. For example, the purpose of statin drugs, which reduce cholesterol, is to reduce heart attacks. Rather than measure the heart attack rate, researchers could instead measure cholesterol levels. Cholesterol levels would be the surrogate for heart attack rates, a contested one we might add.

Geographic Information Systems

Geographic information systems (GIS) are computer-based methods for mapping and analyzing spatial data. They add a new type of data (spatial) and a new way to visualize data (mapping) to the social researcher's conceptual and analytical tool kit. To date, most social science research has underemphasized spatial (and temporal) attributes of the cases studied. Some of that neglect is due to the fact that coding and analyzing spatial (and temporal) data is much more difficult than coding the kinds of variables that occur at one point in time and that do not usually take place/space into consideration, such as answers to survey questions, replies to interview questions, and reactions to experimental treatments. Spatial variables can be difficult to model, but they are basic to understanding in the social science disciplines; people inevitably do what they do in places and spaces. GIS are very new and cutting edge, but what is truly new about them are the technological advances, especially computational speed and other software developments; these enable researchers to do many more types of analysis much more quickly than in the past. But the basic idea of integrating geographic variables into social research is fairly old. For example, John Snow's 19th-century study on the causes of cholera, which we have discussed as the original natural experiment,[94] was also heavily dependent on Snow's mapping of the incidence of the disease.

GIS-based studies are not inevitably built upon archival data, but most of them are, because collecting geographic data oneself is usually very demanding; that is why we discuss GIS approaches in this chapter. Even if you conduct a traditional study and merely stick colored pins in a map, you probably will not draw the map yourself. And finding the right map for your research question can be a daunting archival task. For some studies, such as the history of land development in a city, you might need to do considerable archival searching to find appropriate maps. Fortunately, some important database archives for geographic data exist. Among the most extensive is the U.S. Census; its data are organized into about 8 million geographic areas called **census blocks**.[95]

Many research questions can easily be expanded to include a spatial or geographical component. Can you tie your study's cases or variables to locations? If so, a GIS-based supplement to your study is an option. Where do the respondents to your survey live, and are certain types of responses more likely to be given by people who live in different places? For example, in a study of a city population's attitudes about crime, you might compare the attitudes about crime with the crime rates in different neighborhoods or blocks. This approach would give you a new and important way of visualizing survey data and enable you to possibly see new associations among your variables. An example that gained attention, because of the debate over gun permit laws, was an article in a local newspaper. The *Journal News* (Westchester County, New York) published an article and accompanying map titled "Where are the gun permits in your neighborhood?"[96] The paper used a Freedom of Information request to obtain the names and addresses of all pistol permit holders in a three-county area and plotted the results on a map, with each dot representing an individual handgun permit holder.

---

[94] Snow (1855); for discussions see Vogt et al. (2012, Chs. 3 and 9).

[95] For the census, see *www.census.org*. For an organization that provides many useful resources for GIS users, see *www.csiss.org*, which is the website of the Center for Spatially Integrated Social Sciences.

[96] At the time of this writing, it could be downloaded at *www.lohud.com* (see January 7, 2007, p. B5).

A good example of innovative research using GIS mapping can be seen in an article that investigates neighborhood social, economic, and environmental conditions that lead to heat-related deaths in cities. The authors used some 2,000 Census blocks in the greater Phoenix, Arizona, area as their geographical units. Data from remote sensing of vegetation and land surface temperatures were combined with data on mortality to identify "hot spots," that is, places where residents were more vulnerable to heat-related deaths. The article illustrates how mapping makes patterns clearer and how mapping data can be integrated with more traditional tabular data to produce a more powerful analysis. We cannot reproduce the relevant maps here, but they can be viewed online.[97]

We have warned earlier in this book about data mutilation, about reducing the level of specificity of one's data—for example, by categorizing a continuous variable.[98] But such reductions are inevitable in mapping; otherwise, the map would have to be as large as the entity being mapped. Without scaling and discarding data, a map of Los Angeles, for example, would have to stretch over 400 square miles. One of the biggest coding decisions to make in GIS work is deciding on the appropriate measurement scale; this involves a trade-off between area and detail. If you want to depict a large area (e.g., Canada) on a map 30″ × 30″, you'll have to sacrifice much detail; you can have much more detail on a map of the same size if you are representing a smaller area (e.g., Toronto). These spatial trade-offs are closely parallel to more traditional quantitative ones, and they require at least as much care. All maps are a form of data compression, often much more radical compression than reducing a continuous quantitative variable into high, medium, and low. You can typically avoid making your data more coarse-grained in quantitative scales, but never in map-based data. Maps are models of 3-dimensional space reduced first to 2 dimensions and then reduced in scale by many thousands of times. For example, depicting 20 miles by 1 inch on a map is a reduction of over a million to one, but using that scale would result in a map of the United States about 15 feet wide, still too large for most purposes.

Deciding on an appropriate scale is hardly the only problem with GIS work. The majority of work in a GIS-based study involves data preparation. Even though many data are available online or from other archival sources, it can come in different file formats that require considerable work to make compatible, and data often have to be repurposed by recoding. When coding or recoding, one key choice is whether to use **vector** or **raster** models. Vector models are topographical; they look like maps. Rasters are pixel-like squares; a raster map usually looks like a very low-resolution digital photograph. With the raster model, the picture is less clear, but the computation is much faster. As with pixels for photographs, so too with rasters for maps: The more you have, the more computing power you need. And you need even more for vector mapping.[99] Finally, the data have to be made compatible with the version of GIS software you are using. Choice of software can be quite complicated for GIS work, and differences among types of software are typically more important than differences in statistical and qualitative analysis software programs. As usual, before you purchase anything, unless you are part of a user group that has already decided on its software, we recommend

[97]Harlan, Declet-Barreto, Stefanov, and Petitti (2013); it is available at *www.ncbi.nlm.nih.gov/pmc/articles/PMC3569676.*

[98]See Chapter 3.

[99]For an overview of this and other basic issues, see Steinberg and Steinberg (2006).

that you start by exploring software options in the freeware R.[100] Freeware is great for the independent scholar with limited resources, but for university students and faculty a better option may be the software your university licenses. Often universities provide instruction and user groups. This can be easier than trying to learn how to use freeware on your own. On the other hand, R has become the standard in many fields, so user groups and instruction also exist for it in many universities.

The genus of big data contains many species, each with numerous individuals. One definition of a species is a group whose individual members can mate and produce offspring. That is certainly true of the varieties of big data, which are often used in conjunction to increase sample size and to cross-validate findings. Coding and analysis of such data is sometimes called **analytics.**[101] In part, this is just new jargon for quantitative analysis, but it also connotes analysis of Web traffic, which is the topic of our next section.

CODING DATA FROM THE WEB, INCLUDING NEW MEDIA

Included in the Web-based data coding topics we discuss in this section are:

- Network analysis.
  - Attributes coded in network analysis.
  - Network graphing and visualization.
  - Types of network ties.
  - Coding e-mail as a data source.
  - Coding and analyzing research citations: an example.
- Blogs.
- Online social networks (OSNs).

Web-based and social media data can be researcher-created rather than archival. For example, researchers routinely conduct surveys,[102] interviews, and experiments using social media (see Chapters 1 and 3). In this chapter on archival data, we focus on data mined from the Web,[103] including from new social media, rather than on data created using the Web. What do we mean by "new"? Essentially, "new" means after the beginning of the broad use of the Web. The Web is a system of Internet-linked Web pages and other sites. It was initiated in 1990, and by the mid-1990s, enough Web-based data, such as e-mail messages, had been accumulated that it was possible to start using them

[100] For a YouTube video illustrating the GIS uses of R, see *www.youtube.com/watch?v=mMaMmaTfsQE*.

[101] Siegel (2013) is a popular overview; Carlberg (2013) provides practical steps for the would-be user.

[102] Among the most innovative approaches is the wiki survey; if you have a research question in a compatible format, you can create your own by going to *www.allourideas.org*.

[103] A note on terms: The Internet is a network of computers; the World Wide Web is a network of Web pages. Essentially the Internet is the hardware, the Web is the software. As is common, we sometimes use the terms interchangeably.

as sources for social research. Growth in the Web was at first modest, and using it was painfully slow for a few years (some contended that "www" really stood for world wide *wait*), but improvements in computer speed and in search algorithms, especially PageRank,[104] enabled the data deluge we have seen since the early years of the 21st century. Blogs were initiated in 1998, Facebook in 2004, and Twitter, a microblogging site, in 2006.

It is important to distinguish, on the one hand, the Web as a *source* of data that can be coded in various ways and, on the other, using Web resources as *methods* to access those data. The sources are the archival data on the Web that you can access and study using the Web; they are the stuff that is there. Of course, quite a bit of what you can find on the Web is also available elsewhere, or it used to be. But most Web sources did not exist before the Web. The methods side of the distinction refers to research activities you can undertake using the Web. But distinctions between sources and methods become murky when you realize that the work you do on the Web will, in turn, likely become available on the Web so that others can consult it as a source. As with other forms of data, so too with Web data—coding is a bridge between design and sampling and between concepts and analysis. These are two-way bridges—or, for Web data, a better linking metaphor is probably a cloverleaf interchange (a.k.a. a highway traffic clover).

One of the first kinds of coding is sorting among, naming, and classifying (coding) different types of Web sources. Just as with traditional text data, which need to be coded as primary, secondary, and tertiary so that the reader can assess their value, so too with Web data. It is not appropriate merely to say of a source, "I got it off the Internet," or "I Googled it," any more than it suffices with traditional sources and data to say, "I got it from a bookstore" or "I read it in the library." As sources proliferate—and some of them will surely be unfamiliar to some readers—you need to specify the provenance of your sources. The first thing to provide is a location for the Web data. This is given by the URL, or uniform resource locator, a form of document location invented in 1994. Because the URL includes server names and domain names, it also is a form of document identification. But URLs change, and documents may no longer be available at a particular URL. A more stable form of document identification is the DOI, or digital object identifier; this system was invented in 2000. The DOI is not universal, as many Web documents do not have a DOI, but most reliable ones with good research credentials do.[105] Current citation practice in scholarly publications is to use the URL, but if the documents you cite have a DOI, we recommend including it, and we predict that doing so will become widespread as researchers seek better ways to describe the origins, location, and quality of their sources. Coding for quality is important. For example, there is a big difference between citing a table on Paul Vogt's blog and citing a table from the American Community Survey's Web page.

The Web is so vast, and there are so many possible approaches to it, that, as with other sections of this chapter, we try to cover a great deal by using a few topics and examples that we believe to be illustrative of broader coding issues and strategies. In our discussion of coding Web-based data, we focus primarily on **network analysis.** We do this because the Web is itself a network and because data from the Web are often used

[104]For a nontechnical discussion of this and other important algorithms, see MacCormick (2012); for a more technical discussion, see Wu et al. (2008).

[105]Technically, the URL is a form of uniform resource identifier (URI). For the DOI, see *www.doi.org*.

to study other types of networks. Network studies do not have to be done with archival data, but in fact very many of them are.

Network Analysis

Network analysis was invented well before the Web. Although sociologists and others studied social networks prior to the existence of the Web and before easy-to-use software enabled the drawing of complex network diagrams,[106] the study of networks expanded dramatically and developed in new ways thanks to the Web and computer software.[107] Studying a network starts with two basic kinds of data that have to be coded: **nodes** (or vertices) and **links** (a.k.a. ties, lines, or edges) that connect pairs of nodes. The nodes can be people, organizations, books, or any other entity that can be understood as related to other entities in webs of association. The initial research question in such studies is typically descriptive or exploratory: In a given population, how are relationships between members of a field structured?

The theory tested, or the assumption guiding much of this research, is **homophily**, often referred to as "birds of a feather flock together," or the tendency of like to affiliate with like. Often, it is not clear whether homophily is a descriptive generalization, an assumption, or a theory. How do you know whether these birds are "of a feather" unless they are flocking together? In other terms, your research question could be to determine whether similar people associate, or it could aim at finding out who associates with each other and conclude that because they associate, they must be similar. Are network links configured as they are because the nodes are similar, or do you use links to investigate the nature of similarities you did not already know about? Do nodes connect with others in an expected way, or does the behavior of nodes help you find unexpected links? Whatever the case, much of the data coding for network information is the same. Among the attributes of the network you can look for and code are those concerning particular nodes, the network as a whole, or subgroups in the network. Network features are often derived by summarizing the features of the individual nodes and their relations with other nodes.

The following list of attributes, which are often coded in network data, is a sample of what is possible. The terms for particular concepts to code can vary by research tradition and analysis software. We list here some of the most basic and frequent.[108]

Attributes Commonly Coded in Network Analysis

- **Degree** of a node: How many ties does a particular node have to other nodes? For the network: What is the average degree (number of ties) of all the nodes?
- **Closeness/centrality** of a node: What is the distance between a node and all the

[106] Granovetter (1973) is a classic reference, and it was built on an extensive basis of prior scholarship—including even more classical scholarship, such as Simmel (1908/1955).

[107] Both commercial and freeware programs exist; among the latter, one of the more widely used is Pajek, available at *http://vlado.fmf.uni-lj.si/pub/networks/pajek*. Users of Excel might prefer the freeware node XL.

[108] A frequently cited general resource that requires some background but not extensive expertise is Scott (2000).

other nodes? Obviously, nodes near the center of the network are closer on average to all the other nodes.

- **Betweenness** of a node: How important is a node for linking other nodes? How many paths between other pairs of nodes go through this one?
- **Density** of a network (or of subgroups in a network): What is the proportion or percentage of actual links to the total links possible?
  - **Subgroups or cliques** are subsets of nodes with comparatively strong numbers of links, for example, higher than the mean number. These subgroups are also often called **communities**.
  - **Transitivity of triads** (three nodes). The preceding concepts are for coding and measuring all links between *pairs* of nodes. With groups of three nodes (triads), the number of possible kinds of relations is greater. If the links are **undirected** (the direction of a link is not specified), there are four possible types of relations in a triad (0, 1, 2, and 3 ties). The relative frequency of each of these in the network can indicate quite a bit about the network, such as: How many of the nodes are isolated? How many are linked in couples only? A related issue is the prevalence of "structural holes," in which one node is linked to two others but those two are not connected to one another. If the links between the nodes are **directed** (the direction of the relationship is specified), then 16 types of triad linkages are possible.

This list is far from complete, but it illustrates the main types of relationships and attributes you can code when studying networks. Some of this kind of network research could be done by human coding, but it ranges from impractical to impossible when the number of nodes and connections is more than a few dozen. Many of the basic attributes, such as the center of a network, can be discovered only by using network mapping software. Unlike the kind of mapping discussed in the earlier section on GIS, in network mapping, distance is a metaphor; it is not a scaled-down picture of actual physical distance. In network analysis, physical distance is a way to symbolize social distance and/or a number of links. You might live the same distance from your best friend and from your meter reader, but in a network diagram, your friend would be graphed as closer to you; your meter reader would be further away. Your mother might live in a completely different region of the country, but if your ties with her were frequent, she might be graphed closest of all.

Network visualization is a key part of network analysis; social network analysis all but requires visual presentation in what are often called *sociograms*. Network data are entered in the normal quantitative pattern of a grid, with the rows and columns representing the cases (nodes); the software then produces an initial diagram using the concepts just discussed, such as centrality and degree, to shape the diagram. Sometimes, upon visual inspection of the initial network diagram, unexpected relationships jump out at you. But at other times, particularly when the network is composed of many nodes with many ties, you find yourself squinting at a blur of overlapping lines. And unless there is something quite striking about the resulting structure of the network (e.g., it is mostly a ring or wheel with low density and low betweenness [no spokes]), we have often found ourselves at a loss for words to describe the result.

Graphing and Network Visualization

Visualization aids, such as zoom-in windows, can help, but when the relations among the nodes are complicated, eyeballing a graphic can be frustrating and fruitless.[109] Most network analysis software packages allow you to explore your data by displaying nodes and links in different colors and sizes. There is often as much art as science in this work, and the graphs, though indispensable, are seldom sufficient. We have found it most useful to code and present quantitative data such as density, closeness, and centrality both in tables and visually. Each complements the other.

Figures 5.1 and 5.2 present two rudimentary diagrams to illustrate some basic concepts and relationships. Figure 5.1 is an undirected graph; this means that the direction (or any other information) about the nature of the links is not provided. Say Figure 5.1 represents a network of authors who, over a 5-year period, either do or do not cite one another. Because it is an undirected graph, we do not know, for example, whether 4 cited 6 or 6 cited 4. Looking at the diagram, we can see that the *degree* of node 4 is 1. Only one tie links it to the other nodes in the network. The degree of node 5, by contrast, is 3: It is linked to nodes 1, 2, and 6.

More information is available in a directed graph. Figure 5.2 is an example of a directed graph with the same 6 nodes and one more tie, which we inserted to illustrate some additional concepts. The direction of each arrow indicates who is citing whom. Two-headed arrows, such as the one between nodes 1 and 2, mean that the researchers have cited one another. A one-headed arrow, such as that between nodes 4 and 6, means that 4 has cited 6, but 6 has not cited 4.[110]

It is clear that node 4 is an isolate; it cites 6 but is not cited by any of the other nodes. Node 1 is somewhat less isolated; it is cited by node 2 but none of the others. The *betweenness* of node 2 is the greatest. It is linked to the most other nodes and is on the shortest path from 4 to 1. Nodes 2, 3, 5, and 6 form a little community or clique of mutual citers. In that clique, node 2 is clearly the dominant. Its *degree* is the greatest; everyone has a direct citation to node 2 except node 4. Indeed, node 4 is outside the network to such an extent, one might conclude, that it doesn't even know enough to cite its dominant member. Note also that node 3 is also uncited, but node 3 cites the two most cited members of the network. The real community or clique is made up of nodes 2, 5, and 6. Again, these kinds of relations are easy to see with 6 nodes and 8 links, but a solely visual interpretation is often impossible with hundreds or thousands of nodes and links. Visualization can be improved by making nodes with more links (greater degree)

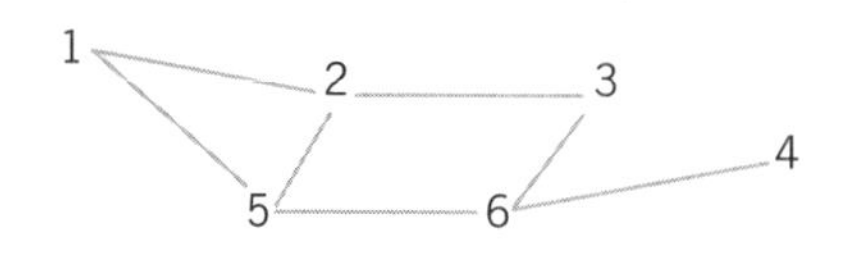

FIGURE 5.1. A network (undirected) with six nodes and seven ties (edges).

---

[109]It can help to view articles online so that colors can be seen and images magnified. Yang and Sageman (2009) recommend "fractal views," which allow information reduction and clearer visualization.

[110]For a fuller discussion, see Wikipedia's article on directed graphs at *en.wikipedia.org/wiki/Directed-graph*.

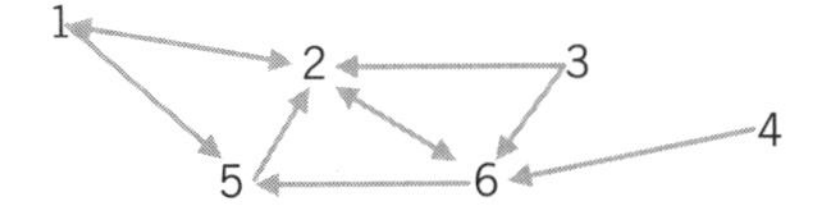

FIGURE 5.2. A directed graph of a network with six nodes and eight ties (edges).

larger. Stronger ties can be indicated by making the lines thicker or by assigning them a numerical weight.[111]

Types of Network Ties

There many types of ties that can be studied from the perspective of network analysis. The ones you select will depend on your research question but also, importantly, on the kinds of data that it is possible to collect and code. Similarities among nodes are one option: for instance, gender, political party, memberships, and interests. Social relations are also very important, of course, and include variables such as friendship, competition, and family relations. Interactions are also codable: e-mail links, texting, telephone, and so on. In addition to the types of ties, there are descriptions of their structures: centrality, betweenness, degree, overall shape of the network (circle, wheel with hub, chain, etc.). And each of these has effects on the nature of the network and its ability to act in particular ways. Your coding will be influenced also by your research question. Do you focus mainly on network structures and what gives rise to different types of structures, or do you highlight the ways that network structures influence the individuals and groups (people, organizations, etc.) within them? This is basically a version of the macro–micro emphasis: Do you generalize about networks, or do you try to understand nodes and the relations among small groups of them?[112]

Among the networks that researchers have frequently studied are networks of researchers and/or of researchers' works. Networks of articles citing other articles are among the most important of these studies, and they antedate the Web by decades.[113] This kind of self-study by researchers sounds somewhat narcissistic, and it may be, but the link between citation counts and other forms of network analysis can be strong. Especially close are the parallels between studying patterns of relations among research articles and similar patterns of links among Web pages. Such links and their strength are at the heart of searching the Web. Search engines use a kind of citation count procedure in their page-ranking algorithms; these determine which pages you see first when you search. For example, to go back to the directed graph in Figure 5.2, if you are joining the group as a new node, number 7, and are cited by node 2, who is cited the most, that will count for much more in your ranking among the nodes than if you are cited by node 4, whom no one else cites.

The ties between the two types of citation become even closer as new forms of Web-based publication become increasingly important. Citation networks have focused

---

[111]See Opsahl, Agneessens, and Skvoretz (2010) for more options.

[112]For a short but remarkably thorough review, see Borgatti, Mehra, Brass, and Labianca (2009).

[113]Examples include Garfield (1955); Small and Griffith (1974); and Mullins, Hargens, Hecht, and Kick (1977).

mainly on research articles published in scholarly journals, but increasingly to understand research networks one has to include other outlets for research, such as blogs. Researchers write blogs (and there is a Research Blogging site that coordinates some of these). Of course, researchers also have Web pages and even talk about their work on their Twitter accounts. And communication among researchers, like everyone else, is often by e-mail.

Coding E-Mail as a Data Source

E-mail is the oldest Web-based data source, and e-mail networks among researchers have been studied, although not as often as citation networks and blogger networks (see the later discussion). Getting people to give you access to their e-mail accounts is not impossible, especially if you can guarantee them privacy. To ensure privacy you can, at minimum, download the data and strip accounts of their identifying information. If you are using an analysis package that focuses on words rather than traditional content, then you can randomly jumble the texts; it makes them meaningless but does not eliminate the possibility of word-frequency analysis.[114] Studying e-mail networks formed, for example, of contact lists and links among them is much more challenging without breach of privacy.[115] We discuss some ways privacy has been dealt with in studies of Facebook and Twitter later.

There is a downside to using e-mail to study relations among researchers. Although e-mail makes much more data potentially available than ever before, the data tend to be less permanent, more ephemeral, than other forms of mail that scholars studying researchers have typically used in their work. In short, e-mails may be less likely to be archived than some older forms of communication. This is a concern among historians and sociologists of science, who worry that the documentation in the unpublished record that once made it possible for them to reconstruct paths of discovery will no longer be available. Electronic records could easily be stored, but currently there seems less incentive to do so than there was for paper records a generation ago when paper notes, memos, lab notebooks, and mail were often archived.[116] Care in preserving paper data seems inversely related to recency; it was stronger in the past. For example, in the 16th and 17th centuries, researchers would carefully write letters on high-quality paper, which would be circulated among members of the scholarly community, and many of these are still preserved. Tracing networks of these circulated letters helps specify past scholarly communities and the links among their members. These circulated letters were an early form of publication. The return of the letter-writing approach can be seen in the use of new media in scholarly communication, but the return to care in preserving records of communications seems less robust.

What we think of as traditional research publications and modern methods of citing the works in them became increasingly common in the 18th century, but traces

[114]See Pennebaker (2011) for an example.

[115]See Mok, Wellman, and Carrasco (2010) for a study of social networking pre- and post-Internet that concludes that e-mail geographically expanded distances between nodes but not by much. A similar study of Twitter networks showed the continued importance of geographical proximity and the possibility of face-to-face interaction (Takhteyev, Gruzd, & Wellman, 2012).

[116]Ferry (2013).

of the letter-writing approach to scholarly communication are still visible in the fairly large number of publications that carry names such as *Environmental Research Letters, Geophysical Research Letters*, and *Operations Research Letters*. All three of these are regular peer-reviewed journals, but they differ in ways interesting for our topic. Although the geophysical and operations research journals are traditional journals, the one on environmental research is a type of new media in that it is free *to readers*; it is funded by an article publication charge paid by the authors rather than by readers' subscriptions. And the per-article charge is substantial ($1,600 as of this writing).[117] Some universities may pay these costs for their faculty members, or research grants may cover them, but it is a dramatic difference from the traditional system in which the main publishing expenses for an individual submitting a research article were photocopying and postage. Coding for this difference—available to subscribers only versus available to all and paid for by authors—is increasingly important as types of works that can be cited in a network analysis multiply.

There are costs to online publication, and they must be paid by someone. The patterns in how they are paid are important codes/variables for archival research on citation frequency. Sometimes a host institution covers the costs, sometimes it is paid by membership fees in an academic institution, and sometimes it is paid for by public funding (tax revenues).[118] When citing articles from journals, it is potentially important to code for the kind of journal, such as refereed or not, subscription or author funded, open access or not. These could be important variables for understanding networks of citations, authors, and journals.[119]

Networks of relations among producers and consumers of research have been studied in many ways besides citation counts. Coauthorship is one of the most frequent of these; another approach is coeditorships of research journals; a third is readers of articles in a journal's online archive.[120] Most studies of networks—whether the networks are composed of people, websites, blogs, or research articles—raise similar issues for coding and analysis. The first issue is a sampling question with implications for coding: How do you define the population of nodes so that you can study the links among them? The second is, How much do you need to know—that is, how much data do you need to have coded—about the nodes in order to understand the network? The third is, How much data do you need to have about the nature of the links between nodes, and how will you code it? We pursue these issues by continuing to examine the study of citation counts as a way to understand network research in general.

Coding and Analyzing Research Citations: An Example

The most instructive reading we have done on this set of issues is a discussion in a recent article on consensus in citation networks, a critique of that article, and a response

[117]Public Library of Science (PLOS) journals charge from $1,350 to $2,900, depending on the journal; for details, see *www.plos.org*.

[118]Wikipedia solicits charitable contributions. The freeware R is supported by a community of volunteers, whereas Facebook, Twitter, and many blog sites are paid for by advertisements.

[119]See Bohannon (2013) for a sobering exposé of some "predatory publishers" of open-access journals.

[120]Respectively, Newman (2004); Baccini, Barabesi, and Marcheselli (2009); Carolan and Natriello (2005).

to the critique.[121] In the original article, Shwed and Bearman discuss a method for detecting the development over time of scientific consensus on a research topic. In their reply, Bruggeman, Traag, and Uitermark offer several methodological critiques and an alternative approach. These two articles, together with Shwed and Bearman's (2012) response, clarify what is at stake using different coding and methodological approaches to studying network issues in similar populations, and they very nicely illustrate the "cloverleaf interchange" that links design, sampling, data collection, coding, and analysis in research on the Web and other networks.

We begin with a list of some general network analysis questions, the answers to which shape coding and analysis. Then we discuss how these are treated in the example articles.

1. How is your population of nodes defined?
2. Is your emphasis on discovering macro-level structures of the entire population of nodes or on discovering communities or subclusters within the overall structure?
3. Is your goal to discover communities within the general population that you can study more closely?
4. How much do you need to know about the members of the population of nodes before you can meaningfully investigate or interpret the ties among them?
5. Should you, or can you, code the value, direction, or valence (these are similar concepts/terms) of the ties? For example, are citations positive, neutral, or negative? Are they strong or weak? And how do you make these judgments?

The population of nodes must be defined before you can begin investigating the links among them. After the population of nodes is defined and the links among them are established, it is possible to infer, using network analysis, the overall structure of the network and to identify subgroups within it. Typically a researcher puts emphasis on one or the other. The more you need to know about the nodes and ties—for example, authors and citations—the more finely grained and qualitative your coding decisions are likely to be. For example, if you need to determine whether the article citations are positive, negative, or neutral, you will have to study each article in detail.

All of these issues came up in the debate covered in the example articles. The original article in the series (by Shwed and Bearman) addressed what might be thought of as the life cycle of scientific debates as they moved from contention to consensus. The authors looked at a broad range of topics in which scientists moved from disagreement to agreement. Shwed and Bearman focused on "the macro-structure of scientific citation networks." They developed a method that allowed them to study these macro-structures across disciplines and topics in ways that do not demand that the researcher (e.g., a sociologist) have expert knowledge of a topic (e.g., the effects of ultraviolet radiation). When the citation analysis indicates the prevalence of distinct communities in the general field of citations to a topic, this shows that the field has contentious subgroups. Communities are defined by **modularity**, which is a measure of the proportion of links

[121] Shwed and Bearman (2010, 2012); Bruggeman, Traag, and Uitermark (2012).

within a community to the possible links that you would expect in a random network of ties. In brief, modularity measures how much communities stand out in the network.

The populations analyzed were composed of all articles indexed in the ISI Web of Science[122] that dealt with each topic. Shwed and Bearman's approach is exemplary in that they provided the search code of keywords used; being thus a model of clarity, they make it possible for other researchers to replicate and assess their work. Because Shwed and Bearman's research includes the study of change in consensus over time, it was possible for them to identify the time at which consensus in a scientific field emerged. This can be distinct from consensus in nonscientific writing on the same or other topics. For example, consensus among scientists on human causes of climate change emerged by the early 1990s and has not waned since. Similarly, the consensus that vaccinations do not cause autism has long persisted among scientists. Popular controversies about these or other topics can be very different, and studying them requires examining other sources, such as blogs, Web pages, editorials, and so on. Shwed and Bearman were formally agnostic about whether scientific consensus settles anything; they note that "consensus, of course, has nothing to do with 'the truth'" (p. 834).

Bruggeman, Traag, and Uitermark's main objection to the work of Shwed and Bearman is that the latter did not study the importance of negative links in the formation of communities (subgroups). They claimed that the presence of even a small number of negative ties can change the outcome of a network analysis. The problem with studying negative ties is that to do so you need to read and understand the articles (or at least the abstracts) so that you can code each link as positive, negative, or neutral. This requires expert judgment when reading thousands of articles. Bruggeman et al. did not actually attempt this, and, thus far, there is no software that can do it reliably. By contrast, mere citations can easily be tallied with computer software, and doing so does not require subjective judgment.

To illustrate the importance of negative ties, Bruggeman et al. examined a public debate in Belgium about immigration issues. They selected articles from a newspaper database and human-coded them, which is the only way positive–negative coding can really be done. Also, their study of the valence of the nodes (e.g., newspapers' editorial policies) was qualitative, though probably not difficult to determine. Bruggeman et al. showed that, in this area of research, not including negative citations in a public debate about political issues can be a big mistake. But, as Shwed and Bearman replied, and we concur, public debate about a political issue cannot be assumed to have the same structure as scientists' contestation on scientific questions. They might have the same structure, but whether or not they do is a question that has to be assessed empirically.

Shwed and Bearman replied to their critics by emphasizing that the main advantage of their approach is that by using it one can conduct comparative studies of networks of citations without having field-specific scientific expertise. Bruggeman et al. replied that some way of determining negative citations is needed but admit that they don't know

[122]This is part of the bibliographic and citation database service of Thomson Reuters. It has changed name and ownership over the decades and is much improved since the 1980s, when parts of it were riddled with errors; for an example of early problems, see Vogt (1993). For an up-to-date overview, see *http://thomsonreuters.com/products.*

how to do it.[123] Shwed and Bearman also suggested that, in academic references, the border between negative and positive citations can be blurry. For example, Bruggeman et al.'s critical article of Shwed and Bearman's research probably served to make it better known than it otherwise would have been. Indeed, we ourselves might have missed it as an example of network coding had it not been for the debate triggered by the "negative" citation of Bruggeman et al. Does that mean that Bruggeman et al.'s critique should be regarded as positive? As Shwed and Bearman point out, "negative citations imply recognition" (p. 1065) and may indicate at least partial approval. Citing an article so as to criticize it at least admits that it is worth debating—or, perhaps, to quote another field of endeavor, there is no such thing as bad publicity. In the last analysis, we can conclude that there is broad agreement that most citations are positive. But we are unsure how much coding a comparatively small number of negative citations would change the overall structure of the network or the number and nature of communities within it.

Blogs

Academic citations are decades older than blogs, and they have a longer history of being studied, but the research on blogs and other new media has been catching up very rapidly. Blogs have broad appeal as objects of study in part because there are blogs about nearly everything, because most of them are interactive, and because network analysis provides new ways to examine this font of popular culture.[124] Some commentators imagined that blogs and other new social media would tie people together in new kinds of networks that would lower barriers between heretofore isolated groups. The question of whether homophily would be reduced, whether birds would more often flock with birds of a different feather, has been studied quite often in the context of political blogs. The strong subgroups or communities found in political blogging networks make it clear that the political "online social network appears to be strongly homophilous and polarized."[125] People seem much more likely to reinforce their beliefs through blogging than to broaden them, and this tendency seems rather stronger for conservative than for liberal bloggers. So although there is broad agreement that most citations of researchers' articles are positive, the same might not be true in political blogs—except within politically segregated communities or cliques. A parallel between the political and academic worlds is that *readers* (rather than citers) of research literature can also be segmented into distinct readership groups.[126] How much this kind of segmentation can be generalized to other groups and other media is among the questions we address as we turn to research on even newer social media, specifically Facebook and Twitter, which are definitely the biggest and probably the most researched of all examples of new media.

---

[123]See Leskovec, Huttenlocher, and Kleinberg (2010) for a discussion of using computer algorithms to identify positive and negative links in social networks, which is distinct from the positive and negative content of research articles.

[124]For a history of blogs, see Siles (2011); for an examination of how traditional news outlets incorporated blogs into their agenda setting, see Meraz (2009).

[125]See Christakis and Fowler (2009, p. 206) for the quotation and throughout for a very comprehensive but nontechnical discussion of social networks and network analysis.

[126]Carolan and Natriello (2005).

Online Social Networks

Hundreds of online social networks (OSNs)[127] contain available data that the archival researcher interested in network analysis can code. There is considerable diversity among OSNs; they allow users to do different things.[128] These uses are sometimes called "affordances"[129] by researchers—for example, one affordance of a cup is to drink coffee; another is to store pencils on your desk. Of course, what particular sites allow and what their users can do determine what you as a researcher can do. When users make their networks visible, researchers can access them; when the networks are restricted only to subscribers, this often limits the kinds of data researchers can collect and code. OSNs are generally public; the connections are to one degree or another accessible—unlike, say, e-mails. You may often e-mail me, but I can't see your list of contacts or your mailbox; however, if you link to me via an OSN, I can usually see at least some of your other links.

OSNs link people, usually people who have previous contacts. They are not generally geared to helping one meet strangers; rather, they are used to make contact with friends and perhaps friends of friends. They are usually organized around networks of individuals, not common interests. By contrast, many websites, blogs, and micro-blogs such as Twitter are organized mainly along the lines of common interests and secondarily by networks of followers.

We have not conducted a systematic review of the literature on social media, but it is our *impression* that in the decade or less since their appearance (as of this writing in 2013) studies of OSNs have surpassed studies of citation networks. It would be challenging to conduct a systematic review because it is also our *impression* (again that pesky word) that a much larger proportion of high-quality research on social networks is published in outlets that are not indexed in the ISI World of Knowledge. More of such research can be found in Google Scholar, but we are not sure how much more, because Google does not fully reveal how its "citees" are determined. We are sure that one thorough and very highly informative recent review of research on Facebook[130] does not cite all the sources we used when researching Facebook for this chapter. Be that as it may, what does research on the two new SNS giants, Facebook and Twitter, look like, and what can we learn from that research about the issues of coding relatively new forms of archival data? As always, we are only indirectly interested in substantive conclusions drawn by the authors of the research itself; our discussion of findings is meant as a context for the consideration of methodological issues of coding, measurement, and analysis.

OSNs are among the biggest kinds of archival big data, especially big data likely to be of interest to social researchers. As well as providing an opportunity to study massive networks with sufficient data that might mirror or parallel real or offline networks (the

---

[127] Some researchers refer to these as SNS, or social networking sites.

[128] See Boyd and Ellison (2010) for an overview.

[129] It is hard to see what is gained by using this term—except a word that is two syllables and seven letters longer than users—but it is used ("affordanced") in some research traditions.

[130] Wilson, Gosling, and Graham (2012). One difference between their search and ours is that they included only articles that were peer reviewed. The authors have a helpful website on which citations to new articles are posted: *www.facebookinthesocialsciences.org*.

good news), OSNs confront the researcher with serious sampling problems (less good news). Researchers who specialize in searching and sampling from the Web often have computer science or physical science backgrounds; without considerable technical background, the task can be daunting for a social scientist. As big data, new media or otherwise, become ever more predominant, combined methodology backgrounds or teamwork will become increasingly necessary. **Web crawling** seems all but indispensable. A Web crawler is a computer program for automated searching of the Web, and using one also usually requires considerable hardware resources. There is little alternative to Web crawling when you want to sample or collect data from hundreds of millions of users.[131]

One of our criteria for big data, you will recall, is that they compel use of computer programs to assist in the research. Thus OSNs fit in the categories of both big and new media archival data. In practice, what this means for researchers is that, unless you work for or with someone from the corporate headquarters of an OSN firm, you will most likely have to gather your data through Web crawling. Other options include recruiting participants in one way or another—perhaps even through the OSN. For example, you can create a survey or other application on Facebook and use it to collect data from users.[132] The advantage of Web crawling, which collects public information, is that it does not require actions and permissions from "participants." But what you can collect by crawling depends on what is available publicly, and that changes as privacy rules for each OSN are altered.[133] We have briefly addressed the ethical considerations involved in using such sources elsewhere.[134] Most of the ethical questions revolve around issues concerning the appropriate use of publicly available information; it may contain many details about the private lives of individuals—albeit information made public by the individuals themselves. Should such information be considered public or private? Researchers disagree. You will need to decide, and your decisions will determine whether and how you code particular kinds of information.

If your research question leads you to focus on the content of the messages in the social networks, you then have to decide how you want to code that content. The general procedure is to identify groups, cliques, or communities and then use one form or another of textual content analysis. The type of content analysis you plan to do will greatly influence the size of the sample of messages you can code and analyze. For example, in one study of Twitter messages (tweets) aimed at learning the extent to which Twitter users were exposed to or opened themselves to ideological messages of varied content, the authors used human coding with intercoder reliability checks to determine political orientation of message content and cluster homogeneity. The clusters were samples obtained and initially analyzed using social network software, but the

[131]Useful articles describing Web crawling techniques for Facebook are Catanese, De Meo, Ferrara, Fiumara, and Provetti (2011) and Gjoka, Kurant, Butts, and Markopoulou (2010); for crawling Twitter, see Bruns and Steiglitz (2013) and Kwak, Lee, Park, and Moon (2010). Carlberg (2013) shows how to retrieve and code Web data using Excel; it can be quite easy.

[132]For a particularly successful example, in which participants are able to take personality and intelligence tests and get the results, which the researchers can then use, see Stillwell and Kosinski (2011).

[133]In one study of Web crawling Facebook, data from about one-quarter of users were unavailable because of their privacy settings (Catanese et al., 2011). In a study of Twitter users, about 8% of data were unavailable (Cha, Haddadi, Benevenuto, & Gummadi, 2010).

[134]Vogt et al. (2012, Ch. 17).

contents of the messages were then human coded. The total number of messages was 5,000, somewhat less than half of which were in the main clusters that were coded and analyzed.[135] This is an unusually small sample in published studies of Twitter networks and messages. A somewhat similar, but more in-depth approach was used by one author who conducted an extensive comparative textual discourse analysis of three quite different OSNs—Facebook, LinkedIn, and ASmallWorld—and found interesting differences among them.[136] Although much more text was analyzed in this study than in the previous one, the number of cases for each OSN was in the hundreds, which, again, is small by some standards. At the other end of the spectrum was a study of the daily mood cycles of 2 million Twitter users and 500 million of their tweets.[137] Not surprisingly, the content analysis in this case was conducted entirely using a computer analysis program—one already briefly discussed in the section on big textual data. What made such a vast sample possible was that no coding beyond the categories already embedded in the software was required.

One of the most important issues in studies of OSNs, as in studies of traditional networks, is influence: Who is influencing whom, and how can you tell? There are many theories of influence, but it is hard to test them in real social networks. Researchers have had to make do with laboratory simulations or survey research collecting after-the-fact reports. With OSNs it is possible to observe real (not simulated) interactions and thus study networks of influence more directly. Influence is not all that easy to define, and therefore it can be difficult to code; the concept raises tricky questions of cause and effect. Etymologically, an influence is an in-flowing of . . . well, something, which *causes* a change in or has the power to affect actions, thoughts, feelings, decisions, and so on. If a book sells many copies, is it influential? Perhaps people buy it but do not read it, or, if they read it, they might find it diverting, but it has no important effect on their thoughts and actions, or it may have different effects on different people. Because influence is a slippery concept, decisions about what you decide to code as a marker of influence can have a big . . . well, influence on the rest of the study.

Most strategies for determining influence in OSNs are versions of citations; what is studied are the effects of citations on citations. For example, a study of political blogs' influence on agenda setting (deciding on what topics to discuss) in other blogs used citations (hyperlinks) to Web addresses (URLs) of other blogs to determine the influence of those blogs; frequency of citation was the measure of influence.[138] Amounts and kinds of influence are frequent research questions in studies of Twitter. This micro-blogging site (limited to 140 characters per post) has many features that make it a good source of archival data to study influence in blogs. Several kinds of data from Twitter can be used to gauge influence. To collect and code it, you'll need to know quite a bit about the site to understand how it works. Unlike archival data prepared by researchers for researchers (census data, GSS, etc.), you have to be familiar with an OSN to determine what might be useful and to figure out how to extract it. When you open a Twitter account, among the first steps is to select some other members whose tweets (micro-blogs) you want

[135]Himelboim, McCreery, and Smith (2013).

[136]Papacharissi (2009).

[137]The study was conducted by Golder and Macy (2011) using software developed by Pennebaker (2011).

[138]Meraz (2009).

to follow; when one of your "followees" posts a tweet, you are notified. If you follow someone, they do not necessarily follow you. Indeed, most do not.[139] This means that some of the links between members of the site are directed links. When you receive a tweet, you can simply read it or forward (retweet) it; but you can also respond to it, mention it in one of your tweets, comment on it for anyone to read, or send your comments only to a particular individual. There are, in short, many types of actions that you can take; some are directed links to other members of the network, and some are not. These actions are the source of the network links that get studied. What parts of such a social network matter? One way to define "what matters" is to say that it is most important to study "people who actually communicate through direct messages with each other, as opposed to the network composed of declared followers and followees."[140] Others cast a broader net and try to weigh the importance of various kinds of network links.

Many of the archives we have discussed in this chapter are fairly easy for diligent researchers to become familiar with by devoting several days to reading online manuals and tutorials. This is especially true of those sites that are designed with researchers in mind. But proprietary sites, such as Twitter, are designed with users in mind. Much research is done, but it is in-house research that is aimed at improving the business model. Before you tackle one of these proprietary sites, you will probably need guidance from more experienced researchers. You don't want to try to be the first kid on your block to do a dissertation on one of these. Fortunately, for those who would like to investigate Twitter, there is very good guidance in two excellent articles. One article focuses on the familiar theme of measuring user influence, and the other devises a systematic catalogue of coding and analysis metrics for studying Twitter activities.[141] We think that a researcher would be ill advised to study Twitter without perusing these first. Much of what can be learned there would also be applicable to coding, measurement, and analysis issues in other OSNs.

CONCLUSION: CODING DATA FROM ARCHIVAL, WEB, AND NEW MEDIA SOURCES

Reviewing the research literature on a topic partly involves discovering a network of interrelated research sources, and those networks are increasingly Web based. Pooling the results of a set of research articles increases the power of conclusions by expanding the amount of data from which they are drawn. Thus literature reviews, like all archival data, tend to be built on big data. Big data tends to come mostly from the Web or is accessible through it. Despite all these links among the chapter's parts, we have maintained the separate categories in the concluding Summary Table on coding in literature reviews, big data, and Web-based data, because coding problems in the three types of archival data can be distinct and because individual researchers rarely engage in all three activities at once. By way of tying together some strands in the chapter, we discuss similarities and differences among the three in the next few paragraphs.

[139] For example, Paul Vogt follows the Twitter posts of Bill Gates and Barack Obama, but, somewhat surprisingly, they do not follow his.

[140] Huberman, Romero, and Wu (2008).

[141] See, respectively, Cha et al. (2010) and Bruns and Stieglitz (2013).

First, there are many other Web-based phenomena that generate archival data that a researcher could investigate. These include archives from computer dating services, prediction markets, and Google Trends.[142] These are all important examples, but most of our conclusions concerning scholarly citations, network analysis, and OSNs are applicable to those phenomena as well. They all generate, and make variously available, data that are codable using similar graphic, verbal, and numerical techniques.

A key issue in coding for just about every archival source we have discussed in this chapter is **keywords**. These provide the main way that you can categorize (code) archival information by relevance, whether the data are research articles for a systematic analysis or blog posts for a study of political networks. One of the first coding jobs for work in any field is learning its keywords. One way to do so is to become familiar with the literature in your field in order to learn its codes and their quirks (see the discussion of the multiple meanings and codes in the earlier section on relevance of works in a literature review). More systematically, you can consult a thesaurus. Most of the major indexing services have a thesaurus of terms. Well-known discipline-based examples with thesauri include PsychINFO, Sociological Abstracts, Medline, and ERIC. Keywords are also used when searching big data archives to find relevant data sources.

Sometimes you have to devise your own keywords because they are not provided in any systematic way. When reviewing a large body of textual data, your first round of coding is essentially to create keywords, categories into which you can place portions of your data and by which you can index them. In OSNs the keywords may be created by users. A good example is the use of "hashtags" in Twitter; these keywords are preceded with the number sign #, also called a hash mark. The availability of keywords varies from one archival source to the next and ranges from none at all to thorough and highly systematic. In the latter group are the keyword glossaries or thesauri used by research journals. A discipline's set of keywords tends to define its field of research. Because of that you need to be sure to use the right keywords to describe your own publications and posts. You might be lured by the pleasure of coming up with a cute title and innovative descriptors for your research or blog posts, but doing so could cost you citations and other markers of influence; people may not be able to find your work.

Web-based sources, including OSNs, are moving targets. They change because their owners change them by adjusting privacy options, membership rules, data collection methods, and so on. OSNs evolve when their members use them in new ways. They change when new kinds of users (such as those from different demographic groups or nations) join the pool of members. Such changeability makes it tricky to study OSNs longitudinally without taking into account such changes in owners' rules, users' activities, and members' social composition. Trying to follow the old adage, "if you want to study change, don't change the measure," requires considerable effort with moving targets. However, it is often well worth it to try to make the needed adjustments, because OSNs are among the largest sources of data available to social scientists for studying change over time in network behavior.

One advantage of studying OSNs is that, despite their changeability, it is comparatively easier to capture OSN data than it is, for example, to gather data from face-to-face interactions when conducting a participant observation. The stationary character of the evidence in an OSN is true of textual data and of archives in general. By contrast, when

[142] See, respectively, Rosenfeld and Thomas (2012), Wilson (2012), and Gaddis and Verdery (2012).

Goffman studied the presentation of self to others, he had to make his observations on the fly because he was working undercover as a participant observer.[143] Conversely, because of their comparative stability, OSN data provide new options for studying how people present themselves in everyday life.

A final feature of social network analysis of OSNs and academic citation networks that make them particularly interesting are the close parallels between what the researchers are doing and the activities the people being studied are engaging in. The way we study networks is influenced by the people engaged in networking. This kind of reciprocity is true to one degree or another of most types of research about people. You want to understand them, but they also want to understand themselves, and their self-understandings are topics of research, as well as providing good clues for the researcher. One often thinks of archival research as exempt from interaction with the participants, but there can be a kind of delayed interaction between the users of OSNs and the researchers who study them.[144] What each group does and learns can influence what the other does and learns. A third group participating in these interactions is composed of the in-house researchers working for companies such as Twitter, Facebook, and Google, and their internal studies are sometimes available to users and researchers.

As always, we close this chapter with a Summary Table. Like the chapter, the table has three distinct sections, but, as we have stressed in this conclusion, the overlap among them is considerable.

[143]Goffman (1961).

[144]The speed of the interactions in OSNs is slow by face-to-face standards but fast by archival standards.

SUGGESTIONS FOR FURTHER READING

One useful way to keep up with developments in literature reviews is to consult the new journal *Research Synthesis Methods*, established in 2010. It is the only scholarly journal we know of aimed specifically at the methodology of literature reviewing. Although the intended scope is general and includes "narrative analysis and synthesis of qualitative data," the published articles as of this writing have been on topics in meta-analysis or other types of quantitative research synthesis. Among the most thought-provoking articles on meta-analysis in that journal, or indeed anywhere else, is the presidential address by John Ioannidis (2010) entitled "Meta-Research: The Art of Getting It Wrong." Also extremely thought-provoking on research syntheses is an issue of the *Educational Researcher*, Volume 37, Number 1, on "Perspectives on Evidence-Based Research in Education." This contains a lead article by Robert Slavin (2008), five "Comments on Slavin" by prominent researchers, and Slavin's "Response to Comments."

Three popular and highly readable books by well-known scholars round out our recommendations. The discussion in each book is elementary and requires little if any background knowledge, but each provides a serious overview of its field, respectively: prediction, networks, and computer science. In *The Signal and the Noise*, Silver (2012) describes the use of (mostly) archival data to make predictions in many fields. It is a broad-based primer on predicting, with particular emphasis on the perils of prediction and why so many predictions are worthless (economists come in for especially severe criticism). Silver provides a set of small steps that researchers can use to improve the quality of predictions. In *Connected: How Your Friends' Friends' Friends Affect Everything You Feel, Think, and Do*, Christakis and Fowler (2009) review a huge amount of research, some of it their own, on social networks. They provide a great deal of technical detail, but always with a light touch; the book is the easiest way we have seen to get an introduction to both the findings of and the research methods in the field of network analysis as applied to many areas of study. Finally, in *9 Algorithms That Changed the Future*, MacCormick (2012) does more to demystify computer science than any other work we know of. Most of the algorithms discussed are specifically tied to using the Web, and they are described with a clarity that is truly beautiful.

CHAPTER 5 SUMMARY TABLE

CODING AND MEASUREMENT IN LITERATURE REVIEWS	
When doing this	**Then code**
Reviewing to guide practice (p. 140)	• By focusing on findings that are agreed upon, on what is known.
Reviewing to guide research (p. 140)	• By focusing on what is unknown or gaps in the literature.
Introductory reviews (pp. 140–141)	• Sources for: o Recency. o Importance. o Breadth.
Traditional/ narrative reviews (pp. 141–142)	• Sources as you would code interview transcripts and fieldnotes (see Chapters 2 and 4).
A theoretical review (pp. 142–143)	• To synthesize established theories by focusing on points of agreement and/or to generate new theories by focusing on gaps.
A meta-analysis (pp. 143–144)	• Data that enable you to calculate effect sizes.
A meta-synthesis (pp. 144–145)	• Using methods of grounded theory or qualitative comparative analysis.
A comprehensive literature review of any type (pp. 145–149)	• Sources for: o Relevance. (pp. 145–146) o Redundancy. (p. 147) o Roles. (pp. 147–148) o Quality. (pp. 148–149) o Diversity. (p. 149)
	o Biases of authors and/or the methods they use. (p. 149)

A meta-analysis (pp. 149–156)	• Sources for sample size. • Whether the IVs and DVs are categorical or continuous. (pp. 149–151) • Any changes in coding/measurement practices in sources. (p. 152) • Intra- and intercoder reliability when using multiple coders. (p. 153) • Information from sources about whether it is better to use fixed/common effect models or random/variable effects models. (p. 154) o Use random/variable effect models when unsure. (p. 154) • Any biases in primary sources. (pp. 154–156)

CODING AND MEASUREMENT FOR BIG DATA

When doing this	Then code
Coding big data in general (pp. 159–160)	• The methods used to select the data from the archive. • The meta-data or methodological documentation of your source. • Whether you have used the entire dataset or sampled or used methods of data reduction. • Any potential biases in the archival data.
Coding big textual data (pp. 160–165)	• Describe the provenance of your sources. • Your sources as primary, secondary, or tertiary. • Specify the qualitative decisions you have made that guide your computer-driven selection and coding. • Use human coding as a validity check on a sample of results from computer software. • Whether your software is general purpose or is dedicated, containing built-in codes.
Coding survey and census archives (pp. 165–171)	• Or recode the coding system of the data source. • Any recoding such as combining items into scales. • How you have recoded into common codes so as to combine or merge data from more than one source. • Missing data from the original sources and/or missing because of incompatibilities in the multiple sources you have used. • The level of data aggregation—e.g., individual case level or group or aggregate data.
GIS data (pp. 172–174)	• The software used and whether you have used vector or raster coding.

CODING AND MEASUREMENT FOR WEB-BASED DATA	
When doing this	**Then code**
Studying Web-based networks (pp. 174–188)	• The keywords used to guide your searching and categorization of the data. • The provenance or source of the data. • How the population of nodes is defined and sampled. • The software used and its algorithms for coding variables such as degree, centrality, density, and so on. • Whether ties are directed or undirected. • The valence (value) of the ties, such as positive, negative, or neutral. • The valence of nodes, such as liberal, moderate, or conservative. • How subgroups in the network are coded/defined. • Contextual variables pertaining to the nodes, e.g., demographic attributes. • Whether coding required expert/subjective judgment or was entirely machine-driven.
	• Change over time in the makeup of the nodes and the nature of the ties.

PART II

Analysis and Interpretation of Quantitative Data

In this Introduction to Part II we:

- Present an overview of analyzing different types of data.
  - Quantitative, qualitative, graphic, and combined/mixed.
- Provide a brief summary of chapter contents of Part II.
- Review the key concepts: theory, model, hypothesis, and variable.
  - Discuss types of relations among variables and the labels used to describe them.
  - Illustrate interaction effects with two graphs.
- Conclude with suggestions for further reading and a note on software.

INTRODUCTION TO PART II

Eagerness, even excitement, about making your analysis decisions is natural. After a long series of forks in the road (design, sampling, ethics, and coding), you are finally ready to select the methods you will use to make sense of your evidence, draw some conclusions, and offer some interpretations. Of course, researchers usually have a preliminary analysis plan quite early on when they write a research design or proposal. And analysis choices are strongly influenced by previous decisions about design, sampling, ethics, and coding. Coding, in particular, often directs the researcher to a fairly short list of specific analysis options. However, even after coding, there remain important choices that are not easy to make. Changing your mind and going back and reanalyzing (perhaps recoding, too) after you've done some preliminary work is common. Things you learn in the early exploration of the data can lead you to rethink your approach. And that's a good thing.

Coding decisions result in specific types of data: quantitative, qualitative, visual, or some combination; those types of data lead to categories of analysis. Now that coding decisions have been discussed in Part I, the rest of the chapters in this book are organized by types of data and data analysis. Part II addresses analysis methods to use when your data are quantitative or when you want to analyze qualitative data quantitatively. Part III addresses parallel questions for qualitative data, analyses, and interpretations, as well as for analyzing combined/mixed data. In both parts, discussions of visual data and analyses are integrated into every chapter.

Although we organize the chapters of Parts II and III by the ways coding has shaped data, we don't mean to overemphasize the distinctions between numerical, verbal, and graphic data. Although the three are distinct, they are commonly joined. Indeed, our emphasis on multimethod and mixed method research throughout the book makes it clear that we think they *should* often be joined. We find it nearly inconceivable to keep them separate in any moderately complex research project. For example, it is often possible, and sometimes advisable, to recode verbal data numerically or to recode numerical data qualitatively. Visual data are sometimes created by recoding numerical or verbal data; at other times, numerical or verbal data are created by recoding visual data. Recoding can be difficult and time-consuming, and it frequently involves some loss of information and/or creates a need to collect more data. But recoding can provide new perspectives on your data. In sum, although types of data coding do importantly limit the range of appropriate techniques, the distinctions between quantitative and qualitative are not absolutely determinative, because many kinds of data—textual, categorical, and ranked—can be studied with either quantitative or qualitative methods. Finally, conclusions arrived at using one type of data are routinely described using another; for example, a network diagram may be described by the number of links or a statistical inference may be described in words—for example, when the p value of .06 is described as "not significant."

As mentioned in previous chapters, we've added the category of visual data to the two most common ways data are coded (verbal and numerical). Visual data include examples such as maps, satellite images, videotapes, photographs, and X-rays, as well as a rapidly growing set of computer-generated descriptive and analytic techniques. In part because visual data are often converted into verbal and/or numerical data (and vice versa), coverage of visual data is interwoven with sections on numerical and verbal data. Indeed, until recently, visual data had mostly been used in social research to graphically represent verbal and numerical data; examples include concept maps, causal diagrams, and bar charts. Today the images brought to mind by the term *visual data* are exceptionally various and range from pencil sketches in fieldnotes to depictions of information networks constructed with graphics software or highly detailed maps to guide survey sampling constructed with GIS technology. And, when the raw data that social scientists investigate are physical artifacts, these are usually translated into verbal, numerical, and/or visual codes. For instance, cultural anthropologists might study a region's pottery by photographing its decorations, measuring its dimensions, and discussing how its use of religious symbolism evolved over time.

Reasoning about evidence, whether for purposes of description, explanation, prediction, understanding, causality, or generalization, uses the same conceptual tools regardless of whether the data are names, ranks, numbers, or pictures. Whatever their form, data are mute on the question of what they are to be used for. The data do not speak for themselves. We have to speak for them, no matter what the symbols used to collect and record them. The analysis chapters of Parts II and III discuss how different methods may be used to understand and speak for the data. The analysis chapters are separated into two parts: Part II, analysis and interpretation of quantitative data, including graphic representations of these; and Part III, analysis and interpretation of qualitative and combined/mixed data, including visual depictions of these. Of course, researchers may wish to use both types (including visual) in their investigations. Methods for doing so are explored in Chapter 13 on combining methods of analysis in multimethod or mixed method research.

To organize our discussions of numerical data in Part II, we use three basic classes of quantitative analysis techniques: descriptive, inferential, and associational. Some writers of texts and reference works discuss only two categories: inferential techniques, which are used for drawing conclusions about populations based on data from samples, and descriptive techniques, which cover everything else. We include the third category, associational methods, to refer to ways of analyzing complex relations among variables based on statistical associations among them. This is actually the largest category, both in our coverage in this book and in use by social science researchers. We devote two chapters to it. Although associational statistical models usually can be tested for statistical significance, such testing is often fairly incidental to the main lines of analysis and interpretation.

The three classes of analysis methods—descriptive, inferential, and associational—are closely related. Associational statistics can be used descriptively, and inferential methods are often applied to descriptive and associational statistics. The three types of statistics often build on one another. For the reader, this means that it is harder to understand an individual chapter on quantitative techniques in isolation from the others. This is especially true of the later chapters in Part II. They do not quite require mastery of the content in the earlier chapters, but they are considerably easier to read if you have a good grounding in the earlier chapters.

Descriptive statistical data and analyses (discussed in Chapter 6) are nearly ubiquitous. Only textual forms of data are more widespread. Even studies focused mainly on collecting qualitative data typically include some descriptive statistical data and analyses, for example: "Interviews of 90 minutes to 2 hours were conducted with 22 informants whose ages ranged from 64 to 77 years." Or "The team visited 27 classrooms over the course of the year, logging close to 400 hours of observation, which is an average of about 15 hours in each classroom." Methods of analyzing and presenting descriptive statistical data are important for virtually all researchers, not only those whose data are primarily numerical. They can provide a key part of the narrative describing the research and allow early data explorations that give important clues for later in-depth analyses. Descriptive methods are not necessarily simple; advanced associational methods and intricate graphic imaging can be used descriptively. Among the descriptive techniques discussed in Chapter 6 we include effect sizes, particularly those based on standardized mean differences.

Inferential statistical methods (discussed in Chapter 7) are used to generalize about populations (a.k.a. universes). The generalizations are based on data gathered from samples. Inferential statistical techniques are quite specifically confined to use with numerical data. Inferences using verbal and other qualitative data are also very widespread, of course (see Part III), but inferential statistical techniques are of limited use in that work. The most common inferential methods (based on null hypothesis significance testing, or NHST) have come in for a great deal of criticism in recent decades. Chapter 7 discusses these criticisms and presents alternatives to NHST. The inferential techniques of NHST are compared with methods for effect-size estimation and confidence intervals (margins of error), as well as with methods of Bayesian analysis and resampling methods.

Virtually all techniques of statistical analysis are ultimately based on the associational methods of correlation and regression. These, addressed in Chapter 8, are the foundation of the general linear model. Correlation and regression provide means to analyze complex relations among variables. In the absence of random assignment, statistical associations among variables are used to draw conclusions. Complicated experimental data from field experiments are also often analyzed using multiple regression. The appropriate use of the numerous types of correlation and regression depends largely on the way the data being analyzed have been coded and on the presumed relations among the variables being studied. A main theme of the chapter is, *Which* of the methods can be used most effectively with *particular* data codings and for specific types of research question? Also, the chapter reviews a range of effect-size statistics based on correlation and regression.

Methods for analyzing numerical data with advanced, computer-intensive procedures are discussed in Chapter 9. These methods extend the basic tools of correlation and regression, some of which are over 100 years old. The computer-intensive methods discussed in Chapter 9 are of more recent vintage and are still under development. We first discuss multilevel modeling (MLM), which is used for nested variables. Most variables in the social sciences are, in fact, nested. Then we turn to structural equation modeling (SEM), which combines regression analysis of the relations among variables with factor analysis for their measurement, particularly when the variables are latent and difficult to measure; and many variables in the social sciences are difficult to measure. A special wrinkle on MLM and SEM is mixture modeling, which addresses categorical latent variables. Although these procedures are quite recondite and mathematically challenging, they build directly on more basic and more broadly understood methods discussed in Chapter 8. This means that answers to the initial questions of when to use them and what they might be used for can be addressed even while bypassing much of the technical detail.

We conclude our discussion of quantitative analysis and interpretation with a discussion of building and assessing quantitative models in Chapter 10. This chapter is a natural extension of the model-building methods discussed in Chapters 8 and 9 (on regression, MLM, and SEM). In Chapter 10 we step back briefly in order to reconsider what it is to build a model and when it is useful to do so. Then we move forward to consider the most advanced (not necessarily most technically difficult) methods that can be used to analyze and interpret quantitative data using multimodel inference; these methods are based on using the idea of multiple working hypotheses. Rather than testing individual null hypotheses, the multimodel approach uses maximum likelihood estimation to rank competing models from most to least effective. Although this approach is somewhat more computationally complex, it has several advantages. One of them is that most people, including researchers, find it more intuitive. It seems more relevant to investigate how well the data fit theories (models) in which one is interested than to attempt to reject (null) hypotheses, which, by definition, have no substantive import. This approach also, as a side benefit, helps avoid pesky triple negatives, such as the researcher describing the results of a successful experiment saying, "Eureka! No, there was not no difference!"

CONCEPTUAL AND TERMINOLOGICAL HOUSEKEEPING: THEORY, MODEL, HYPOTHESIS, CONCEPT, VARIABLE

We conclude this introduction by sorting out the terms used to label several important ideas. When we used these terms earlier in the book, we assumed a sort of rough-and-ready common understanding of what was meant by them. But they are contested terms, and particularly so in research emphasizing quantitative data, so we try to be more explicit here. These terms are important because they codify central ideas in data analysis and interpretation.

The terms *theory, model,* and *hypothesis* are used in several overlapping ways. Consensus among researchers about their proper definitions is far from perfect. Discussions of these terms contain quite a lot of dogmatism, with researchers sometimes insisting on the "correctness" of particular definitions. Although we see subtle differences between theory, model, and hypothesis and appreciate some of the distinctions our colleagues have suggested, we tend to use the terms loosely, if not quite interchangeably. One solution that has considerable appeal, because it can help avoid hairsplitting and doctrinal disputes, is to think of them all as different **types of theoretical expression.**[1]

We use these different varieties of theoretical expression as follows. **Theories** are broad explanations of the relationships among phenomena; they are usually expressed verbally. **Models** tend to be constructed for the purpose of guiding a specific research project and are usually described graphically or with equations; for example, a path model depicts the causal relations postulated in a verbal theory. So models are descriptions or depictions of the relations among concepts; they are used both to summarize empirical findings and to guide further research.

Hypotheses are bits of a model (or a theory) that we want to examine or test. Like many people, we use the word *hypothesis* in two ways: (1) formally, to mean an empirically testable statement derived from a theory (or a model); (2) less formally, to mean an idea that has not yet been examined or verified. Of course, in general discourse, theory is also used in this second way, as in "it's just a theory."

We use the term **concept** as the most general term to describe the phenomena studied. *Concept* includes quantitative variables such as age, qualitative attributes such as gender, and **constructs** such as prejudice. Like many terms in research methods, *concept* and *construct* have various meanings. Both are ideas of something; the idea can be one that is used in ordinary language, or it can be constructed for the purposes of research. The lay concept and the more formal research concept often have the same name and have much in common substantively.

For example, if you were researching the relations among marriage and employment and how these differ between men and women, you would probably use the terms in much the same way as they are used in ordinary discourse (e.g., Are married men/women more or less likely than single individuals to be employed?). But you would also need to specify your concepts to make sure that they were clear for identifying, coding, and analyzing. Does your definition of the concept of marriage include domestic partnerships? Does employment include part-time incidental work? Will you have more than two categories for gender, for example, to include transgendered people? In brief, you have to refine your concepts in order to do research using them. You can label the

[1] Jaccard and Jacoby (2010).

refined concepts *constructs*, as many psychologists do; or you can continue to call them *concepts*, as many political scientists do;[2] or you could call the specified concepts/constructs the **operational definitions** of your variables, although that term has fallen from favor in some camps.

Variable is another term researchers use to discuss the phenomena they study and relations among them; a variable is, naturally, something that varies, that changes with conditions; the opposite of a variable is a constant. There are many types of and labels for variables. While some scholars insist on particular labels for particular types of variables, others use the labels rather loosely. Although many researchers use the term *variable*, others object, especially if they mostly analyze qualitative data.[3] And some readers may not like the idea of causal relationships implied in the term *variable*. We use causal language in Table II.1, which describes relations among phenomena, because we see no way to avoid it.

In any case, the concepts are exceptionally important—the labels, less so. Still, it is helpful to have a quick summary of the typical labels for variables one is likely to encounter when reading research reports. This is provided in Table II.1. The multiplicity of different labels for the same or similar concepts is in part due to the fact that usage differs by discipline and research tradition.

The basic set of relations described in Table II.1 is as follows: Changes or differences in a **cause** (Column 1) will lead to changes or differences in an **effect** (Column 3). These changes are often indirect and occur through **causal links** (Column 2). Finally, the pattern of relations among the causes, links, and effects can themselves be affected by various kinds of **influences**. It is also helpful to see this graphically in Figure II.1.

An example, discussed in a bit more length in Chapter 9, can briefly illustrate. People with higher incomes tend to live longer on average. Income fosters longevity, but it does so indirectly, for example, by improving access to medical care. That pattern

TABLE II.1. Variables: Concepts and Labels

	1 Cause	2 Causal Link	3 Effect	4 Influences
Labels	Independent Predictor Explanatory Regressor Attribute	Intervening Mediating	Dependent Outcome Criterion Response	Control Antecedent Moderating Suppressor Effect modifier Interaction effect
Examples	Income	Access to medical care	Longevity	Age, gender, education

Note. All of the labels are called variables—independent variable, intervening variable, and so forth—except for effect modifier and interaction effect.

[2]Goertz (2006).

[3]One useful distinction is that researchers investigating quantitative data are "variable oriented," whereas those studying qualitative data are "case oriented." Both study processes, including causal processes.

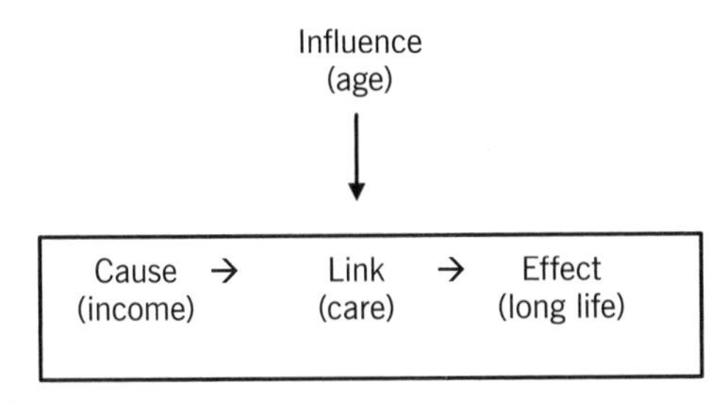

FIGURE II.1. Example of a moderator variable with an interaction effect.

of income leading to better medical care, which in turn increases life expectancy, is probably influenced by many other variables, such as age. For instance, access to high-quality medical care may be especially important for young children and octogenarians, but somewhat less so for people of other ages. The researcher would want to *control* for age, which would be a **moderator** variable (a.k.a. **effect modifier**) and which would likely have an **interaction** effect[4] with access to medical care's influence on longevity. In Figure II.1 we see that the basic relation is that income leads to medical care, which leads to long life. That *set* of causal relations, indicated by the box, is influenced by individuals' ages.

Another way to illustrate these kinds of interactions among variables is presented in Figure II.2. Here the outcome variable is probability of death in a given year; the moderating variable is age, specifically two age cohorts: Infants less than 1 year old are compared with young adults ages 15–24. With increases in access to health care, the probability of death goes down for both. But it goes down further and at a faster rate for infants.[5] The interaction effect arises from the different rates of decline in probability of death for the two groups; it is a joint or combined effect.

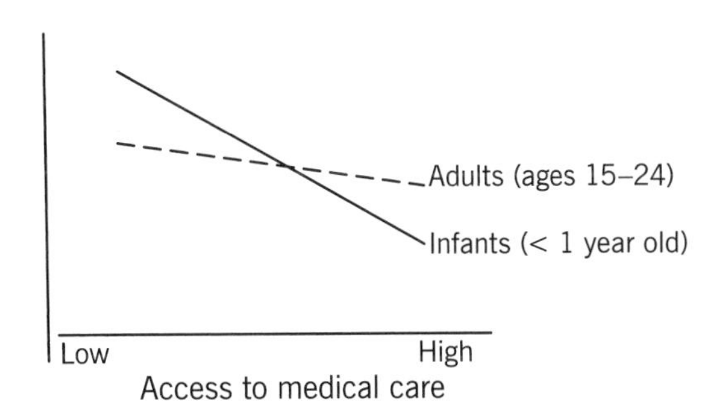

FIGURE II.2. Example of an interaction effect. Probability of death in a given year: by age cohort and by access to medical care (hypothetical/illustrative data).

[4]Interaction effects are conceptually and analytically tricky, which makes them easy for beginning researchers to misinterpret; see Brambor, Clark, and Golder (2006) for a handy, though technically advanced, review. The differences between controlling for a variable, such as age, and testing its interaction in a causal relation are important (see Chapter 8).

[5]The relations depicted here are illustrative only, but they are realistic. Many of the major causes of death in young adults (accidents, homicide, and suicide) are much less influenced by access to good quality health care than are the main causes of death for infants, most of which are related to complications at birth.

The terms and concepts listed in Table II.1 are discussed in more detail at various points throughout the upcoming chapters in Part II. The most complicated of these concepts are in the fourth column, the influences. The terms in the other three columns (for cause, link, and effect) are used more or less synonymously. Here the table presents, for ready reference, those clusters of labels.[6]

What does this proliferation of concepts and the labels used to describe them have to do with research practice and the analysis of your data? How does it relate to taking advantage of the large array of choices awaiting you as you get ready to analyze and interpret your data? You begin with your research questions; these emerge out of and continue to evolve into a sort of dialogue with the theories you are using. Modeling your theory is an important step in making your ideas concrete enough to investigate. When you model your theory, you translate your concepts and your hypotheses about how they are related to one another into variables. The specification of your variables helps make them explicit enough that you can analyze and interpret the data you have collected. Without this kind of specification of the phenomena you are studying and how you conceive of the relationships among them, it is difficult to make sense of your data.

[6]For different accounts of these sets of labels and the concepts they denote, see Jaccard and Jacoby (2010, Ch. 7).

SUGGESTIONS FOR FURTHER READING AND A NOTE ON SOFTWARE

Our suggestions here are less about what you might be interested in reading and more about useful tools. Modern quantitative analysis is inconceivable without statistical software. The history of how data analysis and computer software interacted—with analysis needs driving the creation of hardware and software and new computer devices suggesting new possibilities for analysis—are brilliantly described in Dyson's *Turing's Cathedral: The Origins of the Digital Universe* (2012).

There may be pedagogical advantages (opinions differ) to learning how to do some computations by hand (brain) before availing yourself of statistical packages. But real work, as opposed to school exercises, will always be done using statistical software, and many advanced techniques are literally impossible (in one lifetime) to do by hand. Not only is statistical software faster, but it is also—and this can be more important—much less likely to make mistakes. Today, errors in computation are all but nonexistent. Rather, the errors with the most serious consequences occur when the analyst chooses an inappropriate method. The software will do what it is told. It doesn't know better; therefore, we must. Although statistical analysis software is indispensable, it will make one a good statistician only to the extent that word processing software will make one a good poet.

All of the major statistical analysis packages are solid. Most people we know have in fact "chosen" among them by picking the one they encountered first, the one their professors used, the one their university made available at no cost, and so on. All of the major statistical analysis packages (R, SPSS, SAS, and STATA) are very good, each has various strong points, and users have strong preferences; it really doesn't matter which one you use. On the other hand, if you are going to use a *spreadsheet* to do your statistical analyses—and this is an increasingly common practice, especially in business organizations—then it does matter, because the quality and accuracy of the major spreadsheet packages do vary among packages *and* between earlier and later versions of the same package. At the time of this writing (2013), the best review of spreadsheet packages is Keeling and Pavur's (2012) "Statistical Accuracy of Spreadsheet Software."

We usually avoid software recommendations because they can quickly go out of date and because blanket recommendations are hard to make for different users with different needs. And once you have become familiar with one statistical package, it might not seem worth the effort to learn another, even if it might be better at some tasks. However, if we were advising young people who had not yet invested much time in learning particular softwares and the only considerations were quality and cost-effectiveness, the choices (as of this writing in late 2013) would be very clear. For all-purpose statistical analysis software, the open-source freeware package R is not only the best, but it is also the most quickly updated, and it is totally free to anyone with an Internet connection. The Comprehensive R Archive Network (CRAN) can be accessed and the software downloaded at *http://cran.r-project.org*. R can be somewhat difficult to use, especially for users who have grown accustomed to drop-down menus and pointing and clicking rather than typing in commands. Many R users first record their data in a spreadsheet and then import them into R. What spreadsheet might you use? Any spreadsheet is fine for data *entry*, but for data *analysis*, probably the best spreadsheet as of this writing is also freeware: Gnumeric. It is available at *www.gnome.org*.

CHAPTER 6

Describing, Exploring, and Visualizing Your Data

In this chapter we discuss:

- What descriptive statistics are.
- An overview of the main types of descriptive statistics and their uses, including measures of:
  - Central tendency, dispersion, relative position, association, effect size, and likely error.
- When to use descriptive statistics to depict populations and samples.
- What statistics to use to describe the cases you have studied.
- What descriptive statistics to use to prepare for further analyses.
  - An extended example using graphic methods.
    - Stem-and-leaf plot.
    - Boxplots (a.k.a. box-and-whisker diagrams).
    - Error bars around population estimates.
    - Skewness and kurtosis.
    - Histogram with normal curve superimposed.
    - Normal P-P plot.
- When to use correlations as descriptive statistics.
  - Using scatterplots to examine data for linearity, bivariate outliers, and equality of variances.
- When and where to make the normal curve your point of reference.
  - What to do when your data do not come from a normally distributed population.
    - Distribution-free statistics.
    - Robust statistics.
    - Removing or trimming outliers.
    - Transforming your data.
      —Using *z*-scores, square roots, logarithms, and reciprocals.

- When can you use descriptive statistics substantively?
  - Using the effect size (ES) as a descriptive statistic.
    - Different effect sizes for data coded differently.
    - An example illustrating some common effect sizes.
    - When to use descriptive statistics to prepare to apply missing data methods.

Researchers should begin their data analyses by thoroughly exploring and describing their data. This is true both for qualitative and quantitative data. When the data are quantitative, graphing the data distribution is almost always an indispensable element of these exploratory descriptions. Description of your data can be an end in itself; it can also suggest hypotheses to test; and it is a necessary component of many more complicated analyses. Finally, examining the data distributions to see whether they conform to the assumptions of the analytical techniques you plan to use is a crucial step both for inferential analyses (Chapter 7) and for multivariate regression-based models (Chapters 8 and 9).

Crucial to almost all research, descriptive statistics are sometimes slighted in texts and reference works for researchers. The reason perhaps is the emphasis texts usually put on statistical inference and significance testing; this can overwhelm consideration of descriptive statistics. The difference between descriptive and inferential statistics is that descriptive statistics portray *actual* data, whereas inferential statistics are used to estimate *probable* values.

Slighting descriptive statistics in favor of inferential statistics and significance testing is unfortunate, because many research questions can be answered with descriptive techniques and do not require statistical inference. Also, the two types of statistics are often linked. The basic inferential question is, What is the probability of *this result*? "This result," the one that is being tested for significance, is almost always a descriptive statistic—a mean difference, a change over time, a correlation, or any of numerous other measures. Researchers use descriptive statistics as the basis of their inferences.

Descriptive statistics also have a key *diagnostic* role in quantitative research. They are used to identify problems with the data that require changes in the inferential and/or multivariate techniques you might want to employ, especially assumptions about the shape of population distributions—including how you might need to transform your data to align them with those assumptions. Finally, descriptive statistics have a central role in identifying the scope of and patterns in missing data.

WHAT IS MEANT BY *DESCRIPTIVE STATISTICS*?

The term *descriptive statistics* is usually defined by contrast, by what descriptive statistics are not: not inferential, not multivariate, or not causal. Defining descriptive statistics by what they are not implies a lack of importance, as in *merely* descriptive. This derogation is unmerited.

The most common definition of descriptive statistics is "not inferential." Thus any statistic that is not inferential is, by default, descriptive. Inferential techniques are used to draw conclusions (make probabilistic inferences) about populations, using data from probability samples (selected by random sampling or random assignment) to do so. Researchers not attempting to generalize from a sample to a population—because they are studying a convenience sample or because they are studying the whole population—would, by this definition, be using descriptive techniques.[1]

In addition to "not inferential," a second definition of descriptive statistics is "not multivariate"—that is, not describing relations among two or more variables. Third, descriptive statistics may be said to differ from techniques used to draw causal conclusions from data. It is common to combine these two definitions to imply that descriptive statistics are used for research that examines only one variable at a time and/or that does not examine relations among the variables being studied. Few statistics found in actual research meet these criteria. We have seldom—if ever—seen published studies that study only one variable at a time and that investigate no relations among variables.

If we use the definition "not inferential" for descriptive statistics, their number and range of uses is substantial. Nearly all statistics can be used descriptively. The main exception is methods used to compute *p*-values and confidence intervals, which are exclusively inferential.[2] Although it is common practice to define descriptive statistics negatively, by what they are not, we offer the following positive definition: **descriptive statistics** are methods used to portray the cases in a collection of data, to depict patterns in the data, to explore the distributions or shapes of the data, and/or to summarize the basic features of the data.

Descriptive statistics may themselves be described as falling into six different categories. Most studies of any complexity can productively use them all, and, as we show in this chapter, most of them are much more effective when complemented by graphic representations of the data being described.

OVERVIEW OF THE MAIN TYPES OF DESCRIPTIVE STATISTICS AND THEIR USES

1. Measures of **central tendency**, such as the mean, median, and mode. These are used to identify the typical or middle **score**[3] in a distribution.
2. Measures of **dispersion**, such as the variance and the standard deviation (*SD*). These describe the amount of deviation from the central tendency, especially from the mean.
3. Measures of relative **position**, such as the percentile and the *z*-score. These describe the location of a given score in a distribution of scores.

[1] There is some controversy about whether it is appropriate to use inferential statistics with whole populations; this issue is discussed briefly in the next chapter.

[2] An increasingly common way to describe these distinctions—stemming from the growing importance of data mining and machine learning—is "unsupervised" and "supervised" learning from the data. See Hastie, Tibshirani, and Friedman (2009).

[3] As is fairly common practice, we use the term *score* as a generic label for any quantitative value; thus score includes values, such as income and number of siblings, that are not often described in ordinary language as scores.

4. Measures of **association,** such as the correlation. These describe how the values of two or more variables vary together, or covary. These measures are discussed extensively in Chapter 9; here we focus on their descriptive uses.
5. Measures of **effect size** (ES), such as Cohen's *d*. These are used to describe magnitude. Many statistics describe magnitude, but the term *effect size* is typically reserved for statistics that do so using standardized measures. In other words, ES statistics are usually expressed in or calculated with *SD* units.
6. Measures of **likely error** (or margins of error), such as the **standard error** (*SE*) and **confidence interval** (CI). These are used to estimate the likely range of probable error of estimation in other statistics. They are basically inferential measures (see Chapter 7), but because they also have some limited descriptive uses, we discuss them briefly in this chapter.

When to Use Descriptive Statistics to Depict Populations and Samples

The most widespread use of descriptive statistics in research reports is to tell the reader about the **cases** studied.[4] Researchers should always thoroughly describe who or what was studied and how cases were selected. How many cases were selected? What were their characteristics? These and related questions have to be answered in considerable descriptive detail so that readers can intelligently interpret findings and so that interested researchers could attempt to replicate the results or use the results in a meta-analysis.

Providing sufficient information for interpretation and replication is an ethical obligation of social and behavioral scientists. This obligation does not arise only with numerical data; it is increasingly common for interview and other verbal data to be made available to other researchers, for example, by placing them in archives. We believe that in research analyzing quantitative data, the full dataset should usually be described and made available for researchers wishing to examine results in detail. Independent archives exist in which researchers can deposit their data and the codes they used to analyze them. Doing this is required by most major economics journals, and similar requirements would be an important advance on practice in other fields.[5] Current policies in most journals in social research merely *encourage* researchers to provide their data. All too often, researchers merely say in a footnote something like, "those who want to see the data should contact the author." That puts the burden on the consumers of the research to ask for the data; it should be on the authors of the research to supply the data.

If you are not going to make your full dataset available to other researchers, at minimum you should provide basic descriptive statistics such as means, standard deviations, and the correlation matrix of all variables. These make it possible for readers to critically analyze the results and/or to conduct meta-analyses. If your study uses numerous variables, a full correlation matrix (or a variance–covariance matrix) will take up

[4] *Cases* is used here as a generic term for participants, subjects, informants, respondents, units of analysis, and so on, all of whom find their position in the rows of the data matrix. Cases are often persons, but they also include other units of analysis, such as schools, clinics, cities, businesses, and so on.

[5] See Freese (2007) for details on how this can be done and for a persuasive rationale for doing so.

more room than most journals are willing to supply. If this is the case, see whether the journal has a website for posting such data. If not, establish your own website or blog and make the data available there.

What Statistics to Use to Describe the Cases You Have Studied

Descriptive statistics are used in all designs to describe the cases being studied, particularly how the cases compare with the population to which the researcher wants to generalize. The exact approach varies by design. It can be quite formal in survey research when comparing known data about the population with data describing the sample. In experimental research, you should compute statistics to describe the control and experimental groups to determine whether the groups are similar. In interview and observational research, this descriptive work tends to be less formal, but it can still be quite important. For example, if you are interviewing or observing clients of a social service agency, you may want to discuss the range in the ages of those you are interviewing or observing or to determine whether your interviewees' ages are close to the typical age.

The full range of descriptive statistics can be applied to the fundamental job of describing cases and how representative they are, whether that means comparing samples with populations, experimental and control groups, or informants with the groups to which you want to generalize. Measures of central tendency—means, modes, and medians—are most commonly used. Measures of dispersion—such as the *SD*—are also important for understanding central tendencies. Increasingly, measures of association, particularly correlations, are also used for descriptive purposes. In most instances, it makes sense to provide all descriptive statistics, and, as mentioned earlier, we think that providing them is an ethical obligation that researchers have to the audience for the research. With the exception of the correlation matrix, it usually requires no more than a few lines of text to present this essential information.

The **mode** is the most frequent score in a series of scores. For nominal data, the mode is the *only* appropriate measure of central tendency. Use it with highly skewed distributions, as well as for nominal or qualitative data. There may be more than one mode in a distribution of scores; if there are two, the distribution is described as **bimodal.**

The **median** is the middle score in a ranked series. Thus it divides the series into two equal parts—half of the scores above and half below the median. Like the mode, the median is stable even when a distribution contains extreme values. The median and the mode tend to be more accurate for, and should be used for, skewed distributions.

The **mean** is what most people mean by "average": the total of all the scores divided by the number of scores. But the term *average* is used loosely. Descriptive statistics—such as the "average income for a family of four"—are often reported as medians, not means. Thus it is crucial that you specify exactly what measure you are using. Say *mean* or *median*, not *average.*

A common joke runs, "in our town, all the children are above average." It's a joke because it is widely believed that, by definition, half the scores are above and half below average. This is always true of the median, but only sometimes of the mean. Although all of the children cannot be above average, most of them can be. Say that the town has nine kids and that on some measure they got the following scores: 97, 85, 82, 82, 82,

82, 51, 33, 18. The mean is 68. Six of the kids (two-thirds) scored above that average. The mean isn't a very good description of this particular set of scores. The median and mode are each 82. In this distribution, the median and mode more accurately describe the group. In a balanced or "symmetrical" distribution, such as a normal distribution, the mean is the middle score, because the mean and median (and usually the mode, unless it is bimodal) are identical. But many of the natural distributions that researchers encounter in their work are not normally distributed. In brief: When describing your cases, report all three measures of central tendency.

The most important of these three measures is the mean, despite the fact that it can be a misleading descriptive statistic in some distributions. Its importance stems from the fact that the mean and measures of deviation from the mean are the foundation for most advanced statistics. The two key measures of deviation from the mean are the **variance** and the **standard deviation** (*SD*).[6] The *SD* is the square root of the variance. It is hard to overemphasize the extent to which the most common statistical techniques are built on the mean and deviations from the mean. The variance is important for calculating many statistics, but the *SD* is more useful for descriptive purposes. The *SD* is essentially a measure of how much, on average, the scores differ from the mean. A large *SD* means a lot, a small *SD* means a little. For example, say the mean salary of a group of workers is $40,000. If the *SD* is $1,000, there is only moderate variation in how much the workers make; the mean tells most of the story. But if the *SD* is $32,000, workers in the group have much more diverse salaries. The *SD* tells you a lot, which is why it should always be reported. It provides a good indication of how accurate the mean is as a summary statistic. An *SD* has to be interpreted in context. For example, a large *SD* for the scores on a 100-point exam might be 40, whereas that for the salaries in the preceding example was $32,000.

Measures of association have an important role to play in describing the cases used in research reports. Perhaps the most commonly used measure of association for this purpose is the Pearson *r* correlation. A correlation matrix of all variables is useful in many ways. It allows researchers to look for patterns of relationships between pairs of variables. The correlation matrix is not reported as often as measures of central tendency and the *SD*. This is in part due to tradition and also, undoubtedly, because a correlation matrix can be unwieldy if the number of variables is large. With 5 variables, there are 10 correlations to be reported; with 10 variables, the number is 45; with 15, it is 105—too many to squeeze onto one page. Nonetheless, it is irresponsible for researchers to neglect making these data available to other researchers. The correlation matrix helps other researchers to understand the relations among your variables and to interpret your results. Also, given the correlation matrix, other investigators can more easily use your research in a meta-analysis, as well as in conducting their own factor analysis or building their own structural equation models. Providing these descriptive data is crucial. In the words of the old saying: "In God we trust; all others must show their data."

---

[6]There are several ways to abbreviate these important measures; the two most common among statisticians, when referring to a sample, are s^2 for the variance and s for the standard deviation. When referring to a population, statisticians usually use σ (Greek sigma) and σ^2, respectively.

WHAT DESCRIPTIVE STATISTICS TO USE TO PREPARE FOR FURTHER ANALYSES

Descriptive data are useful for the readers of your research, particularly other investigators. But they are equally important for your subsequent, more complicated analyses. Descriptive statistics are what you use to begin to get to know your data, their features, and their oddities. You need to get a "feel" for your data. That's why it is often *not* a good idea to delegate your data handling work to others. You lose the intimate connection with your data by ceding control of them. Researchers working with qualitative data usually know this. Researchers new to analyzing quantitative data are sometimes unaware of the need to become intimate with their data. In any case, you are ill advised to have a passive relationship with your data by letting them be cared for by someone who, in all likelihood, has less of an interest in getting it right than you do.

You need a subjective sense of your data, their "personality." This needs to be supplemented, of course, by more objective measures. First, look for extreme scores or **outliers**. A common definition of an outlier is a score that is 3 or more *SD*s above or below the mean. A looser but useful definition is an **influential observation**, that is, any observation or score that can, by itself, importantly influence the outcome of an analysis. What is "importantly"? That is usually a matter of judgment and depends on your research question.

Many outliers are mistakes in data entry. Even so, it is important to identify them, because a few outliers, or sometimes even just one, can wreak havoc in an analysis. If the outlier is a mistake, you correct it. But if it is not a mistake, your decision is more complicated; statisticians sometimes disagree about what to do. On the one hand, your outliers can be your most interesting cases, ones that merit special attention. On the other hand, if answers to your research questions require accurate generalizations about *groups*, and if your analytical technique is heavily dependent on the mean and deviation from the mean (and most are), you should probably delete the case from the dataset before doing the analysis.[7] An extreme score can distort the mean, and therefore the variance and *SD*, and therefore every statistic based on them, including *t*-tests, analyses of variance (ANOVAs), correlations, and regression coefficients. There are several ways to delete outliers. Statistical packages will often provide a "trimmed mean" as part of the descriptive output. For example, a 5% trimmed mean would be the mean calculated after deleting the upper and lower 5% of the values from the distribution. If you use a partial dataset, such as a trimmed mean, it is good practice to provide all analytic conclusions, both with the full dataset and with the reduced version.

An Extended Example

Rather than continuing to discuss in general terms when to use which descriptive statistics, we illustrate some main points using descriptive techniques we applied to the analysis of data generated by a quasi-experimental study. The study evaluated the effects on learning of a new method of teaching computer programming to college students.[8] The

[7]Osborne and Overbay (2004).

[8]Hosack et al. (2012).

dependent or outcome variable was scores on common final examinations over two semesters. The study was a quasi-experiment because the 302 student participants were not randomly assigned to treatment and comparison groups. Instead, they enrolled in class sections using whatever criteria they happened to follow. Treatments were assigned to some of those sections, and the students in those sections were the treatment group; students in the other sections served as the comparison group.

One disadvantage of this and other quasi-experiments is that the researchers had no control over the *assignment* of students to experimental conditions. Also, because the learning experiment was not a laboratory simulation but occurred in ordinary classes, the investigators had less control over the *delivery* of the instruction than they would have had under controlled laboratory conditions. A potentially offsetting advantage of the study design was that the participants were real students in real courses, not volunteers for a laboratory simulation. It could be argued that the reality of the setting made it more likely that what was learned in the research could more appropriately be generalized to other real students in real courses.

Our goal here is not to describe the study fully but to use it as an example of how descriptive statistics can be applied in data analysis. Despite the study's relatively simple design, which included only a modest number of control variables, we used a wide range of graphic and descriptive techniques to explore and describe the data.

In our study, as in all quasi-experiments, without random assignment, it is crucial to check for the equal distribution of nontreatment variables in the control and experimental groups. Even had the assignment to sections or groups been random, it would still have been important to check for the equal distribution of variables that researchers knew from literature reviews could influence the outcome variable. The covariates we examined were students' cumulative grade point averages (GPAs), their genders, their academic majors, and their class ranks. All of these, but especially cumulative GPA, have been shown in previous research to be linked to success in course outcomes in STEM (science, technology, engineering, and math) disciplines.

We compared the distributions of these variables in control and experimental sections and found no large or statistically significant differences between the two. The students self-assigned in a way that very closely approximated random assignment, at least on these four variables.

We began with **stem-and-leaf plots** (see Figures 6.1 and 6.2). The beauty of the stem and leaf, and why it is a good graphic technique for you to begin with, is that it combines graphic visualization with a full frequency distribution. It retains *all* of the data while enabling the researcher to see it depicted in a kind of bar graph—specifically, a bar graph in which the bars are constructed out of numbers. A general rule to follow when picking graphic techniques to display and visualize your data is to select those that use or depict the most data. This rule makes the stem-and-leaf among the very best techniques, as it can often display all of the data.[9]

Stem-and-leaf plots are not often reported in the published literature, perhaps because they take up a lot of space, but they are very useful for researchers exploring their data. The "stem" in this example is the number before the decimal point; the "leaf" is the number following it. For example, in Figure 6.1 we can see that 1 female

[9]When the data are several digits long, as they would be, for example, for individuals' annual incomes or cities' population sizes, then the data have to be rounded in order to be depicted.

Frequency		Stem & Leaf
3 Extremes		(= <.0)
3	0 .	689
1	1 .	2
6	1 .	567799
12	2 .	000112223344
6	2 .	577899
22	3 .	0000000001111222224444
14	3 .	55555667788999
5	4 .	00000
Stem width:	1.00	
Each leaf:	1 case(s)	

FIGURE 6.1. GPA, cumulative stem-and-leaf plot for females (*N* = 72).

had a GPA of 1.2 and 6 females had GPAs from 1.5–1.9, specifically: 1.5, 1.6, 1.7, 1.7, 1.9, 1.9. Most important, for this analysis, we learned from this graphic/frequency distribution that the data, supplied by the university registrar, contained several extreme and improbable scores (see the first rows of Figures 6.1 and 6.2, "Extreme Values"). The graphic suggested that we needed to reexamine the data. We found several GPAs of 0 in the dataset; we determined that they were missing data, not real scores. Although it is possible for a student to have a GPA of 0—all grades of F—a student with those grades does not last very long at a university. In any case, there can be a big difference between a GPA of 0 on the one hand and "don't know" or "missing" on the other. It is a mistake,

Frequency		Stem & Leaf
11 Extremes		(= <.5)
5	0 .	66689
9	1 .	122233333
22	1 .	5556667778888889999999
52	2 .	0000000111111112222222222222333333333333333444444444
56	2 .	55555555555555566666666666777777777777788888999999999999
45	3 .	000000000011111112222222222223333333344444444
23	3 .	55555566666666677777788
7	4 .	0000000
Stem width:	1.00	
Each leaf:	1 case(s)	

FIGURE 6.2. GPA, cumulative stem-and-leaf plot for males (*N* = 230).

for example, to say that a person whose height we do not know is 0 inches tall. That's why we converted the 0's to missing values and used this "trimmed" dataset for the rest of our analyses. Although this reduced the number of datapoints for a key covariate, the eliminated data were errors that it made no sense to retain.

Because the two groups (male and female students) differed in size, it was hard to use the stem-and-leaf to compare their distributions, so we constructed a **boxplot** (a.k.a. **box-and-whisker diagram**). This can be much better for comparing distributions side to side (see Figure 6.3).

We can see in Figure 6.3 that the two distributions of GPAs by gender are similar but not identical. The dark bars in the middle of each box show the distributions' medians. When the median line is not in the middle of the box, as in these examples, the distribution is skewed. The top and bottom of the box represent the distribution's 75th and 25th percentiles; the distance between them is called the **interquartile range,** or IQR.[10]

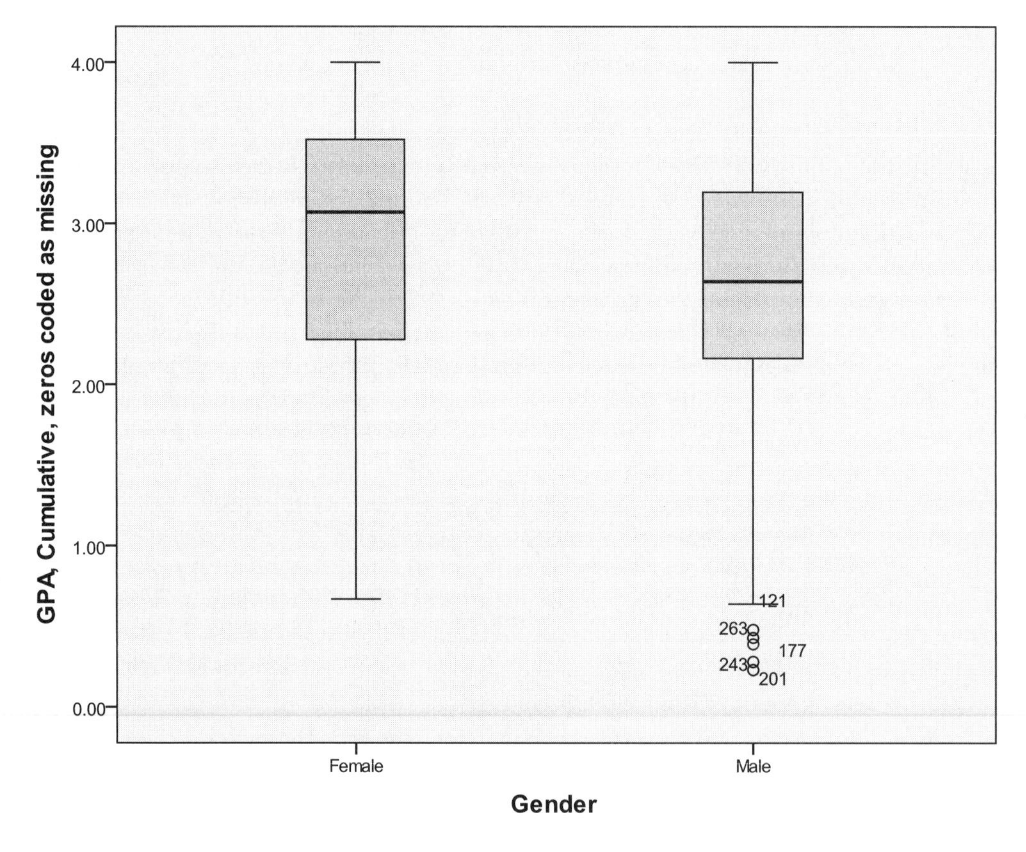

FIGURE 6.3. Boxplot of cumulative GPA by gender (missing data deleted; outliers marked with a case number, extreme outliers also with a circle).

[10]Popular statistical packages compute the values for the boxplot in somewhat different ways. Be sure you know how your software does it, and inform your readers what package you used; the graphics in this chapter were all drawn with SPSS versions 18 and 20.

The lines extending from the boxes (the **whiskers**) end at the highest and lowest scores, except for any outliers. Outliers are identified by their case numbers, and extreme outliers are marked with a circle (O). The case numbers make it easy for you to go back to the dataset to examine them. For example, O 201 at the bottom of the graphic for males tells you that this value is for case number 201. Comparing the two datasets, we can see that the female cases had a higher median GPA, a broader and higher IQR, and no outliers.

A very important comparison in either experimental or quasi-experimental research is between the distributions of the data for the treatment (experimental) and comparison (control) groups. Ideally, these would be very similar. This similarity is usually well accomplished by random assignment, but because this study was a quasi-experiment with no random assignment, it was doubly important to check. Figure 6.4 enables us to do so.

The boxplot in Figure 6.4 tells us whether the distributions of students' GPAs in the treatment and comparison groups were similar at the outset of the study, when they enrolled for the course. The comparison group is called "Traditional" in the boxplot, and the treatment group is labeled "Web Services." It is easy to see that the two are quite similar, and similarity of the treatment and comparison groups is very important

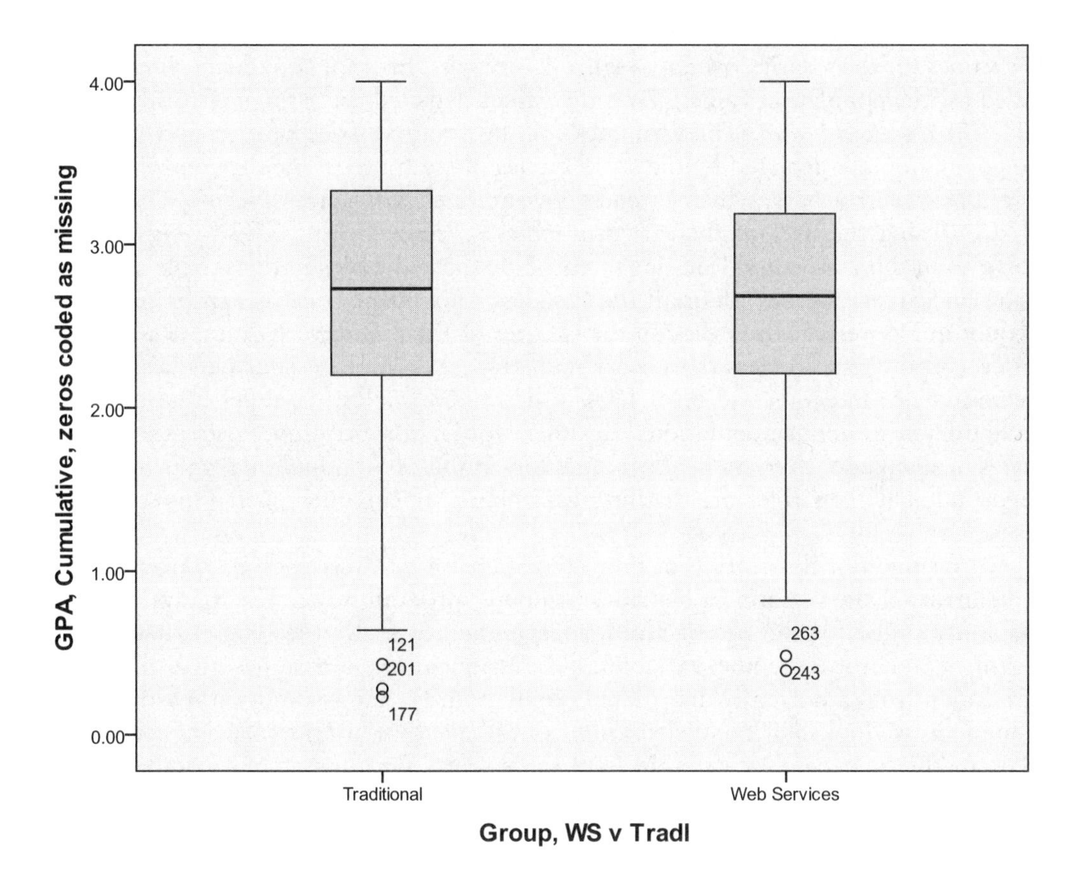

FIGURE 6.4. Boxplot of cumulative GPA by treatment group (Web Services) and comparison group (Traditional); outliers indicated by case numbers; extreme outliers by a circle.

to the success of an experimental study. Note that we could have conducted a *t*-test to see whether there were statistically significant differences between the two groups, and doing so is common practice. But a *t*-test is designed to test the hypothesis that two *randomly assigned* groups differ from the null hypothesis (see Chapter 8). As discussed previously, membership in these groups was not determined by random assignment; therefore, a *t*-test or any other test of statistical significance would be less appropriate than descriptive statistics.

It is important not to forget this distinction between random samples and randomly assigned groups for which inferential techniques are appropriate and nonrandom groups, for which they are not. We illustrate this graphically. The boxplot, used in Figures 6.3 and 6.4, is a descriptive technique. By contrast, a graph of confidence intervals is an inferential technique. It looks somewhat similar to a boxplot, and beginning researchers often confuse them. Both have important uses, but it is equally important not to mistake one for the other.

We illustrate the differences between boxplots and confidence intervals using a different dataset: a random sample of 50 faculty members and their salaries drawn from a population of about 800 in the 1990s.[11] Because it is a random sample, it is appropriate to compute confidence intervals with error bars; it is always appropriate to create a boxplot to describe the values in a sample.

Figure 6.5 is a boxplot of the actual values *in the sample*. It describes the sample. The values for the salaries overlap. Figure 6.6 graphs the 95% confidence intervals estimated for the population values. Thus the values depicted are estimates of the plausible values *in the population*. The estimates for the mean salaries of men and women in the population are depicted by the small circles in Figure 6.6. The margins of error are shown by the error bars, which extend above and below the circles.

Confusing the uses of these two graphic techniques could lead to big mistakes. Doing so in this case could lead one to conclude that all males in the sample and population had higher salaries than all the females. This is not true, as can be seen in the boxplot in Figure 6.5. Even though the salaries of the males were dramatically higher, not every woman made less than every man. The take-home lessons here are: (1) don't use confidence intervals and error bars to describe samples; (2) don't use boxplots to make inferences about populations. In other words, don't confuse descriptions of *real values* in samples with *hypothetical values* (or estimates) of population values. Both are important, but their roles are distinct. Error bars are for inference. Whiskers are for description.

To resume our illustration of preparing data for analysis, we return to the quasi-experiment on the method of teaching computer programming. The analysis plan for this study called for the use of multiple regression to study the relation between the treatment and the outcome variables. Regression analysis assumes that the sample was drawn from a normally distributed population. Is that assumption reasonable? To examine it, we looked at the distributions of the most important covariate, cumulative GPA, and of the dependent variable, final exam score. We illustrate with both statistical and graphic methods, beginning with the descriptive statistics in table form.

Table 6.1 provides some basic descriptive statistics for the control variable, cumulative GPA, and Table 6.2 shows the same information for the outcome variable, final

[11] For details about this sample, see Vogt (2007).

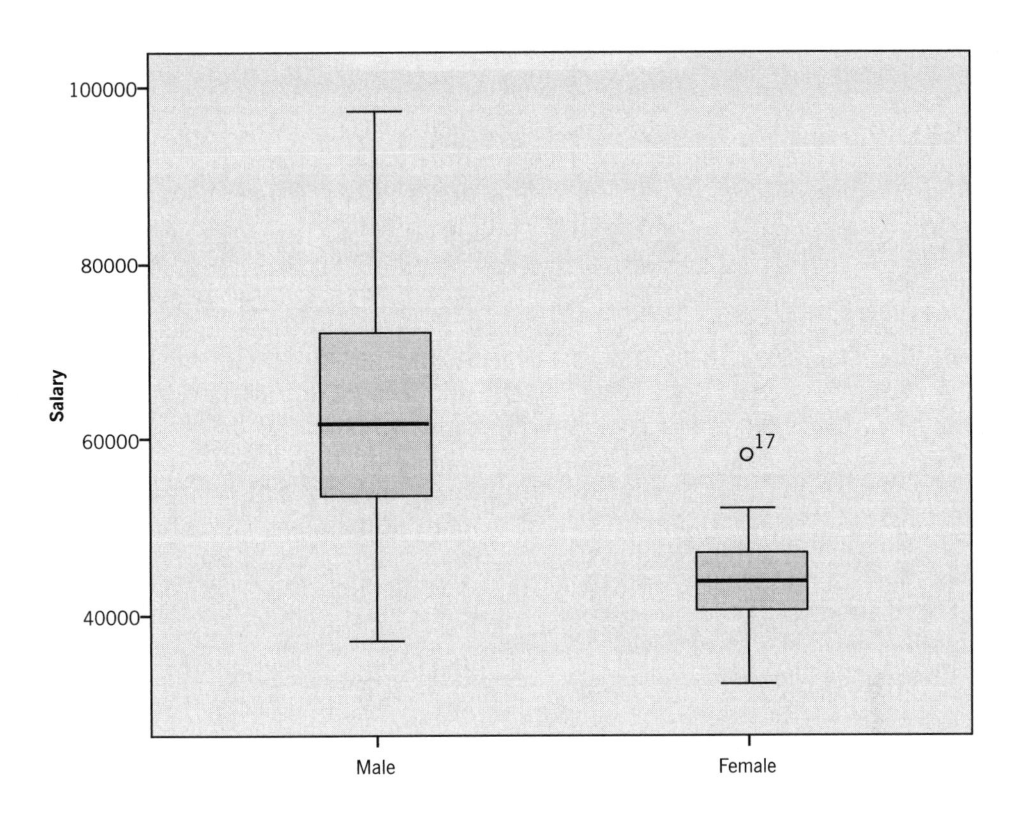

FIGURE 6.5. Boxplot describing the sample of salaries for male and female professors.

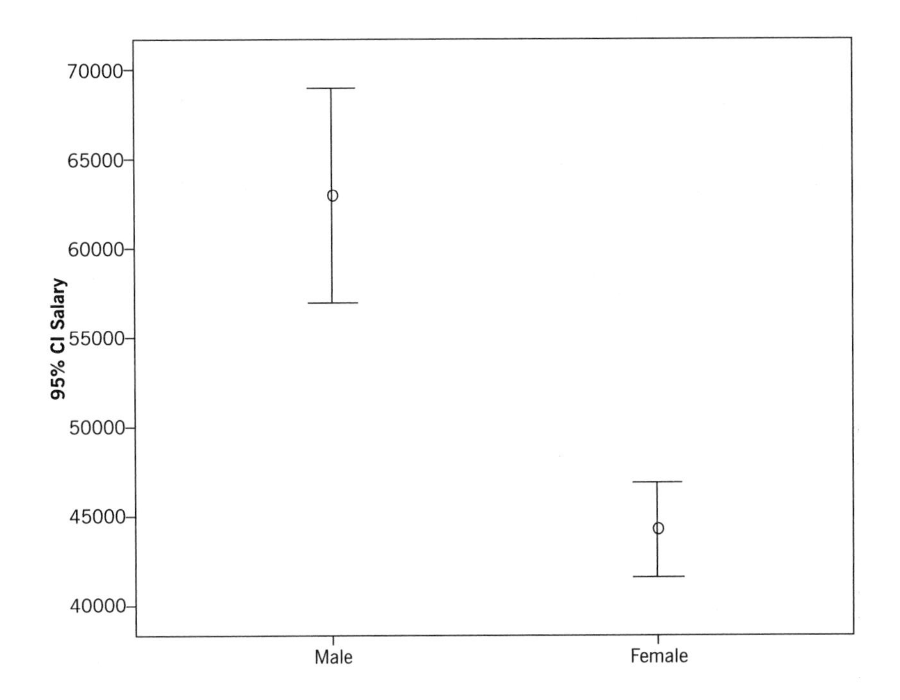

FIGURE 6.6. Confidence intervals and error bars around population estimates of means in salaries of male and female professors.

TABLE 6.1. Descriptive Statistics, Cumulative GPA

	N	Mean	Std. Deviation	Skewness		Kurtosis	
	Statistic	Statistic	Statistic	Statistic	Std. Error	Statistic	Std. Error
GPA, cumulative	293	2.6725	.81013	–.591	.142	.211	.284
Valid *N* (listwise)	293						

exam scores. The most important statistics for checking on the assumption of a normal distribution are the skewness and kurtosis; these are located on the right of the table.

The **skewness** statistic summarizes how symmetrical the distribution is. Symmetrical distributions, such as the normal curve, are not skewed, and their skewness statistic is 0. The distribution for cumulative GPA (Table 6.1 and Figure 6.7) is "left skewed," or negatively skewed. This means that the infrequent scores are on the left, or low, side of the distribution. The skewness statistic is negative (–.591), about 4 times as large as its standard error (.142). We discuss standard errors and their interpretation more fully in Chapter 7; here we just mention some basics.[12]

A **standard error** (*SE*) helps you estimate how much you are likely to be wrong if you use a sample statistic to estimate a population parameter. Another way to put it is that the *SE* estimates how much a statistic is likely to vary in other samples drawn from the same population. Obviously, researchers usually hope for small *SE*s, because that means that their estimates are precise and the margins of error small. As a rough rule of thumb, if a statistic is more than double its *SE*, it is statistically significant at the .05 level; in the case of the skewness statistic, it is over 4 times as large. Because we were hoping to avoid a skewed distribution, this news—statistical significance—was *not* good news.

Kurtosis is a measure of how flat or pointy a graph of a distribution is. A normal curve has a kurtosis of 0. If the distribution of the statistic is pointier than a normal curve, as in this case, the kurtosis statistic is a positive number. In Table 6.1, it is .211. Given that this is not a large departure from 0, especially as compared with the *SE* (.284), kurtosis is not much of a worry in this analysis.

Like the distribution of GPA, the distribution of the scores on the final exam is left skewed (see Table 6.2). The skewness statistic is smaller, and its *SE* is somewhat bigger. The kurtosis is somewhat flatter than a normal distribution. The confidence interval would be wide, and the *p*-value would not be statistically significant. It is important to remember one of the things this example shows: Statistical significance is not always the goal. If you hope your data distribution is normal, you want departures from that norm to be small and statistically *non*significant.

You can also judge normality visually. There are numerous ways to do this. Most common is probably the histogram. Histograms for GPA and final exam scores are shown in Figures 6.7 and 6.8. A normal curve is superimposed on the histogram so that

[12]The standard error of the mean (*SEM*, not to be confused with structural equation modeling) is also often reported in descriptive statistics output. For cumulative GPA, it is .047; for the final exam grade, the *SEM* is 1.09.

TABLE 6.2. Descriptive Statistics, Final Exam Scores

	N	Mean	Std. Deviation	Skewness		Kurtosis	
	Statistic	Statistic	Statistic	Statistic	Std. Error	Statistic	Std. Error
Final exam grade	227	72.945	16.4545	–.406	.162	–.390	.322
Valid *N* (listwise)	227						

the researcher can see how close the empirical distribution (the bars) comes to the normal curve. It looks "pretty close." That's nice to see, but is "pretty close" close enough? The data in Tables 6.1 and 6.2 are probably more useful for making that judgment.

Another graphic representation of normality is the **P-P plot**. P-P stands for probability–probability. The probability of values in a normal curve is compared with the values in the sample data. If the sample data (the dots or circles in Figure 6.9) are close to a normal curve, they will come close to the diagonal line. They are fairly close,

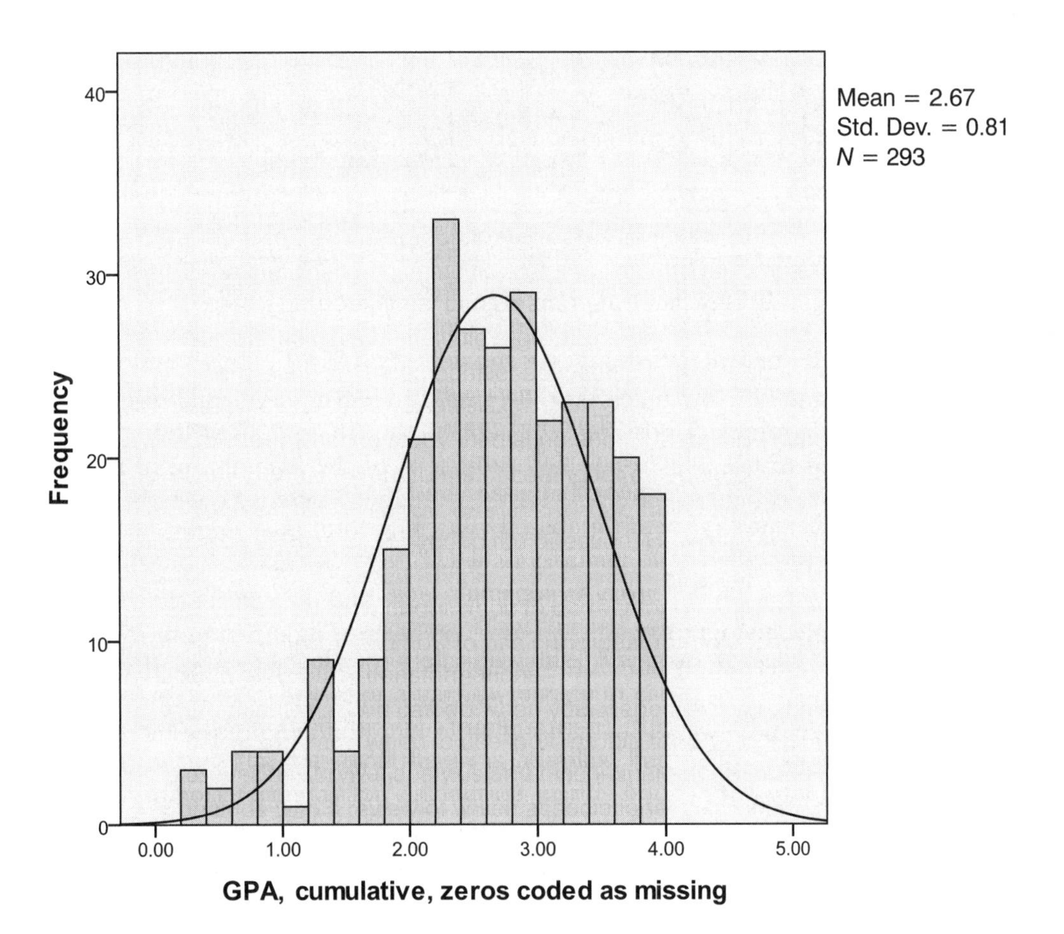

FIGURE 6.7. Histogram of cumulative GPA.

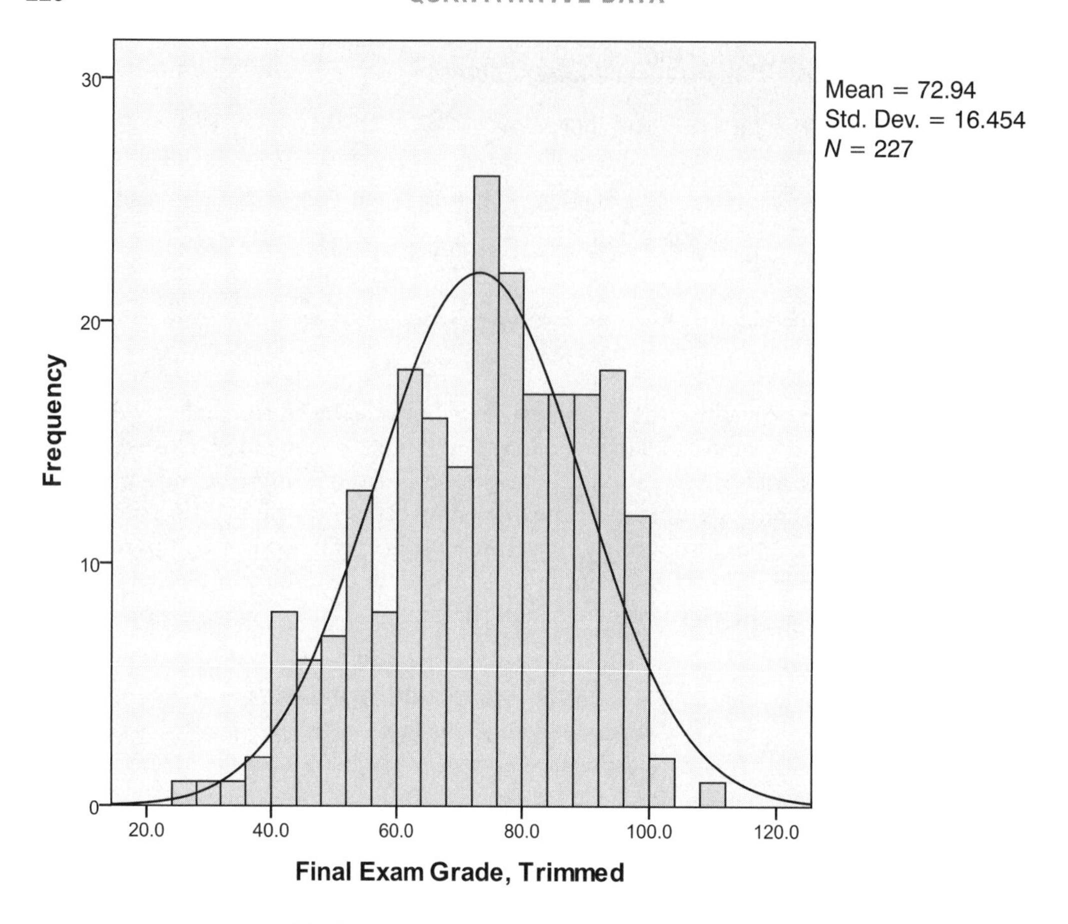

FIGURE 6.8. Histogram of final exam scores.

but they are not identical. How much do these departures from a normal distribution matter? Do they undermine our possibilities of conducting an analysis? Most statistical methods we planned to use are "robust to" violations of the assumption of normality—*if* the sample size is big enough. How big is "enough"? There is no simple answer, but the smallest N we have—227 for the final exam scores—is larger than most rules of thumb would suggest.[13]

Which of these graphic methods is better? The results and the picture can vary considerably. For example, histograms and stem-and-leaf plots using different intervals can look quite different; don't simply accept those supplied by default by your software, but consider broader or narrower intervals. Our advice is to explore various ways to display your data and ponder the results. The more of this work you can do, the more angles from which you look at your data, the better you know them, which is a very important thing. Choosing the method to use to present your work in a research report is much more a matter of judgment about what is useful than a question of right or wrong.

When in doubt, follow the general rule: Select methods that use and depict more rather than less data.

[13]See Chapters 8–10 for discussions of sample sizes in specific contexts.

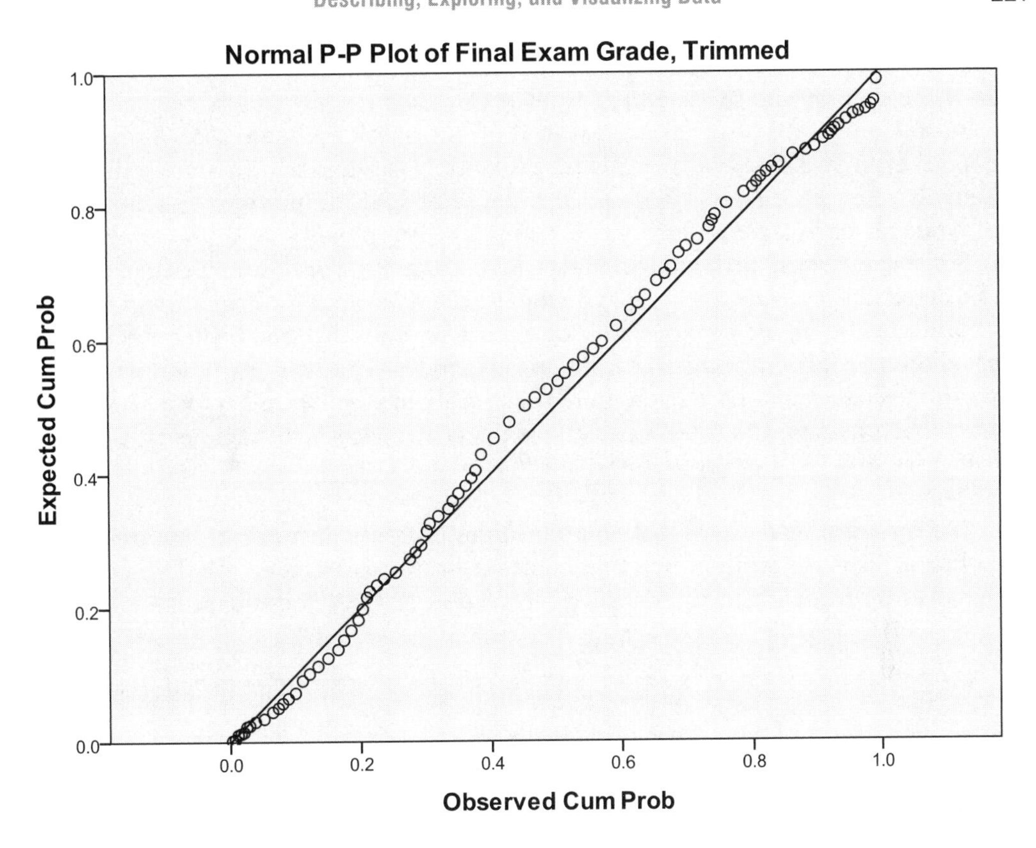

FIGURE 6.9. Final exam scores, P-P plot.

WHEN TO USE CORRELATIONS AS DESCRIPTIVE STATISTICS

One final descriptive statistic we consider is the correlation. It describes the relation between a pair of variables. It can be expressed both numerically and graphically, and the graphical depiction does much to assist in the understanding of this oft-used measure. In addition to describing relations between pairs of variables, it is also essential for checking assumptions that have to be true for the proper use of other techniques. Chief among these are the assumptions of linearity and the equality of variances, also known as homoscedasticity. When these assumptions are not met, nonparametric, or distribution-free, statistics are often required (see Chapter 7).

Several varieties of correlation can be used (for a review of when to use which type, see Chapter 8). When the word *correlation* is used without qualification, the **Pearson *r*** correlation is what is usually meant. It is a measure of the extent to which two continuous variables tend to form a straight line when plotted on a graph—in other words, it indicates the extent to which the relation between the two variables is **linear**. Because the Pearson r measures the linear relation between variables, a nonlinear relation, even a strong one, will have a low r. The correlation between students' cumulative GPAs and their scores on the final exam in our quasi-experiment was $r = .502$. This is statistically significant at the $p < .01$ level, which means that the probability that the correlation was due to sampling error is less than 1%. Of course, because these data are not drawn from a random sample, the *p*-value is not very informative, but the *r* remains a good description of the sample, and the scatterplot of the values can be even more helpful. The scatterplot in Figure 6.10 provides a great deal of information. One reason a scatterplot is a good way to visualize your data is that (like the stem-and leaf) it shows all the data. Although you are unlikely to publish it because of space limitations in scholarly journals, you can learn a great deal by examining a scatterplot.[14]

Scatterplots such as the one in Figure 6.10 are useful for describing linearity (or its lack), detecting bivariate outliers, and viewing the assumption of equality of variances. The latter is also called *homogeneity of variances*, and also (the biggest spelling challenge) **homoscedasticity**, which literally means tendency to scatter in the same way. We discuss correlation and regression more thoroughly in Chapter 9; here we briefly review some of their uses for descriptive basics, particularly concerning: (1) linearity, (2) bivariate outliers, and (3) equality of variances.

1. ***Linearity.*** Note that Figure 6.10 includes not only data points but also a **regression line.** This is the straight line that comes closest on average to the data points. The line moves up from left to right, which means that as GPA goes up, scores on the final

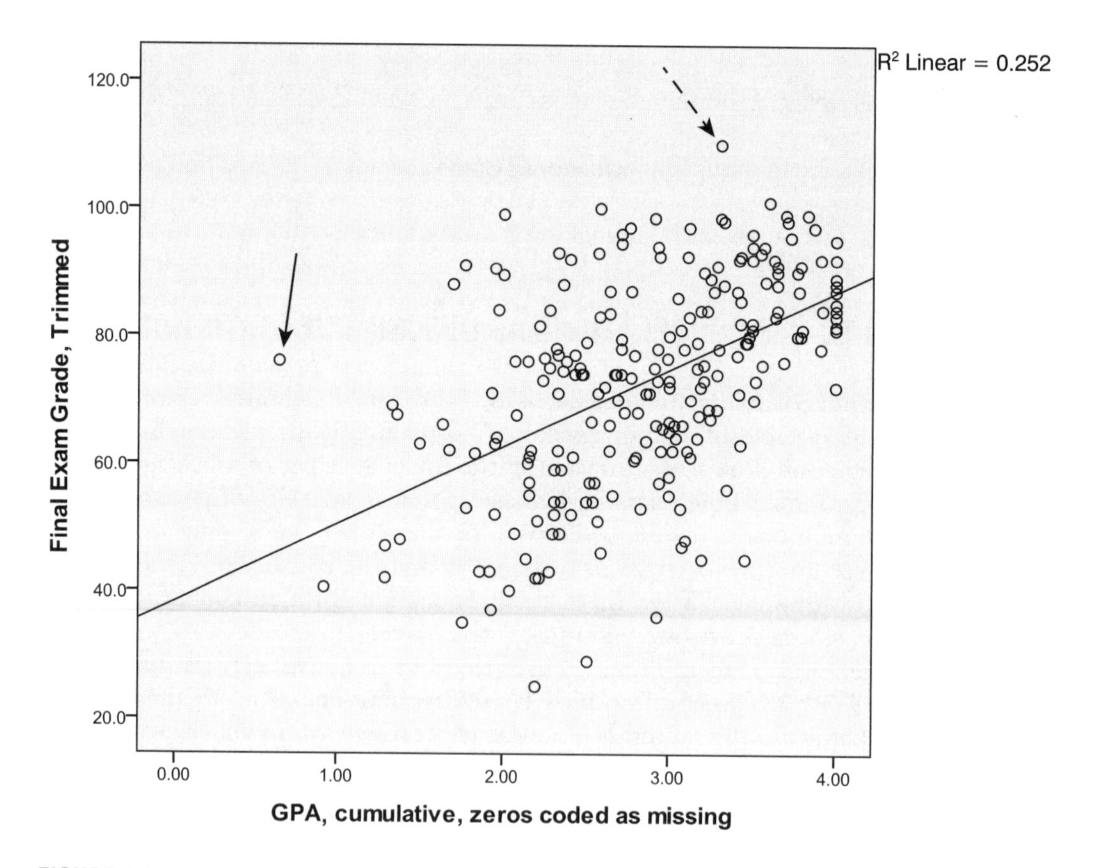

FIGURE 6.10. Scatterplot showing correlation of GPA and final exam scores; regression line added.

[14]Many statistical packages have a 3-D option for scatterplots, usually for depicting one IV and two DVs.

exam tend to go up; the correlation is positive. The strength of that tendency is described by the slope or angle of the line. If the relation (regression) were stronger, the line would slope more sharply upward. If the correlation were stronger, the dots would be closer to the line. If the correlation were perfect ($r = 1.0$), all the dots would be on the line.

2. ***Bivariate outliers.*** When discussing outliers, we usually mean an extreme score on one variable. But bivariate outliers are equally important and can be seen in a scatterplot. For example, the leftmost datapoint (indicated by the solid arrow) in Figure 6.10 represents a student who got a 76 on the final exam. This is not an unusual score; it's a little higher than average, but pretty close to the mean (73) and median (74). However, it is a bivariate outlier because that grade of 76 was earned by a student with a GPA of 0.64. The highest final exam score in the scatter diagram is 110 (indicated by the dashed arrow toward the upper right); it was earned by a student with a GPA of 3.3. This is a high GPA, but it is the combination that is unusual. We thought the score was probably a typo, but upon investigation, we learned the unusually high score was earned because the student got extra credit on the exam.

3. ***Equality of variances.*** Scatterplots are also helpful for seeing the assumption of equality of variances. The statistics for testing equality of variances are not very intuitive or easy to interpret,[15] but the concept is simple to grasp in a scatterplot. Equality of variances is a fundamental assumption upon which many parametric statistics are built. It basically means that the variances in the populations from which you have sampled are substantially equal; for continuous variables, it means that the variance in the dependent variable will be similar at all values of the independent variable. Equality of variances can be fairly easily seen by examining scatterplots. Looking at Figure 6.10, we can see that the dots are quite a bit closer to the line at high values. When the GPAs are high (say, above 3.0), then so are the final exam scores. When the GPAs are low (say, below 2.0), they are more widely scattered, farther from the line. That difference (low scatter at high GPAs and high scatter at low GPAs) shows *in*equality of variances.

All in all, Figure 6.10 shows a relationship between GPAs and exam scores that is only somewhat linear; it does not have many extreme outliers (or influential observations); and it does not violate the assumption of equality of variances too badly. We could "improve" the correlation, the linearity, and the equality of variances by trimming some of the extreme scores, but given that our sample size is large ($N = 227$), there is probably no need to take this step. And throwing away inconvenient data always makes us uncomfortable.

The data in Figure 6.10 are fairly typical in research of this type. But it is not all that unusual to see data that depart much more radically from basic statistical assumptions of normality, linearity, and equality of variances. Figure 6.11 depicts the ages and weights of visitors to a health spa and exercise facility over a 2-day period in 2010. The data are real, but they are not necessarily representative of the relation between age and weight, even at the facility at which they were gathered. We picked this dataset simply to illustrate that real data can look weird. Visitors' ages are plotted on the horizontal axis and their weights on the vertical axis. The correlation between the two variables is very low and negative (the regression line slopes downward from left to right): $r = -.087$

[15] A common one is Levene's test. See the discussion in Chapter 7.

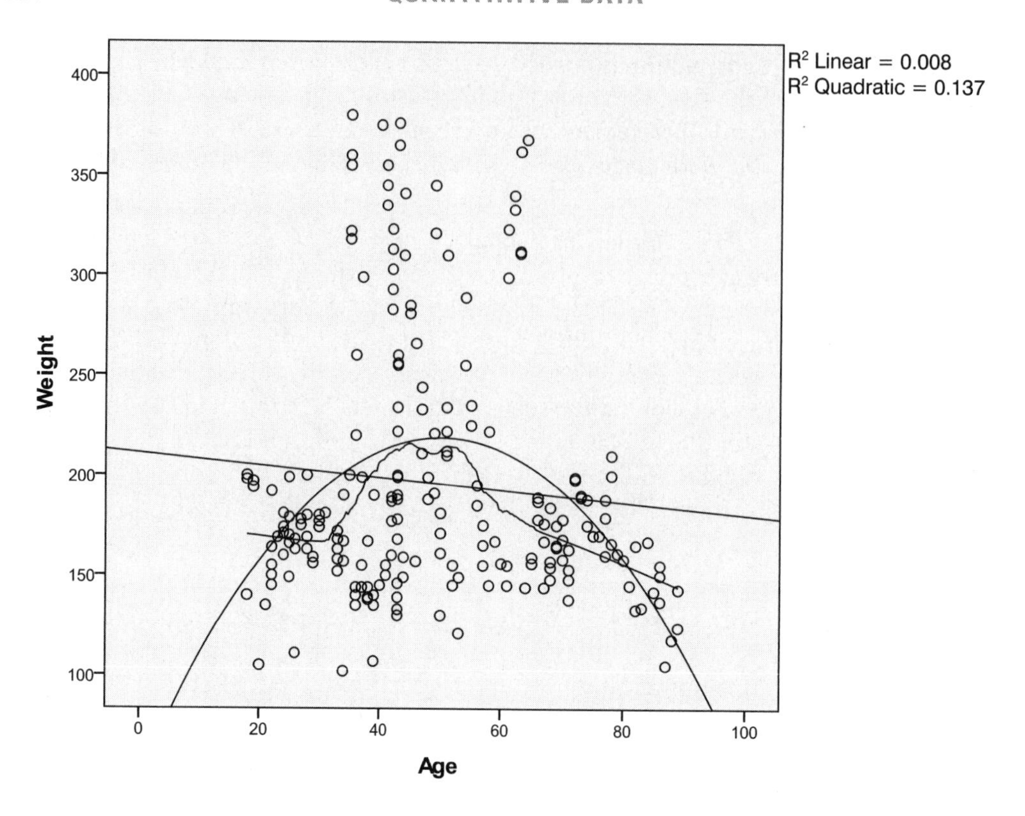

FIGURE 6.11. Ages and weights of visitors to an exercise facility.

(p-value .212). The r^2—which indicates how much of the variance in the Y variable (weight) you can predict with the X variable (age)—is .008, less than 1%. The straight regression line does not fit the data well at all. We tried two nonlinear options: the **quadratic** (which means regression with one bend in the line) and the **lowess** (which means locally weighted regression). Both of these were better than the straight line, but not by a great deal.

What all this means in brief is that the data are a sort of jumble, not easily summarized by a line (whether straight, curved, or wiggly) or by a statistic. But, when looking at the scatterplot, there *are* patterns that stand out. First, and most obvious, all the very high weights occur in the middle of the age range, from roughly 35 to 65. Second, the assumption of equality of variances is not met, because there is a much bigger scatter of scores in the middle of the age range than at either end. So you would not want to use any analytical methods for which the assumption of equality of variances was important.

If you used only the summary statistics (correlation and regression slope), you would not see (literally) the interesting peculiarities of this distribution. It is hard to emphasize enough how important it is to examine your data visually—*always*. The classic illustration is called Anscombe's quartet, after the statistician who devised it. Anscombe presented four short and simple data distributions of two variables. The means and *SD*s for each variable were *identical*, and so were the correlations between them. But when the four distributions were examined visually in a scatterplot, it was immediately obvious that they had nothing at all in common,[16] a fact that is completely missed by using only the summary statistics.

If you want to try it yourself and see the surprising results, graph the four data distributions using any statistical software or spreadsheet. The data are in Table 6.3.

Graphic representations of data can be crucial for reporting results in ways that nonstatisticians can understand. We have also found them necessary in teaching; for example, students have frequently remarked that they never really understood correlation, regression, and the relation between them until they saw data depicted in scatterplots with regression lines. The importance of graphic representation goes beyond reporting and teaching; it is also indispensable for some forms of analysis. Network analysis (see Chapter 5) is a clear case in point.

We have illustrated these points about the advantages of visually examining your data using only fairly conventional statistical graphics. Some researchers say that this is missing the fundamental opportunities that have arisen as a result of recent advances in computer graphics. They believe that mere statistical graphics, the kind produced with typical statistical software, are insufficient in the 21st century. Sometimes this point of view is expressed as the "battle" between graphics and visualization, with the latter referring to the most modern, tech-driven developments. What is the difference between

TABLE 6.3. Data for Anscombe's Quartet

X1	Y1	X2	Y2	X3	Y3	X4	Y4
10.0	8.04	10.0	9.14	10.0	7.46	8.0	6.58
8.0	6.95	8.0	8.14	8.0	6.77	8.0	5.76
13.0	7.58	13.0	8.74	13.0	12.74	8.0	7.71
9.0	8.81	9.0	8.77	9.0	7.11	8.0	8.84
11.0	8.33	11.0	9.26	11.0	7.81	8.0	8.47
14.0	9.96	14.0	8.10	14.0	8.84	8.0	7.04
6.0	7.24	6.0	6.13	6.0	6.08	8.0	5.25
4.0	4.26	4.0	3.10	4.0	5.39	8.0	12.50
12.0	10.84	12.0	9.13	12.0	8.15	8.0	5.56
7.0	4.82	7.0	7.26	7.0	6.42	8.0	7.91
5.0	5.68	5.0	4.74	5.0	5.73	8.0	6.89

Note. There are four datasets: X1–Y1, X2–Y2, X3–Y3, and X4–Y4. To see the surprising results when graphing these four pairs of variables, plot each dataset to make four scatter diagrams and have your software add a regression line to each.

[16]The data and the graphs, originally described in Anscombe (1973), became better known when they were discussed in Tufte (1983) and are widely available on the Web—for example, in the Wikipedia entry on "Anscombe's quartet."

graphics and visualization—beyond four syllables? We have used the terms more or less interchangeably.

The key point is that many new options have become available in recent years, and researchers would do well to take advantage of them.[17] Although some of the new data pictures produced using new technologies are "chart junk" and "eye candy," others are important contributions to exploration, analysis, and communication of data. These technologies give you new ways to investigate your data. Just as important, they provide you new ways to communicate with your readers—readers who are increasingly likely to see what you have to say on computer screens rather than on printed pages. Among the advantages for readers are the opportunities to see graphics in full color, to be able to magnify the portions of the graphics that they want to see more clearly, and to interact with the data by "drilling down" or using "sliders" to explore in depth.

WHEN AND WHY TO MAKE THE NORMAL CURVE YOUR POINT OF REFERENCE

Many of the descriptive statistics we have discussed in this chapter center on the question of whether and to what extent the empirical distribution of scores in your sample match the theoretical normal distribution. Why does this matter? For two reasons: (1) if it doesn't match, this violates a key assumption on which the validity of many more advanced statistics is built; (2) if it does match, this tells you a lot about your empirical distribution. We know a great deal about the normal distribution, so if your empirical distribution is approximately normal, you'll know a lot about it, too.

The normal curve is a **theoretical distribution**. It describes the distribution that *would* result from the *infinite* repetition of a *perfect* **random process**, such as a fair lottery or rolling perfectly square dice. A perfect random process is impossible, but statisticians have found ways to come close.[18] In contrast, the distribution of students' GPAs we examined is an **empirical distribution**. Comparing the empirical with the theoretical can be very informative. When a distribution of a variable is approximately normal, this suggests that the data are not biased, or, in other terms, that the variable is a random variable generated by a random process (also called **stochastic** variables and processes). It is important to note that the randomness here has to do with the process, not the variable itself. The students did not get their GPAs in a lottery, but the selection of students into the quasi-experiment and their assignment into control and experimental groups was close enough to normal to have no obvious biases and close enough to normal to use what are called **parametric techniques**, that is, statistics appropriate for continuous scales when the data approximate a normal distribution.

An empirical distribution can never be more than approximately normal. The bell-shaped curve of the normal distribution is a theoretical continuous curve. It is smoother than anything that can be observed in the empirical world. Even when the variables we are studying can in theory be measured on a continuous scale, such as participants' ages, we have to round off to the nearest year, month, or day. Rounding makes the

[17] For overviews, see Grant (2013) and Yau (2011) and Yau's blog at *www.flowingdata.com*.

[18] An excellent way to generate a random distribution for your research is to go to the website *www.random.org*.

measure discrete, not continuous. And some variables, such as group size, are inherently discrete. There can be 17, 18, or 19 members of a group, but not 17.3, 18.8, or 19.5.

Options When Your Sample Does Not Come from a Normally Distributed Population

What do you do when your sample seems *not* to come from a population that is normally distributed? First, remember that you don't *know*—you only know about your one sample, not the population. If you had the population data, you could study them directly and not bother with sampling. In any case, samples from normal populations may not look normal, but they are more likely to look normal than samples from non-normal populations. So if it's likely that your sample is from a population that is not normal (the graphics look lopsided and the skewness and kurtosis statistics are high), what do you do? There are four broad options.

1. Use **distribution-free** statistics. Also known as **nonparametric** statistics, these methods that make no assumptions about the distributions of the data.
2. Use **robust statistics**. Robust means that the statistics are "strong" enough to be able to withstand violations of the assumptions of normality.
3. Remove or trim outliers.
4. Transform your data.

The first two of these (distribution-free and robust statistics) are used mainly in statistical inference, so we discuss them more in the next chapter. We discussed outliers briefly earlier. Here we repeat the most important point about outliers: You should not use descriptive graphic and statistical techniques simply to pick off inconvenient outliers. You should use a systematic procedure and explain what you have done and why you have decided to do it. Ideally, you should have decided what you will do about outliers *before* you collect the data. Still, you'll have to decide on a case-by-case basis. If you sample 1,000 households to measure mean incomes and the Bill and Melinda Gates household happens to fall into your sample, that's really going to mess up your statistics, and it could be legitimate to delete this one (very interesting but radically atypical) case.

Sometimes you know, in advance, that your sample and population data cannot be normally distributed because of the nature of the variables and the way they have been coded and measured. Consider the data we've been looking at—GPAs and scores on a final exam. Raw scores on final exams were OK in terms of how they were coded. GPAs certainly look like continuous data measured at the ratio or interval level, and they are often reported to two or three decimal points. But GPAs are not ratio or interval level—emphatically not. Instructors' judgments, which may be more or less objective, are used to sort students into five **ranks**—A, B, C, D, F. These are given numbers—such as 4, 3, 2, 1, 0—that are then treated as though they were measured on a continuous, ratio-level scale. This is a *deeply flawed* procedure, one that violates just about every standard practice taught in elementary statistics and measurement courses. The data are not even equal-interval data. For example, the gap between an A and a B has an unknown relation to the gap between a D and an F. It is usually unknown in any one course. And it is even more uncertain between courses, between professors, and over time. Averaging this mess into one cumulative GPA raises a lot of questions, to say the least. Still, cumulative GPA is a fairly strong predictor of the outcome variable in many studies, including ours.

Using z-Scores

Some of the problems with this fundamentally unsound system of measuring student achievement could be reduced by reporting grades as *z*-scores. We skip discussions of educational reforms to illustrate with a simple grading-based example that demonstrates how it could be useful to use *z*-scores to transform and describe your data.

The ***z* statistic** is a measure of a score's rank in a distribution of scores. It is measured in *SD* units. Because it is measured in *SD* units, it can be compared across very different distributions. It is often called *the* standard score, perhaps because, although there are many other standard scores, the *z*-score is crucial to understanding them all.[19]

Say you are a university student. In three of your courses you have taken final exams, and your three professors list the students' final exam scores on their office doors. Your scores are 91, 68, and 110. You'd like to know how your grades rank from class to class, but it's hard to compare these scores—for many reasons. The number of questions on each exam isn't the same, and the point systems your professors use are different. Also, and probably most important, you suspect that some of your professors are harder graders than others. The *z*-score can come to the rescue.

Think of the ***z*-score** as the *zero* score. It is equal to the number of *SD*s from the mean; the mean has a score of 0. If you get a *z*-score of 0 on a test, this tells you that you scored exactly at the mean. If your *z*-score is +2.5, this means that your score was 2.5 *SD*s above the mean, and you were pretty close to the top of the class. If your *z*-score was –3.0, this means that you were at or near the bottom of the class (3 *SD*s below the mean). To convert your score into a *z*-score, you need know only the mean and the *SD* of the distribution of scores. You subtract the mean from your score and divide the answer by the *SD*. Understanding the principle behind the *SD* and the *z*-score is important, so we show the calculations in Table 6.4. By transforming the raw scores into *z*-scores, you can compare your scores on tests that would otherwise be nearly incomparable. Using *z*-scores can be extremely useful in many situations in which the data would otherwise be difficult or impossible to compare.

Because the *z*-scores computed as in Table 6.4 are standardized, you can compare them, you know what they mean, and you can interpret them. Your score of 68 on Wednesday was very good ($z = +2.07$); your score of 110 on Thursday not as good, a little subpar, in fact ($z = -0.67$). Just as you can better understand your exam scores when they have been converted into *z*-scores, the readers of your research can better interpret the scores in your distributions if you provide them with the mean and the *SD*. They can compute their own *z*-scores.

SD scores are the bedrock of most comparisons across distributions and across studies, most important, perhaps, in ES measures and standardized regression coefficients. ES measures are discussed in the next section. For standardized regression coefficients, see Chapter 8.

---

[19]For example, IQ, SAT, and GRE scores are all *z*-scores that have been transformed for public consumption—mostly, one assumes, to avoid negative numbers and decimals.

TABLE 6.4. Computing *z*-Scores for Exams in Three Classes

	Your score	Mean (*M*)	Difference = Your score minus mean	Standard deviation (*SD*)	*z*-score = Difference ÷ *SD*
Tues. exam	91	80	+11	10	+11 ÷ 10 = +1.10
Wed. exam	68	37	+31	15	+31 ÷ 15 = +2.07
Thurs. exam	110	130	–20	30	–20 ÷ 30 = –0.67

Turning your raw scores on the final exam into *z*-scores is an example of a **data transformation**. You can do the same with a distribution of scores rather than simply a few individual scores. Taking a distribution of scores and transforming them into *z*-scores means that the distribution has a mean of 0 and an *SD* of 1.0. By turning the formula for the *z*-score around, you can transform the *z*-scores back into the original raw scores. Even very odd distributions, such as our previous example about the weights of visitors to a health club, can be transformed in this way, but using *z*-scores does not change the shape of the distribution. It doesn't matter if you graph the original scores or the scores transformed into *z*-scores; the scatterplot looks the same. Of course, *z* transformations, and all the others we discuss, can be accomplished with a few keystrokes or mouse clicks using any standard statistical software.

Other common transformations do change the shape of the distribution. They are used to prepare your data for more advanced analyses, such as multiple regression, by making the distribution closer to the normal distribution. The most frequently used of these in the social sciences are (1) taking the square root of each score, (2) taking their logarithms, and (3) converting each into its inverse (also called its *reciprocal*). The latter means dividing the scores into 1, so that 2 becomes ½, 3 becomes ⅓, and so on. When and why would you want to convert your data from its original form?

These transformations can make the dataset more amenable to statistical analysis by making it more normally distributed. Furthermore, transformations do this without spoiling or mutilating the data, as lopping off outliers might. Transformations change each piece of data in the same way. When you do that, statistics computed with the transformed data will yield the same results. For example, if you doubled all the scores[20] in Figure 6.10 describing the correlation between GPA and final exam scores, the correlation would be identical, and the scatter diagram describing it would look exactly the same. This is only true of linear transformations. Nonlinear transformations will produce different statistics because they do not preserve the linear relationships, and this will make the correlation different.[21]

Data transformation can sound awfully mysterious until you realize that you have probably transformed data without giving it a thought when you converted raw data into percentages. Say that of the 83 female students taking a course using a new method, 58 thought that the new approach was an improvement; by comparison, of the 176

[20] Or you could divide each by 43 or take any other similar action, as long as it was done consistently for each score.

[21] We thank one of our anonymous readers for reminding us of this important qualification.

males taking the course, 109 thought it was better. How do you make that comparison? By transforming the scores into percentages, you find that 70% of the females thought it was an improvement, whereas 62% of the males did. To revert to the original numbers, you take 70% of the 83 females and 62% of the 176 males. The *principle behind all transformations* is the same. You *change the data to make it easier to use without losing any information*, and you can change it back to the original when needed.

Data transformations are an increasingly routine part of preparing for your data analysis (and the work is easy because it is conducted with computer programs). As the authors of one standard textbook put it, "with almost every data set in which we have used transformations, the results of analysis have been substantially improved."[22] As mentioned earlier, the three most common transformations used in the social sciences are square roots, logarithms, and inverses. That list is in the order of the departure from normality that they can handle: some, quite a bit, and a lot, respectively. Researchers often try them in that order: If the first (square root) doesn't work to normalize the data sufficiently, try the second (logarithm), and if that doesn't, try the third (inverse).[23] One warning is useful at this point. Although all of the work is done by computer programs, different programs use somewhat different procedures, so be sure to specify in your research report the program you used. And regardless of the program you use, make sure, before you transform, that your dataset contains no zeros, because zeros don't behave well when you try to transform them. The typical way to avoid the problem is to add 1 to every score in the dataset, so that 37 becomes 38, 86 becomes 87, and, most important, 0 becomes 1. Leaving in the zeros will probably get you a disconcerting error message from your software.

WHEN CAN YOU USE DESCRIPTIVE STATISTICS SUBSTANTIVELY?

The question asked here is when can descriptive (noninferential) statistics stand on their own and, for example, be the main method you use to report your research findings? Most of what we have said in this chapter treats descriptive statistics as a preliminary step, not as the way to conclude the analysis and build the interpretations of your study. But there are circumstances in which descriptive statistics are the method of choice. First, when you are studying an entire population rather than a sample from which you hope to generalize, your parameters are descriptive. You don't have to make inferences about the population parameters because the descriptive statistics already tell you what they are. Important national statistical data are frequently reported for entire populations, rather than for samples from which inferences have to be made. Vital statistics (births, deaths, diseases, etc.), crime reports, and economic trends are often considered too important to trust to sampling; a study based on the entire population is required. For example, a study of trends in teen pregnancy in the United States over the last two decades concluded that although teen births fell by over one-third since 1991, the rate is still dramatically higher in the United States than in most other industrialized countries.

---

[22]Tabachnick and Fidell (2001, p. 81).

[23]To be more efficient, the order in which you try them should be influenced by whether the data are left vs. right skewed. A helpful tip sheet for deciding about transformations is available at *http://seismo.berkeley.edu/~kirchner/eps_120/Toolkits/Toolkit_03.pdf*.

The report is thorough and nuanced and provides important data for causal modeling, but it is wholly descriptive; it draws no inferences about the population because the population is known.[24]

In addition to their use in reporting official national data, descriptive statistics can be used to convey information about the entire populations of smaller organizations, such as businesses, universities, and clinics. Researchers use descriptive statistics to report findings more often than many people realize. For example, in a year-long observational study of elementary students in eight different schools, a team of researchers kept track of the amount of time students actually spent learning the curriculum. Detailed observations were reported using straightforward descriptive statistics that revealed that some 40 out of 180 instructional days each year were devoted to noninstructional tasks.[25] Another area of educational research that mainly reports descriptive statistics for full populations is assessing student learning using state-level achievement tests. A telling example of academic performance in the entire population of public schools in Colorado came to definitive findings using descriptive statistics (and no inferential statistics) concerning the reasons for the fluctuations in students' academic performance from year to year. Most changes were due to haphazard shifts in attendance patterns that had little or nothing to do with differences in educational policies or practices.[26]

These three examples—trends in teen pregnancies, educational practices in schools, and state policy making using performance-based data—are distinct methodologically. But the analytical data reporting was similar in important ways. The studies investigated significant policy issues but used comparatively simple descriptive statistics to present and analyze data and arrive at persuasive conclusions. Sometimes rookie researchers want to show off what they have learned in their advanced research methods courses and believe it is necessary to use recondite techniques in order to be taken seriously. And they may sometimes be right about what you have to do to get noticed. But the quantitative techniques you will need to handle the data you've collected to answer your research question, even a difficult research question, need not necessarily be complicated or inferential. As a general principle, it is best to start with the most basic type of analysis and increase the level of complication *only as needed* to answer your research question. Whatever approach you take, descriptive statistics will always have a fundamental role to play.

Effect Sizes

For reporting your research results, the most important of all the descriptive statistics is the effect size (ES). As we saw in the discussion of meta-analysis (Chapter 5), ES indices are the main tool for comparing quantitative results across studies. Even when you are not comparing across studies but are simply reporting the results of your own study, doing so using ES statistics is good practice.[27] The number of ES indices is large, with

[24] Pazol et al. (2011). The article also analyzes some data from sample surveys.

[25] Smith (2000).

[26] Linn and Haug (2002).

[27] For a single dataset, a handy summary is the coefficient of variation, which is the *SD* divided by the mean; the result is often multiplied by 100, although this is an unnecessary step.

a dozen or so in common use, and they date back to Pearson's 19th-century work.[28] Choice among them is not straightforward because, compared with many other choices, there is less agreement among researchers about which indices are better for what purposes. Strong traditions of use exist within disciplines and subfields, so when in doubt, it is advisable to use the ES measures of your "clan." Note, however, that differences among perfectly reasonable and mathematically equivalent choices can matter greatly when it comes to *reporting* your results.

The basic idea behind the ES is simple for anyone who has ever compared two or more results using percentages, which are scores standardized by putting them in the same per-100 metric: the winning record of this team is 60%, and that of its main rival is 70%; I answered 90% of the questions correctly on the first exam, but only 80% on the second; and so forth. Nothing could seem simpler, but approaches to reporting such differences can have a big rhetorical impact. Good researchers should prefer accuracy to rhetoric, but sometimes there seems to be no unloaded, unbiased choice.

For example, in 2011, the state income tax in our state, Illinois, was increased from 3 to 5%. Was that an increase of 2% (3 + 2 = 5), or was it an increase of 66% (2 ÷ 3 = .66)? The answer is that it's both 2% *and* 66%. Mathematically, there is no basis for choice. One is not more accurate than the other. Let's say that the rate had gone from 3 to 6%. Is it better to say that it doubled or that it increased 200%? The answers given to such questions, say in editorials and blog posts, are almost fully predictable: If you were opposed to or outraged by the increase, you say 66% or 200%; if you were in favor of the increase, you'd say 2% or doubled. When there does not seem to be a neutral choice, when one method of reporting is no more accurate than another but the equivalent reports "sound" different, the only fair strategy is to report results both ways.

The same is true of ES reporting. Different indices computed with the same data "sound" different. Many effect sizes are standardized using the *SD*. For comparing two or more variables, several types of ES index are available. We briefly discuss the most common types of ES index used to report on the relation of two or more variables, especially when one of the variables is thought of as the independent variable (IV) and the other as the dependent variable (DV). We repeat in Table 6.5 some information from Chapter 5.

ES indices are computed using sample data; they are not inferential estimates of population parameters. Inferences about populations can be drawn from ES statistics, but they need not be. This distinction—between describing samples and making inferences about populations—is very important, as we saw when comparing a boxplot with a graphic representation of the CIs for the *same data* (Figures 6.5 and 6.6). The CIs describe the *probable* range of values in the population; the boxplots describe the *actual* values in the sample. In this chapter we focus on statistics that describe the actual values.

The first two ES indices in Table 6.5 are the correlation and the standardized mean difference. Both are standardized using the *SD*. For reasons discussed shortly, the third—the odds ratio—is not. Choice between the correlation and the standardized mean difference (SMD) is influenced by your research question. When you want to see how two variables vary together, the correlation is the one to use because it is a measure of association. When you want to see how two variables differ, the SMD is the natural, but not inevitable, choice. Correlations are the more flexible of the two, because various kinds of correlations can be used when the IVs and DVs are coded using categorical, continuous, or ranked data.

---

[28]For a broad-ranging overview of ES indices, see Huberty (2002).

TABLE 6.5. Different Effect-Size Indices Used for Data Coded Differently

	Independent variable	Dependent variable	When to use
Correlation	Continuous	Continuous	To see how two variables vary together.
Standardized mean difference (SMD)	Categorical	Continuous	To see how two variables differ.
Odds ratio (OR) and relative risk ratio (RRR)	Dichotomous	Dichotomous	To predict one dichotomous variable with another.

Example: Using Different ES Statistics

Rather than discussing these indices abstractly, we illustrate with the simple dataset in Table 6.6.

The dataset in Table 6.6 shows scores of 20 students on two 10-item quizzes. The mean score on Quiz 1 was 7.6, and on Quiz 2 it was 6.3. So Quiz 2 was harder—1.3 points harder on a 10-point scale. To standardize that difference you could use an SMD; **Cohen's *d*** is a popular one. You divide the difference between the means of the two quiz scores by the common or pooled *SD* for all the scores: $7.6 - 6.3 = 1.3 \div 1.894$, which gives you $d = .686$. A *d* statistic of .686 would usually be considered a medium to large ES. Why use *d*? Because it gives you an index that you can meaningfully compare with any other *d*, such as *d* scores computed on any other two measures.

If the data in the table were not two quizzes, but two groups of students, an experimental and a control group, who took the same quiz, we might want to use one of the other SMDs, such as **Glass's delta**. For purposes of comparison, delta uses the *SD* from the control group; it results in an SMD of .743. Some think that Glass's delta is a better measure of how much the experimental and control group differ and that Cohen's *d* is better when control and experimental groups are not specified. Most important is for you to specify which SMD you have used when reporting your findings.[29]

Or, say our question were not focused on the *differences* between the two quizzes, such as which one was harder, or between two groups, such as whether the experimental group got a higher score than the control group. If the question were focused rather on *consistency* of performance of the students across the two exams, we could use the correlation as an ES index.[30] So, although students as a whole did less well on the second quiz than on the first quiz, the question here would be: Did the students who did well on one also tend to do well (or poorly) on the other? The correlation between students' scores on the first and second quiz is $r = .511$. The $r^2 = .261$. The r^2 is better for reporting differences such as these. It indicates how much better you can predict scores on one exam if you know scores on the other—26% better in this case, specifically, 26% better than using the mean.

We have now looked at ESs for these data in two ways, with standardized mean differences and with correlations. Both are based on the *SD* (or the variance, which is the squared *SD*). But one cannot calculate the variance or the *SD* with dichotomous data.

[29] Another widely used SMD is Hedges's *g*; for a discussion, see Card (2012).

[30] For fuller discussion of correlations, see Chapter 8.

TABLE 6.6. Example Data for Computing Effect Sizes

Case	Groups	Variable 1 (Quiz 1)	Variable 2 (Quiz 2)	Pooled (1 + 2)
1	1	4	5	9
2	1	8	8	16
3	1	9	7	16
4	1	6	5	11
5	1	7	7	14
6	1	9	7	16
7	1	7	6	13
8	1	6	7	13
9	1	10	8	18
10	1	7	7	14
11	2	9	4	13
12	2	9	3	12
13	2	10	8	18
14	2	8	6	14
15	2	7	7	14
16	2	3	2	5
17	2	7	7	14
18	2	9	7	16
19	2	9	9	18
20	2	8	6	14
Totals		152	126	278
Mean		7.6	6.3	6.95
SD		1.847	1.75	1.894

For the dichotomies, a different approach has to be used to standardize scores so that they can be compared across samples and studies.

Let's say that the quiz was a test of mastery, or competency. To have mastered the topic, to be competent, students needed to get a score of 7 or higher. In that case, the quizzes could be graded as "pass" or "fail." Using the same data, with scores of 7 or higher converted into "pass" and those 6 or lower scored "fail," we get Table 6.7.[31]

[31]We have often argued against categorizing continuous data in this way, but doing so can make sense for minimum competency tests, as in this example.

TABLE 6.7. Passing the Quizzes

	Quiz 1	Quiz 2	Total
Pass	16	12	28
Fail	4	8	12
Total	20	20	40

When variables are dichotomous, calculating an ES based on *SD*s from the mean isn't very meaningful. The most common ways of reporting dichotomous results is to use probabilities *or* odds—and, often, to also use the ratio of two odds or the ratio of two probabilities to one another.[32] Although it is easy to convert probabilities into odds or odds into probabilities as ways of describing the same data, the two can have quite different impacts. And they can easily be confused with one another in ways that can muddle analysis and presentation.

On Quiz 1, the *probability* of having passed is 16 *out of* 20, or .80 (80%); the probability of failing is 4 out of 20, or 20%. But the *odds* of passing are 16 *to* 4—expressed as 16:4, or reduced to 4:1, or, simply, 4. The odds of failing are 4 to 16, or 1:4, or .25. Note the differences: the probability of passing is .80; the odds are 4:1. These relations are summarized in Table 6.8.

Examining the last column in Table 6.8, we can see that the probability of passing Quiz 1 is 1.33 times as large as that for passing Quiz 2; this 1.33 is the **relative risk ratio (RRR)**.[33] But the odds of passing Quiz 1 are 2.66 times as great; that 2.66 is the **odds ratio (OR)**. One of the reasons for this difference is that when a probability is used, no effect = 0. But when odds are used, no effect = 1. Which is better, the ratio of two probabilities or the ratio of two odds? There is no better or worse; they are different ways of expressing the same relation. One can easily be converted into the other. And one can easily be mistaken for the other.[34] Despite their differences, both measures can be used to compare across datasets and across studies.

TABLE 6.8. Probabilities and Odds of Passing Quiz 1 and Quiz 2

	Quiz 1	Quiz 2	Ratio = Q1/Q2
Probability	0.80	0.60	1.33
Odds	4:1 = 4.0	12:8 =1.5	2.66

[32] And if you multiply a probability by 100, you get a percentage.

[33] This is sometimes called the relative risk or the risk ratio, both abbreviated RR. Measures of risk are more likely used to describe the risk of failing than the chances of passing.

[34] For some evidence that they are in fact sometimes confused in published research and for an example of how heated feelings can be about analytical choices ("down with odds ratios!"), see, respectively, Schechtman (2002) and Sackett, Deeks, and Altman (1996).

Odds and odds ratios have many nice properties, and they are used more widely than the probability-based alternatives. For example, the range of odds ratios is essentially infinite, and they have an approximately normal distribution—when they are transformed by taking their logs.[35] ORs are common in medical fields, and the odds-based method of logit regression is frequently applied in social research (see Chapter 9). One of the disadvantages of ORs is that they can seem less intuitively accurate than the probability-based RRR. Ultimately, choice is a matter of the researcher's preference and how the audience for the research is used to learning about findings.

As is the case everywhere in this book, we do not describe how to conduct varieties of categorical data ESs except as brief illustrations meant to define the methods.[36] Our focus is on choosing the most effective methods. ESs are quite similar in their ability to facilitate comparisons across studies, but odds and odds ratios have a bit of an edge for categorical data because of their uses in more advanced techniques. However, odds often seem to make less sense to the general public—except perhaps for gamblers. As elsewhere, when more than one method can be used to report results, we recommend the **principle of inclusion**. Report and discuss the descriptive statistic you think is most relevant, but include all the others. In the case of ES indices, doing so requires no more than a line or two.

WHEN TO USE DESCRIPTIVE STATISTICS PREPARATORY TO APPLYING MISSING DATA PROCEDURES

Thus far we have discussed what statistics to use to describe the data you have. We now turn to what to use to describe data you do not have—missing data. Except in the smallest and simplest studies, missing data are inevitable. You need to do something about missing data and to inform the reader what you have done and why. If you aren't careful, your statistical package will do something by default, and what it does might not be appropriate. Your statistical program's default "solution" could create more problems than it solves. There are dozens of missing data procedures. Unfortunately, most of the easy and common ones, ones that are the default settings in some statistical packages, aren't very good. As Paul Allison put it, "all the common methods for salvaging information from cases with missing data typically make things worse."[37] Some methods are better than others, and some of the weak methods can work well in certain limited circumstances. Decisions must be made, and they are not easy. There is almost never a straightforward statistical solution or an algorithm or a decision tree that the researcher can unambiguously apply. If there were good algorithms, computer programs could make choices much better than they currently do.

Choices among methods for handling missing data are usually much better if they are built on a thorough knowledge of the dataset. This emphasizes once again the importance of descriptive statistics and knowing your data well. Choices should also be based on a strong understanding of the relations among the variables of interest in the

[35] On transformations and the normal distribution, see the earlier section, "When and Why to Make the Normal Curve Your Point of Reference."

[36] A thorough text reviewing methods of computation is Agresti (1996).

[37] Allison (2002, p. 12).

population, as these are related to the study's methods of gathering data. For example, if data are missing from a longitudinal study because people have dropped out, knowing why they have dropped out is crucial: Is the attrition random? (You wish!) Do people leave because they find the program unsatisfactory? Or do they leave because the program has worked for them and they no longer need it? Are older people more likely to drop out, and does that matter for interpreting the results? These are not statistical questions, and computers won't know the answers without your help, but the answers to these questions can be summarized using descriptive statistics. There may be a statistical fix, but knowing which fix to apply requires substantive knowledge of the phenomena and of the people being studied. Because the main methods for addressing missing data problems are inferential, we deal with them in Chapter 7, on inferential statistics. We mention them here because of the central role descriptive statistics play in diagnosing problems and in choosing solutions to them.

CONCLUSION

We have seen that descriptive statistics have a wide range of uses, wider than most other categories of quantitative data analysis techniques. It is easier to imagine a study that does not use inferential and associational statistical methods (Chapters 7 and 8) than one that eschews descriptive statistics altogether. The Summary Table displays the main goals that descriptive statistics can help you accomplish. It does not specify the statistical and graphical methods you can use to accomplish those goals for the simple reason that any and all of them can be employed in the pursuit of the goals listed.

SUGGESTIONS FOR FURTHER READING

Most work on the approach to descriptive statistics we have taken in this chapter goes by the name of *exploratory data analysis* (EDA). This insight into the field of descriptive statistics was pioneered by John Tukey. His classic, *Exploratory Data Analysis* (1977), is still very much worth reading. A good brief account of EDA is Hartwig and Dearing's *Exploratory Data Analysis* (1979).

In the last decade, EDA has often been linked with computer-intensive data mining. A good example of this approach is Myatt's (2007) *Making Sense of Data: A Practical Guide to Exploratory Data Analysis and Data Mining.* Because data mining is heavily dependent on computer software, many books about how to do it are linked with particular software packages. A good example is Torgo's (2011) *Data Mining with R: Learning with Case Studies.* A good popular account with more emphasis on presentation than on analysis is Few's *Show Me the Numbers* (2nd ed., 2012).

Making wise choices when deciding which statistical methods to use is a matter not only of analysis but also of presentation. It is at the presentation phase that the popular phrase "lies, damned lies, and statistics" (attributed variously to Benjamin Disraeli and Mark Twain) is often brought to bear. It is certainly true that statistical summaries can deceive, whether intentionally or not. On the other hand, if the history of dishonesty is any guide, it is easier, and far more common, to prevaricate with words than with statistics. Examples range from the forged "Donation of Constantine" in the 8th century through the fabricated "Protocols of the Elders of Zion" in the 20th century to the denials of Lance Armstrong in the 21st. No statistics were involved in these famous falsehoods.

It may be easiest of all to be misleading with graphics—and being misleading includes fooling yourself. There are many pitfalls, and graphic presentation is as much art as science. The problems of misleading graphics and how to use visual approaches effectively are big themes in the work of Howard Wainer, who edits a column called "Visual Revelations" in *Chance* magazine. Many of these columns have been collected in his *Graphic Discovery* (2005) and *Picturing the Uncertain World* (2009). These books combine statistical sophistication with entertaining and instructive advice. As essential as graphic displays of data are, they require the same vigilance in presentation as do verbal and numerical results.

CHAPTER 6 SUMMARY TABLE

GOALS THAT CAN BE PURSUED USING DESCRIPTIVE STATISTICS
Getting to know your data, to get a feel for their traits and peculiarities.
Exploring data and discovering hypotheses to test, if not with the current dataset, then in subsequent research.
Visualizing patterns in your data—shapes, outliers, and gaps.
Determining whether necessary assumptions hold for use of inferential and associational techniques; important assumptions include normality, linearity, and homogeneity of variances.
Transforming your data so that non-normal distributions can be analyzed.
Providing information that other researchers can use for replication, interpretation, and techniques such as meta-analyses and structural equation modeling.
Comparing control and treatment groups to see whether they are similar before the treatment.
Comparing a population and a sample to see whether it is reasonable to assume that the sample is representative of the population.
Answering research questions, particularly questions about populations that do not require inference from samples to populations.
Uncovering patterns in missing data so as to choose appropriate techniques for handling missing data.

Note. It is difficult to specify page numbers for this table for the reason given in the Conclusion: "Any and all [methods] can be employed in the pursuit of the goals listed" (p. 237).

CHAPTER 7

What Methods of Statistical Inference to Use When

In this chapter we:

- Introduce you to statistical inference.
- Explain the use of null hypothesis significance testing (NHST) with:
  - random sampling and with random assignment.
  - advice about how to report the results of statistical significance tests.
  - some dos and don'ts when reporting *p*-values and statistical significance.
- Review which statistical tests to use for what, including:
  - The *t*-test.
    - When to use what type of *t*-test.
  - Analysis of variance (ANOVA).
    - Which ANOVA multiple comparison to use for what.
  - A comparison of ANOVA "versus" multiple regression analysis (MRA).
- Suggest when to use confidence intervals (CIs).
  - Describe standard deviation, standard error, and margin of error.
    - Explain how the standard error is influenced by standard deviation and sample size.
  - Consider how CIs should be interpreted.
  - Provide reasons to prefer CIs to *p*-values.
- Discuss when to report the power and precision of your estimates.
  - Explain and compare power, precision, sensitivity, and specificity.
- Clarify when you should use distribution-free, a.k.a. nonparametric, significance tests.
  - Describe some common distribution-free NHSTs.
- Review when to use the bootstrap and other resampling methods.
- Consider the pros and cons of Bayesian methods.
  - Describe four advantages of the Bayesian approach to inference.

- Summarize with a review of which approach to statistical inference you should take and when.
- Discuss missing data, the "silent killer" of valid inferences.
  - Review the main classes of methods for addressing missing data: deletion and imputation.
    - Explain why imputation methods are better and compare the two main approaches: maximum likelihood (ML) and multiple imputation (MI).
- Illustrate, in Appendix 7.1, several worked-out examples of some common methods for statistical inference.

Methods of statistical inference are a subclass of the broader category of logical inference. *Inference* means drawing conclusions based on reasoning or evidence. Making an inference is moving from one conclusion believed to be true to another conclusion that follows from the first. *Statistical inference* refers to using known quantities to draw conclusions about the probability of unknown quantities. Inference is important in research. It is also frequent in daily life, in which nonstatistical is much more common than statistical inference.[1] Even in research, nonstatistical inference is widespread, specifically in research using data that are not quantitative. For example, evidence from a case study can be used to draw inferences about similar cases. Statistical inference is distinct in that its methods have the special property of enabling the researcher to systematically estimate margins of error and how likely the inferences are to be well founded or, conversely, not. It is through statistical inference that researchers may decide that conclusions built upon evidence from comparatively small samples might apply to large populations—or that they do not.

Statistical inference is so central to research involving quantitative data that finely honed routines have been developed to handle it. Many statistical packages automatically provide inferential statistics (p-values, confidence intervals) for any statistic you compute. Despite such routinization, statistical inference is remarkably controversial. Controversies concern *which type* of inferential statistics should be computed;[2] *how important* inferential statistics are as compared with other kinds of statistics (such as effect sizes); and, in some situations, *whether* it is appropriate to compute inferential statistics in the first place. Add to these controversies the fact that there are different schools or philosophies of statistical inference—classical, Bayesian, and resampling—and two things are clear: (1) that researchers have many choices available to them; (2) that the choices will often involve controversy. Although many textbooks present the topic of statistical inference in a cut-and-dried way, few of the choices open to you are beyond dispute. Any advice, including ours, can be open to challenge by knowledgeable critics. Although there is a mainstream or traditional approach, controversies abound even within the dominant paradigm.

---

[1]For example, "She averted her eyes when she said that, so she might not be telling the truth."

[2]Many aids to help choose the "right" statistical test are available. One handy source, containing an amazingly wide range of helpful pages, is *http://statpages.org*.

Here is our first controversial paragraph on this topic. Inferential statistics are fundamental in reporting experimental results when experimental participants have been randomly assigned to experimental (treatment) and control (comparison) groups. These statistical techniques are also crucial in survey research for generalizing from random samples to the populations from which those samples were drawn. However, and this is the controversial part, in research not employing random assignment or random sampling, the classical approach to inferential statistics is inappropriate. Classical inferential statistics are routinely abused by being overused. Here is the most fundamental point about inferential methods: They are based on probability theory. If the experimental and control groups have not been assigned using probability techniques,[3] or if the cases have not been sampled from a population using probability methods, inferential statistics are not applicable. They are routinely applied in inapplicable situations, but an error is no less erroneous for being widespread.

The two main approaches to inferential statistics are **null hypothesis significance testing (NHST)** and **effect sizes with confidence intervals (ESCI)**. Both are probability methods based on the same statistical theory, but they differ considerably in how they report the results of experiments, surveys, and other designs collecting quantitative data. We consider each in turn and then compare them.

NULL HYPOTHESIS SIGNIFICANCE TESTING

NHST was long the standard textbook approach to inference and quantitative analysis, and it probably still is. Although it is usually discussed as a unified set of approaches, and although we do so here, there were sharp differences between its founders and early practitioners[4] that have been "resolved" into the uneasy amalgam we call NHST—or often, for short, either significance testing or hypothesis testing. Although NHST is still the main approach used by most applied researchers, many methodologists (including us) and professional organizations recommend replacing or supplementing it with the confidence-interval approach. Our summary of NHST is brief. We describe NHST and discuss some of the options within it.

Dozens of significance tests exist. The different tests are designed for use in different situations, and we discuss some of those later. But they all share certain features. The final outcome of a significance test is usually a ***p*-value**. The *p* stands for *probability*, specifically the probability that a result *in a random sample* would have been obtained if the null hypothesis were true of the population from which the sample was drawn—or, more briefly and informally, the probability that this result is just a coincidence. The **null hypothesis (NH)** is usually (although *not* inevitably) a hypothesis of no effect or zero difference or no relationship—that is, there is no effect of the IV on the DV, or no difference between the control and experimental groups, or no association among the

[3]Strictly speaking, the pool of experimental participants should first be randomly sampled from a clearly identified population—such as all college students in a state or all Medicare recipients—before members of this sample are randomly assigned. This step is usually ignored in experimental practice.

[4]In discussing the battle between the two founding branches of what has come to be described as NHST, statisticians have differed about whether the two are reconcilable or whether the combined approach is intelligible. See Lehmann (1993) and Gigerenzer (2004) for opposing overviews.

variables. What is tested in significance testing is the null: If the null were true, what is the probability of the result we have obtained in our study? Of course, the researcher usually is looking for a small *p*-value, a small probability that there is zero effect. More formally, the *p*-value is the probability of obtaining a result in a random sample as large as or larger than the one obtained if the NH were true of the population.

What would the *p*-value mean when computed for a nonrandom sample? The short answer is, nothing. Part of the definition of a *p*-value is "the probability of a result in a random sample. . . ." Researchers may find it useful to know something like the following: *If* this had been a random sample drawn from *some* population that I had been able to specify, *then* here is what the *p*-value *would have been.* Or, *If* I had been able to randomly assign cases to treatment and comparison groups, here is what the *p*-value *would have been.* We do not find that kind of information very valuable, but given the frequency with which it is reported, it is clear that many people do value it. Also, it is worth noting that you might have trouble getting your research published or getting it past members of a dissertation committee or having a granting agency take your results seriously if you fail to include this information. Our compromise, when we think that there will be a demand for inappropriate inferential calculations, is to report them, usually in a footnote, but to avoid emphasizing them.

Another circumstance in which calculating *p*-values is meaningless occurs when you have data for the whole population. Having such data is fairly common. For example, you might calculate the average difference between public and private college tuition in the 50 states or the relation between mean education level and birth rate in all member nations of the United Nations. You do not need to make inferences to the population or to talk about the confidence intervals of plausible values in the population. You *already know* what the population values are. There is *nothing to infer.* Nonetheless, in this, as in other inappropriate circumstances, the *p*-value is routinely calculated. Again, perhaps some readers find it helpful to know, for example, that if the United States had 700 states and if the study were based on a random sample of 50 of those 700 states, then here is what the *p*-value would have been. This strikes us as an awfully fanciful thing to compute, but such computations are often made and reported. The *p*-value is an extremely handy statistic, but that does not mean it should be calculated in all circumstances. The same considerations apply to confidence intervals (CIs). Inferential statistics are often crucial; it would be a mistake to omit them when they are applicable, but it is also a mistake to use them when they are inappropriate.

There are many other assumptions that need to be true for the proper use of specific inferential tests[5]—such as equality of variances of different samples—but these are secondary to the fundamental assumption of randomness, specifically that probability methods were used either in sampling and/or in assignment of cases. Assuming that probability techniques were used to sample from the population and/or to assign cases, we can now turn to methods of statistical inference.

We only briefly discuss the basic logic of hypothesis testing here. No topic is better covered in the textbook literature.[6] Instead, we focus on when to use significance testing and, when using it, which particular techniques to use. We begin by illustrating with the

[5] A classic source is Glass, Peckham, and Sanders (1972).

[6] Among recent accounts, we like the one in Murnane and Willett (2011) because of its clarity and because it is included as an introduction to the more advanced methods often used by researchers.

two most common circumstances in which hypothesis testing is used: random survey samples and randomly assigned experimental groups. Then we discuss specific types of tests and the circumstances to which they can be effectively applied. (Some basic tests are illustrated in Appendix 7.1 at the end of this chapter.)

Statistical Inference with Random Sampling

Random sampling provides the simplest context for discussing inference. We have already reviewed the main methods of random sampling in survey research in our companion volume.[7] Here we discuss those parts of the topic relevant to statistical inference, specifically, drawing conclusions about populations based on evidence about samples. For example, in surveys, after computing the value of a sample statistic, such as the percentage of the respondents with a particular opinion, the researchers then compute the statistical significance of the sample statistic, which means they answer the following question: If the null hypothesis were true of the population, how likely would we have been to obtain a sample statistic this large or larger in a sample of this size? Say your survey asked college student respondents how many hours they spent studying in a typical week and also for their overall grade point averages (GPAs). Then you calculated the correlation between the two (hours of study and GPAs). It turned out to be $r = .39$ in the sample, and the p-value of that sample statistic was $p = .02$. This means that only 2 times out of 100 would we get a correlation of .39 (or bigger) *in the random sample* if there were no relation (null hypothesis) *in the population* between GPA and hours spent studying.

Statistical Inference with Random Assignment

Experiments rarely use random sampling. Instead, experiments use, and are virtually defined by, random assignment.Although random assignment and random sampling are very different activities, the logic of statistical inference is quite similar in the two cases, but most people find the underlying logic of the process to be a little less clear in experiments. In surveys, the samples are drawn from known populations. In experiments, the usual practice is to make more hypothetical assumptions about unknown and unknowable populations. The goals of random sampling and random assignment are different.[8] But, as a practical matter, the process of random assignment is quite straightforward. Researchers compare data from experimental (treatment) and control (comparison) groups and ask the question: If the null hypothesis were true about the difference between treated and untreated groups, how likely is it that we would have obtained a difference between them this big (or bigger) when studying treatment and comparison groups of this size? For example, say the treatment was "noninvasive brain stimulation";[9] the dependent variable was the score on a problem-solving test. The treated group answered 60% of the questions correctly on the test, whereas

[7]Vogt et al. (2012, Ch. 7).

[8]Random sampling aims at external validity, while random assignment is concerned with internal validity; see Part I, especially Chapters 1 and 3.

[9]This example is based on Chi and Snyder (2011).

the comparison group answered 20% correctly; say that the p-value of the difference between the two groups was $p = < .01$. The question answered by this p-value is, How likely is the difference between the scores of these *randomly assigned groups* if the differences between them were due to random error in the assignment to the groups rather than to differences in the effects of the treatment? In this case, the likelihood was less than 1 out of 100.

How to Report Results of Statistical Significance Tests

Tests of statistical significance result in p-values. By tradition or convention, a p-value of less than or equal to .05—or 1 chance out of 20—is considered statistically significant; one greater than .05 is not. This is an arbitrary but convenient and very widely used dividing line. Another convention is to identify statistically significant results with asterisks. In a table with multiple results, these are often marked with increasing numbers of asterisks as the p-value gets smaller. A footnote to the table is often in this form: $^{*}p < .05$; $^{**}p < .01$; $^{***}p < .001$. A statistic in the table without an asterisk is not statistically significant. Although reporting is largely a matter of convention or tradition,[10] there are some practices that are dos and don'ts.

Dos and Don'ts in Reporting *p*-Values and Statistical Significance

- ***Always report exact p-values.*** By convention p-values are rounded off. And by another convention you should specify in advance a cutoff p-value (technically an alpha). This is considered good practice to keep you from fudging your results; *if* you are going to use cutoff scores, it is definitely good to state them in advance. Still, we think it is important also to report exact p-values. They are helpful for interpretation and can enable other researchers to use your results in a meta-analysis.

- ***Never report p = .000.*** You sometimes see this value in published research. Literally, it means that there is no probability at all that the result could be due to random error. But there is *always* some possibility that a result is due to random error. Such reporting arises from the fact that some statistical software will report results this way, and the researchers simply copy the output. But a computer output of $p = .000$ does *not* mean that there is zero probability that the difference between the null and the result is due to random error. Rather, what the computer output means is that when computing the exact p-value, the software stopped after .001 and did not carry the calculations to the fourth decimal point and beyond. When we get computer readouts with .000 as the p-value, we convert them to < .001, because that is what they actually mean. This practice is recommended by some professional organizations, such as the American Psychological Association.

- ***Always specify type of significance.*** The word *significant* alone can mean practically or clinically important, not only *statistically* significant. But it is quite possible for a statistically significant result to be too small to be of interest in practice. Practical value is more a matter of judgment by experts in a field of activity. Statistically

[10] For a revealing history of the evolution of this practice in sociology, see Leahey (2005).

significant results that are not practically significant occur most frequently in studies based on very large samples.[11] In brief, because there are distinct types of significance, use the word with the appropriate qualifier—statistical, practical, clinical, and so forth.

WHICH STATISTICAL TESTS TO USE FOR WHAT

There are many types and subtypes of statistical tests. Entire books are devoted to the question of choosing among them. One popular title is *100 Statistical Tests*.[12] And more general volumes devote many pages to statistical tests in specific situations.[13] Although the varieties are numerous, their underlying logic is similar; and they all end in a p-value. The two most commonly used significance tests are (1) the t-test and (2) the F-test, usually known as analysis of variance, almost always abbreviated ANOVA.[14] There are several forms of each used for different types of research design. They are the main workhorses of NHST.

The *t*-Test

The t-test has largely replaced the older z-test; the t-test is more versatile because it is more accurate for small samples, and there is no practical difference between the z- and t-tests when the samples are large.[15] The t-test is most commonly used to study two groups defined by one categorical independent variable, such as large and small classes, and how those two differ on average on one continuous dependent variable, such as scores on an achievement test. One mnemonic device—largely accurate and a good place to start—that our students have used is: "t for two." The t-test is for two groups. And if the resulting t-statistic is 2.0 or larger, it is statistically significant ($p < .05$).

Great care is needed in selecting the correct form of t-test. If you pick the wrong one, the software will usually follow your instructions and produce an inaccurate analysis. The choice of test is made more confusing because there are several names for the types of t-tests. The test itself is often also referred to as the Student's t test; "Student" was the pseudonym of the statistician who devised the test in the early 1900s. The basic rules for selecting among t-tests are simple, perhaps deceptively so. We outline the most common rules. But you should keep in mind that for more complicated designs and more advanced work, there are many more options than we can list here. Consult the sources in the footnotes for more guidance about choices and controversies.[16]

[11] For discussions of practical and clinical significance and guidelines for measuring them, see Thompson (2002).

[12] Kanji (1999).

[13] Myers, Well, and Lorch (2010).

[14] The chi-squared test is used for categorical variables; it and some modern replacements are discussed in Chapter 8.

[15] The z-test, based on z-scores (see Chapter 6), assumes that the scores on the DV are normally distributed, as they tend to be with large samples.

[16] On t-test alternatives, especially the Wilcoxon–Mann–Whitney test, see Fay and Proschan (2010); McElduff, Cortina-Borja, Chan, and Wade (2010) explore regression alternatives (see Chapter 8); and Curran-Everett (2012) suggests permutation options, including the bootstrap (see later in this chapter).

As with other significance tests, a preliminary question is, Will your test be **directional** or ***nondirectional***? The answer must also be entered into software before executing the t-test. (A directional test is also called ***one-tailed***; nondirectional tests are called ***two-tailed***.) The significance test is used to determine whether your research result is significantly different from zero (or other NH). If you have good reason to believe beforehand that you know the direction of the difference—that it will be bigger or that it will be smaller than zero—you can use a directional test. If your question asks, Is it significantly different, whether bigger *or* smaller, then use the nondirectional (or two-tailed) test. The advantage of using the directional test is that it's easier to pass; it is easier to obtain a low p-value. But it is not often used. The reason is that researchers can rarely be sufficiently certain *in advance* that they know the direction of any difference from zero. And you must *know* in order to justify using a directional test. The more cautious or conservative approach, and the one that is usually recommended, is to always use a nondirectional test; and this is the option usually provided by statistical software packages. Finally, it is always bad practice first to look at the result and then decide, on the basis of that information, to use a directional test. It's dishonest to conduct a nondirectional test, see that it didn't work out, and then claim that you planned a directional test all along.

When you use software to conduct a t-test of your study results, you usually are given three basic options: a one-sample t-test; a two-independent-samples t-test; or a two-dependent-samples t-test.[17] Like other significance tests, the purpose of the t-test is to learn whether a statistic—such as a mean difference—is significantly different from zero (or from some other NH). A significant difference has a small p-value; the cutoff between small enough and not small enough to be significant is determined in advance by the researcher—by convention it is 5%.

The t-test was devised for experimental research with control and treatment groups. Typically, what is compared is the difference between an experimental treatment and no treatment. If the samples (control and experimental group) are independent because they have been created by random assignment, then you use the two-independent-samples t-test, which was devised for this situation.

In many research situations, the samples are not independent. Then the dependent-samples t-test is used. This test has several alternate names, and they indicate the research designs in which it is used: paired samples, correlated samples, within-subject/within-group, and repeated measures t-tests.[18] The repeated measures example is the clearest. Say that the treatment is training to raise skill level on some task. The participants are tested to determine their level of skill, they engage in the treatment/training, and then they are retested to see whether their skill levels have increased. The pre- and posttreatment participants in the study are hardly independent samples or groups; they are the same people. The dependent-samples t-test is used to answer the question, Is the difference between the mean on the pretest and on the posttest significantly different from zero?

---

[17]Be sure not to confuse one-*sample* and two-sample t-tests with one-*tailed* and two-tailed tests; to avoid confusion when teaching, we generally use *directional* and *nondirectional*, respectively, for one- and two-tailed tests.

[18]These different names for the dependent-samples test reflect subtle differences. Some cynics have also pointed out that this proliferation of synonyms provides lots of work for statistics teachers.

Finally, a version of the *t*-test is available when you have only one group or sample that you have described with a sample statistic. For example, if your NH is that there is no correlation between body mass index (BMI) and amount of daily exercise in a population (say, senior citizens) and in your random sample from that population, you find that there is a correlation of $r = -.13$ between the two, you would use the one-sample *t*-test to obtain the *p*-value for that finding. By contrast, if you had two samples—one of senior citizens over 65 and the other of adults ages 30 to 49—and your NH was that there is no difference between the two populations, then you could use the independent-samples *t*-test to assess any difference between them. See Table 7.1 for a summary of when to use various types of *t*-test.

Analysis of Variance

The subtypes of analysis of variance (ANOVA)—also known as the *F*-test— follow the same logic as the types of *t*-tests, with the most important distinction being between independent groups and repeated measures designs.[19] The repeated measures ANOVA requires different analytical methods because the data are correlated. For example, if a group of people took a strength training course, measures of their strength following the course might be influenced by the course. But the measures after the course would also surely be influenced by how strong they were before the course. Repeated measures designs (a.k.a. within-subjects designs) usually lead to more precise estimates because participants serve as their own controls; that is why repeated measures studies are more likely to lead to a statistically significant result whether assessed with a dependent-samples *t*-test or a repeated measures ANOVA/*F*-test. The advantage of the ANOVA/*F*-test is that it provides an overall within-groups measure as well as the between-groups measure, while the *t*-test provides only the latter.[20]

Like the *t*-test, ANOVA is used with categorical IVs and a continuous DV. When ANOVA and the *t*-test are used on the same problem, they give the same answer, that is, the same *p*-value. But ANOVA is more versatile and can be used with a greater

TABLE 7.1. When to Use What Type of *t*-Test

Type of test	When to use
One-sample *t*-test	To determine when a statistic, such as a mean, which has been calculated on one sample, is significantly different from the NH.
Two-independent-samples *t*-test	To determine whether a statistic, such as a mean difference between control and experimental groups, is statistically significant.
Two-dependent-samples *t*-test	To determine whether the difference between two nonindependent samples, such as in a repeated measures design, is significantly different from the NH.

[19]For a full account of the many varieties of types and uses of ANOVA, see Hancock and Mueller (2010, Chs. 1 and 2). On the issue of repeated measures in general, see Weinfurt (2000).

[20]On longitudinal designs in general, an excellent source is Singer and Willett (2003).

variety of research designs.[21] The difference between the *t*-test and ANOVA is that ANOVA can be applied to more than one IV at a time, and the IVs can have more than two categories. For example, say you were studying factors leading students to decide to become engineering majors. If two of your IVs were gender in two categories and ethnicity in four categories, then your study would be called a 2 × 4 design. You could study whether there were statistically significant differences between genders, among ethnicities, and between any combinations of gender and ethnicity. The effects of the two IVs separately—gender and ethnicity—are main effects. Combined effects are called *interactions*. Was the effect of gender stronger for different ethnicities—and was it statistically significant? Was the effect of ethnicity stronger for one gender or the other—and was it statistically significant? You would examine whether there were differences among all the pairs of groups—Hispanic females, African American males, and so forth. It is important to note that when you have combined or interaction effects, main effects are difficult, often impossible, to interpret.

You could also use the *t*-test to study differences among each pair of groups using one *t*-test after another, but this would be a poor analysis strategy. The eight separate *t*-tests would run an increased risk of finding a "significant" difference between some pair simply by chance, known as Type I error. If the chance for one comparison is 1 out of 20, or 5% ($p < .05$), then the chances of finding a "significant" result for 10 comparisons is roughly 10 times as great: not 5 but 50%. The process of making multiple comparisons is more efficient when you use ANOVA. ANOVA does not eliminate the multiple-comparisons problem, but adjustments for it are more effective. The details are complicated, but the principle is simple. If you want to achieve a *p*-value of < .05 and are making multiple comparisons, you divide the *p*-value by the number of comparisons. So, if you are making 10 comparisons, you divide by 10; the *p*-value needed to reach statistical significance becomes $p < .005$—not 5 out of 100, but 5 out of 1,000.[22]

Statistical packages may offer a dozen or more adjustments for making multiple comparisons, each for a specific design. Some of them have more than one name.[23] The four most commonly used multiple comparison tests are Tukey's HSD (honestly significant difference), Bonferroni's, Dunnett's, and Scheffé's. The main point is that if you use ANOVA and have more than two groups in your IVs, you *must* conduct multiple comparisons. The basic ANOVA output gives you an overall significance level, called an **omnibus** result. It tells you that in the comparisons being made—in our example, between the effects of gender and ethnicity separately and together and for each of the gender–ethnic groups—there is a significant effect *somewhere*. To know where and what it is, and to meaningfully interpret the result, you need to go into more depth. That is what the multiple comparison procedures are for. Table 7.2 sketches the most commonly used methods for multiple comparisons; these are applied following a statistically significant omnibus ANOVA test. (For an example, see Appendix Table 7A.7.)

[21]As we show in Chapter 8, regression analysis is even more versatile.

[22]Also relevant to the type of statistical tests and methods of multiple comparisons you use is whether your comparisons are theory-driven and planned before the data are collected or examined after differences have been discovered (called *post hoc* comparisons). See Table 7.2.

[23]Here as elsewhere it is crucial to report the kind of software used in your analysis. For a striking demonstration of the effects on outcomes of using different statistical packages, see Altman and McDonald (2003).

TABLE 7.2. Which ANOVA Multiple Comparison Procedure to Use for What

Procedure	When to use
Tukey's HSD	To test all possible pairs of means; this is the most general of the tests.
Bonferroni's inequality	To test planned, theory-driven contrasts; this also is a very general test.
Dunnett's procedure	To test each experimental group against each control group.
Scheffé's test	To test comparisons suggested by the observed results.

Although ANOVA was developed for testing experimental results, it is also a fairly general method that can be used to analyze data collected with a variety of designs. For many researchers, it is the go-to design, the one they think of first. The basic logic of ANOVA is fundamental to experimental designs. It is important to understand that logic, because it is also the basis of other significance tests. The outcome of a significance test using ANOVA is an ***F*-ratio**. This is a measure of what you can explain as being due to the experimental treatment divided by what you cannot explain as due to the treatment. The more the explained variance outweighs the unexplained variance, the more effective the treatment, the more impact the IV has on the DV. For example, if the *F*-ratio is 8.5, that means the variance in scores in the dependent variable that you *can* explain as due to the experimental treatment is 8½ times greater than the variance in the DV scores that you *cannot* explain by the IVs.[24] In other words, if what you can explain is a lot bigger than what you can't explain, your results are more likely to be statistically significant than if what you can explain as due to the treatment is small. The *F*-ratio is used to calculate the *p*-value, which, as always, tells how likely it would be for you to obtain the results in your sample if the NH were true of the population. Another way to put it is that the *F*-ratio is the ratio of what you'd expect if the null were true compared with what you actually get. The probability of that ratio is the *p*-value.

ANOVA "versus" Multiple Regression Analysis

ANOVA can be expanded to include covariates, or control variables, by adopting the methods of **ANCOVA (analysis of covariance)**. But ANCOVA is generally less flexible in this regard than regression analysis. When you have more than a few independent and control variables, multiple regression analysis (MRA) is almost always the better choice (see Chapter 8). Such comparisons have led some researchers to see a sort of battle between ANOVA and regression, but this is not a very helpful way to look at the differences between the two. Statisticians have long pointed out that ANOVA is a special or limited case or type of MRA—a type in which the IVs have to be categorical and the DVs have to be continuous. MRA is more general. Anything you can do in ANOVA or ANCOVA, you can do with MRA, but the reverse is not true. MRA can easily accommodate numerous variables, and each of them, independent or dependent,

[24]Specifically, to get the *F*-ratio, the variance between the groups is divided by the variances within them.

can be either categorical or continuous. Still, the two—MRA and ANOVA—are more complementary than not. For example, to test the statistical significance of the total variance explained by a regression equation, one typically uses ANOVA.

When you report the results of an ANOVA-based analysis, it is now common and correct practice to report more than the *F*-ratio, the *p*-value, and the steps used to arrive at these. It is also important to report an ES, such as a standardized mean difference (SMD; see Chapter 6), and CIs around that effect size (see the next section in this chapter). Remember that a *p*-value is *not* a measure of the size of an effect. To repeat, it is the probability of obtaining an effect of a given size in a sample if the NH were true of the population—for example, the probability of obtaining a correlation of $r = .27$ or larger in a random sample of 200 if the NH of no correlation were true of the population. Finally, in addition to an ES, you should also include a measure of association that describes the proportion of the variance in the DV explained by the IV. The two most common measures of association used with ANOVA are omega-squared and eta-squared (see Chapter 8 for further discussion).

WHEN TO USE CONFIDENCE INTERVALS

Most research methodologists (but not all) recommend using confidence intervals (CIs) rather than or in addition to NHST. And some major research organizations, such as the American Psychological Association (APA) and the American Educational Research Association, also strongly encourage the use of CIs.[25] We agree with those recommendations for the simple reason that ESs with CIs (ESCIs) provide everything that *p*-values provide, plus additional information that is useful for interpreting your data. But most practicing researchers still use the basic NHST methods and report statistical significance in terms of *p*-values. This is a long-established and familiar tradition. For those researchers reluctant to abandon familiar reporting methods, we recommend supplementing them with CIs. In the following paragraphs we first briefly describe what CIs are. Then we list the reasons to prefer them over NHST *p*-values.

It is important to begin by noting both CIs and *p*-values are built on the same underlying statistical theory. Both assume that the sample statistics have been computed on random samples and/or randomly assigned groups. And both are built on the **standard error**, which is a theoretical value based on the idea of an infinite number of random samples. A standard error (*SE*) is an estimate of sampling error. When multiplied by (approximately) 2, it gives you a **margin of error (MOE)** for a 95% CI. In general terms, the *SE* answers the question, How far are you likely to be wrong if you use a sample statistic to estimate a population value? The goal, of course, is to design a study with a small standard error or a narrow margin of error.

*SE*s can be computed for any sample statistic. The most frequently discussed is the *SE* of the mean. The statistical theory is complex, but the calculation is easy. Although we rarely report formulas for calculation in this book, the formula for the *SE* of the mean is so fundamental to basic inferential statistics that we make an exception. Say

[25] Wilkinson (1999) summarized the recommendations of the APA; they were a turning point in research psychology.

that for a given city in a given year the researchers estimate that the mean family income is $40,000. This estimate is based on a random sample of 900 residents. Say that the sample data for income have a standard deviation (*SD*) of $6,000. That's all you need to compute the standard error. The formula is

$$SE = \frac{SD}{\sqrt{n}}$$

For our data, that would be

$$SE = \frac{6000}{\sqrt{900}}$$

or

$$\frac{6000}{30} = 200$$

The standard error is the basis of the MOE. You double the *SE* to get the CI on either side of an estimate.[26] The brief conclusion, somewhat rounded off, is that we could be 95% confident that the value of the mean in the population is $40,000 plus or minus $400, or between $39,600 and $40,400.

This is a very narrow CI. It is narrow because of the comparatively small *SD* and the fairly large sample. Samples this large are common in surveys, but rather rare in experiments. What would happen if the sample were smaller? Say it were 100, not 900. Then the *SE* would be 600, and the CIs would range between $38,800 and $41,200. If the sample size were 25, the *SE* would be 1200, and the CIs would range from $37,600 to $42,400. You gain in the precision of your estimate when you use a larger sample size, and you lose precision when you use a smaller one.

In short, the *SE* is a population estimate calculated on the basis of two measures, the size of the random sample and its *SD*. We illustrate these relationships in Table 7.3 with data from the preceding example and from a second example, a city with the same mean income but much more income inequality and therefore a larger *SD*, $30,000. Table 7.3 illustrates two basic facts: (1) the larger the sample, the smaller the MOE; (2)

TABLE 7.3. Standard Error as Influenced by Standard Deviation and Sample Size

Example 1: *SD* = $6,000	Example 2: *SD* = $30,000
sqrt of 900 = 30; 6000 ÷ 30 = 200 MOE = 400; CI = 39,600 – 40,400	sqrt of 900 = 30; 30,000 ÷ 30 = 1000 MOE = 2000; CI = 38,000 – 42,000
sqrt of 100 = 10; 6000 ÷ 10 = 600 MOE = 1200; CI = 38,800 – 41,200	sqrt of 100 = 10; 30,000 ÷ 10 = 3000 MOE = 6000; CI = 34,000 – 44,000
sqrt of 25 = 5; 6000 ÷ 5 = 1200 MOE = 2400; CI = 37,600 – 42,400	sqrt of 25 = 5; 30,000 ÷ 5 = 6000 MOE = 12,000; CI = 28,000 – 52,000

[26] In a *t*-test, you divide the mean difference between two samples by the *SE* to get the *t*-statistic.

the larger the *SD*, the larger the MOE. These can lead to very different estimates. With a sample of 900 and an *SD* of $6,000, the range of plausible values represented by the CI would be $39,600 to $40,400, a very precise estimate. But with a sample of 25 and an *SE* of $30,000, the CIs would be $28,000 to $52,000, a much less precise estimate.

Remember the distinction between the *SE* and the *SD*. The *SE* is inferential. It uses sample data (sample size and sample *SD*) to calculate the probable error of a population estimate. As we have seen, *SE*s (and their associated CIs) vary with sample size; but *SD*s, which are sample statistics, do not. In short, *SDs are facts about samples; SEs are inferences about populations.*

The goal of both NHST and ESCI is to make inferences about populations using data from samples. Does it make sense to compute CIs for an entire population or for a nonprobability sample? As with computing a *p*-value for a population or a nonprobability sample, there is a debate among experts, but there is no doubt that the conceptual basis of the CI approach is random sampling/assignment. We think that if you are going to compute CIs for a population, it is preferable to use resampling methods such as bootstrapping.[27] (See the later section on resampling methods.)

Whenever the NHST approach is possible, so is the ESCI approach. The best way to see the difference between the two is to start with the kind of hypothesis or research question on which each is built. In the NHST approach, one begins with an NH, such as: There is no statistically significant difference on the DV between the control and experimental groups. Of course, the researcher usually expects, or hopes, to be able to reject the NH and thus indirectly confirm that there is a difference due to the experimental treatment—in the predicted direction. In the ESCI approach, one asks a research question such as, What is our estimate of the size of the effect of the DV, as measured by the difference between the control and experimental groups, and how big are the margins of error around that estimate?[28] To many people, the starting point of the ESCI approach seems more direct and natural than the NHST approach. ESCIs are aimed at answering questions we are really interested in: How big is the effect? How accurate/precise is our estimate of that effect?

How Should CIs Be Interpreted?

What's the best way to describe what a CI tells you? Those who use CIs differ on the question.[29] Say we computed the mean difference between two randomly assigned groups on some 10-point measure. Say the mean difference between the samples is 4.75, and the 95% CI is [1.61, 7.89]. So the sample mean difference is 4.75, and the lower limit of the 95% CI is 1.61, while the upper limit is 7.89. The MOE is the amount that gets added to and subtracted from the estimate to produce the CIs; it is approximately 2 *SE*s (see earlier discussion). In this case the MOE is 3.14. To get the lower bound or limit,

[27]See Yu (2008) for a discussion.

[28]When a statistic, such as a sample mean, is used to estimate a parameter, such as a population mean, it is often called an *estimator*. When a statistic is an *unbiased estimator* of a parameter, it is called the *expected value* and is symbolized *E*. For example, the mean of some measure, such as age, of a random sample is an unbiased estimate of the mean of the population parameter; it is also the expected value.

[29]Cumming (2012) discusses six ways to characterize the same CI.

you subtract the MOE (4.75 – 3.14 = 1.61); to get the upper bound or confidence limit you add the MOE (4.75 + 3.14 = 7.89). The information in this example can be described in the following four ways.

1. The CI is the range of plausible values for the population statistic. Values inside the confidence limits (between 1.61 and 7.89, in this case) are plausible. It is reasonable to conclude that we can be 95% confident that this range—1.61–7.89—contains the population value. Values closer to the estimate (4.75 in this example) are more plausible than those at the limits of the CI. This is the description we favor, but it makes some strict constructionists uncomfortable.

2. If we took an infinite number of random samples from a population and computed the mean and CI for each one of those samples, 95% of those CIs would capture the population mean, and 5% would not. This is the strictest interpretation, the most technically correct, and probably the one most favored by mathematical statisticians. More applied researchers may resist it because it contains the same kind of mouthful of hypotheticals and conditionals that many dislike about NHST.

3. The CI (based on the MOE) tells you how precise the estimate is; this precision is likely to be important for practical purposes. Saying, as some incautious researchers might, that the value is 4.75 and that there is only a 5% ($p = .05$) chance that it is not the true value is a *serious* misinterpretation. That statement is much more precise than what we actually know.

4. You can use CIs to come to NHST conclusions. For instance, in our example, if the null hypothesis was a zero mean difference between the two groups, the NH can be rejected at the $p < .05$ level because the CI range (which extends from the bottom confidence limit to the top confidence limit) does not include zero. Conversely, if the CI range did include zero, then the null would not be rejected; the estimate of 4.75 would not be statistically significant. If the CI range included zero, we would be 95% confident that the NH could not be rejected.

The estimate is the same in NHST and ESCI. It can be a mean, a correlation, or any other sample statistic. NHST tells you how likely you would be to obtain that sample statistic if the NH were true. ESCI adds MOEs on either side of the estimate to give the CIs. (See Appendix 7.1 at the end of this chapter for tabular and graphic depictions of CIs.)

Note that there is nothing fixed about the 95% confidence interval. Like the .05 or 5% p-value, it is a handy tradition. Just as in some cases you might want to set a more stringent p-value, say .01, or a lower threshold, say .10, so too with CIs. In addition to the 95% CI, 99% CIs are sometimes used, and occasionally the 90% CI is used as a confidence level. If you are willing to be less confident, say 90%, you will get a narrower confidence interval. Conversely, the more certain you want to be, the wider the CI has to be. To be 100% certain, the CI would have to range between negative infinity, through zero to positive infinity. To be 100% certain, your range of plausible values would be infinite; they could be anything—which tells you nothing, of course. Though we take this reasoning to logical extremes, this is an important point. We researchers cannot be 100% certain of, nor can we prove, anything in the empirical sciences. This is one of the reasons we prefer the ESCI approach. *The ESCI approach specifies our degree of uncertainty and the range of probable error in our estimates.*

Reasons to Prefer CIs to *p*-Values[30]

1. The CIs for a statistic contain all the information that the *p*-value for a hypothesis test contains, but the reverse is not true. If the 95% CI does not include the NH value (usually zero), the estimate is significant at the $p < .05$ level. If the 99% CI includes zero (or other NH value), the estimate is not significant at the $p < .01$ level.

2. The CIs make the degree of uncertainty in statistical estimates much clearer. By contrast, NHST encourages dichotomous decisions (*yes*, it is, vs. *no*, it isn't significant). Dichotomous thinking implies much more certainty than is realistic about the results of social research. *ESCI puts uncertainty up front where it should be.* Somewhat paradoxically, perhaps, we think that clearly describing uncertainty is more accurate. Any study is always a simplification of reality. CIs make that clear.

CIs put uncertainty on display by providing margins of error or ranges of plausible values. For example, in the sample of male and female faculty salaries discussed in Chapter 6 (see Figure 6.6), the sample value, and therefore the population estimate, was that female professors made $18,686 less than their male colleagues. The 95% CI was [–$11,628, –$25,744]. The MOE was $7,058. That range of values is much more informative than just giving the estimate followed by $p < .05$.

3. CIs are very informative about the likely replicability of study results, whereas *p*-values are almost useless for predicting replicability.[31]

4. The ESCI approach helps with some of the more troubling issues of causation in social research. It makes discussions of cause probabilistic rather than absolutistic.

An ES implies a causal relation. It does so by definition, because the noun *effect* is defined in any dictionary as something that is caused; and the verb *to effect* means to cause something to happen. If you are uncomfortable with this, you should probably abandon the term *effect size* and replace it with other terms, such as the *estimate* or the *size of the relation*.

Most discussions of cause at some point encounter the debate over whether only randomized experiments can identify cause. Fortunately, the choice between ESCI and NHST is irrelevant to that debate. CIs around estimates are routine in the reporting of experimental results in the natural sciences. This means that they are much more credible because they are less likely to use the language of "proof," which is really only appropriate in mathematics and logic. It is better for researchers to simply state the facts and to say, for example, "we did a randomized controlled experiment; we found a difference of such and such a size between the control and experimental groups; our margin of error for that difference is thus and so."

---

[30]For an argument that more can be salvaged from the practice of NHST than we suggest here, see Wainer and Robinson (2003).

[31]This point is thoroughly demonstrated in a superb article by Cumming (2008). If we had to recommend only one article on the NHST-ESCI debate, this would be it.

WHEN TO REPORT POWER AND PRECISION OF YOUR ESTIMATES

Power and *precision* are related concepts, as well as statistical measures; they are used, respectively, in NHST and in ESCI. They are also related to several other concepts and measures—and the terms used to label them are not perfectly consistent. Here we focus on the basics, with references to more advanced concepts and calculations. Power is essential in planning NHST work. And precision is equally important in planning a study in which you will take the ESCI approach to data analysis.

Power is the ability to detect an effect.[32] More specifically, power is the probability of rejecting a false NH, which is one that you ought to have rejected. If you don't reject a false NH, you have committed a Type II error. A Type I error, by contrast, is rejecting a true NH, one you ought not to have rejected. These labels have confused generations of students, mostly because they involve double and triple negatives. But the concepts are important in dichotomous decision making, and some decision making is inevitably dichotomous. And avoiding one type of error increases the chances of the other. Think of a smoke detector. There are two ways it can commit an error. The alarm can go off every time someone cooks something, or the alarm will go off only when the house is already engulfed in flames. The only way to make sure that the second won't happen is to put up with some false alarms.

Precision is easier to define. It is the ability to estimate an effect accurately, or precisely, with narrow margins of error or CIs.[33] The narrower the CI is, the more precise the estimate. The trade-off in ESCI is parallel to the Type I–Type II trade-off in NHST, but in ESCI it is between level of certainty and level of precision. The more certain you need to be, the less precise the estimate can be. Thus 99% certainty requires a wider CI than does 95% certainty.

Related concepts used for *bivariate* diagnostic tests are *sensitivity* and *specificity.* These are used mostly in medical research and practice, but the concepts are broadly important for thinking about what your research or diagnostic results tell you. The **sensitivity** of a test is the true *positive* rate, for example, the rate at which it correctly identifies people with a disease. **Specificity** of a test is the true *negative* rate, for example, the rate at which it correctly identifies people as *not* having the disease. As with Type I and Type II errors in hypothesis testing (and with certainty and precision in CIs), there is a trade-off between the two.[34] If you want to be highly confident that you are going to identify everyone with a given disease, so you can begin treatments promptly, you'll probably misdiagnose (false positive) some people as having the disease who in fact are healthy. Conversely, if you want to be sure that you do not incorrectly identify individuals who are ill as not having the disease (false negative), then you will surely miss some folks who have it and who could have benefited from treatment.

Such questions, trade-offs, and decisions in analytic techniques are among the key choices researchers have to make. Where do you set your cutoff *p*-value, how much risk

[32]Power calculations are best made using software. A popular freeware package is G*Power. See Parker and Berman (2003) for a general discussion and Lan and Shun (2009) for more technical but very compact and practical details.

[33]For a very readable case for precision over power, see Cumming (2012); Maxwell, Kelley, and Rausch (2008) provide more technical details—and call the concept accuracy, not precision.

[34]A classic source is Altman and Bland (1994).

of Type I error can you take to avoid Type II error, and which type is more important for your study? What matters more for your study, precision or confidence level? Is your research question one in which precision or certainty is more important?

Although power is relevant only in the context of NHST and precision is used only in conjunction with ESCI, their similarity can be seen in the fact that researchers can increase either power or precision by taking the same steps—most certainly by increasing sample size. That means that researchers taking either an NHST or an ESCI approach will confront the same economy of choices. Increasing sample size is not costless for either the researchers or the research participants. You want your study to have sufficient power or precision to tell you something useful, but you don't want to waste your time and other resources trying to attain unnecessarily high levels of power or precision. You don't want to waste the time of research participants, either. It is especially important not to overdo sample size when the research poses some risk to participants. If the study poses no risk, you still might be better advised to conduct a second study rather than to use your resources to recruit and study unnecessarily large samples of participants.

One final note: You may be required to compute the power of your intended study even if you have decided to conduct no statistical tests and have chosen instead to take the ESCI approach. Many ethics review boards require that you produce power calculations in order to justify the sample size of your planned study. In our experience, many review boards have not adjusted to the fact that precision for confidence intervals is a better alternative—or, at minimum, an equally acceptable one. In that case, we recommend selecting a value for an alternative hypothesis, specifying the power the study needs, and calculating the appropriate sample size. Then, as a supplement, provide the better information about the required precision of the estimate and the sample size needed to achieve that level of precision. Perhaps the additional information will have some educational value for board members.

WHEN SHOULD YOU USE DISTRIBUTION-FREE, NONPARAMETRIC SIGNIFICANCE TESTS?

The significance tests discussed thus far all require that assumptions be met about how the variables are measured and how the values of those variables are distributed. The same is true of CIs. Variables need to be measured on continuous scales and distributed normally. When these assumptions are not met, the researcher has a range of options among distribution-free alternatives, also called nonparametric statistics.[35] **Distribution-free** means free of assumptions about the shape of the distribution; inferences are correct regardless of the shape of the distribution. Sometimes the normality assumption can be met by transforming your data (see the discussion in Chapter 6), but when the data are categories or ranks, normality is impossible. Normality requires continuous distributions. So if your data are categories or ranks, by definition, they cannot be normally distributed. For example, if your DV is dichotomous and has only two values, such as *yes–no* or *pass–fail*, scores on that variable cannot be normally distributed. The same is true of rank-ordered variables, such as on Likert scales: *How much do you*

[35]This chapter discusses distribution-free significance tests; for distribution-free measures of association, see Chapter 8.

agree with this statement: not at all, a little, somewhat, a great deal, or completely? When you do not know about the distribution of values in a population, it is safer to use methods that do not require that you make assumptions. Distribution-free methods are *robust* to violations of assumptions. So why don't people use them all the time?[36] Because there is a cost—distribution-free methods often have less statistical power (see the previous section).

Because there is at least one distribution-free alternative for most parametric significance tests, the number of options is large. We briefly describe the most common alternative and explain when to use it, and a few others, in Table 7.4. Then one special category of distribution-free statistics is discussed in a separate section: the bootstrap and other resampling methods.

The oldest and most familiar of the distribution-free significance tests is the **chi-squared test**, also called the Pearson chi-squared test[37] or the χ^2 test. It is used when all the variables are categorical. Because the data are categorical, the mean is not meaningful, so the test uses counts or frequencies. For example, the IV might be membership in the control or experimental group; the DV might be the number or percentage of those in each group who passed or failed a test. The data are usually displayed in a **contingency table**—so called because the idea is to see whether the variables in the rows are contingent on, or whether they are independent of, the variables in the columns. You calculate what the values in the table *would have been* if the IV had had no effect (NH) and compare this with what the observed values in fact were. The bigger the difference between the observed and the expected values, the larger your chi-squared value. The calculations to obtain the chi-squared value are simple enough to do by hand. Once you obtain the chi-squared statistic, you convert it (or your software does) into a p-value. Like the F-ratio and the t-statistic, the bigger the chi-squared statistic, the more likely the relation is to be statistically significant (have a small p-value).

Generally, you use distribution-free significance tests when you have no alternative. They are resisted mostly because they have less statistical power than parametric tests (briefly, "power" is the ability of a test to detect an effect; see the earlier discussion). However, there are some circumstances in which you might want to convert your continuous data into categories or ranks and analyze them using a distribution-free statistical test. This is especially the case when continuous data are naturally divided. Say, for example, that the dependent variable was attained education level of adults 40 and older. If the education level was measured in years of education completed, *depending on your research question*, you might want to recode years of education completed into categories such as college graduate (yes or no) or into ranks, such as less than high school, high school graduation, some college, and college graduation. The natural breaks in the system of education, such as graduation, tend to be more important (e.g., for job eligibility) than do differences such as those between 10 and 11 years or 13 and 14 years of schooling.

Entire books are devoted to the subject of distribution-free tests, so if Table 7.4 does not cover your situation, it is important to search in one of these.[38] Table 7.4 lists the

[36]Note that distribution-free statistics do *not* eliminate the assumption of random sampling and/or assignment.

[37]It is also used as a goodness-of-fit test; see Chapter 9.

[38]Corder and Foreman (2009) and Wasserman (2007) are good sources.

TABLE 7.4. Some Common Distribution-Free Null Hypothesis Significance Tests

Test	When to use; what parametric test it replaces
Chi-squared (χ^2) test	When all variables are categorical so that summary statistics are counts or frequencies.
Mann–Whitney–Wilcoxon (MWW); a.k.a. Mann–Whitney *U* test	When you would use independent samples *t*-test.
Wilcoxon signed-rank test	When you would use the *t*-test for dependent samples or repeated measures.
Kruskal–Wallis test	When you would use the independent-samples one-way ANOVA; it extends the MWW to three or more groups.
Friedman test	When you would use a repeated measures ANOVA.

chi-squared test and other distribution-free tests that are equivalents of parametric tests such as the *t*-test and ANOVA.

In conclusion, we point out that all the topics we have discussed thus far in this chapter are methods of traditional or **classical statistical inference.**[39] Although they are still quite dominant, there has been considerable discontent with these NHST methods in recent decades. One way that discontent has been expressed is in the increasingly heeded call for the broader use of CIs and ES measures. But, as we have seen, ESCI and NHST are based on the same paradigm, the same model of probability statistics. Bayesian methods are based on a distinct approach with a distinct philosophical foundation. The bootstrap and other resampling methods are built on a different computational foundation. We cannot examine these two alternatives in great depth. As with all topics in this book, our goal is to provide enough detail about research methods and their potential benefits and drawbacks to help you make good decisions about whether to pursue them further.

WHEN TO USE THE BOOTSTRAP AND OTHER RESAMPLING METHODS

Bootstrap methods are an alternative to classical statistical theory. They get their name from the expression "to lift yourself up by your own bootstraps," which refers to the fairy tale of the boy who pulled up on his own bootstraps so hard that he could fly. Bootstrappers rely on their own sampling resources rather than on the assumptions of classical statistical inference. Bootstrap methods replace the theoretical sampling distributions of classical statistical inference (infinite number of random samples) with empirical sampling distributions drawn by computer from one random sample. Bootstrapping is a nonparametric or distribution-free method because it makes no assumptions about the parameters of the population distribution.

However, bootstrapping does not eliminate the need for randomness. First, the initial sample upon which bootstrapping is built should be a random sample from the

[39]This is also called *frequentist*, especially in contrast with Bayesian and resampling methods; see the next two sections.

population to which the researchers wish to generalize. Second, the subsequent resampling is done with random computer (Monte Carlo) methods. Bootstrapping is conceptually simpler than either classical or Bayesian analysis, but it is very computationally and computer intensive. The basic procedure is as follows:

1. The researcher draws a random sample from a population and computes the statistic of interest, such as a mean or a regression coefficient.
2. Repeated resamples—*of the same size as the original sample (and sampled with replacement)*—are taken from the original sample, and the statistic is computed for each resample. The statistics from these resamples form an empirical sampling distribution, not a theoretical one; this sampling distribution is used to compute inferential statistics, such as *p*-values and confidence intervals.

It is important to stress that the samples are taken with replacement: Each time a case is selected, it is replaced in the pool and thus could be selected again. Without replacement, each resample would simply be the original sample over and over again. Because the samples are done with replacement, they will rarely duplicate the original sample. Indeed, with only 5 cases, there are more than 3,000 distinct resamples possible ($5^5 = 3{,}125$). With a sample of 8, there are more than 16 million. The procedure is easier to understand by looking at an example. Table 7.5 presents a sample of 5 cases. They are scores on a test taken by a large number of students and are randomly resampled 8 times.

The mean of the original sample is 57.2. The means of the resamples range from 36.6 to 69.0 (see Table 7.5). Those resampled means form the sampling distribution for the statistic (see Figure 7.1). The number of cases in the sample in this example and the number of resamples is unrealistically tiny. Usually you would want 30–50 cases in the original sample and to take at least 1,000 resamples. As the speed of computers has increased, the number of resamples one can find in the literature is not infrequently huge; 10,000 or more seems the norm. Despite the small sample and number of resamples in this example, it gives the flavor of the procedure and also illustrates why assuming a normal distribution of the population can be mistaken. The bootstrap sampling distribution in Figure 7.1 is not centered on the mean and is not approximately normal.[40]

Bootstrapping works because, in brief, when the "sample is a good approximation of the population, bootstrapping will provide a good approximation of the sampling distribution."[41] For the sample to have a good probability of being a good approximation of the population, it should be a random sample. Then the resampling from the sample provides an estimate of what the sampling distribution would have been had one resampled from the population. In studies comparing bootstrap sampling distributions to known distributions, bootstrap methods have performed quite well. The empirical sampling distribution derived through bootstrapping is often very different from the sampling distribution that would be assumed in classical statistical inference.

Statistical packages that can perform bootstrapping are now fairly widespread. As is often the case, the freeware package R contains one of the best of these, and, of

[40] Note that the bars in Figure 7.1 are in ascending order of the size of the mean—not in the order in which the samples were taken.

[41] Mooney and Duval (1993, p. 20).

TABLE 7.5. Eight Resamples of an Original Sample of 5

	Original sample	1st resample	2nd resample	3rd resample	4th resample	5th resample	6th resample	7th resample	8th resample
Case	a-69	b-96	a-69	e-43	d-67	b-96	d-67	e-43	a-69
Case	b-96	b-96	a-69	b-96	e-43	e-43	e-43	e-43	e-43
Case	c-11	a-69	e-43	b-96	a-69	b-96	d-67	e-43	d-67
Case	d-67	c-11	d-67	d-67	d-67	a-69	a-69	e-43	e-43
Case	e-43	e-43	b-96	e-43	a-69	c-11	b-96	c-11	d-67
Total	286.0	315.0	344.0	345.0	315.0	315.0	342.0	183.0	289.0
Mean	57.2	63.0	68.8	69.0	63.0	63.0	68.4	36.6	57.8

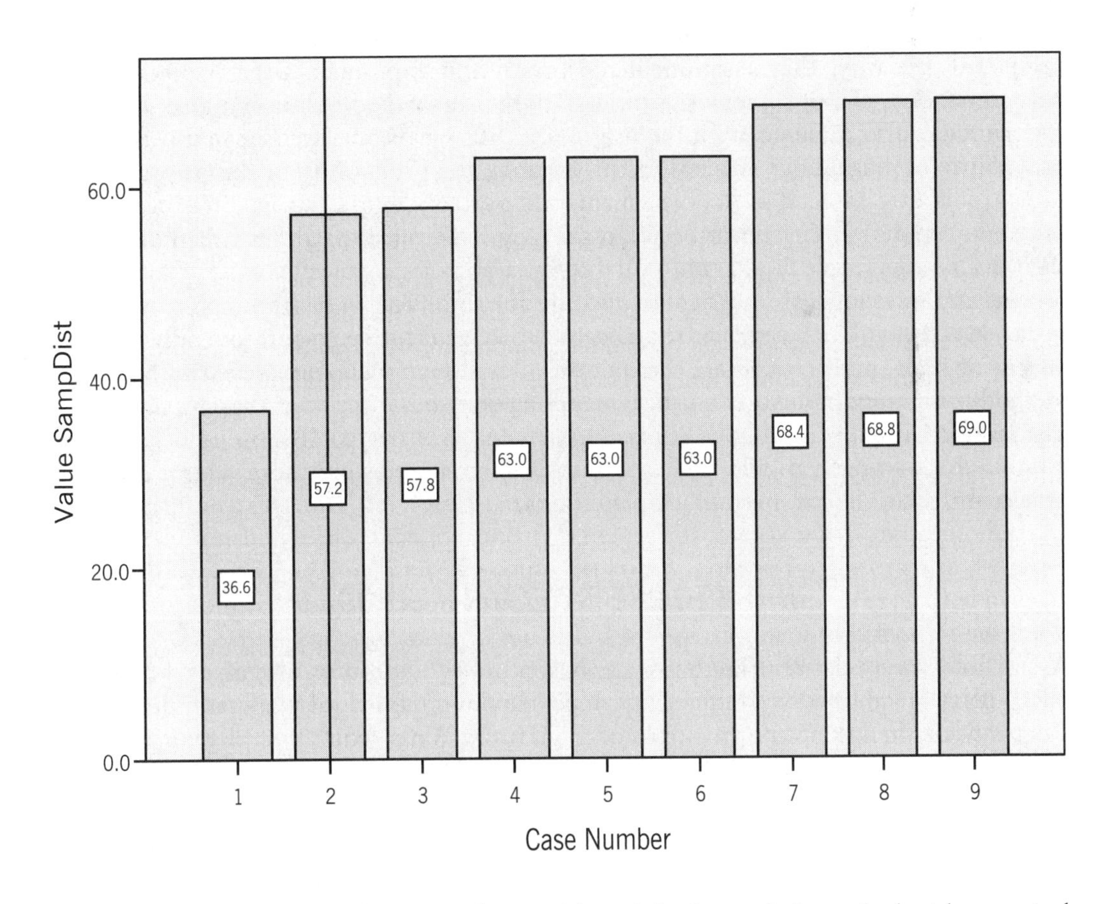

FIGURE 7.1. Bootstrap Sampling Distribution (the original sample is marked with a vertical line).

course, the price is impossible to beat. As with Bayesian statistics, bootstrapping has become generalized; virtually all of statistical inference can be done using resampling methods such as the bootstrap.[42]

Other Resampling Methods

Two resampling methods are less widely used than the bootstrap, and we discuss them only briefly: the *jackknife* and *permutation* methods. In the **jackknife**, samples are taken on subsamples. Each subsample is one case smaller than the original sample; the samples are taken without replacement. Jackknife techniques were a precursor to bootstrap methods; they are simpler to execute and usually give similar results, but they are not often found in the research literature today. As computer power and speed increased, the jackknife was superseded by the bootstrap.

Permutation tests (also known as **exact tests** and rerandomization tests) are resampling techniques to calculate an exact p-value directly—as distinct from using test statistics, such as a t-test or chi-squared test, which yield values that are interpreted to obtain a p-value. For example, in an experiment one could compute the means for the control and experimental groups. These then become the original data to use in the permutation test. Then one would look at *every* possible permutation (or a very large sample) of the ways that assignment to control and experimental groups could have been done. For each of these permutations, the means would be recalculated. Comparing the recalculated means with the original means yields an outcome that is the exact probability of getting the original mean—that is, the probability of the data given the sample.[43] For example, if 14% of the mean and control group samples differ by as much as or more than the difference between the original control and experimental groups, then the p-value would equal .14.

Permutation tests are particularly handy for small samples. Although invented by Fisher in the early 20th century, they became practical for large datasets only with the advent of high-speed computers. Permutation tests have the same appeal as bootstrap methods—they are based on empirical sampling distributions rather than on theoretical assumptions about sampling distributions. Except for very small samples or when the number of cases per variable is small, bootstrap techniques are more widely used and are generally superior to permutation methods.

WHEN TO USE BAYESIAN METHODS

As we have seen, classical methods are based on an understanding of probability as based on long-run relative frequencies, which is why classical methods are often called **frequentist.** Often this is put in terms of a question: What would be the case if an infinite number of random samples had been taken? How probable would the outcome be in the one sample actually taken, using information from the theoretical frequency

[42] Good (2005a) illustrates the generality of resampling methods. Yu (2008) provides a good introductory overview. See Moran (2006a, 2006b) for examples using bootstrapping to study income inequality among nations.

[43] For further details, see Good (2005b).

distribution? Frequentist probability theory is used to close the gap between the actual sample taken and the infinite number of theoretical samples that result in probability distributions.

Methods of Bayesian statistical inference are a radical departure. They are based on a **subjectivist** rather than a frequentist understanding of probability. "Subjectivist" in this context means that a Bayesian researcher begins with a personal assessment of uncertainty called a **prior probability**. This could be, and often is, based on prior evidence, but it is personal (subjective) in that it may vary from one researcher to the next. This prior probability is often described as the opinion of a rational individual given the evidence or as the decision of a rational person expressed as a probability or probability distribution. This is sometimes thought of as a bet: The prior probability is what a rational person would be willing to bet his or her own money on.

Bayesian methods *formally* combine this prior probability with data obtained from research—often called the **likelihood**—to reach a revised assessment of uncertainty called the **posterior probability**. The key difference between Bayesian and classical analyses is the formal (in the formula) use of prior information. Without priors there can be no Bayesian analysis. Researchers combine what they know before the study with what they have learned in the study to come to a revised conclusion. Of course, most researchers do this, for example, by considering their results in the context of their literature review. What is distinct about Bayesian methods is that, using Bayes's theorem, it is done formally.[44]

Although Bayes's theorem dates from the 1760s, it was not often used as a foundation for statistics until the 20th century. One of the first modern applications of Bayesian methods to a real problem with a substantial body of data occurred two centuries after Bayes's theorem was published. This was Mosteller and Wallace's book[45] examining the authorship of the *Federalist Papers*. Bayesian methods gained in stature in the research community by the 1990s, particularly as specialized computer software became available for handling some of the intricate problems of its application to multivariate research.[46] Since the 1990s Bayesian methods have evolved into an approach to the whole of statistics and are no longer confined, as they tended to be before the 1990s, to alternative ways of computing confidence intervals.[47] Statistics teaching, especially in applied fields, has had trouble keeping up with these developments in Bayesian methods, to the point that this is recognized as something of a crisis in the training of researchers in the social sciences. As one faculty member put it, "our PhD students can't even read their own literature."[48]

Bayes's theorem (or rule) is a formula that combines prior degree of belief, expressed numerically, with evidence from new data collected for a study. Thus prior

[44]Modern Bayesian methods are very mathematically challenging, but a kind of practical Bayesian analysis is possible; see Silver (2012) for some straightforward examples.

[45]Mosteller and Wallace (1964/2007).

[46]The two best-known programs are both freeware: *winBUGS* is available at *www.mrc-bsu.cam.ac.uk/bugs*; bayesm is part of the R package and is available at *www.r-project.org*.

[47]For an informative and thoroughly nontechnical history of Bayesian statistics and its surprisingly important role in several fields, see McGrayne (2011).

[48]The quotation is from a special section of *The American Statistician* (2008, Vol. 62, pp. 189–205) "Teaching Bayes to Nonstatistics Graduate Students" (Westfall, 2008).

information—information external to the data collected—is rationally incorporated into the statistical analysis. The prior belief is then updated using the theorem to unite it with the data collected in order to compute the posterior probability. The posterior probability replaces the traditional *p*-value. The correctness of the theorem has never been in doubt, but its appropriate application has been hotly disputed. The posterior probability is computed after the data are known. The prior probability is stated prior to the time that the data are collected and known, and that is the source of some critical reaction against Bayesian approaches.

What can be the value of subjective prior information, stated before data are available? The first clarification is that the priors are often based on expert opinion or on previous research; in the latter case the method is referred to as **empirical Bayes**. The general idea of empirical Bayes approaches is to base the prior probability as much as possible on data and as little as possible on subjective opinion.[49] In a series of studies, posteriors from the first study can be used as priors in the second, and so on. Both Bayesian approaches, standard and empirical, provide the researcher with formal ways of incorporating prior judgment or information into the process of making statistical inferences. In so doing, the inferences are improved in several respects, chief of which is more precise estimates, such as narrower confidence intervals (sometimes called **credible intervals and regions** in Bayesian work).

The key point is that because it is rare, except in the most radically exploratory studies, not to have some prior information on which to base a judgment or to narrow down the possibilities, the Bayesian advantage of being able to incorporate this prior knowledge into the calculations is a formidable one. That advantage can be especially apparent when the researchers are subject-matter specialists who are usually able to use prior knowledge to omit from consideration absurdly improbable priors.

There are four main advantages of Bayesian methods that could lead researchers to consider using them.

1. The use of priors can lead to estimates that are more precise—the better and more informative the priors, the more precise.

2. The use of priors makes the researchers' assumptions more explicit; prior distributions "bring the subjective aspects of the analysis out in the open for everyone to see."[50] And, as Bayesians are wont to point out, all research contains such subjective elements, such as assumptions about population distributions. In Bayesian work researchers must make explicit assumptions; Bayesian analysis cannot be done otherwise. Such explicitness is always to be preferred.[51]

3. The interpretation of statistical inferences using Bayesian methods is more straightforward, as is the language that can be used to express them. Because NH testing is not used, the double and triple negatives of classical statistical inference—"no, we did not fail to confirm the null of no difference"—are eliminated. As for CIs, it is legitimate to say of a Bayesian CI, for example, that "we are 95% confident that the graduation rate in the population is between 62 and 78%." Statisticians often contend

[49]Efron (1986) referred to this as "trying not to put more information than necessary into the prior."

[50]Iversen (1984, p. 67).

[51]Gill (2008).

that this is *not* the correct way of expressing a CI in classical statistical inference. There the correct locution is: "Were we to have taken an infinite number of random samples of graduation rates from this population, 95% of the means of those samples would have fallen in the range from 62 to 78%." The difference is not only a matter of stylistic preference, though it is that, too. Rather, it expresses a fundamental difference in the kind of inferences and interpretations it is appropriate to make.

4. Because Bayesian methods are not tied to the assumptions of classical theory, they can be applied to problems with nonrandom samples and with samples that would be too small for classical inference.[52]

Rapid developments in Bayesian methods mean that they are not now, as they once tended to be, merely a potentially better way of computing CIs. Rather, the Bayesian approach has become a complete statistical system. The scope and nature of Bayesian analyses have changed dramatically in recent decades. One barrier to their wider adoption was that some of the calculation problems associated with doing the analyses were intractable. These problems have been circumvented by the use of methods of computer simulation. Textbooks presenting the Bayesian approach to the whole of quantitative analysis are becoming more widely available.[53] Some researchers predict the triumph of Bayesian methods; others see the inevitable increase in the use of Bayesian methods and some sort of reconciliation of the competing mathematical foundations (classical frequentist and Bayesian) of statistical inference.[54]

We think that in applied work, a large increase in the use of Bayesian methods and/or a merger with traditional or classical methods will be slow to arrive, for two reasons. First, traditional methods have staying power simply because they are traditional. Consider how slow researchers have been to adopt the ESCI approach, and it is just a wrinkle on the familiar traditional classical, frequentist approach. Second, the old routines are comparatively easy to apply and interpret, but Bayesian methods are more difficult. There really are no elementary Bayesian textbooks, in part because Bayesian methods are more mathematically advanced. Despite the fact that it is easier to put Bayesian inferential conclusions into ordinary language, arriving at those conclusions is mathematically more challenging. Even though software is now freely available and many of the more intricate problems of applying Bayesian methods have been solved through the application of MCMC (Markov chain Monte Carlo) methods of simulation, doing Bayesian analysis is still no simple matter for an ordinary researcher who is not well versed in mathematical statistics.

A Note on MCMC Methods

The computer simulations behind **Monte Carlo methods** (named after random chance in gambling) are increasingly important not only in Bayesian analysis but also in bootstrapping and imputation methods for missing data (see the discussion later in this chapter).

[52]Buckley (2004) provides a persuasive example of how Bayesian inference can be used on small samples with qualitative data.

[53]Gelman, Carlin, Stern, and Rubin (2003) is one of the most widely used of these; another is Rossi, Allenby, and McCulloch (2005). Perhaps the most comprehensive is Gill (2008).

[54]Berger (2000).

The basic idea is wonderfully simple; it arose from the thinking of a mathematician who played solitaire while convalescing from an illness in the 1940s. He wondered what the probability of winning a game was. Because there are billions of possible hands, he found it impossible to answer the question with mathematical analysis.[55] But it was possible to get a good approximation of an answer statistically by simply playing solitaire many times and observing the number of wins. The next step was to realize that you didn't have to play thousands of games; you could program a computer to do it. Thus was MCMC born, and it revolutionized data analysis in many fields.

WHICH APPROACH TO STATISTICAL INFERENCE SHOULD YOU TAKE?

All four methods of statistical inference—classical (NHST and ESCI), Bayesian, and resampling—build mostly on data from one sample. They differ in terms of what they do with it. Classical statistical inference interprets the sample using frequentist probability theory; if the sample is random, this is a persuasive approach. Bootstrapping uses resampling methods on one sample to compute a sampling distribution that is independent of assumptions about the population parameter. Bayesian methods formally combine prior information (probability) with new data from a sample to compute a posterior probability. All four allow one to compute p-values and confidence intervals (or equivalents). But the interpretations of these differ.

Deciding whether something is worth it is ultimately subjective. The basics of the four methods have been reviewed, and some advantages of each are outlined in the Summary Table for this chapter (see the first section of the table). One piece of advice is that, if you are at a relatively early stage of a career in which you think you will be conducting quite a bit of quantitative research, it would be almost irresponsible to ignore Bayes and the bootstrap. On the other hand, if you are toward the end of a career, we might advise consulting with a specialist on those occasions when you thought one or another of these alternative approaches could be valuable. For many research problems, it seems too limiting to use the classical methods without also considering these alternative universes of analysis. We would not advise abandoning classical statistical inference or the *langue du pays* in which it is expressed, but we do suggest supplementing it with the Bayes and bootstrap methods and, when appropriate, reporting the results of all four methods.

Even after reviewing the advantages and disadvantages of the four approaches, deciding which inference method to use is no simple matter, unless one simply follows tradition. Both classical and Bayesian methods build upon assumptions: Classical methods are based on assumptions about the normality of the distribution of the statistic in the sample; Bayesian methods are built on assumptions about prior distributions. Bootstrapping tries to minimize all such assumptions. Bootstrapping is more work than using traditional statistical inference. So, if you have a random sample which comes from a population that is known to be randomly distributed or that can reasonably be assumed to have come from such a population, classical statistical inference may be a better option. If you do not know or are unwilling to make an assumption about the population distribution of a statistic, resampling is a better way to go. Some researchers

[55] See Ulam (1991).

have combined bootstrapping with Bayesian and classical statistical inference. Such combined approaches have considerable promise.

Choice of inference method is not merely a matter of personal preference or taste, although it is *subjective*, which means in this context that different people can and do reasonably disagree. We have repeatedly argued that it is very ill advised to use classical methods of inference when it is unreasonable to assume normal distributions and when random samples or random assignment have not been used. Bootstrapping is *fundamentally* sounder for many research projects in which the researcher has no indication that the population distribution is approximately normal. And in head-to-head comparisons, Bayesian methods have sometimes been shown to be quite simply better than traditional inferential methods. The most famous example was in the field of data imputation, which involves using methods of inference for "filling in missing data with educated guesses to produce a complete data set."[56] Imputation is necessary because missing data can cripple multivariate analysis (see the next section). The head-to-head comparison was in the form of a friendly contest between Bayesians versus non-Bayesians imputing missing data in a national health survey. At the annual meeting of the American Statistical Association in 1993, the Bayesians were declared the winners.

The premise of this book is that a reasonable researcher will not avoid choices among research methods or act as though there are no choices and simply follow familiar routines. Custom and tradition are important aspects of social life. They should hold less sway in research than in day-to-day living.

THE "SILENT KILLER" OF VALID INFERENCES: MISSING DATA

Missing data are a problem relevant at every stage of a research project—from design, sampling, and ethics through coding/measurement, analysis, and interpretation. Missing data problems are equally serious regardless of your analytical model: classical, resampling, or Bayesian. It is a rare research study (we've never seen one) that avoids missing data problems altogether. And it is hardly a problem confined to numerical data. Audio recordings of interviews have inaudible sections, texts contain illegible passages, clients stop attending counseling sessions, or participant observers are distracted and miss a key event. These and other sources of gaps in the data are discussed in the appropriate chapters. In this chapter on statistical inference, the focus is on missing numerical data, particularly as they raise problems for making statistical inferences. When do you use which techniques to make a dataset more usable so as to improve your inferences from that dataset to a population? Or if you are studying a population rather than a sample, which techniques better enable you to describe that population?

There are many techniques from which to choose. Unfortunately for the researcher wanting to make a good and timely decision, the majority of options, including the typical default methods in most software packages, are not very good—or worse. This makes the decision about which techniques to use a fairly straightforward one, because you can quickly eliminate most of the options. The price you pay for this easy decision is that the effective techniques are a lot more complicated than the poor ones, which

[56]Krenzke and Judkins (2008) describe the differences between Bayesian and non-Bayesian approaches and are very interesting on the whole subject of imputation.

are often models of simplicity. There is an unusually high degree of consensus about the appropriate techniques to use.[57] But it is also important to review and briefly explain the shortcomings of the less effective techniques because these are so widely used. There is a tendency to assume that the ineffective techniques must be OK because they are very popular and examples of their use can be found in respectable journals in many fields. Researchers can hardly be blamed for following practices that grace the pages of journals in which they aspire to publish, but in this case, at least, that is not a reliable standard to use.

How big a substantive problem is missing data? Why do they matter? How much can they influence a conclusion? Probably more than most researchers assume. Most statistical analysis techniques *assume* complete datasets. Using the techniques with incomplete data runs the risk of serious misinterpretation. By reducing sample size, missing data reduce statistical power and precision, they increase the p-values associated with a statistic, and they widen CIs and MOEs. Finally, except in those rare cases in which the data are missing at random, they introduce bias.

As an exercise in one of our (W.P.V.'s) classes we deleted, *at random*, 12 values out of a total of 200 (or 6%) from a small dataset. The idea behind the exercise was to demonstrate to the class that when data are missing at random, it does not introduce bias. The results were not reassuring for anyone who wants to breeze over missing data problems. Although the univariate statistics for the variables in the dataset were largely unchanged by randomly deleting 6% of the cases, the ultimate multivariate conclusion of the study changed dramatically—from a substantively large and statistically significant outcome to a trivially small and statistically insignificant one.[58]

How could this happen? The percentage of missing data was small, much smaller than in most real studies, and the data were missing *completely* at random, but the conclusion was radically altered. The problem occurred for three reasons. First, anything can happen at random; although it is not *likely* that data missing at random will substantially influence outcomes, it is *possible*. Second, the sample was small (50 cases and 4 variables), too small for the method of analysis, multiple regression, in which small samples can lead to unstable estimates. Third, the method used to handle the missing data was *listwise deletion*. This is almost certainly the most common method,[59] and computers do it by default. But listwise deletion is one of the least satisfactory methods and will often produce a disaster. Perhaps the most important lesson from this example is that missing data add a booby trap to your study. You might try to avoid the trap, but it is hard to know whether you have succeeded. Researchers using samples with real missing data—rather than simulations in which the missing data are known—*do not know* how much of a difference has been made by the missing data. In short, missing data are a study limitation, they should induce researchers to be cautious about what

[57]For good general reviews see Cole (2008), McKnight, McKnight, Sidani, and Figueredo (2007), and Newman (2009). A more detailed and technical overview is Allison (2002). The ultimate source for advanced techniques is the second edition of Little and Rubin (2002).

[58]See Vogt (2007, pp. 175–179) for details.

[59]In one study of articles in major political science journals, over 90% used listwise deletion (King, Honaker, Joseph, & Scheve, 2001). Perhaps practices have changed in the 21st century, but we still encounter too many articles, especially in second-tier journals, using discredited methods.

they conclude, and they require remedial action. The two broad classes of remedy are (1) **deleting** cases or cells with missing data or (2) **imputing** values for the missing data.

Deletion Methods

Listwise deletion is the most common and usually one of the worst solutions to a missing data problem. In this procedure, any case with any missing data is deleted from the dataset. Because all data for the case are eliminated, the method is also called **casewise deletion,** or sometimes "the complete case method." All experts agree that this is hardly ever a good procedure. Many nonexperts do not know this, and they tend to cite one another, so listwise deletion remains shockingly widespread. There is also a tendency to assume that, because listwise deletion is the default setting in several popular statistical packages, it cannot be all that bad. The reason that listwise deletion is usually a poor choice is that it dumps the maximum amount of data. In a big dataset with many variables, it is not uncommon to discard more than half the cases, because it is a rare case that is not missing data on at least one variable. Decimating your sample is the quickest way to reduce statistical power and precision.

A sometimes preferable alternative to listwise deletion is **pairwise deletion** (a.k.a. the "available case method"). This method removes a case from the calculation of a correlation or other bivariate statistic when one of its values is missing. The rest of the case's data are not eliminated from the dataset. Rather, the case is set aside when the correlation with missing data is calculated, but the rest of the data remain available for computing other statistics. Thus more data are retained for analysis than with listwise deletion. Although that seems like a good idea, there is a big problem with this approach: When you use it, the number of relevant cases per variable is then no longer constant; this means that you cannot use procedures based on correlation (or covariance) matrices, such as factor analysis or structural equation modeling. Also, when studying several variables using pairwise deletion, your correlations could be based on different groups of cases. If the correlation between variables *A* and *B* is different from that between variables *G* and *H*, the reason could be that they are based on different cases. In short, although it could be possible to imagine exceptions, and although using pairwise and listwise deletion might not always be harmful, using either is most often bad practice.[60] In short, *the most common practices are bad practices.*

Imputation Methods

In ordinary English, *imputation* means attributing responsibility or blame. In statistics it means using existing data to calculate likely values for missing data. With imputation methods, cells in a grid containing data are used to estimate missing cell values. The chief advantage of the imputation methods is that *no data are discarded.* All the data are used. This means that all imputation methods, even the less effective ones, tend to be preferable to deletion methods. There are numerous imputation methods and statistical packages available for implementing them. Usually the data that are estimated pertain to the independent and control variables, not to the dependent or outcome variables.

[60] See Cole (2008), McKnight et al. (2007), and Newman (2009).

The oldest, simplest, and best-known of the imputation methods is the worst. It is called **mean substitution** or **mean imputation**. The researcher replaces all the missing values for a variable with the mean of that variable. The mean is a reasonable estimate if the values are missing randomly, but this is not likely to be the case very often. For example, if the data are missing because several respondents skipped a sensitive survey question, then those who skipped the question are not likely to be a random sample of all respondents. And even if skippers were a representative sample of all respondents, substituting the mean for missing values reduces a variable's variance. Variance is a measure of difference from the mean, so if, for example, 30 values for a variable were missing, substituting 30 means would reduce the variance. The goal of most research is to explain the variance in one variable by the variance in another. Reducing variance reduces the ability to explain the relations among variables.

Numerous imputation methods exist. But like mean substitution (and like deletion methods), they are mostly antiquated and ineffective. It is typical to review them to explain why they are out of date and weak alternatives. Also, it is helpful to remind researchers when *not* to use what, especially when inadequate procedures are remarkably widespread. That said, it will be more useful for most readers to move to modern and effective methods of addressing missing data. These methods date from the 1980s and have been under development since that time. They have also been underused since that time. Four key works transformed the way researchers address missing data problems; they were all published in 1987.[61]

There is little doubt that one of the imputation methods, **multiple imputation** (MI), is the current standard of best practice according to most statisticians. Another method, nearly as widely advocated by experts as MI, is a **maximum likelihood** (ML) approach; it is closely tied to structural equation modeling (SEM) methods and software, such as AMOS or M-plus. Although it can be important to review some of the other extant imputation methods[62] to illustrate the superiority of MI and ML approaches, it is more useful in a brief overview such as this one to address which of these two to use in what circumstances. There is some disagreement among experts about which is better for what, but no disagreement among experts that together MI and ML offer a suite of methods that render the traditional methods *thoroughly* obsolete.[63]

Both approaches employ the same terms to describe the character of the missing data. The different ways data can be missing determine the applicability of MI and ML to problems of missing data. It is useful for us to briefly clarify the slightly quirky language used to describe types of missing data because that terminology is in all but universal use. The types are defined by the *mechanisms* by which the missing data were produced. There are three key terms. The first two are perfectly clear.

First, data may be **missing completely at random** (MCAR). Such missing data pose the fewest problems for the analyst because, by definition, MCAR data will add no *systematic* bias. Data are not often MCAR, and it is not easy to know when they are, although Little has devised a test of "MCARness."[64] If data are MCAR, then the only

---

[61]The MI works are Little and Rubin (1987) and Rubin (1987). The ML works are Allison (1987) and Muthén, Kaplan, and Hollis (1987).

[62]McKnight et al. (2007) provide a very thorough and accessible review.

[63]The best one-volume overview of MI and ML approaches to missing data is Enders (2010).

[64]Little (1988).

disadvantage of using listwise deletion is reduction of statistical power. This is no small disadvantage, especially when the number of cases deleted from the list is greater than some low threshold—5% is one common rule of thumb, but many say even 5% is too large.

Conversely, data may be **missing not at random** (MNAR). As the name implies, the data are missing in a way that systematically biases the results of the analyst using it. Statistical adjustments are impossible if the data are fully MNAR (also called *nonignorable*). Randomization techniques cannot be used to impute missing data when they are MNAR. MNAR data are surely more common than MCAR data, although there is no definitive test. MNAR data will fail Little's MCAR test, but so will data in the third and most important category.

It is for the third category of mechanisms of missing data that the solutions provided by ML and MI methods are most effective. We would call this mechanism missing ***partly*** at random, but it is referred to in the literature on the subject simply as **missing at random** (MAR). The confusion arises because "missing at random" sounds to many readers (including several of our annoyed students) as if it ought to mean the same thing as MCAR. The term used to describe it may not be ideal, but the concept is crucial, particularly to distinguish it from the other patterns of missing data. Briefly, if the data are missing *not* at random (MNAR), there is not much the analyst can do. If the data are missing *completely* at random (MCAR), there may be little the analyst needs to do.

When the data are missing (partly) at random, or MAR, the following kind of situation pertains. Say you are conducting a survey and you notice that female respondents more often skip a question than do male respondents. This is a response pattern that is clearly not random, but it can qualify as "missing [partly] at random" (MAR) if, within each category, male and female, the data are missing at random. Men differ systematically from the women in their missing data, but the men's missing data differ from one another only randomly. And the women's missing data differ from one another randomly. More generally, when data are MAR, the probability of a case's missing data on a particular variable is not related to the case's score on that variable—after controlling for the other variables in the dataset. In brief, when data are MAR, other variables can be used to estimate the missing values.

In practice, what many analysts do is first apply Little's MCAR test. If the data fail that test, which is quite common, the analyst assumes (hopes) that the data are MAR (not MNAR) and therefore that they are susceptible to missing data techniques. The big question then becomes which of the two dominant families of techniques to use—ML or MI? The two methods have grown up together and will often produce similar results. Our impression is that most applied researchers choose according to the software with which they are most familiar. ML is easily applied using one of several SEM packages, such as AMOS or LISREL or M plus. A widely used MI program can be found in S-Plus. Software features change rapidly, so there is little point in providing numerous details that may be out of date by the time this volume is printed.[65] Suffice it to say that if you

[65] Many readers will probably start with one of the freeware programs in the R package: NORM assumes multivariate normality in the population data. MICE (multiple imputation with chained equations) is better when you cannot safely assume a normal distribution in the underlying population; it is also available in STATA. There are others, but NORM and MICE are two of the best known, along with AMELIA, discussed shortly.

want to improve your dataset and the parameter estimates you make with it by using ML or MI, software for doing so is pretty readily available.

It is important to understand the features of these two approaches to know what each offers and the advantages and disadvantages of each. Both techniques are iterative and highly computer intensive. The goal for both MI and ML techniques is *not* to recreate an approximation of the original sample dataset with no missing data. Rather, the goal is to use the dataset to estimate population parameters.

ML, unlike MI, was not originally developed to handle missing data problems. Rather, it is a more general set of statistical procedures used extensively, for example, in SEM. The general idea is to use an iterative procedure to discover the *unobserved* population parameters most likely true of the population given the *observed* sample statistics. ML estimation "systematically searches over the different possible population values, finally selecting parameter estimates that are most likely (have the 'maximum likelihood') to be true given the sample observations."[66] When the program arrives at a point at which further iterations do not significantly improve the estimates, then the procedure is said to have **converged** on a single solution.

Briefly, MI uses computer randomization techniques (MCMC) to impute several datasets, usually 5–10, not just one. This is the first step. Then each dataset is analyzed and parametric statistics are computed. Then the multiple parametric estimates (such as regression coefficients and their associated standard errors) are combined by taking their means to make a final estimate. MI is not one technique, but a family of related techniques from which the researcher must choose. And the researcher must also choose the variables to be used to impute the missing values.

It seems to us that MI is generally preferable. It handles small sample sizes and large numbers of variables better than ML. MI also has fewer problems than ML with larger proportions of missing data (up to one-third or more). And MI requires fewer distributional assumptions. Although no writers on the subject dismiss ML as inadequate or inappropriate, it has few advantages (except perhaps a certain ease of use) that compensate for being less adept than MI in dealing with smaller samples, larger numbers of variables, and greater proportions of missing data. Whichever of the two methods you choose, it is important to choose. That is perhaps the most important conclusion of this section. Choose your method. Do not rely on the software default choice in commercial statistical packages; it is not likely to be a good one. Unfortunately, the choice is complicated by the fact that the programs for implementing MI have not been easy for nonexperts to use, and they can be slow. This partly explains the continued popularity of the execrable listwise deletion.

Although we avoid making software recommendations because of the speed with which they become obsolete, once in a while an exception to the rule may be in order.[67] One set of data imputation procedures in one particular program is considerably more user-friendly than others. It is called AMELIA (named after Amelia Earhart) and is based on bootstrapping techniques. Available as freeware since the late 1990s, it is both faster and easier to use than the most common MI and ML alternatives.[68] In 2008 it

---

[66]Eliason (1993, p. v).

[67]See Horton and Kleinman (2007) for a review of missing data software.

[68]Honaker, Joseph, King, Scheve, and Singh (1999).

became accessible as a package in R. It is the easiest to learn and use of the acceptable procedures.

Finally, what do you do once you've chosen a missing data technique and applied it? What outcomes do you report? It can be a good practice to first briefly report your analysis of the original dataset (with the missing data) and then report the full results after having used the data imputation. Following the *principle of inclusion*, some recommend systematically discussing any differences between the two—both the substantive differences, such as effect sizes, odds ratios, or regression coefficients, and inferential differences, such as *p*-values, standard errors, or CIs.[69] Others think it is sufficient, and this is the more common practice, to describe the missing data that have been imputed. For example, explain how many cases had missing data imputed (and for how many variables) and whether the cases with missing data significantly differed on any key variables from those that did not have missing data.

It is also important to explain to the reader how data came to be missing in your study. Missing data can be caused by a poor design but reduced by a good one. Variations in sampling methods, such as how often respondents accidentally or intentionally skip a survey question, can influence the amount of missing data.[70] Ethical concerns can lead to not collecting certain data or not collecting them in the detail researchers might otherwise prefer. Some measurement techniques can reduce or increase the likelihood of data problems, whereas other approaches to measurement, such as dividing continuous variables into categorical ones, lose information by intentionally discarding data.

CONCLUSION

Methodological choice is the theme of this book. That theme is particularly salient when the topic is statistical inference. Choices are legion, and disputes between schools of thought can be intense. We have tried to provide food for thought on questions that seem as yet unresolved. When we believe that there are clear advantages of one approach over another—such as ESCI over NHST or imputation over deletion methods for missing data—we have said so forcefully. But no belief about appropriate methodological choices is completely beyond dispute. Our recommendations are reviewed in several tables and lists throughout the chapter, and again in the Chapter 7 Summary Table. As always, these are meant to be guides to—not substitutes for—further thought.

Appendix 7.1. Examples of Output of Significance Tests

For readers who like to see examples of what the output of significance tests look like—to look under the hood, as it were—we give the following examples of tests discussed in the chapter. They were calculated using SPSS version 20.

Table 7A.1 gives the number of cases (20) and the correlation between two variables, called variables 1 and 2. (See the data in the tables in Chapter 6.) The correlation is $r = .511$. The exact

[69]See King et al. (2001) for examples.

[70]See "Missing Answers to Your Survey Questions," which can be found on Vogt's blog: *http://vogtsresearchmethods.blogspot.com/.*

TABLE 7A.1. Correlation

	N	Correlation	Sig.
Pair 1 Variable 1 and Variable 2	20	.511	.021

p-value (labeled "sig." in the table) is $p = .021$. This figure was arrived at with a one-sample *t*-test of the null hypothesis that the correlation in the population was $r = 0$.

Table 7A.2 reports three *one-sample t-tests of means*. The NH in each case is that the mean in the population = 0. The two-tailed significance tests all give a *p*-value of .000. As discussed in the text, this does not mean that there is no probability, only that the software stopped calculating it after three decimal places. The 95% confidence intervals give the plausible range of values for the population means. For example, the population estimate for Variable 1 is 7.60, with a likely range of from 6.74 to 8.46.

Table 7A.3 compares the difference in the means between variables 1 and 2 and tests the mean difference with a *paired-samples t-test*, which is appropriate if, for example, variables 1 and 2 were pre- and posttests. Plausible values for the mean difference in the population from which these 20 cases were drawn range from .467 to 2.133. The exact *p*-value is .004. In case you are interested, the *t*-statistic is calculated by dividing the mean by the standard error of the mean: $1.30 \div .398 = 3.266$.

Table 7A.4 is the *t*-test for the mean differences between *two independent groups*, different academic majors; these groups are the first 10 cases (1–10) and the second 10 cases (11–20). These two groups are compared on two dependent variables: 1 and 2. The difference between the two groups on variable 1 is –.600; for variable 2 it is +.800. Not surprisingly, these small differences in these two small groups of 10 each are not statistically significant; the *p*-values are .482 and .320, respectively—much larger than the conventional cutoff of $p < .05$.

To see the relation between the CI and the *p*-value, note that when the 95% CIs contain the value of the NH, this means that the *p*-value for the difference is less than .05. In this case, the NH = 0, and the CI contains 0. For example, the lower and upper bounds of –2.358 and +1.158 include 0. (Think of the temperature on a thermometer on a cold day rising from 2 below 0, passing through 0, to reach a high of 1 degree above 0.)[71]

TABLE 7A.2. One-Sample *t*-Tests; Null Hypothesis, mean = 0

	Test Value = 0					
					95% confidence interval of the difference	
	t	*df*	Sig. (2-tailed)	Mean difference	Lower	Upper
Variable 1	18.404	19	.000	7.600	6.74	8.46
Variable 2	16.098	19	.000	6.300	5.48	7.12
Pooled	19.879	19	.000	13.900	12.44	15.36

[71] Full SPSS output for this table is not included here in order to concentrate on some central points; see the discussion of equality of variances in Chapter 6.

TABLE 7A.3. Paired Samples Test

	Paired differences					t	df	Sig. (2-tailed)
				95% confidence interval of the difference				
	Mean	Std. deviation	Std. error mean	Lower	Upper			
Pair Vars 1 and 2	1.30	1.78	.398	.467	2.133	3.266	19	.004

TABLE 7A.4. *t*-Tests for Mean Differences of Independent Groups on Two Variables

	t-Test for Equality of Means						
						95% confidence interval of the difference	
	t	df	Sig. (2-tailed)	Mean difference	Std. error difference	Lower	Upper
Variable 1	–.717	18	.482	–.600	.837	–2.358	1.158
Variable 2	1.023	18	.320	.800	.782	–.842	2.442

Table 7A.5 uses ANOVA to compare the same groups (majors) as did Table 7A.4. This illustrates that, although the calculations are quite different, p-values are identical—.482 and .320—when the t-test and ANOVA can be used on the same problem.

ANOVA is also used in Table 7A.6 on a different dataset. It is used to compare the scores of six classes of students, each taught by a different professor, on a common final exam. The NHST question addressed in Table 7A.6 is: Were there statistically significant differences among the professors' students? The "Sig." column gives the p-value of .000, which should be converted to $p < .001$. So there is a significant p-value; there is some kind of significant difference or differences among the professors, but the basic ANOVA output does not specify what it is.

To see which among the comparisons is statistically significant, you need to examine the table of **multiple comparisons**, Table 7A.7. This lists all possible comparisons among all pairs of the six professors, gives the mean difference between each pair, the p-value of that mean

TABLE 7A.5. ANOVA for Difference between Independent Groups

		Sum of squares	df	Mean square	F	Sig.
Variable 1	Between groups	1.800	1	1.800	.514	.482
	Within groups	63.000	18	3.500		
	Total	64.800	19			
Variable 2	Between groups	3.200	1	3.200	1.047	.320
	Within groups	55.000	18	3.056		
	Total	58.200	19			

TABLE 7A.6. ANOVA of Students' Final Exam Scores, Six Professors

	Sum of squares	*df*	Mean square	*F*	Sig.
Between groups	27971.146	5	5594.229	17.054	.000
Within groups	144004.756	439	328.029		
Total	171975.902	444			

difference, and the 95% confidence interval for that difference. For example, on the top line, we see that Professor 1's students scored 12.6085 points higher than Professor 2's students; the *p*-value of that difference is given as .000; and the 95% CI for that difference ranges from 7.432 to 17.786. On the next line we see that Professor 1's students scored 2.5894 points lower than Professor 3's. That difference is not statistically significant at the .05 level, because there is no asterisk and because the confidence interval includes 0 as it ranges between –8.466 and +3.287.

There is inevitably a lot of repetition in multiple comparison tables, but it is needed to examine differences between all pairs. For example, going down four lines, we can compare the student scores of Professor 2 and Professor 1. Of course, all the numbers are the same—12.6085 and so on—as when comparing Professor 1 with Professor 2. But there is a change in the signs of some: The mean difference and the CIs become negative, because Professor 2's students scored lower than Professor 1's.

Finally, to get a good overall picture of the differences when making multiple comparisons, it is often very helpful to examine them graphically. One way of doing this is provided in Figure 7A.1. In that figure, the CIs around the mean are given for the six professors. A striking

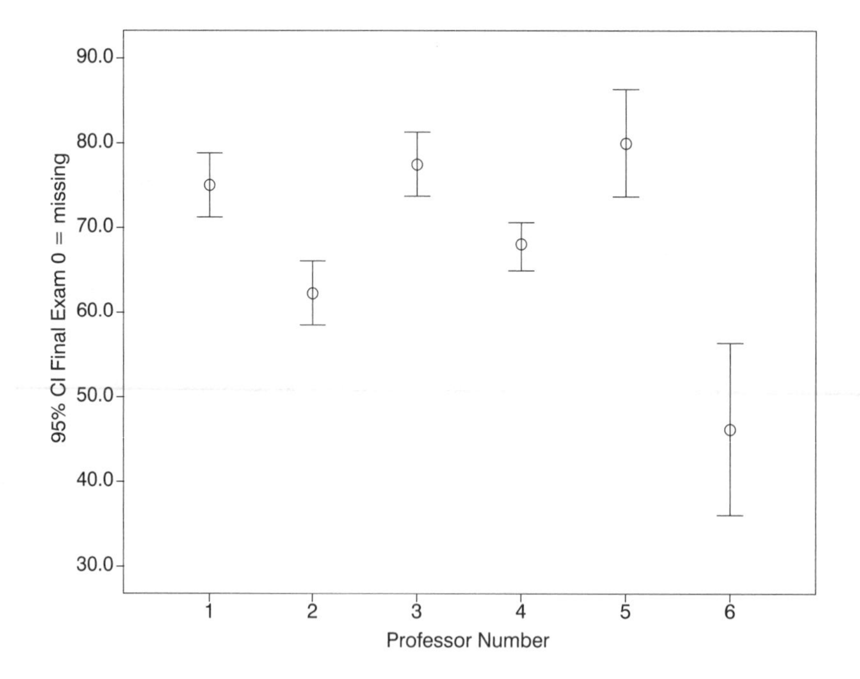

FIGURE 7A.1. Ninety-five percent confidence intervals on the student exam scores of six professors.

TABLE 7A.7. Multiple-Comparisons (LSD) Dependent Variable: Final Exam Scores

(I) Professor number	(J) Professor number	Mean difference (I–J)	Std. error	Sig. *p*-val.	95% confidence interval	
					Lower bound	Upper bound
1	2	12.6085*	2.6341	.000	7.432	17.786
	3	–2.5894	2.9899	.387	–8.466	3.287
	4	7.0206*	2.4619	.005	2.182	11.859
	5	–5.1693	4.6945	.271	–14.396	4.057
	6	28.5572*	4.0535	.000	20.591	36.524
2	1	–12.6085*	2.6341	.000	–17.786	–7.432
	3	–15.1979*	2.8722	.000	–20.843	–9.553
	4	–5.5879*	2.3175	.016	–10.143	–1.033
	5	–17.7778*	4.6204	.000	–26.859	–8.697
	6	15.9487*	3.9674	.000	8.151	23.746
3	1	2.5894	2.9899	.387	–3.287	8.466
	2	15.1979*	2.8722	.000	9.553	20.843
	4	9.6100*	2.7152	.000	4.274	14.946
	5	–2.5799	4.8321	.594	–12.077	6.917
	6	31.1466*	4.2121	.000	22.868	39.425
4	1	–7.0206*	2.4619	.005	–11.859	–2.182
	2	5.5879*	2.3175	.016	1.033	10.143
	3	–9.6100*	2.7152	.000	–14.946	–4.274
	5	–12.1899*	4.5244	.007	–21.082	–3.298
	6	21.5366*	3.8553	.000	13.959	29.114
5	1	5.1693	4.6945	.271	–4.057	14.396
	2	17.7778*	4.6204	.000	8.697	26.859
	3	2.5799	4.8321	.594	–6.917	12.077
	4	12.1899*	4.5244	.007	3.298	21.082
	6	33.7265*	5.5534	.000	22.812	44.641
6	1	–28.5572*	4.0535	.000	–36.524	–20.591
	2	–15.9487*	3.9674	.000	–23.746	–8.151
	3	–31.1466*	4.2121	.000	–39.425	–22.868
	4	–21.5366*	3.8553	.000	–29.114	–13.959
	5	–33.7265*	5.5534	.000	–44.641	–22.812

*Significant at the .05 level.

difference really stands out: Professor 6's students scored much lower than all the others. The difference can also be seen in the bottom rows of Table 7A.7, but the strengths of a graphic depiction are very obvious in this example. The graphic better calls attention to the most important difference.

Although space limitations in your final research report may mean that you cannot include multiple comparison tables, graphics of CIs, and other helpful displays of your data, you would almost always benefit from examining them as you engage in your interpretation.

Incidentally, one of the advantages that dissertations have over most other forms of research report is that they usually are not confined by space limitations. Writers of dissertations have more freedom to include all that is useful, more freedom than they will likely ever have again. The greater completeness of dissertations also means that, when conducting reviews of research, dissertations are often the reviewer's best sources for full information about a research project, even when they have been revised and published as journal articles.

Note. Data for tables are provided in Table 6.6 (p. 234).

SUGGESTIONS FOR FURTHER READING

We focus here on the more readable works written in the same spirit as our approach. We always emphasize the questions of *which* methods you should plan to use and why; the textbook literature tends to be thin on that question. We devote less attention to *how to* apply those methods once you've decided to use them; how-to books are easier to find.

There are huge numbers of general books on statistical inference. Among these is Motulsky's *Intuitive Biostatistics: A Nonmathematical Guide to Statistical Thinking* (2010). We have enjoyed it, and our students have found it helpful. It discusses a very wide range of topics, including some fairly advanced ones, but always in a lively manner and in a way that nonspecialists can (usually) follow.

The CI approach is nicely laid out in Cumming's (2012) book, *Understanding the New Statistics*. It is very accessible to nonspecialists. It also pursues its topics to rather advanced levels, yet it still remains readable by nonstatisticians. That is accomplished in part by the free demonstration software the book uses to illustrate its points. Called ESCI (Effect Size Confidence Interval) it makes the concept come alive. You can use the author's data, simulations, and/or your own data to investigate such helpful visuals as the "dance of the CIs." Finally, the book ties the CI approach to statistical inference to meta-analysis and even more fundamentally to meta-analytic thinking. The key point is that *meta-analysis is not just for literature reviews anymore*. The only limitation is that the book gives little direct guidance about data that have not been gathered in a randomized experiment. But CIs are much more widely used than with experimental data alone. Also Cumming's work is thoroughly frequentist, so it includes no discussion about how to interpret CIs other than in that framework.

One book on distribution-free (a.k.a. nonparametric) statistics is Corder and Foreman's *Nonparametric Statistics for Non-Statisticians* (2009). It provides a good how-to overview. Another is Wasserman's *All of Nonparametric Statistics* (2007), which is more thorough, advanced, and technical, but worth the effort, as it goes well beyond the usual basics.

Most general books on resampling methods are tied to software packages, and many have been written by Good. His most recent (published in 2013) is *Introduction to Statistics through Resampling Methods and R*.

McGrayne's popular history of Bayesian analysis, *The Theory That Would Not Die* (2011), gives the reader an easy way to get started in a field that is difficult but important to know. A more advanced, but mostly nontechnical, discussion can be found in an article by Gelman and Robert (2013), as well as comments by several others in the *American Statistician, 67*(1), 1–17. Silver's *The Signal and the Noise* (2012) contains some practical examples of how Bayesian calculations can be done by hand and applied to simple problems.

The most general and accessible volume on missing data analysis is by Enders, *Applied Missing Data Analysis* (2012). It covers both MI and ML approaches.

CHAPTER 7 SUMMARY TABLE

ADVANTAGES OF DIFFERENT APPROACHES TO STATISTICAL INFERENCE

Approach	Advantages
Classical statistical inference (NHST) (pp. 242–243)	• Based on well-substantiated statistical theory. • Is widely known in the community of researchers.
Confidence intervals (ESCI) (p. 255)	• Based on the same statistical theory as NHST. • Provides margins of error and plausible ranges of population values. • Provides useful indication of likely results in a replication.
Bayesian statistical inference (pp. 264–265)	• Formally combines prior knowledge with that gained from the research and makes statistical assumptions explicit. • Avoids the double-negatives of hypothesis testing. • Allows for more straightforward interpretations of confidence intervals.
Bootstrap/ resampling methods (pp. 259–260)	• Avoids the need to make assumptions about unknown population distributions. • Uses computer simulation to generate empirical rather than theoretical sampling distributions.

DOS AND DON'TS IN REPORTING *P*-VALUES AND STATISTICAL SIGNIFICANCE (p. 245)

Practice	Reason
Always report exact *p*-values.	When using a cutoff *p*-value (specified in advance), also include exact *p*-values when you can obtain them; they are helpful to other researchers using your results.
Never report $p = .000$.	A computer output of $p = .000$ means that the software stopped after .001 and did not continue to the fourth decimal point and beyond. Convert computer readouts with $p =$ or $< .000$ to $p < .001$.
Always specify type of significance.	The word *significant* alone can mean "practically" or "clinically" important, not only *statistically* significant. Use the word *significance* with the appropriate qualifier—statistical, practical, clinical, etc.

WHEN TO USE WHAT TYPE OF *T*-TEST (pp. 246–248 and Table 7.1)

Type of test	When to use
One-sample *t*-test	To determine when a statistic, which has been calculated on one sample, is significantly different from the NH.

Two-independent-samples *t*-test	To determine whether a statistic, such as a mean difference between control and experimental groups, is statistically significant.
Two-dependent-samples *t*-test	To determine whether the difference between two nonindependent samples, such as in a repeated measures design, are significantly different from the NH.

WHICH ANOVA MULTIPLE COMPARISON PROCEDURE TO USE FOR WHAT (pp. 248–250 and Table 7.2)

Procedure	**When to use**
Tukey's HSD	To test all possible pairs of means; this is the most general of the tests.
Bonferroni's inequality	To test planned, theory-driven contrasts; also is a very general test.
Dunnett's procedure	To test each experimental group against each control group.
Scheffé's test	To test comparisons suggested by the observed results.

REASONS TO PREFER CIs TO *P*-VALUES (p. 255)

The CIs for a statistic contain all the information that the *p*-value for a hypothesis test contains, but the reverse is not true.

The CIs make the degree of uncertainty in statistical estimates much clearer; they put uncertainty in the foreground.

CIs are informative about the likely replicability of study results; *p*-values are of little use for predicting replicability.

The CI approach makes discussions of cause probabilistic rather than absolutistic/dichotomous.

WAYS TO INTERPRET CIs (p. 254)

The CI is the range of plausible values for the population statistic.

In an infinite number of random samples from the population, 95% of those CIs would contain the population statistic; 5% would not.

The CI is an indication of the precision of the estimate; the narrower the CI, the more precise.

CIs can be used to draw NHST inferences. For example, if the NH is zero and the CI does not include zero, the NH is not confirmed. If the CI does include zero, the NH is rejected.

COMMON DISTRIBUTION-FREE NHSTs (pp. 258–259 and Table 7.4)	
Test	**When to use; what parametric test it replaces**
Chi-squared (χ^2) test	When all variables are categorical so that summary statistics are counts or frequencies.
Mann–Whitney–Wilcoxon (MWW)	When you would use independent-samples *t*-test.
Wilcoxon signed-rank test	When you would use the *t*-test for dependent samples or repeated measures.
Kruskal–Wallis test	When you would use the independent-samples one-way ANOVA; extends the MWW to three or more groups.
Friedman test	When you would use a repeated measures ANOVA.

CHAPTER 8

What Associational Statistics to Use When

In this chapter we:

- Introduce correlation and regression using graphics and warn about incautious causal phrasing.
- Discuss when to use correlations to analyze data and review when to use which particular types of correlation.
    - Describe related measures of association based on the chi-squared statistic and proportional reduction of error (PRE) measures of association and when to use them.
- Discuss when in general to use regression analysis, as well as standardized and unstandardized regression coefficients.
    - Examine when to use multiple regression analysis and examine the types of questions that can be answered with multiple regression.
    - Review the uses of multiple regression.
    - Address the so-called conflict between multiple regression and multiple correlation analysis.
    - Consider when to study mediating and moderating effects.
    - Outline the different forms of coding for categorical variables and when to use them.
    - Discuss ways of answering the question, How big should your sample be?
    - Give suggestions about when to correct for missing data.
    - Illustrate when and how to use curvilinear (or polynomial) regression, as well as other transformations.
    - Examine what you can do when your dependent variables are categorical and when to use logit, probit, tobit, or Poisson regression, as well as survival analysis and discriminant analysis.
- Conclude with a review of which associational methods work best for what sorts of data and problems.
- And, lastly, address the *most* important question: When to include which variables and the related question of what kinds of relations among variables to consider.

Many methods exist for depicting the associations among variables. Most of them are types of correlation and regression. Although differences in the way the data are coded and measured require different types of correlation and regression, a conceptual understanding of the basic types carries over into the more specialized and advanced forms. In the next few pages we use examples to make several points about correlation and regression. First, correlation and regression have many uses in social research, particularly in nonexperimental research, and some disciplines use them almost exclusively. Second, correlation and regression are closely tied to one another. Third, they both can be better understood when the patterns they describe are studied visually, as well as statistically. And, finally, the two are the foundation stones of nearly all advanced analytical techniques for quantitative data.

Correlation and regression are closely related. To illustrate their relation, we use data from the United Nations (UN) and other international agencies concerning education levels, birth rates, average incomes, and homicide and suicide rates. The data are real, which means that coding and reporting problems abound and many gaps in the data occur. We use these data because they are typical, not ideal. As discussed in our coding chapters, in order to compare variables, they have to be coded and reported in the same way. The UN does a good job collecting comparable data, but there are always missing data. For example, poorer nations and Islamic nations often did not report suicide rates. And even when the data are reported, coding is always an issue: Was the car crash or the drug overdose a suicide or an accident?

The links between correlation and regression can be most easily seen graphically. Figure 8.1 shows the association between the average educational level of adults and the average income per person in 100 nations.[1] Each dot represents the intersection of two values for a nation: average education level of adults in the country and the average income per person in the country (gross domestic product [GDP] divided by the population). For example, the dot in the upper right of the graph represents Norway, with mean education level of 11.8 years and a mean income level of $56,984. The cluster of dots in the far lower left represents countries, including Mali, Mozambique, and Niger, with average adult education levels of around 1 year and incomes about $1,000. The pattern in the dots is clear. More education is associated with more income. But the association is not perfect. The United States has the highest level of education (12.0 years), but in income it ranks about $10,000 below Norway. Both Singapore and Kuwait have higher mean incomes than the United States, but education levels of only 7 years. The relation between education and income is a little tighter at the low end, but there are some surprises there, too. The pair of dots just above 8 years of education represents nations with somewhat more education than Singapore and Kuwait, but dramatically less income: they are Fiji and the Philippines. Overall, the correlation is strong, about as strong as we see in the social sciences: $r = .803$. If the relation between education and income were perfect, it would be $r = 1.0$. The relation is positive (represented by a positive number) because the two variables move in the same direction. When one goes up (or down), so too does the other. The **R^2 statistic** (0.645) on the upper right just outside the graph is the square of r of .803. This R^2 is very important

[1]The data used in this and the other examples come from various international agencies, mostly UN sponsored. To get an idea of the complexities involved in collecting and analyzing such data, see United Nations Office on Drugs and Crime (UNODC; 2011), especially pages 83–89 on "data challenges."

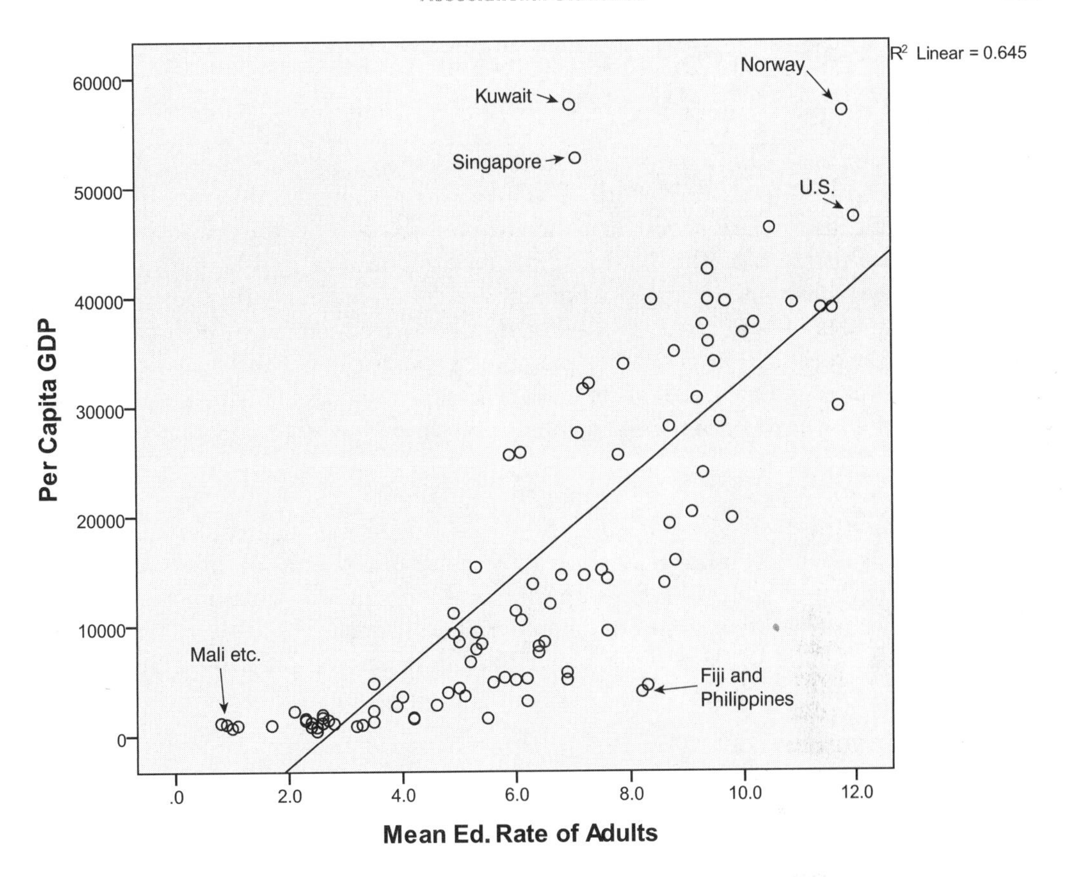

FIGURE 8.1. Scatter diagram with regression line: Adults' mean education level and per capita GDP.

because it indicates how much better you can predict income if you know education. Here the R^2 is .645, so you can predict 64½% better. (The predictions are better than they would be if you used the mean to estimate the associations.) In other terms, you can explain 64½% of the differences (variation) in income by differences in education, but you can't explain the other 35½%.

The line in Figure 8.1 is the **regression line**. The regression line is the straight line that best fits the dots (comes closest to the most dots). The steeper the slope of the regression line, the stronger the regression effect. The correlation is a measure of how close the dots are to the line; the closer the dots, the stronger the **correlation**. Much like the chicken and the egg, so too with correlation and regression: You can't have one without the other. You can't fit the line to the dots unless you have the dots, and you can't measure the distance of the dots from the line unless you have the line.

Note that it is important to consider both the regression coefficient and the correlation coefficient. The regression coefficient indicates the steepness of the trend line, or the *strength* of the average effect. The correlation coefficient indicates the *consistency* of the trend. In this case, the trend is fairly consistent. Some of the dots are very close to the line, but some are not. The line is a better summary of the dots at the lower levels of education than at the higher. This illustrates why it is very important to consider correlation and regression together *and* to examine your data graphically. We can see this even more clearly in the next two examples.

Note: Incautious causal phrasing. In an earlier paragraph, we said, "When one goes up (or down), so too does the other." This *implies*, though it does not quite *assert*, that there is a causal relation between the two variables—education and income. But that is not demonstrated by the data. For instance, it could be that higher rates of educational achievement cause average incomes to be higher, *or* that higher education levels lead to higher rates of per capita income, or that both are fostered by a third unnamed variable, or that there are several other possible explanations for the statistical association. Although it is common and acceptable when speaking casually to talk causally, it is inappropriate to draw casual conclusions *solely* from statistical associations such as these.

The relation of average adult education level and national birth rate (per 1,000 population) is shown in Figure 8.2. Here we see that the regression line slopes downward, meaning that as education goes up, the birth rate goes down—on average. More precisely, it means that higher rates of educational attainment are associated with lower birth rates. The relation is slightly stronger than that between education and income:

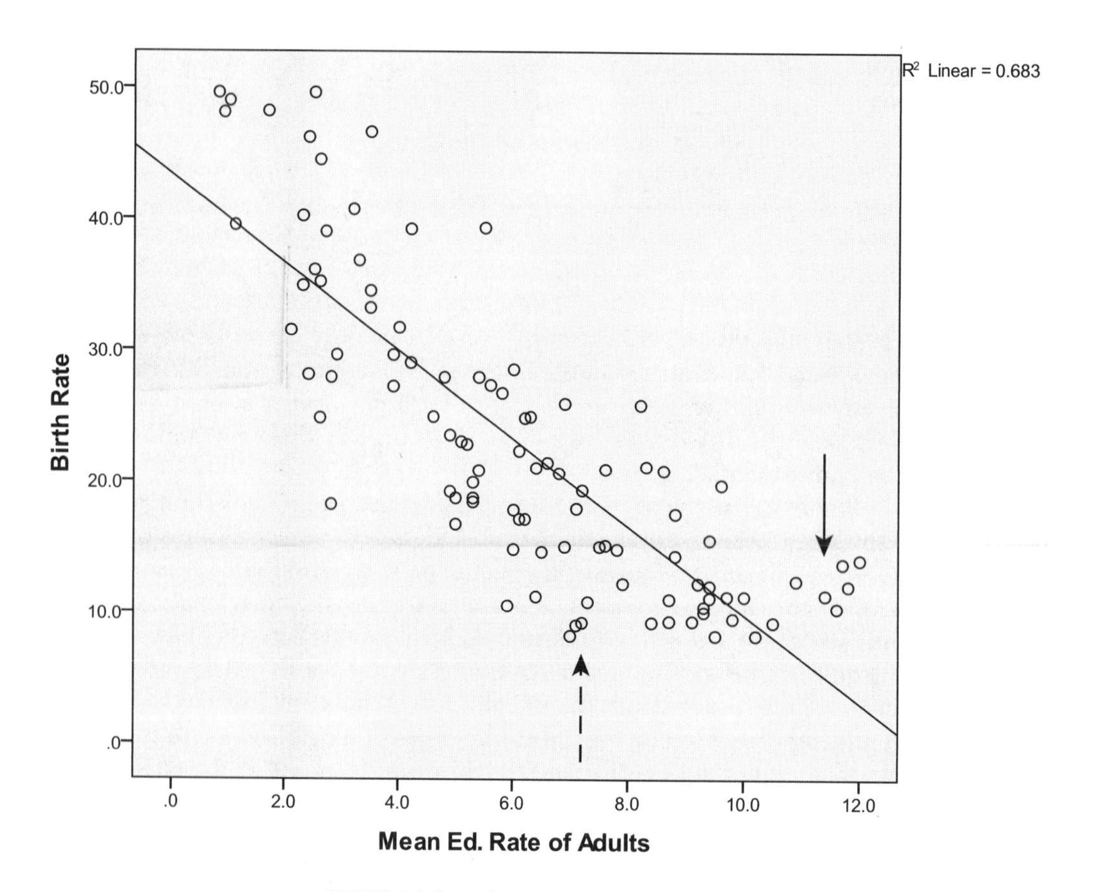

FIGURE 8.2. Education and birth rate.

The steepness of the slope is sharper and the dots are generally closer to the line. But even here there are exceptions.

For example, a cluster of six dots on the far right side of the graph represents nations with birth rates higher than we would expect if we used the regression line to make our prediction.[2] Those six are the United States, New Zealand, Norway, Canada, Sweden, and Australia. On the other hand, a cluster of three dots just above 7 years of education represents nations with birth rates lower than most others at that level of education. They are Slovenia, Singapore, and Italy. A **regression coefficient** (calculating regression coefficients is discussed later in the chapter) tells you about the slope of the line, which is a measure of the size of the relation between the outcome variable (here birth rate) and the predictor variable (education in this example).[3] The regression coefficient is usually represented by the letter b. Here the coefficient $b = -3.4$. This means that for every 1-year increase in the education level, the birth rate is lower by 3.4—on average.

Our last graphic example presents a murkier picture. When we make birth rate the predictor variable and look at the relation between it and per capita income (Figure 8.3), we see a weaker association. The r and the R^2 are quite a bit smaller than in the two previous examples: $r = -.638$ and $R^2 = .407$. These are still high correlations by social science standards, but by looking at the scatter diagram, you can see that "high by social science standards" does not always paint a clear picture. Even more important than the modest correlations is the fact that a straight line does not describe the relation very well. If you didn't look at the scatter diagram, you probably wouldn't know this. A curved line with one bend (a so-called quadratic line) captures the relation better, but only somewhat: It raises the R^2 from .407 to .464.

Finally, let's consider the association between education as a predictor variable and two often studied outcome variables: homicide and suicide rates. In the interest of saving space, we produce only one of the graphics here.[4] The correlation between nations' education levels and suicide rates is $r = .410$, and the regression coefficient is $b = 2.01$, which means that for every 1-year increase in the average educational level, the suicide rate goes up by 2 persons. That sounds like a lot, but it is 2 per 100,000 persons. The homicide rate is the other way around. The correlation $r = -.313$ and the regression coefficient $b = -1.75$.

The homicide numbers are negative because higher levels of education are associated with lower levels of murder. These are figures for national rates, not for individuals, although the general pattern for individuals is the same: As education goes up, so does the probability of suicide, but the likelihood of homicide goes down. These are not strong associations; you can only explain (using the R^2) about 17% of the suicide rate or about 10% of the homicide rate with education. But they are strong in a different way. They have been remarkably persistent. Ever since Durkheim first extensively discussed these relationships in the 19th century, they have been consistently confirmed by other

---

[2]Using regression lines to make predictions is common, which is why the regression line is sometimes called the prediction line and why regression equations are also called prediction equations.

[3]Regression coefficients are affected by units of measurement. For example, they will be bigger if you measure height in inches rather than in feet. See the later discussion on standardized regression coefficients.

[4]Figure 8.4 is on page 294. The other, depicting the association of national education levels and murder rates, is on Paul Vogt's blog: *http://vogtsresearchmethods.blogspot.com/*.

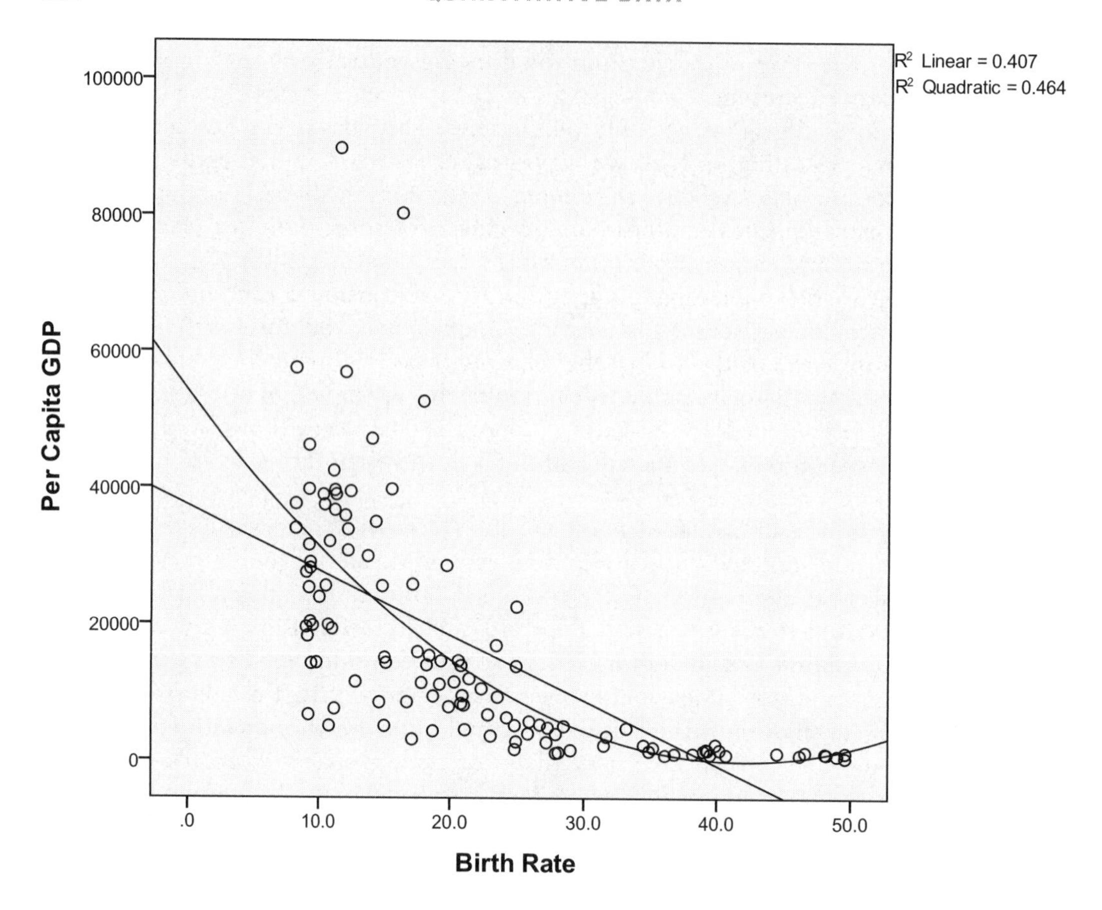

FIGURE 8.3. Birth rate and per capita income.

researchers. If you live in a society with a high education rate, your neighbor is more likely to kill himself—but he[5] is less likely to kill you.

A word of caution is in order here. Using data about groups to draw conclusions about individuals is inappropriate. Doing so is known as the **ecological fallacy**. For example, if crime rates were higher in neighborhoods with higher concentrations of the elderly, you would commit an ecological fallacy to conclude, therefore, that old people were more likely to commit crimes. Another example would be to conclude, from the data in Figure 8.1 on national educational levels and national average incomes, that you would increase your income if you got more education. You might well do so, but the data in Figure 8.1 are not valid evidence for drawing conclusions about the effects of an individual's education on his or her income.

Despite the possibilities for misinterpreting correlations, virtually all quantitative analytical methods are at base correlational.[6] All are built using variances and covari-

[5]We say "he" here not through any insensitivity to gender equity but because both suicide and homicide are more likely to be committed by males.

[6]Thompson (2000).

ances, and most multivariate techniques are built upon correlation and/or covariance matrices. One way to persuade yourself of the basic unity of methods is to spend an afternoon computing some statistics by hand: a few correlations, *t*-tests, analyses of variance (ANOVAs), and regression coefficients ought to be enough to make the point. Even through the fog of the tedium this computing exercise will induce, you will note that regardless of the statistic that you are computing, you are doing the same kinds of calculations over and over again: averaging the scores, subtracting the average from each score, squaring the result of the subtraction, summing the squares, and so on. The statistics are all versions of the same basic algorithm, the same *general linear model*. Despite this unity, there are many choices concerning which statistics to use for particular purposes. But it is important to remember the underlying unity; you need not buy into the false dichotomies about which statistics to use for what that are still surprisingly common in textbooks.

There are important differences in the effective use of correlation and regression. Correlations are **nondirectional**, or symmetric, which means that the direction of any causation is not specified. The correlation between height and weight is the same as the correlation between weight and height. The question addressed by correlation is, What is the degree of association between variables? By contrast, regression assumes a causal direction; therefore, it is called **directional**. The question addressed by regression is, What is the effect of one variable on another? If you know, or can reasonably assume, a causal direction, regression is the better associational statistic to use. If not, correlation is. One knows whether to assume a causal direction not by the statistic but by an understanding of the relation of the variables. For example, as children get older and taller, they almost always get heavier. But getting heavier, say by eating junk food, does not make children taller or older, nor do children who lose weight become shorter or younger. Hence, in a regression model, height and age would be the independent or predictor (or causal) variables, and weight would be the dependent or outcome (or effect) variable.

WHEN TO USE CORRELATIONS TO ANALYZE DATA

When the association between two variables is of interest, studying it with a correlation is a natural choice. The choice is *not* dependent on design. There is some confusion here because it has been traditional in research methods textbooks to contrast experimental designs with so-called correlational designs. This confusion needs to be cleared up, because belief in the categorical difference between experiments and correlations is not uncommon. It is among the more basic of the false dichotomies that limit our analytical options.

Correlations are a method of analysis. As such, they are applicable to a wide range of designs. They are quite useful for describing the strength of the effect of an experimental treatment, which is why the common practice of contrasting correlations with experiments is confusing at best. A correlation makes a good effect size (ES) measure in an experiment; it can be used to measure the association between scores on the dependent variable (DV) and assignment to experimental and control groups. This correlation is tested for statistical significance with the *t*-test. A more common way to report experimental results is a *t*-test of the difference between the means for the experimental and control groups. The two ways of reporting results are more similar than is sometimes believed. For example, a *p*-value computed with the *t*-test for the mean difference will be identical to the *p*-value for the correlation. The mean difference is a useful measure of the size of the effect; the correlation provides a *standardized* measure of ES, one that can be compared across studies; it is a good complement to other standardized measures, such as the *d*-statistic (see Chapters 6 and 7).

The other element in the supposed incompatibility between experimental and correlational methods relates to the oft-repeated slogan that correlation does not imply causation. Indeed, it does not. Nor does any statistic. Causal inference is built upon design. We can draw good inferences about cause in an experiment if we have randomly assigned participants to groups and if we have controlled the administration of the independent variable (IV). Whether we measure the effect of the IV by a mean difference, a *d*-statistic, or a Pearson's *r* correlation is mostly a matter of which of these conveys more information about the variables. We recommend reporting all three. Each can provide a helpful perspective on outcomes.

The point about the distinction between causal inferences and the statistics used to make them cannot be too strongly emphasized. Drawing causal conclusions has almost nothing to do with particular statistics. Just as drawing a conclusion from something you have seen is not mainly about the mechanics of vision (e.g., the retina and the optic nerve), coming to a conclusion based on statistics is not mainly about computational procedures. Drawing conclusions about cause is based more on reasoning about evidence than on the particular method of coding and analyzing the evidence.

The many types of correlation are all read in the same way. Briefly, correlations range from +1.0 to –1.0. A correlation of 0 means that the variables are not statistically associated; knowing about one variable provides no information about the other. A positive correlation indicates a **direct relationship**, which means that values on the two variables tend to move in the same direction, such as nations' education levels and average incomes. A negative correlation describes an **inverse relation**, which means that the two variables tend to move in opposite directions, such as nations' education levels and birth rates.

When two variables are studied (or when several are studied two at a time), many bivariate correlations are available. Choice among them has mostly to do with the way the data are coded. The original correlation, and the workhorse among them, is the Pearson correlation,[7] or **Pearson's *r*.** Many of the other correlations are special cases of *r*. For instance, the point-biserial correlation is Pearson's *r* between one dichotomous and one continuous variable; Spearman's rho is Pearson's *r* between two sets of data that are in rank order. Several of the other correlations were mostly designed to make calculations easier when the data were not continuous. Today, with the advent of computers, many of these have lost their importance for making calculations. Others retain their importance for special uses, and all are still occasionally reported in the research literature. Table 8.1 gives the circumstances in which various correlations are used and their characteristics. In other terms, it describes when to use what.

[7]The full term for this is the "Pearson product–moment correlation," but this longer expression is not commonly used.

TABLE 8.1. When to Use Which Types of Correlation

Name	Measurement	When to use
Pearson *r*	2 continuous variables	When the data are continuous and the relation between them is linear, *r* is the best choice.
Correlation ratio, eta (η)	1 categorical and 1 continuous variable	When the data are not assumed to be linear, eta, which is independent of the form of the data, may be used.
Spearman's rho (ρ)	2 rank-order variables with no tied ranks	Continuous data may be converted to ranks when they are not normally distributed and/or if they contain large outliers.
Kendall's tau (τ)	2 rank-order variables	Better than Spearman's rho, especially when the data contain tied ranks; three versions exist; tau-c is the most flexible.
Point-biserial correlation	1 dichotomous and 1 continuous variable	This kind of Pearson *r* is often used to report experimental results.
Biserial correlation	1 dichotomized and 1 continuous variable	Used when 1 continuous variable is dichotomized by the researcher, usually not a good practice.
Tetrachoric correlation	2 continuous variables that have been dichotomized	Dichotomizing continuous variables might be useful for data with many gaps.
Widespread biserial correlation	1 dichotomized and 1 continuous variable	Used when the researcher is interested in extreme scores on the variable, not the middle range of the scores.

When to Use Measures of Association Based on the Chi-Squared Distribution

Another class of measures of association is based on the chi-squared test statistic. The chi-squared-based measures of association for categorical variables are widely used for data in contingency tables when all the variables are categorical. The unadjusted chi-squared statistic is not a good measure of association because it is strongly influenced by sample size. Three measures of association adjust the chi-square for sample size. They are the phi coefficient (Φ), Cramér's *V*, and the contingency coefficient (C), also called Pearson's contingency coefficient. A disadvantage of these measures is that the three give different answers to the same problem, and there is no certain way to tell which one is more accurate. All range between 0 and 1.0 and are read like correlation coefficients. The best of the three measures is generally **Cramér's *V***, but it is probably the least used. Its advantage is that, unlike the contingency coefficient, it can attain a maximum value of 1.0 when two variables are perfectly associated, and unlike the phi coefficient, it cannot exceed the value of 1.0. (See Table 8.2.)

By far the most popular of these measures is the **phi** (Φ) coefficient. It is so popular that it is often referred to by its nickname: "phi-co." The big problem with the phi coefficient is that in tables with more than three rows and three columns it can produce

TABLE 8.2. Measures of Association Based on the Chi-Squared Statistic

Measure	Advantages/disadvantages
phi coefficient (Φ)	Highly associated variables may have a value greater than 1.0.
contingency coefficient (*C*)	May not attain the value of 1.0 even for perfectly associated variables.
Cramér's *V*	Applicable to the widest range of problems.

meaningless results; specifically, it can be larger than 1.0—which would mean bigger than completely, totally, perfectly correlated. To avoid this absurd result, Cramér's *V* is used to adjust phi downward. The *p*-values for the same data will be identical regardless of which of these measures of association is used.

When to Use Proportional Reduction of Error Measures of Association

One of the disadvantages of the chi-squared-based measures is that they do not always have a clear interpretation. By contrast, the measures that indicate the **proportional reduction of error** (**PRE**) are models of clarity. The question they answer is, How much better can you estimate one variable if you know the values of another variable? Another way to put it is that PRE measures tell you the percentage of the variance one variable explains in another. In other words: How much better can you predict an outcome (dependent) variable if you know the values of a predictor (independent) variable? How much better than what? For the Pearson *r*-squared correlation, the answer is: better than the mean. For lambda, it is: better than the modal category. In either case, the

TABLE 8.3. When to Use Which PRE Measures of Association

Measure	Variable coding	Causal direction and comments
Lambda (λ)	Both categorical	Asymmetric; reduction of error is from the modal category as the best estimate.
Goodman & Kruskal's tau (τ)	Both categorical	Asymmetric; indicates proportion of one variable correctly predicted by another.
Gamma (γ)	Ordinal variables	Symmetric; ranges from –1.0 through +1.0.
Somers's *d*	Ordinal variables	Asymmetric; it is an asymmetric version of gamma.
Eta squared (η^2)	Categorical IV and continuous DV	Asymmetric; often used as an ES measure after a significant *t*-test or ANOVA.
Omega squared (ω^2)	Categorical IV and continuous DV	Asymmetric; it is an adjusted eta squared and is always smaller than eta squared or *r*-squared for the same data.
r-squared (r^2)	Both continuous; one may be dichotomous if coded 1 and 0	Symmetric; reduction of error is from the mean as best estimate.

answer is always expressed as a proportion ranging from 0 to 1.0—or a percentage ranging from 0 to 100.

PRE measures are categorized according to two main criteria: (1) whether the variables are coded as categorical (nominal), ordinal (ranked), or continuous; and (2) whether the correlation is symmetric or asymmetric. *Symmetric* measures are the same regardless of which variable (if either) is thought of as independent (predictor) or dependent (outcome); the correlation between A and B is the same as the correlation between B and A. *Asymmetric* measures of association, such as regression coefficients, specify a causal direction and have a different value depending on which variable is thought of as the predictor (independent) and which as the outcome (dependent). For example, an association between scores on a reading test and on a math test would be symmetric; either (or neither) could be thought of as the cause or the effect. By contrast, any association between gender and test scores is clearly asymmetric: No matter how hard you study to improve your score, or how much you slack off, your gender won't change. (See Table 8.3.)

WHEN TO USE REGRESSION ANALYSIS

Regression is and has always been the heart of quantitative analysis in sociology, political science, economics, and related disciplines, such as social work, education, and business.[8] Regression is the all but universal method for explaining or predicting variance in an outcome on the basis of variance in one or more independent or predictor variables. Different types of regression analysis allow one to analyze different types of data. Regardless of these differences, regression analysis always answers one version or another of the same basic question: For every 1-unit increase in a predictor (a.k.a. independent, or X, variable) what happens to the outcome (a.k.a. dependent, or Y variable)? In short, the regression coefficient b is the answer to the question, How big is the effect of the predictor on the outcome?

To return to our earlier examples of international demographic variables, we showed (in Figure 8.1) that the correlation between average education level and per capita income was strong. The correlation was $r = .803$, and the R^2 was .645, meaning that education "explains" 64½% of national differences in income. On the other hand, the correlation between education and female suicide rate is much more modest: $r = .304$ and $R^2 = .09$, meaning that you could explain 9% of the variance in female suicide rate across countries by education—the other 91% would have to be explained by other variables. The differences between these two relations can be more clearly understood by looking at them graphically. We present the scatter diagram with a regression line for the relation between education and female suicide in Figure 8.4. Comparing this figure with Figure 8.1, two things stand out: (1) the line slopes up more steeply for education and income than it does for education and suicide (for which it is nearly horizontal); (2) more dots are closer to the income line than to the suicide line. The steepness of the line tells you how strong the relation is; the closeness of the dots to the line tells you how consistent it is. The steepness of the line is measured by the regression coefficient,

[8] Regression is also central in psychology and related disciplines, but there the foundational method is comparing mean differences and testing them for statistical significance.

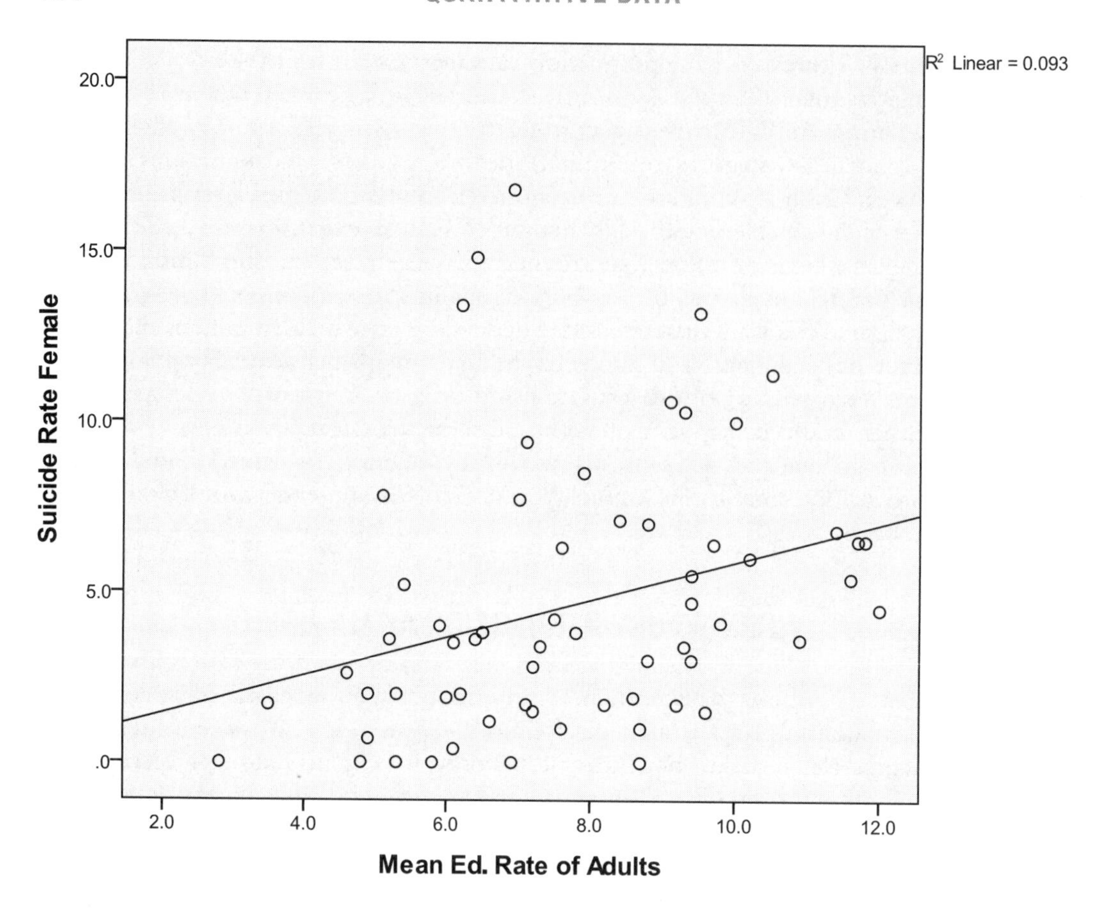

FIGURE 8.4. Mean national educational attainment rates and national suicide rates per 100,000 population.

usually summarized with the letter *b*. The regression coefficient for female suicide is *b* = .56. This means that for every 1-year increase in average education, the average female suicide rate goes up about half a suicide per 100,000. By contrast, the regression coefficient for income is *b* = 4406, meaning that on average 1 year of education is associated with $4,406 in income. The relation between income and education is stronger than that between income and suicide, but the coefficient for income is thousands of times bigger, much bigger than the strength of the association. Why do the regression coefficients differ so much? The reason is in the scale of the outcome measure. The highest female suicide rate is around 16; the highest per capita income is around $57,000. How do you compare the strength of the relations measured on such different scales? You use a **standardized regression coefficient.**

A standardized regression coefficient states the relation in standard deviation (*SD*) units that can be compared across studies (see Chapter 7 on ES measures, which are also standardized). The standardized coefficients, often symbolized by beta (β), are for income and suicide, respectively, .803 and .304. Standardized regression coefficients have many advantages; chief among them is the ability to compare across studies and to say in this case, for example, that the relation between education and income is about

2½ times stronger than that between education and suicide (.803 ÷ .304 = 2.6). But there are both advantages and disadvantages to using standardized coefficients.

When to Use Standardized or Unstandardized Regression Coefficients

Regression coefficients can be in the original units, in which case they are usually labeled *b*. If they are given in *SD* units, they are labeled beta (β).[9] When the standardized coefficient is used, the basic question becomes: For every 1 unit increase in the independent (predictor) variable, how much of a change is there (expressed in *SD* units) in the dependent (outcome) variable? Which is better to use, the *SD* coefficient beta (β) or the unstandardized coefficient *b*? It depends on your goals, not on the technical character of the two measures, as each coefficient can be easily converted into the other. Most computer packages routinely produce both, and it usually makes good sense to report both, because readers with different interests and goals are likely to want to see the results expressed in different ways. The one you use to interpret your results will depend on the nature of your data and your research question. For the income example used before, the unstandardized coefficient *b* will often make more sense, because the interpretation is straightforward: For each year of education, income goes up an average of $4,406. It could just confuse things to report this outcome in *SD* units. But, as we saw, if you wanted to make meaningful comparisons of the relation of education to income and to suicide, the only option is to use standardized coefficients.

The need for standardized coefficients becomes clearer in examples of multiple regression. In multiple regression the researcher uses several predictor (independent) variables to explain or predict the values of the outcome (dependent) variable. The standardized coefficient beta is often useful for comparing the effects of different predictor variables, particularly when the variables are measured on different scales (see later discussion).

When to Use Multiple Regression Analysis

When researchers want to predict or explain an outcome (dependent) variable using two or more predictor (independent) variables—which is most of the time—multiple regression is the most common analytical tool. Despite its peculiar name,[10] regression is *the* foundation for the analysis of quantitative data in the social sciences. *Multiple* regression is much more commonly used than two-variable (bivariate) regression, which we have been discussing thus far. Beginning with two-variable regression is a good strategy, because it makes basic principles easier to discuss. Because most principles are the same in multiple-variable regression as in the simple two-variable versions, it is easy to build on the bivariate examples to generalize to multivariate cases.

Few social science problems can be intelligently studied examining only two variables at a time. The social world is multivariate, with numerous influences affecting

[9]In regression with two variables, the standardized regression coefficient is the same thing as the correlation coefficient, which is always expressed in *SD* units.

[10]Regression was given its name by Francis Galton, after "regression to mediocrity," today called *regression to the mean*. A better name than *regression* might be *slope analysis*, in reference to the slope or angle of the line summarizing the data. *Prediction analysis* or *explanation analysis* would also be more descriptive.

outcomes and events; hence the importance of multiple regression. Relations between two variables may disappear or even be reversed when you control for other variables. For example, the correlation or bivariate regression coefficient between urbanism and academic achievement is negative, meaning that, *on average*, students in cities perform less well on tests of achievement. However, that is mostly because of the high degree of poverty in cities. When poverty is controlled (included as a variable in a multiple regression analysis), the relation between city residence and academic achievement is often reversed: on average, students in urban areas do better on the tests.

Experiments often examine only one IV and one DV, but they do not ignore other variables. They control for other variables by random assignment. Multiple regression allows researchers to control statistically for variables that cannot be controlled through random assignment. For example, we cannot randomly assign students to live in urban areas or to be poor. Multiple regression also enables researchers to study several IVs simultaneously. Researchers using multiple regression attempt to answer three questions:

1. What is the effect of all the predictor variables taken together on the outcome variable? The answer is usually expressed using the multiple R^2 statistic.[11] Like the bivariate r^2 statistic, it is a PRE measure. It answers the question, How much better can I estimate the outcome if I know the predictors? The answer is usually expressed as a proportion or a percentage (e.g., .45 or 45%).
2. What is the effect of a 1-unit increase in one predictor variable ($X1$) holding constant, or controlling for, the effects of the other predictors ($X2$, $X3$, . . .)?
3. Which of the predictor (independent or explanatory) variables has the strongest effect on the outcome (dependent or response)[12] variable? Very often, the emphasis in multiple regression is on comparing the effects of the predictor variables.

In comparing the influence of predictor variables, the standardized coefficient, beta, usually becomes important. Say the outcome you were interested in explaining was annual salaries for workers in a given occupation. Your explanatory (predictor) variables are years of experience (which range from 1 to 45 years in your sample) and average supervisor rating; the scale used is: 1 = poor, 2 = average, 3 = good.[13] It would be very hard to compare these two predictor variables using unstandardized *b* coefficients, because the variables are measured on different scales. An increase in experience from 2 to 3 years probably would not be very important, whereas an increase in supervisor rating from 2 to 3 (from average to good) could easily matter quite a lot. The basic regression question is, What is the effect of a 1-unit increase? To compare the effects of two variables, the phrase "1-unit increase" has to mean the same thing for each.

---

[11] Using the ***adjusted R^2*** is standard practice.

[12] Multiple terms are used for the same concepts in regression analysis, and there are differences of opinion about which are the "correct" terms to use. Although there are subtle distinctions, we use *predictor*, *independent*, and *explanatory variable* interchangeably to mean *causal variable*. For the effect variable, equivalent labels are: *outcome*, *dependent*, *criterion*, and *response variable*. Compare Table 8.9.

[13] This is an ordinal scale that we are treating here as continuous merely for the purposes of illustration. In actual practice we would convert it into three dummy variables (see Table 8.5); this would not eliminate the problem of comparing two variables measured on different scales.

Multiple Regression Analysis "versus" Multiple Correlation Analysis

Much of the work of multiple regression analysis in studying the effect of several explanatory variables on one outcome variable can also be done with multiple correlation analysis. For example, the so-called partial correlation examines the correlation between two variables after holding constant ("partialling out") the effects of one or more control variables. Most researchers report their results using multiple regression, but multiple correlation analysis can also often be used, and in some cases it may be preferable,[14] although the differences are fairly minor.

A more important use of correlation is to help examine the relations among the independent (predictor) variables in a regression analysis. An important IV might appear in a regression analysis to have only a small relation with the DV simply because it is highly correlated with another of the IVs. This correlation among the IVs is called **collinearity.** It is even possible that a variable that appears to have a positive relation might actually be negatively related (or vice versa) because of a **suppressor variable.** Problems with the interpretation of a multiple regression analysis can be addressed by looking at the pattern of the correlations among the IVs and the correlations between each of the IVs and the DV and between the correlations of each of the IVs with the *predicted value* of the DV.[15] The importance of correlation in the correct interpretation of regression is a further indication that the two analytical techniques are natural allies, as well as being closely related.

When to Study Mediating and Moderating Effects

When will or should researchers employing multiple regression analysis inquire into mediating and moderating effects? Almost always, especially as these are driven by your research questions. The study of mediating and/or moderating variables is often one of the chief goals of investigators using multiple regression analysis.[16]

Mediating variables are often called **intervening** variables because they come between an independent and a dependent variable; they provide a causal link. For example, there is a strong association between income and longevity: Rich people tend to live longer than poor people. The cause is surely indirect or mediated by other variables. Otherwise, a person on his death bed who wins the lottery would be immediately cured. Being prosperous leads to something; it is that "something" that, in turn, leads to longevity. It might be access to better health care, safer working conditions, better environment, better nutrition, or all of the above.[17] Using multiple regression analysis, you can examine these potential mediating/intervening variables to assess their effects, both individually and jointly.[18]

---

[14] Huberty (2003).

[15] For details, see Thompson (2006, Ch. 8).

[16] For a thorough account, using somewhat different labels for types of variables, see Aneshensel (2002).

[17] Or perhaps becoming prosperous is caused by the same variables that lead to good health and longevity. See Krieger et al. (2008) and Link et al. (2008) for discussions.

[18] More advanced techniques, beyond what we can cover in this chapter, are often used to conduct mediation analyses; see Chapter 9 and MacKinnon (2008).

Moderating variable is a blanket term that covers two distinct but related concepts: **effect modifiers** and **interaction effects**. These, along with mediating effects, are often confused. Although the mathematics used to study them can be the same, they are conceptually distinct.

Effect modifier is one of the truly clear terms in quantitative analysis. A variable is an effect modifier if it influences a causal link between two or more variables. For example, say that income can be shown to increase access to health care and that this access increases longevity.[19] Access is then a **mediating** (or intervening) variable, as depicted in the following graphic:

Income → Access to Health Care → Longevity

An *effect modifier* would be a variable that influences this effect. It might be that gender is an effect modifier. That would be the case if the strength of the effect were different for men and women; if, in other words, increases in income increased access to health care at different rates for men and women.[20]

An **interaction effect** is also called a *multiplier* or *joint effect*. A joint effect is distinct from the effects of the variables taken singly and added together. Drug interactions are a clear example. Two drugs that are harmless when taken individually can be dangerous, or more powerful, when taken together. Or exercise and calorie reduction might each have a separate effect on weight loss, but their combined or joint effect could be greater than the sum of their individual effects. Interactions in the social sciences are sometimes less clear, but they are often very important. For example, in the case of the effect of income on longevity through access to health care, age might interact with the other variables. Perhaps access to good health care is more important for infants and senior citizens than it is for adolescents and young adults. Unlike in the drug interaction example, choice or caution is not an option. You can avoid taking two drugs together, but you can't avoid having an age.

It is vitally important to check for interaction by including interaction terms in the regression analysis. Researchers often do this, but it is also easy to make mistakes and misinterpret the results. Empirical analysis of published articles in well-respected journals has shown that "errors are common,"[21] especially in interpreting the main or independent effects of variables that have a significant interaction effect. Once it has been shown that two variables interact and have a joint effect, their independent effects are *not interpretable*. For example, there are no separate effects of two interacting drugs when they are taken together. You can avoid the interaction by not taking them together, but when taken together they no longer have separate effects.

It is obviously crucial to good research using regression to include variables that allow you to investigate (1) causal links or mediating variables, (2) effect modifiers, and (3) interaction effects. A common approach to the mediating variables and to effect

[19]Trends in the association between income and longevity (and between poverty and premature death) in the United States are reviewed in Krieger et al. (2008).

[20]See Figures II.1 and II.2 in the Introduction to Part II.

[21]Brambor, Clark, and Golder (2006). For ease of interpretation, interaction terms should be **centered**, which means setting the means of the scores for the interacting variables to zero; see Jaccard, Turrisi, and Wan (1990).

modifiers is to first calculate the effect of the main IV on the DV.[22] Then add the next variable to see how much the coefficient is altered when the next variable is added. In our example, longevity is the DV and income is the main or target IV. Table 8.4 shows four clusters of variables, or *models*, used to understand the relation between income and longevity.

Model 1 shows the simple basic model with one independent variable, income. Model 2 adds the intervening variable of access to care. To test for mediation, you calculate whether the change in the regression coefficient between Model 1 and Model 2 is statistically significant. Model 3 expands Models 1 and 2 by including gender as an effect modifier. Interaction effects are multiplier effects, so when interactions are entered into the equation in Model 4, you multiply the variable values for age by those for access. If the coefficient for the interaction of *X*2 and *X*4 is significant, it can be interpreted, but then the two variables cannot be analyzed individually. It is also possible that a three-way interaction exists among age, gender, and access. Interactions of three variables are very difficult to interpret. More than three interacting variables are, according to most researchers, virtually impossible to decipher.

How do you know whether gender, age, and access to health care are effect modifiers, mediating/intervening, or interacting variables? Not by statistics alone, but rather by your knowledge of the subject matter. Knowledge of (or beliefs about) the subject matter, including the relations among variables, is what most researchers call *theory*. This is the reason that a review of the literature is so important. Reviewing previous research helps you develop your theory, your understanding of how the world might work, and thus it provides clues about how to structure your regression models. These models are the statistical description of how you think the variables might be related; they are a form of your theory. You use the models to assess or test the theory (see Chapter 10).

TABLE 8.4. Variables in the Equation for Mediating, Moderating, and Interaction Effects

Model 1	Model 2	Model 3	Model 4
*X*1 Income (independent)	*X*1 Income (independent)	*X*1 Income (independent)	*X*1 Income (independent)
	*X*2 Access to care (mediating/intervening)	*X*2 Access to care (mediating/intervening)	*X*2 Access to care (mediating/intervening)
		*X*3 Gender (effect modifier)	*X*3 Gender (effect modifier)
			*X*4 Age (interaction variable)
			*X*4 × *X*2 (interaction of access and age)
			*X*4 × *X*2 × *X*3 (interaction of all three)

Note. Dependent or outcome variable = longevity.

TABLE 8.5. When to Use Different Forms of Coding for Categorical Variables

Type of coding	Uses
Dummy coding	Use to compare the mean of one category with the means of all the other categories.
Effects coding	Use to compare each group's mean to the overall mean.
Contrast coding	Use to make planned comparisons between groups.

Finally, what if your interacting variables, mediating variables, and effect modifiers are categorical, such as gender or ethnicity or religious preference? Categorical variables in regression and other methods can be coded in different ways depending on your purposes. The main options are listed in Table 8.5.

How Big Should Your Sample Be?

Simple formulas and computer routines for determining sample size focus mostly on the issue of *statistical power*. This means determining a sample size big enough to detect relationships. Specifically, power is the ability to reject the null hypothesis (NH) when it is false. Although the formulas are simple and easy to use, there is always a lot of guesswork involved. One has to plug into an equation numbers that are not available until *after* you have done the study. But the whole idea was to help you determine how big your sample had to be before conducting the study. The almost exclusive emphasis on statistical power for determining sample size has been criticized, and persuasive alternatives have been proposed,[23] but these good suggestions have not been widely adopted. The chief among these good suggestions is to focus more on statistical *precision*, which is the degree to which an effect is measured accurately—with small margins of error (see Chapter 7 for a discussion).

The short answer to the question about sample size in regression analysis is: All else equal, the bigger the better. It never hurts statistically to have more cases. Larger samples reduce error and increase power. It may be a waste of your time to collect vastly more cases than needed, but that is an *economic*, not a methodological, problem. If you study human participants, it is a waste of *their* time to collect many more cases than needed. That is an *ethical* problem. But in terms of quantitative analysis, the more cases, the more accurate the estimates and inferences. In regression analysis, the emphasis tends to be more on accurate estimates rather than on hypothesis testing and statistical power.

For ordinary least squares (OLS) regression, which is the most common kind, an often recommended minimum for the number of cases is 50 plus 8 times the number of IVs. Comparatively larger samples are required for the effective use of logit regression (see discussion later in this chapter), in which one rule of thumb is at least 50 cases per IV, but another is at least 100.[24] Thus, for a problem with four independent variables,

[23]Parker and Berman (2003); Kelley and Rausch (2006); Strug, Rohde, and Corey (2007).

[24]Osborne (2008, Ch. 20). Also, the more uneven the number of cases in the categories of the DV, the bigger the sample needed.

OLS regression would require a minimum of 82 cases, but logit regression would require 200 to 400. Remember, these are *minima*. That means they are just barely adequate, not fully acceptable. For more advanced regression-based techniques discussed in Chapter 9, such as multilevel modeling,[25] sample sizes usually need to be even larger. We recommend erring on the side of a sample that is "too" big. It is always sad to see a months-long study spoiled because the researcher was too busy or too frugal to devote a few more days to collecting data.

When to Correct for Missing Data

One of the worst ways your sample can become too small is through missing data. It is a universal problem. Experimental participants drop out, survey respondents fail to answer questions, research assistants lose data sheets, and so on. The most conservative way to handle missing data is to delete cases for which any data are missing. This not only reduces sample size, but it is also likely to bias your results, because the cases and data are seldom likely to be *missing at random*. For example, on a survey some questions may not be answered because they are sensitive, or some respondents may be less likely to answer questions than others. Eliminating those questions and those respondents will bias your results.

As discussed in Chapter 7, it behooves the conscientious researcher to examine patterns in the missing data, to adopt a strategy for dealing with the missing data, and to reveal the results to the reader. Most statistical packages have routines for helping with this work. Old methods, now usually considered too primitive, are eliminating cases with any missing value (casewise deletion) and replacing missing values with the mean for the variable (mean substitution). The two state-of-the-art methods are highly computer intensive but far superior to the traditional methods. Maximum likelihood (ML) is one; the other, and by many accounts the best, is multiple imputation (MI).[26] A somewhat simpler method, using the AMELIA freeware, is based on bootstrapping. See the discussion in Chapter 7.

When to Use Curvilinear (or Polynomial) Regression

The type of regression discussed thus far is **ordinary least squares** (OLS) regression. The *most important* statistical assumption for the correct use of OLS regression is that the relation among the variables is linear. The assumption of **linearity** means that the line that best summarizes the dots on a scatter diagram is a straight line. But what if it isn't? In our example of age as an interacting variable in the relation of income and long life, it was suggested that the effect was more important for infants and for senior citizens. The effect could be strong in the early years and in the later years but weaker in the middle years. The effect was, in other words, nonlinear. See Figure 8.3 for a graphic depiction of another curvilinear relation—between birth rate and per capita income.

---

[25] Maas and Hox (2005).

[26] For a general overview see Tabachnick and Fidell (2001, Ch. 4) or Cohen, Cohen, West, and Aiken (2003, Ch. 11). For more advanced accounts, including comparisons of maximum likelihood (ML) and multiple implementation (MI), see Cole (2008) and Howell (2007).

The most common solution for this particular violation of assumptions, as well as many others, is to *transform the data*. Specifically, if you suspect that the line that best describes the pattern of relations between the IV and the DV is a curved line with one bend, you add a new term to the regression equation; you square the IV and perform **quadratic regression**. If you want to check for a curve with two bends, then you add a variable to the regression equation that is made up of the original values cubed. What you do is transform the IV to make it more amenable to the analysis of your particular data.

We are able to do such manipulations because one can multiply or divide series of scores by a constant without affecting statistics computed on the series of numbers. For example, if we took the data from any of our preceding examples (e.g., education and income), doubled all the scores so that the highest average education level was 24 years and the highest per capita income was $115,000, we would have "transformed" the two sets of numbers. If we then recomputed the correlation r between the two sets, the coefficient would be *exactly* the same. And the regression coefficients b and β (beta) would also be identical. This would also be true if we multiplied each score by 17 or any other number, or if we divided each score by 103 or any other number. We wouldn't do that, of course, because those transformations would simply make for more tedious calculations. However, some transformations greatly expand our opportunities to analyze data well. Squaring the values of a variable or taking their square roots or their logarithms are three of the more common transformations (see the discussion in Chapter 6).

To see how it works, consider an example from data on tuition as a percentage of family income. One specific research question in this example was whether recessions had a lasting effect on the cost of public higher education for students and their families. There is no doubt that since the late 1970s the cost of public higher education increased markedly both for states and, the focus of this study, for students and their families. One theory is that recessions have contributed to this trend. Ground is lost in state funding of higher education during a recession that is never regained when the recession is over; the costs are transferred to students and parents.[27] But there have been fluctuations over time and important differences among the states.

To test for the presence of a recession effect, we can construct linear and curvilinear regression trend lines; the latter are constructed using the values of the variable squared. If a recession had no lasting effect, the linear regression would tell the whole tale. On the other hand, if moving from linear to curvilinear (quadratic) regression increases the variance explained (R^2) substantially, this indicates a potential recession effect. The R^2 difference is an estimate of the recession's ES. The recession of 1991 is amenable to this approach because for that recession we had a sufficiently long time series. The 17 years from 1983 through 1999 form a series running from 8 years before through the 8 years after the 1991 recession.

To illustrate, we use the data from New Hampshire (Figure 8.5). The figures on the vertical axis are the percentages of median income that a family would have to spend to cover average public tuition in each of the years studied. In the 1980s the tuition cost of public higher education as a percentage of family income was steady at 10–12% and was even trending downward. Following 1991, which is marked by the vertical reference

[27] Vogt and Hines (2007).

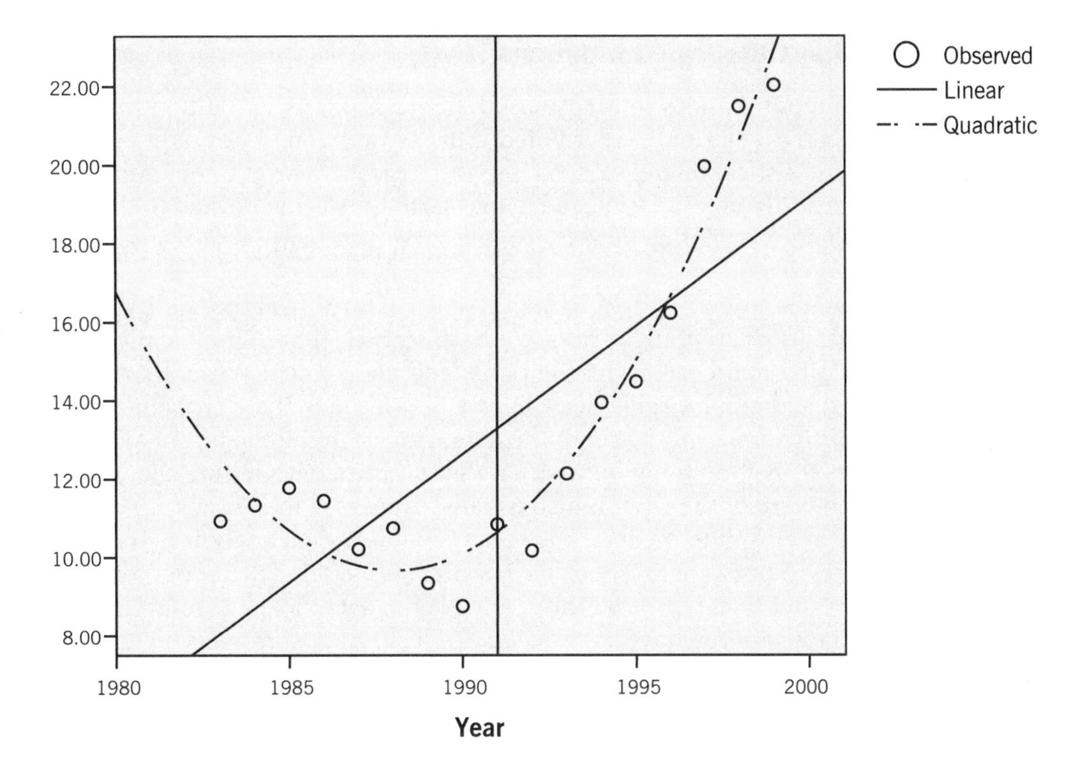

FIGURE 8.5. The cost, over time, of tuition in public higher education as a percentage of the median family income: New Hampshire, 1983–1999.

line, costs increased and did so quite steadily through the end of the period in 1999. The R^2 for linear regression is .62. For the curvilinear, quadratic regression it is .95, an increase of 33% of the explained variance. The curved regression line fits the data very well; the straight line fits less well. Of course, this does not prove that the recession hypothesis is accurate for New Hampshire. Nor would the lack of a bend in the data for other states prove that recession had no effect on the cost of public higher education there. But the data are very consistent with those conclusions. And they nicely illustrate why, when you are conducting a regression analysis, you should check for nonlinear relations and analyze them when you find them. Some research questions are better answered using nonlinear analyses.

Finally, after calculating the R^2 change, the scatterplots and trend lines must be examined visually to see whether the curve began in or after 1991 and whether the change was in the predicted direction. Again, although the presence of a substantial bend in the trend line in 1991 does not prove that the recession *caused* the change, if the recession *did* cause the change, the R^2 difference estimates its size. R^2 change, from linear to curvilinear, is an easily understood and well-established[28] indicator of the size of the possible effect.

[28]Berk (2004); Pedhazur (1997); Cohen et al. (2003).

When to Use Other Data Transformations

The other big assumption besides linearity in OLS regression, as in many other techniques, is that the data are normally distributed. This assumption of normality is especially important for statistical inference, which most researchers want to do, even when it is inappropriate (see Chapter 7). Data can be non-normal by being skewed to the right or left, by being pointier or flatter than a normal curve (kurtosis), or because of the presence of outliers.

It is unconscionable to omit checking for these departures from normality and to fail to report the results of so doing. There are both statistical and graphical ways to investigate and describe non-normal distributions, and good practice usually requires using both statistical and graphic tools (see Chapter 7). Although there are some doubters, most statisticians recommend "fixing" the data, transforming them to make them approximately normal, before doing an analysis. This can involve taking the log, the square root, or the inverse of the data. It also usually requires eliminating outliers. The details are available in most intermediate and some beginning data analysis texts. Here, it is important mostly to insist that responsible researchers examine their data for violations of assumptions and then report on the results. If the data violate assumptions, do something—or explain why you have not done so.[29] The burden of proof is on you. The basics about when to transform which variables are sketched in Table 8.6.[30]

When to Use Analysis of Covariance

Analysis of covariance (ANCOVA) is an extension of ANOVA. It is a hybrid of ANOVA and regression. The regression part of the hybrid is used to partial out (a.k.a. control

TABLE 8.6. When to Transform What in Multiple Regression

Analytical problem	What to transform
When the relation between the dependent and independent variable is curvilinear	Transform the *independent* variable by squaring it for one curve, cubing it for two.
When using standardized regression coefficients, betas	Transform *both* the dependent and independent variables into *z*-scores.
When using logistic regression for categorical dependent variables	Transform the *dependent* variable by taking its natural log.
When correcting for skewness, kurtosis, or other departures from normality	Transform *any* variable, dependent or independent, by taking square roots, logs, etc. (see Chapter 7).

Note. Often (not always) these transformations will be done automatically by your software package, but it can be useful to know what is going on behind the screen.

[29] Osborne (2008, Ch. 13); Osborne and Overbay (2008); Tabachnick and Fidel (2001).

[30] Several statistical tests can be used to help determine whether assumptions have been violated: Shapiro–Wilk tests the hypothesis that the sample data have been drawn from a population with a normal distribution; Kolmogorov–Smirnov can be used for the same purpose.

for) the effects of control variables or covariates. In experiments, a common use of ANCOVA is to control for a covariate such as a pretest measure. All ANCOVA problems can be handled with regression analysis, and computer programs make it very easy to do this. Consequently, the use of ANCOVA has declined in recent decades. In our view, which is not without controversy, ANCOVA adds nothing to regression. ANCOVA is less flexible than regression, and it is suitable for a narrower range of problems. Its decline seems probable.

WHAT TO DO WHEN YOUR DEPENDENT VARIABLES ARE CATEGORICAL

Despite the versatility of OLS regression analysis, there are circumstances in which it is not applicable. OLS regression is appropriate when the DV is continuous (interval or ratio level of measurement). OLS's versatility comes from the fact that the IVs can take any form, from categorical through rank[31] to continuous. When the *dependent* variable is categorical, however, the OLS model needs to be extended, and other forms must be used. And many DVs are in fact categorical: survive or perish, graduate or not, pass or fail, innocent or guilty verdicts, bankruptcy or not, eligible or not.[32]

When the DV is measured with a set of *ordered* categories, or ranks, the researcher has a choice. Judgment is required. OLS regression may be the better choice when it can be assumed that the gaps between the ranks in the ordinal scale are "fairly" even. That would mean that the ordinal scale is close to an interval scale. For example, suppose the DV were measured by answers scored as follows: 7 = *totally agree*, 6 = *agree strongly*, 5 = *agree*, 4 = *don't know*, 3 = *disagree*, 2 = *disagree strongly*, 1 = *totally disagree*. Should we treat this scale as categorical or continuous? Is it an ordinal or an interval scale? It is probably somewhere in between, not merely ordinal, but not quite interval either. When is it "reasonable" to assume that the gap between, say, *strongly agree* and *agree* (from 5 to 6) is roughly the same size as that between *don't know* and *disagree* (from 2 to 3)? The answer is not directly statistical (which is why we have put "fairly" and "reasonable" in quotation marks). The answer depends more on the researcher's knowledge of the topic and the context in which the question is being asked. The simplicity of OLS regression and the comparative ease with which its results can be communicated would make us reluctant to give it up in a context in which it could be appropriate.[33] Also, treating the DV quantitatively rather than categorically increases statistical power, and with increased power you can more easily detect relations among variables. But when the DV is definitely categorical, the choice of methods is more constrained.

Most of the methods for categorical DVs involve expanding or generalizing the linear model of ordinary regression. These expansions are called **generalized linear models (GLMs)**. The *general* linear model is made more broadly applicable (*generalized*) by using what is called a **link** that can be thought of as tying the OLS regression model to

---

[31]Rank order IVs require special treatment. One common but not fully satisfactory method is to treat them as categorical and use dummy coding. See Fox (2008, Ch. 7).

[32]Of course, when one's data are categorical or qualitative, one can use qualitative methods of data analysis, such as qualitative comparative analysis (see Chapter 13).

[33]One of our anonymous reviewers made the excellent suggestion to run the data both ways; if there is no substantial difference in the findings, report them using OLS for ease of interpretation.

a different kind of problem. Common links are **logs, logits** (logistic probability units or logs of odds), and **probits** (probability units). Table 8.7 lists all of the options for analyzing categorical DVs discussed in this chapter.

Bivariate correlations, including the Pearson *r* and its derivatives, can be used on categorical or continuous data. OLS regression can also use categorical or continuous data for the IV, but the DV must be continuous. When all variables are categorical, either chi-squared-based measures of association or log-linear methods (a.k.a. Poisson regression) can be used. The chi-squared method is the oldest, simplest, and most familiar. Unfortunately, it is also the weakest. It is not an associational method, strictly speaking. It is, rather, a statistical test. However, as discussed earlier, some associational measures, such as the phi coefficient and Cramér's *V*, are based directly on it. Log-linear methods are a sharp advance on the chi-squared techniques because they can describe associations and interactions among categorical variables, something that goes well beyond the abilities of the chi-squared test. They are not as widely used as they might be, in part perhaps because applied researchers may have some trouble understanding them and in part because logit (also called logistic) regression can replace them for many problems.

You can improve greatly on simple contingency table methods of categorical data analysis by using regression analysis if you can treat one of the variables as dependent, and it is fairly rare not to be able to do so. Regression analysis enables you to examine both (1) the **total effects** of a large number of IVs on a DV and (2) the **conditional effects,** which are the effects of any one of the variables, while controlling for the effects of the

TABLE 8.7. Measures of Association for Categorical Variables and When to Use Them

Analysis technique	Independent variables	Dependent variables
Pearson *r* and other correlations (see Table 7.1)	Either	Either
OLS regression	Either	Continuous
Eta-squared (η^2)	Categorical	Continuous
Odds ratio and relative risk ratio (see Chapter 7)	Categorical	Categorical
Chi-squared-based measures (see Table 8.2)	Categorical	Categorical
PRE measures (see Table 8.3)	Categorical	Categorical
Log-linear analysis (Poisson regression)	Categorical	Categorical
Logit regression	Either	Categorical
Probit regression	Either	Categorical
Tobit regression (censored regression)	Either	Zero or any positive number
Discriminant analysis	Continuous	Categorical
Kaplan–Meier analysis	Categorical	Time until a categorical event
Cox proportional hazards analysis	Either	Time until a categorical event

Note. "Categorical" in this table refers to both nominal and ordinal variables.

others. However, we stress that the basic form of linear regression—OLS regression—is not appropriate when one is studying a categorical DV. OLS regression is built upon assumptions about the distribution of the DV that simply cannot be true when it has two categorical values, such as *survive*: *yes–no*. OLS regression works with means and statistics derived from the mean, such as variances. But you cannot compute a mean for a categorical variable, such as gender, ethnicity, or survival. There are three main ways to handle research questions with a categorical DV and several IVs: logit regression, probit regression, and discriminant analysis. We review each of these and discuss when it is possible and preferable to use each. Most attention will be paid to logit regression, because it is the most versatile and most widely used.

When to Use Logit (or Logistic) Regression

The answer is: when you have a categorical DV and one or more IVs. The IVs may be categorical, continuous, or a mix of the two. Logit regression transforms the DV, which has been coded 1 for *yes* and 0 for *no*: for example, 1 = *yes, survived;* 0 = *no, died.* The variable is treated as an *odds*, the odds of *yes*. The *log of the odds* of *yes* is used for the transformation. We have already seen a transformation of an IV in the earlier discussion of curvilinear regression. There we squared the *independent* variable to produce a curve that better fit the data describing change in the cost of higher education following a recession. The DV was left unchanged. In logit regression, the *dependent* variable is transformed, and the IVs are left unchanged (see Table 8.6). A different transformation is used, the logit transformation, which takes the natural log of the odds (logit). This results in an *S*-shaped curve.

The kinds of variables for which logit transformations are appropriate are quite common. Examples of categorical DVs include graduate or not, get married or not, visit an emergency room or not, be a victim of a crime or not, or retire or not. When you have a DV such as one of these, logit regression is the preferred method. All the tools of regression remain at your disposal. You need only adjust the way the DV is measured. In OLS regression the idea is to find the straight line that most closely approximates the actual data. When the DV is categorical, a straight line will not fit the data (except in the rare cases in which there are only two data points or in which all cases fall into the same category).

An example helps clarify. Figure 8.6 describes a sample of 100 employees of a large company. The DV is whether members of this sample retired or not in a given year. The IV is the length of time they had worked for the company as of December 31st the previous year. To produce the figure, you put the number of months worked on the horizontal or *X*-axis and "Retirement, yes or no" on the vertical or *Y*-axis.

A straight line could not capture these data well. But a curved, *S*-shaped line can do better. Two kinds of *S*-shaped lines have been most frequently used for this purpose: the logit and the probit. The two provide roughly equivalent curves, although they are derived in mathematically different ways. For regressions with dummy DVs, the logit and probit approaches almost always give highly similar results.[34] We illustrate with the probit curve, as most people find it easier to understand. *Probit* is short for "probability unit." You transform the probabilities of the DV—in this case, the probability

[34]Agresti (1996).

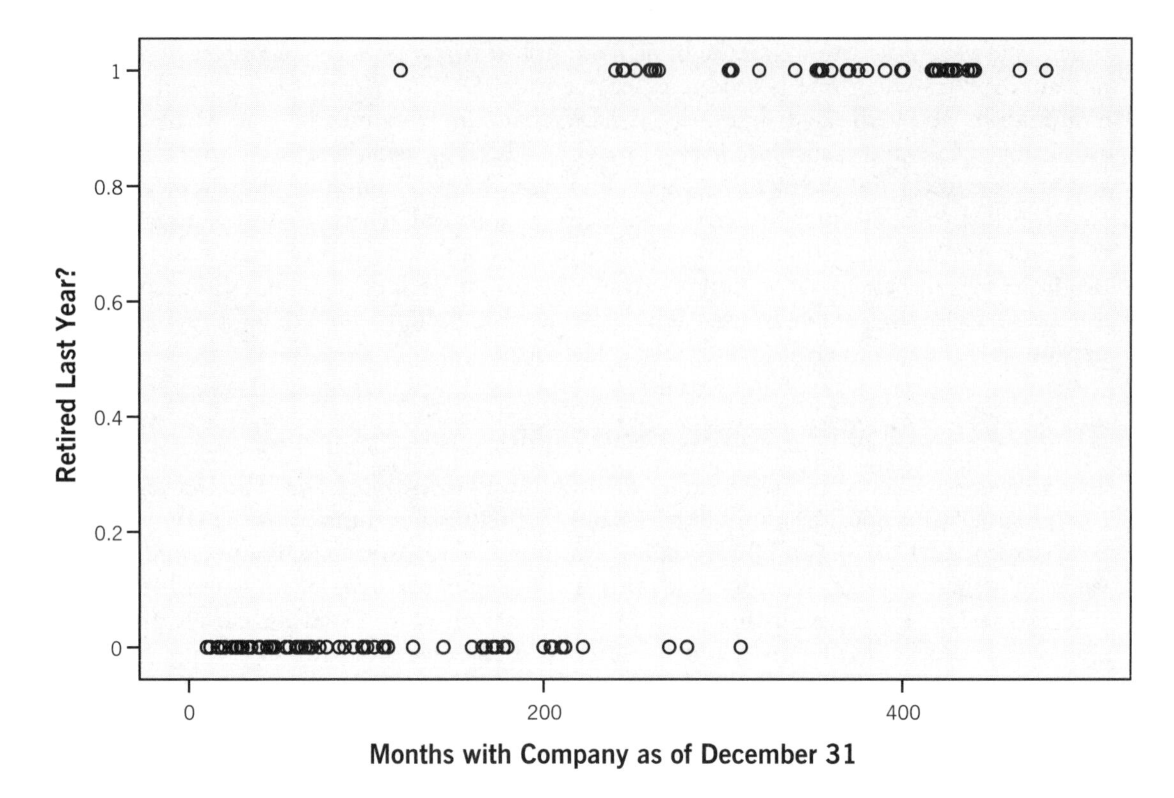

FIGURE 8.6. Retirements and time with company.

of retiring—into *z*-scores.[35] The ***cumulative standard normal distribution*** (CSND) is used to do this. If you remember the normal distribution and its relation to percentile scores, the concept is easy to understand. A score that is 2 *SD*s below the mean ($z = -2.0$) would fall in the 2nd percentile and would have a cumulative frequency or probability of 2%. A score 2 *SD*s above the mean ($z = +2.0$) would be in the 98th percentile and have a cumulative probability of 98%, and so on. The cumulative standard normal distribution looks like the left-hand side of a normal curve (see Figure 8.7), and it also resembles the logit curve.

In logistic regression, by contrast, you use the *odds* of retiring, not the *probabilities*, but the need for a curve, rather than a straight line, is the same. The reason such research problems require an *S*-shaped curve is that an increase in the IV at the extremes of the distribution tends to have much less impact than does an increase in the middle. In our example, the odds of retiring for an employee with 10 months' service in a company are very low, and the odds of retiring are not much higher for an employee with 15 months' or 20 or 30 months' service. Indeed, in this sample, until we got to 120 months (10 years), no one retired. The odds of retirement start to climb around 200 months (15 to 20 years). Then the odds go up fairly sharply. Someone with 25 years' (300 months') service is quite likely to retire. After 25 years of service, the odds are high and remain

[35] You do not actually have to calculate the transformations yourself. When you specify probit regression in your software, the transformations are done automatically.

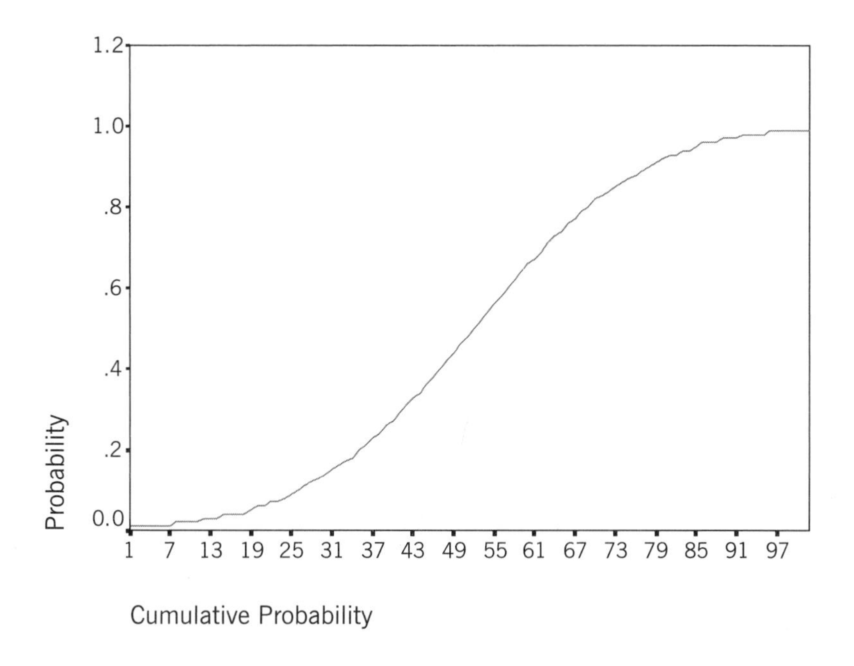

FIGURE 8.7. Cumulative standard normal distribution.

high. The odds of retiring with, say, 35 years are very high. They aren't much lower with 34 years or 33. It is in the middle that we would find that comparatively small increases in the IV are likely to have a big effect on the odds of retiring, roughly in the range of 15–25 years. That's what the curve reflects: slow increase until some threshold, probably around 15 years in this example, then more rapid increase to around 25 years, when the curve flattens out again. A straight line does not fit the distribution, but an *S*-shaped curve does.

How well does the curve fit the data? If the fit to the curve is not good, then little is gained by using it. Does it fit in this case, and how well does it fit? This is where **goodness-of-fit tests** enter the picture. These tests are usually reported as part of the output of a logit regression. There are several of them. What is being tested is a model. The model, in this case the logit curve, is a representation of the data. How good a representation is it? Two frequently used tests for model fit are the Pearson chi-squared (χ^2) test and the log-likelihood-ratio chi-squared test, G^2. When you test for model fit, what you are testing is just the *opposite of the NH*. With the NH you are looking for a significant *difference* between the statistic and the hypothesis. With goodness-of-fit model tests you are hoping that there is *no significant difference* between the model and the data. In significance testing, you want the test statistic to be big and the *p*-value to be small. In model fitting, you want the test statistic to be small and the *p*-value to be big. For the retirement data, we used a goodness-of-fit test called the Hosmer–Lemeshow test. The chi-squared statistic for it is 1.75 (small), and the *p*-value is .998 (large), just as we would expect if the fit were good[36] (see Table 8.8).

[36]We offer only a few specific suggestions about methods of model testing here. It is pursued further in Chapter 10.

TABLE 8.8. Dependent Variable = Odds of Retirement, 1 = Yes; 0 = No

							95.0% CI for Exp(*B*)	
		B	*SE*	Wald	Sig.	Exp(*B*)	Lower	Upper
Step 1(a)	Yrs With	.383	.091	17.689	<.001	1.467	1.227	1.754
	Constant	–7.692	1.860	17.096	<.001	.000		

Note. –2 log likelihood = 33.52, $p < .001$; Hosmer–Lemeshow test: chi-squared = 1.75, $p = .998$.

Once we have a logistic curve that fits the distribution, the interpretation of a logit regression works the same way that it does in OLS regression. You use it to address the same kinds of questions. The main question is, What is the effect on the DV of a 1-unit increase in an IV while controlling for the other IVs? The only difference is that in logit regression the DV is expressed in different units. The DV in a logit regression is the log of the odds, or *logit*. This is arrived at by dividing the probability of *Yes* by the probability of *No* to get the odds.[37] Then one takes the natural log (ln) of the resulting odds. This transformed odds is sometimes symbolized by the letter *L*. The IVs all stay in their original units (years, dollars, GPA, etc.), as they do in ordinary regression. So in ordinary regression we might ask, What is the expected change in *Y* for a 1-unit increase in *X*? In logit regression, the equivalent question would be, What is the expected change in *L* (the log of the odds or logit) for a 1-unit change in *X*?

The statistical significance of each coefficient is not, as in OLS, computed with the *t*-test. Rather, the *Wald test* is used (to test the NH that the odds ratio = 1.0), but the *p*-value derived with the Wald test is read the same way as any other *p*-value. The whole model, which is the effect of all the independent variables taken together on the dependent variable, is not tested with the *F*-test as in OLS regression. Rather, it is assessed with the log-likelihood test. You will often see this reported at the bottom of the regression table (conventions vary); in this case as: –2 log likelihood. For the retirement data, the statistic is 33.52, which yields a *p*-value of <.001.

How strong is the relation of time with the company to odds of retirement? The output is given in Table 8.8. We've converted the monthly data to annual data (dividing months by 12). The figure for *B* of .383 shows that the log of the odds of *X* being 1 (retirement, yes) go up .383 for every 1-year increase in service to the company. The Wald statistic is used to arrive at the *p*-value (called "Sig." in the table) of <.001.

The only problem with this output is that in its original, logarithm-based form, the unstandardized regression coefficient *B* defies interpretation. To get something that can be more easily interpreted, go to the column, headed "Exp(*B*)," which is short for the "exponent of the regression coefficient *B*." In logit regression, the Exp(*B*) is an *odds ratio*. The Exp(*B*) of 1.467 means that for every 1-year increase in years with the company the odds of retirement increase by 46.7% (1.467 – 1.000 = .467). The 95% CI of 1.227, 1.754, means that the plausible range of values for the effect of a 1-year increase in time with the company is an increase in the odds of retiring that ranges from 22.7% to 75.4%.

[37]More commonly this is described by saying you take the probability of *Yes*, or "success," symbolized *P*, and divide it by 1 – *P* ("failure") to get the odds. The formula for the logit would then be: $L = \ln[P/1 - P]$.

In logit regression, as in all odds-based statistics, *1.0 means that there is no effect of the IVs on the DV.* By contrast, in OLS regression, a coefficient indicating no effect would be 0. This "oddity" arises from the fact that we are dealing with odds. If the odds of the dependent variable being *Yes* (retiring) are unaffected by the independent variable, the odds will be 1 to 1 or 50–50—or, expressed as a single number, 1.0. The Exp(*B*), or odds ratio, approach is the clearest way to present the results of a logistic regression, but it is not always provided in research reports. Sometimes only the unstandardized regression coefficient *b*, not the exponent of the coefficient *b*, is reported. All one needs to do to move to the more interpretable Exp(*B*) is enter the value for *b* (or *B*; capitalization practices differ) into a calculator and push the button labeled e^x. Try it with your calculator. Enter .383, push the e^x button, and you get 1.46667. Or enter 1.46667 and push the ln (for log, natural) button and you get .383.

Finally, note that if the relation between the IV and the DVs were inverse, if an increase in the independent resulted in a decrease in the dependent, then the Exp(*B*) would be less than 1.0 (but more than 0, because odds can't be negative). For instance, an Exp(*B*) of .75 would mean that a 1-unit increase in the IV would lead to a 25% (1.0 – .75 = .25) drop in the odds of the DV being *Yes*, 1. The unstandardized *b* coefficient would in such a case be negative. For .75, it would be –.2877.

What about a coefficient of determination, the equivalent of R^2 in OLS regression? The R^2 statistic estimates the percentage of variance in the DV explained by all the IVs taken together. It can be thought of as a goodness-of-fit statistic, or an ES statistic, and it is often one of the first things a reader looks at when examining the results of an OLS regression. There is no exact equivalent in logit regression. There are approximations, often referred to as pseudo-*R*-squared, but there is not much consensus about which of them is preferable—or whether any one of them is useful enough to be reported. The differences between them can be substantial. SPSS reported two versions of the R^2 statistic for our retirement example: "Cox and Snell R Square," which in our example was .639. Also reported in SPSS is the "Nagelkerke R Square," which is always larger. For the retirement data it was .861. The uncertainty about whether or which coefficient of determination to use leads some researchers to use none. More frequently, they are reported, but not emphasized. They are not crucial interpretive tools as is the R^2 in OLS regression.[38]

More useful than the pseudo-R^2 for assessing the overall quality of the model are: (1) percentage of cases the model has categorized correctly, especially with probit regression, and (2) the degree of model fit of different models. You should always report these. What percentage of cases was successfully predicted by the model? Of the 100 cases, 42 retired and 58 did not. The model successfully "predicted" all but 5 of these, for a total of 95%. That is very impressive, but this figure must be qualified by what you could have predicted by chance alone; for example, flipping a coin would have, on average, successfully predicted 50% of the cases. And there is more than one way to define chance in this situation, because the chance analyst does not start out with 50–50, but rather with 42 and 58, which are the actual numbers of retirees and nonretirees. Nonetheless, a 95% prediction rate is quite solid. For the company's personnel department planning for future retirements, this rate would be reassuring.

[38]The search for an equivalent to the R^2 for logistic regression goes on, still without much resolution. See DeMaris (2002) and Tjur (2009).

Comparing models in terms of fit statistics is another useful method for assessing their quality. The basic –2 log-likelihood (–2LL) chi-squared fit statistic compares the constant, which is the model without IVs, with the model with IVs. Say that in comparing two models the –2LL statistic goes down from 41 to 32. This is an improvement in fit of 9.0, and that is the number that is tested with the ordinary chi-squared statistic. To see whether one model is better than another, you can compare them in terms of goodness of fit. You might want to compare the basic model with one IV (years of service with the company) with another model that adds, say, job category—managerial and clerical—to see whether that improves the model fit. If adding that variable reduced the statistic to –2LL = 27, a reduction of another 5.0, and if that were a statistically significant difference, then you could say that the model that included job category improved the fit and was the better model. In sum, there are two strategies for comparing models: comparing percentage of cases correctly predicted and comparing the –2LL statistics.

Even though logit regression can be classified as a nonparametric method, statistical assumptions are not totally irrelevant. One need not worry about the normality of distributions and constancy of variances, because logit regression (like probit regression) is a distribution-free method. But other cautions apply. Outliers can be as much of a problem in logit as in OLS regression. And, as always, the analysis is only as good as the quality of the measurement, so all the checks of measurement reliability and validity have to be done with logit regression, as with any other method of analysis. Even measuring a categorical DV can raise measurement issues. "Survive or die" is a clear outcome,[39] but outcome variables categorized as "eligible" or "ineligible" or "meets standards" versus "fails to meet standards" can require complicated coding and measurement decisions. In general, the more crudely categorized the outcome variable, the greater the loss of statistical power, or the ability to detect effects.[40] Types of logit regression are available for cases in which the DV is ordinal or has more than two unordered categories; these are called ordered LR and multinomial LR, respectively.

When to Use Survival Analysis

When the DV is "time until a categorical outcome occurs," extensions of logit regression techniques are needed. The general class to which such methods belong is called **survival analysis,** because it was developed for studying how long patients receiving (or not receiving) a treatment would survive. The same class of procedures in sociology is called **event history analysis**. Probably the most commonly used of these methods is **Cox proportional hazards analysis**. This allows researchers to describe and estimate how long cases (usually people) will remain in a particular state (e.g., employed in an organization) before they change to a different state (not employed there). The DV is categorical; the IVs may be categorical or continuous. A variant is **Kaplan–Meier analysis;** it measures the proportion of survivors in the first state (employed) who have not passed to the second (not employed). Both methods usually present results graphically, with time

[39]Even this is not perfectly clear, because hospitals differ considerably in the extent to which they adhere to the stringent guidelines of the American Academy of Neurologists before declaring a patient "brain dead"; Greer, Varelas, Haque, and Wijdicks (2008).

[40]Taylor et al. (2006).

to event (death, unemployment, graduation, etc.) on the horizontal axis and percentage surviving on the vertical axis.

When to Use Probit Regression

Like logit regression, probit regression is used when the DV is categorical. Although based on a different mathematical model, it is closely parallel in its applications to logit regression. It deals with the problem of a dichotomous DV by fitting an *S*-shaped curve to the data, not a straight line, as in OLS regression. As discussed, the curve used by probit regression is based on the CSND (see Figure 8.7).

The questions addressed with probit regression are the questions addressed in any regression analysis. The answers to those questions are in probability units (probits) rather than in odds (as with logit regression) or in natural units (as in OLS regression). Those questions, in probit regression language, are: (1) What is the change in the *probability* of the DV being 1 (e.g., *yes, survive*) for a 1-unit change in an IV while controlling for the effects of the other IVs? (2) What is the cumulative effect of all the IVs together on the *probability* of the DV variable equaling 1 (*yes*)? Replace the italicized word *probability* in the two questions with the word *odds*, and you have the equivalent questions for logit regression.

Compared with logit regression, probit regression has a few disadvantages, and these have led to a decline in its use as compared with logit regression. In most circumstances, the two methods will give similar results. One circumstance in which that is not true is when the categorical DV has more than two categories, especially when those categories cannot be ranked in any way. For ranked DVs, logit regression is superior to probit,[41] and logit regression has no comparable disadvantages.

When to Use Tobit Regression

Tobit regression is used when your dependent variable is in one of two categories: zero or any positive number.[42] For example, the amount of money individuals spend on buying a car in any given year will either be 0 or it will range from hundreds to thousands of dollars. Tobit regression is a type of **censored regression**, which is used for data in which some values for the *DV* are unknown, but the values of the IVs are available. This is similar to **truncated regression** in cases in which observations with values in the outcome variable below or above certain thresholds are unavailable or unknown for *both* the DV and the IV.

When to Use Discriminant Analysis

Our answer to the question of when to use discriminant analysis is: not very often. But, because discriminant analysis was the earliest and was long the favored means of treating problems with a categorical DV, we discuss it in a bit more detail than it might otherwise merit. It is still popular with researchers who went to graduate school a long

---

[41] Borooah (2002).

[42] Tobit regression is named after its founder, James Tobin; *tobit* is meant to be parallel to logit and probit. For an example applying tobit regression, see Wang, Selman, Dishion, and Stormshak (2010).

time ago and, perhaps, with some of their students. Discriminant analysis is used for problems with a categorical DV, such as college graduation (*yes* or *no*). The IVs *must be continuous*, such as parents' income, parents' education, high school grades, and SAT scores. This, of course, is a limitation as compared with logit regression.

Discriminant analysis (DA) helps researchers identify the boundaries between (to discriminate between) cases, such as students who are and who are not likely to graduate. Rather than finding the best *line* that summarizes the relation between continuous variables, as in OLS regression, one uses DA to find the best *cutoff score*. In OLS regression analysis, the question is, How much better can I predict your score on a continuous DV if I know your scores on several IVs? By contrast in DA, the question is, How much better can I predict your group (graduate–nongraduate) if I know your scores on several IVs? In regression you find the equation that minimizes the errors in prediction of scores. In DA you find the equation that minimizes errors of classification—or, in other terms, the equation that minimizes errors in the prediction of group membership.

The idea of discriminant analysis is to classify or categorize cases using data about continuous IVs. If the DV is college graduation and the average graduation rate is 50%, in the absence of any other information, your best guess for any individual case would be 50%. How much better could you predict the classification of cases if you had information about several continuous IVs? DA produces a weighted combination of IVs in an equation. This equation, which is equivalent to a regression equation, is called the **discriminant function**. The equation (function) is used to determine whether the particular cases meet a cutoff score for making it into one group or another. Each case gets a score by having the equation applied to its data. The value computed with the equation is usually symbolized L. This is parallel to the Y in an OLS regression equation. The L statistic either is or is not above the cutoff score, and that determines the classification of the case. Some researchers continue to prefer DA when the goal of the research is determining cutoff scores, as it might be in classification problems.

Two disadvantages of DA have led to its being replaced by the probit and logit regression methods. First, it only works with continuous IVs, whereas probit and logistic regression can handle any combination of IVs, categorical or continuous. Second, and equally serious, DA requires that important assumptions be true of the IVs in the population (e.g., normality and equality of variances). These assumptions can be hard to meet and, worse yet, it can be hard to know whether they have been met. These assumptions and limitations do not apply to probit and logit regression analysis. When the assumptions are met and when the IVs are continuous, then DA will usually produce results closely parallel to those of logit and probit regression, but the range of problems it can deal with is narrower.

When to Use Log-Linear Methods (Poisson Regression)

Log-linear methods are an important analytical advance over chi-squared methods for dealing with a set of categorical variables. Log-linear methods make it possible for researchers to deal with contingency table chi-squared-type problems, but with the statistical power of regression analysis. These advantages over the chi-squared approach are substantial, but log-linear methods are not as widely used as one might suspect. Part of the reason is that much (not all) of what they can do can also be accomplished by the related and somewhat simpler method of logit regression.

Chi-squared tests and related correlations, such as phi, are calculated using actual frequencies/counts or percentages/proportions in the cells. Log-linear methods are able to do more by taking the logarithms of these values. The greater precision and more powerful statistical tests are achieved through transforming the odds and odds ratios by taking their natural logs. This transformation can be used to turn categorical data into linear data. Hence, the name *log-linear methods*. Finally, and another advance over chi-squared methods, log-linear methods allow the study of interactions among variables when all the variables are categorical. Two- and three-way ANOVA can do this, too, but only when the DV is continuous.

The output of a log-linear analysis looks more like a correlation matrix than a regression output. Log-linear methods deal with associations between pairs of variables, but—and this is a big advantage—they can do so while controlling for the effects of other variables. As with correlations, log-linear methods are used when there is no clear IV and DV, which in essence means that all variables are treated as dependent on all the other variables. Log-linear methods are more powerful techniques than simple frequency tables or tables of odds. Still, even when you transform odds by taking their logs, you ultimately cannot avoid some of the problems encountered with any contingency tables or correlation matrices. Chiefly, the number of cells multiplies rapidly as you add variables and can soon reach unmanageable levels.

Log-linear methods are designed to study patterns of association among sets of categorical variables, especially when there is no sharp distinction between IVs and DVs. The variables are related, but there is no clear causal sequence. One well-known example analyzed the use of cigarettes, alcohol, and marijuana by high school students.[43] These three are probably related, but it is by no means clear that one or more of them is the predictor (independent) variable and another is the outcome (dependent) variable. Log-linear methods are good for this kind of exploration. And if you wanted to relate other variables to this set of three, such as gender, ethnicity, and class level, you could use log-linear methods to do so. This is their strength. If there is a clear DV, logit regression is simpler to use. One reason that logit regression is more popular is that in most research studies there is a DV. It is pretty rare for a researcher to gather data on several variables but have no theory, or even a hunch, about how they might be related. It is more typical to investigate an outcome variable in terms of how other variables are related to it.

SUMMARY: WHICH ASSOCIATIONAL METHODS WORK BEST FOR WHAT SORTS OF DATA AND PROBLEMS?

When you want to analyze the association between two continuous variables, the Pearson r correlation is a powerful tool, at least when the association is linear. It is especially appropriate when the two variables are not hypothesized to be in a causal relation, that is, when there is no DV or IV. The Pearson correlation has analogues for categorical data, and these are equally good measures of association for problems with two

[43] Agresti (1996).

variables. Noteworthy about the Pearson r is that it is a standardized measure. This is an advantage in that it allows comparability across studies. A disadvantage is that standardization disconnects the analysis from the original units of measurement. Correlation coefficients are tested for statistical significance using the t-test.

If you want to study the statistical association between one continuous dependent (or outcome) variable and one or more independent (or predictor) variables, then regression analysis is the method of choice. For OLS regression, the DV must be continuous, but the IVs may be categorical or continuous or both. OLS regression is the foundation on which other, more specialized, forms of regression have been built. Regression coefficients may be either standardized or in the original metric, and it is usually a good idea to report them both ways. Individual regression coefficients are tested for significance with the t-test. In a multiple regression the entire model (the relation of the set of IVs to the DV) is tested with ANOVA, or the F-test.

When the DV in a regression problem is categorical, OLS regression is no longer appropriate. Then you need to use one of the three other regression methods: logit regression, probit regression, or DA. The overall form and function of regression analysis is the same whether it is OLS regression or logistic regression or probit regression. Although the measurement units used to report the effects of the predictors on the outcome variables vary—logits, probits, or natural units—the basic form of the questions asked, and of the answers provided, by regression analysis remains the same.

Our advice is to make logit regression your first choice for problems with a categorical DV. Probit regression and DA will often give similar results, but each is less versatile than logit in some circumstances. DA is the weakest of the three because it requires the full range of statistical assumptions about the normality of distributions and constant variances. These assumptions are often not met and, more important, they are unnecessary for the kinds of problems we are discussing. Also, unlike logit and probit regression, DA does not function well with categorical IVs. Finally, logit and probit regression are superior to DA when the numbers of cases in the categories of the categorical DV are very uneven. For these reasons, which add up to an overall lack of versatility, DA is used less often than it once was. Apart from a sentimental attachment to the old ways, there doesn't seem much point in using it.[44]

Probit regression does not share these weaknesses about assumptions and difficulty handling categorical IVs (and it was long Paul Vogt's favorite, probably because he learned it first), but it too is used less frequently than it once was. Part of the reason is that it cannot handle outcome variables with multiple categories as well as logit regression.

The same general rule of thumb, that logit regression is preferable to others, holds for a comparison with log-linear methods, too—if they take the form we are discussing: one categorical DV and two or more IVs. Log-linear methods are used when all the variables are categorical and when there is no clear DV. If there is a single DV, log-linear methods can be used, but they are, in our view, less simple and add nothing to what can be accomplished with logit regression. On the other hand, when you want to explore the patterns of associations among categorical variables in a contingency table, only log-linear methods enable you to do this effectively.

[44]To qualify, we should add that, although the growth of logit regression has been strong, distinguished scholars still use DA.

THE *MOST* IMPORTANT QUESTION: WHEN TO INCLUDE WHICH VARIABLES

Saving the most important question for last is a time-honored tradition. *Which variables should be included?* is the most important question. Even if researchers code the variables well, select the kind of regression appropriate for the kind of coding, and make sure that the data do not violate assumptions such as linearity and normality, it is still possible to do worthless research using regression. The key to good research is including all relevant variables and excluding irrelevant ones. Excluding relevant or including irrelevant variables is called a **specification error**. Avoiding this error and correctly specifying your model starts early in a project. A good model is obviously importantly shaped by your research question and the theory on which it was built, as well as by your research design, your units of analysis, and how you sample them. In this section we consider model specification at the analysis stage. Model building and the assessment of entire models are pursued further in Chapter 10.

No amount of correct statistical procedure will make up for specification errors. But statistical procedures can be useful for *finding* them and suggesting how they might be corrected. That is our main focus in this section, although, in the process of reviewing analytical techniques, we necessarily review some design, sampling, and measurement issues. The two broad types of specification error are ***left-out variable error***, or **LOVE**, and ***redundant added variable error***, or **RAVE**. Each can be serious. The former is more serious because it is harder to diagnose and correct.

If the R^2 for a regression equation is low, that means that the model the equation expresses does not explain a lot. A likely reason is that the equation does not include one or more important predictor variables. Or, in other terms, when the residual of unexplained variance is high, the reason probably is that explanatory variables have been left out. Sometimes analysts try to engage in "residualism," in which the unexplained is held to be caused by an unmeasured variable. After including $X1$, $X2$, and $X3$ in the equation, any unexplained residual "must be" due to $X4$. $X4$ is hard to measure, the argument goes, and it is omitted from the equation, but *if* we could include it, it would account for the unexplained variance. For example, to explain income inequality, say we measured years of experience and education levels and concluded that any income inequality not explained by education and experience must be due to discrimination, which we didn't measure. That *might* be true, but there are other possible explanations, and leaving out variables is no way to discover their influence. In short, the unexplained residual cannot be explained by fiat.

Sometimes the unexplained is given a fancy name. The cutest example is from the history of anatomy: Part of the forebrain is still called *substantia innominata*, literally, unnamed stuff. But a high-sounding label, even a Latin one, will not rescue an embarrassed researcher whose model is inadequate to the explanatory task. In short, the biggest assumptions in regression are not statistical and have nothing to do with the shape of the data distributions. The key issue is modeling. Have all the relevant variables been included and all the irrelevant ones excluded?

Because specification errors are not a matter of statistical procedure, they cannot be fixed with statistical procedures. And indeed the statistical, computer-intensive procedures that are sometimes used to decide what to include and exclude, such as the

stepwise methods of **forward selection** and **backward elimination**, are often worse than the disease they were meant to cure. They replace thinking with a mechanistic computer routine and are appropriate only for the most exploratory work in which researchers have almost no idea about the possible relations among variables. On the other hand, a computer routine called the **best-subsets**[45] procedure has much more promise. It cannot eliminate LOVE, but it is quite effective for handling RAVE. That is, it cannot help figure out what you have omitted that you should have included, but it can help you find variables you've included that you should omit. Our advice is: Never[46] use stepwise methods, but always consider trying the best-subsets procedure.

You might make a case for using computer routines to build your regression model if you have a very large number of IVs and no strong hypothesis to test. This can be a reasonable way to get hints, especially when you have very few strong leads and the research literature does not suggest alternatives to pursue. But one wonders whether it is advisable for investigators with very few ideas to engage in this kind of research. Still, **data mining** in massive datasets is an area in which computer software can legitimately be used, as an exploratory technique, to search for "interesting" variables.[47]

TABLE 8.9. What Kinds of Relations among Variables to Consider

Label	Concept
Antecedent	Earlier in the causal chain that you are interested in; sometimes called exogenous in economics; may need to be controlled.
Control	Something you do not want to investigate in this study; you want to see your results without examining its influence or with its influence subtracted.
Extraneous	Irrelevant to a research question but possibly important to control.
Intervening or mediating	Causal link coming between the IV and the DV. If the regression coefficient for an IV goes down after including this, that is evidence of a mediating effect.
Effect modifier or moderator	A variable that influences the relation between the IV and the DV—or between two IVs.
Suppressor	A variable that has an effect in a contradictory way; if $X1$ and $X2$ have equal and opposite effects, it may appear that both have no effect.
Interacting	Variables whose joint effects are more than or different from their individual effects. Their multiplier effects are more than or different from their additive effects.
Collinear	Explanatory variables that are highly correlated with one another and thus make interpretation difficult. Check for collinearity with tolerance or VIF statistics.

Note. For a thorough and insightful review of these relations among variables in regression analysis, but one that uses somewhat different terminology, see Aneshensel (2002).

[45]King (2003) provides a useful overview. Another useful procedure is "generalized additive models" (GAM), which is a routine in the SAS package.

[46]For a somewhat different view, see Norusis (2005).

[47]See Caster, Niklas-Noren, Madigan, and Bate (2010) and Reddy and Aziz (2010).

Table 8.9 reviews the types of relations among variables that a researcher would do well to consider. The profusion of labels for defining kinds of relations among variables indicates a profusion of possibilities. We list several of them here as a way to conclude the chapter. The table can be used as a sort of conceptual checklist to stimulate thinking about your research problem, perhaps providing ideas about variables to include and how to analyze them.

CONCLUSION: RELATIONS AMONG VARIABLES TO INVESTIGATE USING REGRESSION ANALYSIS

In a way, there are only two kinds of variables in regression analysis: those on either side of the equal sign in a regression equation. On one side of the equation is the outcome or dependent variable. On the other are the predictor or explanatory variables. These predictor or explanatory variables can all be loosely called "independent variables," taking that term as a generic label for any variable that influences the DV, even indirectly. The complications arise among these independent (a.k.a. predictor or explanatory) variables. They can be related to one another and to the outcome variable in several ways. Those ways are what is outlined in Table 8.9.

The labels applied to these variables are not categorical, in the sense of being mutually exclusive. The particular label chosen will depend on the purposes of the researcher and the variable's place in the analysis. An **antecedent variable** is one that precedes the variables of interest to the researchers, but because it may have an influence on the variables of interest, it can still be important to include in the regression equation and, in so doing, to control for it. Economists call such variables **exogenous,** meaning outside of the pattern of relations being examined. For example, in a study of the effects of interest rates on inflation, political control of the Congress (Republican or Democrat) is antecedent; it comes before and is not the main focus of investigation, but it may influence the variables studied and the relation among them. A similar concept is addressed by the term **extraneous variable**, the main difference being that an extraneous variable does not necessarily precede the others as does an antecedent variable. In either case, if you know of such a variable and can measure it, it is usually best to control for it by including it in the regression equation, in which case it becomes a **control variable**.

Unlike antecedent and extraneous variables, *intervening* or *mediating* variables are often included by design in an investigation. Mediating variables are causal links between an IV and a DV or between two IVs leading to a DV. Finding and measuring mediating variables is often a road to progress in understanding. An old but striking example is the association of arthritis and reduced rates of heart attacks. Men who had a heart attack and subsequently developed arthritis were less likely to have a second heart attack than men who did not get arthritis. Somehow arthritis seemed to protect against a second heart attack. The reason was that arthritis sufferers were more likely to take aspirin, which reduced the probability of heart attack. It wasn't the arthritis, it was the aspirin. Aspirin was the mediating variable. Subsequent research has looked for the mediating variable(s) between aspirin and heart attack, perhaps pain relief, perhaps reduction of inflammation. But other pain relievers and anti-inflammatories did not have the same effect, so the search continues. Science often proceeds by searching for ever deeper, more detailed mediating effects. Imagination in research often means thinking of new possible mediators to investigate.

Variables that are **effect modifiers** or moderators are also included in regression models and equations by design. The inclusion of an effect modifier is a way to provide a more precise context in which a relationship occurs and to talk about how it varies from one context to another. For example, small classrooms tend to promote student learning. However, the effect is stronger for students living below the poverty line than for middle-class students. The income level of students' parents is an effect modifier. This in turn raises the question of why the effect is stronger for poor than for well-off students. If the researcher has a theory (or hunch) about the reason, this can be added to the regression equation—possibly as in intervening variable.

A **suppressor variable** is a form of effect modifier that can lead to paradoxical conclusions. If two IVs have a strong effect on a DV, but one has a negative effect and another has a positive effect, the net effect of having both in the equation could be zero. There are several ways the suppressor effect can occur. One example is the effect of education on political values. Individuals' education levels tend to be positively related to liberalism and to be positively related to income level, but income tends to be negatively related to liberalism. Removing a suppressor variable from an equation will increase the association between the DV and the other IVs still in the equation. Should you remove the suppressor? That depends entirely on your research question and the variables it is important to examine in order to answer your research question. The number of possible scenarios with suppressor variables is quite large, and there is serious controversy among statisticians about just what constitutes one.[48]

Interacting variables are predictors that have different effects when acting jointly than when acting individually. If variables interact when together, their individual effects are no longer interpretable. That is why checking for interactions among all predictor variables is wise practice. But it can be a daunting exercise. If your equation has 5 predictors, there are 10 possible two-way interactions to check. Adding one variable, for a total of 6 predictors, gives you 15 possible two-way interactions; add one more predictor and the number increases to 21 possible interactions, not counting any three-way interactions. So, although LOVE is serious, avoiding it by including variables has costs. With each added variable, you need a bigger sample, and when you consider the interaction effects, the necessary increase in sample size can be substantial. As in most decisions about research methods, there are trade-offs. Deciding which trades to make requires judgment. There is no formula.

If there is an important mediating variable or an effect modifier or an interaction effect and one does not include it in one's model at the data collection phase, then it is lost to analysis. For example, it is especially important to remember to collect covariate data when studying the effect of programs on heterogeneous populations.[49] Collecting background information about participants (e.g., age, gender, ethnicity, income, education level) and including it in the regression analysis can help understand how a program works and for whom. For example, a program to promote energy conservation might work better for some groups than others; it may even backfire for some. Such consid-

[48]See Lynn (2003) and David (2009); for a persuasive argument that confounding, mediating, and suppressor variables can be seen as varieties of the same species, see MacKinnon, Krull, and Lockwood (2000).

[49]Manski (2001).

erations attest to the importance of LOVE. So it is easy to argue for including more variables despite the undeniable costs.

This has led some writers to be incautious and to advocate including anything and everything. As discussed, one drawback is the effect on needed sample size. Throwing in the kitchen sink can get you in trouble and reduce statistical power and the ability to detect relationships—in other terms, each additional variable reduces degrees of freedom. You don't want to leave out important variables, but you don't want to include irrelevant ones. Worse than irrelevance is redundancy. It leads to the other main type of specification error: RAVE. If you have a large sample, including an extra variable is not a large problem—*if* it is not redundant. If you find that it is irrelevant and has no effect—individually or as part of the network of control variables—you can later decide to delete it.

But redundancy can be a big problem. An analogy might help clarify. Variables in a regression analysis are like storytellers sitting around a campfire. The entire story can be thought of as all the variance there is to explain ($R^2 = 100\%$). Each storyteller knows part of the story. As they take turns, each gets to tell the part he or she knows, *unless* it has been told already by one of the other storyteller variables. The first storyteller, Albert, gets to tell all that he knows. The second, Betty, adds to what Albert said any new parts of the story not already recounted. If Albert knows 40% of the story, he tells that. If Betty knows 45% but it completely overlaps with (is redundant with) what Albert said, then she can add only 5% more, bringing the total to 45%. The third storyteller, Carol, knows only 10% of the story, but it is unique, so she gets to recount all that she knows, for a total 55% of the whole story. Note that Carol added twice as much as Betty, even though Betty knew over four times as much of the story. Finally, it is David's turn. He knows 50% of the story, but he has already been "scooped" and can say nothing. So even though he knew the most, he had nothing he could say. An unwary listener might conclude that David was the least important raconteur, when, in fact, he knew the most.

One can stretch the analogy only so far, but it helps illustrate several points. First, each multiple regression coefficient is a **partial** coefficient. That means it indicates the association of the predictor variable with the outcome variable after having controlled for the influence of the other predictors. Second, if you follow the analytical strategy of introducing predictors one at a time to see how much each adds to the total explained variance in the outcome (R^2), then the order in which you include the predictors is *very* important. Third, if you have two highly redundant (correlated) predictors, they can cancel out one another's effect, so that it appears that one or both are unimportant. Such redundancy is called **collinearity** in this context (it is also known as **multicollinearity**). For example, two common ways to compute income inequality in counties are using the percentage of poor and the Gini index. These two are frequently so highly correlated that only one of them can be included in the equation. If both are included, the collinearity may inflate the standard errors and lead to nonsignificant p-values for both indicators even when, if considered singly rather than together, they would each be important predictors.

In other words, there are limits to how much you can use statistical controls to study the separate effects of predictor variables, especially when the correlations among the predictors are stronger than their correlations with the outcome (dependent) variable. To check for collinearity among the variables in the equation it is *crucial* that you run one of two diagnostic tests on the predictor (independent) variables in the equation. First, you can compute the **tolerance statistic.** Tolerance is the proportion of the variance in one predictor variable that is not explained by the other variables in the equation. You want the tolerance (unique percentage of the story the storyteller knows) to be high for each variable. Maximum tolerance is 1.0. Some analysts prefer the ***variance inflation factor*** (VIF). This is the tolerance divided into 1.0. So if the tolerance were .5, the VIF would be 2.0. If the tolerance were .2, the VIF would be 5.0. You want the VIF to be small.

What about predictor (independent) variables that are wholly uncorrelated with other predictors? Statements about any specific regression coefficient depend on the other variables in the model, because the other variables are controlled when they are correlated with it. If they were not correlated, you would not need to control for them. But including predictor variables that are uncorrelated with the other predictors but are correlated with the outcome variable can be important, especially when the goal is putting together the strongest overall prediction equation, rather than assessing the influence of the individual predictors. When the goal is forecasting, rather than explanation, as it might be in insurance work, uncorrelated predictors may have considerable value.

Most of the cautions about regression and the steps for dealing with them discussed in this chapter—reviewing whether the right variables are included and the wrong ones excluded, checking for outliers and departures from normality, determining that the relations are linear when the technique assumes it, investigating whether the sample size is adequate for the job—continue to be very important when using the advanced techniques discussed in Chapter 9; these include factor analysis, structural equation modeling, and multilevel models. Most advanced techniques in quantitative data analysis, including some rather recondite ones, are elaborations on the basic correlation and regression methods discussed in this chapter. After reviewing these advanced techniques in Chapter 9, we return again, in Chapter 10, to the most fundamental question: When to include which variables in your models and how to relate them to one another. This provides a conclusion to Part II on the analysis of quantitative data and reminds us that the most important foundation of data analysis is thinking, not calculating.

SUGGESTIONS FOR FURTHER READING

Nearly all statistics textbooks have good chapters on basic correlation and elementary regression. The classic general sourcebook for correlation and multiple regression is Cohen, Cohen, West, and Aiken's (2003) *Applied Multiple Regression/Correlation Analysis for the Behavioral Sciences* (3rd edition). More elementary and very readable is Allison's (1999) *Multiple Regression: A Primer.* Spicer's (2005) *Making Sense of Multivariate Data Analysis* covers a great deal of multivariate ground in a book that assumes little prior knowledge on the part of the reader. An overall four-volume sourcebook on correlation and regression is Vogt and Johnson's (2012) *Correlation and Regression Analysis.*

For categorical DVs, a standard reference is Agresti's (1996) *An Introduction to Categorical Data Analysis.* Liao's (1994) *Interpreting Probability Models: Logit, Probit, and Other Generalized Linear Models* is also an excellent source. For logit regression, Pampel's (2000) *Logistic Regression: A Primer* is probably the easiest for nonspecialists to read.

Because regression-based methods tend to be less familiar to many readers than the hypothesis testing of mean differences, extra care may be required when you present to some audiences your results based on correlation and regression. Miller's (2005) *Chicago Guide to Writing about Multivariate Analysis* is a practical guidebook for researchers who want to explain their results effectively. Reviewing this book on how to present your findings also can be an interesting way to survey the analytical methods discussed in this and the next chapter.

On the key questions of the relations among variables, particularly mediator and moderator variables and effects, see, in addition to the works cited in the notes, Jose's *Doing Statistical Mediation and Moderation* (2013) and Hayes's *Introduction to Mediation, Moderation, and Conditional Process Analysis: A Regression-Based Approach* (2013). Jose's work is more introductory; Hayes's covers more advanced topics.

CHAPTER 8 SUMMARY TABLE

Because this chapter contains several summary tables, we list the key ones as follows in a summary of summaries and indicate the page numbers on which each can be found.

CHAPTER 9

Advanced Associational Methods

In this chapter we:

- Introduce advanced associational methods, explaining how they build directly on the basic methods discussed in the previous chapter.
- Explain the need for multilevel modeling (MLM).
- Describe how path analysis (PA) incorporates causal reasoning into associational methods and illustrate with a path diagram.
- Provide an overview of factor analysis (FA), both exploratory (EFA) and confirmatory (CFA).
  - o Discuss when you would use FA.
  - o Review decision making for an EFA.
    - ▪ Which method of factor identification/extraction will you use?
    - ▪ After preliminary analysis, how many factors should you retain?
    - ▪ Which (class of) factor rotation methods should you use?
    - ▪ How do you interpret and name the factors (latent variables)?
- Probe the differences between EFA and CFA and when you would use each.
- Introduce structural equation modeling (SEM) as the unification in one analysis of path analysis and CFA and illustrate with a basic SEM path model.

In this chapter we discuss advanced and specialized quantitative data analysis methods and why some of them are likely to be more effective than others in specific circumstances. Explaining why a given method can be more effective for addressing a particular type of problem often entails providing detailed descriptions of just what the method is. Still, it can actually be comparatively easy to discuss how to select among these advanced methods, even though they are quite technical and built upon complex math and/or intensive computer work, for two reasons. First, they are all extensions of correlation and regression, so if you have a good grasp of the material in Chapter 8, it is easy enough to understand the nub of Chapter 9's methods. Second, we can be fairly brief because the computational work is all done by computer. Unlike some of the methods discussed in Chapters 7 and 8—such as standard deviations, correlations, standardized mean differences, and so forth—that could reasonably be computed by hand, the methods in this chapter range from very difficult to nearly impossible to compute without using a dedicated computer program.

So computational details are not very helpful for defining these techniques, and the techniques are all based on fairly straightforward work discussed in Chapter 8 on correlation and regression. Our first topic in this chapter, multilevel modeling (MLM), illustrates nicely; the subtitle of a well-known book on MLM is: "It's Just Regression."[1] For other methods, such as factor analysis, we might say, "It's just correlation." Or, for others, such as structural equation modeling, "It's just a combination of correlation and regression."

One important caveat with all of the methods discussed in this chapter is that the principles of good data handling and reporting, discussed in Chapters 6–8, are even more essential with these advanced methods than they were with more basic methods of analysis. The analytical structures that are erected on the data foundations are so elaborate and complex that the foundations need to be particularly sturdy. Sampling methods and sample sizes need to be justified and described in detail. Data have to be screened for outliers, and any methods for handling outliers and skewed distributions should be described and justified. The same is true for methods of identifying and handling missing data. Finally, it is very important with the advanced methods discussed in this chapter, which basically cannot be conducted without software, to report the type of software (and the version) used.

We begin the chapter with a discussion of MLM. It is a conceptually straightforward (but computationally complex) extension of ordinary least squares (OLS) regression, discussed in Chapter 8. MLM extends ordinary regression to problems with nested data, such as individual student data, which are nested within classrooms, which are nested within schools. Then we discuss path analysis. This extends the causal thinking of researchers using correlation and regression by having them build graphic models that specify causal direction. Next we turn to factor analysis, which is a method for finding patterns in correlation matrices that help improve measurement of variables gauged with more than one indicator.

Path analysis (PA) and factor analysis (FA) have fairly long histories dating to the 1920s and 1930s, but they did not come into widespread use until more powerful computers and dedicated software became widely available in the 1980s. These two were united into a combined causal model (PA) and a measurement model (FA) under the name of structural equation modeling (SEM) in the 1980s. Indeed, conceptually, path, factor, and structural equation methods are all part of the same connected suite of *latent variable models*, and "all these methods are at heart one."[2] A **latent variable**, briefly, is one that cannot be observed directly but only inferred from indirect measures, as understanding of statistical concepts might be indicated by correct answers on a statistics quiz.

MLM and SEM are the two foundations of modern quantitative analytical methods. MLM tends to be more familiar to sociologists, and SEM is more closely linked to psychology, but the two are applicable to many of the same problems. Finally, we

---

[1] Bickel (2007).

[2] The quotation is from the superb book by Loehlin (2004), which does more to uncover the common roots of these methods, in a *fairly* nontechnical/nonmathematical way, than any other work we know of.

conclude with several even more specific advanced methods that can be done in the SEM or MLM environment, such as growth curve models, latent class analysis, and latent variable mixture models.

MULTILEVEL MODELING

Building directly on Chapter 8, our first topic is multilevel modeling or MLM—which is also known as hierarchical linear modeling (HLM).[3] MLM is a type of multiple regression analysis applied to variables that can be best understood in context or that can be seen as being in a series of levels of analysis, with each higher level including the lower levels. Such variables are often called **nested**. Paradigm examples include student-level variables, which are nested within classrooms, which, in turn, are nested within schools. Students, classes, and schools are a hierarchy of levels. Because many variables in social research are contextual, nested, or hierarchical, the introduction of MLM in the 1980s addressed a key analytical problem in quantitative analysis. It is important to understand why nested variables give rise to an analytical problem, because that helps you decide when and why to use MLM.[4]

If, for example, you wanted to study the influences on the air quality of neighborhoods, you would have to consider more than just neighborhood characteristics. Neighborhood features, such as population density and local traffic patterns, would be important, of course. But each neighborhood's air quality is also influenced by the city it is in, and each city's air quality is influenced by the region in which it is located. How much of a neighborhood's overall air quality is determined by each of these contexts—city and region—to say nothing of the national and worldwide determinants of air quality? It could be hard to distinguish from one another the effects at each of these levels. One can think of and depict these kinds of variables in several ways: as concentric circles, or nested inside one another, or in hierarchical levels.

Whatever the metaphor, the key point is that studying contextual effects raises specific analytical problems. Contexts matter, and their effects are difficult to study using the kinds of regression analysis discussed in Chapter 8. Why? Because OLS multiple regression analysis assumes that each predictor variable is measured *independently*. But how can you measure the independent effects of phenomena that are unavoidably contextual or nested and dependent upon one another? Neighborhood air quality is influenced by—and it influences—city air quality. City air quality is influenced by—and it influences—regional air quality. When you measure city air quality, you are also partly measuring regional air quality, because the city is part of the region.

Using multiple regression gives you the advantage of being able to examine the effect of each independent variable (IV) while controlling for the others. In OLS regression

---

[3]HLM is also the name of one of the best known software packages for this kind of analysis. The MLM suite of methods is also called *random effects models* and *mixed effects models*, because the models include (mix) both random and fixed effects. The numerous names arose partly because the methods were independently developed and named more or less simultaneously.

[4]For a brief nontechnical account of the logic of MLM, see Vogt (2007). For an extended discussion stressing the links between MLM and ordinary one-level regression, see Bickel (2007). Kahn (2011) also provides an excellent overview.

you can add as many variables as you like to the design, as long as the sample is big enough and as long as the variables are measured independently. What is the effect of IV1 while controlling for IV2? To control for IV2 you use its mean to assume it had no effect, no variation around the mean. So the real question is, Assuming that all participants had the same score, the mean score, on IV2, *what would their score have been on* IV1? Comparing the answer with what their scores actually were gives you an estimate of the size of the effect of IV2. Variables can be empirically related, but they must be *measured* independently. But independent measurement is not possible when the IVs are nested, because then they are not truly distinct. A concrete example helps make this clear.

A topic that did a lot to define the MLM paradigm and one that helps explain the need for MLM methods was the investigation of the variables that lead to student academic achievement in schools. Say we are interested in the effects of two variables on student achievement: their parents' educational levels (IV1) and the per-pupil expenditures of their schools (IV2). The dependent variable (DV) is students' achievement. Student achievement is fostered by having highly educated parents (IV1) and by attending a school that spends more per pupil (IV2) on libraries, laboratories, computers, teachers' salaries, and so on. The comparative importance of these two variables can be a significant practical question because it addresses how much school expenditures matter. Parental education is a student-level variable—a Level 1 variable in MLM terms.[5] School expenditures are a school-level or Level 2 variable. They are not independent because students whose parents have higher levels of education also often attend schools with higher per-pupil expenditures, which can lead to better paid teachers, more computers, and so forth.

If you want to study the separate effects of the Level 1 and Level 2 variables, you have to use MLM. If you don't use MLM, you will almost certainly underestimate the effects of the Level 2 variables.[6] In short, if you do not take context into account by using MLM in your analysis, the variance attributable to contexts—such as the effects of cities and regions on neighborhoods or the effects of school variables on individual students—will be underestimated. Conversely, the influence of Level 1 variables will be overestimated.

These problems were understood to some degree well before they were resolved.[7] Recognizing that there was a problem was a key step toward solving it. Researchers did not devise an effective way to deal with the problems until the 1980s. And the solutions pioneered in the 1980s came into broader use only as more powerful computers and more software options became available in the 1990s. What was a largely unavoidable and dimly understood problem in the 1960s and 1970s—confounding levels of analysis—is today an inexcusable mistake.

---

[5]Levels of variables depend on the research question. In a study of parents' influence on siblings' education, parental variables would be Level 2; a Level 1 variable in that study could be, for example, each child's tested aptitude.

[6]For a striking example reviewing an extensive literature showing how badly outcomes can be measured when group-level effects are ignored or measured at the individual level, see Baldwin, Murray, and Shadish (2005).

[7]See Harder and Pappi (1969) for an early attempt to sort out community-level influences on the intentions of individual voters.

A researcher new to quantitative analysis might want to resist MLM analyses because they are more complicated than the one-level regression. They involve new, more intricate statistics and strange symbols and abbreviations. You need to make several critical choices to conduct an effective MLM analysis.[8] But if you keep in mind two things, MLM is easy enough to deal with: (1) MLM is just an extension of ordinary regression to problems with variables at more than one level; and (2) the choices that you need to make are parallel, if somewhat more consequential and complicated, to those you would make using OLS. And you really do not have a responsible alternative. Fortunately the software needed to conduct MLM is more accessible than ever before, somewhat easier to use, and cheaper, too—sometimes free.[9]

Although conducting an MLM analysis can be demanding, reporting the results is not terribly complicated. One of the more basic outputs of MLM analyses, and one that your readers will often look for first, is the **intraclass correlation,** or **ICC**. This is the proportion of the total variance that occurs at the group level. The remainder, of course, occurs at the individual level. The ICC is routinely included as part of the output of an MLM analysis. The bigger the ICC, the greater is its negative impact on statistical power. Even with the comparatively modest ICCs typical in social research, the impact can be very large, "dramatic" in the words of one very persuasive account.[10] One solution, as always with statistical power, is to increase the sample size, the *N*—both the *N* of clusters and the *N* of individuals so clustered. Increasing either one can help, and you need to code/measure both. But increasing the number of clusters will have a more beneficial influence on statistical power than will increasing the number of individuals in the clusters. In short, it is the sample size at Level 2 of the analysis that matters more. In practice, most MLM studies use only two levels of analysis, but given sufficient numbers of cases three- and four-level studies are possible.

An additional sample-size problem with multilevel analyses is that there will always be fewer cases at the higher, contextual levels—more neighborhoods than cities, more cities than regions; more students than classrooms, more classrooms than schools; and so forth. So if you need to use MLM to address your research question, you'll need to pay attention to sample size, especially at the higher levels. There are two general ways an inadequate number of cases can occur. For example, if you surveyed individuals (Level 1) and also studied neighborhood (Level 2) effects, you might have enough neighborhoods but not enough respondents in each. The problem can occur the other way around—enough respondents in each neighborhood, but not enough neighborhoods. Which of the two problems is the greater one, and what strategies are most effective for dealing with them?

As mentioned before, the number of Level 2 cases is more important than the number of cases in the neighborhood. One way to deal with too few respondents per neighborhood is to cluster the neighborhoods into larger groupings. But this can backfire; it can lead to the underestimation of contextual effects, which was the whole point of

[8] An often-cited overview by Klein and Kozlowski (2000) is very useful, although the analysis section is somewhat dated. Dedrick et al. (2009) provide a methodological checklist, a review of articles using MLM, and a set of guidelines for researcher reports.

[9] As usual, options exist in the freeware R; see *http://cran.r-project.org/doc/contrib/Bliese_Multilevel.pdf.*

[10] Murnane and Willett (2011, Ch. 7). On the ICC see also Murray and Blitstein (2003) and Hedges and Hedberg (2007).

conducting an MLM in the first place. Managing the trade-off between the number of groups and the size of each group is as much art as science. But because the number of groups at Level 2 is more important for accurate estimates than is the number of individuals (Level 1) in each group, the strategy of clustering groups is often a bad idea. You should always report the practice if you have engaged in it, and you should also expect other researchers to provide this information so that you can judge their analyses.[11]

Finally, MLM can be used for a broader range of problems that those we discuss here—measuring contextual (Level 2) effects such as the effects of neighborhood variables on individual-level variables. MLM can be used also to study individual-level variables over time in repeated measures designs. In such cases the observations are Level 1 and the individuals are Level 2 variables. This is one of several cases in which MLM and SEM (discussed later) overlap. Although there are sometimes reasons that one is better than the other for a particular problem, individual researchers often make their choices of method on the basis of disciplinary tradition. For example, psychologists seem more often to choose SEM, whereas sociologists opt for MLM.[12] Although many problems can be addressed in either MLM or SEM, often with identical results, there are some cases in which one is distinctly better than the other.[13]

PATH ANALYSIS

Path analysis (PA) is another extension of the basic correlation and regression models discussed in Chapter 8, but this time including up-front causal and graphic components. Researchers specify, *before* conducting the analysis, the causal model they want to explore or test. The model can include both direct and indirect effects. Each hypothesized causal link is specified by an arrow, and the strength of the relation is indicated by a **path coefficient**, which is a standardized regression coefficient. PA, which puts regression variables into a causal diagram for analysis, was developed nearly a century ago by Sewell Wright.[14] He thought that correlations were clues that could be combined with theory to investigate the degree of causal relations among variables. PA, he said, could "be used to find the logical consequences of any particular hypothesis" (1921, p. 557) about relations among variables. His work was a major step forward in the analysis of causal relations, but it was only rather sporadically applied in the social sciences before the work of Duncan and others in the 1960s.[15]

The widespread adoption of the method awaited the growth of the personal computer industry and dedicated software programs. With the emergence of PA, researchers

---

[11] See the discussion in Clarke and Wheaton (2007); for sample size in MLM with particular attention to statistical power, see Scherbaum and Ferreter (2009).

[12] We don't wish to stereotype; any such differences are only tendencies, and there are many counterexamples. For instance, one of the best overviews of how practitioners can apply MLM is by a psychologist; see Kahn (2011).

[13] For a discussion, see Tolvanen et al. (2011) and the concluding paragraphs of this chapter.

[14] See Wright (1921, 1934). Both are still worth reading, and the 1934 article specifies "path rules" that continue to be used.

[15] See Duncan (1966) for the first systematic account of how to incorporate Wright's methods (developed for use in population genetics) into social research. It remains a valuable reference. See also the much-cited unpublished paper by Garson (2005) for a basic primer of terms and methods.

got bolder about trying to make causal claims and to measure causal effects by using multiple correlation and regression techniques to adjust for the fact that in social research the simple bivariate experiment, foundational in many other fields, is an unrealistic measure of most human thought and action in natural settings.

Today, PA is not much discussed in text and reference books for researchers because it has been subsumed under SEM, in which it functions as the causal part of an SEM model. The path analytic concepts are still there, within SEM, and very importantly so, but the name has faded. The relation between the two is described in several ways, each of which is correct: PA is SEM without the measurement model. Or SEM is PA to which a measurement model has been added. Or PA is the causal/structural part of an SEM. Most commonly, the term *path analysis* is used to refer to causal modeling of single-indicator variables, that is, variables that are measured in only one way—with observed rather than latent variables. SEM is used when there is more than one indicator for at least some of the variables. The most important difference between PA and SEM is that PA assumes that there is no measurement error; with SEM you can use latent variables to account for measurement error.

Whether you use SEM or PA, the question of causation does not really change. You don't make variables "causal" merely by connecting them with arrows. What you can't appropriately do in either method is data dredging to find a handful of correlated variables, put them together in a graphic, and start drawing arrows. Rather, to conduct a path analysis properly, you first specify a causal model and variables. Then you collect data on the variables and insert them into the prespecified places. PA and SEM are examples of how computer software can actually foster organized thinking (not merely brute force number crunching). Using a path or structural equation program first requires you to specify the model before the computer can begin running the program.

Figure 9.1 is an example of a PA diagram. The flow of hypothesized causation runs from left to right. Capital letters depict variables. Single-headed arrows represent a causal relation between variables. Double-headed arrows indicate a simple nondirectional correlation: The two are correlated, but the nature of any causal link is unspecified.[16] Variables *A* and *B*, parent's income and educational attainment, linked by a double-headed arrow, are called **exogenous** variables. This means that they enter the

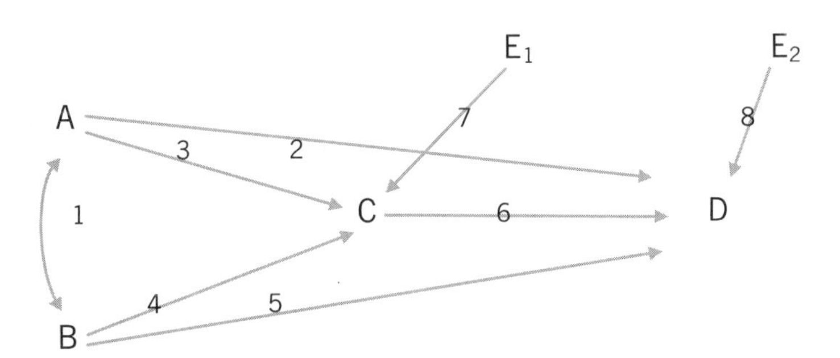

FIGURE 9.1. Basic path diagram. A, parent's income; B, parent's educational attainment; C, child's academic skills; D, child's educational attainment; E, error terms: omitted variables.

[16]The parallels with network analysis diagrams are close. See the discussion in Chapter 5.

causal model from the outside; arrows point *from* them, but not *to* them. By contrast, **endogenous** variables (*C* and *D*) are inside the model; they have at least one arrow pointing to them, as well as sometimes having arrows pointing from them.

The hypothesized causal model is that a parent's income and a parent's education influence the educational attainment of her or his child.[17] The educational influence of parents is thought to be both direct, that is, from parent's education (*B*) to child's educational attainment (*D*), and indirect, that is, from parent's education to child's academic skills (*C*) to attainment (*D*). For example, educated parents might help develop children's educational skills (e.g., writing, listening, and vocabulary), which would then increase the child's likely degree of educational attainment. The influence of income is also hypothesized to be both direct (e.g., high-income parents can pay for college tuition; arrow 2 from *A* to *D*) and indirect (parents with more income can help support acquiring academic skills via a rich home environment, by taking the child on trips to museums, etc.), which then can increase opportunities of educational achievement (arrows 3 and 6, from *A* to *C* to *D*).

Arrows 7 and 8, which represent the effects of *error terms* (*E*), are very important. Error terms are often labeled R for residual (the part left unexplained). These two, E_1 and E_2, specify that there are unexplained causes not included in the model. Error terms, unlike other variables in a path model, can stand for more than one causal variable. Because PA uses observed, not latent, variables, it assumes that variables are measured without error. So in PA the error term refers to unmeasured variables. In SEM, by contrast, the error terms also include sampling error and measurement error. In the path diagram in Figure 9.1, the error term E_1 and arrow 7 indicate that there are more sources of *C*, child's academic skills, than just *A* and *B*. Without the error term, your model would be specifically claiming that arrows 3 and 4 *fully* explained *C*, which would not be very likely in this case.

One could imagine a situation in which different *A* and *B* variables might come closer to a sufficient explanation of *C* (attainment). For example, what if *A* and *B* were heredity and environment? If heredity and environment were defined very broadly, they might work as a full explanation. But you would probably still want to include an error term to account for measurement error, which is inevitable—and rarely negligible in the social sciences. An error term should probably also be included to account for any possible *interactions* between causally linked variables. In practice, almost every endogenous variable in a path diagram, especially one that is part of an SEM, will or should have an external arrow pointing to it from an error term, at minimum, to account for measurement error. As in any model, such as the regression examples in Chapter 8, it is often as interesting to know what is *not* accounted for by the variables as what is. Error terms provide estimates of that important feature of the model. Another way to explain the importance of error terms is to remember that *omitted arrows are part of the theory.* They specifically say that there is no causal link.

In a full PA, the model in Figure 9.1 would also include **path coefficients**; these are written on or just next to each arrow. They are usually[18] expressed in standardized form—they are standardized partial regression coefficients, also known as **beta weights.**

---

[17]We are modeling the effects of one parent's characteristics. Including both would complicate this simple introductory example, as we show later when we discuss SEM.

[18]Conventions vary, and some software packages do not provide beta weights by default.

In this example, all of the path coefficients would probably be positive, but there can be negative as well as positive coefficients. For example, if a variable were included in the model that measured the number of times the parent moved and the child transferred from school to school, the coefficient for that variable would probably be negative. Of course, "negative" refers only to the sign of the coefficient and connotes no evaluation. For example, if the model were the same except that the dependent variable (*D*) were changed to the probability of dropping out, the arrow between academic skills and dropping out would probably be labeled with a negative number, but this would hardly be a "bad" thing because lowering the dropout probability is generally considered a good outcome.

Because the path coefficients are standardized, they are directly comparable, and it is possible to use them to examine many interesting questions. Is the parent's income or education more important? Are the direct effects or the indirect effects more important? The answers are suggested by the size of the path coefficients. If you find a path coefficient that is very small, it is permissible, as in ordinary regression, discussed in Chapter 8, to delete that variable from the analysis and redo the analysis with the variable omitted. It would be even better to use new data to redo the analysis after deleting the variable.

With a path diagram, you put your cards on the table. You say what you think in a clear way that also identifies what you have to study in order to test your ideas. That is the heart of theoretical modeling (see Chapter 10). In some ways, PA adds little to correlation and regression, but its visual component contributes greatly to interpreting regression research results: It makes the assumptions about the causal ordering of the variables clear and helps the researcher keep the interpretations clear and consistent. It enables you to better see direct and indirect effects and separate and combined effects.[19] For all of these reasons, we rarely do regression analysis without bringing in PA. There are many more details about path diagrams that we could include here, but our basic goal has been to indicate how path models and diagrams might be useful in your research. In our view, also discussed in Chapter 10, there aren't many multivariable social research problems that wouldn't benefit from a path approach. Even when the variables are not quantitative, the path diagram or model remains a useful conceptual tool for sorting out one's thinking. Remember that path models almost always begin as a description of the theoretical relationships among qualitative concepts described in words, not numbers. Path analysis has an additional role to play when the concepts are coded and measured quantitatively, but the first steps are theoretical and qualitative.

FACTOR ANALYSIS—EXPLORATORY AND CONFIRMATORY

Like PA, factor analysis (FA) dates to the early 20th century, and like PA it came to be used extensively by applied researchers only in the last few decades when computer programs for conducting its complex and widely varying routines became highly effective and readily available. Today, PA and FA are most commonly used together in SEM. PA functions as the causal part of an SEM, whereas FA addresses its measurement components.

[19]Another classic and much-cited paper on measuring and interpreting direct and indirect effects is by Alwin and Hauser (1975).

Of all the analysis methods we have written about, FA is the most choice-laden. To conduct an FA, the researcher must make a series of decisions. Each decision can be quite consequential in terms of how it affects the outcome of the analysis. There is no type of analysis in which deciding when to use which methods or selecting the right methods has more influence on the analysis and interpretation of results. And there is no wholly uncontroversial choice among the researcher's numerous options. It seems to us and other commentators that many researchers simply use whatever the default choices are in whatever software they are most comfortable with.[20] That is certainly understandable, but we think it better to at least consider the reasons behind the common options so that you don't wind up saying: "I dunno, whatever the computer did." And, ultimately, blaming it all on the computer is not really possible, because most programs ask you to make at least some choices before they can proceed with the analysis. Our account of the myriad choices in FA discusses only some of the most basic ones in order to illustrate what is involved.

There are two broad types of FA. As their names indicate, **exploratory factor analysis (EFA)** is used when researchers are looking for interesting patterns among variables. **Confirmatory factor analysis (CFA)**, by contrast, is used when researchers have theories about the patterns that they want to test. The two are often linked because it is very common to conduct them in sequence—first an EFA to refine theories, then a CFA to test them. Following this order, we first discuss EFA and then CFA. (See the end of this section for more on CFA.)

In either case, FA is correlational. As MLM is just regressions and the associations among them, FA is just correlations and the associations among them. The basic data for an FA is a correlation matrix—or a covariance matrix. Usually either can be used, because correlations are standardized covariances. The correlation matrix need not be one you have generated. Quite a lot of research using FA (and SEM) is archival, in the sense that the researcher did not generate the data. That is one of the reasons researchers are encouraged by many (including us) to make available their correlation/covariance matrices.[21] Doing so makes your work dramatically more usable—both in meta-analysis and in other archival approaches to your subject. Why should you let others have your data? There are two reasons. The first is the implied social contract among researchers: As you have benefited from the research of others, you should repay the community of researchers of which you are a part. Second, more selfishly, when others use your data, you get cited—and citations are, for academics, the coin of the realm, the main currency of recognition and advancement.

As mentioned, FA has roots in the early 20th century and was used most extensively in the field of psychology.[22] From its beginnings the purposes of FA have been to improve the measurement of **latent variables** or constructs that cannot be directly observed; latent variables can only be studied indirectly by using **indicators** of observed variables. For example, in a multi-item measure of traits, the items would be indicators

[20]Bandalos and Boehm-Kaufman (2009) make this point most forcefully. See also Henson and Roberts (2006).

[21]See Zientek and Thompson (2009) for a rigorous argument for including matrix summaries in research reports.

[22]See Thurstone's foundational work (1931), which remains a very readable and informative introduction. Earlier pioneering conceptual work was conducted by Pearson and Spearman.

(or observed variables), and the clusters of questions identified by the EFA would help you identify the **factors** or latent variables, which are the constructs or concepts you seek in your research.

What's It For, and When Would You Use It?

FA can be used for several broad classes of measurement problems, that is, it can help you decide about the reliability and validity of your measurements of latent variables and thus how to analyze and interpret them. For example, imagine that in your research you want to measure participants' self-efficacy or their social tolerance or their attitudes toward a controversial issue. These are latent variables because they cannot be measured directly. Based on previous discussions in the literature, you put together a series of 15 questions, each coded using a Likert scale ranging from *strongly agree* (5) to *strongly disagree* (1).[23] You think these questions tap into the construct (efficacy, tolerance, or attitudes) in your population/sample of participants.

Do your 15 questions represent 15 different variables, which should be analyzed one at a time? Or are all 15 questions aspects of the same underlying variable, and thus summable into one overall scale? Or do subclusters of questions address conceptually distinct aspects of your topic—are you investigating not 15 separate variables, and not 1 variable, but perhaps 3 variables (factors), each represented by 4–6 questions? If this were the case, the variables (questions) making up each factor would be highly correlated, but the 3 factors would not be strongly correlated with one another. Multiitem variables from survey questionnaires are more reliable and often more valid than single-item variables, and FA helps you identify and interpret them. The 3 factors would almost certainly be more analytically powerful than the 15 separate questions.

EFA works by examining a correlation matrix. The 15-by-15 correlation matrix in our example would contain 105 distinct correlations. Each correlation would represent the correlation of respondents' answers to questions: the correlation of answers to Question 1 with 2, with 3, with 4, and so forth, and the correlation of answers to Question 2 with 3, with 4, with 5, and so on for a total of 105 nonredundant correlations. For EFA to be effective, the correlations among the variables should be relatively high, and the sample size should be substantial. If those recommendations sound vague, the reason is that there is debate in the research literature about these questions.[24] First, and most obvious, if the respondents' answers to the questions were not correlated, there would be nothing to factor analyze. Second, if the sample size was not substantial, the chances for a good factor solution are greatly reduced.[25]

Although it is hard to nail down specific recommendations on sufficient sample size, most researchers would agree that it cannot hurt to have too many participants/respondents in the sample—and it can definitely hurt to have too few. So err on the side of too many, not too few. You won't really know how many cases you needed in your sample until after you have conducted your analysis. Only after the EFA has been conducted will you know the communalities and the number of variables per factor; *then*

[23]See the discussion in Chapter 1.

[24]See Tabachnick and Fidell (2001) for a good overview; their recommendation is a minimum of 300 cases.

[25]In certain circumstances, the researcher can make do with much smaller samples; see de Winter, Dodou, and Wieringa (2009) for a discussion.

you can accurately estimate needed sample size—when it's too late.[26] That's why it is better to be cautious and run the risk of collecting data from a sample that might turn out to be "unnecessarily" large. People always want statistical consultants to come up with a hard number for sample size, so here it is: 500 would be enough in most cases; you might be able to get by with 300 in a pinch. You will often find those numbers—500 and 300—mentioned in discussions of sample size for EFA, but they are just a way to try to be somewhat concrete. The basic recommendation about sample sizes is: The more the merrier. This also applies to extensions of EFA, including CFA and SEM. All are very "case hungry."

Steps in Decision Making for an EFA[27]

Many of our colleagues, quite happy with CFA, are uncomfortable with EFA. It seems to them too speculative, subjective, and interpretive. On the other hand, others, including us, are rather fond of EFA precisely because of its highly interpretative character. It should come as no surprise—given its name—that EFA is exploratory, uncharacteristically exploratory for what many researchers are accustomed to in more deductive, theory-testing methods of statistical analysis. EFA focuses on inductively generating hypotheses and building theories rather than conducting inferential tests of existing theories. Of course, some theory guides even the most exploratory of analyses. To return to the previous examples about attitudes toward a controversial issue, social tolerance, or self-efficacy, the 15 questions had to come from somewhere, and they couldn't have just been pulled out of the air—or wouldn't be of much value had they been. Researchers should explain their rationale for the content of the questions, how they were constructed, and on what research literature they were based. We have seen few if any topics of investigation for which one could not obtain, from the research literature, considerable guidance about how to construct variables. If you can't find any, you might not be looking hard enough. Or your search may be too narrowly conceived. Try again. It really won't do to assume that grounding in the research literature can be skipped, because, "after all, we're *exploring*, aren't we?"

After you have determined your sample size, constructed your variables, and gathered your data, there are then a set of clear decision steps, no matter how exploratory the EFA. The choices at each step are far from cut-and-dried, and different respected authorities have opposing ideas about the best procedures. The decision points are obvious, but the decisions themselves typically engender much discussion—and they should. We discuss them in the order in which they usually (not invariably) occur: Which method of factor extraction should you use? How many factors should you retain? Should you use factor rotation, and if so, which method? and How do you interpret the factors you have discovered? Because the analysis is exploratory, it is reasonable to take what you learned from having answered the questions and, having made your first pass through

---

[26]For further discussion, see Hogarty, Hines, Kromrey, Ferron, and Mumford (2005).

[27]For brief, nontechnical overviews of these decision making processes see Williams, Brown, and Onsman (2010); Vogt (2007); and Budaev (2010); the latter also discusses principal components analysis. Bandalos and Finney (2010) is a more advanced but compact account; and Pett, Lackey, and Sullivan (2003) pursue the topic in book-length detail. The table of choices in Brown (2006, p. 38) is full of good information.

the data, to answer the questions differently and reanalyze the data—and/or conduct the analysis with a new dataset.

Which Method of Factor Identification/Extraction Should You Use?[28]

The first question is whether to use **principal components analysis (PCA)** or **FA**. They are in some ways similar, and beginning researchers often confuse them; they will often yield parallel solutions, especially when number of variables is large. But PCA and EFA are based on distinct mathematical models. PCA is mainly aimed at data reduction, that is, on reducing a larger number of variables to a smaller number of components. By contrast, EFA is aimed at identifying and measuring the strength of the latent constructs that undergird the correlations among the variables. Another way to describe the difference between the two is to note that in PCA the variables are IVs, whereas the components are DVs. In EFA this relation is reversed. The factors are the IVs and the variables are the DVs. For example, if the factor or latent variable was an attitude or a personality trait, this attitude or trait would "cause" respondents to answer questions in predictable ways. We think that FA is the more appropriate model for most questions in the social and behavioral sciences. A further advantage of FA is that it, specifically CFA, is at the basis of SEM. As you can discover by reading the sources we cite in the footnotes, this is not a universal opinion. Note also that some software packages start an EFA by first conducting a PCA to identify candidate factors before proceeding with the EFA.

If you have decided to conduct an EFA, then you have to choose among the models for doing so. The two most widely used of these are **principal axis factoring (PAF)** and **maximum likelihood (ML)**. Each has its proponents. We think that PAF is most relevant for an EFA, because it is descriptive and exploratory. ML is definitely best for CFA. ML is an inferential method that focuses on a sample in order to find the factor solutions that would best represent the population from which the sample was drawn. We think that in exploratory analyses inferential methods are somewhat out of place. But some researchers, often because of software convenience, use ML for EFA, and there is no harm in doing so. Again, it is important for the researchers to specify what they have done and why, and also to indicate which software and which version they used.

After the Preliminary Analysis, How Many Factors Should You Retain?[29]

How many factors—that is, clusters of correlated variables—should be retained and used for further analysis? There are several methods of deciding, most of them options in computer packages. The most widely used method, and it is a good, if simple, beginning, is to examine only factors with **eigenvalues** greater than 1.0. In general terms, an eigenvalue is a measure of the amount of variance in all the variables that is explained by a particular factor. In our example questionnaire, there are 15 variables (questions); that means the total eigenvalues for all 15 variables add up to 15. An eigenvalue of 1.0 means that a factor explains one-fifteenth of the total variance; that is the same as the

[28]To examine this and related issues more deeply, see Thompson (2004); he prefers PCA and orthogonal rotations. By contrast, Pett et al. (2003) favor EFA and oblique rotation.

[29]See Ruscio and Roche (2012).

average explained by each individual question. If a cluster is no better than the typical single question, it's not worth much. The 1.0 eigenvalue cutoff is usually merely the first sort. Then you need to look more closely at the factors with eigenvalues greater than 1.0. This is often done graphically, using a technique called a **scree plot**. You use this graphic to eyeball the factors with values greater than 1.0; often a bend in the line of the graphic is fairly obvious and can be used as a criterion. There are more technical and statistical methods than the scree plot, but none is universally acknowledged to be superior.[30]

Remember that because you are exploring it is allowable to use several of the methods of factor selection and see what they suggest. Then—based on your knowledge of the field and on pondering possible meanings of the clusters of correlated variables (factors) the EFA has identified—make judgments about which factors it will be most helpful to interpret further.

Which (Class of) Factor Rotation Methods Should You Use?[31]

Factor rotation is complicated and hard to explain in a few lines. Suffice it to say that rotation is a method for refining the factors identified in the first pass through the data. Rotation improves a factor solution by increasing the correlations among the variables *within* a factor while simultaneously lowering the correlations *between* factors. It originally involved literally looking at graphs of the data from different angles, rotating them to see relationships better.

There are two basic categories for factor rotation; within the categories there are numerous options. The two basic classes of factor rotation methods are **oblique** (correlated) and **orthogonal** (uncorrelated). If you use an oblique approach, you assume that the factors may be correlated with one another. If you use an orthogonal method, you assume that the factors are completely uncorrelated, and the method of analysis constrains the factors to be uncorrelated. It is rarely the case in social research that variables and constructs are uncorrelated, so we think it makes most sense to start with oblique rotation. Also, if the factors actually are uncorrelated, an oblique method will not disguise this fact—but the reverse is not true. However, because the method is exploratory, it is acceptable to try both and explore both orthogonal and oblique solutions. Within the two categories, oblique and orthogonal, there are many subroutines. The choice among them is less consequential than the basic distinction between oblique and orthogonal, and it is acceptable to try various methods of rotation. As always, you need to explain what you did and why and to describe any differences that occurred in the course of your explorations.

How Do You Interpret and Name the Factors (Latent Variables)?[32]

It is at this phase that the subjectiveness of EFA becomes most visible. But there are concrete steps you can take to avoid some common misinterpretations. Because EFA

---

[30]See Bandalos and Finney (2010) for a brief discussion.

[31]See Sass and Schmitt (2010) and Brown (2006).

[32]We omit from this discussion questions of how much emphasis you should put on factor pattern matrices as opposed to structure matrices and other more technical issues. See Thompson (2004) and Schmitt and Sass (2011).

is usually conducted with a Pearson *r* correlation matrix (see Chapter 8), the analysis is more effective when the variables in that matrix meet the basic assumptions of correlational analysis. Although EFA does not require that the variables be continuous and their values normally distributed, noncontinuous and non-normal distributions can affect the results. If the values are ordinal—as in a typical Likert scale ranging from *strongly agree* to *strongly disagree*—this usually poses few problems, unless the number of ranks is less than 5. Skewness (see Chapter 7) can be more of a problem, because variables that are *highly skewed in the same direction* can be strongly correlated and fit into the same factor, even when they are completely unrelated. Missing data and outliers can also influence factor solutions, so it is important to report on them and on what you have done about them—did you impute missing data, delete outliers?—as it is in any analysis. So the most subjective phase of an EFA interpretation should begin with some nuts-and-bolts statistical descriptions of your data.

Inevitably, however, you'll have to think hard about which variables are clustered together into factors and which clusters/factors are distinct from one another—and why. As is sometimes said in other contexts, "the researcher is the instrument," and that characterization is applicable to the interpretative phases of EFA. You ask yourself questions such as, What makes this cluster of variables a factor, and why is it distinct from those other clusters of variables, and why do a couple of the variables not fit into any obvious cluster/factor?[33] You will probably be able to get some hints for answering these questions from the research literature, and it is often helpful to discuss these issues with friends and colleagues. But ultimately you're on your own. EFA is very useful for finding patterns in the data; interpreting and naming them is up to you. Interpretation is the creative part of the process, and creativity cannot be farmed out or reduced to an analysis routine. Go forth and be creative.

Deciding between EFA and CFA

CFA is an element of or a type of SEM, so we consider its uses mostly in the next section. Here we review the differences between CFA and EFA and discuss when you might decide to use one or the other. The first point is that distinctions between CFA and EFA are far from absolute. As mentioned earlier, some theory inevitably guides and is investigated in even the most exploratory of EFAs. And the most confirmatory of CFAs often allow for some exploration, such as the comparison of rival models. Generally, CFA should be used if you have quite strong confirmation from the research literature about the factor structure of the latent variables you intend to study. Often it is best to first conduct an EFA to refine the model you want to test and then, using a separate sample, to conduct a CFA to test the refined model. When in doubt, it makes most sense to conduct an EFA, which allows you much greater flexibility in your analysis options.

Both EFA and CFA are based on the same statistical foundation (the common factor model). The basic difference is that the analysis routines in CFA are constrained or restricted by the researcher. In CFA the researcher must specify in advance the number of factors and identify them by indicating which variables/indicators are associated with what factors. This means that factor rotation does not apply in CFA, because you

[33]The sources cited in footnote 27 illustrate with several examples of understanding and labeling factors. See Hayton, Allen, and Scarpello (2004) for an interesting discussion.

have already identified the factors and the indicators used to measure them. Finally, in CFA it is typical to discuss and interpret your output using one or more goodness-of-fit measures. These measures are designed to indicate the extent to which your model fits the data and is the basic way to begin evaluating the overall model. But in EFA you are trying to discover or build a model; you don't have a ready-made model to evaluate, so goodness-of-fit measures do not really apply.

STRUCTURAL EQUATION MODELING

SEM is currently at the top of the quantitative analysis food chain. Decades ago, simple statistical tests, such as ANOVA, were shown to be limited applications of correlation and regression analysis (CRA). In the same way, the techniques of CRA are special, limited cases of SEM. Essentially, SEM incorporates, into one integrated whole, all other statistical techniques we have discussed in Part II, with the exception of the purely exploratory methods.[34] In basic terms, SEM is built up out of PA, which forms the causal part of its model, and CFA, which forms its measurement parts.

SEM also can easily incorporate more advanced regression problems, such as multilevel data, by adding a multilevel component to SEM. Conversely, MLM can include latent variables and thus incorporate SEM into MLM. This means that MLM, with which we began this chapter, is something of a rival to SEM to win a place as the methodological "category of all categories" in quantitative analysis. Whether one sees MLM being included in SEM's broader suite of methods—or vice versa—is a matter for some discussion.[35] Which of these you wind up doing is to some extent partly a matter of personal preference or tradition in your research speciality and also partly of the availability of easy-to-use software. Our impression, and it is only that, is that for most researchers, SEM is becoming the go-to, all-purpose family of methods. That's why we focus mainly on it to conclude this chapter.

SEM is a group of methods into which increasing numbers of subroutines are being incorporated, particularly into the various software packages used to conduct the analyses. The growth in the capabilities of the software packages gives you an idea of SEM's versatility. The original computer program, dating to the 1980s, for conducting SEM was LISREL (short for *linear structural relations*). Using it was very demanding. Originally, even entering the data required a considerable understanding of matrix algebra. AMOS (short for *analysis of moment structures*) was the first program to allow the researcher to enter the names of variables into path diagrams via a graphical interface. Now, several other programs are available, most providing the option of a graphical interface. The list of programs includes, of course, open-source SEM software available through R.[36] As always, when multiple options are available, it is important for you to indicate to readers of your research reports which version of which program you used to conduct your analysis.

---

[34]For an excellent review of how these different procedures are all "part of an overarching model," see Graham (2008).

[35]See Kline (2011b) and Pituch and Stapleton (2011) for perspectives on the question.

[36]See Kline (2011a) for a review of the major SEM programs, and Fox, Byrnes, Boker, and Neale (2012) for the programs in R.

Our goal here is not to tell you how to conduct an analysis using SEM but to provide you with enough information about it to enable you to decide whether you want to do so and, if you do, what "branch" of SEM is likely to be of most interest. There are two main emphases in or branches of SEM analyses. They correspond to its two main components: One focuses on the causal model and the PA parts of the model; the other focuses on the measurement of latent variables and the CFA parts of the model. Of course, many researchers include both the measurement model and the causal model, but there is a tendency to concentrate more on one than the other. These foci are determined by your research questions and perhaps to some extent by the disciplinary tradition you are most familiar with. A sociologist interested in predictors and causes of outcomes might tend to emphasize the causal (also called structural or directional) part of the model while also being happy to take advantage of the opportunities SEM provides to measure the causal variables more reliably. On the other hand, a psychologist might be mainly interested in identifying the basic structure of latent variables—such as intelligence or self-efficacy—and measuring their components, as well as the associations among them.

Figure 9.2 shows the standard way of depicting these relations and their components. The latent variables are represented by the ovals[37] around *X* and *Y*. The predictor variable is *X*, the outcome is *Y*, and the direction of causality is indicated by the straight, single-headed arrow. *X* has four indicators, x_1–x_4, and *Y* has three, y_1–y_3. By convention these indicators are symbolized by squares. For example, *X* might be parental involvement, measured by four indicators, which is thought to lead to increased student achievement, measured by three indicators.

Note the direction of the arrows from the latent variables (factors) to the indicators; this means that the latent variables are seen as causing the indicators. The small circles represent the specificity or the part of the variance in the score that is reliable and not due to error variance, and the sharply curved, double-headed arrows indicate the vari-ance in the indicator variables. The asterisks are coefficients that have to be

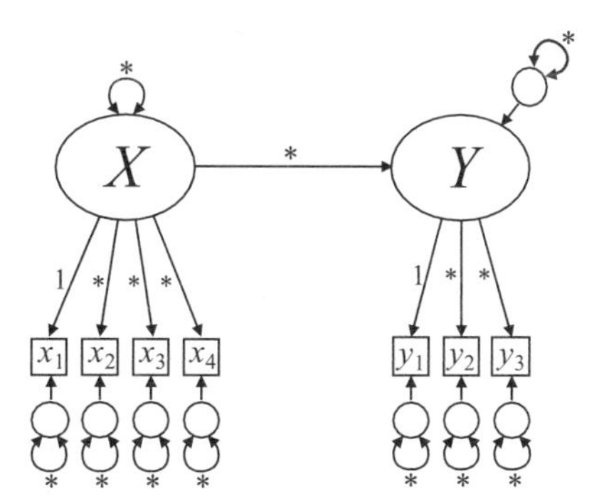

FIGURE 9.2. Basic SEM path model. X, predictor variable; Y, outcome variable; →, direction of causality; *, coefficients to be estimated; O, latent variables; □, indicators; O, specificity, or the part of the coefficient not due to error; ↻, the variance in the indicators. From Hoyle (2012, Fig. 1.1, p. 5). Copyright 2012 by The Guilford Press. Reprinted by permission.

[37]Conventions vary; sometimes the ovals are circles and the squares are rectangles.

estimated. In a completed diagram, the asterisks would be replaced by numbers. It is these numbers, together with fit indices for the whole model and its parts, that would be used to interpret and evaluate the model.

The main difference between the causal emphasis and the emphasis on latent structures can be seen in Figure 9.2. It shows a *causal* relation by the straight single-headed arrow between *X* and *Y*. By contrast, if the emphasis of the researcher was on a latent structure model—for example, *X* could be cognitive sophistication and *Y* could be political tolerance—then *X* and *Y* would be linked by a curved, double-headed arrow. The rest of the graphic would be the same.

Among the biggest advantages of SEM is that it allows researchers to separate (1) measurement error from (2) the size of the causal/structural relations among the variables in the model while also, by using one of several goodness-of-fit indices, (3) assessing the overall fit of the entire model. However, there is still considerable discussion in the literature about which of the measures of fit are best for what particular circumstances, and different researchers often make quite different recommendations.[38] In reviews of the literature, it is quite common to see half a dozen fit indices reported. Determining what fit index to use when is one of the areas in SEM that is still being researched by methodologists.[39] The typical procedure is to first assess the measurement portion of the model (the CFA part) and then to test the causal part (the PA part) by seeing how much the overall fit improves by adding the causal part. It all sounds very clear in theory, but it can be much more problematic than most researchers realize. Goodness-of-fit indices have their limitations. An overall good fit does not mean that all the components of the model fit equally well, nor does it necessarily mean that the predictive value of the model is very high. In brief, because SEM is under development and is subject to adjustments that researchers need to be apprised of, users need to keep up with the methodological literature much more than they might have to do with older, more settled methods.[40]

Most of the applications of SEM that we have seen in our research involve the use of static or cross-sectional models; they do not include variables that measure effects that occur over time. Such static models are certainly the easiest to estimate, and they produce more clear-cut results than models that include time. But the kinds of questions researchers are interested in often imply a temporal element. And time is a necessary condition whenever causation is involved, because cause and effect, by definition, cannot be simultaneous. We briefly discuss two ways temporal variables can be incorporated into the basic SEM model: latent growth curve modeling and **nonrecursive** designs in which variables might have reciprocal effects[41] or effects in a feedback loop.

We begin with **latent growth curve modeling (LGCM)** because it is more commonly used by applied researchers and because it raises fewer technical problems than models

---

[38]We discuss another class of these measures, based on information theory, in Chapter 10.

[39]There are many fit indices and much discussion about which ones are best for which purposes; the uncertainty is indicated by the fact that many articles provide several. A good overview is Schreiber, Nora, Stage, Barlow, and King (2006). See also David Kenny's website at *http://davidakenny.net/cm/fit.htm*.

[40]See Hancock and Mueller (2010) for a fuller discussion.

[41]Jargon alert: in ordinary English, many people take "recursive" and "reciprocal" to mean the same thing, both indicating bidirectional effects. But in stat speak, a reciprocal relation, such as a feedback loop, is called *non*recursive.

with reciprocal effects.[42] You use LGCM when you want to model change over time. A typical example would be the effect of an intervention on individuals, such as an educational program at successive stages. You could also use repeated measures ANOVA for this purpose (see Chapter 7), but it is a far less flexible and powerful method.[43] All the advantages of SEM over ANOVA apply because LGCM is a special case of SEM. The latent variables in LGCM are an **intercept** and a **slope**. The intercept represents the baseline measure of the outcome variable. As in any regression, the slope indicates linear rate of increase over time (for every 1 unit of time the outcome changes by such and such an amount). To conduct an LGCM analysis, you need at least three measures of the time variable, and it is usually better (although there are "work arounds") for the measures to be equally spaced—for example, once a week, once month, once a year, and so forth, depending on the nature of the variable. You can also add covariates to the model to see, for example, whether rates of change are different for different groups; if they are, this would be equivalent of an interaction effect between the group and the causal variable. So if you have a theory of change that leads to predictions of how a predictor will lead to an outcome per unit of increase in time—a trajectory measured at several points in time—such as an increase in test scores per year, LGCM is an excellent analytical approach.

Probably the most challenging problems for causal modelers occur when at least some of the variables in the model are causally reciprocal, for example, when variables form a feedback loop. These cannot be well analyzed using basic SEM methods. If there is a feedback loop, and you use basic SEM, alternate models will often have the same model fit whether you assume that *A* causes *B* or that *B* causes *A*. It is easy to think of examples of reciprocal causation in social and psychological theories and research. Individuals' social prestige and their incomes are probably reciprocally related; people with high prestige in society tend to make more money, and people who make more money tend also to be held in higher esteem. In psychology, negative life events and depressive symptoms are often held to be related in mutually reinforcing ways. And the phenomena of reciprocal causation and debates about them are hardly confined to social and psychological theory. In biology, for example, genetic and environmental variables are often said to be in a feedback loop by researchers arguing for reciprocal causation, whereas advocates of a more traditional approach think it is important to keep ultimate origins in evolution distinct from proximate causes of behavior.[44]

Although social and psychological theorists (and some biological theorists) suggest that reciprocal causation is at play, it has not been easy to analyze theories of reciprocal causation.[45] One reason is that among the traditional criteria for identifying causation, the first, and most elementary, is that the cause must precede the effect—*after* cannot cause *before*. But in a feedback loop, *before* causes *after*; and then, in turn, *after* causes

[42]The following relies on Singer and Willett (2003); Preacher (2010); Biesanz, Deeb-Sossa, Papadakis, Bollen, and Curran (2004); and Little (2013). As mentioned before, similar analyses can be conducted with MLM.

[43]The same limitations apply to extensions of ANOVA, such as MANOVA, in which the several DVs can be formed, using discriminant analysis, into a composite DV.

[44]See Laland, Sterelny, Odling-Smee, Hoppitt, and Uller (2011) for an accessible and up-to-date review.

[45]See Martens and Haase (2006) and for an application, Tang and Robinson (2010).

before—and so on ad infinitum. The problem, of course, is not with the interactions among reciprocal causes, but with the rigid application of the traditional criterion.[46]

CONCLUSION

Finally, we conclude the chapter by once again addressing the account of causation encapsulated in the saying, "correlation does not imply cause." We think it excludes too much. A simple correlation between two variables, *A* and *B*, implies an *unexplained* cause. *A* may cause *B*, *B* may cause *A*, they may both be caused by a third variable, or they may reciprocally cause one another. As can be seen by perusing the summary table for this chapter, causation is always implied in MLM, PA, EFA, CFA, and SEM. Using SEM techniques, we can model competing causal hypotheses and compare the strength (goodness of fit) of the competing models. All this is easier said than done, of course, but SEM and related modeling techniques can be used to narrow the range of competing hypotheses. We pursue this subject from a somewhat different and more general perspective in the next chapter on model selection and inference.

[46] An excellent example of dealing with these issues is Ma and Xu (2004).

SUGGESTIONS FOR FURTHER READING

For PA and FA, we recommend reading the original, historical sources discussed briefly in the chapter. For PA, see Wright's "Correlation and Causation" (1921) and "The Method of Path Coefficients" (1934) and Duncan's "Path Analysis: Sociological Examples" (1966). On FA, see Thurstone's "Multiple Factor Analysis" (1931). After reading these sources we felt we had a better understanding of where and how these methods originated and ultimately, therefore, when and why to use them.

We have not found many easy-to-read books on MLM or on SEM. Neither topic lends itself to nontechnical discussion, which is not surprising given that they are among the more advanced methods of quantitative analysis. On MLM we recommend two works for the beginning researcher: Bickel's *Multilevel Analysis for Applied Research: It's Just Regression!* and Heck, Thomas, and Tabata's *Multilevel and Longitudinal Modeling with IBM SPSS* (2010). Both of these illustrate MLM concepts using SPSS, which more readers are likely to have available than specialized programs such as HLM. Luke's *Multilevel Modeling* (2004) is also helpful.

Useful shorter accounts of MLM include McCoach's (2010) "Hierarchical Linear Modeling" and Klein and Kozlowski's (2000) discussion of a set of critical choices for researchers in their "From Micro to Meso: Critical Steps in Conceptualizing and Conducting Multilevel Research." Dedrick et al. (2009), in "Multilevel Modeling: A Review of Methodological Issues and Applications," provide a methodological checklist, a review of 99 articles using MLM, and a set of guidelines for researcher reports; these guidelines are not very different from what you would see for OLS regression, but because MLM is less familiar to some readers, and because the output is more complicated, such guidelines can be important.

Even more than volumes on MLM, those on SEM are often tied to the use of a particular computer program. An exception is Kline's *Principles and Practice of Structural Equation Modeling* (3rd edition, 2011), which is the best general overview; he also discusses the pluses and minuses of several software brands. Shorter accounts include Vogt's (2007) Chapter 14 in *Quantitative Research Methods for Professionals*, Mueller and Hancock's (2010) Chapter 28 in *The Reviewer's Guide to Quantitative Methods in the Social Sciences*, and Meehan and Stuart's (2007) article, "Using Structural Equation Modeling with Forensic Samples," which contains a nicely worked out example.

Handbooks are common in research methodology, and most of those we know of are quite, well, handy. But occasionally a handbook is published that sets the standard, both as a reference tool and a text for a decade or more. One of these is Hoyle's *Handbook of Structural Equation Modeling* (2012). It passes the "one-book test" (if you could have only one book on a topic, what would it be?) as well as any other volume we know. Whenever we want further clarification about one of the siblings in the family of methods that is SEM, this is the volume we turn to first.

CHAPTER 9 SUMMARY TABLE

METHOD	WHEN TO USE
Multilevel modeling (MLM) (pp. 327–330)	• When your independent variables are nested, hierarchical, or contextual. • When these nested variables cannot be measured independently. • To avoid underestimating the effects of the Level 2 variables. • To study repeated measures over time.
Path analysis (PA) (pp. 330–333)	• To help you manage your thinking about the causal relations among your variables. • To help make clear the relations implied in regression models. • To compare the size of effects: direct, indirect, and total.
Exploratory factor analysis (EFA) (pp. 333–339)	• When you are unsure about how various indicator variables might help you identify and interpret latent variables (factors). • To explore the reliability and validity of the measurement of latent variables. • When you want to explore the latent structure of a multi-item set of potential indicators. • To prepare to conduct a confirmatory factor analysis (CFA).
Confirmatory factor analysis (CFA) (pp. 339–340)	• When you have good data and theory about the factor structure of the latent variables in the model you intend to test and interpret. • When you can specify in advance the number of factors and their indicators.
Structural equation modeling (SEM) (pp. 340–342)	• When you want to combine the strengths of PA (for causality) and CFA (for measurement). • When you want to separate measurement error from the estimation of causal relations. • When you want to be able to assess the overall fit of a model (or alternative models) to the data.
SEM for growth curve modeling (pp. 342–343)	• When you want to model change in the DV over time. • When you have at least three equally spaced measures of the time variable. • When you want to investigate how much change per unit of time a predictor will lead to.
SEM for nonrecursive models (pp. 343–344)	• When at least some of the variables are causally reciprocal, form a feedback loop, or are mutually reinforcing.

CHAPTER 10

Model Building and Selection

In this chapter we:

- Provide a general introduction to causal modeling and how it differs from NHST.
- Discuss when you can benefit from building a model or constructing a theory.
  - Provide an example of using a graphic path-analytic approach.
  - Review the implications of including time as a variable in your model.
  - Note when you might use mathematical modeling rather than or in addition to path/causal modeling.
  - Consider how to determine how many variables you should use in your model, which includes the related issues of model identification and specification.
- Discuss the merits of using a multimodel approach.
  - Review the meaning and use of the Akaike information criterion (AIK).
- Conclude by discussing how the multimodel approach fosters thinking about a research agenda.

Rather than testing a hypothesis about the relation between two variables, when can it be more effective to build and test more elaborate models of phenomena and the relations among them? When is analysis work better done by building models, examining them as a whole, and comparing them with alternative models? We have already begun discussing this approach in the previous chapter on structural equation modeling (SEM) and multilevel modeling (MLM). And the foundations were laid in Chapter 8 in the section that discussed when to include which variables and the use of R^2 as a summary statistic for regression models. Here we build on those foundations. Thus this chapter on model building and testing extends previous discussions. It also serves as a conclusion to Part II on quantitative data analysis and interpretation.

As described in the Introduction to Part II, the basic process of building and assessing models is as follows.[1] You begin with your research questions; these emerge out of

[1]In the Introduction to Part II we devoted a few paragraphs to the various meanings of key terms, including *theory, model, hypothesis, concept, construct*, and *variable*. The reader might want to review those paragraphs.

and continue to evolve into a sort of dialogue with the theories you are using. Modeling your theory is an important step in making your ideas concrete enough to investigate. When you model your theory, you translate your concepts and your hypotheses about how they are related to one another into variables and assumptions about how those variables are related. The specification of your variables helps make them explicit enough to analyze and interpret the data you have collected.

This chapter is devoted mainly to *causal* models. These differ from purely *statistical* models, which can be very important for prediction. Here is a brief example to describe the distinction. Say it's April 10th and you live in Atlanta, Georgia; you are planning a picnic on April 16th, so you want to predict the weather. What will the high temperature be, and what is the precipitation probability in Atlanta on April 16th? Using a purely statistical model, you would investigate to find that over the last 60-plus years the average high for April in Atlanta, Georgia, has been 73 and that it has rained about 30% of the time (9 days out of 30), so your purely statistical prediction is that the high temperature will be 73 degrees with a 30% chance of rain. This isn't a bad prediction, and very often in the social sciences our predictions are like that. You could also take a causal modeling approach. If you have a causal model of which variables are important and how they are related and relevant data that you can plug into the model, you may be able to do better than a purely frequentist statistical model. In the case of predicting the weather for your picnic, information about fronts, barometric pressures, and many other variables can be incorporated into a model of how these affect one another so that you can predict what the weather will be in 6 days. You personally might not be able to do this unaided, but the National Weather Service can routinely beat a purely statistical model for predicting 6 days ahead. It can give an even more precise and reliable prediction 3 days ahead. But it cannot do so 60 days ahead or even 30. When you want to predict that far into the future, a statistical model is your only recourse.

Where do models come from? Model building is often a goal and a product of a literature review. When you review the research literature on a subject, you usually have one of several aims: (1) summarizing outcomes into an overall effect size, as in a meta-analysis; (2) comparing models explaining the same outcome, as in different multiple regressions with the same dependent variable; (3) synthesizing different models into a better, more explanatory, model. The "product" of this third goal is a possibly better model to test or a group of alternative models to test. This third option is potentially the most interesting, or at least the most creative. But it can also be the most challenging. This third approach also allows, and even rewards, combining findings and methods of analysis. The placement of this chapter is likely to strike some readers as odd. The standard description of the research sequence puts theories and model building *before* data collection and data analysis. It is true that collecting the data and only then building a model or constructing a theory to explain them is rightly condemned as post hoc theorizing. It is always possible to come up with some theory to explain the data *after* you have collected them. But it is actually quite common, as part of a research agenda rather than a one-time project never to be revisited, to iteratively collect data so as to refine theories and build more models. You use your literature review and early data collection and analysis to guide model construction, which then is used for further data collection and analysis. This data collection and analysis, in turn, suggests further refinements in your model or models. Descriptions of research proceeding thus iteratively are usually found in textbook accounts of qualitative data analyses, such as grounded theory (GT) and other "emergent" theories. But the iterative approach is also very common among researchers who use quantitative data to investigate questions.

In any case, one thing you can do with your data is build a model. Of course, you often build a model before collecting data. Using data to build a model and then using the *same* data to test it is a tautological process and should be avoided. But cycles of collection, analysis, and theorizing are common and can be very fruitful. The process is often iterative, with a few rounds of preliminary model building, often initially just beginning with a research question that implies a model. Another way of expressing this approach is "training data," which are data used to *build* a model; that model then guides the collecting of further data to *test* the model. Exploratory data analysis, discussed in Chapter 7, is another approach to quantitative data that suggests model building. And Bayesians (see Chapter 7) incorporate the idea of using existing data and conclusions drawn from them into the analysis of data yet to be collected when they include "priors" in their research projects and analyses.

Model building or theory construction can be descriptive in ways that are not radically different from the way grounded theorists want their generalizations to arise out of the data. Path diagrams can not only be built to guide your research but also used inductively to describe hypothesized relations among the data you have already collected. The usual approach to path diagrams/analyses is that these are constructed in advance of data collection. This is a good strategy, but it is not the only way to use path analysis's excellent visualizing tools to describe your concepts and the relations among them (see the discussion of path analysis [PA] here and in Chapter 9).

We tend to be more impressed by the similarities than by the differences among types of theory construction and model building. One might do some preliminary reading of the research literature, think about what one has read long enough to want to investigate a new wrinkle on the original idea, and then return to the literature with a new goal in mind. In GT this is called theoretical sampling, but the same kind of dialogue between ideas and data is involved in all theory construction or model building. You might organize the data as a concept map or as a path diagram or in any of several other ways. Although the subject of this chapter is model building and theory construction using quantitative data and analysis techniques, the basic process does not differ radically from the work done with more qualitative or mixed data (see Chapter 13).

A novice researcher might find the idea of constructing a theory or building a model to be intimidating. The usual advice, and it can be good advice, is *to find* a model or theory that suits, one that is ready-made, off the rack, as it were. The model might have to be altered here and there to fit your problem, but designing a theory from scratch, creating one out of whole cloth, might be foolhardy. But even a novice who is undertaking a major research project, such as a dissertation or thesis, can sometimes afford to be more ambitious than simply adopting someone else's theory. Indeed, it is hard not to be at least a little creative fashioning a theory/model to fit your needs. The main exception occurs when you join an ongoing research project in which the topic, theory, and methods of investigation and analysis are predetermined (often by the terms of a grant award); signing up to work on the project means agreeing to abide by these protocols. This kind of organization of research work is fairly rare in the social sciences, at least as compared with the natural sciences. And even when the project is very highly structured, the data collection and analysis are hardly ever above revision.

In our experience and that of many colleagues, model building usually comes well along in the process of building a research agenda. It can arise out of dissatisfaction with earlier rounds of collection and analysis and a desire to do something more sophisticated. At other times, initial reactions to what you are seeing in the literature can lead to building a model or an alternate model. Finally, the advanced methods discussed in the previous chapter (PA, confirmatory factor analysis [CFA], MLM, and SEM) cannot be conducted unless you postulate a model in advance. Still, model building may often come at the end of an analytical process if you are dissatisfied with the quality of your results.

We focus here on using path diagrams to depict relationships among concepts. It is not necessary to use path diagrams to build a model. But doing so is very handy. In evaluation research, path diagrams are often called *logic models*.[2] In other kinds of research they are called *causal models*.[3] The advantage of the various graphic techniques for depicting relationships among concepts is that it makes it easier to keep something quite complicated straight in your head. We've often found that it is just too hard to sort things out with words and/or numbers alone. The graphic techniques of PA are useful in many ways. Often, as you make your concepts increasingly specific so that you can reach the point of having concepts defined well enough to collect data, you will want to modify your path diagram or write minidiagrams that describe relations among a subset of variables.

What you diagram in a path diagram are the hypothesized *relations* among variables or concepts. You can construct a regression model without specifying the relations among variables in much detail. Instead, you can use only lists of variables to build models. An illustration of that approach is given in Table 8.4 in Chapter 8. But even in that case, the lists of variables imply relations among them. The beauty of a path diagram is that it makes these relations clear, and it helps you (sometimes forces you) to see where you need to further clarify your concepts and how they fit together into a pattern of relationships.

It should also be stressed that the relations among the variables in a path diagram—at least some of them—are *causal*. Many researchers are leery of talking about causes, especially if they are not discussing the results of randomized controlled trials. And many influential statisticians have warned against using nonexperimental data and path diagrams (and, by extension, SEM) to draw causal inferences. As we have said at other points in this book, we find it hard to avoid the concept of cause and the language of causality. Ours is a minority view, but one that some distinguished colleagues share. As one ironically put it, "statistical methods are routinely used to justify causal inferences from data not obtained from randomized experiments," but, "the discipline thriving from such uses assures its audience that they are unwarranted."[4] Another avers that PA and SEM have from their outset been considered "a mathematical tool for drawing causal conclusions from a combination of observational data and theoretical assumptions."[5] Differences over when and how it is legitimate to discuss causation is one of the major rifts in research methodology; we mention this only to warn readers that

[2]Funnel and Rogers (2011).

[3]Morgan and Winship (2007). For a good presentation of the conventional symbols in path/causal models, see Jaccard and Jacoby (2010).

[4]Spirtes, Glymour, and Scheines (2000).

[5]Pearl (2012).

they might wish to take our advice in the coming pages with a grain of salt, although we do not believe it is necessary to share our views on causation to use most of what follows.

WHEN CAN YOU BENEFIT FROM BUILDING A MODEL OR CONSTRUCTING A THEORY?

It can be hard to simply borrow a theory or model and apply it to your research question without modifying it in some way. At minimum, you'll most likely be using the model to guide your data collection in new ways, from new populations, in new contexts. So there is always some creativity involved. No one ever truly starts from scratch—nor should they. In the space between simple borrowing and pure invention is the region in which we all work. We all have to build models to get ourselves going, and we usually have to refine those models to explain our results. Modeling or theorizing is at the heart of the analytical process, and because it involves creativity, it is something of a mystery. There are three general approaches, summarized by the following questions: (1) When do you build a preliminary model to guide initial data collection? (2) When do you use your collected and analyzed data to guide further model building and new data collection? (3) When do you generate alternate models with the goal of comparing them? Whichever of these approaches you take, you have to come up with new ideas. How does one do that? The processes are far from clear, but there are things that people studying creative scientists have found to be true and certain suggestions from cognitive scientists about how to increase your likelihood of being innovative. Jaccard and Jacoby's book is probably the best overall guide. They present and discuss a list of "26 heuristics" for generating new ideas that can be incorporated into a theory or model. They also discuss numerous "influential systems of thought" and suggest that trying to look at your problem through the lens of more than one of these can be very helpful.[6]

When possible we recommend modifying a model not only to suit your research purposes but also to at least flirt with the idea of *multimodel inference*, discussed later in this chapter. Multimodel inference can be somewhat informal and a route to flexible thinking, or it can be much more formal, using competing mathematical models and statistical tests to evaluate how well each fits the data. As mentioned earlier, we most often recommend a visual approach to modeling. This has often been necessary in our work to keep ourselves from getting lost in intricate paragraphs that are hard to follow, whereas a path diagram sorts out things quite nicely. The main alternative is mathematical modeling (see the brief discussion on "When to Use Mathematical Modeling" on p. 356) in which the set of relationships is described with equations rather than or in addition to diagrams. Note that translating diagrams into equations can be comparatively straightforward. Indeed, most SEM software (see Chapter 9) does precisely this.

Here is a relatively simple example drawn from some of our work. In discussing it, we can illustrate just how complicated the process of causal modeling can become and how many intricate choices may be involved.[7] The research involved studying a new

[6] See Jaccard and Jacoby (2010, Chs. 4 and 11, respectively), for heuristics and influential systems.

[7] Lim et al. (2011) built a model at the end of a 2-year cycle of data collection and analysis as part of the preparations for a longer, more ambitious study.

method of teaching computer programming in introductory undergraduate courses. Specifically, "Web services" (WS) approaches supplemented traditional solutions to programming problems. The designers of the curriculum believed that the WS curriculum had four main advantages: (1) it better conforms to industry standards, that is, to what programmers in the real world are doing, (2) students would be more interested and involved in their programming assignments because they could work on more realistic problems applied to their own interests, (3) it enables students to learn advanced concepts in introductory courses, and (4) students would learn measurably more programming concepts and skills with the new methods than with the standard methods of instruction.

The statements in that paragraph add up to a rudimentary theory: WS instruction will lead to more student interest and more student learning. Initially, there were two main alternative models, A and B (see Figure 10.1).

In the first model (A), the new method influences the two outcomes independently. The second model (B) assumes that the method increases student interest and *thereby* increases student learning. Which of these is more correct? That is the kind of question that comparative model testing is meant to answer. Of course, these are extraordinarily rudimentary models.

In the course of implementing and testing the effects of the new methods of instruction, we gradually refined the theory and redrew the models. At the end of a 2-year pilot study we proposed more elaborate models to guide subsequent data collection and analysis. These are depicted in Figure 10.2.

The first addition to the model was to include background variables. First included were variables that almost surely had some influence on the outcome variable (learning). The most important of these was prior academic achievement as measured by cumulative grade point average (GPA; see arrow 2 in Figure 10.2). We were uncertain about the likely effects of other background variables, including students' gender, academic majors, class rank, and prior experience with computers (these were added as control variables). An additional background variable that also had been shown in prior studies of learning to exert a big influence was student self-efficacy. We wanted to pay special attention to this one because of its documented influences on learning outcomes in a variety of contexts.[8]

Controlling for background variables was very important. Because the project aimed to study real students over a full semester in real courses, random assignment was impossible. It is always a good idea in experiments to examine background variables,

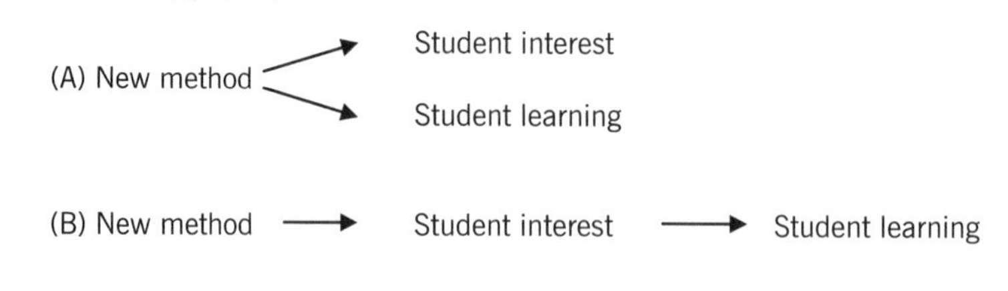

FIGURE 10.1. Two models of the effects of the new method.

[8]Bandura (2006).

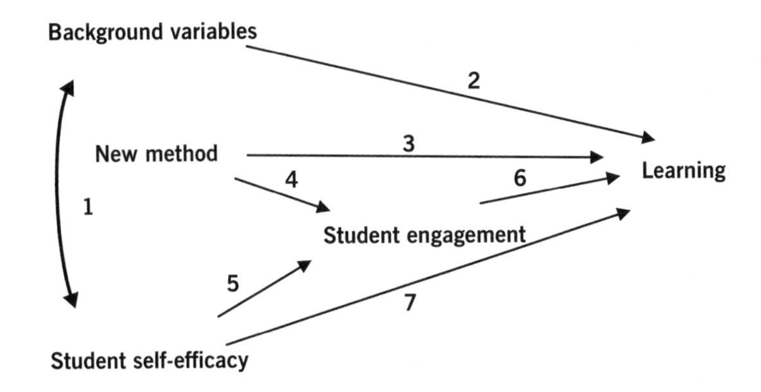

FIGURE 10.2. Path/causal model of effects of new method on learning.

even when one can use random assignment.[9] But it is especially important to do so in a quasi-experiment in which there is, at best, random assignment of treatments to groups.

How should we draw the model, where should the arrows go, what will influence what and in what order in the path diagram? In part, we answered these and related questions through analyses of our pilot study data on 586 students over the course of 2 years. Note that we did not build the model to explain the pilot study data. Rather, we used the data to build the models, which we then planned to test with newly collected data over the next 3 years. We focused on the background variables that were consistently important in the pilot study: cumulative GPA, gender, and student self-efficacy. These three background variables are external to the causal system, that is, they come from the outside; they existed before students enrolled in the course and experienced the curriculum; single-headed arrows point *from* them, not *to* them. They are **exogenous,** in the language of some model builders. The three variables are probably related—correlated—but we do not specify how in this model.

Of course, we don't think that the background variable, cumulative GPA, *causes* learning, but it is a good *predictor* of learning as we measured it in the study. Most likely, GPA is an indirect and partial measure of learning. Whatever causes GPA (effort, ability, etc.) and the learning it symbolizes is also likely to lead to learning in our quasi-experiment. It was a strong predictor in the pilot study data. On the other hand, self-efficacy may be a direct cause of learning in its own right and may also have a positive influence on GPA; and both of these are probably correlated to some degree with student gender. The model does not reflect these possibly complicated relationships (except for the double-headed arrow, arrow 1). The model could very easily wind up looking like a spider's web rather than a causal diagram if we included all possibilities. There is a cost to adding causal paths (each one increases the needed sample size), and the relationships among antecedent variables were not our focus in this study. There is also a cost to omitting causal paths that should be included. By omitting them you are fixing them to be zero or not related, and that will decrease the fit of the overall model. The

[9]See the discussion on experimental design in Chapter 3 of Vogt et al. (2012) and of coding experimental data in Chapter 3 of this volume.

general point is that you can add or erase arrows. Each time you do so you construct an alternative model of how you are claiming the process works.

The visual portrayal of the model helps one keep track of and sort out the various possibilities. Do we think that self-efficacy works independently and that students with more self-efficacy would learn more regardless of the curriculum (arrow 7), or do we think that self-efficacy tends to foster student engagement so that it has an indirect as well as a direct effect on learning? And because engagement is also fostered (arrow 4) by the new method, could there be interaction effects between efficacy and engagement so that they would have a joint influence on learning?

You can usually postulate a prior cause and, in turn, a cause of that cause and usually a possible mediating or modifying variable. For example, we could add intensity of implementation. In the multisite study, all sites incorporated the new techniques into the curriculum, but some sites were more enthusiastic and rigorous in their implementation than others. Do we add a variable for that? It would make sense to do so, especially if we had a reliable method of coding and measuring intensity. But at some point in the process of model building you have to stop. You might have to collect so much data that the analysis could become impossibly complicated. Eventually the theory can get too conceptually complex to be cognitively apprehensible. It can collapse under its own weight.

Note that the model in Figure 10.2 does not specify how the variables are to be coded or measured. It is a causal model (also known in SEM as a structural model). It discusses the relationships among the concepts, not how data on the variables representing the concepts are collected, coded, and measured. SEM always adds a measurement model to the causal/structural model, but we focus solely on the causal model here.

Note also that all of the relations symbolized by the paths in this particular model are presumed to be positive or direct: A change at the base of the arrow will lead to a change *in the same direction* at the tip; an increase in the cause will lead to an increase in the effect, and a decrease will lead to a decrease; a path coefficient (such as +.29) tells you how big the relationship is. Inverse or negative relationships are also indicated by arrows, but they are usually marked with a negative sign and indicated by a negative coefficient (e.g., –.37).[10]

Thus inverse relations are possible and common. Say we include gender in the model, coded *female* = 1; *male* = 0. A review of the literature suggests that an arrow (not shown in the interests of keeping the model simple) leading from gender to GPA would be positive because women tend to have higher GPAs. But the literature also indicates that an arrow (not shown) leading from gender to learning computer programming, as measured by an exam score, would tend to be negative. This kind of duality can lead to a version of the **suppressor effect**, in which the same variable can have opposite direct and indirect effects on the outcome variable.[11] Considerable prior research on academic achievement as measured by GPA indicates that female gender has a positive or direct relation. And GPA has a positive or direct relation on our measure of learning in computer programming. On the other hand, gender is inversely or negatively correlated

[10] If there is no + or – sign, the relation and the coefficient are positive.

[11] There are several types of suppressor effects; they are conceptually tricky, and statisticians are still debating how best to characterize them. For good brief discussions see David (2009), Friedman and Wall (2005), and Lynn (2003). A more introductory discussion is available in Jose (2013).

with some measures of learning in computer programming courses. Which effect will be stronger—the positive effect of gender through GPA or the negative effect of gender on exam score? Or will the two simply cancel one another out? Such are the kinds of alternate models that could be assessed given sufficient data.

Whether to Include Time as a Variable in Your Model

In a path diagram, such as the one in Figure 10.2, *time* is often an unmodeled variable. Causes do not have instantaneous effects. The effects may happen quickly, too quickly to measure easily, but, by definition, they take time. In our case, the effects of the new method on student engagement occurred over the course of one semester. Indeed, instructors noticed some early resistance to the new method and found that it didn't start having the predicted effects for a few weeks.[12] Also, the effects of engagement on learning take time. Note that the model does not specify *how* engagement fosters learning, just that it does so (this assumption comes from the literature review and is not tested). Furthermore, the effects of the new method on engagement and on learning could have effects that extend beyond the time covered by the study; the learning could lead to other learning, for example, if increased engagement leads students to take more courses in the field. None of this is specified in the model. Because time is not specified in the model, it is simply assumed that all these causes have their effects at some unspecified rate over the course of the semester. Further modeling could focus on what happens *between* the variables in the model. One could ask, What happens "inside" the arrow's shaft? Do the gains all come early in the course of the semester and then level off, do they build continuously, or does it take several weeks before they begin to appear?

Time can also raise measurement complications. In the example we have been discussing, student involvement comes earlier in the model than learning, but it is measured at the same time. That is another way that time is not modeled; it is omitted from the model. One additional time wrinkle should be mentioned at this point: autoregressive effects. These could occur if the score on a variable at Time 1 influences the score on that variable at Time 2. This could happen, for example, if involvement differed among students at the outset of the course and if those differences influenced the later development of involvement quite apart from the treatment's effects on involvement. Time is often not modeled by beginning researchers because doing so requires the use of advanced techniques.[13]

Time enters in one final way, in the actual process of model building. This is often done "backward." It is common to start with the outcome that interests you and build your model working back through its possible causes.[14] Then one asks: What are the causes of my causes? If you work that way, the time sequence implied by the direction of

---

[12]These effects were discovered in interviews and open-ended survey questions.

[13]See Singer and Willett (2003).

[14]Of course, some investigations are more exploratory; the idea could be to discover outcomes rather than postulate causes of predetermined effects. There is even a tradition in experimental research, perhaps best developed in social psychology, to conduct an experiment to see what happens. Zimbardo, Garfinkel, and Milgram were exponents of this approach. This approach is briefly discussed in Chapter 15 of Vogt et al. (2012).

the arrows will be the opposite of the one you used when you constructed your model. Conversely, if you write a narrative to *summarize* your project and work your way forward following the arrows, this may not be a good description of what you did to *build* your model.[15]

Model building usually involves an additional round of complicating questions about *mechanisms* of change that activate the causes implied in the model. *How* do my causes bring about their effects: directly, indirectly, in concert with others, as modified by others, or reciprocally? These questions about causal mechanisms can be examined by altering the path model, but they are often better answered using qualitative methods such as interviews and direct observations.

The complications just discussed emerged when we pondered a relatively simple project, one that contained only a handful of variables. The example illustrates how central the process of model building is to good analysis. Pondering alternative models is almost always time well spent. Little is as potentially valuable as sketching your ideas, trying to think about them from new perspectives, and then spending a lot of time pondering your sketch and redrawing it—sometimes dipping into the literature to refresh your thinking. Various models devised in these ways can be compared and tested, as is discussed in the section on multimodel approaches.

When to Use Mathematical Modeling Rather Than or in Addition to Path/Causal Modeling

Often researchers move to mathematical modeling when straight lines no longer capture the relations among variables. Then the *shapes* of those relations become most interesting. Those shapes can be captured with equations or functions; doing so is the heart of mathematical modeling. But it is not easy to incorporate such shapes (*S*-shaped curves, *U*-shaped curves, etc.) into a path model. Of course, both the shapes and the causal relations are important, and eventually one needs to put the two together. Do increases in the cause influence the effect very slowly at first? Then at some point is there a rapid increase, followed by another threshold at which there is a rapid leveling off? If so, the *S*-shaped curve might best be modeled using the logistic function, as is done in logit regression (see the discussion in Chapter 8).

How Many Variables (Parameters) Should You Include in Your Model?

When deciding how many variables to include in your model, there is a trade-off between completeness and usefulness. As is usual with trade-offs, judgment is involved, and there is no one right answer. The answer depends on the uses to which you want to put your model; in other words, it depends on your research question. Although there is no such thing as a perfectly complete model (the model would have to be the very thing it was trying to represent), a model can almost always be made more complete by adding variables. But at some point, adding more variables will result in a model that is too cumbersome to use. Take the example of a map of a big city. How much detail should

[15] Ethnographers are more often forthright about such methodological intricacies. By contrast, researchers analyzing quantitative data (and probably their readers) seem less interested in such "confessional tales." See Van Maanen (2011).

it include? If you are interested in driving from the western to the eastern suburbs on major highways, a relatively small map with most of the streets omitted might be just what was needed. On the other hand, if you were planning a 3-day walking tour of the city's famous buildings, you would probably need a much bigger map and one that depicted many more details.

As with any theory, so too with a model, which is, in our usage here, a picture of a theory: You want a clear, simple model that explains a lot. What you don't want is a difficult, complicated model that explains very little or that confuses you. There is a very direct trade-off between completeness and clarity. A model can be too incomplete or too detailed. As one key text summarizes, "All model selection methods are based to some extent on the principle of parsimony."[16] In general, parsimony means using the fewest number of variables possible that gets you to an effective representation of your data. Where judgment enters is deciding on what is "effective" for your data and your purposes. To continue with a similar analogy, here are two sets of driving directions:

1. Go straight ahead for about half a mile to the first stop sign. Turn left. Go two blocks. Turn right. The store is the third building on your left.
2. Go straight ahead on Maple Street for about half a mile to Third Avenue, which is your first stop sign. If you get to a big green gas station, you've gone too far, which people sometimes do because there are a lot of bushes that make the street sign hard to see. At Third Avenue, turn left; follow that street for two blocks to Oak Street. Turn right on Oak Street. The building is the only store on the block; the others are apartment buildings. The store is white with red trim; it is the third building on the left.

Evaluating the differences between these two sets of directions is in part a matter of taste. Some people want the minimum necessary; they find the details confusing. Others like fuller directions; they find the details reassuring. Does the second set of directions contain useful information or merely confusing redundancy? Picking the most effective level of detail inevitably involves some trial and error—and judgment about what will ultimately be most useful, and for whom or what purpose.

The two basic strategies for deciding how much should go into a model are easy to state, though harder to implement. One strategy is to start with the full model and then see what you can delete without losing too much of importance. Another strategy is to start with the minimum model and see what other helpful information you can add without complicating things too much.

The terms most often used to describe the criteria for categorizing and judging a model are the related concepts: specification, fitting, and identification. **Identification** is the most technical and is usually discussed in the context of SEM. An **underidentified** model has no unique solution; indeed, it has an infinite number of solutions. This makes it useless for most purposes except sometimes to clarify things in the early stages of model building. A **just-identified** model has a unique solution. An **overidentified** model contains more than one feature of the model that can be used to estimate parameter

[16] Burnham and Anderson (2010, p. 31).

values; it contains more knowns than unknowns. For example, in the context of SEM, this could mean having three measures of a latent variable, not only one.

Specification means converting a theory into a model by choosing variables and the relations among them. **Fitting** refers either to curve fitting—for example, deciding that a relation is *U*-shaped rather than linear—or to selecting variables to include in the model. The latter is our main focus here. **Underfitting** a model essentially means leaving out important variables—*left-out variable error*, or LOVE, as discussed in Chapter 8. **Overfitting** means making the model too complex—*redundant added variable error*, or RAVE, as discussed in Chapter 8. Overfitting and underfitting are problems when building a single model. They become even more important to consider when building and comparing multiple models. As always, the problem is the right balance between the two. Multimodel inference, described in the next section, provides methods that are more reliable than the usual "Goldilocks" approach we have all had to use with single models—not too much and not too little, but just right.[17]

WHEN TO USE A MULTIMODEL APPROACH

Of all the challenges to null hypothesis significance testing (NHST), none is more fundamental than the multimodel approach. As one of its proponents put it, "I consider the various null hypothesis testing approaches to be only of historical interest."[18] Much more useful is an approach using multiple working hypotheses. Modern information theory and statistical adaptations allow one to rank these multiple models in terms of how well they explain the data. The intuitive appeal of this approach is great, especially as compared with collecting a large number of null hypotheses that we have failed to reject. In NHST you test only the model you are *not* interested in. By contrast, in multimodel inference, you test and rank the models you are interested in. Note that this approach is based on maximum likelihood estimation (MLE), not the simpler, more familiar least-squares approach used in hypothesis testing.[19]

If we know the correct model of the relations among the phenomena we wish to study, then it is usually a fairly simple matter to estimate, using standard least squares statistical methods, the parameters (values of the variables) in that model. But that is precisely the question: What is the correct model? Among various possible models, which is the best one to use? Answering this question includes both variable selection (see the discussion in Chapter 8) and specifying the relations among the variables.

The alternative approach to comparing various models is based on information theory and is often referred to as **information theoretic (I-T)** analysis. The question is not simply the goodness of fit of a particular model using the kinds of measures mentioned in Chapter 9. These indices are mainly for assessing the model once it has been selected. But the information criterion methods discussed here are for selecting among *candidate* models. Thorough knowledge of the field and the particular problem are used

---

[17]An exceptionally thorough but compact "how to" article on model specification and fitting is Jaccard, Guilam-Ramos, Johansson, and Bouris (2006).

[18]Anderson (2008, p. ix).

[19]The least squares (LS) method was long popular because it is easier to do by hand; but it is a very limited special case of MLE, which has become widespread with the availability of cheap, fast computing.

in conjunction with much discussion and critical thinking to identify a set of plausible models, which can then be ranked from best to worst. The set of models should include all plausible candidates, but both the models and the list of models should be "reasonably" parsimonious. Judgment and knowledge are required to determine what is plausible and what is reasonably parsimonious.

This process is not at all the same thing as collecting data on a large number of potentially relevant variables and using computer software to identify models that meet various thresholds for inclusion. Doing that is very likely to identify spurious relationships. What is an acceptable procedure in certain kinds of data mining and exploration of huge databases[20] becomes unacceptable "data dredging" when stepwise methods are used to wander among variables in the hopes of finding interesting relationships. An often-used computer-assisted method of dumpster diving is "forward selection" for a regression model. First, a computer program examines a set of independent variables (IVs), selecting the one with the strongest correlation with the dependent variable (DV); second, the remaining variables are examined to find the one that, when paired with the first, produces the highest R^2; third, the remaining variables are examined to find a variable that forms a trio with the highest R^2; and so on until the search no longer finds variables that produce a statistically significant increase in the R^2.

Using computer software to dig around in some data until you find "something significant" and then using a set of "significant somethings" to build a model remains a widespread practice, in part because it is easier than thinking. And it is faster, too. All the main computer packages have routines for doing it. You can construct a model this way that will "fit" (describe) the data well. But this will be a poor foundation for making inferences to a population. It is much better to build a model based on knowledge of the topic and the research literature on it. There are few topics on which statisticians agree so completely as the inadvisability of brute force searching for "significant" relationships. Trying out dozens of models (combinations of variables) will often yield several relatively "good models," for example, regressions with good R^2 values, but there will be no reasonable way to select among them. This is especially likely to happen when the predictor variables are highly correlated, as predictors very often are in the social sciences.

The difference between random hunting for associations and building a model can be, to some extent, a matter of degree. The difference between thoughtful exploratory data analysis and mindless data foraging is not always clear or uncontroversial. One researcher's exploratory data analysis is another's data dredging. What is fine in exploration is dubious practice in causal inference and generalization to broader populations. It is usually best to think in terms of iterative processes: You can do more exploring after you've made your inferences and generalizations, which prepares you then to build a new model to test with new data.

An iconic example of the problems of model selection concerns real data on a study "with 13 predictor variables and 8,191 models."[21] Data were collected on 252 participants. The goal was to find a simple model with easily measured variables that could be used to estimate percentage of body fat. The best, most accurate measure at the time these data were collected involved a complicated and expensive underwater weighing procedure. Could this be replaced, with little information loss, with simple

[20] For an instructive example of data mining, see Caster, Niklas-Noren, Madigan, and Bate (2010).

[21] See the discussion and worked-out example in Burnham and Anderson (2010, pp. 268–284).

indicators such as various body circumference measures? Using stepwise regression and other computer-intensive—rather than knowledge and thought-intensive—measures produced a huge number (thousands) of possible models. Brute force approaches testing all subsets of variables constitute "reckless data dredging," which does little to resolve the issues of model selection. Several analysts have shown how to do much better using this dataset as an example by applying more thoughtful and more advanced model selection techniques.[22]

Our recommendations closely follow the discussion in Burnham and Anderson's book.[23] They recommend, and we concur, using the **AIC (Akaike information criterion)**[24] as the simplest and most effective method of model selection. However, they also discuss other related approaches, including bootstrapping methods and the Bayesian information criterion (BIC).[25] Briefly sketching the AIC gives the basic idea. For most researchers it is a very practical way to enter this important area of data analysis and interpretation. The preliminary analyses you need to use the AIC are included in most of the typical software packages as options for analyzing models in regression analysis.

The AIC is used to estimate the best model in a set of models the researcher has put together. The researcher is not relieved of the burden of building good models to compare using the AIC. If the set is poor, the AIC will (usually) still pick the best of a bad lot. There are different versions of the AIC. We don't discuss these except to say that the AIC_c (*c* for corrected) is usually preferable. It is roughly parallel to the adjusted R^2, briefly discussed in Chapter 8, which is usually better than the unadjusted statistic.

The AIC is built on information theory, which, for model building, focuses on how much information is lost when using a model to measure reality. The difference between complete reality (assuming one could know it) and imperfect models (all models are imperfect) is assessed with the AIC. The AIC statistic is an estimate of the information lost using each model. By comparing the estimates, we can select the one that loses the least.

The AIC produces a relative rank order of a set of models, not an absolute measure of a model's quality. It ranks models on how well they perform as explanations of a specific set of data. When the set of data is inadequate, it can be impossible to obtain an unambiguous ranking of models. One solution to that problem is **model averaging**. The first step is to use multimodel inference and AIC to pick the *best* model (as always, from your set, not in any absolute sense). You can also eliminate some clearly inadequate models and then use the rest to do model averaging and multimodel inference. One ranks alternative models and assigns them weights according to their rank; then they can be averaged. This allows you to draw inferences from all models in the set.[26]

---

[22]In a very instructive article, Morgan (2004) compares five reasonable models of the same phenomena and shows how model selection can *dramatically* influence interpretations.

[23]Burnham and Anderson (2010) is the single most comprehensive work on the subject. Anderson (2008) provides a briefer and more introductory account.

[24]The mathematician Hirotugu Akaike called it *an information criterion*; he did not name the AIC after himself, but subsequent researchers have changed the name to give him proper credit.

[25]They find the BIC a poor criterion; see Burnham, Anderson, and Huyvaert (2011).

[26]On model averaging and how it helps analysts avoid some types of model selection bias, see Lukacs, Burnham, and Anderson (2010).

A general description of this procedure makes AIC sound similar to the stepwise methods we have just condemned. The goals are similar, but there are two key differences. First, the AIC is not a statistical test, and statistical significance is irrelevant to the procedures and outcomes of an AIC analysis. Second, with AIC, researchers work with a set of *models*, constructed according to the researchers' knowledge of the problem, not as in stepwise methods, which use a set of *variables* in search of a model.[27] The basic point here, as with most quantitative analyses, is that even with advanced techniques such as AIC, computations are the easy part. The hard part is knowing enough about the phenomena under study to develop not just one model but several good candidate models. You do this before the data collection. After you get the data, you apply the AIC. Here, more than elsewhere, no statistical routine can come to the rescue and save you from the need to think and to think well. This means that part of the methodology section in your write-up may be a discussion of the thought processes you used to build your models. At minimum, keep a journal in which you record these for your own use.

CONCLUSION: A RESEARCH AGENDA

Model building requires a wide range of skills and methods. Quantitative models can be built on preliminary explorations of your data. These data can be described using exploratory and graphic approaches, as well as effect sizes and confidence intervals. Most modeling is done with one form or another of regression analysis (and related correlational methods). Researchers often start with relatively direct linear regression models and then build on these to include nonlinear problems (polynomial regression, logit regression, etc.). The two chief questions are (1) what variables to include and (2) the shapes (linear or otherwise) of the distributions of those variables. A third issue, very important for many research questions, is assessing the relative importance of the variables in the model. The models become more complicated as driven by the needs of the research problem. You can advance through PA, factor analysis, MLM, and SEM before finally reaching the pinnacle: theory construction and model building.

Selecting variables effectively and building good models requires knowledge of a problem (e.g., gained thorough familiarity with the research literature) and rigorous thinking about the implications of the models. We think that all this thinking is not just good for you in some long-term sense, like aerobic exercise or eating whole grains, but in a very direct and immediate sense of being related to the success of a research project. This is especially the case when your research is not a one-time thing, as with a school exercise, but is research in which you care about the outcomes because you plan to do more of it—in other words, when you have a research agenda. There are many reasons that some contributions to research are influential and others are not, but surely one of them is the conceptual foundation on which good research is built.

Conceptual foundations—theories, assumptions, and ideas about the relationships among variables/conditions—are all qualitative, ideational. Models and research agendas, even the most quantitative ones, have a qualitative foundation. That is why the next part of the book, on the analysis of qualitative data, in addition to being very important in its own right, also helps uncover the substructure of the analysis of quantitative data.

[27] On approaches to model building and selection see Doherty, White, and Burnham (2012).

SUGGESTIONS FOR FURTHER READING

One of the most frequently cited sources by writers who discuss theory construction and model building is Platt's 1964 article, "Strong Inference." This article in turn cited, and brought to the attention of more modern readers, Chamberlin's 1890 article "The Method of Multiple Working Hypotheses." Both articles are short, nicely argued, and freely available on the Web (just type the author's name and the title in Google Scholar). They are a good antidote to any notion that the importance of thinking hard before gathering data about multiple alternative hypotheses is a fad that will eventually blow over so that we can all relax and go back to testing the null.

The best modern text on model building and selection that does not require that readers have extensive statistical backgrounds is Jaccard and Jacoby's *Theory Construction and Model-Building Skills: A Practical Guide for Social Scientists.* We often recommend it to our beginning doctoral students and have relied on it extensively when thinking about how to structure this chapter. A more advanced work is Murnane and Willett's *Methods Matter: Improving Causal Inference in Educational and Social Science Research.* It is an exceptionally wise and accessible overview of causal modeling and advanced quantitative models available to researchers. The authors place more emphasis on econometric and experimental approaches than we do, so their work presents a "plausible alternative model" to ours. And, most important, they give in-depth consideration to the most fruitful approaches to take when experiments are not possible, as is often the case.

There is some controversy about the reliability of Wikipedia entries, but in the case of the article on the AIC (*http://en.wikipedia.org/wiki/Akaike_information_criterion*), the article is very clear, concise, and accurate.

The works of Kenneth Burnham and David Anderson were central to our understanding of the information-theoretic approach described in this chapter. Their work is perhaps less known among social researchers than it might otherwise be because it has mostly been published in biology journals. A very useful overview is their article (with K. Huyvaert) on "AIC Model Selection and Multimodel Inference in Behavioral Ecology: Some Background, Observations, and Comparisons" (2011). This is available at *www2.unil.ch/popgen/modsel/biblio/BurnhamBES11.pdf.*

CHAPTER 10 SUMMARY TABLE

When is it more effective to study a model or models rather than variables? (pp. 351–356)	• When the research literature is rich with theories and findings relevant to your question. • When current models/theories seem to you insufficient or flawed. • When you want to be as explicit as possible about, and keep track of, the ideas guiding your research.
When is it useful to compare alternate models rather than study models one at a time? (pp. 358–361)	• When you have a research agenda that can guide you in testing an initial model with data and use what you have learned to modify subsequent models and test them with new data. • When you have enough knowledge of the field to generate plausible candidate models.
When should you consider mathematical modeling? (p. 356)	• When you believe that the relations among the variables in your model may not be linear.
When constructing a model, how do you find the middle ground between underfitting and overfitting? (pp. 356–358)	• Make an informed judgment about the relative importance of completeness and parsimony in your model.

PART III

Analysis and Interpretation of Qualitative and Combined/Mixed Data

In this Introduction to Part III we:

- Discuss varieties of qualitative data analyses and some of their common features.
- Introduce the distinction between inductive and deductive approaches.
- Review possible combinations of deductive, inductive, qualitative, and quantitative data analyses.

INTRODUCTION TO PART III

Writing about any topic requires that authors use categories. The task of devising a set of workable categories for describing qualitative data analysis is complicated by the proliferation of different terms researchers in the field use to describe their work. A common term may denote more than one method, and very similar methods may have different names. Although a parallel naming problem exists in quantitative data analysis, it is exacerbated in qualitative data analysis because the methods are much less codified and routinized. Less codification and fewer agreed-upon terms are natural because researchers collecting and analyzing qualitative data require and demand more flexibility in the methods they use. However, this flexibility in what they *do* does not mean that qualitative researchers should have more latitude in reporting what they *have done*. Indeed, just the opposite is the case; because there are fewer routine shorthand ways of reporting that coincide with well-known procedures, it is especially important for qualitative data analysts to describe in detail the methods they have employed.

There are many varieties of qualitative research and just as many political orientations or perspectives on or approaches to it (e.g., feminist, neocolonial, postpositivist, critical theory, action research). These important orientations are usually most salient in the early shaping of a study's research questions and in the final interpretations of its data. Between the initial orientation and concluding interpretations, researchers tend to apply a common core of coding and analysis methods. As authors of well-respected texts have put it, "many common research procedures . . . underlie qualitative studies that may in other respects differ strongly in their philosophical orientation and research design." Because of these common coding and analytical procedures, "it is possible to develop practical standards—workable across different perspectives—for judging the goodness of conclusions."[1]

Although it can sometimes be hard to find the common analytical ground because the labels given to the methods vary considerably, we are more impressed by the commonalities than the differences. It is often not very productive to spend a great deal of time distinguishing among the subcategories of methods for qualitative data analysis. Students in particular tend to overlook the forest (common methods) and to be distracted by the large number of trees (variants) and to worry too much about finding the "right" label for their research.[2] This is understandable because the "research literature is replete with characterizations of the diversity of approaches to qualitative research . . . , and various authors have attempted to provide lists or even typologies of them."[3] When this happens, an approach can easily become open to the kind of criticism the mathematician and physicist Henri Poincaré leveled at sociology: It is "the science with the most methods and the fewest results."[4]

In Part I, we drew distinctions in qualitative data handling and coding procedures depending upon whether the data came from interviews (Chapter 2), naturalistic observation (Chapter 4), or archival/secondary sources (Chapter 5). But once the data have been collected and put in "codable" form, such as interview transcripts, fieldnotes, or text files, differences in analytical methods are much less determinative. Qualitative data analysis methods (like quantitative methods) are portable across data that have been collected in various ways. (A partial exception is the distinction between deductive and inductive approaches to data analysis, discussed later.)

One reason for the portability of analysis methods across perspectives and designs is that qualitative data have a common feature: They are mostly textual. Many research projects generate their own textual data, whereas others use the enormously rich archives of textual data that await analysis. Analysis of data from interview research is often built upon transcriptions of recordings or upon the researcher's summary notes. Observational researchers analyze fieldnotes and often add published and unpublished documents to their data sources. Even survey researchers and experimenters not infrequently collect verbal data from participants and put it into textual form amenable to qualitative analysis.

Methods of textual analysis to be examined in the following chapters and discussed in terms of when those methods might be most effective range broadly. At one end of the spectrum are traditional methods—reading, underlining, and making notes in the margins. On the other is the application of computer-assisted qualitative data analysis software (CAQDAS). Quantitative techniques for textual data are also widespread and are discussed briefly in Chapter 13 on combined/mixed coding and analysis. Here we note that using multiple methods—traditional, CAQDAS, and quantitative—on the same text is one way to bridge the quant–qual gap (should you wish to do this). And comparing analyses using the three classes of methods is often an excellent source of insights and new interpretations.

---

[1] Yin (2011, p. 15); Miles and Huberman (1994, p. 5).

[2] For a persuasive approach that puts more emphasis than we do on the differences among approaches, see Wertz et al. (2011).

[3] Coffey and Atkinson (1996, p. 12).

[4] Poincaré (1920).

Another nearly universal feature of the analysis of qualitative data is that you not only analyze what you have recorded (such as interview transcripts or fieldnotes) but also your own interpretations of what you have recorded. These interpretations become part of your data for subsequent analysis (Level 2 data, as it were). In some circumstances, upon further analysis, you might interpret your Level 2 interpretations to achieve a third level of data to be analyzed. Whether a fourth level is possible—or desirable, if possible—is a subject of some dispute that we can leave to philosophers and cognitive psychologists. What we do know is that thinking about what you have observed and recorded, *and* thinking about your thoughts, is as important as the initial data collection, whether from interviews, field observations, or documents. We believe this is also true in the analysis of quantitative data and doubly so when analyzing qualitative and quantitative data together.

Qualitative data analysis rewards deep, careful thinkers, people who are meticulous about their use of language and who like to and are able to reflect on their reflections. But it also draws people who are more intuitive and expressive in their approach to research. Intuitiveness and expressiveness are largely beyond our scope in this volume. We don't know how to advise people about how to become more intuitive and expressive. As Camus said in a different context, those who lack character have to make do with methods. Alas, whether or not we agree with Camus, our book restricts itself mainly to methods.

While recognizing the overriding unity in the wide spectrum of qualitative data analysis methods, we have used one distinction to structure the following chapters: the differences in logical approaches and analytical purposes indicated by the terms **inductive** and **deductive.**[5] We mean nothing very complicated by the distinction between inductive and deductive approaches. As Yin summarizes, "inductive approaches tend to let the data lead to the emergence of concepts; deductive approaches tend to let the concepts . . . lead to the definition of the relevant data that need to be collected."[6]

One common misconception among beginning researchers is that the type of data you collect automatically dictates the type of analysis that you can do. For example, some researchers may believe that if your data are textual in nature, you are restricted to qualitative methods and that if they come from experiments, they must be analyzed using quantitative methods. In fact, all types of data can be analyzed in a variety of ways. Data may be transformed from quantitative to qualitative or vice versa, and both may be displayed and analyzed graphically. Finally, data variously transformed and combined can be investigated using any or all of the three possible approaches illustrated in Figure III.1: inductive, deductive, or a combination of the two.

Often the difference between inductive and deductive approaches can be most clearly seen in the relationship of the researcher to the review of the research literature on the topic of investigation. For example, an **inductive approach** to studying intergroup relations would be to find good settings in which to study interacting groups, to go into the field to gather data with which you can carefully describe the interactions, and then, as part of the process of preparing the final analysis and presentation of your results, to review the literature relevant to your interpretations and place your conclusions in the

[5]This distinction is also relevant for quantitative methods, as in the difference between exploratory data analysis (Chapter 7) and model building and testing (Chapter 10).

[6]Yin (2011, p. 94).

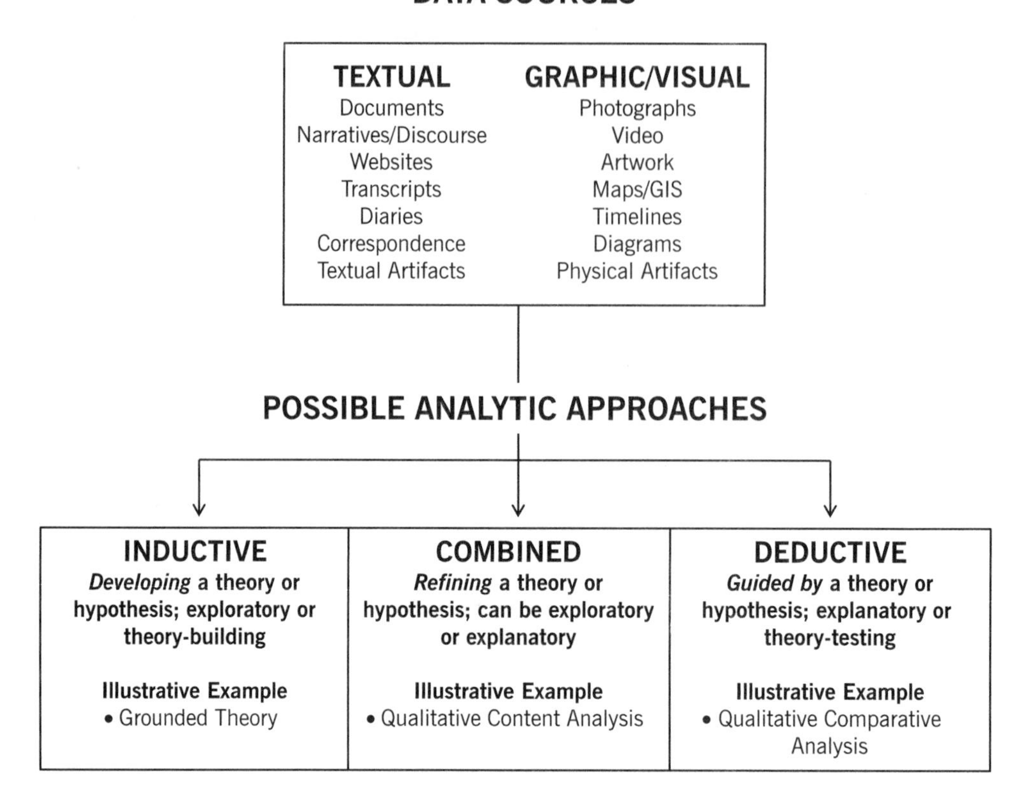

FIGURE III.1. Using data of various types in three possible analytic approaches.

context of that literature. An example of a **deductive approach** to studying intergroup relations would be to review the research literature looking for credible theories and generalizations about intergroup relationships and to select one or more of those theories for investigation; then you would find appropriate settings for observation to see whether the theory holds up upon close examination.[7] In case studies, the inductive–deductive distinction tends to show up in the purpose behind the selection of the case(s) to study. Do you study a case inductively because it is importantly unique and needs to be understood in detail, or do you study a case deductively because it is a case *of something*, of some phenomenon, and you want to gather data relevant to understanding that phenomenon?

Most social research, and probably all, is some of each—part deductive, part inductive. It is hard to imagine investigating human thought and action in either an exclusively deductive or inductive way. Purely inductive research, undertaken with no preconceived ideas to direct one's attention while observing, is impossible—or, were it possible, it would put us into what William James famously called a state of "blooming, buzzing confusion." Purely deductive research might be possible in formal fields, such as some branches of mathematics and logic, but is largely irrelevant to social researchers who

[7]Of course, one could also interview people in the setting or, alternatively, survey them.

study people in places. Our perspective throughout this volume is to focus on ways of gaining usable knowledge. Induction and deduction are both necessary to gain that knowledge, which is why we give them equal weight and why we discuss how they may both be used deliberately in the same study. However, most researchers emphasize one more than the other, and these differences in emphasis have important consequences for analysis and interpretation of data. Although we give each equal emphasis, there is little doubt that among the community of people conducting qualitative research, the inductive approach predominates, both in sheer numbers of studies and in terms of a place of honor in the canon.

In the history of the social sciences, the main founders of inductive qualitative research, such as Boas and Malinowski, conducted ethnographic fieldwork among the people they studied. By contrast, the foundations of deductive qualitative research were built by scholars such as Weber and Durkheim, who conducted comparative case studies using mostly archival data; they worked among other scholars in universities. These two strands of qualitative data analysis are the themes of Chapters 11 and 12, in which we use brief discussions of ethnographic fieldwork and comparative case studies to introduce two modern examples of research in these traditions. These two methods of qualitative analysis have been quite systematized by their users: **grounded theory (GT)** and **qualitative comparative analysis (QCA)**. We employ them as paradigm examples or ideal types to highlight issues pertinent to a broad range of methodological questions.

GT emphasizes an inductive approach but is hardly theory-free. Although QCA takes a more deductive approach, it evinces great respect for empirical evidence. A community of researchers has grown up around each; this has facilitated methodological discussions that are more advanced than in many other branches of methodology for qualitative data. Our example of the inductive approach, GT, emerged out of in-depth interview research by sociologists in the 1960s and is discussed in Chapter 11. GT has been widely used and developed since the 1960s; the developments include the appearance of textbooks, handbooks, and rival schools. Our example of the deductive approach, discussed in Chapter 12, is QCA. It originated in the 1980s in the study of issues in comparative sociology and political science. QCA has mostly focused on the study of large-scale social and political events and structures and has also been adopted by a growing community of researchers who have published texts, guidebooks, and software.

The followers of both GT and QCA have attempted to introduce systematic methods and terminology into qualitative analysis. Of the many attempts to do this, these two have caught on more than most and have attracted a great deal of methodological discussion. Thus GT and QCA provide a good entry point for reviewing most issues about qualitative analysis. Among the issues that concern many qualitative analysts who examine either GT or QCA is the question of the extent to which an approach remains "truly" qualitative when its methods have been quite systematized. Some of the practitioners of these methods employ what look like, at first blush, algorithms that undermine the spirit of qualitative analysis. Qualitative researchers have sometimes resisted attempts at systematizing their methods, and that is understandable, but it gives writers of reference and textbooks on research methods very little to say. GT and QCA have given us quite a lot to say in Chapters 11 and 12.

After the discussions of inductive and deductive approaches to qualitative analysis, we turn our attention (in Chapter 13) to combining them with methods of quantitative data analysis. We focus on modeling and combining various qualitative approaches to data analysis with various quantitative ones, including, as always, visual approaches. By combining qualitative and quantitative approaches, one also sometimes combines inductive and deductive types of research. This is illustrated in Table III.1, which displays prominent examples of the kinds of analysis methods that might be combined into more mixed approaches. The fact that combinations are possible and, we believe, desirable makes it clear that we view the categories—inductive–deductive and qualitative–quantitative—as tendencies, not rigid classifications. All combinations are possible, both in theory and in practice, as the examples in Chapter 13 illustrate.

The examples in each row of Table III.1—inductive and deductive—have much in common and provide the natural starting points for linking qualitative and quantitative approaches. For instance, it is easy to see how GT and exploratory data analysis (EDA) have a clear family resemblance, as do QCA and structural equation modeling (SEM). The examples in each column (qualitative and quantitative) also provide many opportunities for finding analytical links. For example, QCA analyses can be conducted on data gathered and initially analyzed using GT, and the ideas for model testing in SEM often arise out of EDA. It would seem more difficult, but potentially more rewarding, to make links on the diagonals: GT and SEM or QCA and EDA. One promising link might be, for example, inductive–qualitative → deductive–quantitative (GT → SEM). Another could be inductive–quantitative → deductive–qualitative (EDA → QCA). These and others are theoretically and, perhaps, practically possible. The barriers to linking, for example, GT and SEM often arise out of research specialization. It is uncommon (but not impossible) for researchers to have the combination of skills and interests needed.[8]

Finally, in the concluding chapter, we attempt to bring together a broad range of ideas. We discuss the problem of how to make effective choices among myriad analysis options, and we also emphasize some guiding principles of social research that transcend specific options. Not only do we focus on the diversity in the choices researchers confront as they select their analysis methods, we also highlight the common themes that can guide them as they do so. When writing this book, as we discussed various drafts, we routinely engaged in dialogues that went back and forth between, on the one hand, the vast number of alternatives open to researchers as they selected their methods of analysis and, on the other, a substantial cluster of common methodological principles. It is likely that most researchers, as they work through their research projects, will participate in similar dialogues (sometimes internal). We know that we do so in our research. In sum, while selecting among remarkably numerous methodological alternatives, one is usually guided by common themes. From these come Chapter 14.

TABLE III.1. Paradigm Examples of Qualitative–Quantitative and Inductive–Deductive Approaches

	Qualitative	Quantitative
Inductive	Grounded theory (GT)	Exploratory data analysis (EDA)
Deductive	Qualitative comparative analysis (QCA)	Structural equation modeling (SEM)

[8]For an example of the combined use of GT and SEM, see Rosenbaum (2011).

Rather than conclude in Chapter 14 with a linear summary—which the reader could easily obtain by reviewing the Summary Tables in each chapter—we have adapted a literary genre unusual in methodological discourse: aphorisms. We tried other ways of presenting our concluding ideas but found that a collection of aphorisms allowed coverage as complete as but more readable than the alternatives we considered—chief among them being a many-branched taxonomy. We started down the taxonomy path, and the *process* was quite interesting. But the *product* of the work was irremediably dull. Before long we couldn't read it, and it became so intricate that we couldn't graph it, either. On the other hand, we had lively discussions about the aphorisms. That led us to choose them as the way to wrap up the book.

CHAPTER 11

Inductive Analysis of Qualitative Data

Ethnographic Approaches and Grounded Theory

In this chapter we:

- Review the foundations of inductive social research in ethnographic fieldwork.
  - Discuss the origins of the standard model of ethnography.
  - Review the emic–etic distinction and its implications.
  - Discuss studying what you know and theory testing as alternatives to the standard model.
- Introduce grounded theory (GT) as an inductive approach to theory building and provide a general description of GT.
  - Discuss analytical categories and themes relevant to GT practitioners, including:
    - How your goals influence your approach.
    - The importance of prior research.
    - Forming categories and codes inductively.
      —Abduction, or where do you get ideas?
    - GT's approaches to sampling.
    - The question of using multiple coders.
    - The use of tools, including software.

Inductive approaches to data analysis work from the particular to the general, or from the data to concepts and theories. The idea is to begin with data gathering, move gradually to coding and categorizing the data, and from there to generalizations and theories. Although inductive approaches exist in quantitative methods (see the discussion of exploratory data analysis in Chapter 6), inductive methods are most commonly seen in the work of social researchers who collect, analyze, interpret, and theorize about qualitative data. Some social researchers who analyze qualitative data take a more deductive approach and are more guided in their investigations by preexisting theories that they want to assess; these researchers are discussed in the next chapter. Here we focus on researchers who use induction to pursue goals that are more descriptive than theoretical or who aim to construct new theories rather than to assess existing ones.[1] By far the largest and most paradigmatic category of such work is ethnography, broadly defined.

THE FOUNDATIONS OF INDUCTIVE SOCIAL RESEARCH IN ETHNOGRAPHIC FIELDWORK[2]

In earlier chapters on interview and observational research, we mentioned the work of Herodotus. His book *The Histories* has been claimed to be foundational for the modern disciplines of history, political science, folklore, and ethnography. Here we focus on the last of these. About 2,500 years ago, he wrote what is arguably the first book-length piece of social science research; it was based on interviews and fieldwork. He sought cultural explanations of how the Greeks and Persians came to be locked in a devastating series of wars that some see as having continued intermittently to the present day (Europe and its allies vs. Iran and its allies). His work shares one important characteristic with other early ethnographic approaches to inductive qualitative data: Herodotus's descriptions seem to the modern reader to be an odd mix of straightforward credible, almost mundane, accounts on the one hand and preposterously fantastic tales on the other. A careful review of his work leads to an explanation. When he was describing what he had directly seen and heard, his accounts were ordinary, detailed descriptive narratives. But when he related what he had heard secondhand about people from distant lands inhabited by "others," his histories (stories) were often wildly absurd.

This duality remained a feature of proto-ethnographic writing for many centuries. Unknown peoples were described as beasts and monsters, not really human. When one thinks of the cultural stereotypes still prevalent in nations at war, this kind of demonizing of the other is perhaps not behind us. The first systematic attempts to do something like modern ethnography—to describe a different people accurately, based on firsthand knowledge—date to European writers in the 16th century. Not coincidentally, this was also the time of a huge expansion of European colonial empires. The expansion continued in fits and starts well into the 20th century, as did the constant stream of quasi-ethnographic writing. Early writers of credibly descriptive ethnographic accounts, from the 16th through the 19th centuries, were usually soldiers, colonial administrators, or missionaries—and it is often difficult to distinguish among these three roles.

Until well into the 20th century, ethnographic fieldworkers were rarely methodologically self-conscious. Or if they were they didn't share their reflections with readers. Although, by the 1920s and 1930s, examples of a recognizable methodology had appeared, they were accompanied by little if any methodological discourse. Malinowski was among the first to provide a model of how it should be done, and his work almost immediately became a highly influential model.[3] Ethnography, or anthropology, was to be based on intensive fieldwork. The researcher was to live with the people being

[1]We have already discussed data coding methods used by inductive qualitative researchers in Chapters 2 and 4 on coding interview and observational data. See also Vogt et al. (2012, Chs. 4, 10, 16) on observational research design, sampling, and ethics.

[2]We use the terms *ethnography* and *fieldwork* somewhat loosely and interchangeably, because this is how they are used by anthropologists and others describing this form of inductive data gathering and analysis.

[3]Malinowski (1922).

studied, learn their language (not rely on translators, as Boas[4] had), participate as much as possible in their activities, and describe their beliefs and practices in great depth; only then would the ethnographer know enough to make any generalizations. Finally, because of the need to study practices and beliefs in detail, the social groups studied would necessarily be small.[5] This model remains an ideal type of what an ethnographer should aspire to do.

Whereas early ethnographers described others in detail, they didn't describe their own methods in much depth—except sometimes to claim that there wasn't much to it. As Evans-Pritchard is reported to have said, "anybody who is not a complete idiot can do fieldwork." One explanation of this seeming aversion to methodology is that ethnographic fieldwork's "intense reliance on personalized seeing, hearing, and experiencing in specific social settings has always generated something of a hostility to generalizations and abstractions not connected to immersion in situated detail"—and that includes abstractions and generalizations about research methods.[6] Anthropologists rarely went beyond such statements as, "the fieldworking anthropologist tries to understand alien societies from the inside rather than from the outside" and "to understand how it feels to be a member of the society in question," which is why "it is the details that matter, and the details cannot be discussed in general terms."[7] But anthropologists rarely tried to explain *how* they came to understand what it feels like to be an insider, except to say that it took a lot of time to gather enough data to write a credible description. This emphasis on descriptive details explains why nearly all the pioneering works in anthropological fieldwork were book-length studies. What the scholars wanted to narrate could not be easily summarized within the confines of a typical journal article. Compare the ethnographer's data presentation needs and consequent writing style with the format and style of the works of the pioneers of path analysis and factor analysis. Writing at about the same time in the 1920s and 1930s, their pathbreaking works were articles, and not terribly long ones.[8]

There is also a sociological version of intensive ethnographic fieldwork. Its origins are usually traced to the Chicago School of sociology, which emphasized studying disadvantaged urban groups. The Chicago School had important roots in investigative (or muckraking) journalism. It studied unfamiliar social groups and places—unfamiliar at least to middle-class professors and graduate students—such as gang members, hobos, and thieves who congregated on street corners, in pool halls, and so on. Their approach remains an important tradition in sociology and in many applied fields,[9] but it never gained the discipline-defining status that ethnographic fieldwork retains in anthropology.

What sociologists added to the fieldwork mix is an element very important in contemporary ethnography, anthropological or sociological—studying social groups that

---

[4]Boas was the main U.S pioneer of ethnography; many of his students became famous. One example of his work, on the subject of "primitive" thought, which was of great interest at the time, is Boas (1911).

[5]Firth (1936), for example, wrote many more pages about the Tikopia than there were people in that society.

[6]The quotations are in Van Maanen (2011, pp. 97 and 156, respectively).

[7]Leach (1982, pp. 161, 148).

[8]See Chapter 9 and Thurstone (1931) and Wright (1921, 1934).

[9]See the works cited in Chapter 4.

are much less remote or exotic than those studied by the early founders. This raises a methodological question very important for inductive data gathering and analysis: How inductive or purely observational can your research be when the social group you are studying is not really foreign to you? Experiencing what it feels like to be an insider seems not to be much of a stretch when you can get to the site of your fieldwork on the "El" or on a city bus. Can you truly be inductive in your observations if you already know, to some extent, the culture and language of the social group you are studying? Are extensive field studies worth all the effort when the social groups studied are comparatively familiar?

The counterargument is that you do not really know these more familiar groups until you have studied them using intensive fieldwork methods. You might be studying the police in a city, or the nurses in a hospital, or the teachers in a school, or the workers in a factory, all fairly familiar people and roles, but until you have experienced "being there" for an extended period of time, you will have little genuine insight into their lives. Even when you study more remote and less familiar peoples and places, if you are a participant observer, your goal is to become an insider ("go native"). You may start as an outsider, but your goal is not to remain one.

How important is participant observation in a hitherto unexamined social group? How likely are you to find contained, well-defined communities, such as the Tikopia, confined to one spot and limited in numbers of outside contacts? And even if one were to identify such social groups, is ethnography's assumption that they can be understood best by direct personal experience credible?[10] Whomever you study, you are a visitor, and you need to discover a means of understanding the members of the social group in their terms. Then, in the analysis, it is necessary to decide how to translate those understandings into terms your audience of other scholars can understand. This usually involves extensive coding and analyses of fieldnotes, a process that often takes considerably longer than the observations themselves.

Direct observation and extensive onsite fieldwork is now clearly the distinguishing characteristic of all researchers who would say they used ethnographic methods. If you don't have the time or inclination for intensive fieldwork—coupled with even more laborious deskwork—ethnography is not for you. On this common foundation, ethnographers have built widely diverse, even sharply contradictory, approaches, theories, and conclusions.

Extensive direct observation can also be seen in other kinds of investigations and writing. What differentiates ethnography, whether of the anthropological or sociological persuasion, from other intensive "I-witnessing," such as travel logs or investigative journalism? The key difference is your audience. You are a scholarly writer producing your account for other researchers who work in the same discipline or intellectual tradition. As such, your data analysis, if not necessarily your data collection, is expected to be shaped by the literature of that discipline. You may go into the field largely innocent of any knowledge of the social group you intend to study; perhaps you will not even speak their language. And many would advise that this state of innocence is the best way to be prepared to really see and observe.

---

[10]Feldman (2011) raises these challenging questions and illustrates the uses of nonlocal ethnography in a study of illegal immigrants en route from Senegal to Italy.

But the advocates of this "before the fall" approach have all had a broad range of knowledge relevant to their task. They have been very familiar with previous anthropological and/or sociological writings and theories, and they put their findings into that context. They have also usually had a commitment to one or another type of analytical approach, such as functionalism, structuralism, or cultural materialism. To define them briefly:[11] Functionalists interpret persistent social patterns in terms of how they contribute to the stability of the social group; structuralists search for underlying, perhaps universal, patterns of human language and thought; a cultural materialist is a kind of functionalist, but one who focuses less on group stability and more on how social patterns are related to economic production. In any case, if you are observing as an ethnographer, you will almost certainly enter the field with ideas and theories such as these in your backpack. You may be persuaded by one of them or simply aware of the explanatory strategies used by others who went into the field before you. It is hard to imagine that such prior knowledge and ideas would have no influence on what you see or on which among the things you observe you will pay the most attention to.

There can be escape neither from prior knowledge nor from the symbols, primarily language, which we use to express our thinking. And although we might wish we could study things directly, in the last analysis, all we have is indirect representations and symbols. Ethnographers attempt to learn what others using the "native" language mean, and then they put it into ethnographic language to communicate it to their colleagues. Reflection on this language-bound state of affairs has given rise to various antimethods, such as postmodernism, poststructuralism, and deconstructionism. We admit to being somewhat perplexed by postmodernism and most of the other "Posties." It's easy enough to see what they don't like, but hard to get a handle on what they propose to put in its stead. Their adherents might reply that this uncertainty is exactly the point—they propose to put *nothing* in its stead. At any rate, because they are resolutely antimethod, there is little for us to say about them in a book about selecting methods.[12] A postmodernist approach might be just the ticket in some philosophy or literature departments, but it would be a more risky choice in most social research publications or university departments.

Chief among the theoretical orientations that direct much ethnographic research is the one captured by the distinction between the **emic** and the **etic**. These curious labels are adjectival endings of the words *phonemic* and *phonetic*—which does not help all that much without further explanation. In linguistics phonetics is the study of the objective sounds that speakers of a language make, whereas phonemics refers to the study of the meanings of the sounds to those speakers. Stretching this linguistic distinction a bit, it can be applied to anthropology and ethnographic fieldwork. An *emic* emphasis refers to the perspectives of the members of the social group being studied. By contrast, an *etic* emphasis refers to the perspectives of the social researchers summarizing their findings for other researchers. The meanings that have been assigned to these two labels have drifted since they came into use in the 1950s. We summarize in Table 11.1, ending

[11]Such brief descriptions are inevitably a travesty, but because we are doing so only for illustrative purposes, they can suffice.

[12]Unfortunately, but probably inevitably, the clearest descriptions tend to be critical; the best of these is by Habermas (1990), who coined the term *Posties*; see also Lilla (1998) and Rorty (1987).

TABLE 11.1. The Meanings and Connotations of Emic and Etic

Emic	Insider	Particular	Subjective	Humanistic	Idiographic
Etic	Outsider	General	Objective	Scientific	Nomothetic

with the distinction between idiographic and nomothetic, which we discuss in the next chapter.

Why does this matter? The answer is that researchers are often asked, "What side are you on?" Is it more important for the ethnographer to focus on presenting the meanings of a culture and social group as the members themselves see it? Or should the goal be ultimately to contribute to a general understanding of human culture? One such general understanding, it is ironically interesting to point out, is that human beings are inherently dichotomizers. The world may be continuous, but we understand it using binary categories—sacred–profane, dirty–pure, raw–cooked, animal–human, us–them, and, we would add in this context, emic–etic.[13]

Like many other methodological debates, this one can get out of hand, but the question of which point of view you, as a researcher, choose to emphasize is an important one. Those of an inductive frame of mind tend to emphasize the meanings of the members of the culture. Although by no means are all anthropologists focused mainly on insiders' understandings of their culture, it is our impression that most researchers today doing ethnography in applied fields—such as nursing, education, and social work—think of themselves as taking the emic perspective.

Many anthropologists see no real conflict between the emic and the etic. When talking to the members of a social group to learn about their culture, ethnographers focus on the emic side, but when they are preparing the results of their research to present to colleagues, they emphasize the etic side. Perhaps the most memorable example of the emic–etic distinction occurs in explanations of cannibalism. In the various cultures in which this is practiced, the native explanations (emic) are made using magical and religious categories, and many anthropologists build on theories of magic and religion to build their scholarly (etic) explanations. But one anthropological account (a more radically etic one) notes that societies in which cannibalism is widespread would be grievously short of dietary protein if they abandoned the practice.[14]

We have lingered over descriptions of early ethnographic work because it illustrates what remains a common core. But there have been changes superimposed on that core. Over the last few decades, the methodology of fieldwork has moved from being based on a kind of naive empiricism—just go out there, observe, and record—to a discipline as methodology-crazed as any other. "Epistemopilia" and "epistemological hypochondria"[15] are two of the terms used to characterize what some consider a malady. But others think that greater attention to the theory of knowledge and methodology is

[13]This emphasis on binary codes is a position of many structuralists, the most famous of whom was Lévi-Strauss (1969).

[14]This culturally materialist explanation is Harris's (1980); he also stresses the importance of the emic–etic distinction in anthropological theory and provides one of the more thorough accounts.

[15]Geertz (1988, p. 71).

a welcome recognition of the complexity of the ethnographer's work in describing one culture in terms another culture can understand and of his or her managing to do this without doing violence to the original. As the methodological turn has become more widespread and ethnographers have brought diverse perspectives to bear on their work, it has become quite hard to generalize about just what the term *ethnography* now means. It seems to connote quite a few different things to its many and diverse practitioners.[16]

The standard Malinowski model of ethnography had a kind of purity. You arrived on site with a notebook and pen and tried to gain enough acceptance in the social group that you could become a participant observer. You participated, observed, and wrote fieldnotes. Then you wrote a book. That was always something of a romantic simplification, of course. Most ethnographers were well versed in the social science theories of their day before they went into the field, and, in their write-ups, they added to it. Today's ethnographers, of course, use the full range of data gathering, recording, and coding methods and technologies discussed in Chapters 2 and 4.[17] Because ethnographers come from a wide variety of fields, they bring with them the armamentaria of those fields. But the core of the method is the same. It stresses painstaking, detailed observation of phenomena. The data thus gathered are reviewed to build an inductively based analysis.

In sum, ethnographic research requires a huge commitment of time and often other personal resources, such as travel funds. To get an ethnographic analysis published in most respectable outlets or to get it past most dissertation committees also requires a broad familiarity with a complex theoretical literature, and gaining such knowledge to a credible level is no small thing. Furthermore, it is hard to know in advance whether your efforts will be rewarded. This has led many ethnographers to adopt one or both of two strategies: (1) studying something you know or to which you can gain comparatively easy access or (2) theory elaborating or testing.

Studying what you know—rather than going someplace unfamiliar to observe and participate in a social group you don't know—can be a reasonable option, and one that is used by increasing numbers of ethnographers. The big advantage is that you don't have to overcome such a huge knowledge deficit to get to the point at which you can reasonably suppose that you know what the insiders know and think. Thus you may then be able to get to a deeper level of understanding than might be possible for a researcher who is truly an outsider. We briefly illustrate the study-what-you-know approach with three examples.

One author studied, by joining, a "fight club" in his local community, San Francisco. The fight club phenomenon seems to have become fairly widespread since the movie of that name. The study's goal was to gain a deeper understanding of violence in the definition of "manhood" in contemporary U.S. culture.[18] A second example of studying what you know was an investigation of a Danish town with an aging population and in a state of economic decline; it had been "invaded" by younger, more affluent Danes who had moved from Copenhagen.[19] The author, a fieldwork anthropologist, used network analysis and human capital theory to analyze the data gathered by relatively

[16]See Culyba, Heimer, and Petty (2004).

[17]See Bernard (2000, Chs. 9–11) for a review with a strong ethnographic focus.

[18]Melzer (2013).

[19]Svendsen (2006).

traditional means—participant observation and interviews—to explain why the experience of merging two cultures turned out poorly for nearly everyone. Finally, one of the best known examples of studying the familiar is Hayano's auto-ethnography[20] of poker clubs in which he participated; he essentially became one of the people he was studying. Although the term *auto-ethnography* had been around for quite some time before Hayano's work, his book and research note on the topic are two of the most commonly cited sources. More recently, auto-ethnography seems to have morphed into autobiography—as one commentator put it, "enough about them, let me tell you about me!"

The reasons for studying what you know are many. At minimum, most graduate students in their fieldwork training probably start out this way, and they decide to continue on that path. In any case, even if you are doing participant observation in a remote place with an unknown social group, you may start out as an outsider, but your goal is to become an insider. Once you do, you become a quasi-member of the group, and your ethnographic work may be not so different from that of someone who begins work in a comparatively more familiar setting. The main benefit of the traditional approach of classic ethnographic fieldwork in remote locales may be your personal transformation from outsider to quasi-insider. Many scholars have described this as an essential part of what it means to do ethnographic research.[21]

Another alternative to the classic Malinowskian approach is to go into the field with specific theory-testing goals in mind. Or you may have a data template based on prior research, and the visit to a particular site is guided by the needs of applying that template to the local data—much like using a site visit protocol, as described in Chapter 4. In either case, researchers arrive with much more targeted questions than those suggested only by an intellectual orientation such as functionalism, structuralism, or cultural materialism. Entering the field armed with a fairly concrete plan for collecting data to be analyzed according to predetermined methods makes it possible to write an article-length research report. By contrast, a more detailed inductive approach still often requires a book-length (or dissertation-length) account.

Because this chapter discusses the inductive approach to data coding and analysis, we only illustrate other approaches sufficiently to provide a contrast that makes our target subject clearer. For example, in a study of the lexical features of unrelated languages and peoples, the authors found that commonalities occur at a rate that far exceeds chance and concluded that this provides clues to universals in human language and culture formation. This study was built largely on the fieldwork of others.[22] Two recent examples that required extensive fieldwork by the authors were on the general theme of the impact on women of traditional marriage practices of specific peoples in particular locales in Ghana and Tanzania. Although the authors had highly targeted theories to test, they gathered much traditional data in well-defined, comparatively isolated communities. They used household surveys and survey experiments in which respondents reacted to vignettes.[23]

The details of these three excellent studies matter less than the general point that

[20]Hayano (1979, 1982). For highly informative commentary, see Tedlock (1991).

[21]Duneier (1999).

[22]Brown and Witkowski (1981).

[23]For the Tanzanian study of demographic data, see Borgerhoff Mulder (2009); for the study gathering data with vignettes in Ghana, see Horne, Dodoo, and Dodoo (2013).

field researchers have increasingly used alternatives to "going native." All three studies were very concerned with native practices and beliefs, but the authors knew specifically which practices and beliefs they were interested in and how they were going to analyze them before they collected their data. All three provide a sharp contrast to the more inductive approaches of the traditional ethnographic model, as well as with the topic of our next section, grounded theory. Both the standard ethnographic model and grounded theory are focused on building theory inductively, through intensive onsite observation, rather than on applying or testing preexisting theories.

GROUNDED THEORY: AN INDUCTIVE APPROACH TO THEORY BUILDING

Today the most influential and best-known strand of inductive qualitative analysis is grounded theory (GT). It is important to note that GT is both a suite of methods and an outcome of applying those methods. You use GT methods to construct a GT. It also seems common for some researchers to plan to apply GT methods without intending to construct a theory. This seems odd because the whole point of the method is to build a theory, but it is a testament to the attractiveness of the method as an analytic strategy for a broad group of researchers. In any case, for researchers unsure about how to investigate research questions that demand an inductive approach to data analysis and theory development, GT is an excellent place to start.

Although GT proponents sometimes stress that the method can be applied to almost any kind of data, including quantitative data,[24] in fact it is mainly applied to interview studies and transcripts, with the important supplement of observations of the interviewees and their contexts. The reader might want to review Chapters 2 and 4 on coding data from interviews and observations, because in GT approaches, analysis begins with initial coding decisions and continues throughout data collection. Archival data are also sometimes used by GT researchers. This is less common, but it could be more so.[25] For example, in Chapter 5 we suggested that a GT approach to reviewing qualitative research literature has much promise.[26]

Like the character in Moliere's play who discovered that he had been speaking prose all along without realizing it, many methodologically self-aware researchers studying qualitative data inductively have found that they were doing a version of GT without even knowing it. In one sense, this was true even of the originators of GT. In their foundational classic, *The Discovery of Grounded Theory*, Glaser and Strauss explained the method they had used in their earlier work *Awareness of Dying*, which described intensive interview and observational research with terminally ill patients. Glaser and Strauss's great contribution was systematizing and codifying methods, many of which

[24]As Glaser and Strauss (1967) put it, the distinction between quantitative and qualitative is "a distinction useless for the generation of theory" (p. 9; see also pp. 17 and 18).

[25]Chapter 7 in Glaser and Strauss (1967) is an extended discussion of how to use a "new" source of data: the library.

[26]It would be instructive to compare what a GT-based literature review would look like with a review employing standard meta-analysis methods. In the GT approach, there would be no prior identification of populations and samples of works before the analysis began; the emphasis given to the sources would be more subjective and based on the quality of the sources; and the end point of the study would be determined by saturation, rather than by a statistical guideline. See the later section discussing saturation.

had been applied in one way or another before, and adding some order to the technical vocabulary used to talk about these methods. Most important, they pushed inductively inclined researchers to construct ambitious theories.

GT is both easy and hard to describe accurately. A short accurate version is easy; a long accurate version is hard. Here is a short version. Researchers using GT build theories from the ground up by inductively analyzing their data not only after they collect it but also as they are collecting it. Early coding and categorizing often suggest ideas for further data collection. Analysis begins with preliminary codes and then moves to categories, concepts, themes, and theories. The theories are grounded in the data; they arise out of them and reflect back on them. Throughout this process, the emphasis is on constructing *new* theories inductively rather than on testing previous theories.

It is difficult to accurately summarize GT in more detail than the handful of sentences in the previous paragraph. That is because GT is not one method. It is more a family of methods. Like other families, its members come from different generations, who aren't always very polite to one another and who sometimes aren't respectful of their elders. Major authorities in the field, including its two founders, have had important disagreements, and their students and followers have departed from some of the ideas of the founders. For example, we had always thought of **axial coding** (using one category as an "axis" around which further coding is centered) as being among GT's key methods, but we were surprised to learn, when reading the introduction to the major handbook on GT, that the editors "have not found axial coding to be a productive research strategy."[27] Similarly, some practitioners of GT think that graphic and visual approaches to data analysis are crucial; others think visualization is a distraction. Whereas some GT researchers believe that using computer software gives the researcher indispensable tools, others think that computer assistance may ruin an innovative qualitative method by separating the researcher from the data handling and coding. By reducing fruitful interaction of data and researchers (so goes the argument), computers try to replace thinking with algorithms.

The most important divisions among GT proponents concern objectivity and ambitious theorizing. The founders clearly believed that objective or empirical observation was possible and that it could be used to construct theories. The theories are of two types: **formal theories** are broad in scope, more abstract, and apply to several specific classes of phenomena; **substantive theories** are focused on more specific empirical phenomena. For example, a study of ethnic discrimination in a specific sector of the economy might lead to a focused *substantive* theory dealing with that topic. Through further development and research, it could also lead to a more general *formal* theory of status inequality in the economy as a whole and among other groups (gender, age, etc.) of workers.

Later generations of GT methodologists have often been uncomfortable with efforts to construct formal theories. They have also been uncomfortable with the assertion that theories, formal or substantive, can be supported with empirical data or facts. But Glaser and Strauss persisted in making strong theoretical claims and insisted that the

---

[27]Bryant and Charmaz (2006, p. 9). Axial coding is very much associated with the Straussian wing of GT and was sharply challenged by Glaser.

theories were generated using data.[28] In sum, the debate is over whether formal, general GTs are the natural goal and outcome of rigorous inductive qualitative analyses or whether attempts at such empirically based theorizing go beyond what is possible in qualitative research.

These debates make it complicated for us to give detailed advice about when to use particular GT methods for coding and analyzing your data. Any specific suggestion we give is almost certain to be disputed by at least some important researchers in the field.[29] As usual, our approach is inclusive. We invite all members of the GT family to contribute, at least to some research problems. Depending on your research questions and goals, we think that axial coding, archival and quantitative data, software packages, and objectivist or constructivist approaches to constructing formal, as well as substantive, theories can all be appropriate.

An inclusive approach to GT means that there are many situations in which researchers would do well to apply its methods, but in order to do so they will have to do considerable reading in the literature in the field and then construct their own GT tool kit or package of methods to use in their specific research.[30] It will be hard to reduce the many choices to a clear set of alternatives. Still, if your research question is best approached by close attention to interview and observational data and you are aiming to build a theory rather than test one, GT is usually the best place to begin your methodological investigations. Compared with many qualitative methodologies, which can be vague just where the beginning researcher would like some concrete guidelines, GT gives you a lot you can sink your teeth into. But for some GT advocates, that is precisely the problem.

Indeed, one of the areas of disagreement among established GT researchers and methodologists is how much detailed and specific advice one can or should give about GT, especially to beginners. The fear is that writing succinct guidelines and straightforward textbooks will turn a highly nuanced and thought-driven method into a series of recipes that novice researchers will follow slavishly. But what is the alternative for people who want to learn GT because they are persuaded by the general argument that GT would be a good approach to their research problems? Studying with established masters of the field is one option, and probably the best one, but that opportunity is hardly open to everyone. Ultimately, we see nothing wrong with cookbooks and recipes—if they are properly used. As long as you don't think you can become a great cook or a master chef by consulting a cookbook, using one is not a bad way to get started preparing a dish. Putting together a whole meal will be harder, to say nothing of planning a balanced menu for the week. But you have to start somewhere. At some point as a researcher you'll need rules of thumb; you can't invent everything from scratch every time you go to work. You may devise rules of thumb yourself, and they may be fully ad hoc for the particular project, but it is hard to imagine how all analysis methods can always be improvisational or framework-free.

Strauss and Glaser drifted apart somewhat, mainly in the 1980s, and their followers (and students) have evolved into different camps—the older objectivist and the newer subjectivist or constructivist. Our impression is that despite their differences,

[28]See Strauss (1995) and Glaser (2006).

[29]Such disputes are hardly unique to GT; see, for example, our discussion of factor analysis in Chapter 9.

[30]For the novice, the best books to begin with would usually be Corbin and Strauss (2008) and Charmaz (2006); they represent two fairly different approaches, so they should probably be read together.

Strauss and Glaser had more in common with one another than either did with the constructivist/subjectivist critics of the original forms of GT. In any case, the objectivist–subjectivist conflict is closely related to the realist–interpretivist division.[31] We think of such discordant beliefs more as tendencies or points on continua rather than opposites because it is clear that pure objectivity and pure subjectivity in research methods are not only inadvisable but they are also impossible. Likewise, we think that pure induction and pure deduction are impossible in social research. Practicing researchers would usually do well to operate in the pragmatic middle ground where all epistemological categories are porous, all methods are mixed, and all conclusions are uncertain. Paradoxically, the only thing of which we can justifiably be certain is that unalloyed certainty is impossible—for researchers, if not for true believers.

In short, we find the different approaches to GT to be broadening. They open options to researchers. It is less helpful to think of them as diametrically opposed methods among which one must choose once and for all. That is why we do not prescribe which of the several paths through GT research to take. Rather, we lay out alternative menus of options as food for your thought. Taking differences among various GT methodologists too seriously could splinter GT and weaken one of the most effective approaches to analyzing qualitative data.

In its several versions, GT can accommodate most positions in broader methodological and philosophical debates. But it is important to remember that reasonable people and well-known scholars disagree about the best approaches to take when using GT. Even we (the authors of this book) are not in full agreement among ourselves on all issues.[32] But, perhaps because we work in applied fields, we usually agree on advising our students to avoid lengthy discussions of the epistemological underpinnings of research methodology; these debates can be debilitating by diverting too much time and energy away from selecting methods that could be helpful in the actual conduct of the investigation of a research question. We also find the tone of many epistemological discussions unhelpful because they often turn tendencies or emphases into rigid categories—categories that are not at all based on systematic inductive work. Stereotyping is pervasive in human discourse. It is especially debilitating in research methodology. And it is scandalous when practiced by those who advocate basing generalizations on careful inductive analysis.

We know that many colleagues consider epistemological discourse crucial to qualitative data analysis. This belief seems especially strong among colleagues of a more constructivist bent. Many think of the constructivist "turn," with its stronger emphasis on epistemology (broadly defined), as having added an essential enriching element to GT. Others, of a more empiricist bent, see it as diluting the analytical "punch" of GT methods. Enriching or diluting? You may have to decide, and your decision can importantly influence the shape of your research using GT.[33]

In sum, GT is appealing to researchers for many reasons. Perhaps the greatest one is that GT encourages you to come up with your own theory, rather than merely test

[31]In her introduction to the third edition of Corbin and Strauss (2008, p. viii), Corbin describes the "assault on my research identity" when she learned that many in GT methodology thought that the idea of "being able to capture 'reality' in the data was . . .a fantasy."

[32]As we have said elsewhere: Don't take our advice—exclusively.

[33]A useful way to orient yourself would be to compare Charmaz (2006) and Corbin and Strauss (2008).

someone else's. This attractive aspect has a potential downside: What if you do not manage to construct a convincing theory, what if a theory does not somehow "emerge" from the data? And what, in fact, would a successful attempt at theorizing include? At minimum, according to standard GT criteria, a theory would have to be *new*, to *fit* the data, and to *work* to predict and explain the aspects of the social world being studied.[34] A possible fallback position from a broad formal GT, especially for a beginning researcher, might be a "middle range" theory.[35]

On the other hand, in theory-validation research, the results of tests of another's theory can be considered valuable whether they support or reject the theory. Either way, it's a contribution, usually a small one, but it's something. By contrast, it can be quite humbling to start out, inspired by GT methodologists, to discover a theory but return from the voyage empty handed. The fallback position for an unsuccessful expedition of discovery into a field of social interaction is the ethnographer's thick description of people's lives, relationships, and stories, which can be considered worthwhile in its own right. Glaser and Strauss probably would not have been satisfied, because their commitment to theorizing was strong, but dissertation committees can be more understanding.

We organize the remainder of this chapter using several categories and themes likely to be relevant to practitioners of GT. They are derived largely from our earlier chapters on coding data from interviews, observations, and archival records. Each category and theme is introduced by a cluster of questions. We discuss how the questions have been answered and, by extension, how you might choose to answer them when applying GT methods to your research questions.

How Your Goals Influence Your Approach

What are your goals in conducting the research? These should be at least implicit in your research question. What are you investigating? Do you intend mainly to describe or to construct/discover a theory, and if so, what kind of theory?

Description is a common objective, at least a provisional goal, for researchers using GT methods, but the main focus is usually on discovering or building an explanatory and/or predictive theory. By contrast, if you want to test or attempt to validate a theory, GT probably is not for you, for two reasons. First, good practice when testing a theory requires that you state, in advance, rules about what evidence or findings would lead to a confirmation or confutation of the theory; but this kind of approach cannot easily be reconciled with GT's inductivism. The second reason GT does not lend itself to theory testing is that. if you apply GT methods and use data to establish a theory, you need to use different, independent data to test it. However, you might want to use GT methods to explicate or elaborate on an established theory, such as one that has focused mainly on outcomes but insufficiently on processes. GT could be used in process tracing research (as described in Chapter 12). There has certainly been much emphasis on identifying and clarifying "underlying processes" in GT.[36] Another important goal of interest to many GT researchers is the possibility of developing theories of change that would allow practical intervention; improved prediction can lead to more effective

[34]Glaser and Strauss (1967, pp. 3, 31).

[35]See Merton (1968) and Boudon (1991) for a discussion.

[36]Glaser (1978).

action. This possibility was particularly emphasized by Strauss.[37] It has been less central in GT methodology since the 1990s, but we think it is still a viable option.

The Role of Prior Research in GT Investigations

How much is your research question, and the paths you will follow trying to answer it, based on a review of the previous literature on your subject? How will you decide which previous research is likely to be relevant to your research?

This set of questions is among the most frequently discussed in GT methodology writings because it raises fundamental issues about the inductive approach and how to apply it successfully. The general attitude of predominant commentators on GT methodology toward reliance on the research literature is great reluctance. Their concern is that if researchers are too steeped in the literature, they may be tempted to test the theories of others rather than construct their own. Even worse, researchers may not be able to protect their own emerging theories from being contaminated by others' work. They will be biased by their reading.

This worry is based on a rather low, perhaps insulting, view of the independence of mind of the typical researcher. A competent researcher is not likely to be irredeemably corrupted by learning what others think about the proposed topic of research. We find reviewing the research literature on a subject almost always stimulating. And we certainly have not noticed that reading constrains one to adopt a deductivist, theory-testing approach. Reading the literature contributes to **theoretical sensitivity**—the readiness or ability to use ideas and data to construct theory. Personally[38] we find that reading the literature helps us in constructing better theories, in part because we almost always disagree with some of the literature, occasionally most of it. Reading the literature makes us more sensitive to the theoretical possibilities.

As originally recommended by Glaser and Strauss, GT was not really meant for novice researchers but was aimed at persuading sociological professionals to adopt GT. Such professionals would naturally have a rich store of prior knowledge and a broad familiarity with the research literature in their fields. Glaser and Strauss certainly did. Although GT was not for amateurs, researchers were not to use their prior knowledge to force data into preconceived categories. This resulted in something of a dilemma, perhaps even a contradiction, for GT. As one author argued, "researchers were admonished to generate new theory without being beholden to pre-existing theories, but they still required theoretical sensitivity based on broad familiarity with existing theories to generate new theories."[39] Another complication is that proponents of the recent constructivist turn in GT methodology urge researchers to incorporate their prior theoretical commitments (such as feminism or postcolonialism) into their research. But how purely inductive can you be when you are following a preexisting theoretical or political agenda?

---

[37]Strauss and Corbin (1990). This was much less central in Glaser's work. For a skeptical review of the possibility of precision and predictive capacity that can lead to more effective action, see Bakir and Bakir (2006).

[38]There isn't much else to go on except personal experience because there is little if any research on the subject.

[39]Timmermans and Tavory (2012).

In general, we think that although it is not easy to both know a great deal and simultaneously keep an open mind, a highly informed open mind is precisely what is needed to conduct good research. Familiarity with prior research more often helps than hurts. In dialogue with doctoral students who have conducted literature reviews on topics to be investigated with GT, we often hear something like the following:[40] "My review of the literature suggests that three or four different processes might be occurring; a couple of these have not yet been studied in much depth. None of the accounts in the current literature is fully convincing to me. I'd like to investigate these ideas and descriptions by interviewing people and observing them in the proposed setting using grounded coding, categorizing, and theorizing to see whether I can come up with something better. If I can't improve upon the current accounts, maybe I can partially validate or expand one of them."

Rather than swearing off reading up on your subject before and during the conducting of the research, we think it is better to read broadly and critically, bringing in ideas from several different perspectives. Because there is no way to be devoid of prior knowledge, or at least prior beliefs—there can be, in other words, no immaculate perception—you may as well be systematic in your use of prior knowledge to inform your analyses. Support for this view can be found in the works of GT's founders. In their words, "to be sure, one goes out and studies an area with a particular perspective, and with a focus, a general question, or a problem in mind." You could not begin your study without that initial guidance, but you should enter the field "without any preconceived theory that dictates, prior to the research, 'relevancies' in concepts and hypotheses." In practice, we think that you have to experiment and see what works for you in investigating a particular question. In the words of Glaser and Strauss, some researchers "avoid the reading of much that relates to the relevant area until after they return from the field"; but others "read extensively beforehand." In short, "*there is no ready formula*."[41]

The pragmatic flexibility of the founders seems good advice, but the issue continues to be of great concern for current writers on GT method—if the frequency with which the topic is written about is any guide. Concern about the effective use of prior research seems especially salient when it comes to providing guidelines for beginning researchers. Perhaps some new researchers might believe, after an incautious reading of certain statements in GT methodology, that they need know nothing, indeed that they are better off knowing nothing, before they enter the field. Good published advice countering this know-nothing naive inductivism includes discussions of how students need to demonstrate that there is a problem worth investigating, how to use the existing literature for theoretical sensitizing, how to reconcile opposing beliefs about the importance of literature reviews, how to make explicit use of existing external theories, and even, somewhat paradoxically, how to use GT as a method for conducting literature reviews.[42]

---

[40] This is a pastiche of remarks made by students over the years.

[41] Glaser and Strauss (1967, pp. 33, 253); italics ours. As Francis Crick, a codiscoverer of the structure of DNA, put it in an often quoted statement, "it's true that by blundering about we stumbled on gold, but the fact remains that we were looking for gold."

[42] See, respectively, Hallberg (2010); Thornberg (2012); Dunne (2011); Goldkuhl and Cronholm (2010); and Wolfswinkel, Furtmueller, and Wilderom (2011). On the issue of using GT for literature reviews, see our comments in Chapter 5.

One way to handle the prior knowledge problem in inductive research is to use your intellectual imagination to set aside what you know and/or believe and try to consider how the data would appear to you if you did not have that knowledge and those prior beliefs. This can be called either *bracketing* or *role playing.* In the phenomenologist's **bracketing,** you hold in abeyance prior knowledge and beliefs the better to focus on the effect the phenomena have on your mind.[43] **Intellectual role playing** may be an easier metaphor for most readers. You ask yourself, for example, questions such as: "If I hadn't been here before, but were seeing this place for the first time as an outsider, how would it look to me?" Maybe you'd say "I thought the apartment was OK, but looking at it from a fresh outsider's perspective, I can see it needs a coat of paint, new curtains, and so forth."

Extending this common method of thinking to the research realm, you might say, "Were I a symbolic interactionist, how would I code and categorize these data?" Then you could ask yourself, "How might I code and categorize them from a feminist perspective?" Even if neither symbolic interactionism nor feminist research were your basic approach, as an accomplished researcher, you should still be able to see the data from those perspectives. It is not at all simple to engage in that kind of intellectual role playing. Indeed, it is very demanding, much more so than picking a banner and marching under it, but it is a skill that can be developed. The more you have developed that skill, the more effectively you can handle the problem of prior knowledge. Ultimately, if you cannot imaginatively construct diverse points of view, the scope of your coding, categorizing, and analysis will be limited. As J. S. Mill put it long ago, if you only know your own case, you don't know that very well; you also need to know other perspectives in their most plausible and persuasive forms.

The role of existing, published theory is much greater when it comes to generating more general, *formal* theories using GT. By contrast, most current methodological writing in GT focuses on entering a field for the first time in the hopes of building a more specific *substantive* theory, but formal theory remains a viable option in GT. As Glaser and Strauss put it, one may use theoretical sampling on "someone else's formal theory" in order to generate more formal theory. When there is a clash between someone else's theory and your research observations and categories, you can use a "comparative analysis that delimits the boundaries of the existing theory while generating a more general one" of your own.[44] Such procedures amount to something like independent testing of an extant theory with new data, but the test includes the possibility of building a different theory—or qualifying the original—not merely rejecting or validating an extant one. And we think this is an important and legitimate line of research to pursue using GT.

Forming Categories and Codes Inductively

How do you construct codes and categories, especially without guidance from prior research? How can you build theories inductively from data rather than deductively from concepts?

---

[43] See Wertz et al. (2011, particularly Ch. 5).

[44] Glaser and Strauss (1967, pp. 90, 255).

Two things the researcher needs to watch out for are being too influenced by prior research or theories of others *and* being too influenced by your own prior prejudices. Of the two, you'll have to judge which one is the bigger threat to making valid inductive inferences based on the data. As a GT researcher, you want to ground the codes and concepts in the data. But what exactly does it mean for a category or theory to be "grounded"? What do the terms *grounded category* and *grounded theory* mean—theories or categories that are based on, rooted in, built upon, or derived from empirical data? And what is the process or link between the observation of data and coming up with a code or category? The best tentative answers probably lie in the field of cognitive psychology, but the gap between observation and insight may always remain something of a mystery.

The history of science is filled with accounts of researchers who have been successful by proceeding inductively. One of our favorite examples in this book has been John Snow, who, in the 1850s, demonstrated the value of the natural experiment (see Chapter 3). After years of painstaking investigation, he showed that cholera was transmitted by drinking contaminated water—and not by touch, nor by unsanitary living conditions, nor by breathing foul-smelling air, as most people thought at the time. The work he and his colleagues did could easily be described as a GT approach to understanding the origins of a disease and finding remedies for it. They examined instances of the phenomenon (cholera deaths) and looked for what those who died had in common so as to form categories for further investigation. They repeatedly refined their data-based ideas, which led them to do "theoretical sampling" when, guided by their preliminary ideas, they gathered more data. Their method could be called "constant comparison" of the data with preliminary ideas.[45] During years of observing, interviewing, and reinterviewing they constantly refined the substantive theory about the transmission of cholera, and they contributed to the more formal germ theory of disease.

Although it is not hard to find successful examples of inductively driven science, there is a problem with induction: It is based on extremely shaky philosophical grounds. Research on cognitive psychology has brought the reliability of induction further into question. What has been called the "problem of induction"—essentially, that induction has no solid logical foundations—has been a staple of philosophy at least since Hume and Mill in the 18th and 19th centuries. Constructivists were hardly the first to object to the naive empiricism of advocates of inductive methods. Although induction seems to work sometimes in science, and it is often used in everyday life, it cannot be logically demonstrated either deductively or inductively. As one standard philosophical reference put it, "there is no comprehensive theory of sound induction, no set of agreed upon rules that license good or sound inductive inference, nor is there a serious prospect of such a theory."[46]

When you think about it, the idea that codes and categories simply "emerge" from the data isn't very credible. It's OK as a metaphor, but not as an accurate description of how we form categories. We use categories to classify phenomena and thus to begin building theories. We note similarities and differences among phenomena to form and label categories. These categories, as used in GT, seldom meet the criteria that they

[45] One of the most thorough and highly readable accounts is in Johnson (2006).

[46] See Vickers (2013) for a discussion of the "problem of induction."

be exhaustive and mutually exclusive. Rather, phenomena in an effective category can usually be characterized by having a "family resemblance," to use Wittgenstein's phrase.[47]

Whatever their specific nature, categories do not directly emerge from the data, nor are they produced by the data. Data cannot do anything; *we* do things with data. Inductive researchers generate categories; we don't just watch as categories spring from the data on their own or as categories are spontaneously generated by data. Rather, inspired by a desire to understand what we are discerning in the data, we reflect, ponder, take notes, and think about the notes so as to come up with codes and categories. The processes by which this happens are more than a little unclear.[48] What is clear from modern research in cognitive psychology is that the inferences we make from data can be remarkably untrustworthy and subject to all sorts of influences that Glaser and Strauss did not consider in their pioneering work, no doubt in part because the problems with inference were only just becoming well known. The research of Kahneman and Tversky has been most important for establishing the shakiness of reasoning about evidence—when making either statistical or qualitative inferences.[49] A huge number of well-documented biases can trip up the inductive researcher trying to draw conclusions that are data-based.

One partial remedy for these biases is to use rigorous methods to keep from getting too carried away by the first idea that pops into your head. GT's chief contribution is that it codifies some methods for adding systematic attention to the process of categorizing qualitative data. The codifications of Glaser and Strauss diverged by the late 1980s. Both added more prior knowledge to the mix of what the researcher needed to know in order to construct useful categories. Strauss called his procedures "coding paradigms" and "axial coding"; they were fairly prescriptive about how to proceed. Most students we have worked with have found his (and his coauthor Corbin's) approach to be useful because it is didactic; this is precisely because students do not usually have the kind of rich theoretical background that Glaser's approach (using "theoretical coding" and "coding families") presumes.[50] But the divergence between Strauss and Glaser is less important than their common starting points—the common core of methods for coding, categorizing, and interpreting qualitative data.

The chief methods, on which all seem to agree, are constant comparison paired with theoretical sampling. Before we discuss these "twin foundations"[51] of GT (in the following section on sampling), we address a prior question: Where do the initial insights or ideas come from? One major alternative to, or addition to, the typical GT account is **abduction**.

---

[47]See Dey (2007) for an excellent discussion of the grounding of categories. A promising attempt to address the problem of how the researcher moves from codes to categories to themes and theories can be found in Wasserman et al. (2009).

[48]Glaser and Strauss (1967, Ch. 11) discuss how you move from data to analysis to theory; for a different but interestingly parallel approach, see Jaccard and Jacoby (2010).

[49]One of the best overall summaries is Kahneman (2011).

[50]These points are well elaborated by Kelle (2007b).

[51]Holton (2007).

Abduction, or Where Do You Get Ideas?

Abandoning the notion that ideas and theories spontaneously emerge from the data returns us to the problem of where they do in fact come from. One of the more interesting answers, and one increasingly incorporated into the GT literature, is the old pragmatist idea of **abduction**; this was first elaborated for modern audiences by the philosopher C. S. Peirce. We don't think that Peirce's ideas and the subsequent reformulation of them by modern GT methodologists eliminates the mystery of where good ideas come from. Ultimately, the process always seems to resemble what is called the Feynman algorithm: (1) write down the problem, (2) think really hard, (3) write down the answer. This system worked quite well for Feynman because he was a genius and his answers were often profound. The rest of us have to wonder about how good our conclusions in Step 3 really are. The modern reformulations of the idea of abduction provide some handy descriptions of steps in the process and may even help with evaluating the quality of the ideas thus generated.[52]

The basic process is simple. You examine the empirical world or the data when you are doing research. When you are surprised by something new or confront a seeming anomaly, you try to figure it out. You can do this either by pondering or wandering—thinking hard or letting your mind play with the problem. Either can help you get a new idea or flash of insight. That is the abduction: Your mind is taken away ("abducted") to a new place in order to explain the surprising facts. The next step is *deductive*. Your flash of insight becomes a hypothesis. Using it, you can deduce what would also be true of the data if the hypothesis were true. To test those deductions, you return to the data, which you then examine inductively. So abduction is a creative process by which you generate hypotheses; you flesh out these hypotheses by deduction; then you test them inductively by gathering further data.

Your ability to have good creative insights can be enhanced in many ways. One way might be trying to come to a new problem from a different direction; another could be having a rich store of prior ideas. Prior knowledge sometimes enables you to move, perhaps by analogy, from one realm of understanding or investigation to another in a process that is sometimes called *consilience*, which means the "jumping together" of ideas from different levels of generalization.[53] Ultimately, creative and theoretically sensitive observers who have a broad familiarity with the range of theories in their fields will usually be better at this. But, naiveté might sometimes help, too. To repeat the warning of Glaser and Strauss: There is no ready formula.

GT's Approaches to Sampling

Many issues of sampling in GT are identical to those in any interview, observational, and/or archival study. Which persons, sites, and/or documents should you investigate, and how many of them? What is the balance in your selection of people, places, and texts among studying interviewees and their social contexts and documentary materials related to their situation? In GT, sampling is an ongoing process, so after

[52]The following paragraph is based mostly on Reichertz (2010) and Timmermans and Tavory (2012).

[53]Wilson (1999).

preliminary coding and analysis, the questions recur. Will you revisit persons, sites, and/or documents—and with what goals?

When GT analyses are published in major, general purpose journals, sampling is often dealt with fleetingly in traditional terms of sampling frames and representativeness, and the specifically GT methodology issues are addressed quite briefly.[54] In GT-centered journals and in those specializing in qualitative analyses, one typically sees much more methodologically focused discussions. Sampling questions are then addressed by three key GT methods and concepts: constant comparison, theoretical sampling, and saturation. These are so foundational that they are included as elements of most definitions of GT. They are what set it apart from other methods of investigation and analysis. The general idea behind these three is easy to state and agree with: Use what you learn along the way to improve what you are doing, and then stop when you're done. What could be more natural, especially as compared with ignoring what you learn along the way? But systematically using what you learn along the way takes a lot of work and intensive reanalyses.

GT is an iterative process in which you use what you discover as you proceed to improve what you are doing and integrate what you have learned into what you plan to do. You begin with coding, often coding of your interview transcripts, fieldnotes, and/or documentary data. As discussed in Chapters 2 and 4, coding is, simply, assigning labels and definitions to segments of data in order to make them easier to find and use—and to sort in your mind. Coding is a translating, defining, and indexing process: You put things into your own terms; you can then use the coding labels to find your way through a growing body of data. In the early stages, which are usually referred to as **open coding** in GT, the labels are preliminary and often redundant. These almost always have to be combined, ordered, and revised before more permanent codes are determined. This is an intensive rethinking and rewriting process. As we have stressed before, if you don't enjoy rethinking and rewriting, research on qualitative data is probably not going to work very well for you. The recoding and rethinking work is called either **theoretical coding** (by followers of Glaser) or **axial coding** (by followers of Strauss). In either case, the goal is to rework and reorganize the early codes into more conceptually or theoretically advanced accounts of what is in the data and how you are interpreting it.

The recoding and the gradual development of more refined codes and categories are accomplished through **constant comparison**, which combines coding and analysis; it is always used in conjunction with **theoretical sampling.** Early codes and categories are, in essence, preliminary minitheories. The researcher uses these preliminary theories to guide further sampling; the sample is not determined in advance but is adjusted as you go along and learn more about your field of investigation. Although you do not begin with a theory to test in GT, in the course of the data analysis, theories for testing often emerge quite quickly, and you use these to guide your subsequent sampling. Theoretical sampling "reduces the mass of data that would otherwise be collected"; using theoretical sampling means that "the time taken by most interviews decreases as the theory develops."[55] Your early theories, which direct theoretical sampling, are tested by constant comparison. By bringing researchers back to the data, constant comparison is designed to keep them from turning an early idea into a stereotype. Those early ideas

[54] Good examples are Shiao and Tuan (2008) and Silva (2012).

[55] Glaser and Strauss (1967, pp. 70, 76).

are tested, in part, by looking for negative instances. But constant comparison is not designed mainly to test preliminary ideas; by testing and readjusting and refining the ideas, one discovers new relationships and builds theories.

By contrast, in the typical survey or experiment, you determine the nature and size of the sample before you collect any data. Not doing so is considered essentially dishonest; it is like changing the rules of the game as you play it. The sampling distinctions between GT and experiments or surveys are not quite as sharp as they are sometimes made out to be, because researchers conducting experiments and surveys also learn as they go along. For example, in experiments, rather than change the sample as you proceed with a study, you might take what you learned in one study to conduct new, additional studies. This is quite common; a research report will often contain the results of a series of three or four experiments. In surveys, comparable needs are addressed by the pilot studies and follow-up surveys.The difference between learning as you proceed in one study (as in GT) versus learning in a series of studies (as in experiments) is a real distinction, but it is also a matter of degree.[56] It is the contrast between adjustments made in a single study and those made in a research agenda. Researchers conducting GT studies who use constant comparison guided by theoretical sampling make many more frequent revisions in sampling within one study than do researchers conducting a series of experiments or follow-up surveys.

One important question in GT is: When can you bring "constant" work (discover, adjust, discover, etc.) to an end? How can you know when to stop making "more and better—and always theoretically controlled—comparisons"? In applied research, constant comparison means "continual adjustment and reformulation of the theory . . . necessitated by the realities of practice."[57] Is there a way to use principled criteria to decide about a stopping point? The criterion, in a word, is **saturation.** The point of saturation is reached when no new concepts, categories, or ideas are being generated using constant comparison. The big problem here is determining whether you have truly exhausted the data or whether you have merely exhausted yourself. How do you tell when you've reached the limit of the data or simply your own personal limitations? One warning sign is that you reach the point of saturation very quickly. Generally, to reach the saturation point "dozens and dozens of situations in many diverse groups must be observed and analyzed."[58] GT puts a heavy burden on researchers to try to distinguish their own shortcomings from limitations of the data.

Saturation is an easy idea to grasp and to define in general terms, but not one that is easy to specify in practice. A closely parallel notion in meta-analysis is the fail-safe *N*. If, in order to revise your conclusions in a meta-analysis, you would have to find an improbably large number of studies that pointed you in a different direction, then it is safe to stop looking for more. The parallels with saturation in GT research are close, but, not surprisingly, in GT there is no numerical cutoff based on probability theory. In GT the judgment about saturation is, well, a matter of judgment. Nonetheless, we believe that the researcher should provide evidence that the saturation point has been

[56]In exploratory data analysis and Bayesian statistical analyses, adjustments made as you go along are more frequent than in the standard experimental or survey design. See Chapters 7 and 8.

[57]Glaser and Strauss (1967, pp. 151, 243).

[58]Glaser and Strauss (1967, p. 62).

reached. One way to do this is by an **audit trail** built up from evidence in your **memos.**[59] Neither the audit trail nor memos are discussed in Glaser and Strauss's original work, but they were implied and were quickly developed in later publications by the founders and their followers. The audit trail is the description of how you have proceeded to draw your conclusions—what you've done and why and how you've done it. It is roughly equivalent to a lab notebook in experimental research. The goals of the audit trail and lab notebook are the same—to help you reconstruct what you've done and to document the process for other interested researchers.

Memos are your theoretical and methodological notes on your notes and your notes on your activities while collecting data. They are somewhat like meta-data in quantitative data analyses. By giving these processes of note taking and writing a name, GT methodologists have drawn attention to this important part of qualitative data analysis. The term *memoing* is a neologism devised by GT researchers to describe the key processes of writing, note taking, rewriting, and revision that are at the heart of qualitative coding and analysis; the centrality of memoing is why we have stressed the necessity of setting aside *at least* as much time for writing as for data gathering (see Chapters 2 and 4).

Memos, or notes on your transcripts and fieldnotes, are indispensable when you are trying to write up a report of your research. They are early, partial first drafts of sections of your paper, dissertation, or article. You use them to keep track of what you have done, to make sure you have a record of good ideas you've had along the way, to refine your ideas, and to make sure you don't forget them.

The Question of Using Multiple Coders

How can you achieve reliability and validity in coding deductive qualitative data? Should multiple coders be used?

Another safeguard against the biases that we all bring to our work and another way to avoid the logical pitfalls so often pointed out by cognitive psychologists is to enhance constant comparison and theoretical sampling through teamwork. In our experience,[60] having two or three coders more than doubles or triples the rigor of constant comparison. Unfortunately, it is often hard to introduce this extra rigor into the educational system, which is usually based on judging the work of individuals, not teams. But when possible, we think that it is very helpful to try to make social research more social. Lone researchers have done important work, but the benefits of collective work for coding, categorizing, analyzing, and interpreting are potentially great.

In one example, worth reviewing, the authors described how, over several years, the rigor of their analysis was increased by the cross-validation inherent in having to work up coding procedures on which multiple researchers could agree. The research team members had different backgrounds, and that led to combinations of approaches. They make a convincing case that, although collective coding and analysis slowed the process, it

[59]See Bowen (2008, 2009) for a discussion of saturation and audit trails.

[60]We keep referring to our experience because we know of little if any research on the topic. "Researcher, heal thyself" could be the motto of methodologically committed qualitative researchers. Research findings, rather than tips based on personal observations, would be a welcome change.

also enhanced the reliability of the coding and the validity of the conclusions.[61] Another team described their work as follows: "A team of four researchers conducted an iterative process of identifying a set of thematic codes and then applying them systematically to all interview transcripts. The final coding manual included a total of 78 themes and subthemes." The transcripts were then coded by two researchers and their codes compared for reliability/consistency. This kind of rigorous and time-consuming team approach is very common when GT is used in medical settings, as in this case.[62]

In another instructive example of teamwork in the coding and analysis process, one author pointed out that a typical procedure is for the lead researcher to identify parts of fieldnotes or interview transcripts for the team members (often graduate students working for a faculty member) to code and classify. But it is possible to make the entire process more team-based than hierarchical, and that was done in this example. Again, it requires more effort to use a team approach, but the increases in quality are generally worth the additional resources needed.[63]

A final form of multiple coding is "member checking" (see Chapters 2 and 4), in which study participants participate to one degree or another in the coding and analysis of the data. Member checking allows you to include in your study not only your observations but also the observations of those you observe. As with the other approaches to multiple coding, member checking provides more data for constant comparisons and gives more direction to the process of theoretical sampling. In so doing, it can improve the reliability of coding and the validity or trustworthiness of the analysis and interpretations.

The Use of Tools, Including Software

What combination of recording methods (notes, audio and video recordings, transcriptions) will you use? Will word processing software suffice? Will you also use spreadsheets as an indexing tool, and will you use software designed for qualitative data (CAQDAS)?

The full range of tools, mechanical and intellectual, for handling and manipulating data can be used by GT researchers, although beliefs about what tools are appropriate can sometimes be strong. The use of computer programs for coding and analysis remains controversial among various proponents of GT methods. Although we agree that no computer package "can replicate the complex capacities of the human brain for conceptualization of latent patterns of social behaviour,"[64] we do think that computer aids have a fundamental role in managing the sheer masses of data of the typical GT project. We have used a wide range of tools when analyzing qualitative data, and we tend, as authors, to approach writing and analysis work quite differently from one another. For example, in the precomputer era, one of us arrayed thousands of note-laden 4″ × 6″ cards on a huge sheet of plywood. These cards were sorted and resorted into dozens of piles; the piles represented the shifting schema of the main analytical categories.

---

[61] Weston et al. (2001).

[62] Millery et al. (2011).

[63] Kurasaki (2000).

[64] Holton (2007, p. 287).

Since the advent of word processing, spreadsheets, and graphics software to use in data handling, sorting, and display, none of us has ever thought of going back to hand-sorting reams of handwritten text—although this still has its advocates among our colleagues. And we all still jot in the margins and occasionally mark passages with colored pencils or highlighters, but it seems odd to try to elevate such practices, which are matters of personal style and convenience, into methodological principles. We all use computer programs, from word processing and spreadsheet software to the R CAQDAS program. This does not mean that we think dedicated computer programs are necessary to conduct effective GT analyses. They can have an important place,[65] and they can save much time once the author has brain-processed the data, but we have never seen a program good enough that the author could delegate the actual conceptual work of coding and analysis to it. We avoid sweeping judgments about the use of computer tools (see Chapters 2 and 4 for more discussion of using software in qualitative data coding) and simply say that, like any tools, the quality of computer tools should be judged pragmatically—on the basis of which ones work for what purposes and for whom.

The same pragmatic advice applies to tape recording and interview transcripts. Some in the GT community see them as indispensable documentation, and some regard them as unnecessarily cumbersome steps that get in the way of analysis and interpretation. In some studies we have found causal diagrams, logic models, flow charts, concept maps, and Venn diagrams to be of great help.[66] In other studies, we have used nothing more than paragraphs. The best tools are those that are effective for the purpose and the person using them. No one advocates letting the tools rule one's intellect. Ultimately, as Glaser recently recommended, you need to follow the method, use theoretical sampling to see if your categories work, and if they do, start writing it up.[67] If concept maps or NVivo work for you, use them; if they don't, try to avoid feeling pressured by their advocates.

CONCLUSION

We conclude this chapter with a few comparative remarks about the distinction between inductive and deductive approaches to analyzing qualitative data, particularly as these are related to the paradigm cases of this and the next chapter: GT and QCA. The short version is that, although the differences in emphasis are very real, they do not constitute radical distinctions in analysis.[68] There are inductive components in QCA and deductive elements in GT. For example, if anything characterizes GT, it is theoretical sampling, in which early theoretical categories are used to decide what should be sampled next: "*deductions* from grounded theory, as it develops, are the method by which the researcher directs . . . theoretical sampling."[69]

[65]See Corbin and Strauss (2008) for a nice illustration of the use of one package.

[66]Harry, Sturges, and Klingner (2005) illustrate some of these, as do Dourdouma and Mörtl (2012).

[67]Glaser (2012).

[68]Both methods can be effectively combined with methods from other research traditions. For example, see Magasi et al. (2012) for a persuasive combination of GT and differential item functioning in a study of content validity.

[69]Glaser and Strauss (1967, p. 32). Emphasis added.

There is another crucial similarity in the two methods. The founders of both new methods—Glaser and Strauss and Charles Ragin—repeatedly stress how essential it is to maintain a constant dialogue or interplay between evidence and ideas, between data and theory. And both do this by applying comparative methods. Sometimes the ideas lead the discussion, in which case it is more deductive. At other times the data lead, in which case the dialogue is more inductive. But each method, GT and QCA, in different ways, can be used to link ideas and generalizations to data—in both directions and reciprocally. That is the essence of good research.

SUGGESTIONS FOR FURTHER READING

Glaser and Strauss often described their work as codifying and thus making more systematic methods for deriving theory from data; the methods were not necessarily new, but the codification and the clarity to which it led were quite new. A personal example might be useful. One of us (W.P.V.) was asked to give a talk to doctoral students describing the textual analysis methods used in his dissertation.* The steps were pretty crude and informal:

1. Take systematic notes on what seemed important in the texts.
2. Jot down ideas for organizing the notes on separate "idea cards."
3. Reread previous texts and read new ones with those ideas in mind.
4. Take notes on the notes and re-reorganize them.
5. Decide what to (re)read next based on step 4.
6. Repeat steps 1–5 until out of texts, ideas, and time.

Some years later, when he discovered *The Discovery of Grounded Theory*, he realized (with some embarrassment) that he had been doing a type of GT without realizing it and that he could have probably done a better or more efficient job had he known of GT in advance. Several scholars of his generation have described a similarly surprised self-recognition when reading Glaser and Strauss's foundational book. This kind of self-recognition was even somewhat true of Glaser and Strauss; their methodology derived from their reflections on their earlier work, *Awareness of Dying*. It is still very much worth reading the foundational works of GT. It seldom pays to content yourself with summaries of classic works; it certainly doesn't in the case of Glaser and Strauss's 1967 work. Of course Glaser, Strauss, and their students and colleagues have built on, and occasionally tried to undermine, the foundations laid in that work.

As mentioned in the text, the students of Strauss and Glaser and their followers have evolved into somewhat opposed camps, the older objectivist and the newer constructivist wings. The divisions are rather more complicated than that, but lingering over them isn't very productive. We see these divisions as points on the same continuum, or variants in the same family of methods, rather than as opposites. Two basic standard textbooks that give you an idea of the range of options in GT are Corbin and Strauss (2008), *Basics of Qualitative Research: Techniques and Procedures for Developing Grounded Theory*, and Charmaz (2006), *Constructing Grounded Theory: A Practical Guide through Qualitative Analysis*. The best single volume for getting an overview, as well as detailed discussion of the ins and outs of the method is the *Sage Handbook of Grounded Theory*, edited by Bryant and Charmaz (2007).

We began this chapter with a quick look at ethnographic research in anthropology and sociology. These are important fields in their own right, and they helped us lay the foundations for GT as discussed in this chapter. We suggest three very different works for getting a background in the highly variegated field of ethnographic methods. Each is excellent in its way. Each is a very lively account by a master of case making. Each takes on the whole field of ethnography/anthropology from a sharply distinct perspective. And, finally, each has some unflattering things to say about the others. Van Maanen's (2011) *Tales of the Field: On Writing Ethnography* reviews the rhetorical styles of ethnographic writing and adds some clarity to our understanding of newer trends (the literary turn and poststructuralism). Harris's (1980) *Cultural Materialism: The Struggle for a Science of Culture* makes a distinctively materialist case and does so in the context of classical epistemological debates in the social sciences. Edmund Leach's (1982) *Social Anthropology* goes over some of the same ground, but he does so combining functionalist (Durkheim/Malinowski) and structuralist (Lévi-Strauss) positions. Taken together, these three give you an appreciation for the breadth of approaches included under the rubric, ethnography.

*Vogt (1976b).

CHAPTER 11 SUMMARY TABLE

METHOD	WHEN TO USE
Literature reviews (pp. 386–388)	If you are a student, you may be required to do one to show that you have a worthy topic of investigation. As a more established researcher, you may want to use literature reviews to increase your theoretical sensitivity.
Open coding (p. 392)	Use this early and unstructured form of coding to begin to label, define, and index your data and your ideas about them.
Memo writing (p. 394)	At most phases of the research project, make extensive use of this systematic approach to interpretive reflections and methodological notes on notes, such as fieldnotes and interview transcripts. Memos are crucial for constructing an audit trail.
Software (pp. 395–396)	May be used at any stage of a project, but researchers often find it most useful in the initial data sorting and managing phases rather than in the later interpretive stages.
Abduction (p. 391)	To get initial ideas about surprising or puzzling patterns that you noticed in your data while analyzing them inductively; this is followed by rounds of deduction and further induction.
Constant comparison (pp. 392–393)	To check your initial impressions by comparing them with the data and looking for data that lead you to confirm, reject, or adjust your ideas.
Theoretical sampling (pp. 391–392)	After the early stages of data analysis, theoretical sampling enables you to use your preliminary concepts/theories to guide subsequent sampling of people and places and to target what particular kinds of data you want to gather next.
Axial coding (pp. 382, 390–392)	Use this method of organizing and generalizing your initial codes, especially when you find that a code/concept is central and that more peripheral codes/concepts can be organized around it.
Substantive theory (pp. 382–385)	Aim to use this concrete and focused type of theory building when your research question directs you to in-depth investigations of relatively unexamined territories.
Formal theory (pp. 382–385)	To broaden (or decontextualize) your substantive theory and to link it with other general theories in your field.
Saturation criteria (pp. 393–394)	To determine a justifiable stopping point for your data collection and analyses.
Archival data (pp. 386–388)	Theoretical sampling can lead you to use archival sampling to supplement interviews and direct observations; archival data can be especially helpful when you are moving from substantive to formal theory because they can allow you to broaden the scope of your constant comparisons at relatively low cost.

CHAPTER 12

Deductive Analyses of Qualitative Data

Comparative Case Studies and Qualitative Comparative Analysis

In this chapter we:

- Introduce deductive analyses and case study approaches to them and discuss:
  - Variable-oriented and case-oriented research.
  - Nomothetic and idiographic approaches.
  - The role of necessary and sufficient conditions in causal analysis.
  - How to approach theory in case study research: building, refining, and testing.
- Review when and why to do a single-case analysis.
- Discuss when to conduct small-*N* comparative case studies.
- Examine when to conduct comparative analyses with an intermediate *N* of cases, especially using qualitative comparative analysis (QCA) and topics in QCA, including:
  - Coding conditions in QCA.
  - The truth table.
  - csQCA and fsQCA.
  - QCA compared to quantitative alternatives.
  - QCA combined with other approaches.
- Conclude with general considerations on case study research and QCA.

What we call deductive approaches to analyzing qualitative data have several linked features. They are often most easily described by their contrast with the inductive approaches just discussed in Chapter 11, and we contrast the two throughout this chapter. To review, the distinction between deductive and inductive can be captured by the following questions: Do you use theories/ideas to direct data collection and analysis (a deductive approach)? Do you start with data collection and slowly build up generalizations and theories (an inductive approach)? Although there are important differences of emphasis between theories guiding the data collection and theories arising out of data collection, we think the answers to both questions should be yes. In fruitful research, whether the emphasis is deductive or inductive, there must be a dialogue between ideas and evidence. In the dialogue, one key question is, Who should start or lead the discussion, the ideas or the evidence?[1] In this chapter we discuss occasions when your research question is one that you believe can be better answered if ideas play a comparatively larger role at the outset.

Our linking of case study data with deductive analyses probably seems odd to some readers. It is true that one might not think of case study analysis as being deductive because case studies are rightly associated with intensive, in-depth examination of a small number of cases, sometimes only one. This kind of highly focused work is usually, and rightly, thought of as highly inductive. But an inductive approach to *data collection* is also often the foundation for much more deductive approaches to *data analysis*. Of all researchers focusing on qualitative data, those conducting case studies—particularly comparative case studies—are more often theory-driven. And they have produced numerous nuanced discussions of how to draw causal inferences from data.

CASE STUDIES AND DEDUCTIVE ANALYSES

What, in general, is a case study? The literature on the subject of what constitutes a case study is huge. This is not surprising, because case studies are used in virtually all disciplines, and they employ virtually all methods of data collection and analysis. We see the case study approach as being defined largely by *sampling* and by *depth* of analysis. A case study examines one instance or a small group of related instances (sampling). That instance is studied very closely (depth).[2] When the number of instances or cases becomes large enough that an in-depth study of them is impossible, then the analyst's emphasis necessarily shifts from cases to variables.[3] How large is "large enough"? The answer depends on the complexity of the cases. When the cases involve in-depth analyses of national governments, the number of cases will be small, perhaps three or four at most.[4] When the target of the cases is more circumscribed—such as forms of constitutional control over the executive in democracies or graduate students' efforts to unionize[5]—researchers may be able to handle a few dozen cases, but rarely more than that. Although there is no fixed number, using more than 50 cases in a case study project is quite rare. When researchers have more than 50 cases, they typically shift to a more variable-oriented, quantitative approach.

In any case, the analysis and interpretation of data collected using case study methods raise numerous issues that require researchers to choose among several analytical techniques. These are reviewed in this chapter.

Much of the new literature on case study analysis in the social sciences, especially the deductive approaches we examine in this chapter, has been written by political

[1] For an insightful discussion of the hermeneutical dialogue between theories and cases, see Fritzsche (2013).

[2] We have been guided in what follows by the definitional work in Ragin and Becker (1992) and Gerring (2007).

[3] Of course all researchers study cases. In large-sample quantitative analysis, each case is a row in a data matrix; the variables are the columns.

[4] Skocpol (1979) and Moore (1966) are two often cited examples.

[5] Respectively, Pennings (2003) and Caren and Panofsky (2005).

scientists and comparative/historical sociologists. The units of analysis in their investigations have tended to be nations. The data for these analyses have frequently come from archival sources, including scholarly publications. When political scientists and historical sociologists write about nations, they tend to focus on big systemic or large-event variables, such as nations' political systems, diplomatic actions, military policies, degrees of economic development, extensiveness of their welfare systems, and so on. This focus on the nation-state is mostly a disciplinary focus rather than a necessity of case study work. Researchers following the more inductive branch of case study research have usually conducted firsthand observations and interviews (we reviewed their analytical approaches in Chapters 2, 4, and 11). These have often been single-case studies—such as a street-corner society, a devastating flood, or vendors on a particular stretch of an urban sidewalk.[6]

The distinctions between cases that are small social groups, such as a street-corner society; cases that are nations, such as those with parliamentary forms of government; or cases that are major events, such as an economic crisis, are real distinctions. They can lead to different designs for collecting evidence—such as observational approaches when studying small social groups or archival approaches in the case of studying nations. These distinctions are important in disciplinary traditions, and they help textbook writers sort out the topics. But, as we have discussed earlier, these different kinds of case study often use similar methods of analysis. The main analytical distinction among these methods is between emphasizing mainly inductive versus largely deductive approaches. The latter are our focus here.

The distinction between case-oriented and variable-oriented research is another conceptual organizer that helps highlight the nature of case studies and the methods of analysis appropriate to them.[7] Features of these two orientations are spelled out in Table 12.1. Like all kinds of research studies, case studies work with a nested hierarchy of populations, samples, cases, variables, and observations. The *population* is the group about which the researcher wants to generalize, the *sample* is the group actually studied, the *cases* are the individual members of the sample, the *variables* are aspects or attributes of the cases, and the *observations* are methods of collecting and recording data about the variables. A case study is likely to have a small sample and a small number of variables but a large number of observations. A variable-oriented study typically has a larger sample of cases and sometimes a small number of variables; the variables are often coded for ease of measurement—such as *treatment: yes–no*.

Case-oriented researchers are interested in variables, but they tend to be especially sensitive to differences that arise from cases seen as a whole. And variable-oriented researchers are interested in cases (they collect background variables about each case, for example), but the main targets of generalization are the variables, not the cases. Generally, the larger your number of cases, the smaller the number of observations per case will be. And, conversely, the smaller the number of cases, the larger will be the number of observations per case. If you are studying the case of one national election, you might observe hundreds or thousands of facts about it. Conversely, if you are doing a comparative study of 30 national elections, you might make observations about just a few variables.

[6]Classics include Whyte (1943/1993), Erikson (1976), and Duneier (1999), respectively.

[7]The distinction thus labeled probably originated with Ragin (1987).

TABLE 12.1. Contrasting Variable-Oriented and Case-Oriented Research

Levels of study	Variable oriented	Case oriented
Population	Usually large.	May be large or small.
Sample	Usually intended to be representative, often a probability or random sample.	Usually chosen according to explanatory or theoretical relevance.
Cases	Usually a large number, often in the hundreds or thousands.	Usually a small number, seldom more than a few dozen.
Variables	If the number is large, the variables need to be coded for easy manipulation, often numerically.	The number of variables tends to be large as compared with the number of cases.
Observations	If the number of observations is large, they must be coded to be quickly observed and recorded.	The number is typically very large; researchers examine many facets of the cases and variables.

Note that this distinction between case-oriented and variable-oriented research is not a *design* distinction, at least in the way we have been using the term in this book. Many designs (approaches to collecting data) can be used whether one studies a small number of cases and examines them in depth or whether one studies a larger number of cases and operationalizes the variables so that they can be coded quickly. Because cases vary enormously, many designs can be used in case study work. Even single-case studies vary greatly—from one individual with a rare disease to one complex set of events, such as a national financial crisis. All designs can be and have been used to study cases: document analysis, observation, interviews, and surveys, and very often combinations of these. Experiments are rarer in case study research, but not absent: A set of methods for single-case experimental designs is well developed. Because case studies (small-sample, in-depth investigations) are an important methodological option regardless of the design, we have discussed design and sampling options for them elsewhere.[8] Here we focus on analysis methods for case study data.

A related way to describe the differences we have been discussing is to use the terms *large-N* and *small-N* (number) *research*. Many researchers use these terms to describe what they see as a fundamental trade-off between studies with large and small numbers *of cases*. To investigate a large number of cases in one analysis, one must examine either a small number of variables or study variables that can be reduced to a small number of easily coded dimensions. Looking at it the other way around, to study a large number of variables and/or to study them in depth, only a limited number of cases may be investigated. It is important to emphasize: Small *N* means a small number of cases, not necessarily of observations. Observations for one case may number in the hundreds or thousands, and statistical techniques can be used to describe and analyze them. This means that case study research is not necessarily qualitative. Although much small-*N* research has been inductive and most large-*N* research has been deductive, these tendencies are not invariant traits.

[8] Vogt et al. (2012).

Finally, as with most important topics in research methodology, measurement and coding issues in case study research do not easily resolve themselves into the battle between the quants and the quals. The distinction is largely untenable as a way to categorize case study research. As one author put it, "the *purely* narrative case study, one with no numerical analysis whatsoever, may not even exist. And I am quite sure that there is no purely quantitative case study, utterly devoid of prose."[9]

Should Your Case Study Be Nomothetic or Idiographic?

Another influential way to sort out the complexities of case study analysis is to ask whether your research is *idiographic* (nongeneralizing) or *nomothetic* (generalizing).[10] As we discuss, we think that some generalizing is unavoidable, but there are several varieties of generalization. Researchers study cases in depth the better to make one of several types of generalizations. Chief among these are descriptive generalizations about phenomena, identification of causes, and explanations of causal mechanisms.

Because a case study deals with a case *of something*, the implicit promise of a researcher conducting a case study is that the "something," not just the particular instance examined, will be better understood as a consequence of the research. A case study implies generalization. The first generalization comes when the researcher uses a general category and selects a case or cases that exemplify it. Say you wanted to take a case study approach to the study of race riots. To select your case or cases you will need preliminary generalizations about race riots to help you define them so you can tell whether a potential case qualifies for inclusion in your study. This much is uncontroversial.

Researchers differ, however, on a second type of generalization—whether generalization is a two-way street. Of course, you need a general category of cases from which you select a case, but, after you study the case, can you then generalize about the category? We think the answer is yes, and we don't quite see the point of case studies otherwise. However, some case study researchers are strictly *idiographic* in the approach they advocate; they view their work as descriptive of a singular or unique case from which little if any generalization is possible. Historians and anthropologists are probably most likely to make this claim,[11] often as a point of pride, but fewer case study researchers in other social sciences (sociology, psychology, political science, and economics) view their work this way. By contrast to idiographic research, the so-called *nomothetic* approach seeks to establish universal principles or laws. This goal is, if anything, rarer, though not completely absent, among case study researchers in the social sciences. We think that idiographic and nomothetic are impossible extremes, maybe useful to define end points on a continuum but not likely to occur in their pure forms in actual research.

In short, the majority of case study researchers are neither strictly idiographic nor nomothetic; they neither confine themselves exclusively to one case in which all generalization is forbidden nor use case study results to formulate universal laws of social behavior. The research we reviewed when writing this chapter has mostly been

[9] Gerring (2007, p. 11).

[10] There are clear parallels to the anthropological distinction between emic and etic—including the tendency of scholars to invent obscure labels. See Chapter 11 for a brief discussion.

[11] Lamont and White (2009).

conducted by investigators who have tended to seek (and, indeed, are unable to avoid) a middle ground between these two unattainable extremes. And that middle ground can produce something hugely important in social research, without which it would be impoverished. In case studies we often see a strong and very *fruitful tension between the particular and the general.* Generalizations are tempered by knowledge of specific cases. Specific cases are examined in depth in order to say something about the generality of cases. The researcher's focus often alternates between these two, in a kind of dialogue between the particular instance and the general rule. The middle ground between the particular and the general usually involves the *discovery* of causal relations and/or the in-depth *explication* of causal mechanisms.

For example, the financial crisis of 2008 had things in common with previous crises. Otherwise, how could we identify it as a crisis? But it was also unique in several respects, and these unique features need to be highlighted. However, we are not most likely to study the case just to satisfy an idle curiosity or out of some sort of antiquarian interest in the unique aspects of the recent past. Rather, we think it might have something to tell us about crises in general and perhaps, therefore, about how to avoid or mitigate future crises.[12] When such lessons are learned from case studies, they are *causal* in nature. We use the term guardedly, because it raises hackles, but we see no way to avoid it, especially in deductive analyses. We seek a middle ground between causation enthusiasts and deniers. It does not seem correct to assume with the enthusiasts that causal generalizations about human thought and action are unproblematic. But the second group, the causation deniers, which considers studying causes taboo, doesn't have a very good case, either. In steering a middle course, we try to specify both the limits of and opportunities for causal analysis in case study research.

What Are the Roles of Necessary and Sufficient Conditions in Identifying and Explaining Causes?

General discussions of causation identify three broad types of causal conditions: probabilistic, necessary, and sufficient. Because specifying probabilistic causal conditions requires large samples (and probability-based sampling), they are of limited applicability for most case study research,[13] which is often small-*N* research. By contrast, necessary and sufficient causal conditions are central to many methodological discussions among case study researchers. A **probabilistic causal condition** influences the *likelihood* of an outcome; a **necessary condition** is *required* for an outcome to occur; and a **sufficient condition** is *enough* by itself to bring about an outcome. For example, for it to snow tomorrow, the air temperature must be 32 degrees F (0 degrees C) or colder. But a freezing temperature is not sufficient—it's not enough. Many cold days see no snowfall. Other conditions must necessarily be present, such as moisture in the air. Moisture is also not sufficient, as many moist days are not snowy. Coldness and wetness are necessary but not sufficient.

Those distinctions seem simple enough, but there is a different way to conceive of necessary conditions—they can be seen as probabilities. If the temperature tomorrow

---

[12] See Lo (2012).

[13] Bayesian probability statistics may be used with small samples, but not many case study researchers have pursued this approach.

is going to be above freezing, then the probability of snow is zero. If the temperature will be below freezing, then the probability is higher, nonzero, but not 1.0 or 100%. The same reasoning applies to air moisture. Now, if the air is both cold *and* moist, the probability of snow is even higher—100% if moisture and freezing air were the only two necessary conditions and were together sufficient. It is hard to reconcile these two ways of understanding necessary conditions. Should necessary conditions be thought of as probabilists see them, as continuous variables—specifically as truncated continuous variables, the value of which can either be 0 or any positive number between 0 and 1.0? Or should the necessary conditions be thought of as categorical—as either present or absent with no intermediate conditions? Suffice it to say that most case study researchers tend to think of necessary conditions categorically, not continuously and probabilistically. By contrast, large-*N* researchers usually think of causal conditions as increasing the likelihood of an outcome and may even deny the very existence of necessary conditions in the social world.

A sufficient condition is one that, all by itself, can be enough to bring about an outcome. This might seem a tougher standard to meet. It is, but only if by *sufficient* one means sufficient *and* exclusive. Many sufficient conditions are not exclusive. A patient might die of cancer, a heart attack, an infection, an aneurism, or any of several other ailments. These will not always lead to death, because people survive these conditions (they can be sufficient, but they are not necessary). That fact again gives the probabilist an entry—each of these sufficient conditions increases the probability of death but does not inevitably bring it about.

On the other hand, retrospectively, each of these ailments may be a sufficient *explanation* for a death. Thus a condition that is sufficient to explain may not be sufficient to predict. Many case study researchers doing causal analysis are categorical data analysts who think that necessary and sufficient conditions can be identified, coded categorically, and used to analyze social life. When these researchers study necessary or sufficient conditions that are naturally continuous variables, such as temperature, those variables often have clear thresholds, the attainment of which is necessary or sufficient.

Necessary conditions are easy to identify in the social world, but finding *important* necessary conditions is not so easy. For example, for two parties to come to a formal agreement, it is necessary that they have a language in common (if only through a translator) and that they have some means of communication (face-to-face, e-mail, telephone, etc.). Although those two conditions are certainly necessary, we wouldn't think much of a prediction or explanation that said, "The parties were bound to agree; after all, both of them spoke English and had telephones." So a common language and a means of communication are necessary but trivial. They should probably be thought of as antecedent or background conditions. Or, to take a second example, researchers might be interested in the cause of a particular riot or of riots in general. If the researchers defined a riot as a violent civil disturbance involving three or more persons, one of the necessary conditions would be that three or more persons are gathered. But this is trivial in two ways: first, that necessary condition is true simply because it is part of the definition; second, and more important, although it is true, the necessary condition explains or predicts nothing because the vast majority of meetings of three or more people do not lead to riots.

Sufficient conditions are also easy to find, but finding an *exclusive* sufficient condition, or even one that greatly narrows the range of possible sufficient conditions, is hard.

To continue with the same examples, a shared interest, a common enemy, or compatible strengths may be sufficient to explain a formal agreement between two parties. If the sufficient causes of an outcome are very numerous, then the sufficient conditions are of limited interest: A riot can be caused by a religious conflict, an election dispute, an encounter of opposing football fans, a food shortage, a rumor, or any number of other conditions. When the list of sufficient conditions is long and varies greatly from case to case, the sufficient condition as an explanation for a case does not tell the researcher much. The challenge for case study investigators is to find necessary and/or sufficient conditions that are theoretically interesting—conditions that help researchers to explain or predict by narrowing the range of the likely explanatory or predictor variables.

How Should You Approach Theory in Case Study Research?

In case study analysis, as in all types of research, the choice of theoretical approach is largely determined by one's research question and one's analytical purposes. These should determine how you decide what approach to use when. The analytical purpose with which you approach your research question can be summarized in terms of your assessment of the extant explanations or theories in the field you are studying. If you believe that there are few if any good theories that address your research question, you could do case study research to discover causal relations among variables in the case(s) so as to begin to *build a theory*. If you think that one or more explanations of your outcomes of interest are probably correct but that they are underdeveloped, you could do case study research with the aim of *refining the existing theories*. Finally, if your field and the theories in it are organized around a relatively small number of well-elaborated but competing explanations, you could undertake case study analysis with the aim of *testing one or more of these theories*.

These three broad purposes—theory or explanation building, refining, and testing—often coincide fairly closely with the number of cases you plan to analyze. If you are aiming to discover relations among variables in order to begin building a theory, you are probably going to work with only a few cases, and perhaps only one. If you wish to specify or refine an existing theory, a middling number of cases, perhaps 4–15, could work well. Finally, if you are going to attempt to test a theory, a comparatively large number could suit your purposes—as many as you could manage while still retaining in-depth knowledge of the particular cases. For an individual researcher, this number can rarely exceed 20–25, and even that many may be a stretch. But teams can often handle more.

These relations between your research question and purposes, the number of cases you use, and the methods of analysis you employ are summarized in Table 12.2. It is important to say at the outset that these distinctions are tendencies; the categories tend to merge, and it is possible to pursue more than one of these purposes and use more than one of these methods. But if you are a solo researcher—working on your dissertation, for example—it is almost certainly a good idea to pick one purpose and a corresponding method. Moving from one purpose to another means changing or adding research questions; it may be best thought of in terms of a long-term research agenda. Finishing a project requires making choices. The choices are perhaps especially pressing with case study research. Because case study research by definition requires in-depth knowledge of the cases, it is very time-consuming. The three types described in Table 12.2, and

TABLE 12.2. Purposes, Number of Cases, and Methods of Analysis

Analytical purpose	Number of cases	Analytical methods
Discovering relations, building theory	1–5	Intense observation; process tracing
Refining, specifying, elaborating theory	3–15	Taxonomies and typological theories
Testing explanations or theories with data	10–40	Qualitative comparative analysis

with which we conclude this section, also introduce the final three sections of this chapter: single, small, and intermediate numbers of cases.

WHEN TO DO A SINGLE-CASE ANALYSIS: DISCOVERING, DESCRIBING, AND EXPLAINING CAUSAL LINKS

What can researchers learn by studying single cases? Quite a lot, many researchers seem to believe, because the single-case study is probably the most common of all case study types. One reason that the single-case study is very common is the need for the researcher to know the cases in depth: It is difficult to know more than one case really well. Single-case studies often do not seek to test a theory or hypothesis, or even to generate one. Rather, they aim to *understand* a single case. In short, use a single-case study when you want to understand one instance of a phenomenon in depth, with the ultimate goal of understanding similar cases and the general phenomenon. Single-case studies often do not seek to test a theory or hypothesis, or even to generate one; however, in deductive approaches they do usually seek to further understand or elaborate upon existing theories.

Historians and anthropologists often think more in terms of understanding cases than of drawing generalizations from them.[14] And single-case studies are often written by historians or anthropologists and others using ethnographic methods. When political scientists and sociologists conduct single-case studies, they frequently build on the work of historians, though they sometimes collect their own archival data. It is hard to overemphasize the historicity of social science data and the fact that it is always embedded in a temporal context, as well as in social, economic, political, and geographic contexts.

All data presented in research reports are historical. We may want to generalize about the future, but our evidence comes from the past. And the present is constantly receding into the past—this very instant (2:00 P.M.) moves into the past before I finish typing this sentence (at 2:01 P.M.). As one researcher in the cutting-edge field of machine learning and predictive analytics put it, "By the time the programmers deployed my predictive . . . system, the data over which I had tuned it was already about 11 months old."[15] Even researchers conducting observational case studies, in which the processes investigated are ongoing while the investigators study them, write about the past when they compose their research reports.

[14] Lamont and White (2009).

[15] Siegel (2013).

Observational case study researchers can influence their cases while gathering data. This is not possible when social scientists build upon secondary works written by historians. For historians and other archival researchers, the case or event is over before the researchers begin gathering data. They know how it turned out. They cannot intervene. But the same is true of the observational case study. At some point one must cease observing and analyze one's case notes. At that point one is using historical data, albeit sometimes it may be historical data from the very recent past.

Using a single case to test a theory is most likely to be productive if the theory states that some causal condition is necessary. If a particular condition is thought to be necessary to produce a given outcome and you find a case in which the outcome occurred without the particular condition, then the case has tested and disproven—or at least qualified—the theory. Or if the theory claims that a causal condition is sufficient to produce a given outcome and a single case shows that it does not, this also disconfirms the theory.[16] In brief, in single-case analysis, *disconfirming* instances convey the most information. A single case that conforms to the theory adds a little to the credibility of the theory, but typically not much. A single case can be instructive in a very rudimentary theory on which very little empirical work has been done or a theory about which a great deal of skepticism has been expressed. Then a single case can constitute a "plausibility probe,"[17] and a confirming instance could suggest that the theory is worth further inquiry.

Even less is conveyed by a single case if the theory specifies a probabilistic link between the condition and the outcome. The main value of single-case research for theory testing—finding a disconfirming instance—is useful mostly for deterministic theories that postulate necessary and/or sufficient conditions. The value of a single case for theory testing is reduced to almost nothing if the theory is probabilistic. If the theory states that the presence of X, or an increase in X, increases the probability of Y, then a single case, whatever the values of X and Y, tells the researcher very little. Probabilistic theories can be tested only with relatively large probability samples. Small-N case studies have limited applicability to probabilistic theories.

More typically, one uses single-case research not to test a theory but to build a theory. There are other ways to build a theory than through case study research. Probably the most common is the literature review, in which the researcher systematically surveys the available evidence and tries to rethink it. But case study research has a central role in theory building. Case studies can help by discovering a new variable or by suggesting a hypothesis that could be tested with multiple-case research. Perhaps the most important type of theory building done with single-case research is examining and explaining the functioning of causal links or causal mechanisms—what are usually called *mediating variables* in variable-oriented research.

For example, most of the causal mechanisms explaining the *democratic peace theory* arose out of case study research. Briefly—and we are summarizing a huge literature[18]—the theory (or observation) holds that democratic nations never or hardly ever go to war *with one another.* Democracies do go to war with considerable frequency, but

[16] An often cited example is Lijphart (1975), who used the single case of the Netherlands to disconfirm a widely believed political and social psychological theory.

[17] The term is from George and Bennett (2005).

[18] Examples are Levy and Razin (2004) and Mansfield and Snyder (2005).

not with other democracies. Presuming that one accepts that this observation (theory) is accurate, the causal mechanisms, the mediating links, between democracy and peace become important. Perhaps peace between democracies persists because democracies tend to be prosperous and prosperous nations tend not to go to war *with one another.* Or perhaps decision making in democracies is fairly transparent, and this facilitates successful bargaining among them. Those are two of several examples of causal mechanisms (intervening or mediating variables) that have been postulated using single-case research and examined with multiple-case-study research.

The range of types of single-case studies is enormous. Some examples can help make the preceding generalizations clearer. Three single-case studies suggest the breadth of species variation in this genus. The first is from medical research, which is the home of origin for single-case research; here the method is often intensive study of a single patient. In this example, one group of physicians described a new method of diagnosing a rare disease; the method of diagnosis and subsequent treatment were developed with one patient. Previous problems in diagnosing the disease had led to overly aggressive treatments that caused unnecessary harm. In brief, improved diagnosis led to improved treatment of the disease, and those methods of diagnosis and treatment, the authors argued, should guide practice in subsequent cases.[19] This degree of clarity about the implications of case study findings is rare in the social sciences.

A second example used intensive study of a single case to illustrate a methodological approach in the social scientific study of science and knowledge. In the early 20th century, most members of the dominant group of sociologists in France rather abruptly abandoned the study of their own society (and other European societies) for the study of non-Western "primitive" societies. To explain this dramatic shift, the author of the case study proposed a method of analysis that combined necessary (but not sufficient) political, professional, and substantive conditions that led to the result.[20] Although the case was perhaps interesting in its own right, it was offered mostly as a way to examine the origins of other changes in the development of academic disciplines.

Our third single-case study comes from the sociology of health and social behavior, in which there is a long-standing observation (a.k.a. theory) that rich people tend to be healthier and live longer than poor people. The most important research task to explain this fact is to specify why and how this comes to be so; the issue is one of mediating variables. The authors studied the case of cholesterol levels over time (1976–2004) and in relation to socioeconomic status (SES). Their study advanced our understanding of the link between SES and longevity. In brief, in 1976, rich people tended to have higher levels of cholesterol than poor people. By 2004, the relation was reversed, and poor people tended to have higher levels. The change was brought about by the development of statins in the 1980s, to which individuals with higher SES had more access.[21] Again, although the authors found the specific case to be interesting in itself, the goals of the case study were to explain the relationship between SES and longevity by providing a mediating variable and also to illustrate a method for studying the diffusion of technological change, such as the development of a new drug therapy, in the health fields.

---

[19] Abern, Benson, and Hoeksema (2009).

[20] Vogt (1976a).

[21] Chang and Lauderdale (2009).

These three examples of single-case studies vary in many respects. The first involved a single patient with a rare disease who sought treatment at a university medical center. The second focused on a few dozen sociologists from the last century; they were studied using historical techniques and data. The third employed a nationally representative sample of 36,000 individuals to explicate the relationship between cholesterol levels and SES. Although these uses of single-case studies are strikingly different, they also have much in common. Each of the cases is substantively intriguing in its own right, but the researchers studying the cases aimed to make broader points, both about the population of other cases and about methods of studying them; about the disease and how to diagnose and treat it; about a change in scientific knowledge and how to explain it; and about a change in the relation between health and SES and how to investigate it. All three case studies were interested in causes—not only what happened, but how and why it happened and what generalizations could be drawn from that causal knowledge to apply to future research and practice.

In the social sciences, one method for finding and explicating causal mechanisms is often called **process tracing.**[22] Process tracing is a case study method more aimed at multiple causes than at multiple cases. With process tracing one usually examines a chain of causation in a single case. The idea is to identify and explain the causal pathways that led to an event, outcome, or condition. In that sense, process tracing involves kinds of narrative analysis similar to those used by historians, journalists, attorneys, and others putting together a narrative account of how an outcome came about. As such, process tracing tends to be inductive, though it is often used as a method to follow up on conclusions drawn with more deductive approaches. The idea behind process tracing has been to formalize this traditional and natural method of research and to make it more "methodological," that is, by adding more thinking about issues of method than is typical in explanations using natural narratives.

It is hard to specify in advance the criteria or the sequence of steps in a process tracing analysis. At least we cannot do so in the way that we have done for many other methods, such as case selection, writing effective survey questions, matching statistical models to experimental designs, and so on. The goal of process tracing is clear enough—to identify and explain a causal chain in a single case. And a successful process tracing study is easy enough to recognize, but it is hard to give good general advice about how to go about conducting an effective one apart from the obvious, such as be smart, work hard, and examine the case in depth so as to get very familiar with it. The best way to get ideas about how to do a process tracing investigation study is to study good examples. As is fitting, case studies are the best way to learn how to do this kind of case study analysis.[23]

When processes have been identified and an explanatory theory has been built or refined, another sometimes useful approach is **counterfactual reasoning**. When the number of cases is limited, counterfactual reasoning and thought experiments are the only

---

[22]This sense of the term was coined by George (1979) and has since come into wide use. The term is also used in psychology to describe the cognitive processes decision makers use. The two are linked in Lau and Redlawsk (2001) .

[23]A good review of successful instances of process tracing can be found in George and Bennett (2005). A more recent text is Beach and Pedersen (2012).

way to "find" cases for comparison. If a particular event or sequence of X's is crucial to understanding how an outcome occurred, one way to "test" this idea is to conduct a thought experiment: What *would have* happened had the event not occurred, or had the sequence of mediating variables not been present? You can make a case that outcome Y would be inconceivable without $X1$ and $X2$—or that even in the absence of $X1$ and $X2$, Y probably would have occurred anyway. Many researchers object to counterfactual reasoning as being far too hypothetical, but it is a key ingredient in all research, even experimental research, in which it is usually labeled as a thought experiment. In experiments, the same participants cannot be in both the experimental and the control group at the same time. Random assignment is a counterfactual approximation of what would happen if you could give a group a treatment, record what happens, then rewind history and observe the same group without the treatment.[24]

Research on a single case can be done using a wide range of designs, running from the historical to the experimental.[25] Regardless of the design, single-case research is usually focused on description, illustration, and discovery and tends to be most productive in those realms. So, if your research question leads you to want to describe or illustrate a phenomenon or discover relations, single-case research may be the best choice for you. For testing or confirming a theory, or elaborating and specifying a causal relation, comparisons among multiple cases are often needed. Comparisons can be undertaken with a small number of cases or with an intermediate number (see the next two sections).

WHEN TO CONDUCT SMALL-*N* COMPARATIVE CASE STUDIES

Not surprisingly, you use comparative case studies when you want to make comparisons among more than one case. There seems little point in working with multiple cases unless some sort of comparison of similarities or differences is intended. Even in single-case studies, comparisons are imbedded in the case narrative. Indeed, it is probably impossible to think or even describe without implicit comparison. But the comparisons when working with multiple cases are explicit and often carefully planned. Explicit comparison allows a wider range of research questions to be addressed than does the single-case study. With small-N comparative studies, the goal is sometimes theory testing but is more often theory elaboration.

An older use of the term *comparative studies* harks back to the day when "comparative" usually meant comparisons among countries. This use and practice is still very widespread, but there is no need to limit comparisons to nation-states.[26] As we discuss in this section, comparative case study techniques can be applied to many different sorts of units of analysis. Nonetheless, the tradition of international comparisons is strong—as our first two examples illustrate. As with single-case studies, so too with multiple-case comparative studies: The range of possibilities is enormous.

[24]This influential argument comes originally from Rubin (1974, 1986).

[25]Kennedy (2005).

[26]An even older terminology used *comparative* to mean another nation. A single nation's political or educational system would be described, and this would be comparative only in an implicit sense—often "like us versus not like us." Such articles abound in older back issues of excellent journals, including the *Comparative Education Review* and the *Journal of Comparative Politics*.

We begin with a two-case comparative study of the growth of a field of knowledge. Demography as a systematic discipline emerged in the 19th century. England and France were two of the main loci of this emergence. A two-case comparative study of the development of this discipline highlights the different paths demography took, which helps explain some of the features it retains today. The analytical strategy adopted by the author[27] involved using published historical sources to focus on differences in the development of demography in the two national contexts. Of course, because the two cases were cases of the same thing, there were a good many similarities, too. And the two cases really were not independent cases because trends in each country influenced those in the other. A different strategy for this topic could have been to focus on the largely simultaneous development of demography in the two nations and to point to the broader intellectual, social, and economic factors contributing to its rise. But this would not have facilitated the fine-grained understanding of the aspects of demography that the author sought.

A second example of small-*N* comparative case studies also involves the nation-state as the unit of analysis. Israel, Taiwan, and Ireland, though small, played disproportionately large roles in the development of innovations in the production of computer hardware and software in the late 20th century. The author[28] used a 3-by-2 comparison to conduct the analyses: three nations and two industries, hardware and software. In all three nations, government intervention to encourage economic growth was important in the software and hardware industries. Using extensive archival and interview research, the author focused on differences in economic activity fostered by different government technology policies. Although global and local market forces shaped the economic development of the software and hardware industries in these three nations, government decisions had an important, sometimes defining, impact. Different policies and differences among the people who implemented the policies also had significant consequences. The conclusion was that there is no general model for success except a model that stressed adaptability to differences.

Our third example emphasizes similarities in what at first would seem widely disparate cases: deforestation in Ecuador's Amazon basin and suburban sprawl in New Jersey. The author[29] considers these to be cases of how people transformed landscapes in the late 20th century. The most common explanations have emphasized market forces, such as how individuals calculate the value of land; these calculations are influenced by factors such as distance from central cities. Calculations of the value of economic "rent" are important, and so are the social and political elements of land transformation, which have been omitted from most theoretical accounts of land use. Both deforestation and suburban sprawl were importantly fostered by government actions (from incentives for individuals to building infrastructure, especially roads). These government actions made it easier for local elites to profit from dividing large tracts of land into smaller units, which they sold for increasingly intensive uses. By understanding two apparently very different cases as instances of the same, more general phenomenon, the study improves our knowledge of each and shows how similar social and political forces can be enacted in very different cultural and economic settings. And these generalizations

[27]Schweber (2006).

[28]Breznitz (2007).

[29]Rudel (2009).

can be expanded to other cases—a good example being the transformation of millions of acres of grassland into a dustbowl in the United States in the early 20th century.

This brief look at examples of small-*N* multiple-case studies makes it clear that they can deal with many topics, such as academic disciplines, government industrial policy, or environmental depredations. The methods ranged from a historical comparison of the development of demography in France and England to a comparative analysis of state intervention in computer industries in Israel, Taiwan, and Ireland to extensive fieldwork on radical increases in population density in Ecuador and New Jersey.

As with most comparative case study research, the *fact-to-generalization ratio* is very high in all three of these studies—many facts, few generalizations. Enormous erudition, taking years, sometimes decades, yields what some social scientists would think of as a strikingly disappointing number of general conclusions. These studies are characterized by great in-depth knowledge and attention to detail. But they are not narrow studies; they are breathtaking in their scope—multiple languages, extensive travel and fieldwork, impressive familiarity with different social and political contexts are all in evidence. Comparative case study research is not for the faint of heart, and perhaps not for someone wanting to finish a dissertation quickly or who would be uncomfortable with a high fact-to-generalization ratio.

Note that in our first two exemplars of small-*N* comparative case studies, the authors examined quite similar issues (the field of demography and the computer industry) in quite similar nations, but their analyses stressed differences. The study of Ecuador and New Jersey, on the other hand, stressed the similarities of phenomena that are not often thought of together: deforestation and suburban sprawl. Those two approaches illustrate John Stuart Mill's methods of similarity and difference, which are the building blocks on which have been erected most comparative studies. Basically, the question is, Do you select similar cases/sites and focus your analysis on differences, or do you choose different cases/sites and concentrate analytically on similarities? Your research question determines the answer, which, in turn, shapes your strategy for case selection. There is no more important issue in case study research.

Are the cases or outcomes being contrasted different enough—are they really distinct? Are the cases or outcomes being compared really similar enough? As a researcher you will inevitably be confronted with one or both of these questions. They will always be relevant, because limits to difference and to similarity can always be found. Everyone knows that, by definition, generalizations are only generally true. But when a critic points out that your generalization is not universally true, this can carry a sting, and some critics will consider it decisive. Are deforestation and sprawl "really" comparable outcomes? Are Ireland, Israel, and Taiwan really comparable nations? The answer is clear: yes and no. It depends on your analytical purposes. Be aware that whatever you do, you will probably be faced with this kind of criticism. A deforestation scholar will usually say that suburban sprawl is too different; an Ireland specialist will typically stress those phenomena that make it distinct from Taiwan or Israel. You will be accused, no matter what you compare, of "comparing apples and oranges." But, for many purposes, it is quite natural to compare apples and oranges: They are both round, grow on trees, are good sources of vitamin C, are important agricultural products, and so on. The charge is usually that you are treating apples and oranges as identical. But what you are claiming is simply that, for a specific research question, they are similar enough for analytical purposes.

A good example of the validity and the limits of the "you can't really compare that" challenge comes in the well-known field of international comparisons of educational achievement. This is an area of study that has become mostly variable-oriented rather than case-oriented. Regardless of the orientation, the issue of comparable cases is the same—it's the age-old battle between the splitters and the lumpers. Some researchers (splitters) stress differences and question whether large international studies such as PISA and TIMSS (see Chapter 5) really make sense. Can you make meaningful comparisons among separate national education systems with different levels of social and ethnic diversity, different amounts of poverty, and varying degrees of selectivity in the school systems? If secondary education is universal in one nation and highly selective in another, can you really compare secondary school students' scores on the same math test? On the other hand, contend the lumpers, the students are all about the same age, and math (unlike, say, literature or philosophy) is fairly international in its language and methods. For example, one of us (W. P. V.) had the opportunity to observe the teaching of algebra in Cyprus, Yemen, and the United States. Even with major language barriers and very noticeable cultural differences, the observer could follow the lesson fairly well and make comparisons about teaching methods in the three nations. The observer believed that it was reasonable to make comparisons. Individual differences have to be respected, and analyzing them is very instructive, but cases do not have to be clones in order to be comparable.

WHEN TO CONDUCT ANALYSES WITH AN INTERMEDIATE *N* OF CASES

Use an intermediate number of cases when you want to maximize the number of comparisons across cases and when you want to analyze multiple causes and/or interactions of categorical variables. With an intermediate number of cases (perhaps 10–40) the researcher will necessarily have to trade some depth for breadth. The advantages and disadvantages of doing so need not be elaborated on at length. Suffice it to say that to address some research questions, a larger number of cases might be available and may be necessary. Finding the "right" balance between breadth and depth usually requires that you explore potential cases to understand them well enough to decide whether to include them. Rarely are there clear sampling rules that you can apply. The number of cases you settle upon will importantly influence the analysis options that are effective. As always, your research report should clearly articulate your sampling logic and justify the final case selection.

As with the earlier examples discussed in this chapter, so too with researchers who employ an intermediate number of cases: Most investigators typically devise their own methods of analysis. They tend to be created ad hoc—literally "for this" case. The research is usually produced using an artisanal approach rather than a formal system. To say that something is artisanal does not mean that it is of low quality, of course. Artisanal cheese or bread is often made to higher standards than mass market competitors. But being artisanal, the methods of production usually cannot easily be standardized and scaled up for use by a larger community of producers.

In scholarship, a particular work might be admired or highly influential without leading to the development of a disciplinary consensus around which a community of researchers can form. The formation of methodological working groups allows a method to last more than a few years, perhaps more than one generation. Such methodological communities can share and develop a common set of methods. In the last chapter, we saw that one such community has formed around the cluster of methods known as grounded theory—mostly applied to interview research.

Another such community—mostly applied to case study research—centers on **qualitative comparative analysis (QCA)**. QCA is not the only type of comparative case analysis, but it is a very well formulated approach to the problems of comparing cases. It has been under systematic development for two decades. And it is characterized by a detailed and rigorous analysis system that includes dedicated analysis software. We use QCA as our main example for discussing the analysis of an intermediate number of cases because it is a state-of-the-art method (if not necessarily *the* state-of-the-art method) that uses a deductive, theory-guided approach to analyzing case study data. As with all other topics in this book, we follow the literature. Methods that are not currently discussed extensively in the research literature are given less coverage than those that are. Following the shape of the research literature in our discussions is inevitable, and it can also be a useful guide when you select your analysis methods. When you make your choices, you may decide that it is advisable or reassuring to select methods that have been used and tested by others. Be that as it may, QCA's usage rate is substantial, it has increased greatly in recent years, and it has been applied by investigators working in several fields.

QCA has been around long enough and used extensively enough to merit retrospective reviews. QCA was first used in a published article in 1984. By 2011, more than 300 articles applying QCA to data analysis (not just summarizing or mentioning it) had been published in peer-reviewed journals, most of them since 2002.[30] There is an international working group called Comparative Methods for Systematic Cross Case Analysis (abbreviated COMPASSS), and several versions of QCA software have been developed.[31] Since its initial development in the 1980s, QCA has been mostly applied to comparative sociology and politics. Applications in other fields, such as management studies and educational evaluation, have become more common since the turn of the century.

It is not infrequent in QCA studies for the "sample" to be the entire "population," such as all states in the United States, all nations that are members of the Organization for Economic Cooperation and Development (OECD), or all European Union members. As these examples suggest, the units of analysis have often been large sociopolitical entities, such as nations. But more recently, smaller organizations, such as grant recipients, manufacturing firms, and political parties, have been studied.

QCA uses categorical variables, both as predictors and outcomes. Variables are usually called either **attributes** or **conditions**, which helps distinguish them from continuous variables used in most statistical coding and analysis. The use of categorical variables is not unique to QCA. Other forms of comparative case study analysis also often code conditions categorically and sometimes as ranks (see later discussion). But distinct from other forms of comparative case studies using categorical coding, QCA

[30]The first article was Ragin, Mayer, and Drass (1984); the first book was Ragin (1987). The most useful review for our purposes is Rihoux, Alamos, Bol, Marx, and Rezsöhazy (2012).

[31]The organization's website is *www.compasss.org*; a recent and thorough review of QCA software can be found in Thiem and Duşa (2013).

makes formal use of **Boolean logic** at the analysis stage. Boolean logic is a form of logic/algebra in which all values are true or false, all attributes are present or absent. It is the basis of the binary (1,0) computer languages we all use.

Boolean logic may be most familiar to readers of this book who have done research literature searches using computerized databases. You identify categories (key words) for your search. These words will either be present in or absent from each item in the literature search. The same logic is used in QCA's investigation of attributes/conditions and whether they are necessary and sufficient conditions for the outcome being studied. The most familiar "operators" in Boolean logic are OR and AND. If you join two topics, such as *X* and *Y*, by "AND," your hits will be restricted to articles that talk about *both*. If you link the two topics with "OR," your hits will include articles that discuss *either X or Y*. For example, if you specify female AND surgeons AND salary you would be aiming for works dealing with the salaries of female surgeons—a fairly focused topic. But if you specified female OR surgeons OR salary, you would be instructing the software to find sources having anything to do with females, salaries, or surgeons—an unmanageable heap of sources, for sure.

QCA has two aspects: (1) a general approach to comparative case research and (2) a specific set of analytical techniques. The first, the general approach, QCA shares with many other qualitative case study methods: in-depth work to identify cases and then to code conditions/attributes. Because QCA is on the more deductive end of the spectrum of qualitative methods, the work to identify cases and conditions is more dependent on predetermined concepts. As with other methods we have discussed in this book, analysis begins in earnest after case selection and coding. It is this second feature of QCA that most sharply differentiates it from other qualitative analysis methods. QCA's set of analytical techniques is quite distinct. By applying formal Boolean logic and set theory to the codes to identify necessary and sufficient conditions, QCA researchers make more formal John Stuart Mill's principles of similarity and difference, which have long been the mainstay of comparative case analysis. Some researchers don't care for the Boolean formality, because they find it no longer "qualitative" in certain senses of the term. Other researchers seem eager to skip the qualitative part and get right to the analysis by applying QCA methods to more traditional quantitative data. Not surprisingly, we advocate a middle ground between these two positions.

We appreciate QCA's mix of qualitative expert coding and formal analyses. We see it as closely related to combined, multimethod, or mixed coding and analysis. That is hardly a new insight, as the subtitle of the first book on QCA was *Moving Beyond Qualitative and Quantitative Strategies*.[32] The qualitative foundation of QCA is traditional comparative case analysis, during which cases can be added or dropped or recoded on the basis of what is learned when studying them in depth.[33] This contrasts sharply with quantitative coding and analysis, in which dropping cases or recoding variables as the investigation proceeds can be thought of as bad practice—tantamount to cheating. Although the analysis stage of QCA is not quantitative, it is very formal and quite tricky to conduct without the use of dedicated QCA software. This formality is what makes it seem nonqualitative to some. And it is true that logic and set theory have some things in common with regression analysis (see later discussion). Although they

[32] Ragin (1987).

[33] The parallels with grounded theory's "theoretical sampling" are quite close; see Chapter 11.

are distinct, what they have in common is that both are typically interested in generalizing to populations—in making causal generalizations.

We provide only a few details of the analysis method—just enough to help readers decide whether they are interested in pursuing the topic further. The most basic element of a QCA analysis is the **truth table**. A truth table is a way of arranging all possible combinations of values of a set of conditions/attributes. These are then compared with the values present in or absent from the empirical cases being studied. The goal of the analysis is to winnow down all the logically possible combinations to the ones that actually pertain. The number of possible combinations can be very large, especially as the number of conditions/attributes increases. For instance, Table 12.3 shows all the logically possible combinations of two binary conditions/attributes. For example, Condition 1 might be unionization of the workforce (*yes–no* or *true–false*), whereas Condition 2 would be public organization (*yes–no* or *true–false*). When put together, the two conditions and two values yield 16 logically distinct combinations. The truth table is used as a sort of template the researcher can hold up to the data to see which among the logically possible combinations is empirically present in the cases. When more conditions are added, the number of combinations increases geometrically.

QCA was designed and continues to be used mainly for an intermediate number of cases, perhaps 20 or 30. An even smaller number of conditions or attributes are studied—usually 4–6. The more attributes there are, the more combinations among them it is necessary to consider in the initial truth table. The case-to-condition ratio is important, just as it is in quantitative analyses. If you want to study more conditions (attributes), you will generally need to add more cases. There are "benchmark tests" of the case-to-condition ratio that you can use to determine whether random data could produce a QCA solution. If random data could produce a QCA solution, the analysis has failed. One way to repair the investigation would be for the researcher to add more cases—or perhaps to find an attribute that could be eliminated from the model.

With a larger number of cases—larger than, say, 30 or 40—adding more cases and/or conditions can make a QCA analysis quite unwieldy. How can one have in-depth knowledge of dozens of cases? With many cases, the researcher may decide to use quantitative methods for categorical variables, such as logit regression (LR). As discussed in Chapters 8 and 9, regression analysis, especially the more advanced forms, is case hungry: 60 cases would usually be too many for QCA, but not enough for LR.

TABLE 12.3. Truth Table of All 16 Possible Combinations of the Values of Two Binary Conditions

C1	C2	1	2	3	4	5	6	7	8	9	10	11	12	13	14	15	16
T	**T**	F	F	F	F	F	F	F	F	T	T	T	T	T	T	T	T
T	**F**	F	F	F	F	T	T	T	T	F	F	F	F	T	T	T	T
F	**T**	F	F	T	T	F	F	T	T	F	F	T	T	F	F	T	T
F	**F**	F	T	F	T	F	T	F	T	F	T	F	T	F	T	F	T

Note. C1, condition 1; C2, condition 2; T, true/present; F, false/absent.

Because QCA methods of analysis require that the number of cases and conditions be limited, selecting appropriate ones is very important. To be effective, the choices have to be based on deep knowledge of the topic, the cases, and the attributes. Having the deep knowledge needed to classify more than two or three dozen cases would be very difficult for a solitary scholar. However, in some cases, it may not be impossible. QCA research is often done using secondary sources rather than primary sources, which can increase the number of cases it is possible to consider.[34]

The problem of too many conditions given the number of cases is especially likely to occur in the second major variant of QCA. When membership in the sets/conditions is a matter of degree or is ordinal, then **fuzzy-set QCA (fsQCA)** is employed. The original dichotomous form has come to be called **crisp-set QCA (csQCA)** to distinguish it from the more recently developed fsQCA, which uses a form of rank order variables. Crisp-set QCA codes attributes dichotomously—such as *member of the European Union: yes–no*. These can be coded 1 for membership in the set and 0 for nonmembership.[35]

In fsQCA, cases do not have only two values (*yes–no, true–false, 1–0*) but usually have five, such as: 1 = completely in a set; 0 = completely out; .5 = wholly ambiguous; .8 = largely in; .2 = largely out.[36] Although the attributes/conditions are ordinal, not dichotomous, the outcome variable must be dichotomous, as in csQCA. It is often true in the social sciences that sets with fuzzy boundaries or varying degrees of membership are more common than are sets with crisp boundaries. Assigning degrees of membership in sets to cases requires that the researcher have in-depth theoretical and substantive knowledge of the cases. This knowledge, often acquired through years of study, is one of the qualitative foundations of the method. Assigning degrees of membership can be much more than a matter of simple classification and coding.[37] For example, in a study of the effects of university governance, a crisp-set condition would be public or private. A fuzzy-set condition would be extent of shared decision making with the faculty.[38]

The fuzzy-set approach has been somewhat slowly adopted by QCA researchers. This may be because it is much more complicated to conduct and leads to conclusions that seem to lack the crispness of the original and still more common dichotomous approach. Certainly, the fuzzy algebra on which fsQCA is based is more complex than the dichotomous Boolean logic of csQCA.

Many suggestions for developing QCA have focused on improving its causal strengths. One article suggested including a temporal variable or condition to ensure that presumed causes preceded supposed effects.[39] A more recent theoretical refinement challenged the sufficiency of QCA when the conditions are causal chains, that is,

---

[34] A remarkable example of the importance of a work based entirely on (a not very large number of) secondary sources is Skocpol's (1979) discussion of the origins of social revolutions. It has been influential, extensively discussed, and cited thousands of times.

[35] In older studies it is common to see membership in the set coded by capital and lower-case letters: MEMBER/member for members and nonmembers, respectively.

[36] The parallel with the Likert scale is quite strong; see Chapter 1.

[37] A multivalue version of QCA has been developed (mvQCA); it has not been widely applied. For a discussion see Schneider and Wagemann (2012).

[38] The decision making in fsQCA is reminiscent of the work of expert researchers applying Bayesian priors; see Chapter 8.

[39] Caren and Panofsky (2005). For a reply see Ragin and Strand (2008).

when some conditions cause others, which lead to the outcome.[40] Another contribution introduced the distinction between proximate and remote causation. This distinction is parallel to that in quantitative causal modeling between exogenous background conditions (remote causes) and endogenous causal triggers (proximate causes). In QCA, the distinction enables the analyst to proceed in two stages and, in so doing, keep the number of variables to a workable total.[41] From these and other suggested methodological revisions, it is clear that causal reasoning is at the heart of QCA.

QCA is showing signs of paradigm maturity on several fronts. For example, in other traditions in qualitative research, the details of coding and measurement are often left to the imagination of the solo researcher; and some see this lack of guidelines as the essence of qualitative research. But in QCA coding and analysis have drawn attention from specialists who have devised goodness-of-fit tests that formally assess the fit between data and causal hypotheses and sensitivity and robustness of QCA results.[42]

Paradigm maturity is also indicated by the growing number of reports in the research literature on applying QCA in areas of investigation in which it had been previously untried. One such area that interests us is program evaluation.[43] Multiple-case-study analysis has been applied by other researchers in program evaluation.[44] The typical approach is to identify as the cases the projects that are part of a broader program, often with common funding, such as a social service or an educational program. When a theory is being tested, it is the "program theory" or the overall causal model of change around which the program is built—such as intervention *X* will lead to output *Y*, which will foster outcome *Z*.

QCA seems nicely tailored to the problems of multiple program evaluation because multiple cases within a single program often aim, by design, to achieve the same outcomes, which may be measured the same ways, as well as employing many of the same input variables. Those who fund programs often insist on these commonalities. But funders rarely require that all projects be implemented the same way. Thus the projects differ, and it is because projects differ that we can learn by studying them. For example, we are applying this approach in a combined design that links QCA to prospective meta-analysis (PMA). The cases are 24 projects in a program to improve undergraduate instruction in computer programming. Each of the projects is a quasi-experiment. For each project, effect sizes are computed, and these are summed using PMA to achieve an overall program assessment. QCA is then applied to identify the attributes of programs that lead to success (as identified by an effect-size [ES] threshold).[45]

In the conduct of the multiproject program evaluations, we always see the tension between the individual project or case and the overall program—between the particular and the general. For example, in another multisite educational program evaluation in which we have been involved, the same general program theory was applied in quite different contexts—for example, urban versus rural and elementary versus secondary

---

[40] Baumgartner (2013).

[41] Schneider and Wagemann (2006).

[42] Respectively, Eliason and Stryker (2009) and Skaaning (2011).

[43] See Vogt et al. (2011).

[44] Stake (2006).

[45] Vogt et al. (2013).

schools. Of course, were there no such variance, there would be nothing to study by comparative case analysis. All the cases could be lumped into one super case. *Variance is the portal to findings.* We learn by noting differences, such as that some parts of a program were easier to implement and/or were more effective in some contexts than others. Each case is interesting, first in its own right, and second because it belongs to a general class of cases. It is the second that is more important from the standpoint of either usable evaluation knowledge or social science knowledge. The individual case study is instrumental in seeking broader knowledge.

Funding sponsors and researchers usually seek generally usable knowledge. They want to know what is common across cases, not what is unique to particular cases. However, how a generalization might vary in specific contexts is also crucial information. It is crucial because it indicates how broadly the generalization may be applied in particular settings. Still, although the analysis is built up empirically from a study of individual case studies, it is part of a "highly reductive process of cross-case analysis" in which the researcher "expects to lose much of the particularity of each case."[46]

Because detailed knowledge of cases is needed, multiple-case studies are almost necessarily parasitic on single-case work. In the context of an evaluation of a multisite program evaluation, multicase research often involves division of labor among teams. In political science and sociology, multiple-case-study comparisons are more often built upon systematic use of secondary sources. The works of historians are a favorite source. The constant question in multiple-case-study research is, How does one go about building the general out of the particular, while remaining grounded in the particular?

Are Quantitative Alternatives to QCA Available?

The chief alternative to QCA drawn from the quantitative data analysis tradition is **logit regression (LR)**. It is widely used in the social sciences for analysis problems with a categorical dependent variable (DV) and several independent variables (IVs); the IVs may be categorical or continuous (see Chapter 8 for an overview). Logit regression's advantage over QCA is that it can handle large numbers of cases and numerous IVs measured at any level. But like other forms of regression analysis, it is built on the variable-based statistical model that Ragin has criticized as inappropriate, especially as compared with the case-based Boolean model. If you are persuaded by the applicability of Ragin's critique to your research question and data, the presumptive advantages of logit regression will not be very appealing.

No consensus has emerged about how QCA compares as an analysis strategy with LR. One reason is that head-to-head comparisons of the two methods are not common because their data requirements are usually rather different. One exception is a study of party preference (a categorical DV) in which it was possible to compare QCA with LR using the same data. The author found that the two methods led to similar analytical conclusions.[47] The case is not perhaps widely generalizable, but it does indicate a possible region of overlap between the two methods. There may be some situations in which

---

[46] Stake (2006, p. 44). See Sager and Andereggen (2012) for a persuasive example of the application of mvQCA to evaluation research; the article also provides a succinct account of mvQCA, a more advanced method, which we have not discussed in this chapter.

[47] Grendstad (2007).

either could be used and, even more promising, each could be used to cross-validate the conclusions of the other. Other examples were less encouraging about possible areas of overlap. One researcher concluded that QCA requires that the researcher incorporate dubious measurement assumptions into the analysis; others found that QCA can be preferable to LR when causation for groups of cases is complex.[48] Some aspects of each of these arguments are persuasive, but not, we think, decisive. Thus it is hard for us to make a firm recommendation except to say that LR requires a larger sample to be effective. The 20 or 30 cases of the typical QCA would hardly ever be enough to conduct an LR or any other type of regression analysis.

The biggest theoretical difference between QCA and regression analysis is the assumption in QCA that causality can be **asymmetric**—that is, a cause leading to the presence of an outcome can be fully distinct from a cause leading to its absence. In regression analysis, by contrast, if *X* causes *Y*, then absence of *X* leads to absence of *Y*. The key to this difference is necessary and sufficient conditions, which are based on the logic of Mill's method of difference and method of agreement. Rather than using additive variables as in regression analysis, in which an increase in a predictor leads to a proportional increase in an outcome (or a decrease leads to a proportional decrease), the presence of an attribute is a condition for the occurrence of an outcome. In QCA "cases are best understood as configurations of attributes resembling overall types; and . . . a comparison of cases can allow a researcher to strip away attributes that are unrelated to the outcome in question."[49]

Despite the caveats about the difficulty of combining QCA with other methods, it is increasingly common for researchers to attempt to do so, including combining QCA with regression-based methods, as well as more qualitative approaches. Despite the fact that Ragin uses many of these other methods as a conceptual foil, especially regression-based methods, he seems to welcome this methodological pluralism. (This, of course, is an important bridge to the topic of our next chapter on combined methods.) As examples of this pluralism, recent articles have included attempts to devise methods for linking QCA's set theory approach to data analysis with more qualitative approaches, such as process tracing; to link QCA to social network analysis; to combine QCA with PMA to improve the evaluation of multisite programs; and, finally, to apply hermeneutic methods to QCA analyses.[50]

CONCLUSIONS

An enormous variety of methods for analyzing case study data are available. Because of that variety, many decisions confront the researcher planning to analyze case study data. Indeed, the interpretation of case study data raises nearly all the analytical issues discussed in this book. We have reviewed many of these in this chapter's Summary Table. Big questions include how to strike a balance between inductive and deductive approaches and the related issue of what kind of dialogue you want to promote between evidence and ideas. Additional perennial issues raised in case study analysis include:

[48]See, respectively, Seawright (2005) and Grofman and Schneider (2009).

[49]Fiss (2011, p. 402).

[50]See, respectively, Schneider and Rohlfing (2013), Fischer (2011), Vogt et al. (2013), and Fritzsche (2013).

What will be your relation to theory? Will you be guided by theories, attempt to discover theories, build them, refine them, or test them? Will your analysis aim to address issues of causality, and if so, will you aim to discover causes or explain causal processes? And, at the end of the investigation as well as at its beginning, you usually have to reexamine the question of which cases are truly comparable.

A more technical analytical question is, How high does the fact-to-generalization ratio have to be, or how high should it be, to make valid inferences? In other terms, how much do you need to know before you are entitled to generalize—assuming you are not an idiographic generalization denier? The ratio is usually quite high in the in-depth analysis of a small number of cases (many facts/observations, few generalizations). By contrast, the ratio of facts to generalizations tends to be more moderate in the method we have examined in somewhat greater depth in this chapter—QCA.

QCA uses qualitative or categorical variables and is based on in-depth study of the cases to determine whether the attributes are present or not. In that respect it is very similar to traditional comparative case analysis. What QCA adds at the analysis and interpretation phase is the rigor of Boolean logic. This emphasis on the analysis phase of the research strikes us as quite different from the methodological guidance in most qualitative approaches, which tend to be more directive about the early phases of the research, that is, collecting and coding data, but then rather vague about the later analytical phases. QCA instead focuses much of its methodological attention on the methods of analysis. Like grounded theory (GT), it provides would-be researchers with guidance about what to do with the data once you've collected it and coded it. Initial coding is, of course, a stage of analysis, but many discussions of the analysis of qualitative data seem to us to fizzle out after the initial stages are described. The big exceptions to that generalization are GT and QCA.

Although QCA is most usually fruitful when it is based on an in-depth knowledge of the cases, it has also been applied to survey data concerning hundreds of anonymous respondents, when the theory in the field seemed to demand study of logical configurations of categorical characteristics.[51] Because QCA uses set theory analysis of categories, not a statistical analysis, to uncover causes, it can be applied to less in-depth data if those are best coded categorically. When the causal model is more probabilistic, statistical approaches are likely to be more relevant than QCA.

Of course, it is important in QCA to explain the principles that guided the case selection and the coding of attributes—categorical as in csQCA or ordinal values as in fsQCA. But in-depth explanation is also needed at the end of the analysis, when the researcher discusses the causal mechanisms that were uncovered. These discussions usually feature explanations of how causes work out in specific cases. Thus the analysis begins with in-depth discussion of cases and ends with it, too.[52]

Tackling the complex issues involving causation may require more background than most beginning researchers are likely to have. But QCA methods are fairly accessible if your research question is straightforward and your conditions/attributes/variables can reasonably be coded as dichotomies. Still, you will need guidelines to apply the method.

[51] Fiss (2011) is a good example, and his article very carefully lays out the steps of a QCA analysis in ways that would probably be helpful to many researchers new to the method.

[52] For an excellent discussion of the differences between the logic-based set theory causal models of QCA and additive, probability-based statistical models, see Mahoney, Goertz, and Ragin (2013).

More works providing guidance are available now than were accessible just a few years ago.[53]

We conclude by reemphasizing one key point, which is based on one of the first decisions to make about your analysis. The most important coding and analysis questions about which methods to use concern the world—that part of social reality you plan to investigate. The main questions do not—or should not—focus on the kind of coding and analysis methods you would prefer to work with. Before thinking about your "druthers," first ask whether the conditions, attributes, or variables that you intend to study are *naturally* categories, ranks, or continua. It's OK, when necessary, to bend the analyses to fit the world. It's much less OK to bend the world to fit your analytical preferences. So the big questions are about the world. To use QCA, aspects of the social world need to be naturally categorical. Naturally continuous variables can be categorized, of course, but doing so is fraught with possibilities for data mutilation. This is true both of the outcomes and of the conditions or attributes used to predict or understand the outcomes. Some are naturally categorical or ranked. Some continua can be categorized or ranked without doing violence to their underlying reality. But some cannot.

The classic example of the categories-versus-continua problem in the early history of research methodology comes from genetics. The basic issue was how genetic traits were passed on from parents to descendants. Are continuous attributes blended, as you might mix colors of paint? Or is what gets passed on determined by a process more like shuffling a deck of cards—6's and 8's don't get averaged into 7's; they are rearranged. When Mendel crossbred tall and short pea plants, he did not get plants of medium height; rather, the outcome was predictable proportions of tall and short plants. The attribute of height in peas was categorical, and it could not fit into a continuous statistical model. A huge debate about these issues involved most of the leading biologists and statisticians in early 20th-century England, and studying it makes a wonderful case study of what can be at stake in the battle of analytical models.[54] The issue was settled not by picking the right analysis methods but by gaining deeper understanding of the world. Some traits are inherited by dichotomous processes, as Mendelian genetics affirmed. But other genes are "averaged" or blended. Different statistical models have to be used to study the two types. The actual state of the world should determine the correct model. It is a fundamental error to try to squeeze the world into your favorite model. But, and here is the conundrum, how are you to learn about the "actual state of the world" except by attempting to apply a model to it?

---

[53] See Schneider and Wagemann (2010, 2012), respectively, for concise "standards of good practice" and a more detailed book-length overview.

[54] Two interesting accounts are Rosenwein (1994) and Henig (2000).

SUGGESTIONS FOR FURTHER READING

We often recommend reading examples of how methods were applied, in addition to methodological works. The case study approach to research methods is, of course, particularly appropriate for this chapter. We have briefly discussed and cited several of these in the chapter; see the appropriate sections for specific readings.

On case study research in general, one of the most readable and informative texts is Yin's (2008) *Case Study Research: Design and Methods*. Of more general interest, and very relevant to case study investigations, is his *Qualitative Research from Start to Finish* (2011). Also very useful, particularly when the cases studied are being evaluated as programs, is Stake's (2006) *Multiple Case Study Analysis*. These three are rooted in the psychology and education tradition of research.

The other main branch of case study methodology is rooted more in sociology and political science. Three of the most interesting volumes in that tradition are George and Bennett's (2005) *Case Studies and Theory Development in the Social Sciences*; Gerring's (2007) *Case Study Research: Principles and Practices*; and Brady and Colliers's (2004) *Rethinking Social Inquiry: Diverse Tools, Shared Standards*.

The body of literature on QCA is large and growing. For QCA, it is probably best to begin with Ragin's volumes; the one that first formalized the methods is *The Comparative Method: Moving Beyond Qualitative and Quantitative Strategies* (1987); the volume that highlights subsequent developments in QCA is *Redesigning Social Inquiry: Fuzzy Sets and Beyond* (2008).

CHAPTER 12 SUMMARY TABLE

When to use deductive case study methods (pp. 401–408)	• When you are testing, refining, or elaborating an existing theory. • When you are looking for causal mechanisms to explain a phenomenon, including necessary and sufficient conditions. • When in-depth knowledge of particular cases is needed to investigate the tension between knowledge of the general and the particular.
When to use a single case (pp. 408–412)	• When you want to understand one instance of a study phenomenon in depth, with the ultimate goal of understanding similar cases. • When a theory can be disproved by a single disconfirming instance. • When your main goal is process tracing.
When to use small-*N* comparative cases (pp. 412–415)	• When you want to find patterns of similarities and differences among cases to identify potentially causal conditions. • When you want to refine, specify, or elaborate on a theory.
When to use intermediate-*N* comparative case studies, especially QCA (pp. 415–421)	• When you want to maximize the number of comparisons across cases in order to refine and test theories. • When you want to combine qualitative expert coding with a formal method of analysis. • When you have a moderate number of attributes/conditions, perhaps 4–6. • When causation can be asymmetric in the theories you examine. • When you want to analyze multiple causes and/or interactions of categorical variables. • When the attributes/conditions of the cases are categorical or ranked. o Use csQCA when conditions are categorical. o Use fsQCA when they are ranked or matters of degree.
When to use quantitative alternatives to QCA (pp. 421–422)	• When *N* is greater than 20–30 cases. • When the dependent variable is categorical and the independent variables may be categorical or continuous. • To examine QCA and quantitative analyses for cross-validation.

CHAPTER 13

Coding and Analyzing Data from Combined and Mixed Designs

In this chapter we:

- Compare and contrast "simple" and combined research designs.
- Illustrate various combinations of data sources, coding, and analysis options.
- Discuss the choice between separately coding and analyzing data from various components of your research and then merging findings at the end of the study; and "transforming" your data so it can be merged and analyzed holistically.
- Emphasize the importance of coding reliability and consistency in combined and mixed designs, including intercoder reliability.
- Explore coding and analysis considerations for deductive (theory testing) and inductive (theory building) combined designs, and for those studies that take both approaches.
- Explain sequential and concurrent coding and analysis, including:
  - Coding considerations for sequential analysis.
  - Data transformation/data merging in combined designs.
    - Qualitative → quantitative data transformation.
    - Quantitative → qualitative data transformation.
- Consider the capacity of a combined design study to support useful and valid inferences.

In other chapters throughout this volume, we have focused on specific designs, such as surveys, interviews, observations, and archival research. In this chapter, we look at ways these designs may be combined and particularly at some of the special considerations that arise for coding and analysis of, and inference from combined data. Many research questions are relatively straightforward and thus may be addressed using single-method research designs. Other research questions, by their very nature, have multiple components and require more complex, multimethod research designs.

For example, if your research interest is college access and completion, a straightforward research question might be: How does the 6-year first-time/full-time baccalaureate degree attainment rate compare across gender, racial, and socioeconomic groups? This question implies that you will define and acquire a single point-in-time dataset of student degree completers, which you would code by gender, race, and socioeconomic status. You would then compare percentages of completers: male versus female, across racial groups, and across socioeconomic categories. You might also want to analyze differences among subgroups, such as white males versus black males. Depending on the size of the dataset, the analysis work itself could be time-consuming, and you may need to address such complications as missing data. However, the research design, coding, and analysis are essentially "simple."

In contrast, suppose your research question is, What effects does a specific student support program have on student motivation, performance, and 6-year baccalaureate completion rates? This question has multiple parts (motivation, performance, completion), as well as cause-and-effect implications (the student support program causing—or not causing—changes in motivation, performance, and completion). Immediately, you can see that this type of question will involve several data collection, coding, and analysis methods and will certainly require you to use both quantitative and qualitative data. You could compare program participants and nonparticipants in some type of quasi-experimental design, which could potentially involve controlling for extraneous variables through a method such as propensity score matching. You may need to interview and/or survey students and support service providers. You will need to analyze quantitative motivation, performance, and completion data and link those data to program participants and nonparticipants. To address this research question will obviously require a combined or mixed research design.

As the second example illustrates, when your research question leads you to combine designs, you will most often collect different kinds of data. The data must be coded in ways that allow them to be linked so that they can be analyzed. Different types of data—verbal, numerical, or graphic—can also be collected within one design. A familiar example occurs when surveys include both forced-choice questions that generate quantitative data and open-ended questions that yield qualitative data. Whether the different data types are generated within one design type or by combining designs, linking the data so that they can be analyzed raises intricate problems that touch on virtually all the topics discussed in the previous chapters on coding and analysis. And in each of our previous chapters, we have discussed examples in which researchers have combined designs and mixed data types. Because it brings together all of those topics and discusses them at a somewhat higher level of complexity, this chapter is also a good way to conclude our discussions of coding and analysis.

Combined designs are fairly common, whether one calls them multimethod research[1] or mixed methods research.[2] We use *combined* as a generic label to include all combinations, including those that do not necessarily cross the quantitative–qualitative divide. For example, if you were studying an organized social movement, your data might include interview transcripts (Chapter 2), fieldnotes from your participant observations (Chapter 4), and documents from the organizations' archives (Chapter 5). Although all three of these are verbal and textual (qualitative), their origins differ enough that great care has to be taken when combining them. There are fundamental differences between

[1]Brewer and Hunter (2006).

[2]Creswell and Clark (2010).

participants' speech that you have transcribed, your observations that you have turned into fieldnotes, and documents that were produced without your involvement. And even documents can vary greatly—official mission statements versus e-mail correspondence, for instance. No one would recommend blithely treating interview transcripts, fieldnotes, mission statements, and e-mails as the same kinds of evidence. The differences in their origins are more important than the fact that they are all coded with verbal symbols. In some instances, it might be much easier to cross the quant–qual divide and study only one of these—for example, to conduct a combined statistical and textual analysis of an organization's e-mails.

The number of possible combinations—both of data sources (interviews, experiments, surveys, documents, etc.) and of symbols used to record the data (words, numbers, or pictures)—is truly enormous. For example, it has been demonstrated that there are 84 reasonable ways that three sources—focus group interviews, individual interviews, and surveys—could be combined, and finding examples employing these combinations in published articles is not difficult.[3]

Let's belabor the point a bit more because it is very important. We begin with our five designs or methods of collecting data—survey, interview, experimental, observational, and archival designs. To simplify, we'll ignore subtypes such as focus group interviews, quasi-experiments, and participant observations. One may collect either verbal or numerical data with each of these methods. To further simplify, we'll ignore graphic data and analyses. So, after simplifying, we are left with 10 approaches—five designs multiplied by two ways, words or numbers, to symbolize evidence. These 10, like any 10 entities, can be combined in a total of 45 different ways.[4] And that number does not take *order* into account: which part of the combination you do first.[5] Further, it does not take into account that you might repeat a method, for example, interviewing people so as to write better survey questions, then surveying a broad sample, and then interviewing some select members of the sample so as to better understand their responses. Of course, you could combine more than two, conceivably all 10, and you could do so in various orders. In that case, if you look at how all 10 can be combined, there are over 3 million combinations and permutations (10! = 3,628,800). Finally, our list of 10 methods does not take into account that we might want to combine and analyze data collected with newer, less familiar methods, such as social network analysis and qualitative comparative analysis (QCA).[6]

Given that it is not possible to discuss all the conceivable combinations, not even all those that have actually been used by social researchers, we have adopted a more general strategy to discuss which analysis methods to use with different types of data collected in different ways. Basically, we discuss fairly typical problems and provide examples that illustrate general principles.

If you have made the decision to use a combined design to answer your research question, you have, by definition, decided to tackle coding and analysis issues from at

---

[3]Vogt (2008).

[4]If we included graphic coding and raised the number of types of sources and coding to 15, the total number of nonredundant combinations would be 105.

[5]Nor whether you do one first or do them together—*sequentially* or *concurrently* in mixed method terms; see Clark and Plano (2011).

[6]Fischer (2011).

least two of our previous chapters. Regardless of which methods you are combining, you will have to make coding decisions that not only work for each component of your design but that also work together overall. Otherwise, you run the risk of conducting two parallel studies rather than one combined study.[7] The need to code different data in compatible ways will be true whether you employ both quantitative and qualitative methods or whether you use either multiple quantitative or multiple qualitative methods. The basic issues you will need to address are the same as for coding overall: validity, judgment, reliability, choice of coding symbols, persistence, and justification (see the discussion in the Introduction to Part I). With combined data from a combined design, the potential interactions (and opportunities for conflicts) among these basic choices is multiplied. Coding and analyzing data from combined designs at minimum *triples* the coding choices and the analysis choices you have to make. For example, if you combine data from experiments and interviews, you have to make choices about the data from each of those two designs; you must devise codes to link the two sets of data; and you must utilize the two datasets appropriately in your analysis.

Even using one design, with one data collection instrument such as a survey, can yield mixed data that need to be combined. In our study of the effectiveness of a new method of teaching computer programming (discussed in previous chapters), we collected on the same survey three kinds of data about students' learning: student self-assessments using ordinal forced-choice questions coded on a Likert scale; student self-assessments using qualitative open-ended questions; and a "content knowledge survey" (essentially a test) on which the answers were coded by the researchers as right or wrong.[8] Coding and analyzing any one of these three was relatively straightforward, but coding them so that they could be meaningfully (not merely impressionistically) compared was more challenging. Cross-validating the measures of student learning involved matching answers and recoding answers on specific topics that had been coded in three ways: on a 5-point scale completed by students, in sentences written by students in response to the open-ended questions, and with scores on a multiple-choice test graded by faculty. The end result of our coding was three rank order scales. As we have discussed previously, rank order scales often make a natural bridge between verbal and numerical codes. On most topics, the three scales were composed of the students' rankings, the researchers' ranked coding of the students' open-ended responses, and the number of questions on a given topic that students answered correctly. The combined analyses interpreted these variables as measured on rank order scales.

At least two basic options exist for data analysis in combined designs: You can decide to conduct the components separately and merge the separate data analyses at the end, or you can decide to merge your data when collected and analyze them holistically. Coding and analysis from the earlier phases can inform the later phases. For example, if you conduct interviews and observations, you can code and analyze the interview data, then code and analyze the observational data, then compare your results—thus merging your findings at the end in order to draw conclusions. Conversely, you can code the interview data, apply parallel codes to the observational data, merge the two datasets, and then do your analysis on the new "merged" dataset.[9] A basic distinction here is

---

[7] Yin (2006).

[8] Lim et al. (2102).

[9] For a detailed discussion of these options and some variations on them, see Caracelli and Greene (1993).

between **sequential** and **concurrent** coding and analysis: respectively, first one and then the other, or both at the same time. The distinction is a matter of degree because, strictly speaking, concurrent coding is impossible unless you use a fairly loose definition of "at the same time." If, for example, your data are gathered from surveying participants in the fall and interviewing some of them the following winter and spring, then, when you try to put the data together in the summer, the possibility of history effects should always be considered.

Using multiple coders is often a good option when the codes assigned require more than minimal judgment, and judgment is very likely to be required when coding data of different types, especially when the types have to be coded in compatible ways so that they can be analyzed together. When using multiple coders, it is essential to compare and pool their coding in a systematic way. Having coders code the same data and comparing the results is essential; merely dividing the labor among coders is second best. When the level of disagreement among coders is greater than a predetermined minimum (e.g., 10%), the coders should discuss differences to see whether they can reconcile them and devise a common standard. The goal is consistency (reliability) in coding; without it, validity is compromised. Consistency can be best gauged by computing intercoder reliability measures. We have discussed several of these at various places in this volume. A versatile intercoder reliability measure is Krippendorff's alpha, but there are others.[10]

CODING AND ANALYSIS CONSIDERATIONS FOR DEDUCTIVE AND INDUCTIVE DESIGNS

When you designed your study, you likely made a choice between two basic approaches: Either your study is *deductive*, and you are testing a theory or hypothesis based on prior research, or your study is *inductive*, and you are exploring a phenomenon to develop a theory. In a deductive approach, before you ever collect your data, you will have some idea of possible ways to code and analyze them. Prior research on the study phenomenon, which you examined during a literature review, reveals variables of interest that will influence your coding and analysis decisions. In an inductive approach, you are open to emerging variables of interest and therefore will not make a priori coding and analysis choices. (We have discussed analysis implications for deductive and inductive designs in detail in the Introduction to Part III, as well as in Chapters 11 and 12.)

An example of a deductive theory-testing research study examined CEOs' "social responsibility" characteristics. Interview data were coded using predetermined categories from the research literature: moral–legal standards of conduct, inner obligation, concern for others, negative consequences, and self-judgment. The interviews were transcribed and the texts reviewed for statements corresponding to the five predetermined categories. For example, if a CEO responded to a question by saying "I felt responsible for that decision," the response would be coded as "inner obligation." A response stating, "I wanted to help an employee with family problems by offering time off from work" would be coded as "concern for others." Researchers then used a survey of company employees to test the CEOs' self-reports, using the same categories to code employee responses regarding their CEOs' behaviors. By using the same categories,

[10] See Chapters 2 and 4 and Hayes and Krippendorff (2007).

comparing results from the two methods became a relatively straightforward process.[11] In this example, the two datasets were not merged but rather compared during the analysis phase to find similarities and differences in the responses.

There are several ways to approach deductive, theory-testing combined methods strategies. For example, one researcher systematically reviewed the quantitative literature on the influence of teachers' qualifications on their teaching practices. The conclusions drawn from this literature review were then used as hypotheses to investigate using qualitative data.[12] In another example, a political scientist developed a "nested" strategy for combining mixed method data in comparative politics. The basic idea was to use data from large quantitative datasets to test hypotheses. Small-*N* data typical of comparative case studies would then be nested within the large-*N* studies and used to improve the causal specificity and quality of the conclusions.[13]

In an example of an inductive study, a researcher examined the role of school leaders in supporting the mathematics progress of students who were English language learners (ELLs). She employed both interviews and a survey and used an inductive approach to develop coding categories for the interview and open-ended survey responses. Coding categories that emerged included curriculum, instruction, testing, the role of teacher professional development, and cultural considerations. The inductive process and the coded categories it revealed then informed additional analysis and interpretation of the forced-choice survey questions.[14] Another inductive approach to combining data investigated the effects of using private-sector physicians (rather than university-based researchers) to run clinical trials on new drugs. The authors combined evidence from observations at 25 private-sector research organizations with interviews with physicians and others working in those organizations. The fieldnotes and interview data were combined, coded, and analyzed using no specific hypotheses; rather, the authors proceeded inductively based on the tenets of grounded theory.[15]

Another study investigated the role of performance feedback in nurses' self-assessment of their practice. Data sources included focus group interviews and archival document analysis. In this study, researchers combined a priori coding based on a theoretical framework with emergent codes from the qualitative data, in effect combining both inductive and deductive approaches.[16] For example, a preexisting coded category can be paraphrased as "working relationships with others," and an emergent code was "trust and respect." Although these categories are related, they are not identical. Analyzing participant responses and archival materials using the expanded coding scheme, with both established and emergent codes, allowed for richer analysis and more detailed findings in relation to the research question.

In sum, whether your study is deductive or inductive or combines both approaches, attention to coding issues at the outset will vastly improve subsequent analysis options. Having a coding strategy will help you collect and analyze evidence in one combined/

---

[11]DeHoogh and Den Hartog (2008).

[12]Kennedy (2008).

[13]Lieberman (2005).

[14]Rosa (2010).

[15]Fisher and Kalbaugh (2012).

[16]Fereday and Muir-Cochrane (2006).

mixed study, rather than being left with few options other than attempting to impressionistically link evidence from what are actually two or more distinct studies.

CODING CONSIDERATIONS FOR SEQUENTIAL ANALYSIS APPROACHES

Using separate, sequential analysis of datasets in combined research designs is far more common than merging data before analysis.[17] If you have decided to keep the components of your research study separate until your final analysis, you may think that you don't have to worry about interactions among your coded data. Not true! Many a naive researcher has been unpleasantly surprised when parts of a study do not "match up" and cannot be made compatible or comparable in the final analysis phase.

Let's consider a hypothetical example. You want to evaluate workers' reactions to the installation of a new computer system in a large company. Management's hypothesis is that the new system will make work easier and boost productivity. You choose a common approach: to conduct surveys and interviews to see whether your findings support the hypothesis. You first design a survey questionnaire with items that reflect identified variables of interest: Can employees work faster, more collaboratively, with less downtime due to technical problems and so forth? In the first phase of the study, you conduct a census survey of all computer system users, get a very respectable return rate of 84%, then code and analyze the results. You find that although the majority of survey respondents report that the system does help them work faster and with less downtime, a substantial number of employees report concerns with their capacity to work collaboratively online. This finding triggers a second study component: a round of interviews with randomly selected employees in which participants report a range of positives and negatives with the system: better speed, more software features, file-sharing difficulties, limited access to shared databases, and so forth. They also report a range of positive to negative views of the new system overall.

A casual researcher might now file a report saying that the system is generally well liked but has some glitches that need fixing. Here's the problem: Without coding the survey responses to link with interview responses, there is no way to tell whether those who initially reported the problems were the same people who detailed what the actual problems were perceived to be. Were the problems departmental or widespread? Why conduct random interviews when specific follow-up with selected survey respondents would have yielded more targeted findings? In this case, the company could spend time and money on widespread "fixes" when the problems might actually be localized. In this hypothetical case, a coding mismatch made it impossible to place the findings in context and could actually steer management in the wrong direction.

A way to "fix" the problems with this study while still keeping analysis separate until the end might look like this: First, conduct interviews with representatives from all relevant work divisions. Through coding the response data, identify significant themes: for example, positive features and negative features of the new computer system. Then use the coded themes to develop a survey questionnaire asking employees about those system features, with coded responses representing a range of possible answers from positive to negative. Include a department code and also include the opportunity for

---

[17] Bryman (2006).

respondents to comment on their positive and negative answers. In this way, explanatory information can be coded along with positive and negative responses by department, adding context to the responses and potentially pinpointing trouble areas. The interview and survey data are never actually merged but are sequentially coded and are thus linked by their sequential development.[18]

This type of sequential coding and analysis can apply to other combined designs. An actual study one of us conducted used a two-phase approach. In the first phase, we identified key demographic and performance variables for public schools within a state. We then developed coded categories: socioeconomic quintiles (lowest 20%, 21–40%, etc.) and 3-year state test score quintiles in reading and mathematics. We then used the data to identify a group of "outlier" schools: those with significant poverty levels (above 20%) and high performance (above 80% in both reading and mathematics).

In the second phase we took a deductive approach, developing a case study protocol with coded categories for key variables of school operations identified from previous research: curriculum, instruction, staffing, monitoring/assessment, interventions, and school culture. We then conducted case studies of both the outlier schools and the lower performing but demographically similar schools. Through onsite observations, interviews, and artifact analysis, we were able to identify features shared by all the outlier schools—features that were not present or only partially observed in schools with lower performance. These included a strongly aligned "technical core" of curriculum–instruction–assessment, a student-centered school culture, strict attention to continuous analysis of student data to improve outcomes, and high expectations for faculty and staff performance. The data coding was sequential in both phases of the study, and data were not merged, but the first phase of coding led logically to the application of qualitative coding in the second phase.[19]

Overall, for combined studies with separate analysis components, coding choices should allow linking of data across components as necessary to perform the analysis and answer the research question. As in the hypothetical workplace computer study described previously, failure to code properly in one component can severely hamper the analysis potential in another component.

DATA TRANSFORMATION/DATA MERGING IN COMBINED DESIGNS

For mixed methods studies, data transformation for concurrent analysis generally refers to one of these scenarios: changing qualitative data to quantitative data so that statistical analyses can be applied or changing quantitative data to qualitative data in order to use it in a qualitative analysis. Another possibility is to transform text or statistics into categories or ranks, which you can use to conduct Boolean analyses, as in QCA (see Chapter 12). Either way, the ultimate goal is to unify all data types so that they may be analyzed as a single set.

[18] For an example of a similar study that describes problems with data analysis that caused the researchers to recode and reanalyze, see Kaplan and Duchon (1988).

[19] Haeffele, Baker, and Pacha (2007). For other studies taking a similar sequential approach, see Newman, Smith, Allensworth, and Bryk (2001) and Legewie and DiPrete (2012).

Qualitative → Quantitative Data Transformation

Transforming qualitative data to quantitative data is called "quantitizing."[20] The process involves assigning numerical values (codes) to various qualitative data elements. One of the first challenges in recoding qualitative data into numbers is determining that you have sufficient qualitative data to transform, enabling the appropriate application of statistical methods. You could go through a long process of numerical recoding only to realize that you have a sample too small or too purposive to validly apply statistical analysis. For example, one study first used QCA to generate hypotheses and then used the QCA-generated categories as units of analysis in statistical tests of those hypotheses. A problem was that the number of cases/categories was sometimes insufficient for statistical analyses, especially when the number of hypotheses was large in relation to the number of cases.[21] On the other hand, if you do have a very large and randomly selected dataset, there are computer-assisted qualitative data analysis software (CAQDAS)[22] programs that can do the recoding for you in fairly short order—provided you tell the program exactly what to do.[23]

This brings us to a second challenge: deciding which elements of the qualitative data are relevant to the research question. For example, let's say that you have a large set of interview responses that you want to quantitize in order to merge the data with survey responses. You also have a software program that you can use to assist you in coding the transcribed interview response texts. However, you are the one who must tell the software what to code and how. On the one hand, it is possible that you conducted the interviews in order to gather information *not* provided through the forced-choice survey questions. If you now reduce the qualitative data to the same coded categories as the survey responses, what have you actually gained—and lost? On the other hand, it is possible that, if the interviews covered the same questions as the survey but were conducted with *different* respondents, you could justify this transformation as adding more data to your pool. Either way, you will have to provide the coding instructions, and you must decide how to do so validly and reliably.

In a hypothetical example, you might gather interview data from a randomly selected group of school superintendents about a range of services offered by a state education agency. Examples might include financial advisement, curriculum resources, and professional development opportunities. For each service that participants have actually used, you ask them about the quality of the service and about the importance of the service to their school districts. Quantitizing their responses could involve ranking them numerically, and the data from such a ranking could then be used in an analysis of variance to determine which services, for example, were highly important but of low quality, prompting the state department to consider necessary improvements. These results could be merged with results from a census survey administered to all the state's school district superintendents. The survey would ask the respondents to rank the same

[20]Sandelowski, Voils, and Knafl (2009).

[21]Hellström (2011).

[22]This is variously called QDAS and CAQDAS. See Chapters 2 and 4 for brief discussions and Bazeley (2006) for a discussion of the role of software in integrating different types of data.

[23]See the discussions in Chapter 5 of textual analyses using the approaches of Pennebaker (2011) and Franzosi (2010).

services as to quality and importance. The original interview responses could be further coded qualitatively to look for themes to identify and clarify problem areas and guide improvement efforts.[24]

Quantitative → Qualitative Data Transformation

Quantitative data can, of course, be analyzed statistically if the dataset is large enough and collected using appropriate sampling. However, quantitative data can also be used to identify coding categories that can then be used to analyze quantitative and qualitative data in the same study. In effect, patterns in the quantitative data can provide "clues" for coding and analyzing qualitative data. For example, let's say descriptive statistics using income data show a trimodal distribution for engineers' salaries; that is, three clear frequency peaks in the salary ranges $35,000–$45,000, $70,000–$85,000, and $130,000–$150,000. These three categories of low–medium–high salaries can be used to investigate qualitative data on the engineers: comparing educational preparation, specialty fields, market demand versus availability, and other characteristics. In this case, the quantitative data provide a "clue" that specific characteristics may be shared by the members of each salary peak and that, in order to move to a higher salary range, specific characteristics may be necessary.

Our general advice, repeated often in this volume, is to avoid creating artificial categories from continuous data. However, when those data actually show very distinct patterns or clusters (such as the trimodal salary distribution just described), creating categories and studying them further can be very illuminating. The techniques of exploratory data analysis (EDA) are particularly helpful in such investigations.[25] Classification and regression trees (CART) are another way to use quantitative data to make qualitative categorizations. The general idea behind CART is repeated reanalyses of the same dataset; earlier passes through the data are used to inform later ones (this process is called "statistical learning"). The goal of the classification analyses is to identify qualitative categories. CART is partly also a graphic technique, and the data are often presented graphically.[26] These visualizations are a key part of quantitative data presentation and interpretation.

Some of the most interesting visualizations of data are being done by journalists such as Amanda Cox, who won the 2012 award for excellence in statistical reporting given by the American Statistical Association. As Edward Tufte said, her work "integrated traditional news reporting with high-resolution . . . graphics, and makes no distinction among words, numbers, graphics—the idea is whatever it takes to explain something."[27] The illustrations on her blog are also frequently interactive, allowing readers to examine parts of the evidence of most interest to them. As graphic techniques continue to develop, they hold much promise for the integration of qualitative and quantitative evidence.

For example, when using network analysis, qualitative data—such as, Does Alana follow Brittany on Twitter, and does Cindy follow either or both of them?—are used

---

[24] For examples of studies, see Sandelowski et al. (2009).

[25] See Chapter 6 for a discussion of EDA.

[26] See Berk (2006) for a wide-ranging overview.

[27] Quoted in Champkin (2012). Cox is a reporter for the *New York Times*, and her work, including fascinating interactive graphics with sound, can be found on the *Times*'s website.

to draw diagrams indicating the ties among them. The same data are used to construct quantitative measures such as *degree* and *density* of connections, and these measures are used to identify subgroups whose messages are then studied qualitatively.[28] For instance, in a study combining network analysis and QCA, qualitative data on links between individual cases were transformed into graphic depictions of networks, which were also described quantitatively, enabling the researcher to identify several clusters within the network structures, which were then analyzed with QCA. The researcher moved from the graphic and statistical findings of the network analysis to a theory testing phase conducted with QCA.[29] By contrast, another researcher studying political party positions moved from hypotheses generated by QCA to testing them with statistical methods.[30]

CONCLUSIONS

If you have decided to combine different types of data from different kinds of designs and to confront the coding and analysis challenges discussed in this chapter, we applaud your decision. Experience and logic convince us that uniting sources of evidence and types of information is the most likely path to drawing valid inferences and obtaining usable knowledge. Although coding and analyzing various kinds of data (words, numbers, and graphics) require different kinds of knowledge, experience, and skills—and these are truly distinct areas of expertise—many of the most heated clashes between the "quants" and the "quals" are ludicrous.[31] We all have our preferences for the kinds of problems that intrigue us and the kinds of evidence we like to analyze. But because all sources and forms of evidence have both positive attributes and proven limitations, the best work in social research is most likely to be accomplished by scholars who can combine approaches to improve the quality of explanations, understandings, and predictions. The idea is, in John Tukey's phrase, to "borrow strength" from as many forms of evidence as possible and to pool evidence from parallel but distinct sources.

In implementing combined data analyses, you have an obligation to consider data coding early and often in the research process. Decisions you make early on will affect your options for later analysis. Among the decisions you will make are the following:

- Whether to develop codes in advance through a deductive approach (as in theory-testing designs) or to allow codes to emerge from the data in an inductive approach (as in theory-developing designs)—or both.
- Whether to analyze coded data from study components simultaneously, possibly requiring data transformation, or sequentially, merging findings at the end of the analysis.

---

[28] See Chapter 5 for a discussion of network analysis.

[29] Fischer (2011).

[30] Hellström (2011).

[31] A strong theme in a popular book by one of the best known "statheads" is that predictions can be importantly improved by combining subjective, nonquantifiable data with statistical data (Silver, 2012).

- How to link coded data as needed from separate study components, such as linking survey responses to interview responses.
- Determining whether data transformation serves the purpose of your study; whether you will lose potentially valuable information in the transformation (as from qualitative to quantitative codes); and whether you have sufficient qualitative data to make quantitative analysis feasible and valid.

In addition to considering these decisions for combined designs, you will also need to heed the coding guidance we provide for the individual design components discussed in Chapters 1–5 and the analysis issues discussed in Parts II and III.

The obvious purpose of any research project is to seek answers to research questions. When those questions are complex in nature, as they often are in the social sciences, they usually call for research designs that combine various approaches. When conducting these types of studies, you will ultimately combine your findings into some type of conclusion—the answer to the research question, as best you have determined. The validity of that answer will depend on many factors: the quality of your research design, its capacity to address the research question, the rigor with which you conduct the study, the consistency with which you assign data codes, and the fidelity with which you apply your analyses. To a much greater extent than with simple research designs, in combined designs your capacity to produce high-quality inferences will be complicated by virtue of the many "moving parts" of your study. In this chapter, we have provided discussion and examples of the many ways to approach coding and analysis in combined designs, with the ultimate goal of improving the quality of inferences you derive.

SUGGESTIONS FOR FURTHER READING

One of the best and most compact overviews of the discursive field of mixed methods research is by Johnson and Onwuegbuzie (2004), "Mixed Methods Research: A Research Paradigm Whose Time Has Come." It treats the many complicated questions of combing methods through the lens of pragmatism, and it is quite influential (highly cited).

For a good example of data coding in a mixed methods sequential data analysis that combines both inductive and deductive approaches, see Ivankova, Creswell, and Stick (2006), "Using Mixed-Methods Sequential Explanatory Design: From Theory to Practice."

For a general discussion of how to combine quantitative and qualitative coding methods (and the potential pitfalls of doing so), see Driscoll, Appiah-Yeboah, Salib, and Rupert (2007), "Merging Qualitative and Quantitative Data in Mixed Methods Research: How to and Why Not."

For a typology of designs and a thorough discussion of the implications of using concurrent and sequential designs and coding, see Teddlie and Tashakkori (2006), "A General Typology of Research Designs Featuring Mixed Methods."

On the question of measurement validity, Adcock and Collier's (2001) "Measurement Validity: A Shared Standard for Qualitative and Quantitative Research" identifies 37 different types of validity discussed in the research literature and offers criteria uniting them into one common set of validity types useful for both qualitative and quantitative data.

Sandelowski, Voils, Leeman, and Crandell (2012) tackle what is perhaps the most difficult area of combining methods in one analysis: synthesizing research literature employing quantitative and qualitative data and methods. Their "Mapping the Mixed Methods–Mixed Research Synthesis Terrain" is the most successful of the several attempts we have seen.

Bail's (2012) "The Fringe Effect: Civil Society Organizations and the Evolution of Media Discourse about Islam since the September 11th Attacks" is a remarkably ambitious example of how a researcher can combine vast amounts of data from highly disparate sources and bring them together in a unified analysis mixing qualitative, quantitative, and graphic techniques.

Finally, an excellent source for a general discussion of mixed methods research that applies general principles to a fascinating example in several in-depth articles, see the special issues of *Health Services Research* (December 2013, Vol. 48, No. 6.2, pp. 2125–2267) on "Integrating Mixed Methods in Health Services and Delivery System Research."

CHAPTER 13 SUMMARY TABLE

Coding and analysis decisions for deductive combined designs (pp. 431–432)	• Determine whether similar (preselected) codes can be applied to all parts of the research. • Decide whether codes can be/need to be linked for the final analysis.
Coding and analysis decisions for inductive combined designs (pp. 432–433)	• Decide how codes will emerge. • Determine whether/how codes will apply across the various methods.
Considerations for sequential or separate analysis in combined designs (pp. 433–434)	• If participants are common across design components, make a plan to link participant data. • Decide whether to cross-code by theme. • Determine which features of earlier analysis will inform later analysis.
Considerations for data merging in combined designs (pp. 434–437)	• The ultimate purpose is to unify data types so that they may be analyzed as a single set. • If quantitizing qualitative data, determine whether sample size and random selection allow valid use of quantitative analysis methods. • Determine whether converting qualitative data to quantitative will result in harmful data loss. • Be cautious about converting quantitative data to qualitative categories; this usually results in data loss. However, sometimes natural and "real" categories emerge that can lead to further investigation and should not be ignored (e.g., outliers, bimodal data distributions).
Considerations for drawing inferences in combined designs (pp. 437–438)	• Quality of your research design. • Capacity of the research design to address the research question. • Rigor of the study. • Consistency in assigning data codes. • Fidelity of analysis methods.

CHAPTER 14

Conclusion

Common Themes and Diverse Choices

This book is about options and alternatives. There are many alternatives, and it is important to select wisely among them. Selecting wisely is not easy, because the options are numerous and contradictory advice is fairly common. That is the choice *problem*, and it is one of our central themes. The other side of the coin, and a second theme, is the choice *opportunity*. Because there are so many alternatives, it should be possible to find methods that fit your specific research question well. To benefit from that opportunity, the researcher has to exert effort in making choices to find the best methods for particular questions. So the book is all about zeroing in to almost microscopic levels, while remaining aware of the wide range of choices. Making effective selections requires attention to detail *and* a panoramic perspective so that you don't get lost among the details. We bring the dialogue between these themes—the magnifying glass and the wide-angle lens—into a common perspective in this concluding chapter.

As we review the methods we have discussed in this volume, as well as in our companion volume on research design, we are awestruck by the range of wonderful methods of analysis with which to study human thought and action—and by the limits of any one of them. We cannot imagine insisting, as some researchers purportedly do, that there is one best method for all research problems. All are limited, and the only hope for learning is to combine them in various ways. But the dilemma is that, for any particular research project to succeed, the researcher has to select one method or a small handful of methods. We must specialize in a highly variegated world.

We have not tried in this conclusion to recap the previous chapters. The best way for you to do that, to get an overview of the book, would be to skim the Summary Tables for each chapter. Rather, we present some broadly applicable principles in what we believe is a memorable way—a collection of aphorisms that can be consulted at will. This approach is unusual enough to require some justification. We offer three broad classes of explanation: tradition, flexibility, and brevity.

Tradition is a justification for an approach only by indicating that it is feasible, that it has been done in the past. And aphoristic writing does have a long and honorable history, from Hippocrates ("Life is short, art long, opportunity fleeting, experience deceptive, judgment difficult") to Wittgenstein ("Whereof one cannot speak, thereof one must be silent"). Some aphorisms are austere and carry the tone of pronouncements from on high. Others are more informal and playful, such as Oscar Wilde's "Experience is the name we give our mistakes."

Flexibility is enhanced because the aphoristic method puts few restrictions on the writer's efforts to cover a subject. This flexibility is useful in a field such as ours that resists systemization. The aphoristic genre allowed us to take a nonlinear approach, if not quite a herky-jerky one, to a subject that is hard to traverse following a straight path. The flexibility of aphoristic writing gave us ways to describe the narrow slot canyons as well as the broad plains in the terrain of methodological choice, and to do so in a fairly readable way. We have been able, we think, to discuss difficulties in choosing among the intricate pathways while trying to keep an eye on the satellite view from 100 miles up. Most of the time there is no uniquely correct answer when deciding among research methods. That is why we conclude with aphorisms, not algorithms. One reader suggested that this makes the chapter a "postmodern" approach to the topic. That could be an apt description of the form, if not necessarily the content, of this chapter.

Brevity is the hallmark of aphorisms; the dominant writing convention is to make them short, pithy. But because this is a methodology book, we have sometimes been, well, methodical and have included longer explanations and even footnotes with citations.[1] We are reminded of one of Nietzsche's aphorisms about aphorisms (paraphrased), namely, to understand a good aphorism one has to subject it to exegesis.

The aphorisms are clustered into three broad and somewhat overlapping groups. The groups are overlapping because one kind of selection influences the other as you survey the vast array of methodological options. The three groups are:

1. *Common themes:* perennial issues that recur when one does research of almost any kind.
2. *Diverse choices:* the types of analytical choices that confront the researcher.
3. *Strategies and tactics:* tricks of the trade and tips for data analysts.

You can read the aphorisms straight through, from top to bottom, or sample them at will. Some early readers thought it might be better to start at the end, with the more specific and concrete topics in the concluding pages and move toward the more general and theoretical ones in the early parts of the chapter. Either approach is reasonable. Use what works best for you.

COMMON THEMES

The answer lies in remembering the question—the research question, that is.

The research should steer your decisions through all phases of a research project, from the initial design through sampling, coding, analysis, and interpretation. The research question is the rudder to use to keep on course. Keep it foremost in your mind.

[1]There is, of course, quite a lot of scholarship on the topic of aphorisms, their cognitive impact, and their use by various scholars. We have found the following interesting: McGlone and Tofighbakhsh (2000), Alter and Oppenheimer (2009), and Swedberg and Reich (2010).

If it's not worth doing, it's not worth doing well.[2]

The research question is your rudder, but it has to be a good one. You can't rescue a poor question—one that is vague or ambiguous or that deals with a trivial topic—by using excellent methods of sampling, coding, and analysis.

An orientation to theory, often implicit in your research question, provides a guideline for keeping your work on course.

Two common theoretical orientations are theory building and theory testing. If you want to build or construct a theory, you are more likely to use descriptive and exploratory techniques such as exploratory data analysis or grounded theory. If you want to test or confirm a theory, you are more likely to use techniques that would allow you to judge whether the data are consistent with what we would expect if the theory is true. These would include effect sizes with confidence intervals, various model fit statistics, and qualitative comparative analysis.

It can be comforting to tether yourself to a methodological pole.

Whether it's randomized controlled trials, ethnomethodology, or feminist theory, being tethered reduces the burdens of choice. The price for this security is constraint on your creativity and flexibility. However, by running in the path defined by the limits of your tether, you might go far in the academic world; at least it is rumored that some in academe do well by sticking to a narrow track.

We may want our generalizations to apply to the present and future, but they are based on the past.

All data are historical; at best, they come from the very recent past. All accounts of research describe the past. Social researchers frequently put things into social, political, and economic context, but they often neglect temporal contexts.

Open competition among methods is better than rules in restraint of trade.

This does not mean that markets are infallible or that they display "wisdom" or even that they are inevitably "efficient." But open exchanges of ideas are far better than textbook pronouncements that discourage consideration of alternatives.

Tolerance for other points of view is a precondition for progress in research methods.

Intellectual tolerance guards against assuming your own infallibility. As one 16th-century pioneer of tolerance[3] put it (in slightly updated English): "Remember you are human; deem it not impossible for you to err."

---

[2]This one is sometimes attributed to John Tukey.

[3]Hooker (2013).

The world is complex; studies, by comparison, are simple.

Studies will always investigate only some aspects of a complex phenomenon, use only some of the variables among a larger set that could be examined, or try out explanations using a limited sample of research participants. Other studies, using different variables and participants, might, and often do, come to different conclusions.

Proving causation is impossible in social research.

But identifying some potential causes as more likely than others is an attainable goal. A cause can never be directly observed; causation is a concept, a theoretical construct. What we can observe is whether things are as we would expect them to be if a cause is at work. If increased aerobic exercise caused better heart health, we would expect to find a relationship between, for example, jogging and blood pressure. Different measures of exercise and indicators of health might find a different relationship.

A correlation does not imply causation—nor does any other statistic, such as $p < .05$.

A researcher must make a case for causation by constructing an argument built on evidence; making causal inferences is fundamentally a matter of qualitative judgments, although, in order to make them, a researcher may use quantitative as well as qualitative evidence in coming to those judgments. Although a correlation does not necessarily imply causation, if two variables are causally related, they will be correlated.

A fruitful tension between the particular and the general characterizes much good research.

Generalizations are tempered by knowledge of specific cases. Specific cases are examined in depth in order to say something about the generality of cases. The researcher's focus often alternates between these two, in a kind of dialogue between the particular instance and the general rule.

Dialogue between ideas and evidence is fundamental to effective research.

In the dialogue, one key question is, Which should start or lead the discussion, the ideas or the evidence? In deductive approaches the ideas start; in inductive approaches the evidence does. But even in the most deductive studies you usually have some empirical data in mind; and in a highly inductive study you usually have a few orienting ideas.

Doing research entails the idea that there is something to learn.

There is no point in doing research unless you are uncertain or curious about what you might find. Doing research also makes sense only if you believe that through systematic investigation you can come to more or less justifiable conclusions that add to what is known and, usually, if you believe that what you learn can be conveyed to others.

The comparative method is all but universal in social research.

The comparisons may be of many types, from experiments using treatment and comparison groups to case studies examining cross-national instances of a phenomenon. The main purpose in the comparisons is to eliminate otherwise plausible explanations. Without a comparison, you have no way of judging whether your explanation is merely a peculiarity of the one group or case you have studied.

It is quite natural to compare apples and oranges, despite the old saying.

They are both round, grow on trees, are good sources of vitamin C, are important agricultural products, and so on. Thus it is reasonable to say that, for specific research questions (e.g., about vitamins or crops), they are comparable for analytical purposes. The mistake would be treating apples and oranges as identical, but who would ever do that?

Thinking hurts.[4]

It can at least be inconvenient. It is generally easier to follow the traditions in your research specialty than it is to think through the range of methods from which you could conceivably select different methods. Making choices, selecting among the many options in research methods, can have costs. Although we argue here that the benefits outweigh the costs, it may be that the benefits for the field of research are greater than the benefits to an individual making the extra effort.

Political and social orientations are very important for defining a topic of investigation and interpreting the outcomes, but they aren't methods.

Given your value orientations, you are more likely to be interested in some problems or questions. But you can pursue these with the full suite of *methods*, from focus groups to factor analysis. It is natural for beliefs to direct one to particular problems and questions, but they should have much less influence over the analysis of evidence.

Generalizations are only generally true, hence the name.

To criticize a statement for being "just a generalization," one that admits of several exceptions, is thus an odd thing to do. It is hardly a telling criticism to say something that is true by definition. The key question is whether the generalization is useful, more useful than a more particularistic descriptive summary. Useful for what? For answering your research question.

Relativism contains the seeds of its own destruction.

If the statement "all truths are relative" is true, it applies to itself. Relativism is thus much like the "liar's paradox," which takes the following form: If the statement "this sentence is false" is true, then the sentence is false, which is a contradiction. Conversely, if the statement "this sentence is false" is false, then the sentence is true, which is also

[4]This one is from Georg Simmel.

a contradiction. One common form of relativism in methodological discourse is social constructivism. Another, and probably the most widely referenced form, is postmodernism. This is essentially undefinable, which, according to its proponents, is exactly the point. Like other forms of extreme relativism and skepticism, it logically contradicts itself by presupposing that which it denies, that is, it argues that you can't make arguments.

When not taken to their logical extremes, social constructivism and social relativism are defensible.

The statement that "all conclusions are *influenced* by their authors' political and social contexts and therefore not certain" is reasonable; it does not contain the seeds of its own destruction through logical contradiction. By contrast, the statement "all conclusions are *determined* by social and political contexts and therefore not certain" does contain a logical contradiction. Relativism and constructivism are incompatible with determinism.

Limited skepticism is healthy; when taken to its logical extremes, it is, like relativism, incoherent.

Radical skepticism would lead one to doubt the reliability of one's own senses and to conclude that one could justifiably know or assert nothing. A skeptical argument for a philosophical position—including skepticism—would be meaningless. How could you be certain that you knew nothing? But skepticism as an attitude, as a general tendency to wonder about knowledge claims and to question whether they are accurate, is a foundation on which rational investigation is built.

Fallibilism is a reasonable middle way between skepticism and certainty.

Fallibilism is the position that anything we believe could be wrong—it might not be, but it could be. Unlike with skepticism, with fallibilism we need not abandon a belief that knowledge is possible, but we do need to be aware that conclusions we currently accept as true could be overturned by new evidence.

Objectivity and subjectivity are always paired; each is defined in terms of the other.

Pure objectivity and pure subjectivity in research methods are not just inadvisable, they are unattainable. Objectivity and subjectivity are impossible extremes. However, they may be useful for defining end points on a real continuum.

One mark of objectivity is a convergence of beliefs, but this can also be a mark of an intellectual virus.

To indicate objectivity, the convergence has to be attributable to evidence or analyses, not only agreement. The level of agreement on any difficult problem will never be complete, which is why pure objectivity is impossible. An example is several researchers coming to agreement on common codes for a set of interview transcripts. Other examples include the conclusion that global warming is partly caused by human activity and the judgment that vaccines do not cause autism. Dissent exists about these conclusions, but the level of convergence based on evidence is about as high as human beings can achieve. Such consensus can be thought of as objectivity, or at least as intersubjectivity.

Because there can be no certainty, it does not follow that everything is equally likely.

Abandoning research and reason because knowledge cannot be perfectly certain seems like overdoing it. On the other hand, the absence of total certainty should not lead to credulity, to believing things on the basis of little or no evidence.

Certainty is a state of mind, not a characteristic of research conclusions.

Certainty is best seen as a psychological phenomenon, not a feature of research on the empirical world. Psychologists have collected quite a lot of evidence suggesting that most of us tend to be overconfident in our beliefs, and some of this research has investigated the beliefs of researchers, not only college students. Research methods can help us not merely to come to conclusions but to guard against overconfidence in them. Confidence intervals (margins of error) are the obvious example, but many other research practices, such as subjecting one's findings to the critique of colleagues, can have the same salutary effect.

Uncertainty in research findings could be due to the nature of the world, our concepts, or our knowledge.

If our interpretations lack clarity or specificity, the reason could be that the world is inherently chaotic, and our interpretations follow suit. Or, it could be that our concepts, language, and symbols for describing the world are inadequate. Or, it could be that the world is clear enough and that our linguistic and conceptual tools are OK but that we need to gather more data. There is probably no way to know which of those three is true, but to do research one might have to decide, at least provisionally.

THE CHOICE PROBLEM

Which randomized controlled trial (RCT) demonstrates that RCTs are the most effective method?

Of course, there is no such trial; the superiority of RCTs is argued for, using logical criteria and statistical theory, not demonstrated by experiment. Actually, the best evidence for the strength of experiments is observational. This is more than a little ironic because experiments are often touted as superior to mere observational studies.

Different kinds of models are required for studying different phenomena.

The actual state of the world, the phenomena, should determine the correct model rather than one's preference for a particular type of model. It is a fundamental error to try to squeeze the world into one's favorite model. But, paradoxically, how is one to learn about the "actual state of the world" except by attempting to apply a model to it?

Observing actual social behavior may be more informative than observing laboratory simulations.

Each kind of observation has advantages and disadvantages. You have to weigh observing reality over which you have no control (but that is real) against observing a simulation in a laboratory over which you have considerable control (but that is artificial). Studying reality while retaining control over the independent variable is rarely possible.

Faced with complex problems, we cannot make the *best* decision, but we can make *good* decisions.

The best choice either is not knowable or does not exist. We can review the choices to find options that are *better* than others for our specific purposes, to solve our problem, or to address our research question. Methodological choices involve decision making under uncertainty; there are too many variables involved and no way of assigning a precise weight to each of them to select the one best option. After eliminating clearly erroneous paths, one must at some point "satisfice"—a term meant to combine *satisfy* and *suffice*. To satisfice means making a sufficiently satisfactory decision, the best that we can given our limited resources of knowledge and rationality.

Manners, mores, and morals have little place in selecting methods of data analysis.

A possible exception comes in the area of research ethics, but most ethical issues are settled before analysis—at the earlier design and sampling stages. You make the most ethically consequential choices when deciding what you are going to study, as well as how and with whom you will study it. Protecting participants from harm, ensuring their privacy, and obtaining their informed consent are most salient in the earlier, design and sampling, phases of the study. By comparison, few ethical challenges arise when deciding whether to code and analyze your data verbally, graphically, or numerically.

Methodological discourse is corrupted when people talk about research in terms of moral verities.

It's hard to avoid such talk because terms such as *right* and *correct* and *appropriate*—often used in discussions of research methods—also carry moral connotations. But we agree with George Homans's widely quoted remark that methodology "is a matter of strategy, not morals."

Quantitative versus qualitative in social research is a false dichotomy.

The two are inevitably linked in actual practice. Purely numerical research is impossible in the social sciences; at least, we have never seen any presented in that way. For example, one might collect numerically coded data to test a theory, but the theory itself will most likely be verbal—or graphic. Purely verbal research reports are more feasible, but even they are fairly rare. And many concepts used in predominantly verbal research reports can be expressed in numbers, as well as words. Examples include magnitude (bigger or smaller), order (earlier or later), and proximity (nearer or farther).

All major design types can generate all types of data: words, numbers, and graphics.

Surveys, interviews, experiments, observations, secondary/archival, and combined designs have all been used to collect and then to code and analyze all major types of data: names, ranks, numbers, and pictures. Thus to claim, as is often done, that surveys and experiments are quantitative designs whereas interviews and observations are qualitative is to make a category mistake or to "essentialize," to treat a mere tendency as though it were the essence of a phenomenon.

Selecting research methods is fundamentally a qualitative decision/activity.

This is true even when selecting among various methods for generating and analyzing quantitative data. The choice is based on reasoning about categories and concepts and the likely advantages and disadvantages of selecting particular methods.

Purity of methodological choice and conclusions are impossible in social research.

Practicing researchers do better when they work in the pragmatic middle ground where all epistemological categories are porous, all methods are mixed, and all conclusions are uncertain. Paradoxically, the only thing of which we can justifiably be certain is that unalloyed certainty is impossible—for researchers, if not for true believers.

Although there is no one best method, for specific research questions some methods are likely to be better than others.

Methodological pluralism is not methodological relativism. Pluralism does not imply that any method is OK for any problem; it only contends that for any problem there are several potentially useful methods.

A key criterion for assessing a research method is whether it is progressive.

We define *progressive* in Dewey's pragmatic sense of the term. A method is progressive when it leads to growth in our ability to do things; it is regressive when it constricts our capacity to gain knowledge. Pragmatism is an appropriate standard for methodology, because methods are means of accomplishing ends.

Disagreements are natural in methodology because there is no one best method.

When someone disagrees with you, this can be, well, disagreeable, but if you are genuinely interested in learning, it is wise to value opponents and to treat them with respect. They are, in J. S. Mill's terms, "an indispensable resource" for making supportable decisions.

If research methods were as diametrically opposed as some discourse would lead one to believe, they couldn't be combined.

It is always possible to combine methods on any research question. You may not be able to do so because of limited resources, but there is no reason in principle that they could not be combined. At minimum, research using more than one method on the same problem can be conducted sequentially—first interviews, then surveys, and then interviews again is a common sequence.

Methods do not battle one another, but methodologists often do.

People struggle for recognition and advantage, and methodologists are people. There is no clash between inductive and deductive methods, positivism and interpretivism, or qualitative and quantitative analytical methods—only between people who advocate one of these to the exclusion of the others.

Selecting a research topic and methods for studying it can lead to affiliation with a group.

People with similar interests link with one another in networks, work in teams, and generate group solidarity. This can greatly enhance the quality of research. The other side of the coin is that ingroup solidarity can breed outgroup hostility. Rivalries and clannishness can ensue, which can restrict opportunities to think in new ways. The bright and dark sides of human beings' need to form social groups can be seen as clearly in research as in other activities.

There is no gold standard in research methodology—nor in intellectual endeavor generally.

As in monetary policy, in which it has long since been outmoded, a gold standard narrows options and stultifies action. When researchers believe in a gold standard, this restricts thinking about viable options. These days we use a variety of credit cards, direct deposits, and electronic funds transfers, which are much more flexible than having to lug around a sack of gold coins.

All samples in prospective studies are composed of volunteers.

This can be a serious limitation if you wish to generalize to an entire population. For such generalization, a retrospective study of archival data—such as health, school, or employment records—can have more external validity or generalizability.

For some problems, natural experiments and quasi-experiments may be preferable to true (artificial) experiments.

In some cases, true experiments (or RCTs) might not be possible because of ethical or logistical barriers. But even when RCTs are possible, natural and quasi-experiments may do better at combining internal validity with external validity (or generalizability).

The number of possible combinations in mixed method or multimethod research is huge.

The number of options is probably not infinite, but it seems impossible to find an upper limit. Possibilities are indefinitely numerous because one can combine different methods of data gathering, sampling, coding, and/or analysis—and they can be combined in different orders.

Combining methods might unite their strengths. Could it also join their weaknesses?

If, for example, you link a method strong on internal but weak on external validity with another weak on internal but strong on external validity, what is to say that you will not end up with an analysis that is weak on both? How does it necessarily follow that the study will be strong on both?

STRATEGIES AND TACTICS

Methodological choices may be strategic or tactical.

The difference between the two is a matter of degree, and they are ultimately inseparable. Strategies involve a smaller number of choices made earlier in a multichoice problem. Tactics are shaped by strategic decisions; they are made later and are more specific. Although there is no firm distinction between the two, confusing them is a source of, well, confusion. Researchers committed to particular techniques may try to treat their tactical decisions as important strategic choices, whereas researchers who brook no discussion may try to claim that their strategic decisions are uncontroversial technical/tactical options.

Making social research more social is easier to accomplish for some activities than others.

A division of labor can be useful at many points of a research project, but this may involve little more than breaking up the tasks into small bits that individuals can handle. Pooling the resources of the group so that they constitute more than the sum of the individual parts seems more easily done in the early design and later interpretation phases of the research.

In one example we studied, computer programmers often had wide-ranging brainstorming sessions when deciding what features a new program ought to have, but the actual coding work was done by "code monkeys" (their term) working alone. In our own work we have often found that deciding how to code data (qualitative or quantitative) was much more effectively done in group work. At the analysis stage, it didn't matter much. When interpreting the analyses, it became important again. In sum, the helpfulness of group efforts can vary with the task.

When choosing among research methods, practical wisdom (*phronesis*, in Aristotle's terms) is often more useful than theoretical wisdom (*sophia*).

Selecting research methods is more a matter of practical wisdom gained by reflection on experience than it is an exercise of theoretical wisdom based on reasoning about concepts or universals. Practical wisdom helps one decide how to achieve a given end, such as answering a research question. Beginning researchers usually do not have much experience to reflect upon, so they could do well to consult experts, who presumably do have such experience.

Relying on experts raises the question of how we know who the experts are.

Deciding who is sufficiently skilled and experienced is mostly a matter of human judgment—made by people who are skilled and experienced, as determined by those recognized as having skill and experience, and so on.

Statistically significant findings may not be important—and important findings may not be statistically significant.

Statistical significance and *p*-values can sometimes provide evidence of an important outcome, but they are not usually the best evidence—even for experiments. Effect sizes and confidence intervals are better for quantitative outcomes. But even these have limited applications—to generalizing about random samples and groups that have been studied with random assignment. A trivial effect can be statistically significant if the sample is large enough. By contrast, an important finding, based on intensive studies of several cases, might not attain statistical significance if the sample is small enough.

Inferential statistical tests (e.g., *t*-tests) are valid only for random samples or for groups that have been formed by random assignment.

This rule is true given the definition of what constitutes a statistical test, but it is widely violated. Textbook writers appear to overestimate the feasibility of random sampling and assignment, which sometimes leads them to spend too much time on how to analyze data from such probability samples—and not enough on how to analyze data obtained in other ways.

If you don't know where you started, you can't tell how far you've come.

Without baseline data, you can't gauge progress or change. It is easy to overlook the obvious importance of baseline data. Think of how often people forget to check the odometer before beginning a trip. When you have no comparison group and are taking a within-groups approach, baseline data provide an indispensable standard for comparison.

If you want to measure change, don't change the measure.[5]

Multiple measurements are good, advantageous even, but to compare before with after, it is best to use the same method. For example, don't use an attitude survey for before and a test of knowledge for after—or vice versa. You could do well, however, to use both methods when measuring change—both before and after.

Data do nothing and say nothing.

We do things with data, and we speak for them—to say "the conclusions emerged from the data" is to make an odd, depersonalized claim. We construct the conclusions, invent them, dig them out of the data.

If you don't code your data, you can't analyze them.

Codes may be names, numbers, or graphical symbols. They enable you to index, sort, and represent your data. Without this categorization, the data remain an unanalyzable collection of bits and pieces—data in the original sense of the term: words, numbers, and images before you have done anything to them.

To collect useful evidence, it helps to know what you are going to collect.

Ironically, a plan can be useful for discovering something new; it prepares you to be surprised. If you want to be surprised, you have to have expectations.

Everyone loves a good story, but nobody trusts stories very much as evidence.

Narratives are essential for describing causal processes and for narrating or illustrating the results of a study. But narratives are not very effective for establishing that outcomes occurred or for estimating their size.

Researcher, heal thyself.

One of the best ways to improve the quality of research is to conduct more research on researchers' practices. Especially helpful would be research comparing the consequences of different practices. Consulting research on the effectiveness of different research methods allows you to use evidence rather than tradition or whim as the basis for your methodological selections. At least begin by undertaking informal studies of your own practices.

A perfectly unbiased summary of biased evidence will itself be biased.

This is perhaps most obvious in literature reviews and meta-analyses, but it pervades all efforts to combine data into an analyzable whole. The provenance of the evidence matters as much as or more than your skill in accurately summarizing it.

[5]This one isn't ours; it has been attributed to both Otis Dudley Duncan and Albert Beaton.

To decide whether something would make a good natural experiment, use Snow's criterion.

John Snow's criterion is: "no experiment could be devised that would more thoroughly test the effect" than does the naturally occurring event.

Exact measurement is impossible to attain, but we can usually get more precise.

A striking example is from the National Bureau of Standards.[6] Standardized national and international weights ultimately refer to objects. If something you buy weighs 10 grams, it weighs as much as an actual 10-gram object—called the NB 10—held by the National Bureau. From time to time, the Bureau weighs the NB 10, and the weight is different every time. The differences show up only in the fourth or fifth decimal places, but the inconsistency shows that there is no error-free measurement even under the most rigorously controlled conditions. It is a sobering example for social researchers who cannot even begin to attain the National Bureau's degree of control over or exactness in their measurements.

A baby whale is much bigger than a jumbo shrimp.

Interpreting any measurement is relative to a context.

If you are indifferent about the outcomes, it's OK to delegate coding and analysis to others.

Too much is lost by ceding control of coding and analysis. In certain kinds of huge studies, division of labor may be unavoidable, but, when possible, the labor should be divided among colleagues. Assigning important tasks to part-time assistants who may not understand or care about the purposes of the research carries considerable risk.

Using data about groups to draw conclusions about individuals—and vice versa—is inappropriate.

Doing so is known as the *ecological fallacy.* Using information about individuals to draw conclusions about groups is known as either the fallacy of composition or the *atomistic fallacy.* The atomistic fallacy seems to be less often mentioned in methodology books. One way to help avoid either of these mistakes is to use multilevel models.

Social researchers seldom do pure research with no practical aims in view.

They usually try to pursue usable knowledge, at least indirectly. Given this, it is often helpful to think about the potential practical or applied consequences of your findings as you plan an analysis and decide how to report results. Of course, generalizing from research to practice is not without problems, in large part because research studies

---

[6] Our account follows that in Freedman, Pisani, and Purves (1998).

are, by design, much simpler than practice in the real world. For example, researchers control for (hypothetically subtract the effects of) confounding variables that cannot be controlled in the real world.

Analyze not only your data but also your analyses of them.

Whether your data are transcripts, scatter diagrams, survey replies, documents, or measurements on a psychological scale, your analytical steps and preliminary interpretations constitute more data for analysis. Your analyses of, or reflections on, these analyses of analyses could, in turn, be further grist for your analytical mill. Although at some point you have to worry about getting sucked into "a black hole of introspection,"[7] it is usually worthwhile to systematically review the thought processes you used to draw your conclusions and to review your choices to see if they have provided valid findings. They are as much evidence as data screening, member checks, audit trails, or any other procedure for going over what you have done. Think of analyzing your analyses as a kind of cognitive interview—of yourself.

If your question could be answered using more than one method, consider combining them.

If you cannot combine them in one study, you could in a series of studies. You might establish that a relationship exists using one method (say interviews or surveys), and then try to confirm or look more deeply into it using another (such as focus groups or observations). Each of these would generate different types of data that could be coded in compatible ways in order to combine or mix the analyses. Or you could simply combine the interpretations drawn from the different types of data.

A research question is often built "backward," starting with your outcome variable.

You begin with a likely outcome (dependent variable) and then work backward, thinking about what might cause this outcome—and what might cause those causes. Next you might consider links among the causal variables—intervening or mediating variables. In so doing, you have, in the course of composing a detailed research question, essentially developed a theory—an explanation for how a set of phenomena are related. However, if your theoretical orientation and research question are exploratory, then working in the other direction is possible—you start with independent/predictor variables in order to investigate what happens as these are altered.

Because all research findings are uncertain, always describe the sources of and your degree of uncertainty.

For quantitative findings, confidence intervals are a good beginning, and it is irresponsible not to report them. But the range of plausible error in a quantitative estimate is

[7]The phrase is Van Maanen's (2011).

only one step. Uncertainty also arises from imperfections in the implementation of the research plan—and no research plan has ever been implemented perfectly.

If you discuss the uncertainty of your findings, you'll be doing better science, but it could cause a public relations problem.

Potential consumers of your research—such as policy makers, journalists, and even other colleagues—are sometimes impatient with the expression of qualifications and limitations. Even including confidence intervals, which indicate the range of plausible values, can take the zing out of a conclusion. A mean value accompanied by the words "statistically significant" is more likely to garner attention, but presenting your data only this way is incomplete and less accurate.

Poorly designed or executed research is usually unethical.

If the research has no potential benefit to anyone, then even minor risk or inconvenience to research participants is not justifiable, nor is wasting resources that could be better spent.

The sins of the doctors have been visited upon the social researchers.

Because of some truly horrific experiments by medical doctors, we all now have to put up with ethics review boards, such as IRBs. Although it is on the whole a good thing that we have to obtain informed consent, guard against inflicting harm, and protect the privacy of research participants, there have been few, if any, examples of serious harm to participants inflicted by social researchers. An exception might be studies of anthropologists and other social researchers who have worked with their nations' militaries.

The usual examples of ethical violations by social researchers include Watson's traumatizing one infant (in 1920), Milgram's obedience experiments (starting in 1963), which distressed *some* participants, and Zimbardo's prison simulation (in 1971), which put several dozen undergraduates at risk for 6 days. But all of these pale in significance when compared with the murderous Nazi concentration camp medical experiments, which led to the Nuremberg Code of Ethics and the Tuskegee experiments in Alabama, which as late as 1973 allowed men (and some of their children) to die of syphilis long after the disease was curable. The discovery of the Tuskegee abuses was important in establishing the U.S. Office for Human Research Protections (OHRP) and legislation requiring IRB reviews.

Probably the greatest potential harm to participants in social research is a breach of their privacy.

Remember that there is no researcher–participant privilege, as there is a doctor–patient or lawyer–client privilege. If your fieldnotes are subpoenaed, you'll have to give them up—or risk legal consequences. One of your ethical obligations is to make sure that participants in your studies know that you cannot guarantee their privacy in the same way a journalist, lawyer, or physician can. Of course, the confidentiality of clients of psychologists or social workers in a *clinical* setting (not in a purely research setting) is protected.

You may want to study a theory to point out its shortcomings.

Although many theories in social research have shortcomings, it is not worth challenging one if everyone already knows about its inadequacies.

Try not to confuse the weather with the climate.

In studies of organizations and social groups, the researchers may conduct their investigations over the course of a few weeks. They hope to discuss such variables as organizational "climate" but have only observed the short-term weather.

Categorical coding can encourage stereotyping and lead to interpreting tendencies as essences.

When the categories are natural, it makes sense to use them, but imposing categories on continuous phenomena is inappropriate. For example, we witnessed a workshop in which the trainer wanted participants to say whether they preferred to work alone or in teams and whether they preferred to work on short-term or long-term projects. The idea was to use the answers to divide the participants into four groups—short-term loners, long-term team workers, and so forth. They rebelled; they said it depended on the kind of project; they wanted to place themselves on continua, not in boxes. They didn't want to engage in self-stereotyping.

Every person is simultaneously like *all* other persons, like *some* other persons, and like *no* other persons.[8]

When studying individuals' attributes and characteristics, a researcher (and a research question) will tend to focus either on what all people have in common, on what makes them individually unique, or on what they share with their social groups. When coding and analyzing from one perspective, the other two should be kept in mind. For example, when studying the distinct characteristics of a social group, remember that every member of that group simultaneously is a unique individual and shares a common humanity with everyone.

Operational definitions are useful in most forms of research.

Although the *term* is more used in the study of quantitative data, and although it originated in the Vienna Circle of logical positivists (horrors!), the *concept* is broadly useful. When you operationalize a variable, you specify the procedures you will use to identify it and do so in such a way that someone else can verify or replicate what you have done. Operational definitions are most useful in the study of latent variables—those that cannot be observed directly and have to be inferred, such as liberalism, quality of life,

[8]This paraphrases Clyde Kluckhohn's insight.

prejudice, anxiety, and so on. An operational definition suggests how you will code your data and the methods you might use to analyze the data thus coded.

Constant comparison and theoretical sampling are useful in most forms of research.

Although the terms originated in and are mainly applied in grounded theory, the ideas have broad applicability. Constant comparison (adjusting your theories in light of your data as you analyze them) and theoretical sampling (modifying your sampling plan in light of the adjustments made in your theories) are ready to migrate from qualitative data and analyses to quantitative and beyond. They share a family resemblance with Bayesian methods.

Operational definitions help identify, code, or measure concepts, but they are inevitably imprecise.

A concept often cannot be observed directly, which is the reason operational definitions are used. But the operational definitions never reflect the concept perfectly, just as the concept never reflects the empirical world perfectly.

It does little good to use a method correctly if it is the wrong one for the job.

That is why the logic of choice applied to selecting a method is more important than learning the technicalities of implementing the method once chosen.

Intuitions and hunches are wonderful sources of ideas.

Get ideas from wherever you can—movies, literature, personal experience, conversations with friends. Ideas are the engines that drive the activities of researchers. Moving beyond ideas to knowledge requires disciplined examination of relevant evidence.

Have a stopping plan.

Decide in advance on a criterion or point at which you will no longer collect, code, and/or analyze data. This can sharpen thinking by making the boundaries of the analysis less ambiguous. Examples of stopping points include saturation in grounded theory, the fail-safe number in meta-analysis, convergence on a solution in iterative methods such as maximum likelihood estimation, and sequential stopping decisions in experiments. In the absence of more formal stopping rules such as these, devise your own criterion. That criterion will surely be better than "I ran out of time."

A deadline concentrates the mind wonderfully.

A deadline encourages one to ask the question, What and how much can I do given the time and other resources I have available? This question can stimulate more focused thinking about data gathering, coding, and analysis plans.

It is easy to underestimate the difficulty in conducting mixed method or multimethod research.

It can be demanding to learn one method well. Trying to master two, so as to combine them, can be challenging. And, in order to combine the two, facility in a third method may have to be acquired.

Make sure your computer program does not do something by default that you don't intend it to do.

Computer software packages, whether for analyzing qualitative or quantitative data, often incorporate traditions into their programs and thus reinforce them. A good program will be transparent, that is, you can determine, without too much effort, how it has analyzed your data.

References

Abern, M. R., Benson, J. S., & Hoeksema, J. (2009). Ureteral mullerianosis. *Journal of Endourology, 23*(12), 1933–1935.

Ackland, R. (2013). *Web social science.* London: Sage.

Adcock, R., & Collier, D. (2001). Measurement validity: A shared standard for qualitative and quantitative research. *American Political Science Review, 95*, 529–546.

Afendulis, C. C., He, Y., Zaslavsky, A. M., & Chernew, M. E. (2011). The impact of Medicare Part D on hospitalization rates. *Health Services Research, 46*, 1022–1038.

Agresti, A. (1996). *An introduction to categorical data analysis.* New York: Wiley.

Ahn, S., & Becker, B. J. (2011). Incorporating quality scores in meta-analysis. *Journal of Educational and Behavioral Statistics, 36*, 555–585.

Allenby, G. M., & Rossi, P. E. (2008). Teaching Bayesian statistics to marketing and business students. *American Statistician, 62*(3), 202–205.

Allison, P. (2002). *Missing data.* Thousand Oaks, CA: Sage.

Allison, P. D. (1987). Estimation of linear models with incomplete data. In C. C. Clogg (Ed.), *Sociological methodology* (pp. 71–103). San Francisco: Jossey-Bass.

Allison, P. D. (1999). *Multiple regression: A primer.* Thousand Oaks, CA: Pine Forge Press.

Aloe, A. M., & Becker, B. J. (2011). An effect size for regression predictors in meta-analysis. *Journal of Educational and Behavioral Statistics, 37*, 278–297.

Alter, A. L., & Oppenheimer, D. M. (2009). Uniting the tribes of fluency to form a metacognitive nation. *Personality and Social Psychology Review, 13*(3), 219–235.

Altman, D. G., & Bland, J. M. (1994). Diagnostic tests: 1. Sensitivity and specificity. *British Medical Journal, 308*(6943), 1552.

Altman, M., & McDonald, M. P. (2003). Replication with attention to numerical accuracy. *Political Analysis, 11*(3), 302–307.

Alwin, D. F., & Hauser, R. M. (1975). The decomposition of effects in path analysis. *American Sociological Review, 40*, 37–47.

Anderson, D. R. (2008). *Model-based inference in the life sciences: A primer on evidence.* New York: Springer.

Anderson, L. M., Petticrew, M., Rehfuess, E., Armstrong, R., Ueffing, E., Baker, P., et al. (2011). Using logic models to capture complexity in systematic reviews. *Research Synthesis Methods, 2*, 33–42.

Aneshensel, C. S. (2002). *Theory-based data analysis for the social sciences.* Thousand Oaks, CA: Sage.

Angrist, J. D., & Pischke, J.-S. (2009). *Mostly harmless econometrics: An empiricist's companion.* Princeton, NJ: Princeton University Press.

Anscombe, F. J. (1973, February). Graphs in statistical analysis. *American Statistician, 27*, 17–21.

Austin, J. L. (1962). *How to do things with words.* Oxford, UK: Oxford University Press.

Avery, P., Bird, K., Johnstone, S., Sullivan, J. L., & Thalhammer, K. (1992). Exploring political tolerance with adolescents. *Theory and Research in Social Education, 20*, 386–420.

Baccini, A., Barabesi, L., & Marcheselli, M.

(2009). How are statistical journals linked?: A network analysis. *Chance, 22*(3), 35–45.

Bachman, J. G., & O'Malley, P. M. (1984). Yea-saying, nay-saying, and going to extremes: Black–white differences in response styles. *Public Opinion Quarterly, 48*(2), 491–509.

Bail, C. A. (2012). The fringe effect: Civil society organizations and the evolution of media discourse about Islam since the September 11th attacks. *American Sociological Review, 77*, 855–879.

Baker-Doyle, K. (2011). *The networked teacher: How teachers build social networks for professional support.* New York: Teachers College Press.

Bakir, A., & Bakir, V. (2013). A critique of the capacity of Strauss' grounded theory for prediction, change, and control in organisational strategy via a grounded theorisation of leisure and cultural strategy. *Qualitative Report, 11*, 687–718.

Baldwin, S. A., Murray, D. M., & Shadish, W. R. (2005). Empirically supported treatments or type I errors?: Problems with the analysis of data from group-administered treatments. *Journal of Consulting and Clinical Psychology, 73*(5), 924.

Bandalos, D. L., & Boehm-Kaufman, M. R. (2009). Four common misconceptions in exploratory factor analysis. In C. E. Lance & R. J. Vandenberg (Eds.), *Statistical and methodological myths and urban legends: Doctrine, verity and fable in the organizational and social sciences* (pp. 61–87). New York: Routledge.

Bandalos, D. L., & Finney, S. J. (2010). Factor analysis: Exploratory and confirmatory. In G. R. Hancock & R. O. Mueller (Eds.), *The reviewer's guide to quantitative methods in the social sciences* (pp. 93–114). New York: Routledge.

Bandura, A. (2006). Guide for constructing self-efficacy scales. In T. Urdan & F. Pajares (Eds.), *Self-efficacy beliefs of adolescents* (pp. 307–337). New York: Information Age.

Bateson, G., & Mead, M. (1942). *Balinese character: A photographic analysis.* New York: New York Academy of Sciences.

Baumgartner, M. (2013). Detecting causal chains in small-*n* data. *Field Methods, 25*(1), 3–24.

Bax, L., Yu, L., Ikeda, N., & Moons, K. (2007). A systematic comparison of software dedicated to meta-analysis of causal studies. *BMC Medical Research Methodology, 7*, 40. Available at *www.ncbi.nlm.nih.gov/pmc/articles/PMC2048970.*

Bazeley, P. (2006). The contribution of computer software to integrating qualitative and quantitative data analysis. *Research in the Schools, 13*, 64–74.

Bazeley, P. (2007). *Qualitative data analysis with NVivo.* Thousand Oaks, CA: Sage.

Beach, D., & Pedersen, R. B. (2012). *Process-tracing methods.* Ann Arbor: University of Michigan Press.

Beatty, P. C., & Willis, G. B. (2007). Research synthesis: The practice of cognitive interviewing. *Public Opinion Quarterly, 71*, 287–311.

Becker, C. (1931). Everyman his own historian. *American Historical Review, 37*, 221–236.

Becker, H. S. (1958). Problems of inference and proof in participant observation. *American Sociological Review, 23*, 652–660.

Berger, J. O. (2000). Bayesian analysis: A look at today and thoughts of tomorrow. *Journal of the American Statistical Association, 95*, 1269–1276.

Berk, R. A. (2004). *Regression analysis: A constructive critique.* Thousand Oaks, CA: Sage.

Berk, R. A. (2006). An introduction to ensemble methods for data analysis. *Sociological Methods and Research, 34*(3), 263–295.

Bernard, H. R. (2000). *Social research methods: Qualitative and quantitative approaches.* Los Angeles: Sage.

Berri, D., Schmidt, M., & Brook, S. (2007). *The wages of wins: Taking the measure of the many myths in modern sports.* Stanford, CA: Stanford University Press.

Bickel, R. (2007). *Multilevel analysis for applied research: It's just regression!* New York: Guilford Press.

Biesanz, J. C., Deeb-Sossa, N., Papadakis, A. A., Bollen, K. A., & Curran, P. J. (2004). The role of coding time in estimating and interpreting growth curve models. *Psychological Methods, 9*(1), 30–52.

Blair, J., Czaja, R. F., & Blair, E. A. (2013). *Designing surveys: A guide to decisions and procedures.* Los Angeles: Sage.

Bland, J. M., & Altman, D. J. (1999). Measuring agreement in method comparison studies. *Statistical Methods in Medical Research, 8*, 135–160.

Bloom, H. S. (1984). Accounting for no-shows in

experimental evaluation designs. *Evaluation Review, 8*, 225–246.

Boas, F. (1911). *The mind of primitive man.* New York: Macmillan.

Bohannon, J. (2013). Who's afraid of peer review? *Science, 342*, 60–65.

Bond, T. G., & Fox, C. M. (2001). *Applying the Rasch model: Fundamental measurement issues in the human sciences.* Mahwah, NJ: Erlbaum.

Booth, W. C., Colomb, G. C., & Williams, J. M. (1995). *The craft of research.* Chicago: University of Chicago Press.

Borenstein, M., Hedges, L. V., Higgins, J. P. T., & Rothstein, H. R. (2010). A basic introduction to fixed-effect and random-effects models for meta-analysis. *Research Synthesis Methods, 1*, 97–111.

Borgatti, S. P., Mehra, A., Brass, D. J., & Labianca, G. (2009, February). Network analysis in the social sciences. *Science, 323*(5916), 892–895.

Borgerhoff Mulder, M. (2009). Serial monogamy as polygyny or polyandry? *Human Nature, 20*(2), 130–150.

Borooah, V. K. (2002). *Logit and probit: Ordered and multinomial models.* Thousand Oaks, CA: Sage.

Bosk, C. L. (2008). *What would you do? Juggling bioethics and ethnography.* Chicago: University of Chicago Press.

Boudon, R. (1991). What middle range theories are. *Contemporary Sociology, 20*(4), 519–522.

Bourdieu, P. (1965). *Un art moyen: Essai sur les usages sociaux de photographie.* Paris: Ed. du Minuit.

Bowen, G. A. (2008). Naturalistic inquiry and the saturation concept: A research note. *Qualitative Research, 8*(1), 137–152.

Bowen, G. A. (2009). Supporting a grounded theory with an audit trail: An illustration. *International Journal of Social Research Methodology, 12*(4), 305–316.

Boyd, D. M., & Ellison, N. B. (2010). Social network sites: Definition, history, and scholarship. *IEEE Engineering Management Review, 38*(3), 16–31.

Brady, H. E., & Collier, D. (Eds.). (2004). *Rethinking social inquiry: Diverse tools, shared standards.* Lanham, MD: Rowan & Littlefield.

Brambor, T., Clark, W. R., & Golder, M. (2006). Understanding interaction models: Improving empirical analysis. *Political Analysis, 14*, 63–82.

Brewer, J., & Hunter, A. (2006). *Foundations of multimethod research: Synthesizing styles.* Los Angeles: Sage.

Breznitz, D. (2007). *Innovation and the state: Political choice and strategies for growth in Israel, Taiwan, and Ireland.* New Haven, CT: Yale University Press.

Brown, C. H., & Witkowski, S. R. (1981). Figurative language in a universalist perspective. *American Ethnologist, 8*, 596–615.

Brown, T. A. (2006). *Confirmatory factor analysis for applied research.* New York: Guilford Press.

Bruggeman, J., Traag, V. A., & Uitermark, J. (2012). Detecting communities through network data. *American Sociological Review, 77*, 1050–1063.

Bruner, J. (2002). *Making stories: Law, literature, life.* Cambridge, MA: Harvard University Press.

Bruns, A., & Stieglitz, S. (2013). Towards more systematic Twitter analysis: Metrics for tweeting activities. *International Journal of Social Research Methodology, 16*, 1–18.

Bryant, A., & Charmaz, K. (Eds.). (2006). *The Sage handbook of grounded theory.* Los Angeles: Sage.

Bryant, F. B. (2000). Assessing the validity of measurement. In L. G. Grimm & P. R. Yarnold (Eds.), *Reading and understanding more multivariate statistics* (pp. 99–146). Washington, DC: American Psychological Association.

Bryman, A. (2006). Integrating quantitative and qualitative research: How is it done? *Qualitative Research, 6*(1), 97–113.

Buckley, J. (2004). Simple Bayesian inference for qualitative political research. *Political Analysis, 12*, 386–399.

Budaev, S. V. (2010). Using principal components and factor analysis in animal behaviour research: Caveats and guidelines. *Ethology, 116*(5), 472–480.

Burnham, K. P., & Anderson, D. R. (2004). Multimodel inference: Understanding AIC and BIC in model selection. *Sociological Methods and Research, 33*, 261–304.

Burnham, K. P., & Anderson, D. R. (2010). *Model selection and multimodel inference: A practical information-theoretic approach* (2nd ed.). New York: Springer.

Burnham, K. P., Anderson, D. R., & Huyvaert,

K. P. (2011). AIC model selection and multimodel inference in behavioral ecology: Some background, observations, and comparisons. *Behavioral Ecology and Sociobiology, 65*(1), 23–35.

Butler, J. (2008). The family diagram and genogram: Comparisons and contrasts. *American Journal of Family Therapy, 36* (3), 169–180.

Butterfield, H. (1931). *The Whig interpretation of history*. New York: Norton.

Butts, M. M., & Ng, T. W. H. (2009). Chopped liver? OK. Chopped data? Not OK. In C. E. Lance & R. J. Vandenberg (Eds.), *Statistical and methodological myths and urban legends: Doctrine, verity and fable in the organizational and social sciences* (pp. 361–386). New York: Routledge.

Cafri, G., Kromrey, J. D., & Brannick, M. T. (2010). A meta-meta-analysis: Empirical review of statistical power, type I error rates, effect sizes, and model selection of meta-analysis published in psychology. *Multivariate Behavioral Research, 45*, 239–270.

Calvey, D. (2008). The art and politics of covert research: Doing "situated ethics" in the field. *Sociology, 42*(5), 905–918.

Camparo, J., & Camparo, L. B. (2013). The analysis of Likert scales using state multipoles: An application of quantum methods to behavioral sciences data. *Journal of Educational and Behavioral Statistics, 38*, 81–101.

Campbell, D., & Stanley, J. (1963). *Experimental and quasi-experimental designs for research*. Chicago: Rand McNally.

Capps, C., & Wright, T. (2013). Toward a vision: Statistics and big data. *Amstatnews, 434*, 9–13.

Caracelli, V. T., & Greene, J. C. (1993). Data analysis strategies for mixed method evaluation designs. *Educational Evaluation and Policy Analysis, 15*(2), 195–207.

Card, D., & Krueger, A. B. (2000). Minimum wages and employment: A case study of the fast-food industry in New Jersey and Pennsylvania. *American Economic Review, 90*(5), 1397–1420.

Card, N. A. (2012). *Applied meta-analysis for social science research*. New York: Guilford Press.

Caren, N., & Panofsky, A. (2005). A technique for adding temporality to qualitative comparative analysis. *Sociological Methods and Research, 34*(2), 147–172.

Carlberg, C. (2013). *Predictive analytics*. Indianapolis, IN: Pearson.

Carolan, B. V., & Natriello, G. (2005, April). Data-mining journals and books: Using the science of networks to uncover the structure of the educational research community. *Educational Researcher, 34*, 25–33.

Castells, M. (1996). *The information age: Economy, society, and culture: Vol. 1. Rise of the network society*. Cambridge, UK: Blackwell.

Caster, O., Niklas-Noren, G., Madigan, D., & Bate, A. (2010). Large-scale regression-based pattern discovery: The example of screening the WHO global drug safety database. *Statistical Analysis and Data Mining, 3*, 197–208.

Catanese, S. A., De Meo, P., Ferrara, E., Fiumara, G., & Provetti, A. (2011). Crawling Facebook for social network analysis purposes. Available at *www.emilio.ferrara.name/wp-content/uploads/2011/06/71-catanese.pdf*.

Centers for Disease Control and Prevention. (2012, June 15). Helmet use among motorcyclists who died in crashes and economic cost savings associated with state motorcycle helmet laws—United States, 2008–2010. *Morbidity and Mortality Weekly Report, 61*(23), 425–430. Available at *www.cdc.gov/mmwr*.

Century, J., Rudnick, M., & Freeman, C. (2010). A framework for measuring fidelity of implementation: A foundation for shared language and accumulation of knowledge. *American Journal of Evaluation, 31*(2), 199–218.

Cha, M., Haddadi, H., Benevenuto, F., & Gummadi, K. P. (2010, May). Measuring user influence in Twitter: The million follower fallacy. In *Proceedings of the Fourth International AAAI Conference on Weblogs and Social Media* (Vol. 14, No. 1, p. 8). Palo Alto, CA: Association for the Advancement of Artificial Intelligence. Available at *www.aaai.org/ocs/index.php/ICWSM/ICWSM10/paper/download/1538/1826*.

Chamberlin, T. C. (1890). The method of multiple working hypotheses. *Science, 148*, 754–759.

Champkin, J. (2012). Amanda Cox: A life in statistics. *Significance, 9*(5), 28–33.

Chang, V. W., & Lauderdale, D. S. (2009). Fundamental cause theory, technological innovation and health disparities: The case of cholesterol in the era of statins. *Journal of Health and Social Behavior, 50*, 245–260.

Charmaz, K. (2006). *Constructing grounded*

theory: A practical guide through qualitative analysis. London: Sage.

Cheung, S. F., & Chan, D. K.-S. (2008). Dependent correlations in meta-analysis: The case of heterogeneous dependence. *Educational and Psychological Measurement, 68*, 760–777.

Cheung, S. F., & Chan, D. K.-S. (2009). A two-stage approach to synthesizing covariance matrices in meta-analytic structural equation modeling. *Structural Equation Modeling, 16*, 28–53.

Chi, R. P., & Snyder, A. W. (2011). Facilitate insight by non-invasive brain stimulation. *PLoS ONE, 6*(2), e16655.

Christakis, N. A., & Fowler, J. H. (2009). *Connected: How your friends' friends' friends affect everything you feel, think, and do*. New York: Little, Brown.

Christian, L. M., Dillman, D. A., & Smyth, J. D. (2007). Helping respondents get it right the first time: The influence of words, symbols, and graphics in web surveys. *Public Opinion Quarterly, 71*, 113–125.

Cizek, G. J. (Ed.). (2001). *Setting performance standards*. Mahwah, NJ: Erlbaum.

Clandinin, D. J. (Ed.). (2007). *Handbook of narrative inquiry: Mapping a methodology*. Thousand Oaks, CA: Sage.

Clarke, P., & Wheaton, B. (2007). Addressing data sparseness in contextual population research using cluster analysis to create synthetic neighborhoods. *Sociological Methods and Research, 35*(3), 311–351.

Coffey, A., & Atkinson, P. (1996). *Making sense of qualitative data: Complementary research strategies*. London: Sage.

Cohen, J. (1983). The cost of dichotomization. *Applied Psychological Measurement, 7*, 249–253.

Cohen, J., Cohen, P., West, S., & Aiken, L. (2003). *Applied multiple regression/correlation analysis for the behavioral sciences* (3rd ed.). London: Erlbaum.

Cohen, K. B., & Hunter, L. (2008). Getting started in text mining. *PLoS Computational Biology, 4*(1), e20.

Cole, J. C. (2008). How to deal with missing data. In J. W. Osborne (Ed.), *Best practices in quantitative methods* (pp. 214–238). Los Angeles: Sage.

Cook, T. D., & Campbell, D. T. (1979). *Quasi-experimentation: Design and analysis issues for field settings*. Boston: Houghton Mifflin.

Cooper, H. (2010). *Research synthesis and meta-analysis: A step-by-step approach* (4th ed.). Los Angeles: Sage.

Corbin, J., & Strauss, A. (2008). *Basics of qualitative research: Techniques and procedures for developing grounded theory*. Los Angeles: Sage.

Corder, G. W., & Foreman, D. I. (2009). *Nonparametric statistics for non-statisticians: A step-by-step approach*. New York: Wiley.

Cortina, J. M. (1993). What is coefficient alpha? An examination of theory and applications. *Journal of Applied Psychology, 78*(1), 98.

Creese, A., Bhatt, A., Bhojani, N., & Martin, P. (2008). Fieldnotes in team ethnography: Researching complementary schools. *Qualitative Research, 8*, 197–215.

Creswell, J. W. (2007). *Qualitative inquiry and research design: Choosing among five approaches*. Los Angeles: Sage.

Creswell, J. W., & Clark, V. L. P. (2010). *Designing and conducting mixed methods research* (2nd ed.). Thousand Oaks, CA: Sage.

Cronbach, L. J., & Shavelson, R. J. (2004). My current thoughts on coefficient alpha and successor procedures. *Educational and Psychological Measurement, 64*, 391–418.

Cross, R., & Parker, A. (2004). *The hidden power of social networks: Understanding how work really gets done in organizations*. Cambridge, MA: Harvard Business School Press.

Cullen, J. B., Jacob, B. A., & Levitt, S. (2006). The effect of school choice on participants: Evidence from randomized lotteries. *Econometrica, 74*, 1191–1230.

Culyba, R. J., Heimer, C. A., & Petty, J. C. (2004). The ethnographic turn: Fact, fashion, or fiction? *Qualitative Sociology, 27*(4), 365–389.

Cumming, G. (2008). Replication and *p* intervals: *p* values predict the future only vaguely, but confidence intervals do much better. *Perspectives on Psychological Science, 3*(4), 286–300.

Cumming, G. (2012). *Understanding the new statistics: Effect sizes, confidence intervals, and meta-analysis*. New York: Routledge.

Curran-Everett, D. (2012). Explorations in statistics: Permutation methods. *Advances in Physiology Education, 36*(3), 181–187.

Daston, L. J., & Galison, P. (2007). *Objectivity*. New York: Zone Books.

David, H. A. (2009). A historical note on zero

correlation and independence. *American Statistician, 63*(2), 185–186.

Davidson, F. (1996). *Principles of statistical data handling.* Los Angeles: Sage.

de Winter, J. C. F., Dodou, D., & Wieringa, P. A. (2009). Exploratory factor analysis with small sample sizes. *Multivariate Behavioral Research, 44*(2), 147–181.

Dean, D. R., & Vogt, W. P. (2012). *Truth in tuition: A study of guaranteed tuition's effects on undergraduate students in Illinois public higher education.* Indianapolis, IN: Lumina Foundation.

Dedrick, R. F., Ferron, J. M., Hess, M. R., Hogarty, K. Y., Kromrey, J. D., Lang, T. R., et al. (2009). Multilevel modeling: A review of methodological issues and applications. *Review of Educational Research, 79*(1), 69–102.

Dee, T. (2004). Are there civic returns to education? *Journal of Public Economics, 88*, 1697–1720.

DeHoogh, A. H. B., & Den Hartog, D. N. (2008). Ethical and despotic leadership, relationships with leaders' social responsibility, top management team effectiveness and subordinates' optimism: A multi-method study. *Leadership Quarterly, 19*, 297–311.

DeMaris, A. (2002). Explained variance in logistic regression: A Monte Carlo study of proposed measures. *Sociological Methods and Research, 31*, 27–74.

Denson, N., & Seltzer, M. H. (2011). Meta-analysis in higher education: An illustrative example using hierarchical linear modeling. *Research in Higher Education, 52*, 215–244.

DesJardins, S. L., McCall, B. P., Ott, M., & Kim, J. (2010). A quasi-experimental investigation of how the Gates Millennium Scholars program is related to college students' time use and activities. *Educational Evaluation and Policy Analysis, 32*, 456–475.

DeVellis, R. F. (2011). *Scale development: Theory and applications.* Los Angeles: Sage.

Dey, I. (2007). Grounding categories. In A. Bryant & K. Charmaz (Eds.), *Sage handbook of grounded theory* (pp. 167–190). London: Sage.

Dixon-Woods, M., Bonas, S., Booth, A., Jones, D. R., Miller, T., Sutton, A. J., et al. (2006). How can systematic reviews incorporate qualitative research?: A critical perspective. *Qualitative Research, 6*(1), 27–44.

Dixon-Woods, M., Booth, A., & Sutton, A. J. (2007). Synthesizing qualitative research: A review of published reports. *Qualitative Research, 7*, 375–422.

Doherty, P. F., White, G. C., & Burnham, K. P. (2012). Comparison of model building and selection strategies. *Journal of Ornithology, 152*(2), 317–323.

Dourdouma, A., & Mörtl, K. (2012). The creative journey of grounded theory analysis: A guide to its principles and applications. *Research in Psychotherapy: Psychopathology, Process and Outcome, 15*(2), 96–106.

Dovidio, J. F., Gaertner, S. L., Stewart, T. L., Esses, V. M., ten Vergert, M., & Hodson, G. (2004). From intervention to outcome: Processes in the reduction of bias. In W. G. Stephan & W. P. Vogt (Eds.), *Education programs for improving intergroup relations: Theory, research, and practice* (pp. 243–265). New York: Teachers' College Press.

Driscoll, D. L., Appiah-Yeboah, A., Salib, P., & Rupert, D. G. (2007). Merging qualitative and quantitative data in mixed methods research: How to and why not. *Ecological and Environmental Anthropology, 3*(1), 19–28.

Drometer, M., & Rincke, J. (2009). The impact of ballot access restrictions on electoral competition: Evidence from a natural experiment. *Public Choice, 138*, 461–474.

Drury, J., & Stott, C. (2001). Bias as a research strategy in participant observation: The case of intergroup conflict. *Field Methods, 13*(1), 47–67.

Duncan, O. D. (1966). Path analysis: Sociological examples. *American Journal of Sociology, 72*, 1–16.

Duncan, O. D., & Stenbeck, M. (1987). Are Likert scales unidimensional? *Social Science Research, 16*(3), 245–259.

Duneier, M. (1994). *Slim's table.* Chicago: University of Chicago Press.

Duneier, M. (1999). *Sidewalk.* New York: Farrar, Straus, & Giroux.

Dunne, C. (2011). The place of the literature review in grounded theory research. *International Journal of Social Research Methodology, 14*(2), 111–124.

Durkheim, E. (2010). *Suicide: A sociological study.* New York: Simon & Schuster. (Original work published 1897)

Dyson, G. (2012). *Turing's cathedral: The origins of the digital universe.* New York: Pantheon.

Eby, J., Kitchen, P., & Williams, A. (2012). Perceptions of quality of life in Hamilton's neighbourhood hubs: A qualitative analysis. *Social Indicators Research, 108*, 299–315.

Edgell, P., Gerteis, J., & Hartmann, D. (2006). Atheists as "other": Moral boundaries and cultural membership in American society. *American Sociological Review, 71*, 211–234.

Edwards, J. R. (2001). Ten difference score myths. *Organizational Research Methods, 4*, 265–287.

Efron, B. (1986). Why isn't everyone a Bayesian? *American Statistician, 40*, 1–5.

Ehrenreich, B. (2011). *Nickel and dimed: On (not) getting by in America* (with a new Afterword). New York: Picador Books.

Eliason, S. R. (1993). *Maximum likelihood estimation: Logic and practice*. Thousand Oaks, CA: Sage.

Eliason, S. R., & Stryker, R. (2009). Goodness-of-fit tests and descriptive measures in fuzzy-set analysis. *Sociological Methods and Research, 38*(1), 102–146.

Embretson, S. E., & Reise, S. P. (2000). *Item response theory for psychologists*. New York: Wiley.

Emerson, J. W., & Arnold, T. B. (2011). Statistical sleuthing by leveraging human nature: A study of Olympic figure skating. *American Statistician, 65*, 143–148.

Emerson, R. M., Fretz, R. I., & Shaw, L. L. (1995). *Writing ethnographic fieldnotes*. Chicago: University of Chicago Press.

Enders, C. K. (2010). *Applied missing data analysis*. New York: Guilford Press.

Erikson, K. T. (1976). *Everything in its path: Destruction of community in the Buffalo Creek flood*. New York: Simon & Schuster.

Ezzati, M., Friedman, A. B., Kulkarni, S. C., & Murray, C. L. L. (2008). The reversal of fortunes: Trends in county mortality disparities in the United States. *PLoS Medicine, 5*(4). Available at *www.plosmedicine.org*.

Faul, F., Erdfelder, E., Lang, A.-G., & Buchner, A. (2007). G*Power 3: A flexible statistical power analysis program for the social, behavioral, and biomedical sciences. *Behavior Research Methods, 39*, 175–191.

Fay, M. P., & Proschan, M. A. (2010). Wilcoxon–Mann–Whitney or *t*-test? On assumptions for hypothesis tests and multiple interpretations of decision rules. *Statistics Surveys, 4*, 1–39.

Feldman, G. (2011). If ethnography is more than participant-observation, then relations are more than connections: The case for nonlocal ethnography in a world of apparatuses. *Anthropological Theory, 11*(4), 375–395.

Fereday, J., & Muir-Cochrane, E. (2006). Demonstrating rigor using thematic analysis: A hybrid approach of inductive and deductive coding and theme development. *International Journal of Qualitative Methods, 3*(1), 80–92.

Ferry, G. (2013). Science today, history tomorrow. *Nature, 493*, 19–21.

Few, S. (2012). *Show me the numbers* (2nd ed.). Burlingame, CA: Analytics Press.

Finch, H. (2010). Using item response theory to understand gender differences in opinions on women in politics. *Chance, 23*, 19–24.

Finfgeld, D. L. (2003). Metasynthesis: The state of the art—so far. *Qualitative Health Research, 13*, 893–904.

Finn, J. D., & Achilles, C. M. (1999). Tennessee's class size study: Findings, implications, misconceptions. *Educational Evaluation and Policy Analysis, 21*, 97–109.

Firth, R. (1936). *We the Tikopia: A sociological study of kinship in primitive Polynesia*. London: Allen & Unwin.

Fischer, C. T. (2009). Bracketing in qualitative research: Conceptual and practical matters. *Psychotherapy Research, 19*, 583–590.

Fischer, M. (2011). Social network analysis and qualitative comparative analysis: Their mutual benefit for the explanation of policy network structures. *Methodological Innovations Online, 6*(2), 27–51.

Fisher, J. A., & Kalbaugh, C. A. (2012). United States private-sector physicians and pharmaceutical contract research: A qualitative study. *PLoS Medicine, 9*(7), e1001271.

Fiss, P. C. (2011). Building better causal theories: A fuzzy set approach to typologies in organization research. *Academy of Management Journal, 54*(2), 393–420.

Fortin, M., Dionne, J., Pinho, G., Gignac, J., Almirall, J., & Lapointe, L. (2006). Randomized controlled trials: Do they have external validity for patients with multiple comorbidities? *Annals of Family Medicine, 4*, 104–108.

Fowler, F. J. (1995). *Improving survey questions*. Thousand Oaks, CA: Sage.

Fowler, F. J. (2008). *Survey research methods* (4th ed.). Thousand Oaks, CA: Sage.

Fox, J. (2008). *Applied regression and generalized linear models* (2nd ed.). Thousand Oaks, CA: Sage.

Fox, J., Byrnes, J. E., Boker, S., & Neale, M. C. (2012). Structural equation modeling in R with the sem and OpenMx packages. In R. H. Hoyle (Ed.), *Handbook of structural equation modeling* (pp. 325–340). New York: Guilford Press.

Franzosi, R. (2010). *Quantitative narrative analysis*. Los Angeles: Sage.

Freedman, D., Pisani, R., & Purves, R. (1998). *Statistics* (3rd ed.). New York: Norton.

Freedman, D. A. (2009). *Statistical models: Theory and practice* (rev. ed.). New York: Cambridge University Press.

Freelon, D. G. (2010). ReCal: Intercoder reliability calculation as a web service. *International Journal of Internet Science, 5*, 20–33.

Freese, J. (2007). Replication standards for quantitative social science. *Sociological Methods and Research, 36*, 153–172.

Friedman, L., & Wall, M. (2005). Graphical views of suppression and multicollinearity in multiple linear regression. *American Statistician, 59*(2), 127–136.

Friese, S. (2006). Software and fieldwork. In D. Hobbs & R. Wright (Eds.), *Sage handbook of fieldwork* (pp. 309–332). Los Angeles: Sage.

Fritz, C., Curtin, J., Poitevineau, J., Morrel-Samuels, P., & Tao, F. (2012). Player preferences among new and old violins. *Proceedings of the National Academy of Sciences*. Available at *www.pnas.org/content/early/2012/01/02/1114999109*.

Fritzsche, E. (2013). Making hermeneutics explicit: How QCA supports an insightful dialogue between theory and cases. *International Journal of Social Research Methodology*. Available at *www.tandfonline.com/doi/full/10.1080/13645579.2013.779778#.UnPkkPvD85s*.

Funnel, S. C., & Rogers, P. J. (2011). *Purposeful program theory: Effective use of theories of change and logic models*. San Francisco: Jossey-Bass.

Gaddis, S. M., & Verdery, A. M. (2012, October). *Using Google Trends in social science research: Predicting demographic trends and social movements*. Paper presented at the annual meeting of the American Evaluation Association, Minneapolis, MN.

Gaines, B. J., Kuklinski, J. H., & Quirk, P. J. (2007). The logic of the survey experiment reexamined. *Political Analysis, 15*, 1–20.

Gajewski, B. J., & Simon, S. D. (2008). A one-hour training seminar on Bayesian statistics for nursing graduate students. *American Statistician, 62*(3), 190–194.

Gans, H. J. (1968). The participant-observer as a human being: Observations on the personal aspects of field work. In H. S. Becker (Ed.), *Institutions and the person* (pp. 300–317). Chicago: Aldine.

Garfield, E. (1955). Citation indexes for science: A new dimension in documentation through association of ideas. *Science, 122*, 108–111.

Garfinkel, H. (1967). *Studies in ethnomethodology*. Englewood Cliffs, NJ: Prentice Hall.

Garson, G. D. (2005). Path analysis. Available at *http://scholar.google.com/scholar?hl=en&q=Garson+path+analysis*.

Gauchat, G. (2012). Politicization of science in the public sphere: A study of public trust in the United States, 1974 to 2010. *American Sociological Review, 77*, 167–187.

Gee, J. P. (2005). *An introduction to discourse analysis: Theory and method*. London: Routledge.

Geertz, C. (1988). *Works and lives*. Palo Alto, CA: Stanford University Press.

Gelman, A. (2008). Teaching Bayes to graduate students in political science, sociology, public health, education, economics. *American Statistician, 62*(3), 195–198.

Gelman, A., Carlin, J. B., Stern, H. S., & Rubin, D. B. (2003). *Bayesian data analysis* (2nd ed.). London: CRC Press.

Gelman, A., & Robert, C. P. (2013). "Not only defended but also applied": The perceived absurdity of Bayesian inference (with commentary and replies). *American Statistician, 67*(1), 1–17.

George, A. L. (1979). Case studies and theory development: The method of structured, focused comparison. In P. G. Lauren (Ed.), *Diplomacy: New approaches in history, theory, and policy*. New York: Free Press.

George, A. L., & Bennett, A. (2005). *Case studies and theory development in the social sciences*. Cambridge, MA: MIT Press.

Gerring, J. (2007). *Case study research: Principles and practices*. Cambridge, UK: Cambridge University Press.

Ghani, K. R., Grigor, K., Tulloch, D. N., Bollina, P. R., & McNeil, S. A. (2005). Trends in reporting Gleason Scores 1991 to 2001: Changes in the pathologists' practice. *European Urology, 47*, 196–201.

Gigerenzer, G. (2004). Mindless statistics. *Journal of Socio-Economics, 33*(5), 587–606.
Giles, J. (2012). Making the links. *Nature, 488*, 448–450.
Gill, J. (2008). *Bayesian methods: A social and behavioral sciences approach* (2nd ed.). London: Chapman & Hall/CRC.
Gilpin, A. R. (2008). $r_{equivalent}$, meta-analysis, and robustness: An empirical examination of Rosenthal and Rubin's effect size estimator. *Education and Paychological Measurement, 68*, 42–57.
Gjoka, M., Kurant, M., Butts, C. T., & Markopoulou, A. (2010, March). Walking in Facebook: A case study of unbiased sampling of OSNs. Available at *www.minasgjoka.com/papers/unbiasedsampling-infocom2010.pdf*.
Glaser, B. G. (1978). *Theoretical sensitivity: Advances in the methodology of grounded theory* (Vol. 2). Mill Valley, CA: Sociology Press.
Glaser, B. G. (2006). Doing formal theory. In A. Bryant & K. Charmaz (Eds.), *The Sage handbook of grounded theory* (pp. 97–113). Los Angeles: Sage.
Glaser, B. G. (2012). Stop. Write! Writing grounded theory. *Grounded Theory Review, 11*(1), 2–11.
Glaser, B. G., & Strauss, A. L. (1967). *The discovery of grounded theory: Strategies for qualitative research*. New Brunswick, NJ: Aldine.
Glass, G. V. (1977). Integrating findings: The meta-analysis of research, *Review of Research in Education, 5*, 351–379.
Glass, G. V., Peckham, P. D., & Sanders, J. R. (1972). Consequences of failure to meet assumptions underlying the fixed effects analyses of variance and covariance. *Review of Educational Research, 42*(3), 237–288.
Goerres, A., & Prinzen, K. (2012). Can we improve the measurement of attitudes toward the welfare state? A constructive critique of survey instruments with evidence from focus groups. *Social Indicators Research, 109*, 515–534.
Goertz, G. (2006). *Social science concepts: A user's guide*. Princeton, NJ: Princeton University Press.
Goffman, E. (1961). *Asylums: Essays on the social situation of mental patients and other inmates*. New York: Anchor Books.
Golder, S. A., & Macy, M. W. (2011). Diurnal and seasonal mood vary with work, sleep, and daylength across diverse cultures. *Science, 333*, 1878–1881.
Goldkuhl, G., & Cronholm, S. (2010). Adding theoretical grounding to grounded theory: Toward multi-grounded theory. *International Journal of Qualitative Methods, 9*(2), 187–205.
Goldschmidt, N., & Szmrecsanyi, B. (2007). What do economists talk about? A linguistic analysis of published writing in economic journals. *American Journal of Economics and Sociology, 66*, 335–378.
Gonzalez, R. (2009). *Data analysis for experimental designs*. New York: Guilford Press.
Good, P. I. (2005a). *Introduction to statistics through resampling methods*. New York: Wiley/Jossey-Bass.
Good, P. I. (2005b). *Permutation, parametric and bootstrap tests of hypotheses* (3rd ed.). New York: Springer.
Good, P. I. (2013). *Introduction to statistics through resampling methods and R*. New York: Wiley.
Goody, J. (1986). *The logic of writing and the organization of society*. Cambridge, UK: Cambridge University Press.
Graham, J. M. (2008). The general linear model as structural equation modeling. *Journal of Educational and Behavioral Statistics, 33*(4), 485–506.
Granovetter, M. S. (1973). The strength of weak ties. *American Journal of Sociology, 78*, 1360–1380.
Grant, R. (2013). A life in statistics: Nathan Yau. *Significance, 10*, 32–35.
Greer, D., Varelas, P. N., Haque, S., & Wijdicks, E. F. M. (2008). Variability of brain death determination guidelines in leading U.S. neurologic institutions. *Neurology, 70*, 284–289.
Grendstad, G. (2007). Causal complexity and party preference. *European Journal of Political Research, 46*(1), 121–149.
Grissom, R. J., & Kim, J. J. (2005). *Effect sizes for research: A broad practical approach*. Mahwah, NJ: Erlbaum.
Grofman, B., & Schneider, C. Q. (2009). An introduction to crisp set QCA, with a comparison to binary logistic regression. *Political Research Quarterly, 62*(4), 662–672.
Guzmán, D. (2011). Speaking stats to justice: Expert testimony in a Guatemalan human

rights trial based on statistical sampling. *Chance Magazine, 24*(3), 23–29.

Haahr, M. T., & Hrobjartsson, A. (2006). Who is blinded in randomized clinical trials?: A study of 200 trials and a survey of authors. *Clinical Trials, 3*, 360–365.

Habermas, J. (1990). *The philosophical discourse of modernity: Twelve lectures.* Cambridge, MA: MIT Press.

Haeffele, L., Baker, P. J., & Pacha, J. (2007). The Illinois best practice school study (Research & Policy Brief No. 1-2007). Normal: Illinois State University, Center for the Study of Education Policy.

Hallberg, L. (2010). Some thoughts about the literature review in grounded theory studies. *International Journal of Qualitative Studies on Health and Well-Being, 5*(3), 1.

Hammersley, M. (2010). Reproducing or constructing?: Some questions about transcription in social research. *Qualitative Research, 10*, 553–569.

Hammersley, M. (2011). Objectivity: A reconceptualization. In M. Williams & W. P. Vogt (Eds.), *The Sage handbook of innovations in social research methodology* (pp. 25–43). London: Sage.

Hancock, G. R., & Mueller, R. O. (Eds.). (2010). *The reviewer's guide to quantitative methods in the social sciences.* New York: Routledge.

Harder, T., & Pappi, F. U. (1969). Multiple-level regression analysis of survey and ecological data. *Social Science Information, 8*(5), 43–67.

Harlan, S. L., Declet-Barreto, J. H., Stefanov, W. L., & Petitti, D. B. (2013). Neighborhood effects on heat deaths: Social and environmental predictors of vulnerability in Maricopa County, Arizona. *Environmental Health Perspectives, 121*(2), 197–204.

Harper, D. (1988). Visual sociology: Expanding sociological vision. *American Sociologist, 21*, 54–70.

Harris, M. (1980). *Cultural materialism: The struggle for a science of culture.* New York: Vintage.

Harrison, G. W., List, J. A., & Towe, C. (2007). Naturally occurring preferences and exogenous laboratory experiments: A case study of risk aversion. *Econometrica, 75*, 433–458.

Harry, B., Sturges, K. M., & Klingner, J. K. (2005). Mapping the process: An exemplar of process and challenge in grounded theory analysis. *Educational Researcher, 34*(2), 3–13.

Hartwig, F., & Dearing, B. E. (1979). *Exploratory data analysis.* Newbury Park, CA: Sage.

Hastie, T., Tibshirani, R., & Friedman, J. (2009). *The elements of statistical learning: Data mining, inference, and prediction* (2nd ed.). New York: Springer.

Hayano, D. M. (1979). Auto-ethnography: Paradigms, problems, and prospects. *Human Organization, 38*(1), 99–104.

Hayano, D. M. (1982). *Poker faces: The life and work of professional card players.* Los Angeles: University of California Press.

Hayano, K. (2012, August). *Referents of self-deprecations: Negotiating ownership and responsibility in interaction.* Paper presented at the annual meeting of the American Sociological Association, Denver, CO.

Hayes, A. F. (2013). *Introduction to mediation, moderation, and conditional process analysis: A regression-base approach.* New York: Guilford Press.

Hayes, A. F., & Krippendorf, K. (2007). Answering the call for a standard reliability measure for coding data. *Communication Methods and Measures, 1*(1), 77–89.

Hayton, J. C., Allen, D. G., & Scarpello, V. (2004). Factor retention decisions in exploratory factor analysis: A tutorial on parallel analysis. *Organizational Research Methods,* 7(2), 191–205.

Heck, R. H., Thomas, S. L., & Tabata, L. N. (2010). *Multilevel and longitudinal modeling with IBM SPSS.* New York: Routledge/Taylor & Francis.

Hedges, L. V. (2011). Effect sizes in three-level cluster-randomized experiments. *Journal of Educational and Behavioral Statistics, 36*, 346–380.

Hedges, L. V., & Hedberg, E. C. (2007). Intraclass correlation values for planning group-randomized trials in education. *Educational Evaluation and Policy Analysis, 29*, 60–87.

Hellström, J. (2011). Conditional hypotheses in comparative social science: Mixed-method approaches to middle-sized data analysis. *Methodological Innovations Online,* 6(2), 71–102.

Henig, R. M. (2000). *The monk in the garden: The lost and found genius of Gregor Mendel, the father of genetics.* New York: Mariner Books.

Henson, R. K., & Roberts, J. K. (2006). Use of exploratory factor analysis in published research: Common errors and some comment on improved practice. *Educational and Psychological Measurement, 66*(3), 393–416.

Herrera, Y. M., & Kapur, D. (2007). Improving data quality: Actors, incentives, and capabilities. *Political Analysis, 15*, 365–386.

Hessler, R. M., Downing, J., Beltz, C., Pelliccio, A., Powell, M., & Vale, W. (2003). Qualitative research on adolescents' risk using e-mail: A methodological assessment. *Qualitative Sociology, 26*(1), 111–124.

Himelboim, I., McCreery, S., & Smith, M. (2013). Birds of a feather tweet together: Integrating network and content analyses to examine cross-ideology exposure on Twitter. *Journal of Computer-Mediated Communication, 18*(2), 40–60.

Hoenig, J. M., & Heisey, D. M. (2001). The abuse of power. *American Statistician, 55*(1), 1–6.

Hogan, T. P., & Agnello, J. (2004). An empirical study of reporting practices concerning measurement validity. *Educational and Psychological Measurement, 64*, 802–812.

Hogarty, K. Y., Hines, C. V., Kromrey, J. D., Ferron, J. M., & Mumford, K. R. (2005). The quality of factor solutions in exploratory factor analysis: The influence of sample size, communality, and overdetermination. *Educational and Psychological Measurement, 65*(2), 202–226.

Hollis, S., & Campbell, F. (1999). What is meant by intention to treat analysis? Survey of published randomised controlled trials. *British Medical Journal, 319*, 670–679.

Holton, J. A. (2007). The coding process and its challenges. In A. Bryant & K. Charmaz (Eds.), *The Sage handbook of grounded theory* (pp. 265–289). London: Sage.

Honaker, J., Joseph, A., King, G., Scheve, K., & Singh, N. (1999). *Amelia: A program for missing data.* Cambridge, MA: Harvard University. Available at *http://GKing.Harvard.edu.*

Hooker, R. (2013). *Of the laws of ecclesiastical polity.* Oxford, UK: Oxford University Press.

Horne, C., Dodoo, F. N. A., & Dodoo, N. D. (2013). The shadow of indebtedness: Bridewealth and norms constraining female reproductive autonomy. *American Sociological Review, 78*(3), 503–520.

Horton, N. J., & Kleinman, K. P. (2007). Much ado about nothing: A comparison of missing data methods and software to fit incomplete data regression models. *American Statistician, 61*, 79–90.

Hosack, B., Lim, B., & Vogt, W. P. (2012). Incorporating the use of web services in introductory programming classrooms: Results from a series of quasi-experiments. *Journal of Information Systems Education, 23*, 373–384.

Howell, D. C. (2007). The treatment of missing data. In W. Outhwaite & S. Turner, *The Sage handbook of social science methodology* (pp. 208–224). Thousand Oaks, CA: Sage.

Howell, R. T., & Shields, A. L. (2008). The file drawer problem in reliability generalization. *Educational and Psychological Measurement, 68*, 120–128.

Hoyle, R. H. (Ed.). (2012). *Handtbook of structural equation modeling.* New York: Guilford Press.

Hruschka, D. J., Schwartz, D., St. John, D. C., Picone-Decaro, E., Jenkins, R. A., & Carey, J. W. (2004). Reliability in coding open-ended data: Lessons learned from HIV behavioral research. *Field Methods, 16*, 307–331.

Huber, M. (2012). Identification of average treatment effects in social experiments under alternative forms of attrition, *Journal of Educational and Behavioral Statistics, 37*, 443–474.

Huberman, B., Romero, D., & Wu, F. (2008). Social networks that matter: Twitter under the microscope. Available at *www.hpl.hp.com/research/scl/papers/twitter/twitter.pdf.*

Huberty, C. J. (2002). A history of effect size indices. *Educational and Psychological Measurement, 62*(2), 227–240.

Huberty, C. J. (2003). Multiple correlation versus multiple regression. *Educational and Psychological Measurement, 63*, 271–278.

Hudson, J., & Kühner, S. (2009). Towards productive welfare?: A comparative analysis of 23 OECD countries. *Journal of European Social Policy, 19*(1), 34–46.

Hughes, S., Pennington, J. L., & Makris, S. (2012). Translating autoethnography across the AERA standards: Toward understanding autoethnographic scholarship as empirical research. *Educational Researcher, 41*, 209–219.

Husserl, E. (1962). *Ideas: General introduction to pure phenomenology* (W. R. B. Gibson, Trans.). New York: Collier. (Original work published 1913)

Ibrahim, J. G., & Molenberghs, G. (2009). Missing data methods in longitudinal studies: A review. *Test, 18*, 1–43.

Inbau, F. E., Reid, J. E., & Buckley, J. P. (2011). *Criminal interrogation and confessions* (5th ed.). New York: Jones & Bartlett Learning.

Ingersoll, R. M., & Strong, M. (2011). The impact of induction and mentoring programs for beginning teachers: A critical review of the research. *Review of Educational Research, 81*, 201–233.

Ioannidis, J. P. (2008). Why most discovered true associations are inflated. *Epidemiology, 19*, 640–648.

Ioannidis, J. P. (2010). Meta-research: The art of getting it wrong. *Research Synthesis Methods, 1*, 169–184.

Ioannidis, J. P., & Trikalinos, T. A. (2007). An exploratory test for an excess of significant findings. *Clinical Trials, 4*, 245–253.

Irwin, K. (2006). Into the dark heart of ethnography: The lived ethics and inequality of intimate field relationships. *Qualitative Sociology, 29*(2), 155–175.

Ivankova, N. V., Creswell, J. W., & Stick, S. L. (2006). Using mixed-methods sequential explanatory design: From theory to practice. *Field Methods, 18*(1), 3–20.

Iversen, G. R. (1984). *Bayesian statistical inference*. Thousand Oaks, CA: Sage.

Jaccard, J., Guilamo-Ramos, V., Johansson, M., & Bouris, A. (2006). Multiple regression analyses in clinical child and adolescent psychology. *Journal of Clinical Child and Adolescent Psychology, 35*(3), 456–479.

Jaccard, J., & Jacoby, J. (2010). *Theory construction and model-building skills: A practical guide for social scientists*. New York: Guilford Press.

Jaccard, J., Turrisi, R., & Wan, C. K. (1990). *Interaction effects in multiple regression*. Newbury Park, CA: Sage.

Jacobs, B. A. (2006). The case for dangerous fieldwork. In D. Hobbs & R. Wright (Eds.), *The Sage handbook of fieldwork* (pp. 157–168). Los Angeles: Sage.

Jagsi, R., Guancial, E. A., Worobey, C. C., Henault, L. E., Chang, Y., Starr, R., et al. (2006). The "gender gap" in authorship of academic medical literature: A 35-year perspective. *New England Journal of Medicine, 355*, 281–287.

Jemal, A., Ward, E., Anderson, R. N., Murray, T., & Thun, M. J. (2008). Widening of socioeconomic inequalities in U.S. death rates, 1993–2001. *PLoS ONE, 3*(5). Available at *www.plosone.org*.

Jesson, J. K., Matheson, L., & Lacey, F. M. (2011). *Doing your literature review: Traditional and systematic techniques*. London: Sage.

Johnson, J. M. (2001). In-depth interviewing. In J. F. Gubrium & J. A. Holstein (Eds.), *Handbook of interview research* (pp. 103–119). Thousand Oaks, CA: Sage.

Johnson, R. B., & Onwuegbuzie, A. J. (2004). Mixed methods research: A research paradigm whose time has come. *Educational Researcher, 33*(7), 14–26.

Johnson, S. (2006). *The ghost map: The story of London's most terrifying epidemic*. New York: Riverhead Books.

Jones, D. K. (2001). Researching groups of lives: A collective biography perspective. *Qualitative Research, 1*(3), 325–346.

Jose, P. E. (2013). *Doing statistical mediation and moderation*. New York: Guilford Press.

Kahn, J. H. (2011). Multilevel modeling: Overview and applications to research in counseling psychology. *Journal of Counseling Psychology, 58*(2), 257–271.

Kahneman, D. (2011). *Thinking, fast and slow*. New York: Farrar, Straus, & Giroux.

Kalkhoff, W., & Thye, S. R. (2006). Expectation states theory and research. *Sociological Methods and Research, 35*, 219–249.

Kanji, G. K. (1999). *100 statistical tests* (2nd ed.). London: Sage.

Kaplan, B., & Duchon, D. (1988). Combining quantitative and qualitative methods: A case study. *MIS Quarterly, 12*, 571–586.

Keeling, K. B., & Pavur, R. J. (2012). Statistical accuracy of spreadsheet software. *American Statistician, 65*, 265–273.

Kelle, U. (2007a). Computer-assisted qualitative data analysis. In C. Seale, D. Silverman, J. F. Gubrium, & G. Gobo (Eds.), *Qualitative research practice* (pp. 443–459). London: Sage.

Kelle, U. (2007b). The development of categories: Different approaches in grounded theory. In A. Bryant & K. Charmaz (Eds.), *The Sage handbook of grounded theory* (pp. 191–213). London: Sage.

Kelley, K., & Rausch, J. R. (2006). Sample size planning for the standardized mean difference: Accuracy in parameter estimation via narrow confidence intervals. *Psychological Methods, 11*, 363–385.

Kennedy, C. H. (2005). *Single-case designs for educational research*. Boston: Allyn & Bacon.

Kennedy, M. M. (2008). Contributions of qualitative research to research on teacher qualifications. *Educational Evaluation and Policy Analysis, 30*(4), 344–367.

Kenny, D. A., Kashy, D., & Cook, W. L. (2006). *Dyadic data analysis.* New York: Guilford Press.

King, G., Honaker, J., Joseph, A., & Scheve, K. (2001). Analyzing incomplete political science data: An alternative algorithm for multiple imputation. *American Political Science Review, 95*, 49–69.

King, G., Murray, C. J. L., Salomon, J. A., & Tandon, A. (2004). Enhancing the validity and cross-cultural comparability of measurement in survey research. *American Political Science Review, 98*, 191–207.

King, G., & Wand, J. (2007). Comparing incomparable survey responses: Evaluating and selecting anchoring vignettes. *Political Analysis, 15*(1), 46–66.

King, J. E. (2003). Running a best-subsets logistic regression: An alternative to stepwise methods. *Educational and Psychological Methods, 63*, 392–403.

Klebanov, B. B., Diermeier, D., & Beigman, E. (2008). Lexical cohesion analysis of political speech. *Political Analysis, 16*, 447–463.

Klein, K. J., & Kozlowski, S. W. (2000). From micro to meso: Critical steps in conceptualizing and conducting multilevel research. *Organizational Research Methods, 3*(3), 211–236.

Kline, R. B. (2011a). *Principles and practice of structural equation modeling* (3rd ed.). New York: Guilford Press.

Kline, R. B. (2011b). Convergence of structural equation modeling and multilevel modeling. In M. Williams & W. P. Vogt (Eds.), *Handbook on innovations in social research methodology* (pp. 562–589). London: Sage.

Kohavi, R., Longbotham, R., Sommerfield, D., & Henne, R. S. (2009). Controlled experiments on the web: Survey and practical guide. *Data Mining and Knowledge Discovery, 18*, 140–181.

Kolata, G. (2006, February 5). Pity the scientist who discovers the discovered. *New York Times, Week in Review*, p. 4.

Konstantopoulos, S. (2009). Incorporating cost in power analysis for three-level cluster randomized designs. *Evaluation Review, 33*, 335–357.

Konstantopoulos, S., & Hedges, L. (2008). How large an effect can we expect from school reforms? *Teachers' College Record, 110*(8), 1611–1638.

Kostoff, R. N. (2010). Expanded information retrieval using full-text searching. *Journal of Information Science, 36*(1), 104–113.

Krenzke, T., & Judkins, D. (2008). Filling in the blanks: Some guesses are better than others. *Chance, 21*, 7–13.

Krieger, N., Rehkopf, D. H., Chen, J. T., Waterman, P. D., Marcelli, E., & Kennedy, M. (2008). The fall and rise of U.S. inequalities in premature mortality: 1960–2002. *PLoS Medicine, 5*(2), 227–241.

Krippendorff, K. (2004). *Content analysis: An introduction to its methodology* (2nd ed.). Thousand Oaks, CA: Sage.

Krueger, R. A. (1998). *Analyzing and reporting focus group results.* Los Angeles: Sage.

Krumholz, H. M., & Lee, T. H. (2008). Redefining quality: Implications of recent clinical trials. *New England Journal of Medicine, 358*, 2537–2539.

Krysan, M., Couper, M. P., Farley, R., & Forman, T. (2009). Does race matter in neighborhood preferences?: Results from a video experiment. *American Journal of Sociology, 115*(2), 527–559.

Kurasaki, K. S. (2000). Intercoder reliability for validating conclusions drawn from open-ended interview data. *Field Methods, 12*(3), 179–196.

Kwak, H., Lee, C., Park, H., & Moon, S. (2010, April). What is Twitter, a social network or a news media? *Proceedings of the 19th International Conference on World Wide Web*, pp. 591–600.

Laland, K. N., Sterelny, K., Odling-Smee, J., Hoppitt, W., & Uller, T. (2011). Cause and effect in biology revisited: Is Mayr's proximate–ultimate dichotomy still useful? *Science, 334*(6062), 1512–1516.

Lamb, W. (2004). *Couldn't keep it to myself.* New York: Harper.

Lamb, W. (2007). *I'll fly away.* New York: Harper.

Lamont, M. (1992). *Money, morals, and manners: The culture of the French and the American upper-middle class.* Chicago: University of Chicago Press.

Lamont, M. (2009). *How professors think: Inside the curious world of academic judgment.* Cambridge, MA: Harvard University Press.

Lamont, M., & White, P. (2009). *Workshop*

on interdisciplinary standards for systematic qualitative research. Washington, DC: National Science Foundation.

Lampropoulou, S., & Myers, G. (2013). Stance-taking in interviews from the Qualidata Archive. *Forum: Qualitative Social Research* (Vol. 14, No. 1). Available at *http://www.qualitative-research.net*.

Lan, K. G., & Shun, Z. (2009). A short note on sample size estimation. *Statistics in Biopharmaceutical Research, 1*(4), 356–361.

Lau, R. R., & Redlawsk, D. P. (2001). Advantages and disadvantages of cognitive heuristics in political decision making. *American Journal of Political Science, 45*, 951–971.

Laver, M., Benoit, K., & Garry, J. (2003). Extracting policy positions from political texts using words as data. *American Political Science Review, 97*, 311–331.

Leach, E. (1982). *Social anthropology*. New York: Oxford University Press.

Leahey, E. (2005). Alphas and asterisks: The development of statistical significance testing standards in sociology. *Social Forces, 84*, 1–24.

Leahey, E., Entwisle, B., & Einaudi, P. (2003). Diversity in everyday research practice: The case of data editing. *Sociological Methods and Research, 32*, 64–89.

Lee, R. M. (2004). Recording technologies and the interview in sociology, 1920–2000. *Sociology, 38*, 869–889.

Legewie, J., & DiPrete, T. A. (2012). School context and the gender gap in educational achievement. *American Sociological Review, 77*(3), 463–485.

Lehmann, E. L. (1993). The Fisher, Neyman-Pearson theories of testing hypotheses: One theory or two? *Journal of the American Statistical Association, 88*(424), 1242–1249.

Leskovec, J., Huttenlocher, D., & Kleinberg, J. (2010, April). Predicting positive and negative links in online social networks. In M. Rappa, P. Jones, J. Freire, & S. Chakrabarti (Eds.), *Proceedings of the 19th international conference on World Wide Web* (pp. 641–650). New York: Association for Computing Machinery.

Letherby, G., Scott, J., & Williams, M. (2013). *Objectivity and subjectivity in social research*. London: Sage.

Lévi-Strauss, C. (1969). *The raw and the cooked: Introduction to a science of mythology*. New York: Harper & Row.

Levy, G., & Razin, R. (2004). It takes two: An explanation for the democratic peace. *Journal of the European Economic Association, 2*, 1–29.

Lewins, A., & Silver, C. (2007). *Using software in qualitative research: A step-by-step guide*. Los Angeles: Sage.

Lewis, M. (2003). *Moneyball: The art of winning an unfair game*. New York: Norton.

Liao, T. F. (1994). *Interpreting probability models: Logit, probit, and other generalized linear models*. Thousand Oaks, CA: Sage.

Lieberman, E. S. (2005). Nested analysis as a mixed-method strategy for comparative research. *American Political Science Review, 99*(3), 435–452.

Lijphart, A. (1975). *The politics of accommodation*. Berkeley: University of California Press.

Lilla, M. (1998, June 25). The politics of Jacques Derrida. *New York Review of Books, 45*, 36–41.

Lim, B., Hosack, B., & Vogt, P. (2012). A framework for measuring student learning gains and engagement in an introductory computing course: A preliminary report of findings. *EJEL: Electronic Journal of e-Learning, 10*(4), 428–440.

Lima, M. (2011). *Visual complexity: Mapping patterns of information*. New York: Princeton Architectural Press.

Lindsay, A. C., & Hubley, A. M. (2006). Conceptual reconstruction through a modified focus group methodology. *Social Indicators Research, 79*, 437–454.

Link, B. G., Phelan, J. C., Miech, R., & Westin, E. L. (2008). The resources that matter: Fundamental social causes of health disparities and the challenge of intelligence. *Journal of Health and Social Behavior, 49*, 72–91.

Linn, R. L., & Haug, C. (2002). Stability of school-building accountability scores and gains. *Educational Evaluation and Policy Analysis, 24*(1), 29–36.

Lipsey, M. W., & Wilson, D. (2001). *Practical meta-analysis*. Los Angeles: Sage

Little, R. J. (1988). A test of missing completely at random for multivariate data with missing values. *Journal of the American Statistical Association, 83*(404), 1198–1202.

Little, R. J. A., & Rubin, D. B. (1987). *Statistical analysis with missing data* (1st ed.). New York: Wiley.

Little, R. J. A., & Rubin, D. B. (2002). *Statistical*

analysis with missing data (2nd ed.). New York: Wiley.

Liu, Y., Wu, A. D., & Zumbo, B. D. (2010). The impact of outliers on Cronbach's coefficient alpha estimate of reliability: Ordinal/rating scale item responses. *Educational and Psychological Measurement, 70*, 5–21.

Lo, A. W. (2012). Reading about the financial crisis: A twenty-one-book review. *Journal of Economic Literature, 50*, 151–178.

Loehlin, C. (2004). *Latent variable models: An introduction to factor, path, and structural equation analysis.* Mahwah, NJ: Erlbaum.

Lombard, M., Snyder-Duch, J., & Bracken, C. C. (2002). Content analysis in mass communication: Assessment and reporting of intercoder reliability. *Human Communication Research, 28*, 587–604.

Lombard, M., Snyder-Duch, J., & Bracken, C. C. (2010). *Practical resources for assessing and reporting intercoder reliability in content analysis research projects.* Available at *http://matthewlombard.com/reliability/*

Lukacs, P. M., Burnham, K. P., & Anderson, D. R. (2010). Model selection bias and Freedman's paradox. *Annals of the Institute of Statistical Mathematics, 62*(1), 117–125.

Luke, D. A. (2004). *Multilevel modeling.* Los Angeles: Sage.

Lynn, H. S. (2003). Suppression and confounding in action. *American Statistician, 57*(1), 58–61.

Ma, X., & Xu, J. (2004). The causal ordering of mathematics anxiety and mathematics achievement: A longitudinal panel analysis. *Journal of Adolescence, 27*(2), 165–179.

Maas, C. J. M., & Hox, J. J. (2005). Sufficient sample sizes for multilevel modeling. *Methodology, 1*(3), 85–91.

MacCormick, J. (2012). *9 algorithms that changed the future: The ingenious ideas that drive today's computers.* Princeton, NJ: Princeton University Press.

MacKinnon, D. P. (2008). *Introduction to statistical mediation analysis.* New York: Taylor & Francis.

MacKinnon, D. P., Krull, J. L., & Lockwood, C. M. (2000). Equivalence of the mediation, confounding and suppression effect. *Prevention Science, 1*(4), 173–181.

Macnaghten, P., & Myers, G. (2007). Focus groups. In C. Seale, D. Silverman, J. F. Gubrium, & G. Gobo (Eds.), *Qualitative research practice* (pp. 65–79). London: Sage.

Magasi, S., Ryan, G., Revicki, D., Lenderking, W., Hays, R. D., Brod, M., et al. (2012). Content validity of patient-reported outcome measures: Perspectives from a PROMIS meeting. *Quality of Life Research, 21*(5), 739–746.

Mahoney, J., Goertz, G., & Ragin, C. C. (2013). Causal models and counterfactuals. In S. L. Morgan (Ed.), *Handbook of causal analysis for social research* (pp. 75–90). The Netherlands: Springer.

Major, C. H., & Savin-Baden, M. (2011). Integration of qualitative evidence: Towards construction of academic knowledge in social science and professional fields. *Qualitative Research, 11*(6), 645–663.

Malinowski, B. (1922). *Argonauts of the Western Pacific.* London: Routledge.

Mansfield, E. D., & Snyder, J. (2005). *Electing to fight: Why emerging democracies go to war.* Boston: MIT Press.

Manski, C. F. (2001). Designing programs for heterogeneous populations: The value of covariate information. *American Economic Review, 91*, 103–106.

Markham, A. N. (2007). The Internet as a research context. In C. Seale, D. Silverman, J. F. Gubrium, & G. Gobo (Eds.), *Qualitative research practice* (pp. 328–344). London: Sage.

Martens, M. P., & Haase, R. F. (2006). Advanced applications of structural equation modeling in counseling psychology research. *Counseling Psychologist, 34*(6), 878–911.

Mauss, M. (2004). *Seasonal variations of the Eskimo: A study in social morphology.* New York: Psychology Press. (Original work published 1950)

Max, D. T. (2012). *Every love is a ghost story: A life of David Foster Wallace.* New York: Viking.

Maxwell, S. E., Kelley, K., & Rausch, J. R. (2008). Sample size planning for statistical power and accuracy in parameter estimation. *Annual Review of Psychology, 59*, 537–563.

McCoach, D. B. (2010). Hierarchical linear modeling. In G. R. Hancock & R. O. Mueller (Eds.), *The reviewer's guide to quantitative methods in the social sciences* (pp. 123–140). New York: Routledge.

McConahay, J. B. (1983). Modern racism and modern discrimination: The effects of race, racial attitudes, and context on simulated hiring decisions. *Personality and Social Psychology Bulletin, 9*, 551–558.

McCormick, J., Rodney, P., & Varcoe, C. (2003). Reinterpretations across studies: An approach to meta-analysis. *Qualitative Health Research, 13*, 933–944.

McElduff, F., Cortina-Borja, M., Chan, S. K., & Wade, A. (2010). When *t*-tests or Wilcoxon–Mann–Whitney tests won't do. *Advances in Physiology Education, 34*(3), 128–133.

McGlone, M. S., & Tofighbakhsh, J. (2000). Birds of a feather flock conjointly (?): Rhyme as reason in aphorisms. *Psychological Science, 11*(5), 424–428.

McGrayne, S. B. (2011). *The theory that would not die.* New Haven, CT: Yale University Press.

McKnight, P. E., McKnight, K. M., Sidani, S., & Figueredo, A. J. (2007). *Missing data: A gentle introduction.* New York: Guilford Press.

McPhee, J. (2013, January 14). The writing life: Structure. *New Yorker*, 46–55.

Meehan, J. C., & Stuart, G. L. (2007). Using structural equation modeling with forensic samples. *Criminal Justice and Behavior, 34*(12), 1560–1587.

Mehl, M. R., & Conner, T. S. (Eds.). (2012). *Handbook of research methods for studying daily life.* New York: Guilford Press.

Melzer, S. (2013). Ritual violence in a two-car garage. *Contexts, 12*(3), 26–31.

Menchik, D. A., & Tian, X. (2008). Putting social context into text: The semiotics of e-mail interaction. *American Journal of Sociology, 114*(2), 332–370.

Meraz, S. (2009). Is there an elite hold?: Traditional media to social media agenda setting influence in blog networks. *Journal of Computer-Mediated Communication, 14*(3), 682–707.

Merton, R. K. (1968). *Social theory and social structure.* New York: Free Press.

Miles, M. B., & Huberman, A. M. (1994). *Qualitative data analysis: An expanded sourcebook.* Los Angeles: Sage.

Milgram, S., Bickman, L., & Berkowitz, L. (1969). Note on the drawing power of crowds of different size. *Journal of Personality and Social Psychology, 13*, 79–82.

Miller, J. E. (2005). *The Chicago guide to writing about multivariate analysis.* Chicago: University of Chicago Press.

Miller, W. R., & Rollnick, S. (2013). *Motivational interviewing: Helping people change* (3rd ed.). New York: Guilford Press.

Millery, M., Shelley, D., Wu, D., Ferrari, P., Tseng, T., & Kopal, H. (2011). Qualitative evaluation to explain success of multifaceted technology-driven hypertension intervention. *American Journal of Managed Care, 17*, 95–102.

Minkler, M., Fuller-Thomson, E., & Guralnik, J. M. (2006). Gradient of disability across the socioeconomic spectrum in the United States. *New England Journal of Medicine, 355*, 695–703.

Moffitt, R. A. (2004). The role of randomized field trials in social science research. *American Behavioral Scientist, 47*, 506–540.

Moher, D., Liberati, A., Tetzlaff, J., & Altman, D. G. (2009). Preferred reporting items for systematic reviews and meta-analyses: The PRISMA Statement. *PLoS Medicine, 6*(7). Available at *http://hiv.cochrane.org/sites/hiv.cochrane.org/files/uploads/PRISMA.pdf.*

Mok, D., Wellman, B., & Carrasco, J. (2010). Does distance matter in the age of the Internet? *Urban Studies, 47*(13), 2747–2783.

Mooney, C. Z., & Duval, R. D. (1993). *Bootstrapping: A nonparametric approach to statistical inference.* Thousand Oaks, CA: Sage.

Moore, B. (1966). *Social origins of dictatorship and democracy: Lord and peasant in the making of the modern world.* Boston: Beacon Press.

Moran, T. P. (2006a). Statistical inference and patterns of inequality in the global north. *Social Forces, 84*, 1799–1818.

Moran, T. P. (2006b). Statistical inference for measures of inequality with a cross-national bootstrap application. *Sociological Methods and Research, 34*, 296–333.

Morgan, S. L. (2004). Methodologist as arbitrator: Five models for black–white differences in the causal effect of expectations on attainment. *Sociological Methods and Research, 33*(1), 3–53.

Morgan, S. L., & Winship, C. (2007). *Counterfactuals and causal inference: Methods and principles for social research.* New York: Cambridge University Press.

Mosteller, F., & Wallace, D. (2007). *Influence and disputed authorship: The Federalist* (3rd ed.). Stanford, CA: CSLI. (Original work published 1964)

Motulsky, H. (2010). *Intuitive biostatistics: A nonmathematical guide to statistical thinking* (2nd ed.). New York: Oxford University Press.

Mowbray, C. T., Holter, M. C., Teague, G.

B., & Bybee, D. (2003). Fidelity criteria: Development, measurement, and validation. *American Journal of Evaluation, 24*, 315–340.

Mueller, R. O., & Hancock, G. R. (2010). Structural equation modeling. In G. R. Hancock & R. O. Mueller (Eds.), *The reviewer's guide to quantitative methods in the social sciences* (pp. 371–383). New York: Routledge.

Mullins, N. C., Hargens, L. L., Hecht, P. K., & Kick, E. L. (1977). The group structure of co-citation clusters. *American Sociological Review, 42*, 552–562.

Munday, J. (2006). Identity in focus: The use of focus groups to study the construction of collective identity. *Sociology, 40*, 89–105.

Murnane, R. J., & Willett, J. B. (2011). *Methods matter: Improving causal inference in educational and social science research.* Oxford, UK: Oxford University Press.

Murray, D. M., & Blitstein, J. L. (2003). Methods to reduce the impact of intraclass correlation in group-randomized trials, *Evaluation Review, 27*, 79–103.

Muthén, B. O., Kaplan, D., & Hollis, M. (1987). On structural equation modeling with data that are not missing completely at random. *Psychometrika, 52*, 431–462.

Myatt, G. J. (2007). *Making sense of data: A practical guide to exploratory data analysis and data mining.* New York: Wiley.

Myers, J., Well, D., & Lorch, R. F. (2010). *Research design and statistical analysis* (3rd ed.). New York: Routledge.

Najman, J. M., & Hewitt, B. (2003). The validity of publication and citation counts for sociology and selected other disciplines. *Journal of Sociology, 39*, 62–80.

Needham, J. (1954–1998). *The science and civilisation in China* (Vols. 1–7). Cambridge, UK: Cambridge University Press.

Newman, D. A. (2009). Missing data techniques and low response rates: The role of systematic nonresponse patterns. In C. E. Lance & R. J. Vandenberg (Eds.), *Statistical and methodological myths and urban legends: Doctrine, verity and fable in organizational and social sciences* (pp. 7–36). New York: Routledge.

Newman, F. M., Smith, B., Allensworth, E., & Bryk, A. S. (2001). Instructional program coherence: What it is and why it should guide school improvement policy. *Educational Evaluation and Policy Analysis, 23*(4), 297–321.

Newman, J., Rosenbach, J. H., Burns, K. L., Latimer, B. C., Matocha, H. R., & Vogt, E. R. (1995). An experimental test of "The Mozart Effect": Does listening to his music improve spatial ability? *Perceptual and Motor Skills, 81*, 1379–1387.

Newman, M. E. (2004). Analysis of weighted networks. *Physical Review E, 70*(5), 056131.

Newton, R. R., & Rudestam, K. E. (1999). *Your statistical consultant: Answers to your data analysis questions.* Thousand Oaks, CA: Sage.

Norusis, M. J. (2005). *SPSS 14.0: Statistical procedures companion.* Upper Saddle River, NJ: Prentice-Hall.

Opsahl, T., Agneessens, F., & Skvoretz, J. (2010). Node centrality in weighted networks: Generalizing degree and shortest paths. *Social Networks, 32*(3), 245–251.

Osborne, J. W. (Ed.). (2008). *Best practices in quantitative methods.* Los Angeles: Sage.

Osborne, J. W., & Overbay, A. (2004). The power of outliers (and why researchers should always check for them). *Practical Assessment, Research, and Evaluation, 9*(6), 1–12.

Osborne, J. W., & Overbay, A. (2008). Best practices in data cleaning. In J. W. Osborne (Ed.), *Best practices in quantitative methods* (pp. 205–213). Los Angeles, CA: Sage.

Pampel, F. C. (2000). *Logistic regression: A primer.* Thousand Oaks, CA: Sage.

Papacharissi, Z. (2009). The virtual geographies of social networks: A comparative analysis of Facebook, LinkedIn, and ASmallWorld. *New Media and Society, 11*(1–2), 199–220.

Parker, R. A., & Berman, N. G. (2003). Sample size: More than calculations. *American Statistician, 57*(3), 166–170.

Pawson, R. (2002). Evidence-based policy: The promise of "realist synthesis." *Evaluation, 8*, 340–358.

Pazol, K., Warner, L., Gavin, L., Callaghan, W. M., Spitz, A. M., Anderson, J. E., et al. (2011). Vital signs: Teen pregnancy—United States, 1991–2009. *Morbidity and Mortality Weekly Report, 60*(13), 414–420.

Pearce, L. D. (2002). Integrating survey and ethnographic methods for systematic anomalous case analysis. *Sociological Methodology, 32*, 103–132.

Pearl, J. (2012). The causal foundations of structural equation modeling. In R. H. Hoyle (Ed.), *Handbook of structural equation modeling* (pp. 68–91). New York: Guilford Press.

Pedhazur, E. J. (1997). *Multiple regression in behavioral research: Explanation and prediction* (3rd ed.). New York: Harcourt Brace.

Pellegrini, A. D. (2013). *Observing children in their natural worlds: A methodological primer* (3rd ed.). New York: Psychology Press.

Pennebaker, J. W. (2011). *The secret life of pronouns: What our words say about us.* New York: Bloomsbury Press.

Pennings, P. (2003). Beyond dichotomous explanations: Explaining constitutional control of the executive with fuzzy sets. *European Journal of Political Research, 42*, 541–567.

Pereira, T. V., Horwitz, R. I., & Ioannidis, J. P. A. (2012). Empirical evaluation of very large treatment effects of medical interventions. *Journal of the American Medical Association, 308*(16), 1676–1984.

Pett, M., Lackey, N., & Sullivan, J. (2003). *Making sense of factor analysis.* Thousand Oaks, CA: Sage.

Pfeffermann, D. (1993). The role of sampling weights when modeling survey data. *International Statistical Review/Revue Internationale de Statistique, 61*, 317–337.

Pituch, K., & Stapleton, L. (2011). Hierarchical linear and structural equation modeling approaches to mediation analysis in randomized field experiments. In M. Williams & W. P. Vogt (Eds.), *Handbook on innovations in social research methodology* (pp. 590–619). London: Sage.

Platt, J. (1981). Evidence and proof in documentary research: 2. Some shared problems of documentary research. *Sociological Review, 29*(1), 53–66.

Platt, J. R. (1964). Strong inference. *Science, 146*, 347–353.

Poincaré, H. (1920). *Science and method* (F. Maitland, Trans.). London: Nelson. Available at *www.archive.org/details/sciencemethod.*

Pong, S., & Pallas, A. (2001). Class size and eighth-grade math achievement in the U.S. and abroad. *Educational Evaluation and Policy Analysis, 23*, 251–273.

Poulson, R. F., Gadbury, G. L., & Allison, D. B. (2012). Treatment heterogeneity and individual qualitative interaction. *American Statistician, 66*, 16–24.

Preacher, K. J. (2010). Latent growth curve modeling. In G. R. Hancock & R. O. Mueller (Eds.), *The reviewer's guide to quantitative methods in the social sciences* (pp. 184–198). New York: Routledge.

Presser, S., Couper, M. P., Lessler, J. T., Martin, E., Martin, J., Rothgeb, J. M., et al. (Eds.). (2004). *Methods for testing and evaluating survey questions.* New York: Wiley.

Raffle, H. (2006). *Assessment and reporting of intercoder reliability in published meta-analyses related to preschool through grade 12 education.* Unpublished doctoral dissertation, Ohio University.

Ragin, C. C. (1987). *The comparative method: Moving beyond qualitative and quantitative strategies.* Berkeley: University of California Press.

Ragin, C. C. (2008). *Redesigning social inquiry: Fuzzy sets and beyond.* Chicago: University of Chicago Press.

Ragin, C. C., & Becker, H. S. (Eds.). (1992). *What is a case?: Exploring the foundations of social inquiry.* Cambridge, UK: Cambridge University Press.

Ragin, C. C., Mayer, S. E., & Drass, K. A. (1984). Assessing discrimination: A Boolean approach. *American Sociological Review, 49*(2), 221–234.

Ragin, C. C., & Strand, S. I. (2008). Using qualitative comparative analysis to study causal order: Comment on Caren and Panofsky (2005). *Sociological Methods and Research, 36*(4), 431–441.

Raudenbush, S. W., & Chan, W. S. (1992). Growth curve analysis in accelerated longitudinal designs. *Journal of Research in Crime and Delinquency, 29*, 387–411.

Raudenbush, S. W., Spybrook, J., Congdon, R., Liu, X., Martinez, A., Bloom, H., et al. (2012). Optimal design software for multi-level and longitudinal research (Version 3.01). Available at *www.sitemaker.umich.edu/group-based.*

Reddy, C. K., & Aziz, M. S. (2010). Modeling local nonlinear correlations using subspace principal curves. *Statistical Analysis and Data Mining, 3*, 332–349.

Reichertz, J. (2010). Abduction: The logic of discovery of grounded theory. *Forum Qualitative Sozialforschung/Forum: Qualitative Social Research, 11*(1). Retrieved from *www.qualitative-research.net/index.php/fqs/article/view/1412.*

Reinharz, S., & Chase, S. E. (2002). Interviewing women. In J. F. Gubrium & J. A. Holstein

(Eds.), *Handbook of interview research: Context and method*. Thousand Oaks, CA: Sage.

Rihoux, B., Alamos, P., Bol, D., Marx, A., & Rezsöhazy, I. (2012). From niche to mainstream method?: A comprehensive mapping of QCA applications in journal articles from 1984 to 2011. *Political Research Quarterly, 66*, 1.

Rihoux, B., & Ragin, C. C. (Eds.). (2009). *Configurational comparative methods: Qualitative comparative analysis (QCA) and related techniques*. Los Angeles: Sage.

Rohe, K. (2012). A tale of two researchers. *Amstatnews, 424*, 16–17.

Rorty, R. (1987). Posties. *London Review of Books, 3*, 11–12.

Rosa, M. (2010). *A mixed-methods study to understand the perceptions of high school leaders about ELL students: The case of mathematics*. Unpublished doctoral dissertation, California State University, Sacramento.

Rosenbaum, M. S. (2011). From theoretical generation to verification using structural equation modeling. In V. B. Martin & A. Gynnild (Eds.), *Grounded theory: The philosophy, method, and work of Barney Glaser* (pp. 283–308). Boca Raton, FL: BrownWalker Press.

Rosenfeld, M. J., & Thomas, R. J. (2012). Searching for a mate: The rise of the Internet as a social intermediary. *American Sociological Review, 77*(4), 523–547.

Rosenthal, R., Rosnow, R. L., & Rubin, D. B. (2000). *Contrasts and effect sizes in behavioral research: A correlational approach*. New York: Cambridge University Press.

Rosenthal, R., & Rubin, D. B. (2003). $r_{equivalent}$: A simple effect size indicator. *Methods, 8*, 492–496.

Rosenwein, R. E. (1994). Social influence in science: Agreement and dissent in achieving scientific consensus. In W. R. Shadish & S. Fuller, *The Social Psychology of Science* (pp. 262–285). New York: Guilford Press.

Rossi, P. E., Allenby, G. M., & McCulloch, R. (2005). *Bayesian statistics and marketing*. New York: Wiley.

Roth, L. M., & Kroll, J. C. (2007). Risky business: Assessing risk preference explanations for gender differences in religiosity. *American Sociological Review, 72*, 205–220.

Rousseau, M., Simon, M., Bertrand, R., & Hachey, K. (2012). Reporting missing data: A study of selected articles published from 2003–2007. *Quantity and Quality, 46*, 1393–1406.

Rubin, D. B. (1974). Estimating causal effects of treatments in randomized and nonrandomized studies. *Journal of Educational Psychology, 66*(5), 688–701.

Rubin, D. B. (1986). Statistics and causal inference: Comment: Which ifs have causal answers. *Journal of the American Statistical Association, 81*(396), 961–962.

Rubin, D. B. (1987). *Multiple imputation for nonresponse in surveys*. New York: Wiley.

Rudel, T. K. (2009). How do people transform landscapes?: A sociological perspective on suburban sprawl and tropical deforestation. *American Journal of Sociology, 115*, 129–154.

Rudner, L. M., & Peyton, J. (2006). Consider propensity scores to compare treatments. *Practical Assessment Research and Evaluation, 11*(9), 1–9.

Ruscio, J., & Roche, B. (2012). Determining the number of factors to retain in an exploratory factor analysis using comparison data of known factorial structure. *Psychological Assessment, 24*(2), 282.

Sabates, R., & Feinstein, L. (2008). Effects of government initiatives on youth crime. *Oxford Economic Papers, 60*, 462–483.

Sackett, D. L., Deeks, J. J., & Altman, D. G. (1996). Down with odds ratios! *Evidence Based Medicine, 1*(6), 164–166.

Sager, F., & Andereggen, C. (2012). Dealing with complex causality in realist synthesis: The promise of qualitative comparative analysis. *American Journal of Evaluation, 33*(1), 60–78.

Saldaña, J. (2012). *The coding manual for qualitative researchers*. Los Angeles: Sage.

Sandelowski, M., Voils, C. I., & Knafl, G. (2009). On quantitizing. *Journal of Mixed Methods Research, 3*(3), 208–222.

Sandelowski, M., Voils, C. I., Leeman, J., & Crandell, J. L. (2012). Mapping the mixed methods–mixed research synthesis terrain. *Journal of Mixed Methods Research, 6*(4), 317–331.

Sanders, S. A., Hill, B. J., Yarber, W. L., Graham, C. A., Crosby, R. A., & Milhausen, R. R. (2010). Misclassification bias: Diversity in conceptualizations about having "had sex." *Sexual Health, 7*(1), 31–34.

Sass, D. A., & Schmitt, T. A. (2010). A comparative investigation of rotation criteria within exploratory factor analysis. *Multivariate Behavioral Research, 45*(1), 73–103.

Schaefer, W. D. (2008). Replicated field study design. In J. W. Osborne (Ed.), *Best practices in quantitative methods* (pp. 147–154). Los Angeles: Sage.

Schaeffer, N. C., & Maynard, D. W. (2001). Standardization and interaction in the survey interview. In J. F. Gubrium & J. A. Holstein (Eds.), *Handbook of interview research* (pp. 577–601). Thousand Oaks, CA: Sage.

Schechtman, E. (2002). Odds ratio, relative risk, absolute risk reduction, and the number needed to treat: Which of these should we use? *Value in Health, 5*(5), 431–436.

Scherbaum, C. A., & Ferreter, J. M. (2009). Estimating statistical power and required sample sizes for organizational research using multilevel modeling. *Organizational Research Methods, 12*(2), 347–367.

Schmitt, T. A., & Sass, D. A. (2011). Rotation criteria and hypothesis testing for exploratory factor analysis: Implications for factor pattern loadings and interfactor correlations. *Educational and Psychological Measurement, 71*(1), 95–113.

Schneider, C. Q., & Rohlfing, I. (2013). Combining QCA and process tracing in set-theoretic multi-method research. *Sociological Methods and Research, 41*, 1–39.

Schneider, C. Q., & Wagemann, C. (2006). Reducing complexity in qualitative comparative analysis (QCA): Remote and proximate factors and the consolidation of democracy. *European Journal of Political Research, 45*(5), 751–786.

Schneider, C. Q., & Wagemann, C. (2010). Standards of good practice in qualitative comparative analysis (QCA) and fuzzy-sets. *Comparative Sociology, 9*(3), 397–418.

Schneider, C. Q., & Wagemann, C. (2012). *Set-theoretic methods for the social sciences: A guide to qualitative comparative analysis.* Cambridge, UK: Cambridge University Press.

Schochet, P. Z. (2008). Statistical power for random assignment evaluations of educational programs. *Journal of Educational and Behavioral Statistics, 33*, 62–87.

Schreiber, J. B., Nora, A., Stage, F. K., Barlow, E. A., & King, J. (2006). Reporting structural equation modeling and confirmatory factor analysis results: A review. *Journal of Educational Research, 99*(6), 323–338.

Schuman, H., & Rodgers, W. L. (2004). Cohorts, chronology, and collective memory. *Public Opinion Quarterly, 68*, 217–254.

Schwalbe, M. L., & Wolkomir, M. (2001). Interviewing men. In J. F. Gubrium & J. A. Holstein (Eds.), *Handbook of interview research: Context and method.* Thousand Oaks, CA: Sage.

Schweber, L. (2006). *Disciplining statistics: Demography and vital statistics in France and England, 1830–1885.* Durham, NC: Duke University Press.

Scott, J. (2000). *Social network analysis: A handbook* (2nd ed.). London: Sage.

Searle, J. R. (1969). *Speech acts.* Cambridge, UK: Cambridge University Press.

Seawright, J. (2005). Qualitative comparative analysis vis-à-vis regression. *Studies in Comparative International Development, 40*(1), 3–26.

Seymour, E., Wiese, D., Hunter, A.-B., & Daffinrud, S. (2000, March). Creating a better mousetrap: On-line student assessment of their learning gains. In *Using real-world questions to promote active learning.* Symposium conducted at the meeting of the American Chemical Society, San Francisco. Available at *www.salgsite.org/docs/SALGPaperPresentationAtACS.pdf.*

Shadish, W. R., Cook, T. D., & Campbell, D. (2002). *Experimental and quasi-experimental designs for generalized causal inference.* New York: Houghton Mifflin.

Shermer, M. (2012). Shock and awe. *Scientific American, 307*(5), 86.

Shiao, J. L., & Tuan, M. H. (2008). Korean adoptees and the social context of ethnic exploration. *American Journal of Sociology, 113*(4), 1023–1066.

Shin, Y., & Raudenbush, S. W. (2011). The causal effect of class size on academic achievement multivariate instrumental variable estimators with data missing at random. *Journal of Educational and Behavioral Statistics, 36*(2), 154–185.

Shwed, U., & Bearman, P. S. (2010). The temporal structure of scientific formation. *American Sociological Review, 75*, 817–840.

Shwed, U., & Bearman, P. S. (2012). Symmetry is beautiful. *American Sociological Review, 77*, 1064–1069.

Sidnell, J. (2010). *Conversation analysis: An introduction*. London: Wiley-Blackwell.

Siegel, E. (2013). *Predictive analytics: The power to predict who will click, buy, lie, or die*. Hoboken, NJ: Wiley.

Sigaud, L. (2008). A collective ethnographer: fieldwork experience in the Brazilian northeast. *Social Science Information, 47*, 71–97.

Sijtsma, K. (2009). On the use, the misuse, and the very limited usefulness of Cronbach's alpha. *Psychometrika, 74*(1), 107–120.

Siles, I. (2011). From online filter to Web format: Articulating materiality and meaning in the early history of blogs. *Social Studies of Science, 41*(5), 737–758.

Silva, J. M. (2012). Constructing adulthood in an age of uncertainty. *American Sociological Review, 77*(4), 505–522.

Silver, N. (2012). *The signal and the noise: Why so many predictions fail—but some don't*. New York: Penguin.

Simmel, G. (1955). *Conflict and the web of group affiliations*. New York: Free Press. (Original work published 1908)

Simon, A. F., & Xenos, M. (2004). Dimension reduction of word-frequency data as a substitute for intersubjective content analysis. *Political Analysis, 12*, 63–75.

Simon, H. A. (1991). *Models of my life*. New York: Basic Books.

Simon, S. (2012). *Classrooms First commission: A guide to P–12 efficiency and opportunity*. Report submitted to the Illinois General Assembly: 21, 25. Available at *www2.illinois.gov/gov/P20/Documents/Reports/CFC%20FINAL%20REPORT%2006.29.12.pdf*.

Singer, J., & Willett, J. (2003). *Applied longitudinal data analysis*. New York: Oxford University Press.

Siontis, G. C. M., Tzoulaki, I., & Ioannidis, J. P. A. (2011). Predicting death: An empirical evaluation of predictive tools for mortality. *Archives of Internal Medicine, 171*(19), 1721–1726.

Skaaning, S. E. (2011). Assessing the robustness of crisp-set and fuzzy-set QCA results. *Sociological Methods and Research, 40*(2), 391–408.

Skidelsky, R. (2000). *John Maynard Keynes: Fighting for freedom*. New York: Viking.

Skidmore, S. T., & Thompson, B. (2012). Propagation of misinformation about frequencies of RFTs/RCTs in education: A cautionary tale. *Educational Researcher, 41*, 163–170.

Skocpol, T. (1979). *States and social revolutions*. Cambridge, UK: Cambridge University Press.

Slavin, R. E. (2008). What works?: Issues in synthesizing educational program evaluations. *Educational Researcher, 37*, 5–14.

Slavin, R. E., & Smith, D. (2009). The relationship between sample sizes and effect sizes in systematic reviews in education. *Educational Evaluation and Policy Analysis, 31*, 500–506.

Small, H., & Griffith, B. (1974). The structure of the scientific literature. *Science Studies, 4*, 17–40.

Smith, B. (2000). Quantity matters: Annual instructional time in an urban school system. *Educational Administration Quarterly, 36*(5), 652–682.

Smith, S. K. (1987). Test of forecast accuracy and bias for county population projections. *Journal of the American Statistical Association, 82*(400), 991–1003.

Smyth, J. D., Dillman, D. A., Christian, L. M., & Stern, M. J. (2006). Comparing check-all and forced-choice question formats in web surveys. *Public Opinion Quarterly, 70*, 66–77.

Snow, J. (1855). *On the mode of communication of cholera* (2nd ed.). London: Churchill. Available at *www.ph.ucla.edu/epi/snow/snowbook4.html*.

Song, M., & Herman, R. (2010). Critical issues and common pitfalls in designing and conducting impact studies in education: Lessons learned from the What Works Clearinghouse. *Educational Evaluation and Policy Analysis, 32*, 351–371.

Spano, R. (2006). Observer behavior as a potential source of reactivity: Describing and quantifying observer effects in a large-scale observational study of police. *Sociological Methods and Research, 34*, 521–553.

Spector, P. E. (1992). *Summated rating scale construction: An introduction*. Thousand Oaks, CA: Sage.

Spicer, J. (2005). *Making sense of multivariate data analysis*. Thousand Oaks, CA: Sage.

Spirtes, P., Glymour, C. N., & Scheines, R. (2000). *Causation, prediction, and search* (2nd ed.). Cambridge, MA: MIT Press.

Spradley, J. P. (1979). *The ethnographic interview*. Fort Worth, TX: Harcourt Brace.

Spybrook, J., & Raudenbush, S. (2009). An examination of the precision and technical accuracy of the first wave of group randomized trials funded by the Institute of Education

Sciences. *Educational Evaluation and Policy Analysis, 31*, 298–318.

Stake, R. E. (2006). *Multiple case study analysis*. New York: Guilford Press.

Steinberg, S. J., & Steinberg, S. L. (2006). *Geographic information systems for the social sciences*. Los Angeles: Sage.

Steiner, P. M., Cook, T. D., & Shadish, W. R. (2011). On the importance of reliable covariate measurement in selection bias adjustments using propensity scores. *Journal of Educational and Behavioral Statistics, 36*, 213–236.

Stephens, N. (2007). Collecting data from elites and ultra elites: Telephone and face-to-face interviews with macroeconomists. *Qualitative Research, 7*(2), 203–216.

Stewart, R. (2006). *The places in between*. Orlando, FL: Harcourt.

Stillwell, D., & Kosinski, M. (2011). *Mypersonality project*. Available at *www.mypersonality.org*.

Strauss, A. (1995). Notes on the nature and development of general theories. *Qualitative Inquiry, 1*(1), 7–18.

Strauss, A., & Corbin, J. (1990). *Basics of qualitative research* (2nd ed.). Los Angeles: Sage.

Strube, M. J. (2000). Reliability and generalizability theory. In L. G. Grimm & P. R. Yarnold (Eds.), *Reading and understanding more multivariate statistics* (pp. 23–66). Washington, DC: American Psychological Association.

Strug, L. J., Rohde, C. A., & Corey, P. N. (2007). An introduction to evidential sample size calculations. *American Statistician, 61*, 207–212.

Stuart, E. A., & Rubin, D. B. (2008). Best practices in quasi-experimental designs. *Best Practices in Quantitative Methods*, 155–176.

Sudman, S., & Bradburn, N. (1982). *Asking questions*. San Francisco: Jossey-Bass.

Svendsen, G. L. (2006). Studying social capital in situ: A qualitative approach. *Theory and Society, 35*(1), 39–70.

Swedberg, R., & Reich, W. (2010). Georg Simmel's aphorisms. *Theory, Culture, and Society, 27*(1), 24–51.

Swern, A. S. (2010). A story of evidence-based-medicine: Hormone replacement therapy and coronary heart disease in postmenopausal women. *Chance, 23*, 52–56.

Tabachnick, B. G., & Fidell, L. S. (2001). *Using multivariate statistics* (4th ed.). New York: Allyn & Bacon.

Takhteyev, Y., Gruzd, A., & Wellman, B. (2012). Geography of Twitter networks. *Social Networks, 34*(1), 73–81.

Tang, T., & Robinson, T. (2010). Learning approach and perception of learning context in economics education: A causality test. *International Journal of Learning, 17*(2), 21–40.

Tavory, I., & Swidler, A. (2009). Condom semiotics: Meaning and condom use in rural Malawi. *American Sociological Review, 72*, 171–189.

Taylor, A. B., West, S. G., & Aiken, L. S. (2006). Loss of power in logistic, ordinal logistic, and probit regression when an outcome is coarsely categorized. *Educational and Psychological Measurement, 66*, 228–239.

Teddlie, C., & Tashakkori, A. (2006). A general typology of research designs featuring mixed methods. *Research in the Schools, 13*(1), 12–28.

Tedlock, B. (1991). From participant observation to the observation of participation: The emergence of narrative ethnography. *Journal of Anthropological Research, 47*, 69–94.

Thiem, A., & Duşa, A. (2013). Boolean minimization in social science research: A review of current software for qualitative comparative analysis (QCA). *Social Science Computer Review, 31*, 505–521.

Thompson, B. (2000). Canonical correlation analysis. In L. G. Grimm & P. R. Yarnold (Eds.), *Reading and understanding more multivariate statistics* (pp. 285–316). Washington, DC: American Psychological Association.

Thompson, B. (2002). "Statistical," "practical," and "clinical": How many kinds of significance do counselors need to consider? *Journal of Counseling and Development, 80*(1), 64–71.

Thompson, B. (2004). *Exploratory and confirmatory factor analysis*. Washington, DC: American Psychological Association.

Thompson, B. (2006). *Foundations of behavioral statistics*. New York: Guilford Press.

Thornberg, R. (2012). Informed grounded theory. *Scandinavian Journal of Educational Research, 56*(3), 243–259.

Thurstone, L. L. (1931). Multiple factor analysis. *Psychological Review, 38*(5), 406–427.

Tilly, C. (2006). *Why?: What happens when people give reasons—and why*. Princeton, NJ: Princeton University Press.

Timmermans, S., & Tavory, I. (2012). Theory construction in qualitative research from grounded theory to abductive analysis. *Sociological Theory, 30*(3), 167–186.

Tjur, T. (2009). Coefficients of determination in logistic regression models—A new proposal: The coefficient of discrimination. *American Statistician, 63*, 366–372.

Tolvanen, A., Kiuru, N., Leskinen, E., Hakkarainen, K., Inkinen, M., Lonka, K., et al. (2011). A new approach for estimating a nonlinear growth component in multilevel modeling. *International Journal of Behavioral Development, 35*(4), 370–379.

Tope, D., Chamberlain, L. J., Crowley, M., & Hodson, R. (2005). The benefits of being there: Evidence from the literature on work. *Journal of Contemporary Ethnography, 34*, 470–493.

Torgo, L. (2011). *Data mining with R: Learning with case studies.* Boca Raton, FL: CRC Press.

Torche, F. (2011). The effect of maternal stress on birth outcomes: Exploiting a natural experiment. *Demography, 48*, 1473–1491.

Tsivian, M., Sun, L., Mouraviev, V., Madden, J. F., Mayes, J. M., Moul, J. W., et al. (2009). Changes in Gleason score grading and their effect in predicting outcome after radical prostatectomy. *Urology, 74*(5), 1090–1093.

Tufte, E. R. (1983). *The visual display of quantitative information.* Cheshire, CT: Graphics Press.

Tukey, J. W. (1977). *Exploratory data analysis.* Reading, MA: Addison-Wesley.

Ulam, S. M. (1991). *Adventures of a mathematician.* Los Angeles: University of California Press.

United Nations Office on Drugs and Crime. (2011). *2011 global study on homicide: Trends, contexts, data.* Vienna: Author.

Utts, J., & Johnson, W. (2008). The evolution of teaching Bayesian statistics to nonstatisticians: A partisan view from the trenches. *American Statistician, 62*(3), 199–201.

Vacha-Haase, T. (1998). Reliability generalization: Exploring variance in measurement error affecting score reliability across studies. *Educational and Psychological Measurement, 58*, 6–20.

Van Aalst, J. (2010). Using Google Scholar to estimate the impact of journal articles in education. *Educational Researcher, 39*, 387–400.

Van den Noortgate, W., & Onghena, P. (2003). Multi-level meta-analysis: A comparison with traditional meta-analytic procedures. *Educational and Psychological Measurement, 63*, 765–790.

Van Maanen, J. (1982). Fieldwork on the beat. In J. Van Maanen, J. Dabbs, & R. Falkner, *Varieties of qualitative research* (pp. 103–151). Thousand Oaks, CA: Sage.

Van Maanen, J. (2011). *Tales of the field: On writing ethnography.* Chicago: University of Chicago Press.

Van Staa, T.-P., Leufkens, H. G., Zhang, B., & Smeeth, L. (2009). A comparison of cost effectiveness using data from randomized trials or actual clinical practice: Selective Cox-2 inhibitors as an example. *PLoS Medicine, 6*(12), 1–10.

Venkatesh, S. (2008). *Gang leader for a day.* New York: Penguin.

Vickers, J. (2013). The problem of induction. In E. N. Zalta (Ed.), *The Stanford encyclopedia of philosophy.* Available at *http://plato.stanford.edu/archives/spr2013/entries/induction-problem.*

Vogt, W. P. (1976a). The uses of studying primitives: A note on the Durkheimians, 1890–1940. *History and Theory, 15*(1), 33–44.

Vogt, W. P. (1976b). *The politics of academic sociological theory in France, 1890–1914.* Unpublished doctoral dissertation, Indiana University.

Vogt, W. P. (1993). L'influence de la *Division du travail social* sur la sociologie américaine. In P. Besnard, M. Borlandi, & P. Vogt (Eds.), *Division du travail et lien social: Durkheim un siècle après* (pp. 215–230). Paris: Presses Universitaires de France.

Vogt, W. P. (1997). *Tolerance and education: Learning to live with diversity and difference.* Los Angeles: Sage.

Vogt, W. P. (2007). *Quantitative research methods for professionals.* Boston: Allyn & Bacon.

Vogt, W. P. (2008). The dictatorship of the problem: Choosing research methods. *Methodological Innovations Online, 3*(1), 1–17.

Vogt, W. P. (2012, October). *From surveillance to participation: Evolving evaluator roles in multi-year projects.* Paper presented at the annual meeting of the American Evaluation Association. Minneapolis, MN.

Vogt, W. P., Tsivian, M., Sun, L., Mouraviev, V., Madden, J. F., Mayes, J. M., et al. (2013, October). *Combining prospective meta-analysis (PMA) and qualitative comparative analysis (QCA) in program evaluation.* Paper presented at the annual meeting of the American Evaluation Association, Washington, DC.

Vogt, W. P., Gardner, D. C., & Haeffele, L. M. (2012). *When to use what research design.* New York: Guilford Press.

Vogt, W. P., Gardner, D., Haeffele, L. M., & Baker, P. (2011). Innovations in program evaluation: Comparative case studies as an alternative to RCTs. In M. Williams & W. P. Vogt (Eds.), *The Sage handbook on innovations in social research methods* (pp. 289–320). London: Sage.

Vogt, W. P., & Hines, E. (2007, April). *Analyzing trends in higher education funding using curvilinear regression.* Paper presented at the annual meeting of the American Educational Research Association.

Vogt, W. P., & Johnson, R. B. (2011). *Dictionary of statistics and methodology: A nontechnical guide for the social sciences* (4th ed.). Los Angeles: Sage.

Vogt, W. P., & Johnson, R. B. (Eds.). (2012). *Correlation and regression analysis* (Vols. 1–4). London: Sage.

Vogt, W. P., & McKenna, B. J. (1998, April). *Teachers' tolerance: Their attitudes toward political, social, and moral diversity.* Paper presented at the annual meeting of the American Educational Research Association, San Diego, CA. Available at *eric.ed.gov/?idED423344.*

Vogt, W. P., & Nur-Awaleh, M. (1999, November). *"Whatever the dean doesn't want to do and the janitor refuses to do": The roles and responsibilities of university associate deans.* Paper presented at the annual meeting of the Association for the Study of Higher Education, San Antonio, TX.

Wainer, H. (2005). *Graphic discovery.* Princeton, NJ: Princeton University Press.

Wainer, H. (2009). *Picturing the uncertain world: How to understand, communicate, and control uncertainty through graphical display.* Princeton, NJ: Princeton University Press.

Wainer, H., & Robinson, D. H. (2003). Shaping up the practice of null hypothesis significance testing. *Educational Researcher, 32*(7), 22–30.

Wang, M. T., Selman, R. L., Dishion, T. J., & Stormshak, E. A. (2010). A Tobit regression analysis of the covariation between middle school students' perceived school climate and behavioral problems. *Journal of Research on Adolescence, 20*(2), 274–286.

Ware, J. (2012). Missing data. *New England Journal of Medicine, 367,* 1353–1354.

Warren, C. A. B., Barnes-Brus, T., Burgess, H., Wiebold-Lippisch, L., Hackney, J., Harkness, G., et al. (2003). After the interview. *Qualitative Sociology, 26*(1), 93–110.

Wasserman, J. A., Clair, J. M., & Wilson, K. L. (2009). Problematics of grounded theory: Innovations for developing an increasingly rigorous qualitative method. *Qualitative Research, 9*(3), 355–381.

Wasserman, L. (2007). *All of nonparametric statistics.* New York: Springer.

Webb, E. J., Campbell, D. T., Schwartz, R. D., & Sechrest, L. (1966). *Unobtrusive measures: Nonreactive research in the social sciences.* Chicago: Rand McNally.

Weinfurt, K. P. (2000). Repeated measures analyses: ANOVA, MANOVA, and HLM. In L. G. Grimm & P. R. Yarnold (Eds.), *Reading and understanding more multivariate statistics* (pp. 317–361). Washington, DC: American Psychological Association

Wejnert, C., & Heckathorn, D. D. (2008). Web-based network sampling: Efficiency and efficacy of respondent-driven sampling for online research. *Sociological Methods and Research, 37,* 105–134.

Wertz, F. J., Charmaz, K., McMullen, L. M., Josselson, R., Anderson, R., & McSpadden, E. (2011). *Five ways of doing qualitative analysis: Phenomenological psychology, grounded theory, discourse analysis, narrative research, and intuitive inquiry.* New York: Guilford Press.

Westfall, P. H. (2008). Teaching Bayes to non-statistics graduate students. *American Statistician, 62*(3, Special section), 189.

Weston, C., Gandell, T., Beauchamp, J., McAlpine, L., Wiseman, C., & Beauchamp, C. (2001). Analyzing interview data: The development and evolution of a coding system. *Qualitative Sociology, 24*(3), 381–400.

Whyte, W. F. (1993). *Street corner society.* Chicago: University of Chicago Press. (Original work published 1943)

Wibeck, V., Dahlgren, M. A., & Oberg, G. (2007). Learning in focus groups: An analytical dimension for enhancing focus group research. *Qualitative Research, 7*(2), 249–267.

Wilkinson, L. (1999). Statistical methods in psychology journals: Guidelines and explanations. *American Psychologist, 54*(8), 594–604.

Williams, B., Brown, T., & Onsman, A. (2012). Exploratory factor analysis: A five-step guide for novices. *Journal of Emergency Primary Health Care, 8*(3), 1–9.

Williams, D. W., & Zimmerman, R. H. (1996). Are simple gain scores obsolete? *Applied Psychological Measurement, 20*, 59–69.

Willis, G. B. (2005). *Cognitive interviewing: A tool for improving questionnaire design.* Thousand Oaks, CA: Sage.

Wilson, E. O. (1999). *Consilience: The unity of knowledge.* New York: Vintage.

Wilson, J. L. (2012). Prediction markets: How accurate are they? *CHANCE, 25*(4), 32–38.

Wilson, R. E., Gosling, S. D., & Graham, L. T. (2012). A review of Facebook research in the social sciences. *Perspectives on Psychological Science, 7*(3), 203–220.

Wimalasuriya, D. C., & Dou, D. (2011). Ontology-based information extraction: An introduction and a survey of current approaches. *Journal of Information Science, 36*, 306–323.

Winship, C., & Radbill, L. (1994). Sampling weights and regression analysis. *Sociological Methods and Research, 23*(2), 230–257.

Wolfswinkel, J. F., Furtmueller, E., & Wilderom, C. P. (2011). Using grounded theory as a method for rigorously reviewing literature. *European Journal of Information Systems, 22*(1), 45–55.

Woodward, B. (2008). *The war within: A secret White House history, 2006–2008.* New York: Simon & Schuster.

Woodward, B. (2010). *Obama's wars.* New York: Simon & Schuster.

Wright, S. (1921). Correlation and causation. *Journal of Agricultural Research, 20*(7), 557–585.

Wright, S. (1934). The method of path coefficients. *Annals of Mathematical Statistics, 5*(3), 161–215.

Wu, X., Kumar, V., Quinlan, J. R., Ghosh, J., Yang, Q., Motoda, H., et al. (2008). Top 10 algorithms in data mining. *Knowledge and Information Systems, 14*, 1–37.

Yang, C. C., & Sageman, M. (2009). Analysis of terrorist social networks with fractal views. *Journal of Information Science, 35*, 299–320.

Yau, N. (2011). *Visualize this.* Indianapolis, IN: Wiley.

Yin, R. K. (2006). Mixed methods research: Are the methods genuinely integrated or merely parallel? *Research in the Schools, 13*(1), 41–47.

Yin, R. K. (2008). *Case study research: Design and methods.* Los Angeles: Sage.

Yin, R. K. (2011). *Qualitative research from start to finish.* New York: Guilford Press.

Yong, E. (2012). The data detective. *Nature, 487*, 18–19. Available at *www.nature.com/news/the-data-detective-1.10937.*

Yu, C. H. (2008). Resampling: A conceptual and procedural introduction. In J. W. Osborne (Ed.), *Best practices in quantitative methods* (pp. 283–298). Los Angeles: Sage.

Zhao, S. (1991). Metatheory, metamethod, meta-data-analysis: What, why, and how? *Sociological Perspectives, 34*, 377–390.

Ziegler, M., & Buehner, M. (2009). Modeling socially desirable responding and its effects. *Educational and Psychological Measurement, 69*, 548–565.

Zientek, L. R., & Thompson, B. (2009). Matrix summaries improve research reports: Secondary analyses using published literature. *Educational Researcher, 38*, 343–352.

Zijlstra, W. P., Van der Ark, L. A., & Sijtsma, K. (2011). Outliers in questionnaire data: Can they be detected and should they be removed? *Journal of Educational and Behavioral Statistics, 36*, 186–212.

Zussman, R. (2004). People in places. *Qualitative Sociology, 27*, 351–363.

Index

An *f* following a page number indicates a figure; *n* following page number indicates a note; *t* following a page number indicates a table.

B

C

D

E

F

G

H

I

P

Q

R

S

T

U

V

W

Z

About the Authors

W. Paul Vogt, PhD, is Emeritus Professor of Research Methods and Evaluation at Illinois State University, where he has won both teaching and research awards. Before coming to Illinois State as an administrator and faculty member, he held similar posts at the University at Albany, State University of New York. He has also been a visiting researcher at l'École des Hautes Études en Sciences Sociales in Paris (1980) and at the University of London Institute of Education (1986). Dr. Vogt's areas of specialization include research design and data analysis, with particular emphasis on combining qualitative, quantitative, and graphic approaches. He has also served as principal program evaluator for many funded projects and continues to be active in this field. His publications include *Dictionary of Statistics and Methodology* (4th edition), *Quantitative Research Methods for Professionals*, *Education Programs for Improving Intergroup Relations* (coedited with Walter G. Stephan), and *The SAGE Handbook of Innovation in Social Research Methods* (coedited with Malcolm Williams). He is also editor of three four-volume sets in the series Sage Benchmarks in Social Research Methods: *Selecting Research Methods, Data Collection*, and *SAGE Quantitative Research Methods*. He blogs about research methods at *vogtsresearchmethods.blogspot.com* and is coauthor (with Dianne C. Gardner and Lynne M. Haeffele) of *When to Use What Research Design*.

Elaine R. Vogt, MA, CAS, is certified as a school psychologist in New York and Illinois and has worked as a psychologist in schools and a variety of other public and private institutions. She recently retired from Illinois Wesleyan University, where she taught piano and was a staff accompanist. Ms. Vogt's research interests include cognitive psychology, especially music cognition.

Dianne C. Gardner, PhD, is Associate Professor of Educational Administration and Foundations and a Research Associate at the Center for the Study of Education Policy at Illinois State University. Prior to joining the faculty at Illinois State, she served as a speech diagnostician in early childhood special education. She next was as an instructor at Alverno College, a pioneering institution in postsecondary assessment of learning, where she directed grants aimed at developing Alverno's partnership with the Milwaukee Public Schools. Her research interests include assessment, evaluation of collaborative professional learning systems, qualitative research methodology, and P–20 education systems. She currently serves as a program evaluator for state- and federally funded education programs.

Lynne M. Haeffele, PhD, is a Senior Research Associate in the Center for the Study of Education Policy at Illinois State University and also serves as Education Policy Director in the Office of the Illinois Lieutenant Governor. She provides research, evaluation, policy analysis, and management expertise for various state and federal projects in P–20 education, and has served as a consultant to the U.S. Department of Education. Dr. Haeffele has won state and national awards as a high school science teacher and served as Chief Deputy Superintendent for the Illinois State Board of Education. Her research interests include combining research designs, applying research findings to policy and practice, program evaluation, and the topical areas of college readiness and completion, organizational performance, and school–university partnerships.